Inside the World Wide Web

Steven Vaughan-Nichols

Rob Tidrow

Loren Buhle

Jason Küffer

Noel Taylor

NRP
NEW RIDERS
PUBLISHING

New Riders Publishing, Indianapolis, Indiana

Inside the World Wide Web

By Steven Vaughan-Nichols, Rob Tidrow, Loren Buhle, Jason Küffer, Noel Taylor

Published by:
New Riders Publishing
201 West 103rd Street
Indianapolis, IN 46290 USA

Printed in the United States of America 1 2 3 4 5 6 7 8 9 0

CIP data available upon request

Warning and Disclaimer

This book is designed to provide information about the Internet and the World Wide Web. Every effort has been made to make this book as complete and as accurate as possible, but no warranty or fitness is implied.

The information is provided on an "as is" basis. The author and New Riders Publishing shall have neither liability nor responsibility to any person or entity with respect to any loss or damages arising from the information contained in this book or from the use of the disks or programs that may accompany it.

Publisher	*Don Fowley*
Associate Publisher	*Tim Huddleston*
Product Development Manager	*Rob Tidrow*
Marketing Manager	*Ray Robinson*
Managing Editor	*Tad Ringo*

Product Director
Rob Tidrow

Acquisitions Editor
Alicia Krakovitz

Software Specialist
Steve Weiss

Production Editor
Suzanne Snyder

Copy Editors
Amy Bezek
Gail Burlakoff
Laura Frey
Sarah Kearns
Rob Lawson
Stacia Mellinger
Cliff Shubs
John Sleeva
Steve Weiss
Lillian Yates

Technical Editor
Paul Gudelis

Editorial Assistant
Karen Opal

Cover Designer
Karen Ruggles

Cover Illustrator
Roger Morgan

Book Designer
Fred Bowers

Production Team Supervisor
Laurie Casey

Graphic Image Specialists
Dennis Clay Hager
Clint Lahnen
Dennis Sheehan

Production Analysts
Angela Bannan
Bobbi Satterfield
Mary Beth Wakefield

Production Team
Carol Bowers, Kim Cofer,
Mike Henry, Aleata Howard,
Karen Lyon, Shawn MacDonald,
Joe Millay, Erika Millen,
Beth Rago, Erich J. Richter,
Tim Taylor, Christine Tyner,
Karen Walsh, Tom Wilkinson

Indexer
Bront Davis

About the Authors

Steven Vaughan-Nichols, a mild-mannered historian by training, earns his daily bread as a full-time freelance writer specializing in the Internet and online services. He has been the online services columnist for *Computer Shopper* and has also written for *Byte, Compute, Government Computer News, Internet World, Mobile Office, NetGuide, OS/2 Magazine, PC/Computing, PC Magazine, Windows Sources,* and *SunWorld.* In short, if it's a computing magazine, chances are he's written for it. He is also the co-author of *New Riders' Guide to Modems* and *Riding the Internet Highway, Deluxe Edition.* When he's not plying his trade, Mr. Vaughan-Nichols goes to the theater, listens to music, reads science fiction and mysteries, and pretends—in the Society for Creative Anachronism—that the 11th century isn't over yet.

E. Loren Buhle, Jr., Ph.D. was the creator and cofounder of OncoLink, the winner of the "Best of the Web'94" in all professional services. OncoLink was the first multimedia cancer information resource for patients, physicians, healthcare workers, and other interested parties throughout the world. Loren Buhle has been heavily involved with both hardware and software issues of computing for more than 20 years, focusing mostly on three-dimensional visualization, distributed and portable computing, and medical informatics. As Assistant Professor of Medical Physics in Radiation Oncology, he published more than 30 articles in topics ranging from structural and molecular biology, computer standards, data visualization, and use of the Internet for extending comprehensive and unbiased medical knowledge to the entire Internet community.

Jason Küffer has combined an art and production background for working with computers. He worked at McGraw-Hill Computers as one of the top system sales people. It was there that he developed insight into people's computer needs. As the art director of *Street News,* a publication aimed at helping the homeless, Mr. Küffer took the monthly paper and turned it into a biweekly four-color publication. With a limited budget and many restrictions from a non-profit company, this conversion actually lowered the monthly production costs. Today, he does computer and traditional illustration for major magazines, including *Scientific American,*

and is published in over 12 different countries monthly. Mr. Küffer consults for all areas of publishing and teaches all major graphics programs at Publication Directions and The New School. He currently owns a company called Vyne Communications, Inc., the purpose of which is to help both large and small businesses go online on the Internet.

Rob Tidrow is Product Development Manager at New Riders Publishing. He specializes in operating systems, networking, and communications topics. Mr. Tidrow has edited and contributed to the development of several popular NRP titles, including *Inside Novell NetWare, Inside Windows 3.1, Inside Microsoft Access,* and *Technology Edge: A Guide to Field Computing.* He also is a contributing author of several New Riders books, including *Understanding Windows 95, New Riders Official CompuServe Yellow Pages, Inside Microsoft Office Professional,* and *Riding the Internet Highway, Deluxe Edition.* Mr. Tidrow has created technical documentation and instructional programs for use in a variety of industrial settings and has a degree in English literature from Indiana University. He resides in Indianapolis with his wife and two boys, Adam and Wesley.

Noel Taylor is a freelance writer based in Columbia, Maryland. She has studied at Johns Hopkins University. Ms. Taylor's articles have appeared in such publications as *PC Magazine, Laser Focus World,* and numerous user guides.

Trademark Acknowledgments

All terms mentioned in this book that are known to be trademarks or service marks have been appropriately capitalized. New Riders Publishing cannot attest to the accuracy of this information. Use of a term in this book should not be regarded as affecting the validity of any trademark or service mark.

Acknowledgments

New Riders Publishing would like to express appreciation to Michael Hughes for his timely assistance and countless hours of Web surfing in order to provide the screen captures for the Scrapbook section of this book. Thanks for helping us out yet again, Michael!

Contents at a Glance

Table of Contents

Part III: Using Web Clients

9   Using Mosaic as a Web Client   235

17   Commerce on the Web   393

Part V: Creating Web Documents

18   Writing Web Documents   413

Introduction

H ow do you put a lasso around a running river? When you figure that out, tell us. Then we might be able to apply the same technique to capturing the World Wide Web. The World Wide Web has exploded in the last 12 months. Since its meager and almost invisible announcement in 1992, the World Wide Web has now become a major force in the way businesses communicate, sell, and market their products in 1995.

This book attempts to take a snapshot of the World Wide Web as it existed in early 1995. Unfortunately, by the time *Inside the World Wide Web* hits the stores, new, more powerful applications will have been introduced that are not covered here. The underlying procedures and discussions in this book, however, will still apply to most of these newer applications.

What This Book Discusses

The book is divided into eight parts, each focusing on different aspects of the World Wide Web. The following paragraphs briefly describe each chapter.

Part I: Basics of the Web and Internet

If you are brand new to the Web, you might want to read through the four chapters in this part. These chapters describe the Web and how it relates to the Internet. Each chapter assumes a basic understanding of the Internet and its applications.

Chapter 1. Introducing the Web

Even if you have an idea of what the World Wide Web is, you might want to read this chapter for some up-to-date information with which you may not be familiar. This chapter discusses the history of the Web, hyperlink technology, and the evolution of Web browsers.

Chapter 2. Introducing the Internet

For some, the concept of the Internet is difficult to grasp. Chapter 2 discusses the Internet at large and the way in which the World Wide Web fits. Read this chapter if you want to understand the Internet.

Chapter 3. Usenet Mail and Newsgroups

One of the most widely used applications in the computing industry is electronic mail (e-mail). In fact, today it is the life blood of many large and small companies. Without it, many company managers and executives would not stay connected with their employees. This chapter describes some of the technical components of e-mail as well as Usenet newsgroups.

Chapter 4. Introducing Internet Tools

Although this book focuses on the World Wide Web, many users want to use the Web to access more than just pretty home pages and audio files. Chapter 4 helps readers discover how to take full advantage of their Internet experience, such as understanding FTP, Telnet, and Gopher.

Part II: Examining the World Wide Web

This part is devoted to the mechanics of getting onto the Web. You are shown what you need to access the Web, where to go for access, and how to choose a Web browser. Many of the discussions in this part are rapidly changing, particularly with the emergence of new access providers and the merger of larger companies with smaller ones, such as CompuServe and Spry.

Chapter 5. What You Need to Link to the Web

Are you scratching your head saying, "Just what does it take to be on the Web?" If so, read this chapter for a discussion of the types of applications and computer equipment you need to join millions of other users on the World Wide Web.

Chapter 6. Finding Web Access

After you satisfy the equipment needs to get on the Web, you need to find the best access provider for you. Is it a traditional commercial service? Is it a SLIP or PPP connection? Is it a T1 connection? If you don't know, look at this chapter.

Chapter 7. Examining WWW Browsers

Mosaic. Netscape. Lynx. Internetworks. Air Mosaic. Netlauncher. Which WWW browser is right for you? This chapter examines some of the currently available applications that help you navigate the Web. Again, this is another discussion that is rapidly changing on the World Wide Web frontier.

Chapter 8. Finding Resources on the Web

As you will learn in Chapter 4, "Introducing Internet Tools," there is more to the Internet than just pretty home pages. This chapter takes you deeper into understanding other types of resources and files that you can access by being part of the Web community.

Part III: Using Web Clients

NCSA's Mosaic application helped propel the Web to where it is now. In fact, if it were not for Mosaic, the Web probably still would be a research and academic tool instead of a mass market communication network. Regardless, Mosaic is here, and Part III discusses how to set up and configure Mosaic for your system. Again, be aware that many of the discussions and procedures in this part change rapidly and might be outdated by the time this book hits the stores. Despite this fact, you can apply the basic steps and discussions presented in this section to many of the newer applications and updates.

Chapter 9. Using Mosaic as a Web Client

See this chapter for help on setting up and configuring Mosaic as your Web browser. Many new procedures for version 2 are included as well.

Chapter 10. Navigating the Web for the First Time

This chapter gets you started on the Web and helps you take your first steps for finding new resources and services available on the Web. Once you've touched the surface of the Web, you'll never be the same. In fact, many users find themselves "addicted" to the Web, spending hours and hours at the keyboard traveling from one Web site to another. Prepare yourself for this.

Chapter 11. Finding Out More About Mosaic

This chapter shows you some more in-depth features of Mosaic and how to use them. Because many of these advanced features are included in other Web browsers as well, you can use this chapter to learn more about other browsers.

Chapter 12. Navigating the Web with Netscape

As this book was being produced, another Web browser, Netscape, became the most popular browser available. This chapter focuses on Netscape Communications' Netscape 1.1 Web browser. You'll find out how to navigate the Web using Netscape, how to add sites to the Bookmark menu, and how to customize its interface.

Chapter 13. Using E-Mail on the Web

As you will learn in Chapter 3, electronic mail is the most popular tool on the Internet. Chapter 13 shows you how to use e-mail on the Web.

Chapter 14. Accessing Newsgroups via the Web

This chapter shows you how to integrate your newsgroup activities with your Web browser. Although Web browsers do not handle newsgroups as well as dedicated newsreaders (such as WinVN), Web browsers are beginning to introduce tools that are stronger and better equipped to handle newsgroups.

Part IV: Becoming a Web Site

Now that you know how to navigate on the Web, you might be interested in becoming a Web site or putting your company on the Web. This part discusses some of the basic mechanics of installing a Web server, why you might want to be a Web site, and how other companies are using the Web as a business tool.

Chapter 15. Putting Up a Web Server

This chapter focuses on the technology of installing and configuring a Web server. Some of the topics discussed include how to find the right server for your needs and

the type of equipment and hardware you need. You also will find a step-by-step discussion of how to install NCSA's Windows Web server.

Chapter 16. Putting a Business on a Web Server

In this chapter, you can learn about the type of business procedures and transactions that take place on the Web today. You also will find explanations of different solutions if you are looking for ways to outsource your Web development. You'll find, for instance, that many commercial providers will lease you space on their Web servers. Look at this chapter if you are considering this alternative.

Chapter 17. Commerce on the Web

What are companies using the Web for? Look at this chapter to see the type of businesses and the type of products and literature companies are providing on their sites.

Part V: Creating Web Documents

This part tells you how to create, design, and read Web documents. Chapters 18 through 20 show you how to use HTML to write Web documents. Chapter 21 is an introduction to the way in which many documents are being distributed in Adobe Acrobat and how to read these files.

Chapter 18. Writing Web Documents

If you are brand new to writing Web pages, see this chapter, which breaks down the components of a Web document and shows you how easy it is to understand the HTML format.

Chapter 19. Introducing Hypertext Markup Language (HTML)

Now that you've seen what a Web document is made of, you are ready to start creating your own. This chapter shows you how to write simple HTML documents.

Chapter 20. Writing HTML Documents

For more advanced HTML instructions, see this chapter. It goes into more detail and even includes discussion of how to create and integrate *Common Gateway Interface* (CGI) scripts with your documents. You also are given a brief description of some of the new HTML+ features.

Chapter 21. Using Adobe Acrobat on the Web

As the Web grows, many companies are experimenting with methods of making the Web easier to use. One way is to make the document format more universal; that is, doing away with the HTML standard. Adobe's Acrobat application is one of these solutions. See this chapter for more information on using Acrobat to read Web documents.

Part VI: Emerging Technologies on the Web

What is the future of the Web? Is it the "Information Superhighway" that we keep hearing about? For now, it probably is, but is it for the future? This part examines some of the wishes and wants of what the Web can offer us.

Chapter 22. Looking Toward the Web's Future

This chapter looks at some of the future and not-so-future technologies on the Web. In fact, by the time this book reaches bookstores, some of these future "observations" may be present or past realities. That is how quickly the Web and the Internet move.

Chapter 23. Interactivity on the Web

In many respects, the Web is giving all of us an ability to communicate like we never have before. This interaction is what makes the Web so appealing and dynamic. What happens if you add real-time video to the Web? Is this possible? Do we want this to be possible? Read this chapter for more insight into the way in which the Web enables users to interact with one another. After which, go outside and smell the real world. "Cyberspace" isn't always the ideal place to live.

Part VII: Exploring Web Sites: A Scrapbook

You'll find that using Web browsers is fairly easy. (Setting them up is another story!) After your Web browser is configured and you know it's working, you'll be interested in finding new hot spots on the Web. Use this part as your starting point to the thousands of Web pages available to you.

Chapter 24. Looking at the Best General Sites

Yahoo! You're on the Web. Now what do you do? See this chapter for a list of the common online directories to help you explore the Web. You'll also find the address to Yahoo (see fig. I.1), a popular starting point for many users.

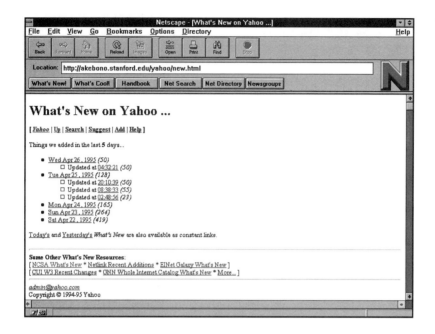

Figure I.1

Yahoo!

Chapter 25. Looking at the Best Technical Sites

Admit it, you're a computer geek or want to be one. This chapter lists some of the most popular computer sites (see fig. I.2), as well as research and science sites. Life can't be full of fun and entertaining things to do all the time.

Chapter 26. Looking at the Best Arts and Humanities Sites

As an English major, I understand the value of preserving the "artistic" side of life (see fig. I.3). This chapter focuses on some of the stuffier and snobbish sites on the Web. You also can find a listing of a graffiti "art" site.

Chapter 27. Looking at the Best Recreation Sites

Now that you've worked a long, hard day, sit back and relax with your favorite hobby. You can find sports, movies, music (see fig. I.4) and other entertaining and cool sites here. Many of these sites also offer audio or video files to clutter up your hard drive. Have fun!

Figure 1.2

The Macmillan USA Information SuperLibrary is a nice place to find computer-related resources.

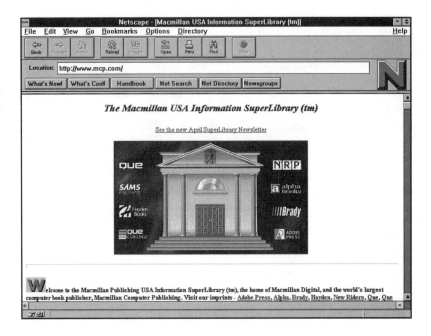

Figure 1.3

"To Web or not to Web?" What would the Bard say about this?

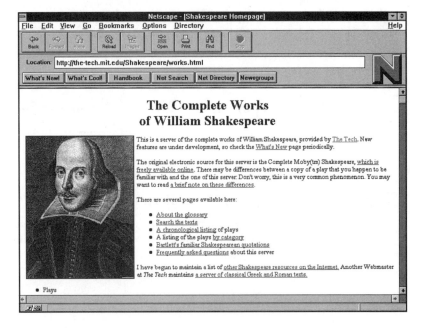

Figure I.4

Adam Curry might not be on MTV anymore, but he does have a presence on the Web.

Chapter 28. Looking at the Best Professional and Government Sites

During the course of your work, you might find the need to access databases of information or understand the complexities of the way a government institution works (see fig. I.5). Use this chapter to begin those journeys. You might find what you're looking for or you might find something completely new and interesting.

Chapter 29. Looking at the Best Commercial Sites

Sooner or later, you knew the Internet and Web would become a vehicle for commercialism (see fig. I.6). It's here, and this chapter shows some of the sites that are already popping up all over the place that pretend to offer "information" but really are intended to sell you something.

Part VIII: Appendix

As with any book, you'll find an appendix that helps supplement the major part of the book. This book is no different. This appendix is devoted to the following topics: installing the *Inside the World Wide Web Bonus CD,* the PDIAL list of access providers, and some of the sources that are available to help you stay up-to-date with the emerging universe of the Web.

Figure I.5

You now can bring the government right into your office or home.

Figure I.6

Shopping2000 assumes you don't want to leave your home to buy your next pair of pants or bra.

New Riders Publishing

The staff of New Riders Publishing is committed to bringing you the very best in computer reference material. Each New Riders book is the result of months of work by authors and staff who research and refine the information contained within its covers.

As part of this commitment to you, the NRP reader, New Riders invites your input. Please let us know if you enjoy this book, if you have trouble with the information and examples presented, or if you have a suggestion for the next edition.

Please note, though: the New Riders staff cannot serve as a technical resource for the World Wide Web or for related questions about software- or hardware-related problems. Please refer to the documentation that accompanies Netscape, Mosaic, or any other application that you might use, or refer to the application's Help systems.

If you have a question or comment about any New Riders book, there are several ways to contact New Riders Publishing. We will respond to as many readers as we can. Your name, address, or phone number will never become part of a mailing list or be used for any purpose other than to help us continue to bring you the best books possible. You can write us at the following address:

New Riders Publishing
Attn: Associate Publisher
201 W. 103rd Street
Indianapolis, IN 46290

If you prefer, you can fax New Riders Publishing at (317) 581-4670.

You can send electronic mail to New Riders from a variety of sources using the following e-mail address:

```
jlevalley@iquest.net
```

NRP is an imprint of Macmillan Computer Publishing. To obtain a catalog or information, or to purchase any Macmillan Computer Publishing book, call (800) 428-5331.

Thank you for selecting *Inside the World Wide Web!*

Part I

Basics of the Web and Internet

Introducing the Web

Before there was the World Wide Web, before there was an Internet, there was the dream of Xanadu. In Xanadu, all human knowledge, all documents, images, sounds, and videos would be instantly accessible to anyone who had a computer, anywhere, anytime.

Xanadu was the dream of Ted Nelson, a computer visionary. He foresaw a world where all information could be linked together in a world-wide web of hypertext and hypermedia. In short, he saw a world where the constant Babel of incompatible data formats and protocols would be replaced by a universal library of information. It would be a world transformed, one that would have as little in common with our world as ours does with the one before Gutenberg invented the printing press.

This chapter introduces you to the World Wide Web and focuses on the following points:

- ◆ Hypermedia and hypertext

- ◆ The evolution of the Web

- ◆ Mosaic and Web browsers

- ◆ Business on the Web

- ◆ Growth issues

Exploring the Web's Foundation

Xanadu was the dream. Today we have a reality: the World Wide Web (WWW). It's not the reality envisioned by Ted Nelson—his Xanadu project soldiers under the guidance of Serious Cybernetics in Melbourne, Australia. But, while the Web may not be quite what Nelson envisioned, it attempts the same grand unification theory of information. It will change the world as perhaps no other invention of man has, save the printing press and the computer.

Those are strong words, but consider this: The Web can link together information from anywhere in the world and make it available to anyone. Grade-school students can jump from Dun & Bradstreet's financial information to a pictorial tour of Croatia's capital, Zagreb, to the state of the Internet in southern Africa, without ever leaving their desks.

There's far more to the Web than just information. You can learn static facts from any encyclopedia. The information stored in the Web is constantly updated. With the Web, you'll always have the freshest information at your fingertips.

The Web also dynamically links information into a seamless whole. You may start your information hunt next door and finally track down your quarry somewhere in Singapore. From where you sit, however, there's no difference between the two online data sources. The Web enables you to move around the world as easily as to the local library—with a click of a mouse.

The Web manages this feat by employing the twin concepts of hypertext and hypermedia. Both concepts date back to Ted Nelson.

Looking at Hypermedia

In hypertext, related information is linked together. Instead of being forced to move linearly from page 1 to page 2 and so on, a hypertext document lets you leap from word to word using *links*.

In a hypertext encyclopedia, for example, you could be reading about Michael Jordan and find a reference to the Chicago Bulls winning the NBA championship in 1992, and that makes you wonder which team won the championship the year before. In an ordinary book, you're stuck; you must either go to the index or continue reading through the book searching for the information you seek. In hypertext, however, a simple click on the phrase "NBA championship" can take you to the next occurrence of the phrase or to a fuller description of the NBA championship's history.

Now, take this concept one step further. With hypermedia, you can link pictures, sounds, and movies to form multimedia documents—not only are words linked together, but images and sounds are bound together as well.

For example, in The New Grolier MultiMedia Encyclopedia, a well-known CD-ROM encyclopedia, you can click your way from an article on the Apollo 11 moon landing to a video of the moon landing. From there, you can click on a caption about the launch and from there continue your study of space exploration.

Hypermedia tries to make computers work the way people think: that is, in jumps rather than always moving straight forward or backward. It is not perfect, of course. A hyperdocument link may lead you far astray from the destination you have in mind. Still, hypermedia can be a great help in chasing down elusive information.

Looking at Hypermedia's History

The first popular use of hypertext was in the Apple Macintosh's and Apple IIGS's application development system: HyperCard. As it happens, HyperCard, created in 1987, was also the first noteworthy use of hypermedia.

Note HyperCard is worth mentioning because some of its strengths and weaknesses mirror those of the Web. For example, both are hard to get a handle on. More importantly, however, HyperCard represented a new way of looking at information, a way that the Web would follow. At first, the concept of multimedia was too difficult for many people to grasp and the hypertext's hardware demands were too high, even by the standards of the 1980s. By the 1990s, however, processor speeds and RAM costs had improved to the point that multimedia's requirements were no longer a barrier. Today, almost all desktop computers can be purchased multimedia-ready. With these developments, multimedia is making serious inroads into the computer world.

From the beginning, multimedia's most important role was in CD-ROM-based applications. These CD-ROM programs run on systems that meet the MultiMedia PC (MPC) specifications.

MPC requirements (see table 1.1) are set by the Multimedia PC Marketing Council, a subsidiary of the Software Publishers Association (SPA). There are two levels of MPC compliance. The first, created in 1990, is the bare minimum to run multimedia and, as it happens, Web applications. Products that are certified by the Multimedia PC Marketing Council as meeting the MPC requirements display the MPC or MPC-2 insignia. While there are no standards for systems to work with the Web, with the exception of CD-ROM and sound requirements, an MPC-2 system is the minimum you need to run a graphical Web browser like Mosaic.

TABLE 1.1
MPC Specifications—Minimum Requirements

Hardware	Level 1	Level 2
RAM	2 MB	4 MB
Processor	386SX/16 MHz	486SX/25 MHz
Floppy disk	1.44 MB 3.5"	1.44 MB 3.5"
Hard disk	30 MB	160 MB
CD-ROM	150 Kbps transfer rate 1 second access time CD-ROM XA ready multisession	300 Kbps transfer rate 400 ms access time
Sound	8-bit, 8 voice synthesizer MIDI playback	16-bit, 8 voice synthesizer MIDI playback
Video	640×480 pixels ×16 colors	640×480 pixels ×64,000 colors
Ports	MIDI & joystick	MIDI & joystick

Recommended Features

Hardware	Level 1	Level 2
RAM	As minimum	8 MB
CD-ROM	64 KB on-board buffer	64 KB on-board buffer
Sound	As minimum	CD-ROM XA audio, support for IMA adopted ADPCM algorithm
Video	640×480 pixels ×256 colors	Able to deliver 1.2 megapixels per second without using more than 40 percent of CPU bandwidth.

Multimedia CD-ROM packages are impressive. For instance, the New Grolier Multimedia Encyclopedia is based on the 21-volume Academic American Encyclopedia. This single CD-ROM can boast 10 million words of text in 33,000 articles—along with comprehensive bibliographies and tables.

Although CD-ROMs excel in logically linking information together, they do not come close to equaling the resources that are available on the Web. CD-ROMs are produced by artists, authors, and editors all working together to form complete works of art. WWW, on the other hand, comes from the efforts of thousands, each adding their own strands of information to the Web.

Looking at the Web's History

In essence, the Web is a worldwide string of computer databases using a common information retrieval architecture. In concept, the Web is a client/server database management system. There's nothing particularly special about this as advanced database designs have been doing it for years.

Perhaps, for example, you want to see if a book is in the Library of Congress. This doesn't pose much of a problem to Net experts; they just set their Gopher clients to connect with a Gopher server at `rs5.loc.gov`. For anyone else, of course, the job is almost hopeless. Not only do you need to know how to run Gopher—by Internet program standards, a very simple program—but you also need to know the Internet address for the Library of Congress' Gopher. It is enough to make users tear out their hair.

Note In the days before the Web, you had to be a Unix wizard to use the Internet's information resources. Unix is the operating system that underlies the Internet. Refer to Chapter 2, "Introducing the Internet," for more information.

The Early Days of the Web

Tim Berners-Lee, a British computer programmer, did something different from that which had gone before. He combined hypermedia with the Internet's vast information resources. Before the Web, you could do an untold number of interesting things on the Internet, but none of them easily.

In 1989, Berners-Lee was working at the European Particle Physics Laboratory (CERN) in Geneva, Switzerland. Berners-Lee faced the eternal problem of getting people the information they needed to work together effectively on many projects in real time.

Berners-Lee's solution uses hypertext technology to form a web of documents. Unlike books or many databases, there is no hierarchical structure to his information web. Instead, there are many possible connections between documents without a beginning or an end. All the messy details of how this information is linked is hidden by a character-based hypertext interface. With the Web, a physicist can jump from an article on particle theory in a local machine to a glossary of nuclear physics terms on a system a thousand miles away. He can do so with less trouble than a reader has paging through a book's glossary for the same information.

Web documents must be written in a special format that enables the hypertext links to work. This format is *Hypertext Markup Language* (HTML). HTML is a subset of *Standard Generalized Markup Language* (SGML). SGML is an *International Standards Organization* (ISO) standard for defining formatting in text documents. Although SGML is meant for desktop publishing, Berners-Lee and his companions seized upon its hyperlink capacity to form the basis of the first Web documents.

To access the first early strands of the Web, you had to use a line-based Web browser, an interface that was so simple that it couldn't even use a full-screen character interface. Rather, it was limited to a single line of information. To get to the interface, you had to telnet to either of the first two Web servers: `info.cern.ch` or `nxo01.cern.ch`. This first version, which you ran with the login www, had only two commands: `start a search` and `follow a link`.

Note A *browser* is a program that enables you to access the World Wide Web. If you like the information superhighway analogy, you can think of a browser as a car that lets you drive from one Web site to another.

The newest text-based version of WWW (see fig. 1.1) is more sophisticated than its ancestor, but it still pales when compared to the Mosaic view of the same resource (see fig. 1.2). Mosaic gives you not only text, but graphics and (note the little speaker symbol) sounds as well.

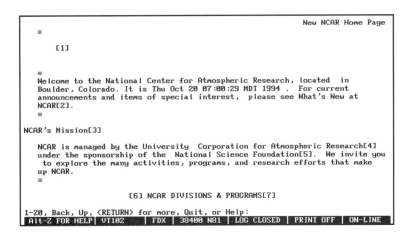

Figure 1.1

An example of a text-based WWW interface.

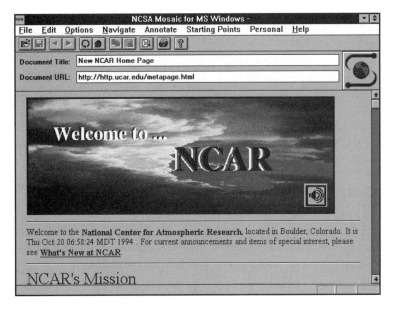

Figure 1.2

An example of a newer WWW interface, NCSA Mosaic, complete with graphics and sound capabilities.

That link ability may not sound like much but it really is. With the introduction of the Web, users had the ability to seek information without worrying about where it was or how to unlock it. Much of the data with which the Web dealt was not in hypertext format, so the hypertext advantage was not clear and the Web often came across as simply another Internet data-hunting tool with a more consistent interface.

The result was that the Web grew very slowly. If you were to ask Internet information jockeys what was hot in Net information retrieval two or three years ago, chances are that most of them would have mentioned Wide Area Information Servers (WAIS). What changed the Web from being an interesting but neglected part of the Internet to being the hottest news ever to hit the Net was Mosaic.

Mosaic

No one set out with a plan to build an interface (a browser) that would free the power of the Web. Instead, Mosaic began as a project by Marc Andreessen, an undergraduate student at the University of Illinois at Urbana-Champaign (UIUC). In 1993, Andreessen faced the same problems at his part-time job at the National Center for Supercomputing Applications (NCSA) that Berners-Lee had dealt with at CERN: many people working on many projects at once who needed to share information. Specifically, Andreessen was working on tools for scientific visualization.

In the course of working toward that goal, Andreessen began to build Mosaic. At first, Andreessen didn't even know of the Web's existence. Not being one to reinvent the wheel, he searched for existing solutions and found the Web. Once he discovered the Web's potential, he began turning Mosaic into a Web browser.

Even by using the existing Web, building Mosaic was not an easy task. Andreessen soon found himself burning the midnight oil to complete the job. Fortunately, Andreessen was joined by Eric Bina, who helped develop the first version of Mosaic.

Note   There's really nothing that difficult about building a Web browser, which is one reason why there are now dozens of them demanding your attention. What was hard was making that first step of seeing how you could show the Web's underlying structure in a way that didn't overwhelm users.

Mosaic established ordinary appeal because it was the first program to do this for a mass audience. Not only was Mosaic free to Macintosh, Windows, and X-Windows, it worked and worked well.

In April 1993, the first version of Mosaic, called *Mosaic 1.0 for the X Window System* appeared. The program took off like wildfire, and the Web's popularity exploded with it. Why? Because, although Mosaic didn't really bring anything new in functionality to Web interfaces, it brought together the best ideas of existing interfaces and gave them an attractive, easy-to-use interface.

If Andreessen and the NCSA had been Microsoft, Inc., you would have heard of Mosaic months in advance of its actual arrival. Instead, Mosaic's popularity boomed solely within the confines of the Internet without the benefit of conventional advertisement. The NCSA, a non-profit government agency, was left in an odd situation—it had an extremely popular product and no intention of marketing it. Because programs made at NCSA were freeware programs intended "for academic, research and internal business purposes only," no one had to invest a dime to try Mosaic.

Because of Mosaic's popularity, the NCSA developed Windows and Macintosh versions of the browser. These programs were released in the early autumn of 1993—just in time for Mosaic to ride the wave of Internet interest to the beaches of broad popular acceptance.

Because the NCSA's resources were meant to provide supercomputer resources to researchers, rather than help Microsoft Windows users navigate the difficulties of setting up Mosaic, the NCSA gave several companies, such as Spry, Mosaic Communications, and Quarterdeck, the right to commercially develop Mosaic.

This proved only a short-term solution as the NCSA found itself in a commercial world that it was ill-suited to deal with. Finally, in August 1994, the NCSA gave Spyglass Incorporated the right to commercially develop and license Mosaic. There continues to be a freeware version of Mosaic, however, which includes some Spyglass improvements.

Although the Spyglass decision washed NCSA's hands of the difficulties of commercializing Mosaic, it also muddied the Mosaic marketplace. With numerous "Mosaics" moving into the marketplace, telling one version from another became confusing. Today, there are several companies developing Mosaic from older versions of Mosaic, while others use Spyglass' Enhanced Mosaic as their base.

Looking at the Web Today

Today there are no fewer than four available versions of Mosaic for Microsoft Windows, including NCSA's Mosaic Version 2 Alpha 2 and 9, Spry's AIR Mosaic, and Spyglass' Enhanced Mosaic. There are also at least as many other Web browsers that aren't based on the Mosaic model. The situation isn't a whole lot clearer in the workstation and Macintosh markets.

Web Browsers

If you are presently deciding between Web browsers, your choice likely depends upon your operating system's needs, plus the performance and features you desire. Although today you can pretty much get data from any Web server by using any graphical Web browser, in the future that will no longer be the case as the Web itself grows more fragmented.

A current problem, but one that is likely to disappear soon, is that most Web browsers are not universal front ends to all Internet services. While any Web client can use Gopher, most of them can't read newsgroup messages, or read and write e-mail. Developers are working, however, to make Web browsers that enable you to do anything your heart desires on the Internet.

Note   And what might your heart desire? Well, how about talking to someone you've just met in a little Web bistro—with full voice and graphics? Or taking a moving tour of the Grand Canyon in which you control where the "chopper" goes? If it's communications, and it can be made interactive, you'll see it on the Web.

Another problem continually being worked on that is specific to PC and Macintosh browsers is the capability to access WAIS databases (see Chapter 8, "Finding Resources on the Web," for more information on using WAIS).

Although 1995 state-of-the-art Web browsers are all very easy to use, they are difficult to set up. If you're a TCP/IP network administrator, you'll find setting up a Web browser to be no trouble at all. If you're not, be ready to earn your power-user stripes because setting up Mosaic is a real job. This situation, however, is changing rapidly. Soon, putting Mosaic into action will be easier on some levels, but others will continue to be difficult for the next few generations of Mosaic.

The Growth of the Web

The Web is continuing to expand at a remarkable rate. If you keep an eye on the Usenet newsgroup devoted to Web servers, `comp.infosystems.www.providers`, you'll see that there's a new Web server coming up every day.

 Note   A *Web site* is an Internet system that holds a Web server. A *Web server* is the software on a site that enables Web browsers to access Web documents sitting on the Web site.

This surge in Web servers springs from several causes. A large part of it can be attributed to the fact that Web servers are relatively easy to set up. As more and better HTML editors and text converters emerge, new Web servers will flood the Web. Equally important, however, is that Web servers enable businesses to enter the Internet.

Business and the Web

In the past, because of the Internet's long-standing acceptable use policies, it was impossible for commercial traffic to use the Net. This changed in 1991 with the beginning of the Commercial Internet Exchange (CIX).

The CIX was created by the Internet service providers behind AlterNet, CERFnet, and PSInet, whose goal was to create a system by which commercial traffic could flow freely through the Internet. The effort was a success, because now businesses in Pasadena, California can use FTP to get to their accounting records in Bangor, Maine. At the same time, however, CIX inadvertently created the expectation that other Internet/Usenet services also could be used for commercial purposes such as selling goods or services.

These early efforts were feeble at best. At their worst, companies engaged in mass e-mail mailing, and using Usenet newsgroups for advertising, were flamed and attacked in mail and newsgroups messages by thousands of Internet users.

The Web, however, offered new ways for companies to venture into the Internet. Here, companies can project an attractive appearance while simultaneously selling their services or goods through Web server hyperlinks. For example, if the traditional Sears and Roebuck mail-order catalog existed on the

Web, it would have text and illustrations just like its paper counterpart. Unlike mere paper and ink, Web catalogs let users find out more about a product than they could ever learn from an ordinary catalog, then enable them to post orders instantly. And that's the least you can do with Web interactions and catalogs. Silicon Graphics' catalogs, for example, let you try their high-end systems from across the Web when you access their catalog.

Other companies, particularly computer companies, can offer technical support services over the Web. The Web lends itself to this use, because users easily can find their way to the solutions for their problems thanks to the hypertext format.

Other businesses are using the Web as a publishing venture. Their magazines and newspapers exist only as electronic text and graphics. While this format may not appeal to all readers, it does offer a way for both old and new publications to easily gain a worldwide online presence without substantial capital investment.

Some companies are venturing into the Internet by building their own Web servers and hypermedia documents. These businesses are enlisting the aid of a new breed of expert, called a "WebMaster" or, more appropriately, "WebWeaver." Whatever the title, the job combines the work of network administrator and desktop publisher.

 Tip   For businesses that are unsure of the new technology, companies like the MecklerWeb, subsidiary of MecklerMedia, offer an all-in-one solution. The MecklerWeb can set your business up with the hardware, the Internet connection, and even the creation of your Web documents and resources.

This process is only continuing to speed up. Companies are leaping onto the Web every day, eager to show and sell you their wares.

Growing Pains on the Web

To make commerce on the Web work, the Web needs secure encryption standards so that a user in Tulsa can send her credit card number to a company in San Francisco without worrying about a cracker in Chicago grabbing the number. To do this, Web businesses are building encryption schemes into their servers to make sure that anyone intercepting credit or debit card numbers will only pick up garbage.

All solutions come with their own set of problems. One such problem is that encryption schemes are not compatible with one another. This could mean that even if you have a secure Web browser, you may not be able to buy things from every secure Web site.

Another problem of which a Web explorer should be aware is that the Internet and the Web are getting very crowded. Many popular Web sites are being mobbed by other users, and as a result they are often unavailable or their performance is very poor.

This trouble is not going to pass away quickly. Whether your connection to the Internet is a 9600 *bits-per-second* (bps) modem or a 64 *kilobits-per-second* (kbs) T3 line, there are times you're going to feel like you're in an online traffic jam.

The only ways out of this jam are an increase in the Internet's data capacity and more, faster Web sites to spread out the load. The first problem is constantly being worked on. For the foreseeable future, however, the bandwidth—the total amount of data that can pass through a network at a given time—isn't going to catch up with the demand. More Web sites, of course, are springing up every day. Because popular sites can be visited by 10,000+ users in a day, wise Web administrators are putting only their most powerful machines on the Web.

In short, today's Web is a confusing, chaotic place. It's a grand place too, with information wonders unlike any that have ever been seen before. Perhaps the best way to look at the Web is to think of the old American West—wild, woolly, and exciting.

Looking Toward the Web's Future

In the next few years, we'll see many Web developments. The Web browser of the year 2000 will be as easy to install as a simple word processor is today. Future programs will combine all Internet services into a single, easy-to-use *graphical user interface* (GUI) that will be both keyboard-/mouse- and voice-activated.

What won't change, however, is that the Web will still be difficult for some kinds of information retrieval. Although there are current efforts to standardize and catalog Web data, there is no consensus on how this should be done. Even if rules on how to catalog the Web's data existed, it seems questionable that these could be in place on the majority of Web servers. The Web will always be somewhat confusing.

Overall, we'll also see faster performance from software and the Internet itself. In particular, *integrated services digital networks* (ISDNs), will increase the throughput speed of modem users from a top of 28,800 bps to 64,000 bps.

In the near future, we're going to see still more Web browsers. In 1995, IBM's OS/2 and Microsoft's Windows 95 will emerge with their own built-in Web browsers. It's impossible to say now whether these will drive Mosaic and the other browsers out of the market. All that is certain is that competition in the browser market is going to be fierce in the coming years.

There also will be some incompatibility problems between browsers and Web servers. Mosaic Communications has added some extensions to HTML. Documents written in this new variant of HTML may not be displayed properly by some browsers.

A more serious problem is that HTML, and its successor language, HTML+, are being challenged by Adobe Acrobat. Acrobat produces documents in the *Portable Data Format* (PDF). While PDF has advantages for document designers over HTML, users must have an Acrobat reader integrated with their Web browser to read PDF documents.

An interesting shift for all Internet users is that commercial online services, like America Online (AOL), CompuServe (CIS), and Delphi are moving onto the Internet. CompuServe already has a Web site, and is considering producing an interface that combines the system specific advantages of their *CompuServe Information Manager* (CIM) with Mosaic to form a combined CompuServe/Web interface.

CompuServe, for example, is also becoming an Internet and Web provider in its own right. Don't be surprised—especially as the free resources of the Internet become more overburdened—if one or more of the online services start up their own FTP, Gopher, and Web servers. These online services will offer better service than the free servers but will cost users either a subscription or a usage fee.

Commerce is booming on the Internet. What once was science fiction, using a computer to order everything from groceries to your wardrobe, is already becoming reality. In the next year we'll see the current handful of online stores grow into the thousands.

Other resources also are pouring onto the Web. By the end of the year, you're likely to be able to get your hometown newspaper, access encyclopedias, wander through virtual museums, look through national want ads, and even use a dating service to meet that special someone—all through a Web browser/access service.

The Web's potential is as unlimited as human communications. The next chapter takes a closer look at the system behind the Web: the Internet.

Introducing the Internet

T he Internet's the biggest network the world has ever seen. Tens of millions use it every day, but few truly understand how it works. This chapter looks under the Internet's hood to see what makes it run.

Defining the Internet

If you're slightly confused about what the Internet is, you're in good company. There's no neat answer. A definition that most experts can live with is that it's a Transmission Control Protocol/Internet Protocol (TCP/IP)-bound network of networks and their common accessible resources.

The Usenet, though often confused with the Internet, is actually only one of its subsets. *Usenet* really isn't a network at all, but a distributed peer-to-peer message distribution system with messages that consist of e-mail, using the Internet's RFC-822 addressing standard, as well as publicly available messages bundled by topic (the Usenet newsgroups). Usenet information travels on everything from lightning fast T-3 (45 Mbps) lines to floppy disks which are hand-carried from node to node. The Internet's traffic, in contrast, always travels by way of a network connection.

Beyond even the Internet and Usenet is what Internet expert John Quartermain calls the Matrix. The *Matrix* is the sum of all networks that can communicate with each other. Every bulletin board system with Internet mail capacity and all important online services, such as AOL, CIS, Delphi, eWorld, GEnie, Interchange, and Prodigy, are all part of the Matrix. In short, the Matrix is the superset of all networks that can communicate with each other—including the Internet.

 Note The Internet is big and it's getting bigger every day. Although much of this growth springs from new "pure" Internet machines coming online, the major commercial online services are also merging with the Internet. America Online, CompuServe, and Delphi are all moving in the direction of offering Internet services up to, and including, TCP/IP connections to the Internet.

The three *metanetworks* (the Internet, the Usenet, and the Matrix) are defined by their standards. An important thing to understand about all three metanetworks is that no one is in charge. In the case of the Internet, the lowest common denominator is the connection of systems by TCP/IP. In the case of the Usenet, it's RFC-822 mail and Usenet news; for the Matrix, it's the use of any e-mail system that enables mail to be transferred from network to network, usually by means of RFC-822; however, the X.400 mail standards also provide a framework for networks to join the Matrix.

Although there's no grand committee of scientists or a government agency in charge of the Internet, there are organizations that guide the Internet. These groups, such as the Internet Society (ISOC), Internet Engineering Task Force

(IETF), and the Internet Architecture Board (IAB), try to direct, design, and approve changes in the Internet. These groups lead the worldwide Internet community by consensus rather then by any dicta or legal authority.

Even the technical rules of the Internet are subject to change. The *Request for Comments* (RFCs) documents that make up the Internet technical standards are working notes, not hard and fast standards.

The Internet is also no one's property. It's an open network that welcomes anyone who can connect with it and obey the rules of the road. You might think of the Internet as being the property of your Internet provider or your Internet software company; it's not. The Internet isn't free—one way or the other, access is always paid for. No company or government has any claim over its totality. Parts, to be sure, are controlled by companies such as IBM or consortiums such as the Commercial Internet Exchange (CIX, pronounced "kicks"), but even the largest group holds only a part of the whole Internet picture.

When you pay a business for access to the Internet, you're not paying for the Internet in the same way that you pay for service on America Online or CompuServe. You're paying for the connection. The Internet itself is made up of tens of thousands of systems working together, most of which your provider has no control over.

Packet-Switching Network Theory

The Internet was born from many fathers, but ARPAnet, and hence the Internet, sprang from the Cold War. The new network was meant to be one that would keep working even if parts were destroyed in a nuclear war. Data would be lost, but communications would continue.

In the late 1960s, the U.S. Department of Defense's *Advanced Research Projects Agency* (ARPA) set about developing a network that tied together geographically distant computers using the then-new technology of sharing data lines by packet-switching.

In a packet-switching network, data is divided into packets. Each packet has a header, which includes an identification number and information about the packet's origin and destination.

Once split up, the packets are sent to their destinations over a web of possible connections. No particular route is laid out for the packets. Instead each packet trundles along to exchange nodes, usually a router or a computer. A *router* simply is a device that routes packets to their proper destinations. At a node, the headers are examined for the packet's destination and then sent along on what at that time is the best possible route. This optimal road might change from moment to moment, and in that case, the packets split up along several different routes. When the packets arrive at the destination, their headers enable the receiving system to reassemble the data into its original form.

Packet-Switching Advantages

Packet-switching has several advantages. First, packets can be sent successfully even when large sections of the network fail, as might have happened if the Soviets had bombed us or, as recently happened in Virginia, when a backhoe took out a major fiber-optic link.

Another advantage of packet-switching is that a message may consist of several packets. If only one packet becomes corrupt, you don't have to re-send the entire message—only that one packet. Thus, even when errors do occur, throughput speed is not significantly slowed.

Each level of the packet contains not only data but a header with directions to assure that the packet gets to its destination. When a packet arrives at a router, the layers are peeled off and the headers are read to ensure proper delivery of the data they enfold. To translate IPs into and out of packets, routers combine packet examination and translation functions with packet-switching technology.

That was the theory. It was not put into practice until the fall of 1969. In that year, four Honeywell 516 minicomputers, located on West Coast university campuses, connected together to form ARPAnet, the Internet's predecessor.

This first network was built around the now obsolete *Network Control Protocol* (NCP). NCP, however, wasn't robust enough to connect with ARPA's other experimental packet-switching networks.

TCP/IP

In the early 70s, work progressed on a network protocol that could handle interconnecting heterogeneous packet networks. The resulting protocol was TCP/IP. Long after the first packet networks became history, TCP/IP's flexibility enabled packet-switching networks to live on.

TCP/IP's great strength is that it easily enables computers of different architectures and operating systems to communicate with each other. The resulting

networks of networks are known as *catenets*. The largest catenet is the Internet. TCP/IP enables network designers to build catenets by encapsulating IPs inside lower level system native network packets. To use the analogy of a letter, Internet mail can be given another network's envelope so that it can be sent through that network's mail system.

TCP/IP encapsulation, packets, or IP datagrams, are made of four separate levels. From top to bottom, these are as follows:

◆ Application

◆ Host-to-host transport

◆ Internet

◆ Network access

Of course, for the systems to make any sense of where a datagram should go, an addressing scheme is needed. In the Internet, each Internet host has a domain name. A domain name consists of labels separated by periods, such as in the author's domain, `vna.digex.net`.

Computers don't understand English. What the Internet hosts use as addresses are IP addresses. An IP address consists of a 32-bit integer that's represented by four 8-bit numbers, written in base 10, separated by periods. Don't get upset if that confuses you. The important thing for you as a user to know is that you can use these numbers with some commands, such as ftp and telnet, to contact a remote system. For instance, `vna.digex.net`'s IP address is 164.109.213.7.

Normally, no one has to worry about IP addresses because the distributed name and address directory program, the *Domain Name System* (DNS), takes care of translating from domain names to IP addresses. This is a significant TCP/IP advantage. Sometimes, however, your DNS server will either be down or its address list will be incorrect. In that case, you need to take things into your own hands by using IP addresses.

Another TCP/IP advantage is that it's not bound in any way to a physical medium. Whether its wireless, token-ring, ordinary phone lines, an X.25 packet-switching network, or smoke signals, if you can transmit data through it, you can use TCP/IP on it.

Although there have been many attempts to replace the TCP/IP design, TCP/IP remains interoperability's shining success story. Most experts agree that the switch-over of ARPAnet and the Defense Data Network (DDN) from NCP to TCP/IP on January 1, 1983 marks the true birth of the Internet.

In reality, the Internet runs on everything from the nearly antique 286 PC with MS-DOS to the Delphi online service's VAX-VMS minicomputers to the National Center for Supercomputing Application's Crays running Unix. Remember, the Internet is not operating system driven; it's defined by the TCP/IP networking protocol.

As TCP/IP was becoming popular, one of the first ports of this protocol was to a DEC PDP-11 minicomputer running Unix, which would prove to be a technology marriage made in heaven. TCP/IP would soon be incorporated into the "free" academic version of Unix, the Berkeley Standard Distribution (BSD). BSD Unix, together with TCP/IP, rapidly became popular throughout the computing world, and, with their growth, the Internet expanded at an explosive rate. Today, Unix, TCP/IP, and the Internet are bound together in the public's view of the Internet.

For a very long time, the TCP/IP sinews of the Internet were limited to 56 kilobit per second (Kbps) main lines, or backbones. By 1987, it was time for an upgrade. The National Science Foundation (NSF) began developing a backbone system fast enough to meet the needs of Internet users accessing supercomputers. This was the birth of the backbone of the NSFnet.

Simultaneously, the NSF decided that rather than have small Internet networks plug directly into the NSFnet, these LANs should go through regional, mid-level networks. Companies and organizations, known as network service providers, sprang up to create and maintain these mid-level networks.

Without realizing it, the NSF was starting the process that would lead to the current Internet market. Today, there are Internet providers for everyone, from major corporations needing T-3 speeds to Joe User with a 1,200 bps modem.

Speeds of the Internet

1,200 to 28,800 bps

↓

56 to 128 KB ISDN

↓

T1

↓

T3

The immediate effects of small networks were seen at higher levels. Advanced Network & Services (ANS), formed by IBM, MCI, and Merit, first connected with NSFnet and then began developing their own high-speed backbone. At the same time, government agencies began building their own backbones. In an attempt to combine efforts, and expedite current data communications technology, the government began working on what became known as the information superhighway: the *National Research and Education Network* (NREN).

This combination of efforts was all well and good, but as more companies and private individuals got on the Internet, thanks to ANS and business customer-oriented network service providers such as PSI and UUNET, usage problems became more prominent. The Internet, until then, had been reserved for research and educational purposes; commercial Internet use was expressly forbidden.

There were some isolated business-related sites on the Internet, such as UUNET's AlterNet, but they were islands surrounded by packet seas that their information could not cross. The solution was clear: there needed to be a commercial Internet backbone. In 1991, the major commercial Internet providers created CIX. With this, you could now conduct business on the Internet.

Connecting to the Internet

There are three different end-user Internet connection levels, all of which spring from Internet Points of Presence (POP). They are as follows:

◆ Unix-to-Unix Copy Protocol (UUCP)

◆ Shell

◆ IP

An Internet *Point of Presence* (POP) is simply a place with modems, routers, and terminal servers that enables outside users to call in and connect to the Internet. When you call a POP, you first connect with a modem. Your signal is then relayed to a terminal server through one of its RS-232 serial interfaces. An *RS-232 port* is just a serial port like the one your modem uses. A *terminal server* is an asynchronous multiplexing device that takes your call and translates it from an asynchronous data stream to TCP/IP packets. The terminal server then sends your transformed data to the local Internet host computer. In return, the terminal server translates the Internet's computer responses into signals that your modem can work with. The local host computer, in turn, uses routers to connect with the rest of the Internet. From where you sit, this process is completely invisible.

What happens next depends on whether you have a shell account or a Unix to Unix Copy Protocol account.

The UUCP Connection

With a UUCP account, such as Computer Witchcraft's Winnet program, your PC and the Internet system copy e-mail and newsgroup messages between the systems. In this arrangement, you write your messages off-line and only connect with the Internet long enough to transfer messages.

For Web users, the problem with UUCP is that, for all practical purposes, there's no way you can access the Web. There are work-arounds using e-mail messages, but they're really not worth bothering with.

The Shell Connection

A shell account is an entirely different kettle of fish. Here, your system becomes a terminal to an Internet host system. As such, you can run such TCP/IP-borne utilities as *File Transfer Protocol* (FTP) and Telnet.

FTP does just what its name says it does—it transfers files. Telnet enables you to log into other computers. Although this is most useful if you have accounts on several systems, as you'll see, it can also be useful in other situations. With a shell account, you don't run these programs on your PC. For instance, if you "ftp" a file from a remote site, the file appears on your host Internet system, not on your PC.

Some Internet shell interface programs, such as Pipeline's Pipeline for Windows and Delphi's InterNav, make it appear that the file is transferred in one smooth operation, but that is not actually the case. Instead, your Internet host is ftp-ing the file to its system while simultaneously copying the file to your PC with an asynchronous data transfer protocol, such as Z-Modem. You can see the difference clearly on systems that require you to transfer the file to your PC manually with Z-Modem or the like.

With a shell account you can access the Web in three ways. The first is to run a local character-based Web browser. The second method is to run the same client remotely, using Telnet. Beside limiting you to a character-based interface, with the exception of special Internet interfaces like Pipeline for Windows, these programs keep you from moving data directly to your computer. Like FTP, when you save a file, the file is only saved to your Internet provider's computer, not to the one sitting in front of you. The third way to access the Web from a shell account is to use a program that fakes an IP connection with a shell account. These programs are Oslonett A/S's Remsock and Cyberspace Development's The Internet Adapter (TIA). One problem with these is that the software must be running on both the host machine and your PC. If your POP won't, or can't, run these programs, you'll be unable to use your copy to connect with the Web.

The IP Connection

Thus far, we have discussed the shell account and the UUCP methods of connecting to the Internet. The third connection option, the IP method, is an actual IP connection with the Internet. Remember that one of TCP/IP's strong points is that it runs on almost anything that carries data, including normal phone lines and modems. This is the usual, but not the only way, to run a Web client like Mosaic on your PC.

There are several advantages to the IP approach. For instance, you can run multiple programs at once. In one Telnet window, you can be chatting with someone using *Internet Relay Chat* (IRC), while at the same time ftp-ing a file directly to your computer in another window. IP connections also enable IP-specific programs, such as most Web browsers, to work.

The oldest modem way to make an IP connection with the Internet is *Serial Line Internet Protocol* (SLIP). SLIP, while still popular, is slowly being overhauled by *Point-to-Point Protocol* (PPP). One advantage that PPP has over SLIP is that it can automatically assign IP addresses, making it a boon to laptop Internet argonauts. PPP can also encapsulate other network layer protocols, such as NetWare's IPX, instead of just IP. The latter makes PPP useful for hooking into non-TCP/IP networks that are connected to the Internet by a router.

With either SLIP or PPP, your machine becomes an actual part of the Internet. To make use of this, you also need TCP/IP programs, such as Telnet, FTP, or Mosaic, to be resident on your computer.

Note The hardest part of setting up a browser is setting up the TCP/IP connection. Vendors are working frantically to make SLIP and PPP easier to set up. Today, however, setting up either one might be the most painful job you'll ever do on your PC. Be sure to read all your network software and POP documentation and set aside lots of time for the job.

Understanding Routers and Gateways

No matter how you get to the Net, the information on the Net itself is transmitted by several methods:

◆ Mail is moved from site to site with *Simple Mail Transport Protocol* (SMTP)

◆ Internet traffic is directed either by dedicated devices, such as Cisco System's *Internet Gateway Routing Protocol* (IGRP) routers or by computers acting as routers

When packets must leave the Internet proper to go to a non-TCP/IP network, a *gateway* computer routes the packets across the network divide, either to their destination or another gateway. Gateway computers also translate information from one native format to another. The most common of these are the mail gateways that bind the Matrix together by translating e-mail address headers and forwarding mail from one part of the Matrix to the next.

Defining the Internet/Web Relationship

"So how does the Web fit into all this?" you ask. Very easily, actually. From a structural point of view, the Web is made up of four parts, as follows:

◆ Browser

◆ Hypermedia Documents

◆ Hypertext Transfer Protocol (HTTP)

◆ Uniform Research Locator (URL)

Before we go into specifics, here are the basics. Like the Internet, the Web isn't under anyone's control. It is simply an open set of standards that work because everyone who uses it agrees to play by its rules.

The World Wide Web Consortium (W3C) guides the Web. The goal of the W3C is to develop the Web into a global information infrastructure capable of supporting commercial as well as research activities. In particular, the W3C intends to make sure that the Web doesn't fragment into incompatible sub-webs. There are other groups that shepherd the Web. Perhaps the most important of them is the same *Internet Engineering Task Force* (IETF) that establishes technical guidelines for the Internet.

The reason for this close relationship between the Internet and the Web is quite simple: The Web can't exist without the Internet. The Web runs on the Internet like cars over two bridges.

Browsers

A *browser* is the client in the Web's client-server model. A *client* program is one that you interact with. The *server*, which you don't touch, supplies information to the client as it relays your requests to it.

To get down to brass tacks, for you, a browser is your gateway to the Web. Everything that you see on the Web passes through the lens of your browser.

A browser can only show you files that it understands. Most files you'll run into will be hypermedia files written in *Hypertext Markup Language* (HTML), and any Web browser will be able to read them.

There will be some files that will completely befuddle your browser. For example, most of the images and illustrations that you'll find on the Web will either be in *Graphics Interchange Format* (GIF) or *Joint Photographics Experts Group* (JPEG). Unfortunately, most Web browsers can't show you JPEG files directly. Instead, the browser must call on another program, a viewer, to display these files to you. A *viewer* is any program that lets you access a file from your browser, even if the file contains sounds or music.

As time goes by, and browsers mature, browsers will doubtlessly integrate viewers. Some viewers are available on the Internet and can be downloaded using FTP. For now, though, be ready to add viewers, some of which are on the enclosed CD-ROM, to your browser.

A related problem is that there's no perfect way of identifying file types on the Web. Files can be plain old ASCII, HTML, GIF, JPEG, PostScript, ZIP, or one of hundreds of other formats.

In the best of all possible worlds, every file type would contain its own unique identification so that browsers and viewers would know exactly how to handle each file. Unfortunately, except for files on the Macintosh operating system, no other popular operating system supports a file identification system.

Tip   After getting your browser, one of your first jobs should be to set up your viewers. Otherwise, sure as shooting, you'll be wandering over the Web and be stopped cold in your tracks by a file you can't read.

This isn't, by the way, much help for Macintosh browser users. The only time it helps is when the file originated on a Macintosh.

Web browsers try to deal with the file type problem by using *Multipurpose Internet Mail Extensions* (MIME). MIME began as extensions to the Internet's Simple Mail Transport Protocol (SMTP) (see table 2.1), enabling mail messages to carry binary data such as programs, sounds, and pictures. Since then, it's become a de facto standard for identifying file types.

TABLE 2.1
MIME Types

MIME Types/MIME SubTypes	Extensions
application/mac-binhex40	hqx
application/msword	doc
application/pdf	pdf
application/postscript	ai, eps, ps
application/rtf	rtf

MIME Types/MIME SubTypes	Extensions
application/wordperfect5.1	May be any
application/zip	zip
audio/basic	au, snd
audio/x-aiff	aif aiff aifc
audio/x-wav	wav
image/gif	gif
image/jpeg	jpeg, jpg, jpe
image/tiff	tiff tif
image/x-portable-bitmap	pbm
image/x-portable-pixmap	ppm
image/x-xbitmap	xbm
image/x-xpixmap	xpm
text/html	html
text/plain	asc, txt
video/mpeg	mpeg, mpg, mpe
video/quicktime	qt, mov, moo
video/x-msvideo	avi

Your browser's configuration file, an .INI file in Microsoft Windows, has a section called the *mailcap* section, in which viewers are linked to file types. Check your browser's documentation for the exact syntax you'll need to get your browser to work in cooperation with your viewer.

Some of the most popular viewers for the file types that you're likely to encounter are listed in table 2.2.

TABLE 2.2
MIME Types and Viewer Programs

Type/Subtypes	Mac Viewers	Windows Viewers
application/msword	MS-Word	MS-Word
application/pdf	Acrobat	Acrobat
application/postscript	Not Needed	GhostScript
application/rtf	MS-Word	MS-Word
application/wordperfect	WordPerfect	WordPerfect
application/zip	StuffIt	PKzip
audio/basic	Sound Machine	WPlany
audio/x-aiff	Sound Machine	WPlany
audio/x-wav (wav)	Sound Machine	WPlany
image/gif	JPEGView	LView
image/jpeg	JPEGView	LView
text/html	Mosaic	Mosaic
text/plain text	Mosaic	Mosaic
video/mpeg	Sparkle	MPEGPlay
video/quicktime	Simple Player	Quick Time Video Player
video/x-msvideo	N/A	Video for Windows

When you start to get information from a server, the server *might* also send along the information's MIME type. If it doesn't, your browser will try to identify the file by its extension, but this isn't a perfect method. For example, a file with the extension 'PIC' could be a Pictor PC Paint file, a Lotus 1-2-3 chart or graphic, or a Macintosh graphics file —none of which are compatible with formats that have the same extension.

If your browser doesn't have an extension, it will fall back on its last resource: identifying the file by its source. In the case of *Gopher*, another Internet client-server database system which is discussed later, your browser will try to use the Gopher file identification system. Unfortunately, if your browser can't identify a file type, chances are that Gopher won't know either. Otherwise, files coming from an HTTP server are assumed to be HTML, and everything is assumed to be plain old ASCII.

What happens when your browser can't determine the file type? It depends on the browser and the file's particular data. Usually, you'll see a blank display or a screen full of garbage. If you try to read a file without the proper viewer, you'll probably get an error message.

Hypermedia Documents

If it weren't for hypermedia documents, we wouldn't have a Web to play on. The vast majority of Web documents are written in HTML. HTML, as you'll see, isn't without its problems for online publishers, so some authors are looking towards other hypermedia authoring languages or systems. The most important of these is Adobe's Acrobat and its *Portable Document Format* (PDF).

Before we discuss conflicting standards, let's take a closer look at HTML and PDF. HTML comes from *Standard General Markup Language* (SGML), ISO 8879h. SGML is a set of rules for creating document grammars—the rules on how a document should be formatted. The specification for the SGML rules is a *Document Type Definition* (DTD). In SGML, documents are written in ASCII text, but may represent anything from a speech to dance choreography.

HTML is a rogue SGML DTD. Although HTML looks and acts like an SGML DTD, HTML doesn't obey all SGML rules. There are efforts afoot to regularize HTML into a true SGML DTD.

HTML and its descendent, HTML+, are far more limited than SGML. In essence, HTML is a small collection of tags for formatting documents. Because of this, HTML lacks the grace and power of even an early model desktop publishing program. In short, an HTML author has only the most limited control over what his reader will see on the screen.

Another problem which is exacerbated by HTTP's limitations, is that you can't pluck a single element from an HTML document. For example, you have a book with the word *obscure* in it, and the document is set up so that the word is linked to a dictionary. If you click on the word link, what will happen—unless the word has its very own tiny HTML file—is that you would get the entire dictionary instead of the word's definition. This isn't exactly what most of us would have in mind when we think of an online dictionary.

 Note For practical purposes, HTML writers divide their text into reasonably sized portions. For example, if this book were available on the Web, it would appear in at least 53 HTML files rather then one huge HTML file.

So why do we use HTML? It's really very simple. HTML is an open standard. Anyone can use it without paying a penny for it. Although HTML editors, such as SoftQuad's HoTMetaL, make writing HTML documents easier, you can write in HTML with any ASCII editor. The HTML rules are publicly available.

Browsers and servers can both be configured to use HTML documents with absolute assurance that any server or browser that comes their way will be able to use their documents. Another important point here is that these documents can be read on any platform. Whether you're using a Macintosh, a PC, or an X-terminal, if you can display graphics, you can read HTML documents.

In response to author and publisher problems with HTML, Adobe is suggesting that their Acrobat 2.0 portable document format editor is the solution. This is no surprise because it's Adobe's intention to make PDF the standard for all electronic documents.

Although Acrobat offers writers and publishers much greater control over the look of their documents, and it's far more powerful for organizing documents and making them searchable, its problems are the reverse of HTML's. Adobe is making free PDF readers available, and the *application programming interface* (API) is an open standard, but you still need Acrobat to write PDF documents. That's not a problem with HTML. A second problem is that the free Acrobat readers only exist for systems running Unix, Windows, and System 7.*x*. Users on other platforms, from Amigas to VAXes, would be unable to read PDF documents until readers came along for these orphan systems. Finally, a PDF document carries along its own collection of fonts which means that the PDF files are bigger and take longer to transport across the Internet.

Another company, SoftQuad, is supporting the use of straight SGML for Web documents. In this same vein, SGML Open, an organization that supports SGML, is lobbying for the next version of HTML, HTML 2.0, to incorporate more of SGML.

There's probably room for multiple styles of hypermedia documents in the Web. It does mean, however, that navigating the Web will become more difficult unless your browser can handle multiple document formats.

Hypertext Transfer Protocol (HTTP)

Hypertext Transfer Protocol is a simple data transfer protocol that binds the Web together. Essentially, the protocol consists of a set of messages and replies for both servers and browsers. In HTTP, documents, files, menus, and graphics

are all treated as *object*s. HTTP relies on the *Uniform Resource Identifier* (URI), enclosed in the *Uniform Resource Locator* (URL), to identify files. As you might recall from the section on browsers, this isn't a perfect system because files can be misidentified or their type not identified at all.

Although it uses the Internet's TCP/IP network protocol, HTTP isn't limited to TCP/IP. HTTP can be implemented to run on other network protocols such as NetWare's *Internet Packet Exchange* (IPX).

HTTP runs on Web servers. Web servers are really fairly tame. A Web server is software that, upon receiving a browser request, sends the requested document back to the browser. If for some reason it can't send the file—maybe the machine that document is on is down for the count with a power failure—the server sends a simple error message. That's it. The server doesn't worry about what the document looks like or how a menu is presented to the client—that's the browser's job.

Even jobs that might appear to be the server's responsibility really aren't. For example, you might believe that getting Usenet news from a Web site is a server problem. It's not. Getting Usenet news through a Web browser is a browser implementation problem. The server might not even get into the act of passing along a request for news to the news server. Instead, the browser might use *Network News Transfer Protocol* (NNTP) directly to get at the latest hot gossip in `rec.arts.tv.soap` or, on the more serious side, the latest development in the Web in `comp.infosystems.www.providers`.

As you might have guessed by now, servers don't place much of a load on their host system. What keeps server systems busy is not the server itself, but the constant requests to send its local files and documents to other browsers.

Tip   The topic of actually setting up a server is covered later in this book. If you want to at least get started, the machine you purchase or designate to be the server should have as large a drive and as fast a processor as you can afford, with lots of memory for caching. Given a choice between a faster processor and more memory, go with the memory. More memory enables faster file input/output, which is what Web servers need to be good at. Processing power is not as important.

Servers do have their share of problems. Until recently, servers have had no way of encrypting information or authenticating users. Secure servers work by encoding sensitive information. The exact method varies from system to system, but the idea is always the same. your private information is encrypted so only the receiver can read it. The companies that make these servers are, understandably, reluctant to explain exactly how they encode such things as credit card numbers and passwords.

This issue of security might not seem very important for most users and most sites to date. However, if you conduct any form of business over the Web, this is vital.

One form of doing business on the Internet is a credit card transaction. Commercial sites must have a way of making sure that a customers credit card number is secure and not accessible to others. Such sites must also make certain that any valuable information they send out can't be read by Internet eavesdroppers or anyone not authorized to receive the information. Business-class Web servers, such as Mosaic Communications' Netsite, can handle these concerns. Freeware servers, however, do not have these capacities.

If security isn't a worry, you might be happy with one of several freeware servers. There are servers available now for almost every operating system. Some of the more important freeware Web servers, their more well-known URLs, and their operating systems are listed here:

Macintosh System 7.x

MacHTTP:

`http://www.uth.tmc.edu/mac_info/machttp_info.html`

OS/2

OS2HTTPD:

`ftp://ftp.netcom.com/pub/kfan/overview.html`

Unix

CERN httpd:

`http://info.cern.ch/hypertext/WWW/Daemon/Status.html`

NCSA httpd:

`ftp://ftp.ncsa.uiuc.edu/Web/httpd/unix/ncsa_httpd`

Windows 3.1x

NCSA httpd for Windows:

`http://www.alisa.com/win-httpd/index.htm#news`

Windows NT

HTTPS:

```
ftp://emwac.ed.ac.uk/pub/https
```

Before charging off to get a file, you'll want to use Archie to check to see if there are any other sites that carry the server you're interested in. If you're wondering why you would want to bother doing this, read the section coming up on how to use the Internet.

Uniform Resource Locators (URL)

*Uniform Resource Locator*s are the addresses of Web resources. Usually, an URL (pronounced like the name *Earl*) leads to a file, but that's not always the case. An URL can point you to a single record in a database, the front-end of an Internet program such as Gopher, or the results of a query you made using veronica or another program. URLs give you more information about your destination than just ordinary file names. Not to remind you of Freshman English, but the following figures demonstrate how to diagram the URL found in figure 2.1.

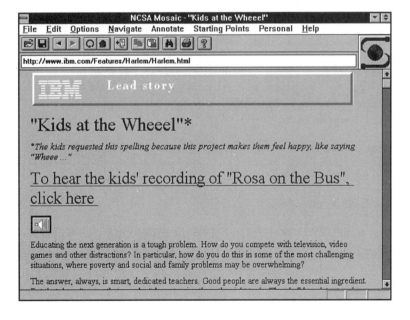

Figure 2.1

A typical Web page with its URL.

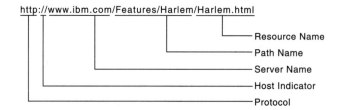

The first section (`http:`) tells you the type of resource you're connecting to. In this case, it's an HTTP resource. All the common resource types are given in table 2.2.

Note When you see *http*, this an example of how the first part of an URL actually looks. *HTTP* refers to the protocol itself.

The double slashes (`//`) indicate that you're talking to a server. If you were accessing a file on your local machine, you would see triple slashes.

Next, you have the Internet domain name and address of the Web server (`www.ibm.com`). When you have a complete address such as this, it's called a *fully qualified* domain name. The letters at the end of the address, depending on the naming style used by the site, either tells you something about who owns the server or where the server is located.

Almost all non-US sites use two-letter country identifiers. For example, `.uk` is the United Kingdom, `.ja` is Japan, and so on. In some countries, notably the UK, the order in the domain name fields are reversed from typical US practice. That is, instead of the following:

`fred@thisplace.somewhere.uk,`

the address in the UK would read:

`fred@uk.somewhere.thisplace`

Both styles are equally valid. In the States, most, but not all, sites use organizational type designators. Some sites do use geographical identifiers, in which case they usually correspond to the site's home state. A few sites mix organizational and geographical domain names. The most well known organizational identifiers are shown in table 2.3.

TABLE 2.3

Designator	Meaning
com	Commercial Site
edu	Educational Site
int	International Site
mil	Military Site
net	Internet Site #
org	Organization Site *

\# These are sites that are meant primarily to enable people connect with the Internet.

* Sites that are run by an organization like the Electronic Freedom Foundation use this designator.

Continuing on, (`/Features/Harlem/`), you see the path to your destination. Windows and/DOS users in particular should note two things.

◆ On the Web, like almost all of the Unix-based Internet, directories use forward slashes instead of back-slashes for directory names.

◆ Both upper- and lowercase letters are used and are significant, which means that 'a.txt' is not the same file as 'A.txt'

At the end of the URL is the actual resource or resource name. This time around, it's a file, and the file extension (.html) tells us that it's an HTML document. Systems that can't deal with extensions longer than three letters, such as MS-DOS or Windows, use exactly three letters instead. For example, a Windows server would list the same file with an extension of ".htm."

Most of the time, you won't have to get down and dirty with typing URLs because you can usually just click on the link. Most browsers also let you cut and paste URLs so you can grab one from a document and drop it into the URL area. Nevertheless, being able to read URLs can tell you more about the file you're bringing in, which can help you if you run into trouble with it.

Putting It All Together

When you put all the components together, the address works in the following manner. The whole network is held together by links. Your browser scampers over the strands of TCP/IP with an HTTP request to an URL. At the other end of the URL sits an HTTP server that sends the requested information back, using HTTP.

If you start with your browser and take it step by step, the first thing you will see is the loading of your default home page. This home page is the document that's been set for you to visit whenever you start the browser. Your browser is actually checking for a network connection between itself and the Internet.

Next, it takes your home page's URL and tries to find the IP address for its Internet site. A browser, like almost all client-server Internet applications, does this by checking with its known DNS. If it can't find the DNS, the program returns an error message, but this usually won't be a problem. Now, armed with the IP address of the destination site, your browser sends out an HTTP request.

If all goes well, this request is received by the server's HTTP program. Normally, HTTP programs run as daemons—programs that are always running in the background and are constantly checking to see if they need to perform their job. After the HTTP daemon receives your request, it relays it to the appropriate service.

When the service required is to fetch an HTML document, The HTTP daemon fetches the document and sends it to you using HTTP. If it's some other resource that HTTP can access directly, it still follows this routine.

HTTP works differently, however, when you call upon other Internet services such as FTP or Gopher. In these cases, HTTP acts as your go-between. For instance, when you transfer a file with HTTP, the HTTP server logs you in with a login id of 'anonymous' and uses your Internet address as a password.

This might all sound terribly complicated, but you really dont need to be concerned. When all you want to do is use the Web, you never see the layers of complexity underlying your browser. This, after all, is the idea of the Web—to make information access easy. What you do need to be concerned with, however, is how you use the tools that the browser puts at your disposal. This is discussed in the next section.

Using the Internet Properly

The tragedy of the commons is a historical concept that explains the economic collapse of medieval English villages. Because everyone in a village tended to overuse and abuse the land held in common (which is where the "commons" got its name), the village commons were ruined for everyone. What does that have to do with the Internet and the Web? Everything.

Like the commons, Internet resources are not infinite. As more and more users crowd into the Internet, the "free" resources of the Internet—from FTP sites to WWW servers—are pushed to work harder and harder. In the immediate future, it will become more difficult to get a quick response from many Web resources. Worse still, you might not be able to use some Internet resources at all because they are too busy.

In this situation, you should be patient. Many of these resources are maintained by volunteers or workers for whom your desire to ftp a file comes way behind the needs of the group that owns the server. Getting pushy will only help bring about the day when some resources are closed to the general population by their owners. Eventually, the Internet's resources will catch up with demand, but the key word is *eventually*. The biggest improvement for the Internet will be the expansion of high-speed backbones. As more of these come online, the net's overall speed will rise to meet demand. In the meantime, practice patience.

 Tip   Don't take out your frustrations on your POP's help desk staff. Most slowdown and blockage problems have nothing to do with your POP.

Learning the Basics

Almost all Internet sites that carry resources do not supply these resources as their primary job. This situation is changing, however. Many Web sites are being set up expressly for the purpose of supplying Web services to users, not to supply the Web with information. For better or for worse, most of these new sites are commercial sites, and you will more than likely experience difficulties if you call on them during normal business hours. Accessing resources will almost certainly be slower, and you're likely to find tighter restrictions on the use of the resource. Nights and weekends are the best times for Internet surfing.

Tip

A good reason for noting a resource site's location is that the closer you are to a resource, the more likely you are to have a connection take only a few jumps. The fewer links between you and another Internet computer, the better your chance of getting a clean, fast connection.

Is your session running slowly? You might want to turn off the inline images feature, using whatever method is appropriate to your browser. You won't get the pretty pictures, but you will get the text much faster.

To avoid the busy, popular sites, look around for *mirror* sites, which contain the exact same information as their primary sites. Once found, mirror sites are great for saving time and energy. which is especially important when you're going file-hunting with Mosaic. As you'll see in more detail later, Archie, the paramount Internet file-hunter, lists the first 20 or so sites that hold your file. Before cheerfully charging at the site at the top of the list, look carefully at the file's address. It's quite possible that the address will be for ".ch," Switzerland, or somewhere else far, far away. Not only will the international link be slower than a stateside connection, but you'll also be slowing down everyone else using the narrow bandwidth that's available for transcontinental links. The Internet is global, but think local whenever possible.

The Web is a delightful place filled with wonders. Walk through it with care, and it will continue to be that way for all of us.

Understanding Netiquette

What is Netiquette? *Netiquette* is online etiquette. In its most essential form, it can be summed up as the Golden Rule: Do unto others as you would have them do unto you.

Netiquette begins with respecting your fellow users. Far too many people seem to think that just because they're online, they've been given license to be rude. Wrong! Insults sting just as hard when written on cathode ray tubes as they do in person. In fact, words often sting even harder in e-mail and newsgroup messages than they do face-to-face. What's written in cold letters of electron fire cannot be softened by a light-hearted tone. On the Internet, no one can see you smile. What *you* think is funny or lighthearted might be taken in deadly earnest. Think twice, and write once—you'll be far happier for it.

Dousing the Flames

Online arguments can get quite heated, but there's never any call to resort to insults. Unlike real life, where sometimes you *can't* walk away from an argument, on the Internet, you can always walk away to cool off.

When online arguments occur in newsgroups and they don't die down, the message threads, or discussions, in which they occur are called *flames*. When things get really out of hand and arguments are breaking out in all discussions, you have a *flame fest*—something you never want to get involved with.

If you find yourself involved in a flame, try to get out of it. Most of the time, you can't win online arguments—you can only pour more fuel on the fire. Unless your idea of a good time is spending every day arguing, the best way to treat a flame is to "just say no." In other words, you could just refuse to respond to the argumentative message, or you could send one last message saying, "I have my view, you have your view, we don't agree; I'm not going to post to you on the newsgroup or the mailing list about this issue anymore." That's it.

If you can't stand hearing from someone again, check to see if your browser's newsreader has an automatic kill function, which is a setting that automatically deletes someone's message based on their Internet address, subject matter, or what have you. That way, you never have to read another word from whoever is annoying you.

Signatures

There are other points of netiquette that are important. First, when you're sending e-mail or Usenet newsgroup postings, you should attach what's called a *signature* to your message. This should be your name, your e-mail address, and perhaps a few words about yourself. What it shouldn't be is long. Resist the temptation to insert long quotes or ASCII art in each and every one of your e-mail addresses. An ideal signature is no more then three lines long. If you want to tell the world more about yourself, you can always set up a personal home page on the Web and include its URL in your signature.

Another no-no is sending a newsgroup message out asking if anyone knows where so-and-so is. Those millions of newsgroup readers *don't* know where so-and-so is and couldn't care less. Because almost all browsers have built-in links to Internet white pages services, there's no need to pester other news readers with your request.

Before posting anything to a newsgroup, you need to ask yourself what would be appropriate for the group and of interest to its members. The only way to know if what you have to say is important is, very simply, to read the newsgroup. Once you have a feel for its subject, then you can start writing. Before posting to any newsgroup, look for its *Frequently Asked Question* (FAQ) file. More on FAQs in an upcoming section.

There are several other related issues. When you reply to a message, don't copy the entire—or even most of—the message in your response. Nothing is more annoying then reading screen after screen of quoted text to see "And I agree" at the end.

You should also resist the temptation to post messages to more than one newsgroup—lest ye be flamed. Find the one newsgroup that's appropriate for your message and send it to that group alone. In the same vein, make sure that your subject line is specific and concise.

Another thing to consider is where your article is going to go. Most of the main newsgroups are distributed throughout the world. If you want to sell your computer, it's not a good idea to post it somewhere where there really aren't any potential buyers. Someone in Zambia should not have to consider whether a thousand bucks is too much for your Apple IIc when it's unrealistic for them to buy it at all. (It's about a 100 times too much, by the way.)

The trick here is to use the distribution feature. When the news system prompts you for a distribution, don't press Enter. When you hit Enter, the system usually defaults to "world," and that's not where you want your ad to go. Instead, after checking with your POP's help feature, type a more appropriate distribution. For instance, many sites have a distribution of just the state that the system is in so that your ad would only go out to people nearby.

Stop   By the way, don't think of actually advertising for a commercial business over the Usenet. It's highly frowned upon. If you want to put your business online, see the later chapters of this book on running a server and putting together a commercial Web site.

Don't Be a Cyberstalker

Many online women, or users with feminine names, get tons of unwelcome attention. All too often, they're constantly bombarded with lewd mail messages or online chat requests from jerks who know nothing about them save they might be female. Okay, guys, in two words: "Stop it!" Acting like an idiot

New Riders Publishing
INSIDE
SERIES

doesn't get you anywhere in the real world, and it doesn't get you anywhere on the Internet either. Yes, you can meet people and make friends on the Internet—even your spouse-to-be—but you don't do it by pounding on every available door. You certainly don't do it by trying to smash through someone's virtual window. No one likes a cyberstalker.

Note Some people with unconventional lifestyles or interests use the Internet as a way of getting to know others with similar interests. Actually, no matter how broad minded you are, chances are you'll find something on the Internet that will offend you. The thing to remember is that whether it's a group devoted to homosexuality, Macintosh computers, or lemurs you have no right to be rude online or to interfere with their activities. If an area or newsgroup offends you, don't go there. It's that simple.

Understanding Frequently Asked Questions (FAQs)

When you were sixteen, did you expect to be able to climb into a car and drive it away into the rush hour crush? No, you probably didn't. You might have understood how the wheel turned, how to push down the gas pedal, and how to slam on the brakes, but you hadn't yet learned the finer, more important details of driving.

Learning how to drive on the Internet highway can be a lot like your first time in a car. You might know the commands to cruise around the Web and how to mail a message to a newsgroup, but that does not mean you're an expert. To answer both basic and advanced questions, users throughout the Internet turn to FAQ files.

FAQs are exactly that: collections of questions and, more importantly, answers. Some FAQs cover the nut-and-bolt details of getting Internet tools to work. Others are about making the best possible use of Internet resources, explaining a newsgroup's theme, or how to behave in certain areas of the Internet. FAQs can tell you everything from what the "T" in James T. Kirk stands for (Tiberius), to how to find a Web server for AmigaOS.

FAQs are invaluable for learning how to be a responsible Internet driver. Whether you're using a new resource or beginning to read a new Usenet newsgroup, one of the first things you should do is look for its FAQ.

You can find FAQs in many places. Most FAQs began in Usenet newsgroups, and that's where the vast majority of them can still be found. In newsgroups,

FAQs are published on irregular schedules. Some are published as often as every week, others are updated perhaps as seldom as once a year.

Two moderated newsgroups, `alt.answers` and `news.answers`, consist entirely of FAQs and other regularly published information of interest to the entire Net community. Even if you're not interested in newsgroups, you should, at the very least, sign up for `news.answers`. If you're new to the Internet, you should also sign up for `news.newusers.questions` and `news.announce.newusers`. Here, you can find all the vital FAQs. The FAQs you can't live without are shown in the following list:

◆ A Primer On How To Work With The Usenet Community

◆ Answers To Frequently Asked Questions About The Usenet

◆ Emily Postnews Answers Your Questions About Netiquette

◆ Hints On Writing Style For Usenet

◆ FAQ: How To Find People's E-Mail Addresses

◆ FAQ: International E-Mail Accessibility

◆ How to Find The Right Place to Post

◆ Introduction to News Announcements

◆ Introduction To the `*.answers` Newsgroups

◆ Internet Services Frequently Asked Questions and Answers

◆ Rules for Posting To Usenet

◆ What is Usenet?

◆ World Wide Web Frequently Asked Questions

All of the above, save the last, can be found in the `news.answers`, `news.newusers.questions`, and `news.announce.newusers` newsgroups. The World Wide Web FAQ is found in the `comp.infosystems.www.users` and `comp.infosystems.www.providers` newsgroups. If you don't have newsgroup access, don't despair. You can go to the following URL for a HTML front-end to the FAQ.

`http://www.cis.ohio-state.edu/hypertext/faq/usenet/FAQ-List.html`

Understanding Requests for Comments (RFCs)

Requests for Comments are the hard and fast standards for the Internet. In the grand, chaotic tradition of the Net, these can range from detailed, technical descriptions of network protocols to poetry.

RFCs are often identified by their number rather than title. For instance, RFC-822 is the RFC that describes the standard format for Internet e-mail messages.

FYIs—For Your Information—are a subseries within RFCs. Normally, these are meant for developers and new users. RFCs tend not to be set in stone. None of the Web protocols have RFCs yet.

Instead, parts of the Web are documented in Internet Drafts, Internet Drafts are usually working documents of the IETF, but they don't have to be from the IETF. They are works in progress which expire six months after they're written. They can also be superseded at any time, even during their six-month life span.

Like the Web, the rules of the Internet are never static; they are always dynamic, ever-changing. RFCs can also be replaced.

The most important thing to remember about this chapter's information is that it is all background information. The Web makes it possible to use Internet resources without knowing the technical details. This, more than anything, is what makes the Web invaluable to accessing the Internet.

Usenet Mail and Newsgroups

T his chapter covers Usenet e-mail and newsgroups. Technically, these tools differ from the Internet tools in that they don't require an Internet Protocol connection to the Net. Practically speaking, e-mail and the newsgroups are the communication tools that bind the users of the Usenet and the Internet together. This chapter covers the basics of using these tools.

Introducing Usenet E-Mail

The application that makes the Internet world go around is e-mail. Unfortunately, e-mail is where Web browsers are the weakest. At this time, there are no browsers with even a decent e-mail front-end, much less a good one. This will change. In the meantime, you'll need an e-mail front-end, as well as a Web browser, to get the most from the Net.

The closest that the browsers come to e-mail is the use of *forms*, which are HyperText Markup Language (HTML) documents that can send fill-in-the-blank messages. Although you could use these HTML documents to build a true e-mail system, it would be rather cumbersome. As you can see from figure 3.1, some Net browsers will let you forward information from the Web to a mailing address.

Note   Most of the documents you'll find on the Web are written in HTML, which is very flexible. Not only can you use it to create documents, but you can use it to make e-mail forms, survey forms, and query forms for databases. For further coverage of HTML, see the chapters in Part V, "Creating Web Documents."

Figure 3.1

The Netscape Send Mail/Post News dialog box. The address lines are at the top of the box; the actual message is in the middle.

Send Mail / Post News
From: "Steven J. Vaughan-Nichols" <sjvn@access.digex.net>
Mail To: sales@netscape.com
Post Newsgroup:
Subject: This is an example
Attachment: Attach...
Of what a form looks like.
Steven
Send   Quote Document   Cancel

Forms are usually used for feedback to Webweavers and for commercial purposes. Forms, for example, might ask you for your opinion on the Web server you're visiting or for your credit-card number when you want to buy something from a Web server.

In the future, e-mail programs will be grafted into Web viewers, making it very easy for you to search the Web and send e-mail. Today, forms can only be used to send mail back to a Web-site–determined address. An e-mail program will let you send mail to anyone. For Telnet, you might use NetManage's Telnet; for FTP, Spry's Air Network File Manager (NFM), and QualComm's Eudora for e-mail.

Note For more information on the various tools introduced in the preceding paragraph, see Chapter 4. That chapter introduces you to basic Internet tools that will help you take full advantage of your on-line experience. For more information on using these tools in Web browsers, such as Mosaic, see Part III, "Using Web Clients."

A few Web browsers currently have some built-in Internet tools. Netscape, for example, has a fine Usenet newsreader, and the Cornell Law School's Cello has a good, built-in Telnet program. In the future, you'll see more applications bundled with Web browsers. Eventually, there will be Web browsers that are all-in-one Internet interfaces.

There are many things you need to know about Internet mail, however, that have nothing to do with the interface. No matter the look and feel of a program, there are many things about Internet mail that are true regardless of your application.

Working with Electronic Mail

E-mail has always been better than using browser forms. It's faster and its hardware is easier to integrate into a PC. E-mail's Achilles heel has been that it's difficult to use. If you can dial a telephone, you can learn to use a fax machine. E-mail, on the other hand, used to require expert-level computer users.

Things are changing. Today's e-mail programs make it possible for even computer novices to send messages across the hall and across the continent. The fall of fax, with its gigantic installed base, won't be quick, but, by 2001, fax machines will seem as quaint as rotary-dial phones are today.

Unfortunately, jumping on the Internet e-mail bandwagon still isn't easy. E-mail interfaces are far more friendly than they once were, but difficulties still abound. The following sections examine some of these concerns.

Mail Problems: Privacy

First, e-mail is not the US Postal Service. Large gray areas exist in the law when it comes to privacy rights and e-mail. If you're using your company or school's Internet system, the system owners may claim that they have a perfect right to peek into your electronic mailbox. Whether they do is still a matter that's being hashed out in the courts.

You might also have a problem with an individual snooping through your mail. This can be a serious threat. Your confidential mail, whether it's related to business or romance, is vulnerable to the online equivalent of a cat burglar.

Another problem is that someone might use your mail address to send bogus messages. In a recent case, someone sent out thousands of racist messages from a college professor's mail account.

 Tip   Sounds unlikely doesn't it? Maybe not. Consider that one rude electronic note to your boss, a colleague, or a client, by someone else's hand—but in your name—could prove disastrous. At the very least, turn off your Internet connection when you're not around.

To combat online Peeping Toms, you must employ some security basics. First, security starts with people. An old cracker joke, that's painfully true, is that the easiest way to break into a system is to make friends with someone in the office. (And in case you are not aware of the difference, *crackers* are hackers with criminal intent. *Hackers* hack for the heck of it.)

If you want to make sure that your secrets don't walk, you can start by making sure that your password isn't easy to guess, changing it on a regular basis, and not telling *anyone* what it is. Equally important, don't write it down on paper on or in your desk. Too many people do this, and every snoop knows it.

Another way to safeguard your privacy is to use an encryption program with your e-mail. By far the most popular of these on the Internet is Philip Zimmerman's *Pretty Good Privacy* (PGP). PGP encrypts your mail so that nobody but the intended recipient can read it.

You can also use PGP to sign your public messages with a unique digital signature. You use this option when you want to make it absolutely clear that

New Riders Publishing
INSIDE
SERIES

you are the author of a particular message. If you want to know more about PGP, look for the FAQ in the alt.security.pgp, alt.answers, or news.answers newsgroup.

Electronic Mail Problems: Addressing

Most people find e-mail addressing to be their biggest headache. For all of e-mail's virtues, getting mail from one system to another can be monstrously difficult to accomplish.

Much of this problem isn't that e-mail addressing is really that difficult. It's just that with dozens of different e-mail systems out there, it can be tricky which method is right for getting the mail from one specific system to another. Sending messages from user to user on the Internet, for instance, is pretty straightforward. On the other hand, sending a message from the friendly confines of the Internet to someone on MCI Mail or CompuServe can be more complex.

The crux of this difficulty is that the "who, how, and what" of e-mail addressing is hard to come by. Most systems hide this vital information away in so-called help files. In essence, addressing really isn't the problem; it's finding the address in the first place. Later in this chapter, you'll deal with this problem. For now, background information on mail addressing might help you get a feel for the issue.

Electronic Mail Addressing Theory

No man may be an island, but e-mail systems certainly can be. Sitting alone in splendid isolation, an e-mail system can make it mindlessly simple to send a message to another on the same system. At the same time, it can be practically impossible to send messages to someone on another system.

Most networks, however, at least attempt to let you send messages to users on other systems. These systems usually use one of two sets of protocols to accomplish this feat: RFC822 or X.400. See Chapter 2 for more on RFC basics.

RFC822 Protocol

The vast majority of e-mail users, whether they know it or not, use the RFC822 protocol. RFC822's real name, *Standard for the Format of ARPA-Internet Text Messages,* gives witness to its age. The ARPAnet was the first network of networks. The late, lamented ARPAnet bound together the systems connected to the Defense Advanced Research Project Agency (DARPA).

Today, RFC822 is still the standard of choice for the Internet, BITnet (Because It's Time Network), and most academic and scientific networks. RFC822 defines not only how messages are addressed, but their formats as well. For instance, RFC822 messages must consist of either ASCII characters, or—on BITnet—EBCDIC (Extended Binary Coded Decimal Interchange Code, an IBM mainframe binary code for representing data) characters.

RFC822 Addressing

The current concern, however, is with addressing. An RFC822 address consists of two parts: a mailbox name and a domain name. This address can be represented in many formats. For example, were I to send you a message from the Internet, my address might read:

```
sjvn@access.digex.com (Steven J. Vaughan-Nichols)
```

or

```
Steven J. Vaughan-Nichols <sjvn@access.digex.com>
```

Whichever way you type it, the important part is the line containing the *at* (@) sign. The name listing is purely an optional convenience so you'll know who's sitting behind an often cryptic address. The following address syntax, for example, works fine:

```
sjvn@access.digex.net
```

The information to the left of the at sign is the mailbox address. On many mail systems, this usually is a version of your name, or in this example, my initials.

Note Some mailbox names contain percentage signs (%) or periods, which usually means that the mailbox name is a forwarding address. When you send a note to a forwarding address, the address is expanded to its full size by the receiving machine. This is frequently the solution used within an internal network. The following address, for example, sends a message to my Lotus Notes mail account, which is connected to the Internet by the `mail.zd.ziff.com` gateway system.

```
sjvn.Notes@mail.zd.ziff.com
```

There are fundamental problems with full names, however. Not only are some mail systems unable to deal with very long names, but some—noticeably BITnet systems—can't handle mixed cases in addresses. A message sent to the hypothetical mailbox, "`Heidi_Patton@testcase.bitnet`," for instance, would generate a "nasty-gram" from the BITnet mailer daemon because it couldn't figure out, or, as we say in the business, *resolve*, the address.

 Note In an address, *mixed case* is simply the use of upper- and lowercase letters in an address element, such as username.

Another concern with mixed case addresses is that these addresses are usually treated precisely. If you sent a message to sjvn@access.digex.net, I would get it; if you sent one to Sjvn@access.digex.net, however, I would never see it because *Sjvn* is not the same thing as *sjvn* to most mailers. To prevent confusion, most users go with e-mail names, or handles, in all lowercase letters. You would be wise to adopt the same convention.

On the right side of the address is the domain address. At the extreme right, you'll find the top-level domain. Other elements in this section of the address are referred to as *subdomains*. These work just like the Internet site addresses you looked at in the last chapter.

Domain addresses normally resemble the US Postal Service system of addressing. The more specific address elements come first, and the more general ones come last. There are thousands of com sites, for instance. The next subdomain, as you move closer to the at sign, tells you more specifically where the user's e-mail account can be found. Table 3.1 shows how postal addresses are similar to RFC822 e-mail addresses:

TABLE 3.1
RFC822 Addressing

Postal Address	E-Mail	Addresses
Steven J. Vaughan-Nichols	sjvn@	sjvn@
123 Some Street	well	access.
New York, New York 21202	sf.ca.	digex.
USA	usa	net

Tip There are two exceptions to address ordering. In the United Kingdom and New Zealand, some mailers read the address in reverse. These systems expect to see something like the following:

example@uk.cambridge.csdept

Fortunately, most modern mailers can handle with either address form.

You'll notice that there can be more than one subdomain, which can represent geographic entities, as you can see from the WELL address with San Francisco, California in table 3.1. A subdomain can also represent a particular computer in a network or a department inside a larger business or organization. For example, another of my addresses reads as follows:

`sjvn@vna.digex.net`

In this case, *vna* is a single computer within the larger digex organization. This is an especially popular addressing scheme in university communities where addresses such as `test@history.mit.edu` are common.

The details of how to route your message to an Internet address are handled by a *nameserver*. This aptly named program seeks among authoritative mail servers on the system to find the most efficient address for your message. These mail servers usually yield not the route itself, but rather directions to the name-server best equipped to know how to direct your message.

In the previous example, the mail server would point your system's addressing inquiry to digex.net. Finally, digex would supply the details on how to send a message first to it and then to the vna computer. The mailer would then deliver your message as directly as possible to the target system. Normally, it does so by using the Simple Mail Transport Protocol (SMTP, described in RFC821), although other protocols can be used.

Other Addressing Formats

Not every system that uses RFC822 style addressing actually uses RFC822 within its own confines. The two most important systems that hide their own address-ing systems behind RFC822 are the UUCP networks (some of Usenet in the US and Europe's EUnet) and BITnet.

The UUCP networks use UUCP to maintain system connections rather than TCP/IP. In practical terms, this means that UUCP network internal addresses look like "test!sample!example!sjvn."

 Note TCP/IP is the networking protocol that binds the Internet together. It determines everything from how the graphics in a Web document reach your machine, to how your e-mail address looks to your Internet provider's machine. If you want to know more about these subjects, see New Riders Publishing's *Inside TCP/IP*.

What that translates into is not an address as such but an actual listing of the path that a message should take to reach sjvn at the 'example' machine. Sounds messy, doesn't it? It's worse than it sounds. A sizable percentage of a UUCP system's intersystem mail is used to update maps of the UUCP topology. These maps are then used by UUCP mailing systems to guide mail from sender to destination. Fortunately, even between UUCP sites, you can normally just use RFC822 addressing and not worry about the precarious underpinning that makes it possible.

BITnet's addressing looks much like RFC822. The only obvious difference is the use of ".bitnet" as the top level domain. BITnet addresses, however, do have quirks. Besides the aforementioned mixed-case problem, BITnet puts an eight-character limit on mailbox names.

Mailing Lists

You might occasionally bump into mailbox names with dashes (-) in them. These are almost always mailing list addresses.

A *mailing list* is simply a single mail address that corresponds to a list of other e-mail addresses. Thus, when you send a message to a mailing list, the message is automatically forwarded to all the people on the list. Mailing lists are used for everything from keeping college friends in touch with one another, to students of heraldry, to serious discussions of the C++ computer language.

If a list's subject matter sounds interesting to you, you can usually ask to be added to the list by sending a message to the RFC822 address:

```
listname-request@domain_name.system_type
```

Note that the word "request" is critical. If you send a message to the list itself, which is what would happen if the address didn't include "request," everyone on the list would get your message. Soon thereafter, you would get mail from many people on the list telling you not to bother them with your requests.

For instance, if you want to join the mailing list devoted to Traveler, a science-fiction role playing game, you'd send a message to the following address:

```
traveler-request@engrg.uwo.ca
```

Other lists use programs to manage their lists. These lists will have mailbox names such as listserv, majordomo, listproc, and mail-serv. Each of these uses a slightly different method to place you on a mailing list. To find out how to join a list, send a message to the list management program consisting simply of the word "help".

Once you're on a list, you'll automatically get all mail sent to the list, including any mail you send. Some systems also enable you to set up your own lists. Check with your Internet provider to see if it's possible. Small lists are easy to maintain and can be invaluable for keeping people with common interests in contact.

 Note The one common name with a hyphen that is not a list is MAILER-DAEMON. Whenever you get a message from MAILER-DAEMON or a similar name, it's almost always an error message from the mail-handling program, or, as they're known in the trade, a *mailer*.

X.400 Protocol

The X.400 standard was to be the universal answer to e-mail interconnectivity. Born from a desire to solve such recurring problems as binary file transfers and to produce a single, consistent addressing scheme, X.400 promised much and, to date, delivers little. Still, X.400 is the one open standard for mail interchange that has the blessing of official standards organizations such as ISO and CCITT.

 Note Binary files, like programs and word processing files, can't be sent through ordinary e-mail. There are two ways around this: Multipurpose Internet Mail Extension (MIME) and uuencode. Both translate binary files into formats that

can be sent through e-mail. MIME is easy to use, but it can only be used if you have a MIME-capable mail program and can't be used to transfer binary files at all to addresses outside the Internet proper. In contrast, uuencode is difficult to use, but can be used with most mail programs and, if your receiver has the right software, can send binary messages to users on Usenet systems. For more information, check your software documentation.

X.400 is one of the Open System Interconnection (OSI) standards family. The OSI standards are meant to make maintaining connections between heterogeneous networks easier.

X.400 Background

In this country, X.400 was given a boost when the federal government mandated its use, rather than RFC822, in government internetworking projects. Government Open Systems Interconnection Profile (GOSIP) has been the driving force behind X.400 in the United States. But because the U.S. government has recently dumped its X.400 requirements, it's likely that X.400 will start a slow decline. The government gave up on X.400 because of the popularity of RFC822.

X.400 tries to be a universal mail standard. Fax, mail, binary files, you name it—in theory there's a way to send it on X.400. In practice, it's another matter. You can't, for instance, send binary files or faxes reliably between networks.

In part, this is due to there being several differing versions of X.400. Although many vendors use the newest updates to the 1988, or "Blue Book" version, other companies are still selling systems based on the older 1984 "Red Book" standard. Other interconnection problems exist because there's enough "looseness" in the standard for incompatibilities to creep in.

X.400 Address Elements

Using X.400 addresses, as opposed to implementing X.400, is easy. X.400 addresses consist of a unique combination of originator/recipient (O/R) names. The O/R's format is "keyword:value, keyword:value." Each keyword represents an address element. There are many possible address elements. The most common of these are shown in table 3.2. Fortunately, you usually need only three to five address elements for a working address.

TABLE 3.2
X.400 Address Elements

O/R Name	Abbreviation	Examples
Administrative Management Domain	ADMD, A, PUB	MCI, TeleMail
Country	C	US
Domain-Defined Attribute	DDA	Id #
First Name	FN	Dan, Susan
Generational Qualifier	GE	Jr., Sr.
Given Name	GN	Jim, Alice
Initial	IN, I	J., K
Organization	ORG, OR, O	GSFCMail, NASA
Organization Unit	OU, UN, O	Chemistry, Editorial
Personal Name	PN	Joe User
Private Management Domain	PRMD, PVT, P, PR	Boeing, GSFC
Surname	SN	Smith, Brown
User Name	UN	sjvn, sam

Some common elements are found in every address. For instance, all X.400 addresses include an Administrative Management Domain (ADMD), which is a public mail system that serves as a message transfer system (MTS). Most of the major commercial e-mail networks—such as AT&T Mail, MCI Mail, and Telemail—support X.400 as ADMDs. Private mail systems (PRMDs)—such as GSFC or NASAMail—or LANs using cc:Mail and Sprint's Sprint Message Xchange (SMX) are attached to an ADMD.

Individuals are uniquely identified in their home mail system by a username, user number, or a combination of first name and surname. Each keyword used

must be assigned a value. A GSFC user O/R, for example, would look like the following:

```
ADMD:Telemail, PRMD:GSFC, ORG:GSFCMail, FN:Joe, SN:User.
```

Keyword and value order, unlike in the RFC822 protocol, does not matter.

Entering X.400 Addresses

What an X.400 address looks like in practice varies wildly. Some systems, such as SMX, hide the address' complexity from the user. The administrator must map from an easy-to-use username to the more complicated X.400 address. The problem with this, of course, is that it keeps X.400 from being an on-the-fly e-mail solution. In short, X.400 addresses are more trouble than they're worth.

On most systems, however, you can manually enter the address in X.400 format. The exact way that you should enter the address varies from system to system. Normally, coming from the Internet, you'll use a gateway system. If you need to send someone mail on an X.400 system, check with your Internet provider.

You should *always* pay attention to the system's punctuation requirements. Some mail systems require a ':' to separate field names and data, while others use a '='. Similarly, most systems don't distinguish white space between O/R elements. You must however, be sure to separate O/Rs with the right delimiter: a comma on some, a semicolon on others. One miskey spells the difference between sending a message to your recipient or the trash can.

Considering how common many names are, your best bet is to go with a user id. In X.400, this field can be represented as DDA:ID:, which stands for *domain defined attribute* and the *identification number.*

DDA fields are what bind X.400 to the RFC822 address formats and other non-X.400 e-mail systems. A DDA can contain the necessary mapping information to ensure that a message can be sent from or to the X.400 world into the larger e-mail universe.

For practical purposes, gateway systems are used to translate between mail systems using the different standards. An ordinary X.400 or RFC822 mail handling system is not equipped to cope with the translation burden. Because of this, some ADMDs, like MCI Mail, offer both types of mailing. In MCI Mail, you can use X.400 to send to services that primarily use X.400, and vice-versa. You're not encouraged to try to send X.400 mail to an RFC822-bound recipient.

The X.500 Directory System

Unfortunately, there is still another hurdle that e-mail must clear to be truly universal; it still is difficult to determine when you must give a more elaborate address to ensure that your message won't disappear into the electronic haze. There are times when you need to know a person's *exact* electronic address before you can send a message to them. There is a solution to this problem, X.500, but it's still a few years away.

 Note   X.500 is directory assistance for the e-mail age. The distributed X.500 DBMS will contain not only e-mail addresses, but telephone, fax, and telex numbers, as well as physical addresses.

The technical, not to mention financial and political, problems of building a network-borne master database have turned X.500 into a lovely mirage always just beyond our reach. Although some prototype X.500 installations are in place, the best way to find someone's e-mail address is still just to ask them.

In theory, you can send binary files—like programs, word processing files, and spreadsheets—across properly equipped X.400 connections. Don't believe it. Test out the connection with a sample file or two before trusting any real data to it.

Finally, if you haven't looked at your system's manuals or online help, do so before venturing into intersystem e-mailing. Besides keeping you informed about addressing quirks, you'll probably discover a host of shortcuts to make intersystem e-mailing easier. For instance, many X.400 and RFC822 sites have ways of condensing long addresses, or even lists of addresses, into single, short addresses. On X.400 systems these methods are often called *nicknames*. RFC822 systems usually call these methods *aliases*. Regardless of the name, the idea is always the same: turning a long, unmanageable address into a short, sweet address.

The Internet relies on RFC822 for its intersystem mailing. You can use Internet gateway systems to send messages on X.400-based systems. Following is an example of how this looks from the user's perspective:

```
/C=US/ADMD=TELEMAIL/PRMD=NASAMAIL/O=NASA/PN=JOE.USER/@x400.msfc.nasa.gov
```

In this case, `x400.msfc.nasa.gov` is a gateway between NASA's X.400 systems and the Internet. Besides being too long to memorize easily, there's a more serious, hidden problem with the address; although Internet mailers won't have any trouble with this address, UUCP-based mailers will likely choke on it. The reason for this is that for security purposes, these mailers won't pass along something that looks like a command. And those of you who know Unix are already ahead of this: that's exactly what an address with a leading "/" looks like.

The upshot of all this is that Internet systems can use X.400 addresses, with the right gateway, but many Usenet sites won't be able to contact these addresses. Users stuck in this situation will need to search for other solutions to this communication problem. For specific details on how to move messages from the Internet to X.400 mail users, see the FAQs in the `comp.protocols.iso.x400` newsgroup.

Using Mail Basics

There are too many Internet e-mail interfaces to go into much detail on how to use them. Nevertheless, here are the basics for two of the basic Internet mail programs: mail and elm. Check your manual or your Internet provider's help desk for more information.

Using mail and elm

Almost all Unix systems give you access to the rather spartan Unix program, *mail*. Mail is about as friendly as a punch in the face, but once you've learned the commands, you can live with it.

Many systems, even if they don't support anything fancier, will have *elm*, which is short for elementary mail. Elm supplies you with an easy-to-use, menu-driven interface, which can be seen in figure 3.2. If you've never run elm at your command prompt, give it a try; you may just be pleasantly surprised at what you find there.

Figure 3.2

There are fancier mail interfaces than elm, but it's a good e-mail program for average users.

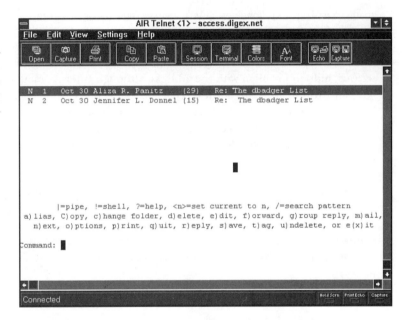

For specific instructions on how to use either mail, elm, or other Internet programs, simply type the following line at your Internet provider system's command line prompt:

```
man program_name
```

This presents you with an online manual for the command. The information provided here is meant for Unix "power users," so be prepared to spend some time studying the manual online. Better still, print the manual pages with your communication program's print option so you can reference it as you start working with the program.

EMACS and vi Text Editors

A wide variety of text editors can work with the mail interfaces. If you're working with a system that gives you a native Unix interface to the Internet, your choice of editors will almost certainly include EMACS and vi. If that's the case, read your Internet provider's documentation on which editor to use

before starting with either one. EMACS is very powerful, but is very complicated. On the other hand, vi has a bare minimum of commands to learn, but its
learning curve is very steep because there's no online help available while it is
running.

Note If you have a more advanced editor as part of your front-end program, use
it rather then vi or EMACS. Although both native Unix editors are very
powerful, they are much harder for average users to learn when compared
to the simple graphical editors of some interfaces such as PipeLine for
Windows or NetCom's NetCruiser.

Troubleshooting Sending Mail

When sending mail, there are several problems that often trip up users. If you
avoid these common mistakes, you'll be on your way to using intersystem e-mail
successfully.

◆ **Why did my e-mail come out as gibberish?** The first thing to
remember is to send only ASCII text. Word processing files might look
like ASCII to you, but they're loaded with formatting codes, which means
they'll be turned into gibberish if you send them as is. If you need to send
a document, first save it into an ASCII format.

You can send binary files, like graphics, programs, and spreadsheets, over
Internet mail, but you can't send them as ordinary mail. That's why trying
to send a WordPerfect document as the text of your message will lead
only to garbage on the other end.

◆ **How do I send binary files?** To send a binary file, you need to use
Multipurpose Internet Mail Extensions (MIME) to send it as an attachment to
your message. MIME is a set of additions to the SMTP format that enables
it to carry digital data. To use MIME, you need a mail interface that
supports it. This brings you to the next topic: picking a mail interface.

◆ **What's a good program for use with binary files?** Your best
move for a mail front-end/editor combination might be QualComm's PC
Eudora or Macintosh Eudora, which come in freeware and commercial
versions at the following address:

`ftp://ftp.qualcomm.com/`

◆ **Is there a good way to find others' e-mail addresses?** Of
course, before you can send someone a message, you need to know their

address. How do you find out what someone's address is? Truly, the best way is simply to ask them or to have them send you a message to your address. Although there is a network Yellow Pages, it's an address book for systems and network connections, not users.

There are several white pages systems available on the Internet. Many Web browsers, including Mosaic and Netscape, have built-in addresses for some of the more popular white pages services. Unfortunately, none of these come close to having complete listings of Internet addresses. Nevertheless, something is still better than nothing. They also are not updated often, so they can be out-of-date.

Figure 3.3

Internet white pages can be useful, such as this searchable one from InterNIC, but they don't have complete listings, and their records are quickly outdated.

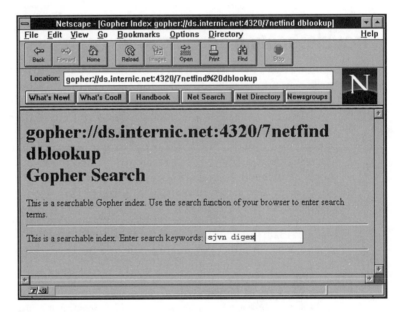

After you've gotten the hang of Net addresses, they're easy to use. You can also use Internet mail to send mail to users on other networks or online services. For the address format for several popular online services, see table 3.3.

TABLE 3.3
Online Service Address Formats

Service Name	Address Format
America Online	user_name@aol.com

Service Name	Address Format
AT&T Mail	user_name@attmail.com
BIX	user_name@bix.com
CompuServe	user_number@compuserve.com *
Delphi	user_name@delphi.com
eWorld	user_name@eworld.com
GEnie	user_name@genie.geis.com
Interchange	user_name@interchange.com
MCI Mail	user_number@mcimail.com
Prodigy	user_number@prodigy.com

*To send mail to CIS users, use a period instead of a comma in the user number.

One final note: Even when leaving the Internet, address case is still important. For example, fred.com is not the same thing as Fred.com. Although some *mailers*—programs that do the grunt work of forwarding mail from one system to another—can cope with mixed-case addresses, older ones still crash at the very thought. You can make the mailer's job easier and ensure that your message will arrive where you want it to go by making sure that your addresses are in the right case.

Getting a Mail Interface

What do you do if you don't want to deal with Unix's character-based applications, and you don't have a native e-mail interface program? You get an e-mail program, of course.

There are several things you should look for in a mail program.

◆ **First, it should be capable of using aliases.** No one wants to type ladeda@somewhere.or.the.other.com every time they want to send a message. A good mail program also has an address book so you can keep all your aliases and addresses in one place. The best mail programs also let you store more than one name to an alias so you can easily send mail to a group of business associates or friends.

◆ **Another important feature is the ability to place your mail in various folders.** If you're on a mailing list or two, it won't take long for your mail to get too unwieldy for a single virtual mailbox. In figure 3.4, for example, you can see that Spry's Air Mail program lets you set up a complete system of mail folders.

Figure 3.4

User-configurable folders in Spry's Air Mail, part of their Internet in a Box package.

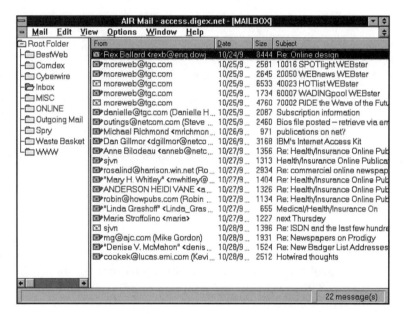

◆ **Be binary-file capable.** Your mail program should also be capable of sending binary attachments with MIME. E-mail is a great way of getting vital documents to people far away.

◆ **Your e-mail should keep working in the background.** If you're like the author, you'll want a mail program that can run in the background and gather your mail automatically on a timed schedule. This way, you always get your mail within minutes of its arrival without having to strike a single key to get it.

◆ **Get a mail sorter.** A good mail program is capable of letting you sort your mail in a variety of ways. Some people like their mail sorted by date order in last-in, first-out order, while others prefer their mail to be listed alphabetically by address.

◆ **Get a mail filter.** The best mail programs filter your mail for you. Say, for instance, that you don't want to read any more junk mail from an annoying correspondent. An excellent mail reader can set up a "twit" filter that will automatically dump these messages into the bit-bucket. An absolutely top-of-the-line mail program could also be set to sort your mail. You could, for example, set your mail program to place mail from your boss in a business folder while putting notes from your significant other in a romance folder.

◆ **E-mail bells and whistles.** There are other bits of chrome you might want for your mail program. One popular option is to have the mail program attach your signature to your messages. Although you're looking for a mail program, you might want to use QualComm's Eudora 1.4. This freeware program, included on this book's accompanying CD-ROM, doesn't do everything, but it comes pretty darn close. Versions of Eudora exist for both the Macintosh and Windows systems. As you can see in figure 3.5, Eudora also is an attractive program.

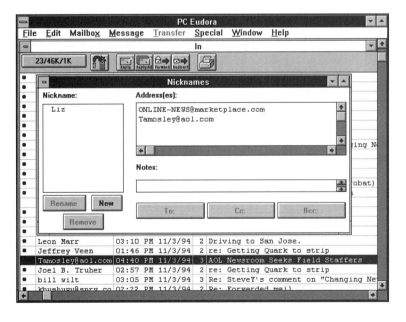

Figure 3.5

Eudora might be freeware, but it includes several advanced features such as mail folders, signature files, and binary transfer capacity.

Working with Usenet News

Now that you're grounded in e-mail, it's time to move on to Usenet news. Like mail, you'll be using an editor to write messages to people. With newsgroups, however, you'll be sending to large groups of people, not just an individual or the folks on a mailing list.

Usenet newsgroups are collections of messages on a single topic, or as closely related as anything can be in the formalized anarchy known as the Internet. For instance, whether you're a fan of the Irish singer Enya, the xBase programming languages, or (like me) both, there's a newsgroup for you.

 Note   Usenet groups, along with RFC822 mail, define the Usenet. Any system that gives users access to newsgroups is part of the Usenet. Any particular system, however, will not carry all Usenet newsgroups. The defining point is not how many—it's whether the system lets you access Usenet news at all.

With thousands of topics, tens of thousands of networked computers, and hundreds of thousands of readers, it doesn't take much to turn Usenet reading into drudgery rather than a joy. There's invaluable information hidden away in Net news; the problem is finding it.

Besides pure volume, Usenet newsgroups have other problems that make them difficult to read. The most common of these are flaming and spamming. *Flaming* occurs when people start arguing online, and the argument goes from disagreement to insults. These online battles can go on forever. The best solution to a flame war is to walk away.

Spamming is when someone sends the same message to numerous newsgroups. It is barely tolerable when the same message is sent to related newsgroups, but it's totally unacceptable when the same message, or a slight variation, is sent to unrelated groups. In two words: Don't spam. Send your message only to the most appropriate newsgroup.

This is where character-based news readers like trn and nn come in. *trn* and *nn* make it possible to wade through the Net news swamp and get only the information you want, instead of spending hours online becoming an Internet zombie. The following section takes a look at trn.

trn Newsreader

trn is a popular Usenet reader that runs on most Internet systems. You don't need a copy of this program. Instead, you simply run it from your provider's command line. If the news program doesn't come up, try running rn (trn's older and less sophisticated brother) or nn (another newsreader that works like trn).

When you run trn, the first thing that happens is that trn searches for your .newsrc file, which contains a list of all available newsgroups and your current subscription status. If trn doesn't find a .newsrc, it makes one for you. The program then makes sure your listing is up to date; if not, trn automatically updates it. You don't need to worry about the process damaging your .newsrc because trn automatically backs up the file when the program starts working.

Note All Unix hidden files have names that start with a period. You can find these files in a Unix directory by running the command *ls -l*.

Due to the sheer volume of news (megabytes a day), many sites don't get all available newsgroups. Even so, you'll find on most systems that you have been subscribed to every available newsgroup. This can be more than a little daunting when you realize just how many newsgroups are around. At last count, the Usenet is closing in on 10,000 newsgroups.

Tip Don't fall prey to the temptation of subscribing to interesting but non-essential newsgroups. You could spend your entire life reading and writing to newsgroups, but only if you want to give up the rest of your life. There's an old Usenet saying that once you start reading news, you can add a year to the time you'll spend in school.

trn Command Levels and Commands

If all goes well, and 99 percent of the time it will, you'll be at the top command level. Most users' confusion stems from trn's use of three different command levels. Which set you're using depends on where you are in reading the news. The order, starting at the top, goes as follows:

Newsgroup selection layer

Article selection layer

Paging layer

The commands are basically the same on each level, and they have about the same effect. The difference is in the scope of how these commands are applied. If you search with the command /fan/h on the newsgroup level, for instance, you're looking for newsgroup names with the word "fan" in them. On the other hand, the same command at the article selection level finds articles, not newsgroups, with fan in the header.

No matter what level you're on, the one command you'll always need to know is 'h' for help. You'll solve more of your trn problems with online help than you will from reading this entire chapter. If you look at figure 3.6, you can see why you might want to keep your right pointer finger near the 'h' key.

Figure 3.6

Quick! Do you know what to do here? If you haven't a clue, you're in good company because learning to use trn takes time.

```
┌────────────────────────────────────────────────────────────────────┐
│ ═                 AIR Telnet <1> - access.digex.net            ▼ ▲ │
│  File  Edit  View  Settings  Help                                   │
│ alt.online-service              130 articles                        │
│ a Tony DeVito        2  E-World                                      │
│   Gopher Nut                                                        │
│ b phil garfinkel     1  Free Med Help/Support BBS                   │
│ d Ron Martin         1  Request N/G: alt.online-service.INN(ImagiNation)│
│ e Janny Corien       2  comparison of services and prices           │
│   Michelle Tessler                                                  │
│ f Dean Hughson       3  Online ways to get a PHD                    │
│   E P Associates                                                    │
│   E P Associates                                                    │
│ g kat                2  Tech/Internet T-Shirts For Sale!            │
│   Unidexter                                                         │
│ i Oracle9999         1  >AOL has gone down for sure                 │
│ j maxwells@delphi.   1  catalog newsletter                          │
│ l Larry Johnson      1  E mail                                      │
│ o J Annamalai        1  Need help regarding Internet provider       │
│ r R. BENCE           1  Internet Investment Opportunity             │
│ s+David O'Donnell    2  PROPOSAL: alt.online-service.marvel         │
│   Jonathan Grobe                                                    │
│ t AGHILI,K           1  Need help Desperately                       │
│ -- Select threads (date order) -- 84% [>Z] --                       │
│                                                                     │
│ Connected                                          Hold Scrn Print Echo Capture │
│ Winsock WWW/FTP-Servers MAILBOX                                     │
└────────────────────────────────────────────────────────────────────┘
```

Note   You might have noticed that I've not said anything about pressing Enter after these commands. This isn't because I'm taking it as a given. It's because trn operates in what's called *cbreak mode*. The important thing to remember about cbreak is that except for commands that take an argument, such as g alt.dolphin.group, which tells trn to go to dolphin_newsgroup you shouldn't press Enter after a command. All that will happen is trn will run the command and do whatever an unadorned return does at that level. Normally, a return moves you down a level, or, if you're already at the page level, it displays the current message's next line. That's not harmful, but it can be confusing.

y Command

If you want to dive in and start reading, just press **y** or the spacebar, and you're on your way. The trn defaults are normally set to start with the earliest messages, place them in thread order, and then work forward from the oldest to the newest ones. This sounds trivial, and it is designed for messages on systems like Ziffnet with a centralized computer. On the Net, however, messages are maintained on hundreds of computers across the world. Keeping messages straight is a big job, but it's one that you as a user don't have to worry about.

= Command

It's one thing to catch up with the latest messages in a low-traffic group such as comp.compression which is about data compression, and another thing entirely to try to read the hundreds of messages that daily pour through the misc.jobs newsgroup. The right way to handle this situation is to use the = command which lists the subject heading for each message. At this point, you've dropped into the article selection layer of the trn cake.

Ctrl+N Command

When you see a message that sounds interesting, just enter its message number and start reading the newsgroup containing that message. If the message strikes your fancy, you can read follow-up messages by using the Ctrl+N command which scans the rest of the current newsgroup for other messages with the same subject. Some messages, however, are cross-posted to several groups. You might, for instance, have a question about using a Solaris-based program, such as FrameMaker, and post your query to both comp.sys.sun.apps and comp.unix.solaris. In this case, Ctrl+N won't find any related articles in cross-referenced news groups.

Unlike many trn commands, Ctrl+N, becomes the default once you've used it. Because there's little point in jumping from subject to subject without rhyme or reason, most users are content with this. Just keep in mind that other trn commands don't work this way.

n Command

At any level you're on, if you don't want to read a group, select an article, or read the rest of an article, you can always move on with the n command. The newsgroups or messages you leave unread will stay marked as unread, which means that the next time you use trn, they will still be waiting for you. The one proviso to this is that nobody, anywhere, has room to store newsgroups online, so messages (or *articles* as they're called in trn) "scroll" off the system into data heaven at a system-determined time.

c Command

If you want to mark a group as having been read, but not actually go to the trouble of reading the messages, use the c command at any level to mark all messages in the current newsgroup accordingly. For more drastic situations, you can use the Ctrl+K command.

Ctrl+K Command and EDITOR

Ctrl+K puts you into a text editor used to edit a file that contains one-line records. The exact editor depends on the value of the system variable EDITOR. If EDITOR isn't set to anything, chances are you're going to end up in the vi editor. The file you would be editing is the kill file, normally located in your News directory. Each record in this file consists of a pattern search in the following format:

`/whatever/j`

Trn takes this to mean that you want it to search the currently subscribed news groups and mark every message with the pattern "whatever" in the header as having been read. This makes it unnecessary for you to deal with messages that you have no interest in.

Say, for example, that you're subscribed to `comp.unix.sysv386`, the font of information about PC Unix, but you have no interest in reading about SCO Unix. The solution is to make an entry in the form given above in the kill file. Unless the subject sneaks in through what's called *topic drift* (the tendency for any online conversation to ramble away from its subject heading), you won't need to read about SCO Unix again.

K Command

Another way of handling message overload on the article selection level is to use the K command, which automatically enters the current article's subject in the "terminate-with-extreme-prejudice" file without any need for manual editing.

$ and 1 Commands

There are other ways of moving around the newsgroups besides pattern searching and moving sequentially through the groups. Say, for instance, you want to get to the last of the newsgroups you read in a hurry. The quick way to do that is to type **$**, which brings you to the bottom of your subscription list. Conversely, to get to the top of the list, you merely type **1**, and there you are.

The same commands also work at the article selection level, except you'll be moving to the last or first unread articles. Similarly, you can move about in trn at either level, as shown in table 3.4.

TABLE 3.4
trn Commands

Command	Newsgroup Level	Article Level
p	Go to previous newsgroup with unread mail	Go to previous unread article
P	Go to previous newsgroup	Go to previous article
n	Go to next newsgroup with unread mail	Go to next unread article
N	Go to next newsgroup	Go to next article

g and l Commands

Another useful command is the g command on the newsgroup level. To use this effectively, first use either a pattern search or the l command, which works like a pattern search except it looks through not only your .newsrc file, but the system's master .newsrc as well. For instance, l pc would find all newsgroups with "pc" in their title.

Armed with this information, you can then subscribe to a newsgroup with the 'g' command. This would look like g alt.internet.services. This example group is an information clearinghouse for questions about advanced Internet use, such as logging into remote databases and services. If you want to explore other IP programs besides Web browsers, check out alt.internet.services.

Pnews News Writer

Okay, you're all set; you've subscribed to the newsgroups you want to see, and you've been reading them for a while. You're finally ready to stop lurking and ask a question of (or better still, provide an answer for) the collected intelligence (that's an oxymoron some days) of Usenet. Here are the techie details of how to do that in trn.

To post a new message to a newsgroup, trn is *not* the program you use. When the programmers said trn stood for "threaded read news," that's exactly what they meant. Instead you use a news writer, Pnews or PostNews, to post original messages.

Pnews is about as easy to use as a program can get. Before using it, however, you should first read the newsgroup thoroughly. Posting a message to the wrong newsgroup wastes not only your time, but the time of every system connected to the network and many news readers.

When you invoke pnews, it asks for the newsgroup names. After that, you are given a choice of distribution areas for the message. These range from your local service to the world. A message about your problems with your e-mail account probably doesn't need to be seen by the whole world, though.

Next, you are asked for a title and subject for your message. You should be concise and to the point. A title like "Web Trouble" doesn't tell anyone anything, whereas "Help: Netscape 1.1 and Large JPEG Images" is much more likely to get you a helpful response.

After this, you are asked if you really want to send the message. If you're not sure, don't bother to continue. Finally, you are launched into your word processor, where you actually write your message. When finished, save and exit as usual, and the program posts your message to your chosen Usenet newsgroup.

Another reason to hold off asking questions, even if you're bursting at the seams, is that your questions may have already been answered. Remember that many questions on a given subject are answered in its FAQ file. Always check the newsgroup's FAQ before posting.

s Command

You can save these or other important articles for future reference by using the s command. s takes a file-name argument. Without one, s saves to a file named by the variable SAVENAME.

If the information you want to save is broken up into several articles, you can append to a single file by simply saving again (using s) to the same file name. Unless set otherwise, the resulting file is placed in your Internet system's current directory.

R and r Commands

Answering newsgroups' messages can be done from within trn with two sets of commands. R and r reply to an article over Net mail services. The distinction between them is that R includes the text of the message you're replying to. In either case, you use your default text processor to write the actual reply.

F and f Commands

The other set of response commands, F and f, work similarly but your message will be posted in the newsgroup. Remember, anything you say can and will be read by perhaps millions of Net news readers. Scary thought, isn't it?

Getting a News Interface

When you go shopping for a news interface, there are several features you should look for. First, the interface must be capable of threading messages. In *threading*, messages are presented to you in conversational order. For example, if you read a conversation between John and Liz about the Web, you would see their responses one after another as their "conversation" continues.

Some news programs only display messages in chronological order, which is something entirely different. In this arrangement, you see the messages only in the order that they were written. This means you would find it much harder to read Web discussions because dozens of other messages might be interposed between the messages you want to read.

The chronological order method is used by most Web browsers with any news-reading capabilities. As you can see in figure 3.7, one Web browser, Netscape, can handle threaded news discussions.

Figure 3.7

*Netscape promises
to be a great
newsreader.*

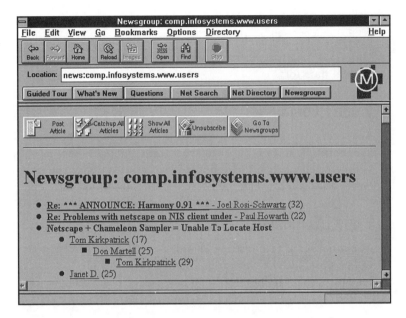

If you want a more sophisticated newsreader, you might want to get a
newsreader program such as NetManage's NEWTNews or Spry's AIRNews. The
difference between these programs and the character-based Unix programs is
that they make it much easier to manage news. The key to enjoying newsgroups
is managing the incredible flood of information that roars through them.

Newsgroup articles, for example, often have what's called a header. In the
header, you'll find useful information, such as the subject of the message; and
some not-so-useful information, such as the number of lines in the message.
NEWTNews gives you the option of deep-sixing this information so that you
never have to see it.

AIRNews, in its turn, lets you organize your newsgroups into newsgroup
sections. That way, you can have your set of newsgroups for fun, when you have
the time for them, and another set for business, which you always turn your
attention to.

In the future, what you'll likely want is a Web browser has full-featured
newsgroup support. For today, you'll need to make do with character-based
interfaces, Netscape's first good stab at newsgroups, or a dedicated newsgroup
program.

Introducing Internet Tools

As you'll see when you start using Mosaic, Netscape, and other Web browsers (see Part 3 for specific instructions on using Mosaic), chances are you'll need to work directly with other Internet tools at some time as well. The day will come when a single universal front-end to the Internet enables you to view Web pages, download files via FTP, read newsgroup articles, and telnet to other sites, but that day isn't here yet. Mosaic, Netscape, and other browsers try to shield you from the complexity of other useful Internet tools, but they're only partly successful. So, for today, it is still helpful to know the basics of programs such as Telnet, FTP, Archie, Gopher, Veronica, and WAIS (Wide Area Information Server).

You can use most of these utilities in two ways. You can either use them in character mode on a remote Internet system or run them as applications on your system. Both ways are covered in this chapter.

Using Telnet

Telnet provides direct communication with other computer systems through a TCP/IP network. In essence, Telnet enables you to log in on other computers on the network.

Although Telnet has been around on the Internet for several years and it is not as graphical as the WWW, you should not feel intimidated by it. In fact, the type of information that is available through Telnet is remarkable. You don't have to be a rocket scientist to recognize Telnet's possibilities. If you're running a complex query on a monster Sybase database but must work on something else as well, you can simply telnet to an idle system and start anew there.

Using Character-Based Telnet

Telnet is spiffy enough when you're working with your own in-house systems, but it also has no distance barriers. If you're logged in to a system in San Francisco, you can telnet into one in Boston as easily as you can to an Internet system in the cubicle right next to you.

Another way to work with Telnet is to use it to run a remote program. If, for example, you're working with a character-based interface and want to visit the Web, but you don't have a local Web browser, you can telnet to a system with a character-based browser and use that. Normally, you do this by logging in as www and, if you're asked for a password, using your mail ID as the password.

To connect to another system using Telnet, simply type **telnet remote.host.name port** at the Unix command prompt. On most systems, the "port" is optional because the Telnet daemon automatically uses a default port (usually port 23). As you can see from figure 4.1, Telnet works like a charm even when you don't specify a port.

For the name of the system you're trying to contact, you usually use the system's host name, such as `access.digex.net`; `princeton.edu`; or `well.st.ca.us`. If that doesn't work, you might need to specify the host's Internet Protocol (IP) address. For instance, 192.132.20.3 is the IP address of `well.sf.ca.us` (a site otherwise known as the Well online system).

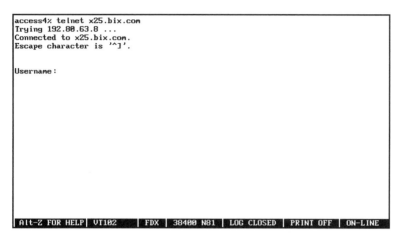

```
access4% telnet x25.bix.com
Trying 192.80.63.8 ...
Connected to x25.bix.com.
Escape character is '^]'.

Username:
```

```
Alt-Z FOR HELP| VT102    | FDX | 38400 N81 | LOG CLOSED | PRINT OFF | ON-LINE
```

Figure 4.1

Telnet may be a plain-jane program, but you can't beat it for working on multiple computers.

The main reason you sometimes have to spell out the IP address is that your system's host files won't have that particular site listed. Another reason might be that your system doesn't have permission to use the stretch of virtual highway on which your target system resides. The most common such case used to be when systems attached to the more commercialized parts of the Internet road tried to reach systems that were on the noncommercial NSFnet. Today, the reason is likely to be that you're trying to get from a Commercial Internet Exchange (CIX) part of the network to a non-CIX Internet site.

Some system administrators also restrict their users' capabilities to use Telnet. If you're having trouble, check with your system administrator before you assume that something is wrong. You simply may not have permission to use Telnet or FTP.

After you've logged in to another system, proceed just as though you were logged in to the computer next door. Everything you type feeds directly into the remote system. If you need to issue a command to the Telnet program, precede the command with the *escape character*, which usually is the Control key and the right bracket key pressed at the same time (shown as Ctrl+]). To quit Telnet and return to your local system, you press **Ctrl+]**.

In addition to using a command line to tell Telnet to open a session across the network, you can run Telnet interactively. To do this, just type **telnet**. Then, to start a session, type **open host_name**, at the `telnet>` prompt.

Depending on the Unix shell you're using and the Telnet implementation, there are other ways to open a session across the network. With some versions of Telnet, for instance, you can connect simultaneously to several systems.

Using Local Telnet Clients

Many companies make Windows and Macintosh Telnet clients. In addition, one Web browser, Cello, already has a Telnet program (see fig. 4.2).

Figure 4.2

Cello's Telnet session is not perfect, but comes ready to go with this popular Web browser.

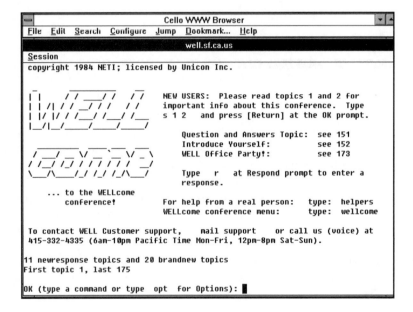

If you don't already have a Telnet program, and you have an IP connection with the Internet, look for the following Telnet features:

- ◆ VT-100 Terminal Support
- ◆ 3270 Terminal Support
- ◆ Adjustable Scroll Buffer
- ◆ Capture Data to File
- ◆ Capture Data to Printer
- ◆ Enable Cut/Paste Operations

◆ Telnet Address Book

◆ Multiple Telnet Sessions

◆ Multiple Terminal Type Support

Note   I'm still looking for the perfect Telnet program. Among the better commercial
programs, I favor Spry's Telnet (see fig. 4.3), bundled in AIR Series 3.0 and
Internet in a Box, and NetManage's Telnet, bundled in their Chameleon
product line. Trumpet Software's shareware Telnet program, included in the
companion CD-ROM, also is a good Telnet client. Mac users should check
out InterCon Systems' TCP/Connect II.

Figure 4.3

*Another
advantage of
Telnet programs
is that you can
use them to
connect with
commercial online
services such as
Ziffnet on
CompuServe.*

Using FTP

Many systems around the world keep file archives (usually in directories named
"pub") for FTP access. The name *file transfer protocol* (FTP) says it all. FTP
enables you to download files from remote systems to your local system over
the network. As with Telnet, this can be done as easily from across the country
as from across the room. FTP is the tool you need to get copies of these files.

Files available for anonymous ftp range from the complete C code for X Window to bawdy song collections to the GNU EMACS editor.

Unlike Telnet, which is often really useful only when you have full-fledged accounts on remote systems, ftp comes in handy even if you just have a single account because many sites allow what's called anonymous ftp. In *anonymous ftp*, you gain access to remote files by logging in with the name "anonymous." Common netiquette is then to use your full mail address as your password. (For example, I'd use sjvn@access.digex.net as my password.)

Using Character-Based FTP

To help you understand FTP a little better, this section shows you some basics of how to use FTP on a character-based interface. The simplest way to use FTP is to enter **ftp** *remote.host.name*.

After you type in the preceding command, you are prompted for a login and password. At this point, you should use the process described earlier to get in. Once in the system, you'll find that you're in the pub (or the local equivalent) directory. From this directory, you can use the ls command to list available files. (Some systems use the dir command for the same purpose.)

On some FTP servers, a file named ls -lR holds this information. In this case, you can use cat, a Unix command that displays data, to read this file of file listings. Another good move is to use ftp to transfer the file to your home page, where you can examine it at your leisure. If additional subdirectories exist, you can investigate them by using the cd (change directories) command. In any case, as you can tell from figure 4.4, ftp has a Spartan interface.

Figure 4.4

The raw character interface for FTP is rather barren.

```
access4% ftp
ftp> open rtfm.mit.edu
Connected to BLOOM-PICAYUNE.MIT.EDU.
220 rtfm ftpd (wu-2.4(24) with built-in ls); bugs to ftp-bugs@rtfm.mit.edu
Name (rtfm.mit.edu:sjvn): anonymous
331 Guest login ok, send your complete e-mail address as password.
Password:
230 Guest login ok, access restrictions apply.
ftp> ls
200 PORT command successful.




Alt-Z FOR HELP| VT102   | FDX | 38400 N81 | LOG CLOSED | PRINT OFF | ON-LINE
```

The command you'll get to know best is get. From the user's perspective, the way the get command works is similar to the way Unix's cp and MS-DOS' copy commands work. Instead of copying a file locally, get copies a file from the remote system to your local Internet system.

Tip In both Telnet and FTP, the question mark is your friend; Unix commands might be cryptic, but help is usually just a keystroke away.

In many ways, FTP's get command is similar to the asynchronous file-transfer protocols of dial-up connections such as X-modem, Z-modem, and Kermit. The critical difference is that FTP works only across network connections. Although it's possible to use FTP over an ordinary modem connection, using Serial Line Internet Protocol (SLIP) or Point to Point Protocol (PPP), these are examples of networking across phone lines rather than the asynchronous connections offered by services such as CompuServe and GEnie.

To use FTP to copy a file, you might use a command such as get nifty.file at the ftp> prompt. For binary files, such as programs or compressed files, you should first enter the binary command at the ftp prompt. To copy the compressed file spiffy.file.zip onto your local system successfully, for example, you would type the following:

```
ftp> binary
ftp> get spiffy.file.zip
```

If you don't use this format, your file will be a garbled mess. By default, FTP sends ASCII files, not binary files. More time has been wasted and tears shed over this simple mistake than any other in the ftp command collection. Some ftp programs also refer to binary mode as *image mode*; in such cases, you can use *image* as a synonym for *binary*.

There's also a chance that you'll find the odd FTP site still running the TOPS-20 operating system. In such cases, you need to set ftp to tenex mode by entering **tenex** at the ftp command line. If this confuses your FTP program, use the command line type **L 8** instead.

Stop You've heard the stories: "Virus causes computer to die a hideous death." There's some truth to these tales. Although you'll more likely get a virus from pirated commercial software than from the Internet's file collections, always use a virus detector to check files you acquire by using FTP.

At some Internet sites, you can get several files simultaneously by using the `mget` command. To download any files with names that begin with `neat.file`, for example, type **`mget neat.file.*`** at the ftp prompt, as in the following line:

```
ftp> mget neat.file.*
```

would ftp down any files with names beginning with `neat.file`. Most FTP sites that support `mget` recognize the standard wildcard characters: the asterisk (*) means any string of characters and the question mark (?) means any single character. Puzzled? The character string `*cat` matches strings such as `alley-cat` and `tomcat`. On the other paw, `??cat` matches neither `alley-cat` nor `tomcat`, but does match `a cat`.

Thanks to sites that permit anonymous FTP logins, anyone with Internet access can download files—if that person knows where to find the files. You can find a comprehensive, if not complete, list of FTP sites in *New Riders' Official Internet Yellow Pages, Second Edition.*

Using Local FTP Clients

Unlike Telnet, you'll really want to have an FTP client. Most Web browsers can transparently ftp files. That's the good news. The bad news is that most browsers are still a bit clumsy at finding and retrieving FTP files. For today, stand-alone FTP programs are still valuable.

Not only is raw FTP somewhat difficult to use, but, unless you're on a direct TCP/IP connection on the Internet, you'll need to move your FTP files to your local PC in a separate operation. Who has enough time to move a file twice? Fortunately, good Windows and Macintosh FTP clients are available that enable you to download files in an easy-to-use manner. The following are some of the most important features to look for in an FTP client:

◆ Automatic Name Translation with User Control

◆ Drag-and-Drop File Copying

◆ File Sorting by Name, Extension, and Type

◆ FTP Site Address Book

◆ Multiple File Retrieval

If you're using an FTP client with DOS/Windows or some OS/2 setups, you should be aware of one problem. If you're using the file allocation table (FAT) file system, you're limited to file names with eight character names and three character extensions. When you bring down a file with a name that exceeds these limits (such as `muchtoolonganamebutthereisworse`), the operating system—unable to deal with such a long name—truncates the name into something it can manage (the eight-character `muchtool`, in this example), which can turn into a problem when you get several files with names that don't change until after the first eight characters. What would happen in such a case is that each file overwrites the last file with the same name as each is downloaded.

Two of the better FTP programs for Windows are Spry's Network File Manager (see fig. 4.5) and John Junod's shareware WS_FTP. On the Mac side of the house, there's Peter Lewis' shareware program, Anarchie (which also is the only decent native Archie client for any PC platform).

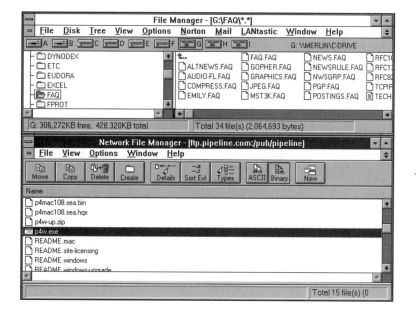

Figure 4.5

In stark contrast to the raw FTP interface, Spry's Network File Manager makes transporting files using FTP as easy as copying files from one directory to another.

File Types

No one who goes file hunting is spared the headache of dealing with a bewildering array of data compression and archive types. This section describes the basic file types you can expect to find and how to open them.

A long time ago, when 300 bps modems were the grooviest things around, people had trouble trading files with each other online. One problem was that moving any file at 300 bps took too long. Another difficulty was that then, as now, many programs required multiple files, and there was no way to package them neatly into one file. Data compression solved the first problem. To settle the matter of bundling files together, people came up with the idea of file archives, or libraries.

An important point that's often missed in the PC/Macintosh world is that these are two problems with two solutions. This is because most of the data compression programs on thcsc platforms do both jobs. On the Internet, however, some file collections are compressed by one program and then tied into one file by another program.

Finally, another file type is used primarily to make shipping binary files through e-mail possible. For FTP users, the most important file of this type is the hqx file, a Macintosh file type known as *binhex*.

 Note   A binhex file is a binary file used to ship programs from place to place.

Data is compressed in two ways. The first method, used for text and binary files, is called *lossless* compression because not a single bit of information is lost. Graphics files, on the other hand, often are compressed with *lossy* programs that help shrink a file by actually getting rid of some data. Both methods work. You simply need to be sure that you use the appropriate type of program whenever you compress a file. A lossy program would make hash of a binary file, whereas a lossless compression program might have little effect on the size of a graphics file. Graphics and JPEG files are the most popular lossy compression file types.

To deal with binary and ASCII compressed files, you need the appropriate software. Table 4.1 shows the different compression file extensions, as well as the corresponding programs and the operating systems. Compressed graphics are covered later in the chapter.

TABLE 4.1
Data Compression/Archives File Types

Compression/ Archive Extension	Program	OS
.arc	arc, pkarc	MS-DOS
	arc	Unix
	arcmac	Mac
.arj	arj	MS-DOS
	unarj	Unix
	unarj	Mac
.cpt	None	MS-DOS
	Compact Pro	Mac
	macutil-20b1	Unix
.exe	None	MS-DOS ^
	None	Mac
	None	Unix
.gz or gzip	gzip-msdos	MSDOS
	macgzip	Mac
	gzip	Unix
.hqx	xbin23	MS-DOS
	binhex	Mac
	mcvert	Unix
.lha or .lzh	lharc	MS-DOS
	maclha2	Mac
	lharc	Unix

continues

TABLE 4.1, CONTINUED
Data Compression/Archives File Types

Compression/ Archive Extension	Program	OS
.pak	pak251	MS-DOS
	None	Mac
	None	Unix
.sea	None	MS-DOS
	None	Mac ^
	None	Unix
.shar*	None	MS-DOS
	None	Mac
	None	Unix ^
.sit	unsit	MS-DOS
	Stuffit	Mac
	unsit	Unix
.tar	tarread	MS-DOS
	tar-30.hqx	Mac
	None	Unix #
.tar.Z, .tar-z, or taz	None	MS-DOS %
	None	Mac %
	None	Unix %
.tar.gz, tar.z, or .tgz	None	MS-DOS &
	None	Mac &
	None	Unix &

Compression/ Archive Extension	Program	OS
.zip	PKzip	MS-DOS
	Unzip	Mac
	zip	Unix
.zoo	zoo	MS-DOS
	maczoo	Mac
	zoo	Unix
.Z	comp	MS-DOS
	macompress	Mac
	compress	Unix

`*.shar` files: type **sh foo.shar** to open these files in Unix.

^ MS-DOS EXE compressed files, Macintosh sea files, and Unix shar archived files can be dangerous. To extract these files, you simply run the program. Most of the time, they merely distribute the files enclosed within them. By design or accident, however, these three file types might run in a way that's hazardous to your system. Always be especially careful when dealing with these files. The one exception to this rule of thumb is that data-compression utilities themselves are often boxed up in these self-extracting files. Even then, be certain to scan the file with a virus detector and run the compressed file in an empty directory.

tar files: opened in Unix with the command line: tar xvf foo.tar.

%. tar.Z files have been compressed with the Unix compress program and bundled together with the tar archiving program. To open tar.Z files in Unix, type **zcat file.tar.Z ¦ tar xvf**; if you have GNU tar, type **tar xvzf file.tar.Z** instead. Mac and MS-DOS/Windows users must first uncompress the program, see the .Z entity, and then unarchive it by using the tar programs.

&tar.gz files: to extract these files you must use two programs (as is true with tar.Z files). Run the command **gzip -cd file.tar.gz ¦ tar xvf** for straight Unix. If you're using GNU tar, use **tar xvzf file.tar.gz** instead. For other operating systems, first pop the file open with the utility you use for .gz files, then untar the file.

Compression programs are in a constant state of flux. To get the latest, most accurate information, get a copy of the comp.compression newsgroup's FAQ (frequently asked questions) file.

When you have a file and its appropriate utility, make sure you have the newest available version of the archiving program. PKzip versions older then 2.04G, for instance, can't deal with compressed files made by 2.04 GB.

The important compressed-graphics file formats are listed in table 4.2.

TABLE 4.2
Graphics Compression File Types

File Extension	Full Name
GIF	Graphics Image Format
JPEG	Joint Photographic Experts Group
MPEG	Moving Pictures Experts Group
PCX	(None)
TIFF	Tagged Image File Format

Graphics users don't have to run through the same steps as other users to decompress a file. Graphics-file viewers always include the appropriate decompression tools and make them transparent to the user. The graphics viewers included on the companion CD-ROM should see you clear.

Using Archie

You can use FTP to search through a public directory for files, but if the files you're looking for aren't in the directory, hunting for them won't do you much good. Worse still, looking for a specific file can be like looking for a needle in a haystack. That's where Archie comes in (see fig. 4.6).

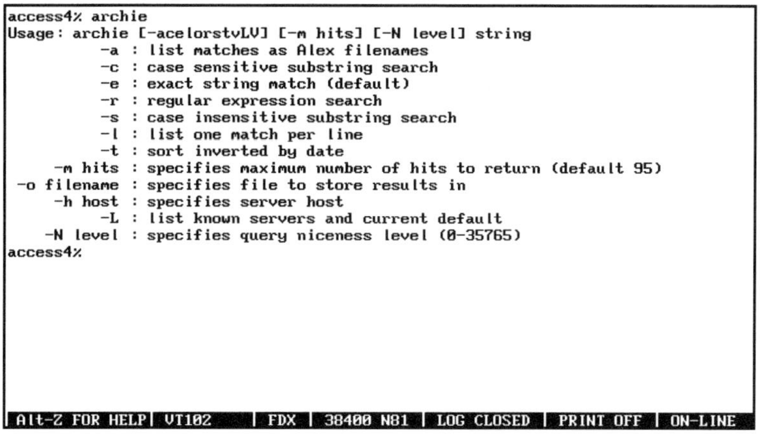

```
access4% archie
Usage: archie [-acelorstvLU] [-m hits] [-N level] string
              -a : list matches as Alex filenames
              -c : case sensitive substring search
              -e : exact string match (default)
              -r : regular expression search
              -s : case insensitive substring search
              -l : list one match per line
              -t : sort inverted by date
          -m hits : specifies maximum number of hits to return (default 95)
       -o filename : specifies file to store results in
          -h host : specifies server host
              -L : list known servers and current default
          -N level : specifies query niceness level (0-35765)
access4%
```
```
 Alt-Z FOR HELP  VT102        FDX   38400 N81   LOG CLOSED   PRINT OFF   ON-LINE 
```

Figure 4.6

One way to get started with an archie program is to enter the archie *command without any parameters.*

The "virtual reality" of cyberpunk science fiction is a tantalizing, yet treacherous world in which a single misstep can lead to a disaster. This mysterious maze has much in common with the Internet today. Fortunately for all would-be network explorers, a faithful guide—Archie—can lead you through the deepest, darkest network nodes. *Archie* is a client-server database program that does the hard work of finding and indexing files throughout the Internet. Instead of tracking down elusive files by blundering blindly from one FTP site to another, you can contact an archie site and use archie to find your elusive quarry.

Only a few Archie sites are scattered across the world (see table 4.3). Although you can use any archie server, use the one for your geographical area. In this way, you not only reduce online time but also, by spreading out the load, are less likely to overburden the service.

TABLE 4.3
Worldwide Archie Server Sites

Internet Name	Area Served
archie.ans.net	Eastern US
archie.rutgers.edu	Eastern US
archie.sura.net	Eastern US

continues

TABLE 4.3, CONTINUED
Worldwide Archie Server Sites

Internet Name	Area Served
archie.unl.edu	Western US
archie.mcgill.ca	Canada
archie.funet.fi	Europe
archie.au	Australia
archie.doc.ic.ac.uk	Great Britain/Ireland
archie.wide.ad.jp	Japan
archie.ncu.edu.tw	Taiwan

Using Archie through Telnet

You can use Archie in one of three ways. The most popular way is to use Telnet to contact the closest Internet site with a copy of archie. To perform a search, enter `telnet archie.sura.net`. The other two ways are through mail and by Gopher.

Then, when you have a connection, log in as archie. You are not asked for a password. The next thing you see is the archie> prompt. From now on, you'll be talking to the Archie program rather than to the operating system (as you normally do with telnet).

At the archie> prompt, enter the show command to display all of Archie's settings. You can ignore most of these settings, but two you might care about are pager and search.

Tip   You might want to use one Archie command: niceness. When you're 'nice'—that is, when you set the Archie niceness level to a high number—your Archie hunt processes more slowly then it normally would. This is the best way to run low-priority searches because while you get your results eventually, more urgent requests can go first.

Pager tells Archie whether you want the program to dump its results to the screen, or whether, after Archie has filled the screen, you want Archie to wait until you press Enter or the spacebar. If you're unable to scroll your screen back to catch something that just disappeared off the top of your display, set the pager on by typing **set pager** and pressing Enter.

Search defines how Archie goes about looking for your entry. Different Archies have different search defaults. Some default to case-sensitive searches, for example, whereas others don't care whether the search string is all upper- or lowercase.

If Archie comes back with a search value of "exact," you know that it's currently set to find exact case matches only (a search for CHess, for instance, would not find Chess). That probably isn't what you want. To set this parameter to your liking, type the following command at the `archie>` prompt:

```
set search exact
```

In addition to exact, you also can choose regex, sub, and subcase. When you use regex, the search string works with wildcards, such as the asterisk and question mark.

If you search using sub, your expedition finds any program names that contain your search phrase, regardless of case. Now, for instance, a search with "CH" uncovers Chess and CHESS, and digs up files with titles that include words such as patches or PATCHES. Although sub is very powerful, it can deluge you with *false hits*—files that contain your search string but have nothing to do with what you're actually looking for. Subcase works much like sub, except that sub is case sensitive.

Regardless of which method or methods you use, the most important thing to do before you begin an Archie hunt is decide, up-front, how you want archie to look for a file. You'll save not only your own time, but everyone's time.

Now you're finally ready to start a search. Simply enter **prog** *search_string* at the `archie>` prompt. Archie proceeds to give you a running score of how many hits it has found and the percentage of the database that has been searched. After that, archie reports on the files that meet your specifications by presenting you with a list, in a multiline format, that describes the files' locations. At the top of each record is the site name for the system with the file. This is followed by the file's directory and, finally, the file's name, along with some size and date information.

You might be able to use archie with a local Archie client. In this case, you would just run Archie from your system's command line. This is the best way to use Archie because it saves wear and tear on the always-too-busy Internet.

Using Archie by Mail

Even without Telnet or a local Archie, you're not out of the hunt. Archie can be used by mail. If you're not in a rush to find a file, using Archie by mail lessens the load on the Archie servers. To perform such a search, send a message to an Archie site, addressed to Archie, as in the following example:

```
archie@archie.rutgers.edu
```

Enter Archie commands in the text of the message. A sample search message might look like the following:

```
path you@your.mail.address
prog what_ever_it_is_you're_looking_for
quit
```

That's it. The first line tells the system where to send its findings. Archie can read your from line and would normally send its results there, but it's safer to use the path command. From lines can be misleading.

The prog line gives Archie its search orders. The default for mail searches is regex, but you can reset it by using the normal commands.

Quit does exactly what it sounds like: It lets the Archie server know that there are no additional commands. Because many people have .signature files, which are automatically added to the end of their messages, using quit is a good idea. Otherwise, you might end up with utterly garbled answers from a very confused Archie, trying to make sense of your name.

When you have a file's name and location, you can use anonymous FTP to retrieve the file. Suppose, however, that the FTP site is always busy (which, with the crush of people on the Internet, is not uncommon at the more popular FTP servers). If you find yourself in this situation, you can use mail to obtain files. This process, although it takes longer than the process of using FTP directly to get a file, is much less frustrating than banging your head against the wall of an always busy FTP site.

There are three ways of using mail to obtain files. Some servers are set up to respond specifically to mail requests for files. Others, especially on BITnet, have listserv servers that use a different method for file requests but, like direct mail requesters, are limited to local files.

In a mail request, you get a file by sending a message to the site with your request in the subject line. Such a request might resemble the following:

```
To: mail-server@some_machine.somewhere.edu
Subject: send /directory/file_name
```

And that's all there is to it. You put absolutely nothing in the text part of the message.

For a BITnet system, your message would look like this:

```
To: listserv@an_ibm_mainframe.somewhere.com
```

You would write get *file_name* *file_type* in the message body. BITnet runs on IBM VM systems, so providing the file type is mandatory.

Generally more useful are ftpmail application gateways, the most popular of which is ftpmail@decwrl.dec.com. Unfortunately, just to make things confusing, this method uses FTP syntax rather than anything that looks like the first two methods. A sample follows:

```
To: ftpmail@decwrl.dec.com
Subject: File Hunt
connect system.somewhere.com
chdir pub/file_location
get file
quit
```

Your subject is actually irrelevant, but it can help you remember what that large, mysterious-looking letter in your mailbox is. The important thing is that you enter ftp commands, one command per line, in the text.

 Stop Take your time and double-check your FTP request. One typo will ruin your attempt.

Presuming that everything goes as it should, you can expect to see your file in anywhere from a few hours to a few days. Speaking of getting it right, you can always get more help by sending the single command, help, to any of the mail servers or to Archie.

Unlike other programs, there are no PC-based Archie clients. The reason for this is that you can access Archie's searching capacity through another Internet tool: Gopher. Mac users, however, might want to use Peter Lewis' outstanding Anarchie for their Archie and FTP work.

Using Gopher

For many users, getting the most out of the Internet isn't easy. Even Archie helps with only one specific area of Net use: finding and downloading files using FTP. Probably more than a few of you have been saying, "The net is neat, but why does finding information have to be so difficult?" Well, these days, with the right software, it doesn't have to be so difficult. Two user-friendly programs—Gopher and WAIS—make using the Internet's resources easier than ever.

Before this dynamic duo showed up, some of the net's most valuable resources were available only to a lucky few in the know. The most important of these resources are the online databases, which provide public access to everything from library catalogs to technical documentation collections. In the past, few people knew how to access these databases. Now, with Gopher at your side, you can liberate this information for your own uses.

Unlike FTP and Archie, Gopher is a general-purpose information tool. Gopher builds on the foundation of FTP, Archie, and other data sources to erect an easy-to-use, menu-driven interface to the net's file and informational resources.

Gopher was born at the University of Minnesota, home of the Golden Gophers. Its name is a bad pun on the name of the University's sports teams and the program's purpose—to "go for" something—hence, the data Gopher!

Unlike Archie, which relies on a centralized Archie database of files, which can be moved using FTP, Gopher doesn't rely on any particular data collection. To use the analogy of a library, Archie is like a card catalog dedicated to publicly available files. Gopher, on the other hand, is like a librarian. Gopher doesn't know where a particular item is, but it does know how to search for hidden information. In computing terms, *Gopher* is a distributed client-server database system.

The best thing about Gopher is that you don't have to have a clue about where some file or bit of information is. IP addresses, file formats, domain names—forget them. With Gopher, you don't need to know Internet esoterica. Gopher does the dirty work. In some ways, Gopher is much more powerful for finding information than even the WWW. All you have to do is pose the questions.

To get Gopher started, you should have a Gopher client on your system. If you don't, you can telnet your way to a site with a publicly accessible Gopher client in the same way you can access Archie. Because the Web browser programs do a top-notch job of using Gopher front ends, you might be perfectly happy using your browser to access Gopher's resources.

When you contact a Gopher server, you're presented with a set of menus. You then select the choice that looks like the best path to your informational destination. You could, for instance, decide that you want to find a library with a copy of the newest Tom Clancy thriller.

In the pre-Gopher days, you did this by telnetting to every computerized library catalog you could think of. Yeah, right—as though everyone knows IP addresses or domain names for automated card catalogs. Even after you found your library and its access point, you then faced the problem of how to log in to the system. Some just let you right in, some required a user id of "guest," others, "anonymous," and so on. If you made it that far, you then had to figure out that system's particular idiosyncrasies. No wonder that, until recently, access to Internet information has been a mystic art practiced only by net gurus.

With Gopher, however, the Gopher server takes care of all this. When you activate your Gopher client, it starts looking for information by first checking for local resources, usually a Gopher server, or by connecting with a preset Gopher service.

Gopher clients often come with a hardwired Gopher server that they look to first for information. This can, and often should, be changed to access the closest available Gopher server. Table 4.4 lists the most important general-purpose Gopher sites (of the more than 5,000 public Gopher servers).

TABLE 4.4
Worldwide Gopher Server Sites

Name	Area Served
consultant.micro.umn.edu	North America
ux1.cso.uiuc.edu	North America
panda.uiowa.edu	North America
gopher.msu.edu	North America

continues

TABLE 4.4, CONTINUED
Worldwide Gopher Server Sites

Name	Area Served
gopher.ebone.net	Europe
gopher.sunet.se	Scandinavia
info.anu.edu.au	Australia
tolten.puc.cl	South America
ecnet.ec	South America
gan.ncc.go.jp	Japan

When you and your client go to the server with a request, the server works on figuring out where to find the information. All you know, sitting at your desk, is that a few seconds after you start your inquiry, Gopher presents you with menu choices that take you closer to your destination.

These choices come in two forms: resources and directories. A *directory*, marked with a slash (/) at the end of its menu item, indicates that choosing this item will lead you to a submenu. *Resources*, as the name indicates, are actual sources of information. As you can tell from figure 4.7, telling them apart is easy. Browsers tend to mark these files in different ways, usually with different colors or icons. In either case, it should be quite clear which is which.

Figure 4.7

Even in plain, old ASCII, Gopher menus are easy to use.

```
              Internet Gopher Information Client v2.0.16

                 Home Gopher server: gopher.tc.umn.edu

 -->   1.  Information About Gopher/
       2.  Computer Information/
       3.  Discussion Groups/
       4.  Fun & Games/
       5.  Internet file server (ftp) sites/
       6.  Libraries/
       7.  News/
       8.  Other Gopher and Information Servers/
       9.  Phone Books/
      10.  Search Gopher Titles at the University of Minnesota <?>
      11.  Search lots of places at the University of Minnesota  <?>
      12.  University of Minnesota Campus Information/




Press ? for Help, q to Quit                                  Page: 1/1
Alt-Z FOR HELP| VT102     | FDX | 38400 N81 | LOG CLOSED | PRINT OFF | ON-LINE
```

New Riders Publishing
INSIDE
SERIES

From the menus, you proceed to narrow down your choices until you can reach an appropriate resource. In the search for Clancy's novel, for example, you can probably ignore card catalogs in libraries thousands of miles away.

Eventually, you end up with what you and Gopher agree is probably a system or program that can provide the information or file you need. At this point, you and Gopher go-fer for it.

When you access a resource, Gopher takes over the job of logging in to the computer and service. Gopher also shields you from the local system. No matter what you're logged in to, you use Gopher's search interface, not the remote systems. If you would rather not use the ASCII form or the browser, you can use a PC Gopher client. Figure 4.8, for example, shows NetManage's Windows Gopher client.

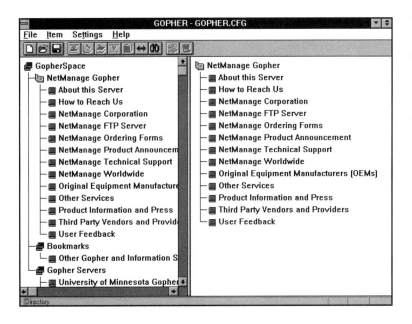

Figure 4.8

For a fancier interface than your browser or an ASCII version, you can use a graphical gopher interface.

Gopher has one great advantage: You never have to learn the ins and outs of a database you might only use once. Gopher's approach has two mirror-image problems. The first is that, although Gopher can perform fairly complicated searches, you might not know whether the software that Gopher is talking to can handle such complexity.

Archie, for example, can search for a single word only. Or you could try searching for, say, "Pentium and PowerPC." Some systems take that as meaning that you want to know about books or articles that contain both words (Pentium and PowerPC). Other systems assume that you want the precise phrase "Pentium and PowerPC." With Gopher you'll only know that your searches are going wrong.

The flip side of this problem is that Gopher defaults to the lowest common denominator while searching. The resource you're accessing might be capable of very precise searches, but you are limited to Gopher's search capacities. Gopher can't tell the difference between lowercase and uppercase, for instance. Although this might not be a big deal on occasional data hunts, big-time information hunters will want to throw Gopher out the window. (At least they'll feel that way until they remember how much work they've done hunting for information without Gopher.)

 Note Another thing you should keep in mind with Gopher is that sometimes Gopher will dig up an information resource that you can't access. The most common example are the news services. Although AP and Reuters news feeds are available at many academic sites, they are inaccessible from many commercial sites—no matter what the Gopher menu says.

One more problem is that Gopher often does not fully identify the resource it's trying to access. Gopher's object types are vague enough to allow room for error. As you can see from table 4.5, Gopher's object definition is quite loose and can lead to a real binary mess when you try to access an item your system can't cope with.

TABLE 4.5
Gopher Object Types

Gopher Object ID	Object Definition
0	Text file
1	Directory
2	CSO (qi) phone-book server
3	Error
4	Binhexed Macintosh file

Gopher Object ID	Object Definition
5	DOS binary archive (ARC, ARJ, ZIP, etc.)
6	Unencoded file
7	Index (often a gopher or WAIS menu)
8	Telnet session
9	Binary file
g	GIF
h	HTML
I	Image type
i	Inline text
M	MIME
s	Sound
T	TN3270 session
+	Redundant or previous gopher server

The next generation of gopher servers, using Gopher+, will clarify these matters by having expanded object-type definitions.

Problems Associated with Gopher Servers

Keep in mind that all Gopher servers are not the same. Some servers might be much stronger in certain areas than they are in others because gopher servers tend to work best when connected to local resources. The original Gopher server at the University of Minnesota, for example, is filled with information resources from that school. One of the neater things about Gopher, however, is that you're not limited to a single server. You can use Gopher to hunt for other Gopher servers that might give you access to information that's more your speed.

Flaws and all, you'll never mistake Gopher for such powerful, single-purpose, online information retrieval engines as Ziffnet's Computer Database Plus. But Gopher does have its good points. Because Gopher brings within reach the almost limitless information resources of the Internet, it is an invaluable tool for any netrunner. As you'll see in the next section, Gopher's not alone in making the Internet a better place for information hunters.

Using Veronica

Veronica is one of the most useful Internet information-hunting tools around. Unfortunately, because it's also the one that has the fewest servers, reaching a Veronica server can be very difficult.

Veronica stands for Very Easy Rodent-Oriented Netwide Index to Computerized Archives. (As you might have guessed, Internet programmers have a warped sense of humor.)

Veronica acts as a server to an index of Gopher objects. This index, which is put together by Veronica in its data-gathering mode, contains information about Gopher objects from almost every publicly accessible Gopher site in the world. Because most Veronica servers update their databases every week or two, their information is usually quite current.

When you access Veronica by using Gopher, a Gopher client, or a World Wide Web browser, you can use keywords to search for information. The advantage of this approach over Gopher is clear. With Gopher, you might have a good idea that a particular Gopher server's menus can lead you to the information you're seeking, but you're unlikely to be sure of this. With Veronica, you cut out the Gopher middleman and go straight to the Gopher resource you want…if Veronica can find it.

Veronica Searches

Most Veronica servers offer two basic types of searches. In the first variant, a keyword-by-title search, you're searching all Gopher resources for your target. The problem with this method is that it takes a long time and can yield an overwhelming number of results.

If you're searching by using common terms, such as "Usenet" and "Web," you're better off using the second type of search: directory titles. With this method, in which you search only the titles of directories, the search is faster and the results are more manageable than with the first method. Narrowing down the hunt takes some effort on your part, of course, because you'll have to open the new-found directories to see exactly what you've lain your virtual hands on.

Most Gopher sites are indexed by Veronica. Because there are so few Veronica servers and so many Veronica users, however, Veronica servers are often

completely swamped. Thus, you're frequently unable to get to Veronica. As always, you should try to use the site closest to you. Don't be surprised, though, if you have to go farther afield. Table 4.6 is a list of Veronica sites.

TABLE 4.6
Worldwide Veronica Server Sites

Name	Area Served
gopher.umanitoba.ca:2347/7	North America
gopher.unipi.it:2347/7	Europe
info.psi.net:2347/7	North America
serra.unipi.it:2347/7	Europe
veronica.nysernet.org:2347/7	North America
veronica.uni-koeln.de:2347/7	Europe
veronica.scs.unr.edu:2347/7	North America *
veronica.sunet.se:2347/7	Scandinavia
wisteria.cnidr.org:2347/7	North America

* The easiest way to get to veronica servers is to use the following line: `gopher://veronica.scs.unr.edu:70/11/veronica`. This command takes you to a gopher menu of veronica sites.

After you fight your way into Veronica, you're ready to start your data hunt. Maybe. Sometimes the only way you find out that the Veronica server is too busy for your search is after you've entered it. Presuming that doesn't happen, the easiest way to begin is to search on a single term. To do this, simply type a single word and press Enter.

After your search is completed, you'll see a Gopher-menu-style display of the Gopher objects, files, directories, and so on, that Veronica has found for you. Then you can simply select any of them to be transported to the actual object.

Veronica is capable of far more than simple one-term searches. The latest version of the program supports Boolean searches in which, for example, you can search by using a hunt phrase, such as "Web AND Mosaic," and dig up only references containing both words. Actually, Veronica is smart enough that you don't even need to use the word "AND." Simply by placing two terms in the search box, you cause Veronica to search for a document containing both terms.

Veronica also supports the NOT and OR operators. (Note that these Boolean terms are capitalized here for emphasis only. Veronica doesn't care whether search or Boolean terms are upper- or lowercase or a mixture of both.) Unfortunately, not all Veronica servers can run these operators. The only way to make sure is to give it a try and see what happens.

Let's assume that your server can work with NOT and OR, and take a closer look at the way this works. Say, for example, that you want to find only items about the Web, not about Mosaic. You would use the search phrase "Web not Mosaic." You could also search for "Web or Mosaic," which would flood your display with items.

Actually, you would get only the first 200 successful searches, or *hits*. To get more hits, you use the -m flag. Say, for example, that you want to search for "frog and prince." To get all the references containing both terms, set the -m flag by itself, as in the following example:

```
frog and prince -m
```

More commonly, the -m flag is used with a number to increase or decrease the number of possible hits.

To use Veronica to make complex queries, use parentheses, as in the following example:

```
web not (Mosaic or Cello)
```

This search finds only items with the word "web" in them, but with no mention of Mosaic or Cello.

Finally, Veronica also has limited support for the use of the asterisk (*) wild-card. In Veronica, you can use the asterisk only at the end of a search phrase (rather than anywhere in the search term). You might, for example, try the following search:

```
NetWa* and TCP/IP
```

Most of the results from this search would be items that include both the terms NetWare and TCP/IP. Thanks to the asterisk, you don't have to spell out the entire word. The asterisk is also useful when you're not sure in what sense

someone might be using a word. The search term wor*, for example, would find references to both work and working.

Tip   If you want to know more about how to use Veronica, look for its FAQ and the "How to Compose Veronica Queries" document at the veronica.scs.unr.edu gopher site.

Using WAIS

WAIS (pronounced wayz) works something like Gopher in that it's a tool for finding information and resources on the Internet. With Gopher, however, you need to point it in a certain direction using its menus. Although Gopher is very easy to use, having an idea of where to find something before you go looking for it is helpful. And Veronica's often too busy to help.

In any case, Gopher and Veronica operate at a *high level of information granularity* (a fancy way of saying that both work at the title level, and neither can help you find a particular word or idea in a document or object). WAIS, on the other hand, works with the words *inside* documents. Clearly, WAIS can't do everything. It's not capable of searching willy-nilly through public directories throughout the Internet universe. (This is fortunate because if it could, it would gobble up network bandwidth like peanuts.)

Instead, WAIS relies on indexed data collections, or *libraries*. These libraries are file collections that consist mostly of informational material. If molecular biology is your meat and drink, for example, several journals on the subject are available online through WAIS libraries. Presently, more than 300 free libraries exist. These data collections generally have been indexed and made available by volunteers at academic sites. Commercial WAIS libraries, such as the Dow Jones Information Service, also are available.

Tip   So how do you find out where these WAIS libraries are? You don't have to. Thinking Machines maintains a directory of servers that all WAIS clients can find. That's the good news. The bad news is that Thinking Machines has run into financial storms, and the future of this service is in question.

Because most libraries are free, WAIS data can be very spotty. Computer science subjects are well covered, for example, but if you want to know something about antique cars, you're out of luck—for now. WAIS libraries keep springing up at a surprising rate, and there's no telling what might be available by the time you read this. During a recent data hunt, I was bemused to discover a WAIS library of technical documentation on the Musical Instrument Digital Interface (MIDI).

WAIS itself is simple to use. The common interface, SWAIS (see fig. 4.9), is a simple character display in which you type your search term. To use SWAIS, you either use a local SWAIS or telnet to a site with a SWAIS client and type `swais`.

Figure 4.9

You can't tell a program by its interface. SWAIS's boring character display hides immense database power.

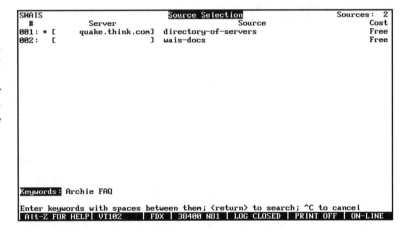

```
SWAIS                          Source Selection                      Sources:  2
  #              Server                        Source                       Cost
001: * [      quake.think.com]  directory-of-servers                        Free
002:   [                     ]  wais-docs                                    Free




Keywords: Archie FAQ
Enter keywords with spaces between them; <return> to search; ^C to cancel
| Alt-Z FOR HELP| VT102     |  FDX | 38400 N81 | LOG CLOSED | PRINT OFF | ON-LINE
```

You could instruct WAIS to search all available libraries, but that would be a waste of time. Searching for information about chess in the WAIS library devoted to the Simpsons (yes, the Fox network cartoon), for example, won't do you any good.

Armed with a library's list, you pick out the most likely targets, and WAIS begins to narrow down its search. If all goes well, you'll be looking at the documents concerning your subject in a matter of seconds.

Note Then again, maybe you won't. WAIS searching doesn't recognize any of the Boolean search terms. In other words, although you can search for references to "Cyrix and 486," you won't get just documents that contain both terms. Instead, WAIS uses an internal weighing system that measures the value of each term for the search, including the "and." Your result would be a table, at the top of which are the most relevant articles (measured by WAIS's 1 to 1,000 score, where higher is the higher priority). WAIS might possibly tag an article that contains many occurrences of "and" and "486"

as more important than a short document with "Cyrix" in the title, but in which all additional references are to c486SLC and c486DLC.

So why use WAIS? Because WAIS does just fine at simple one-term searches. An even more important reason to use WAIS is that it has the unique capability to perform *relevance feedback* searches. Suppose, for example, that you find an excellent article on Cyrix 486 chips. You can pull terms from that document and use them to start a new search. When you're on the right trail, WAIS gives you the ability to spring down the path to other relevant articles. For this capability alone, WAIS—even in its current teething stage—is an excellent information-gathering tool.

WAIS Software

The problem with WAIS, from the point of view of Macintosh and Windows users, is that their browsers presently can't use WAIS URLs directly. Although these programs can access WAIS databases from some gopher sites, the browsers are utterly unable to work directly with WAIS. To date, no one has built a WAIS client or a WAIS client programming library that these programs can use.

This situation will probably change soon. Meanwhile, if you want to access WAIS libraries and you don't want to use SWAIS, you need to get either MacWAIS or, if you're a Windows user, EINet's WinWAIS (see fig. 4.10).

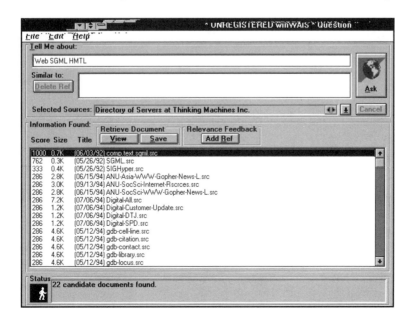

Figure 4.10

Right now, WinWAIS is the only quality Windows interface to WAIS databases.

Part II

Examining the World Wide Web

C H A P T E R

5

What You Need to Link to the Web

Someday soon, hooking into the Internet, and from there to the Web, will be easy. Today is not that day.

By late 1995, the newest version of all operating systems will include Internet connectivity and a Web browser. Unix has always had it, OS/2 Warp already has it, and Windows 95 and the Macintosh's System 8.0 will include it. For the time being, you must have just the right mix of hardware and software to explore the Web. If that were all there is to it, putting together a Web connection would be as simple as following a recipe. Alas, it's not that easy yet. This chapter describes the specific hardware and software you need to hook into the Web.

Specifically, this chapter focuses on the following points:

◆ Modems

◆ Network cards

◆ Systems

◆ Graphics and audio hardware

◆ Network software

◆ Viewer software

◆ Operating systems

Finding the Right Hardware

Most modern PCs are capable of running the software you need for the Web. For acceptable performance, you need (at the very least) the features listed in table 5.1. You can get by with less powerful equipment, but performance will be marginal at best.

TABLE 5.1
Bare Minimum Hardware Requirements

Hardware	PC	Macintosh
Processor	80386SX	68030
Speed	25 MHz	25 MHz
RAM	4 MB	5 MB
Disk space	8 MB	8 MB
Graphics	VGA	Color
Modem (or)	V.32	V.32
Network card	Ethernet	Ethernet

If you're content to use only character-based applications, you can get along by using almost any computer that can talk to a modem and a character-based WWW browser like Lynx. Most users demand more, however. Table 5.2 lists what you need for better than rock-bottom performance in running the software you need for the Web. Finally, if you have the cash, consider getting the Web dream machine outlined in table 5.3.

New Riders Publishing
INSIDE
SERIES

TABLE 5.2
Acceptable Hardware Requirements

Hardware	PC	Macintosh
Processor	80486SX	68030
Speed	25 MHz	40 MHz
RAM	8 MB	8 MB
Disk space	8 MB	8 MB
Graphics	Super-VGA	8-bit, 256-color
Modem (or)	V.32bis	V.32bis
Network card	Ethernet	Ethernet

TABLE 5.3
Optimal Hardware Requirements

Hardware	PC	Macintosh
Processor	80486DX2	PowerPC-601
Speed	33/66 MHz	40 MHz
RAM	16 MB	16 MB
Disk space	8 MB	8 MB
Graphics	Super-VGA	8-bit, 256-color
Modem (or)	V.34/ISDN	V.34/ISDN
Network card	Ethernet	Ethernet

Interestingly enough, except for the modem requirements, there's nothing top-of-the-line about any of these requirements. To run a Web browser, you really don't need a fast Pentium or PowerPC chip. Compared to the demands of most modern programs, Web browsers require very little in the way of resources.

The most critical part of any system you use to explore the Web is your Internet connection. Whether you're using a modem or a network connection, the speed of your Internet connection, more than any other, determines how quickly your Web browser runs.

Modems

To get on the Web, unless you have a network connection, you need a high-speed modem with both data compression and error correction. Don't bother trying to hitchhike on the Net with less than a 14,400 bits-per-second (bps), V.32bis/V.42bis-compliant modem. A V.34 modem, with its 28,800 bps, is better still.

Tip You can connect with slower modems, but whatever you do, don't use a modem without V.42 error correcting and V.42bis data compression. Because *Serial Line Internet Protocol* (SLIP) doesn't include any error correction, the least bit of line noise can knock your network connection for a loop. You need data compression because SLIP has a *high latency* (SLIP takes its own sweet time transferring information). Anything that improves SLIP throughput, which is where data compression comes in, is a good idea.

Before you shop for a modem, check with your Internet provider to see what kind of modems they use. Although most modems work with most other modems, the odds are you'll get more consistent connections (and trouble-shooting is easier) if you and the provider have the same brand.

Furthermore, a rocket-fast 28,800 bps modem won't do you a bit of good if your service supports only speeds of up to 14,400 bps. Even if you decide not to get a twin of your provider's modem, the company can advise you which modems to avoid. Remember, not all modems are created equal.

Note Not all telephone lines are created equal, either. Normal analog telephone lines were never meant to handle high-speed data transfers. Your connection may rarely get up to its theoretical top speed. Go ahead and have your telephone company check your line, but don't be surprised if your speed doesn't improve, even on a "repaired" line.

You might want to consider getting a dedicated telephone line for your SLIP connection. You can use a SLIP connection for many activities—for example, you can telnet your way to such commercial online services as BIX, Delphi, and

CompuServe. Some online services, such as America Online, can now be reached directly through the Internet. All in all, many activities are available online in addition to the wealth of things you can do with the Internet and the Web.

Modem Standards

Modems are governed by arcane standards. You should know the fundamentals of these standards so that you can choose the correct modem for your needs.

Even if you find modem standards mind-numbing, *never* buy a modem that doesn't conform to them. Yes, some modems can fire data at unheard-of speeds—but they use proprietary solutions. And, *proprietary*, in the modem biz, means modems that can only talk to other modems that use the exact same scheme. Even if a modem sounds so good that you think everyone should use it, don't buy it. Proprietary solutions lock you in to that modem only. If your Internet provider changes modems, or the modem manufacturer goes under, you're up the creek without a paddle.

This problem does not occur only with new modems. Every now and again you'll run across a deal for a high-speed modem that sounds too good to be true. Well, chances are it is too good to be true. Older nonstandard modems, even from such top vendors as Hayes, are of little good to an end-user or a computer guru.

The most important modem standards are made by the *Consultative Committee for International Telephony and Telegraphy* (CCITT). This international standards group sets the V-series of standards. Unlike some standards, the CCITT rules are recognized and obeyed by almost every modem and fax manufacturer in the world. The reason is quite simple—rules are necessary even on the datacom autobahn. Without the CCITT's laws, data and fax traffic would slow to a snail's pace.

Note   Other standards are de facto rather than de jure standards. Microcom's *Microcom Networking Protocols* (MNP) are the best known of these standards. Although no standard-setting organization stands behind MNP, almost all modem and communication vendors recognize the MNP standards.

Before launching into communications standards, let's spell out some telecommunication basics. First, what is the difference between *baud* and *bits per second* (bps)? Most of the confusion surrounding these terms arises because, at low speeds, bps and baud have the same value. For instance, a 300 bps modem transmits data at the exact same rate as a 300 baud modem. *Baud* measures the line-switching speed of a communications line. Thus, a 600 baud modem can transmit or receive, in one second, 600 frequency or voltage changes on a line. *Bps*, on the other hand, measures how many bits of data can be sent or received (per second) on a line.

How can a modem pack more information (bps) into a line than a given baud? The secret is in the encoding. By modulating the baud, making changes in amplitude, frequency, or phase polarity of a line's carrier wave, more bps can be stuffed into a single baud. For instance, 1200 bps modems actually use a 600 baud connection. The most common techniques for inserting more bps data onto a baud are *Differential Phase Shift Keying* (DPSK), *Frequency Shift Keying* (FSK), *Quadrature Amplitude Modulation* (QAM), and *Trellis Coding Modulation* (TCM).

The important lesson here for users (as opposed to data communication engineers) is that baud does not equal bps. When you next buy a modem, a quick-and-dirty way to discover whether the salesperson knows about modems is simply to ask for an explanation of the modem's speed rating.

Another point to consider is the difference between simplex, half-duplex, and full-duplex devices. *Simplex* devices can only transmit or receive data in a single session. V.17 fax-modems are an example of this kind of modem. With a *half-duplex* device, or when you operate a modem in *half-duplex* mode, data can be transmitted and received—but only one or the other at any given time. You probably have guessed already that *full-duplex* modems are capable of simultaneously transmitting and receiving data.

For Web runners, the important standards are those listed in table 5.4.

TABLE 5.4
Modem Standards

Designation	Definition
V.22	1,200 bps modem speed
V.22bis	2,400 bps modem speed

Designation	Definition
V.29	9,600 bps fax speed
V.32	9,600 bps modem speed
V.32bis	14,400 bps modem speed
V.32ter	19,200 bps modem speed/Not CCITT
V.34/V.Fast	28,800 bps modem speed
V.FC	28,800 bps modem speed/Not CCITT
V.42	Error correction
V.42bis	Data compression

V.22 Modems

If you started using a modem in the late 1980s, V.22 is probably the first standard that meant something to you. The V.22 standard uses DPSK to provide for modems capable of delivering 600 to 1200 bps. Modems that support this as their highest speed are far too slow for the Web.

What you probably wanted to have since the late 1980s, though, was a V.22bis-compatible modem. V.22bis modems using QAM fire data along the information highway at full-duplex at 2400 bps. If necessary, V.22bis automatically shifts gears to V.22's 1200 bps.

Today, almost all general-purpose modems include V.22bis compatibility as a fallback for when lines are too noisy for higher speeds. If you're having so much trouble that your modem's speed drops to 2400 bps, it's time to disconnect. At this speed, working with the Web is slow torture.

Still, if a modem doesn't include V.22bis compatibility, walk on by. Even today, 2400 bps is an extremely common speed for most value-added, *packet-switching networks* (PSN) and *bulletin board systems* (BBSs).

V.29 Modems

V.29, with its 9600 bps, is one of the most puzzling protocols around. The vendors—not the protocol—are to blame. Some companies advertise fax-modems with speeds of 2400 and 9600 bps. You might think that such a device has a 9600 bps data modem and a 2400 bps fax. Wrong. In this case, the modem is almost always V.29-compliant for the fax (hence the 9600 bps), but the modem uses V.22bis, for a maximum of 2400 bps throughput. When in doubt, always ask exactly what standards the modem supports.

V.29 is great for computer faxing, but you can't use it for the Web. Don't get burned by buying a 9600 bps V.29 device and thinking that it's fine for the Internet. It isn't.

V.32 Modems

With V.32, you start moving into the fast modem crowd. V.32 uses TCM, and optionally TCM encoding, to boost full-duplex data transfers to 9600 bps.

Tip

Some folks still seem to think that they're being financially sensible by sticking with V.22bis modems. This is a case of being penny-wise and pound-foolish.

Although V.32 modems are more expensive than their bottom-rung relatives, the increase in speed—even from services such as CompuServe, that add a surcharge for higher speeds—means that you'll be ahead of the game in the first 100 hours of use. Because you can throughput four times the data with a V.32 9600 bps modem than you can with a V.22bis modem, the former is more than worth its price (double that of the latter). You could use V.22 modems for the Web, but faster is better.

Clearly, if you want your data to fly, you need a V.32bis-compliant modem. V.32bis roars along at 14,000 bps with TCM in full-duplex, and is backward compatible with V.32. In addition to pure speed, V.32bis has *rapid rate renegotiation* to shift the bps speed up or down, depending on line conditions.

If price and speed are your main concerns, V.32bis modems are the ones to buy. Faster modems exist, but you can get by with V.32bis.

Although V.32terbo never really was quite a standard (and never will be), modem manufacturers built modems with it in 1994. Here's the story. The brainchild of AT&T Paradyne, V.32terbo was to be an enhanced version of V.32bis that would push the data speed limit to 19,200 bps. The CCITT gave this recommendation a thumbs down. Nevertheless, despite the CCITT's

rejection, AT&T Microelectronics produced a V.32terbo chip set and major vendors such as AT&T, Multi-Tech, and U.S. Robotics set to work producing V.32terbo modems.

 Stop Only buy modems with CCITT V standards. Otherwise, you will probably be stuck with an incompatible modem.

The problem was that V.34 modems, with top raw speeds of 28,800 bps, were right around the corner. Worse still, a V.32terbo modem cannot connect (at its top speed of 19,200 bps) with a V.34 modem. V.32terbo, like triple-speed CD-ROM drives, was an industry standard that came along too late to win a viable market. As a user, you probably won't find an Internet provider that supports V.32terbo. And without a V.32terbo provider, all you've got is an expensive V.32bis modem. Just say no to V.32terbo.

V.34 Modems

V.34, also known as "V.Fast," takes modems from a top speed of 14,400 bps to 28,800 bps. V.34 was approved in 1994. Some modem manufacturers, irked by the slow-moving CCITT, decided to jump the gun. In July of 1993, Rockwell International, the most important modem chip manufacturer, released its V.FC (V.Fast Class) chipset. Although V.FC is *not* a CCITT standard, it is based on the proposed design of V.34. For example, V.FC uses V.34's multidimensional trellis coding and line probing to produce a top speed of 28,800 bps.

Modem manufacturers jumped on V.FC like firefighters on a fire truck when the alarm goes off. More than a hundred companies, including such major players as Hayes and Supra, are riding the howling-fast V.FC "standard."

But do you really want to buy a modem whose top-speed standard is V.FC? I think not. There's no ironclad guarantee that a V.FC modem will connect with a V.34. Some vendors promise that you can upgrade your V.FC modem to V.34 by replacing a chip or uploading a BIOS upgrade. If you already own a V.FC modem, check with your vendor to see whether you can get the upgrade.

Perhaps your V.FC modem is close enough to the final version of V.34 to be able to connect transparently with V.34 modems at full speed. Don't hold your breath.

Your best move is to upgrade your modem or grit your teeth and buy a new V.34 modem. Whether this upgrade entails a simple update of your modem's initiation string or a complete new chipset is a question that only your modem vendor can answer.

V.42 Modems

The last pair of CCITT standards that are important for modem commuters—V.42 and V.42bis—have confused many people. V.42 defines the use of several error-correction protocols. These protocols attempt (and for the most part succeed) to ensure that no noise creeps into data, no matter how noisy the line.

V.42's primary error-correction protocol is *Link Access Procedure for Modems* (LAPM). LAPM borrows from the X.25 *High-level Data Link Control* (HDLC) protocol; as the names indicate, both protocols correct errors at the data-link level.

When a V.42 modem connects with a modem that doesn't "speak" LAPM V.42, that modem can use the earlier non-CCITT error-correction protocols: MNP Classes 2 through 4. Regardless of the error-correction method, V.42 works with modems that use V.22, V.22bis, V.32, V.32bis, and V.34.

The V.42bis protocol uses data compression to accelerate data communications. V.42bis usually compresses data at a ratio of about 3.5 to 1.

The V.42bis protocol's data-compression ratio leads some modem manufacturers to claim that their V.32/V.42bis-compatible modems can transfer data at 38,400 bps, or even faster. That is a nice theory, and sometimes it's even correct. But most of the time, you won't see anything that even approaches that kind of transfer speed. Why? Because most modem-borne data communications are driven either by your typing speed (and nobody's a 9,600 bps typist!) or by file transfers. What's that you say? Why won't the file zoom from the remote site to your computer? Because most transferable files are already in a compressed format, such as ZIP or ARC. V.42bis can't speed these files along their way by making them smaller. The files are already as small as they're going to get.

Don't dismiss V.42bis. It can help speed things along (it's just not as good as it appears in some advertisements).

Finally, V.42bis is compatible also with the older MNP Level 5 data-compression protocol. V.42bis has one shining advantage over the MNP-5: V.42bis constantly analyzes the data stream and stops trying to compress it when such efforts would be in vain. MNP-5, which doesn't have this feature, can actually slow down the transmission of compressed files by trying to shrink the unshrinkable.

Armed with this information, you should be able to make an informed decision when you buy a modem. Remember, always ask questions about the modem's compatibilities and never settle for wrong or evasive answers. Your modem is your gateway to the online universe. Don't settle for anything other than the best.

ISDN

Even better than any modem is an *Integrated Services Digital Network* (ISDN) connection. This telecommunications standard lays the groundwork for local digital telephone connections capable of transmitting voice, video, and data at a rate of up to 64 kilobits per second (Kbps).

 Note There are ISDN adapters for both PCs and Macintoshes. Many well-known modem companies, such as Hayes, Intel, and ZyXEL, make ISDN adapters.

For high-end users, ISDN is cost efficient. A 56 or 64 Kbps leased line from a data communications company often starts at several grand and moves up from there. Performance Systems International (PSI), a major national Internet vendor, will get you up and running on their InterRamp Internet ISDN service for approximately $500 in hardware. They'll also help you get an ISDN connection from your telephone company, which costs an additional hundred dollars or so. Maintenance expenses for the Internet connection and the telephone line run about $100 a month. If you have a network you want to hook to the Internet, ISDN costs more, but the pricing tends to be lower than traditional lease line costs.

Sounds great doesn't it? There's only one problem: ISDN services can be very difficult to get, even when you have the bucks. Many large metropolitan areas, such as New York and San Francisco, have no ISDN services.

Tip   Because the telephone companies continue to drag their feet in making ISDN widely available, don't hold your breath if your area doesn't have it. On the other hand, it doesn't hurt to check. You may already have ISDN in your area. Remember, however, that even if you can get ISDN, you'll gain no speed advantage at all unless your POP also has ISDN lines.

Someday in the near future, you may also be able to access the Internet through cable television's coaxial cable. Experimental sites have already been set up to test this technology. If it works out—which seems likely—you soon may be able to use cable TV lines to hook into the Internet at true Ethernet speeds of 10 Mbps, or even faster. One Long Island cable television company is experimenting with 16 Mbps speeds.

Network Cards

To connect with the Web through a network, you need an Ethernet-capable network card. For the most part, any *network interface card* (NIC) will do. There are exceptions to this rule. PC users cannot use any proprietary NIC, such as Artisoft's LANtastic/Z product or the Moses LAN NIC. Mac users must steer clear of LocalTalk.

When you shop for a network card, you, or more specifically your network administrator, should check on a few things. First, on PCs, a 16-bit card is faster than an 8-bit card (and either is much faster than even an ISDN connection).

Even faster, if you have a PC with *extended industry standard architecture* (EISA), *Video Electronics Standards Associations* (VL-Bus) or *Peripheral Component Interconnect* (PCI) slots, is a NIC that can use one of these slots. Remember, however, that these standards are incompatible. You can't use an EISA NIC in a PCI slot, and so on.

Note   You must also be certain that the card will work with your LAN's wiring. 10BASE-T cards use wiring that looks like telephone wiring and plug-in connections. 10BASE2 cards use coaxial cable, sometimes called *Cheapernet*, with T-connectors to hook PCs into the LAN. 10BASE5 is obsolete for PC connections to LANs.

Mac users should consider upgrading to a Mac with a PCI bus. PCI cards are much faster than their NuBus cousins. NuBus is the Mac's older bus architecture.

Another feature to look for is memory on the NIC itself. You don't need a great deal of memory on the board, but even 16 KB of memory helps buffer network traffic. NIC memory helps ensure that when your computer is busy with a job in the foreground, it won't lose any Web traffic that's arriving in the background.

System Speed

Believe it or not, system CPU speed is probably the least important factor in putting together a Web-capable system. That's because your overall speed is dictated by the entire system's slowest component, which, on the Web, is almost certainly going to be your modem or the network itself.

But don't dig out your 4.77 MHz IBM PC from the attic. You do need some system speed to be happy with your Web connection. My recommendation is to go no slower than a 25 MHz processor on any PC.

And you don't have to worry about *floating point units* (FPUs), also known as *math coprocessors*. No Internet-related programs use these chips.

On the Macintosh side of the house, you needn't dither over PowerPC computers versus the older 680x0 systems. A fast 680x0 works as well as a slow PowerPC for most practical Web-wandering purposes.

CPU speed is less important than the total amount of memory. Given a choice between a faster processor and more memory, go with the RAM.

CPU speed is important, however, in translating graphic and PostScript files into viewable formats. If you think that you're going to be dealing extensively with these file types, go ahead and get a faster processor.

With a large amount of memory, you can cache more Web pages on your local system, which means that you'll need to access the Web site less frequently. As a result, your system will be much more responsive when you need to move back to a document you were looking at earlier.

A fast hard drive is important, but not vital for decent Web browser performance. Any modern drive with an access speed of 28 milliseconds or less should serve you well.

Another thing you don't need to be concerned about is the drive interface. Whether you're using *small computer system interface* (SCSI), *integrated drive electronics* (IDE), *extended IDE* (EIDE), or an older technology doesn't matter a fig to Web browsers.

Graphics Hardware

Graphics is another area in which speed is nice but not critical. The critical factors you should look at in a graphics card are the following:

◆ Its graphics processor

◆ Its onboard memory

◆ Its interface to the motherboard

A graphics processor, such as ATI's Mach128, essentially speeds up your graphics in two ways. First, it takes the work of displaying graphics away from your main processor. Second, the graphics processor's chips specialize in speeding up the graphic routines that all programs use to display their images.

Tip

No graphics processor will do you any good, however, unless you have the specific software driver for that specific processor. For instance, it doesn't matter how fast a graphics processor is supposed to be if you're an OS/2 Warp user and the card doesn't have a Warp driver. For Warp users, such a video adapter would be about as useful as the cheapest VGA card.

Also, sad to say, you'll need to make sure that the driver works properly. Many graphics vendors have a nasty habit of releasing video cards with new hardware long before the software is ready to take full advantage of the new equipment.

One thing you don't need is a card that specializes in rendering 24-bit color images—99 percent of all Web images are in 8-bit color.

You can still get by with only 1 MB of video memory, because most color images on the Web have only 256 colors and 640-by-480-pixel resolution. As time goes on, this situation will change—to images with up to 16.7 million colors and

1024-by-768 resolution. This change isn't going to happen quickly, however, because even the Internet backbone networks simply don't have the bandwidth to tolerate the sending back and forth of huge, truecolor images. If you want to look toward the future, you should get video cards with 2 MB of RAM. The day is still far off when you'll need 4 MB of RAM on a video card for Web-running.

Generally speaking, cards with *video RAM* (VRAM) are faster than their sisters with *dynamic RAM* (DRAM). Graphics board designers constantly test the limits of memory technology, and having VRAM no longer guarantees that a board will be faster than a twin with DRAM. When in doubt, check reputable computer magazines such as *Byte*, *PC Magazine*, and *Computer Shopper* for the latest hard numbers. Again, keep in mind that without the appropriate driver, a particular card is not worth an extra premium.

The card's connection to the system is the one place where, driver or no, your video card's performance can be choked off. Systems with *industry standard architecture* (ISA), NuBus, and EISA graphics cards will lag behind otherwise identical cards that connect with VL-Bus or PCI slots.

If your machine doesn't have these standards, don't rush out to buy a new computer just so you have a local bus video connection for the Web alone. Although the faster slots make a large difference to most applications, again, what's really going to determine your browser speed is the Internet connection's speed.

Audio Hardware

Audio requirements are perhaps the easiest for Web users to meet. Macintosh users already have all the sound equipment they need to deal with Web audio files. PC users must get Sound Blaster–compatible sound cards. (That's a cinch, because almost all PC audio cards are Sound Blaster compatible.)

Software Requirements

Your software is as important as your hardware. Unless everything works together as a team, you can't connect with the Web.

Web connection software consists of three parts: the networking software, the operating system, and the socket software that enables network applications to connect with the Internet. Let's take a long, hard look at these elements.

Network Software

If you already have a TCP/IP-based network, you're home free. Connecting your network to the Internet will be child's play for any TCP/IP network administrator. If you're running Novell NetWare, Artisoft LANtastic, or Microsoft's Windows for Workgroups (WinWorks), expect some headaches.

Macintosh owners are the one exception to this rule. Because System 7.5 includes MacTCP, hooking up a Mac to a TCP/IP network—although not child's play—is a simple, straightforward operation. That's anything but the case for PC users.

Stop   Be sure that you're running the newest version of MacTCP (2.04 or higher). Older versions, especially the 1.x editions, have a serious memory bug.

If you're a PC network administrator you should ask yourself—before going any farther—whether the people who want Internet can reach it through a dial-up modem connection. If they can get acceptable Internet connectivity by this route, let them. SLIP and PPP software can often run effortlessly over existing network stacks. It's no trouble at all, for example, to run Trumpet Software's SLIP stack over a stack that includes both the Novell *Internet Packet Exchange* (IPX) and NetBIOS. But running Trumpet Software's TCP/IP over the same stack is another thing entirely.

Note   Don't let the Internet in IPX fool you. Although IPX can work with the Internet, IPX itself is not an Internet protocol.

Your chief problem will be getting your current network stack to coexist with the TCP/IP protocols. Your first move should be to make sure that there's a TCP/IP that works with your *network operating system* (NOS). Most major LANs have TCP/IP supplements. For example, NetWare has NetWare/IP and LAN WorkPlace.

The details of how to get each network stack to work with one another vary from situation to situation—too much to get into in this book. To achieve peaceful coexistence between network protocols, you need to rely on your network vendors' documentation. Here, though, are some of the general principles.

New Riders Publishing
INSIDE
SERIES

Network Protocol General Principles

First, there are three basic ways to get dueling network protocols to live with each other on a given card. The oldest is to use a *packet driver*, a program that acts as a translator between your NIC and your TCP programs.

Packet drivers work well…after they're installed properly. That first step can be a doozy. To use them properly you must understand vectors, *Interrupt ReQuests* (IRQs), and I/O addresses.

Note   A *vector* is a number (ranging from 0 to 255) on an x86 architecture chip. Vectors are used by software to communicate with the underlying hardware. Normally, these numbers are expressed as *hexadecimal* numbers—0x10 calls, for example—to the video *basic input/output system* (BIOS). These numbers may also appear as decimal numbers. In either case, the packet driver must have a vector number, from 0x60 to 0x7F, that is not used by another piece of equipment or program. The default number is 0x60.

Your packet driver must also have a free IRQ and IObase address for its work. The *IRQ* is one of 16 numbers (0–15) on an 80286 or higher PC; the hardware uses this number to *interrupt* (get the attention of) the CPU. When the CPU is paying attention, the IRQ is used to communicate data from a modem, a scanner, or (as in this instance) a packet driver to the CPU. The *IObase* is the specific hardware address reserved for a particular piece of equipment or program. If any of the three (vector, IRQ, IObase) are shared by another program or piece of hardware, the TCP/IP session probably will abort. Finding just the right combination of vector, IRQ, and IObase can be a tedious task.

Most network cards come with packet drivers (but if you have one that doesn't, you're still not out of luck). An enormous collection of public domain packet drivers is available in the Crynew Packet Driver Collection, which can be found on the *Inside the World Wide Web Bonus CD*.

In essence, packet drivers work by sharing a network card as if it were a duplex house. That is, the TCP/IP packet driver lives on one side of the house and has nothing to do with the protocol living in the building's other wing.

That's one reason that packet driver solutions are being eclipsed by Microsoft's *Network Driver Interface Specification* (NDIS) and Novell's *Open Data-Link Interface* (ODI). Both are NIC interface standards that support up to four different network protocols on one NIC. Many network companies write drivers for these interfaces. Many network companies write drivers for these interfaces. Companies can write a driver for ODI or NDIS and not have to worry about writing directly to (or building packet drivers for) each card's hardware.

 Stop Avoid older Ethernet cards (more than three years old). They can be more contrary than most in adapting to a situation in which they must run your LAN's native network protocol and TCP/IP.

The one bad thing about ODI and NDIS is that they're not compatible with each other. Although you can use ODI and NDIS NICs on a LAN, a driver written for one will not work with the other. Novell does have a program, ODINSUP, that lets you use some ODI drivers to work with NDIS interfaces. Don't count on being able to pull off this trick.

For Internet users, the standards make running TCP/IP with other NOSs much easier to do. That said, getting different networks to live together on one NIC is still no walk in the park. Always check your documentation and keep the technical support number handy when you're trying to get TCP/IP to work in tandem with another network protocol.

Before you sit down and roll up your sleeves, you can help ensure that your setup goes as smoothly as possible by checking a few things. First, make sure that you have the newest versions of your network software. Network companies constantly update their drivers. The newer the version, the more likely it is to work under the stressful conditions of running multiple protocols.

Next, read the documentation and any readme files. There's almost no one who doesn't have the bad habit of installing first and then reading the manual. With network software, that's a sure path to trouble, especially when you're trying to run more than one NOS at a time.

 Note The best place to find packet drivers is the Crynwr collection. On the Web, you'll find the latest information on where to find them at this address:

`http://www.crynwr.com/crynwr/`

Some NICs, even with ODI or NDIS, still require the use of a packet driver. In this situation, you'll need not only a packet driver, but another program, called a *shim*, which enables the packet driver to connect with the network interface

software. To learn more about how to use Trumpet Software's TCP/IP with another network, read the program's install.doc file on the *Inside the World Wide Web Bonus CD*. As for the specifics of how to get the network software to work with an Internet provider, read on. Those specifics are addressed in the next section.

SLIP/PPP Software

The niftiest Internet applications, like most good Web browsers, have one problem: Your system must actually be on the Internet to use them. You can get to their resources from an ordinary modem connection, as you'll learn in Chapter 6, "Finding Web Access," but to get the most out of a browser, you must have a TCP/IP connection to the Internet.

For companies and educational institutions, having a TCP/IP connection is not a problem. These entities can afford dedicated lines and routers—and the experts to run them—to hook their systems into the Internet. Small businesses and home users can also marry their systems to the Internet by using *Serial Line Internet Protocol* (SLIP) and *Point-to-Point Protocol* (PPP)—TCP/IP protocols that work over ordinary modems and telephone lines.

That's the good news. The bad news is that to get SLIP and PPP connections to work, you need esoteric networking knowledge. That may change soon. Major online companies, such as CompuServe, are getting into the Internet provider business and plan to make IP connections easier. For now, though, hooking your PC to the Net isn't an easy job. But with this chapter in hand, the job is not an impossible one.

SLIP Software

This description of how you can hook into the Internet uses Trumpet Software's shareware SLIP implementation, Trumpet Winsock. Although different in some details from other products, Trumpet Winsock (available on the companion CD-ROM) works well and clearly illustrates the most important SLIP and PPP installation concerns for would-be Internet surfers.

Tip If you ever move up to using TCP/IP on a network, Winsock can handle that job also. Because Winsock also supports NDIS and ODI, you'll be able to connect to the Internet while maintaining links to NetWare servers.

If you're interested in a conventional, commercial SLIP package for a PC, look to SPRY's Internet in a Box and NetManage's Internet Chameleon. For a Mac, you need to get System 7.5, which includes MacTCP; and then, for SLIP or PPP, Synergy Software's VersaTerm SLIP, part of VersaTilities; InterCon Systems' InterSLIP (part of TCP/Connect II); or MacPPP.

Tip
The one vital factor to look for in a SLIP package for a standalone PC is a program that doesn't require a *terminate-and-stay-resident* (TSR) program. TSR TCP/IP network stacks always take up too much memory below the 1 MB mark and can cause oddball problems with other applications. Spry, NetManage, and Trumpet Software all implement the network stack as a Windows *Dynamic Link Library* (DLL).

For Trumpet Winsock, you also need a computer that can run Windows 3.1. Forget about running Windows on machines with only 4 MB of RAM. You can do it, but with a SLIP connection and resource-grabbing applications such as National Center for Supercomputing Applications' (NCSA) Mosaic, you really don't want to. Regardless of your SLIP program, your PC needs a 16550 *universal asynchronous receiver transmitter* (UART) chip in charge of the serial port. With DOS, you can check your serial cards with MD-DOS' msd utility. You can run this from any command prompt. Older serial port chips cannot handle high-speed communications reliably.

When you have everything in hand, it's time to look at your software. Trumpet Winsock includes the three separate programs needed to get SLIP to work in a Windows environment. Every SLIP program includes the SLIP network stack. To make a SLIP connection, however, you also need a dialer and a sockets program.

The *dialer* is a program that simply dials up your Internet provider's data phone. This program also handles the initial login process and starts the SLIP program on the Internet provider's side. You can fake this successfully by using a communications program such as Procomm Plus. For ease of use, it's best to go with a dedicated dialer like Trumpet's Tcpman. Tcpman not only handles making the initial phone calls, but also is the interface program for setting up the rest of Trumpet Winsock.

Sockets are TCP/IP's way of implementing *InterProcess Communications* (IPC). An IPC enables programs to trade information with each other. The most familiar

IPC is Microsoft Windows' *Dynamic Data Exchange* (DDE), which is supported by most Windows programs.

 Note In a TCP/IP network, sockets basically provide a way for TCP/IP-aware applications, such as Mosaic, to communicate through TCP/IP with other TCP/IP servers, such as a Web server. A single socket provides a full-duplex communication tunnel between a local application's virtual port address and its IP address to a remote application's socket. With this in place, your application and its remote server can work reliably with each other.

Specifically, for Windows you also need a copy of the winsock.dll that's version 1.1-compliant. Here, Winsock not only implements socket services, but also provides an *application programming interface* (API) that enables any Winsock-compliant TCP/IP application to work, regardless of its maker. Some older PC TCP/IP software is not Winsock-compliant and should be avoided.

When it comes to sockets, Macintosh users have it much easier. MacTCP includes the necessary sockets software, and all modern Macintosh TCP/IP applications transparently use these resources.

Establishing a SLIP Account

Before you start trying to connect, you must arrange with your Internet provider to set up a SLIP account. This may take several days. Internet providers are notoriously understaffed, and setting up SLIP accounts is not much easier on the provider's staff than it is on you. Be kind—you're going to need these folks' help to get the job done.

With some operating systems, such as OS/2 Warp and IBM's Advantis Internet system, things are much easier. In these systems, all you have to do is click on a single button, and your SLIP or PPP connection is made without fuss or muss.

Some Internet providers, such as Netcom and Performance Systems International (PSI), offer Internet packages that include semi-automatic SLIP/PPP linkups. If all the finicky work required to set up an IP connection gives you the cold sweats, you'll be much better off going with one of these options.

Your provider has information you must have to successfully put up a SLIP connection. Some of this information is the same for every SLIP user for that provider. Other bits of information are specific to your account. Table 5.5 provides the details needed to connect with the Web.

TABLE 5.5
What You Need to Connect with the Web

Item	Where to Find It
Modem	Store, direct market
Network/SLIP software	Store, online service, Internet provider
SLIP phone number	Internet provider
Domain name	You and your Internet provider
Netmask	Internet provider
Account name/Password	Internet provider
Server IP address	Internet provider
DNS server IP address	Internet provider
Time server IP address	Internet provider
CSLIP or SLIP	Internet provider
MTU	Internet provider/Docs
TCP MSS	Internet provider/Docs
TCP RWIN	Internet provider/Docs
COM Port	Check modem connection
Hardware handshaking	Check modem docs

First, you may have to decide on a domain name. If you're only going with a part-time SLIP account, this name probably will be based on your service's address name. For example, my Internet provider's address is `access.digex.net` and my SLIP domain name is `vna.digex.net`.

You may be assigned a random letter or number sequence for your domain name. Don't sweat it. If you have a part-time SLIP operation, no one should ever send mail to your domain address because messages can't reach you when you're off the air.

Note If you elect to get a full-time SLIP account, you can have any address you like, provided that it complies with the Internet naming conventions and doesn't duplicate an existing name. Approval for such names takes approximately two weeks because these names must be approved by the Internet Network Information Center (InterNIC).

Clearly, you need to know your domain name, as well as its corresponding IP address. The IP address is a 32-bit number that's represented as four sets of decimal numbers separated by periods. For instance, the IP address to vna.digex.net is 164.109.213.7. As the Internet grows more crowded, even larger numbers will be required. You may run into other IP addressing systems that further pin down your IP address with a number delimited from the rest of the address by a comma.

The IP address, not your domain name, is your domain's true address. When you move data through the Internet, this address is kept in your datagram's header. In short, the messages, connections, and data transfers you initalize on the Net are identified by your IP address (which is also your system's unique address on the net). If someone wants to telnet to your system or ftp a file from your system, they can do so by using your IP address.

You also need to know your *subnet netmask*, an IP number that's used with your IP number to divide networks into smaller networks. Most SLIP users are assigned either the number 255.255.0.0 or 255.255.255.0. Your Internet provider will use the netmask to organize their network hierarchy. Other than making sure that you enter the right value when you bring up your SLIP account, you'll never need to worry about it again.

Tip If you decide to go with a part-time SLIP account, you should also be certain that you have a shell account on your Internet provider's main service. Why? Because, although you might have a local mail account (mine is sjvn@vna.digex.net), neither of the popular mail program interfaces— *Simple Mail Transfer Protocol* (SMTP) or *Post Office Protocol mail* (POPmail)—will deliver mail to you unless you're online while they're trying to deliver it to your account. If you and SMTP or POPmail never connect, you'll never get your mail.

The moral of the story is that unless you're on the Internet full-time, make sure that your vendor gives you a shell account so that you can use a mail client to get your mail from your account on one of their 24-hour machines.

An important thing to keep in mind is the telephone number to call for SLIP services. This number almost certainly is not one of the main numbers used for other data calls. If you have a full-time account, your number is dedicated for your use alone.

You'll also have a SLIP account name and password. These work just like a shell account's name and password, except that they identify you as a SLIP user to your Internet *Point of Presence* (POP).

Next, you'll need to know the IP address to your *default server*—or, as it's called in Trumpet, the *gateway server*. This is the IP address of the machine you call into, and it's your first link into the Internet.

Then you need the IP address of your *Domain Name Service* (DNS) Server (for Trumpet, the Name server) at hand. The DNS is a distributed database system for resolving host names into IP addresses. For example, if you want to telnet to `delphi.com`, home of the Delphi Internet Service, chances are you'd much rather type delphi.com instead of 192.80.63.8. Without a DNS server to resolve domain and WWW's HTTP addresses, navigating the Net is much more difficult.

Currently, the time server entry is not used in Trumpet, but you might as well get the time server's IP address too, if it's available. A *time server* does exactly what you'd expect it to do: It enables you to reset your system's clock to the server's clock. This may seem trivial, but if you need precise file and document date-and-time stamping, being able to set your system to an agreed upon time standard can be very desirable.

You should also ask whether the system supports Van Jacobson's *compressed SLIP* (CSLIP). Many systems now use CSLIP in place of SLIP but still call it SLIP. You don't have to have this parameter in sync in order to communicate with a plain SLIP system, but you'll achieve higher throughputs if you can both use Van Jacobson CSLIP.

CSLIP is something of a misnomer. Unlike data compression standards, such as V.42bis, CSLIP doesn't try to squeeze down every byte that passes through it. Rather, CSLIP increases throughput by means of two tricks. The first is that it checks whether long series of repetitive fields in TCP headers are being sent in datagrams. This is often the case, and CSLIP doesn't send this duplicate data. CSLIP also analyzes the data stream and arranges it so that packets for interactive applications, such as telnet, are sent before those for noninteractive programs, such as ftp. The result is a pronounced performance boost.

Next, you need to know about parameters that directly control the way SLIP runs between your modem and your POP's modem. These parameters are the *Maximum Transmission Unit* (MTU), *TCP Maximum Segment Size* (TCP MSS), and *TCP Receive Window* (TCP RWIN). You will need to set these parameters by entering them in your Network Configuration Window.

If your Internet provider has suggested values for these parameters, use those numbers. Otherwise, set TCP MSS to 512 for SLIP and less than 255 for CSLIP. MTU should be to set to about 40 above your TCP MSS (552, in the case of SLIP). TCP RWIN should be set to three or four times the TCP MSS value (in this example, to 2048). These numbers represent the sizes, in bytes, for these parameters.

 Note With faster machines and modems, the values can be set higher for marginally faster performance. For example, a 33 MHz 486DX with 16 MB of RAM and a 14,400 bps modem can use the following values:

TCP MSS: 966
MTU: 1006
TCP RWIN: 4096

It's not essential to Trumpet, but if you plan to read Net news, you'll need the IP address of the nearest news server. Trumpet won't call for this number, but you'll need the address when you install a newsreader to work with Trumpet.

No, we're not done yet. There are still other parameters to set. Because you'll be using SLIP, you need to check off the box for Internal SLIP. In the box for SLIP Port, place the number corresponding to the COMM port you'll use for SLIP. Were you to use COM2 for your modem, you'd enter a 2 for that box. The program then asks for your baud rate, which should be set to 57600. This is an error. What the program really wants is bps, not baud, but (wording aside) it works. No, your modem won't actually go that fast, but with data compression and luck you may achieve data throughput numbers in that range.

Last but not least, you need to check whether your modem supports hardware handshaking. The image is rather silly, but if your modem can signal automatically when it's getting too much data and that the other modem should slow down, you'll get much more effective data throughput.

With all this equipment and information at hand, you're almost ready to install. First, however, you'll want to make some changes to Windows. Go to the Windows control panel and double-click on the Ports icon. Then head to the port that's going to be used for SLIP and give it a healthy-sized buffer of 10,000 or so. A buffer of this size will head off any data overflow disasters when five programs simultaneously decide to pour data into your system.

Later, if you run into trouble with simultaneously running Internet programs causing crashes when both try to access the port at once, you'll want to make another change. Head over to the 386 Enhanced Icon in the control panel and set the COMM port's AutoAssign value to 0. This setting causes Windows to respond immediately to the next program asking for control of the COMM port.

Installing Trumpet Winsock

At last—you're ready to begin. First, set up a directory for the SLIP program files. Commercial programs set up their own directories, but with Trumpet you must set up the directory yourself, giving it a name like SLIP or TRUMPET. Then copy the files to the new directory. If, as is likely, the files are in zipped format, you'll need to unzip them first, before using them.

After you unzip the files, you should have at hand the files shown in table 5.6.

TABLE 5.6
Essential Trumpet Winsock Files

File Name	Description
winsock.dll	The TCP/IP driver and winsock.dll
tcpman.exe	Installation program and dialer
hosts	List of host names
services	List of Internet services
protocol	List of Internet protocols
login.cmd	Sample login script
bye.cmd	Sample logoff script

Now start your modem and Windows, and launch Tcpman. Soon you'll see a blank network configuration display similar to the filled-out display shown in figure 5.1.

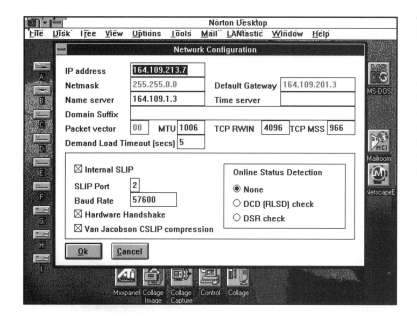

Figure 5.1

The Trumpet Winsock configuration window is complex, but you can use the information in this chapter to fill it out correctly.

You'll notice that some of the fields are blank. Because Demand Load Timeout, Domain Suffix, Packet vector, and Online Status Detection aren't essential to most SLIP connections, those fields have been left blank. If you were using a network connection rather than SLIP, the Packet vector would be important. If you have a new IP address with a number delimited by a comma at the end, you might also need to fill out the Domain Suffix field with the number after the comma.

Always check your SLIP software's documentation to make sure that you have all the information you need. Trumpet covers all the vital bases, but other programs may require more (or less) information.

After checking to make sure that everything here is correct, click on the OK box. By doing so, you automatically bring up the Winsock dialer program. From the Dialer menu, choose the manual login option for your first try at clicking into the Internet.

To do this, you must use Hayes *AT commands*, the standard set of orders for controlling modems. If AT commands are foreign to you, look at your modem manual for a quick summary of them. If you're not sure whether you're talking to your modem, type **AT**. If OK is displayed, you're in touch with your modem.

The following code is an example of a typical manual login, with your input shown in italics:

```
ATDT 982-5658
CONNECT 57600
Express Access (tm) Online Communications Service
301-220-2020)
     Part Time slip dialin only!
slip login: my_slip_id
Password: my_password
SLIP Session from (164.109.201.3) to 164.109.213.7 beginning
```

Press Esc

```
SLIP ENABLED
```

To hang up on this connection, press Esc again and type **ATH**.

Tip

As you can see from the preceding interchange, logging on with a commercial program is a clean and simple procedure. With Trumpet, the process is more complicated. When you know what your Internet system expects from an incoming SLIP call, you must manually write your automatic login script. The following script (in which each comment is preceded by a #) is stripped to the bare minimum.

```
output ATV1X4&C1&D2&K3&L0\13
# Initalizing the modem
input 3 OK
#Wait 3 seconds for the modem to respond with an OK
output ATDT982-5658\13
#Dial the phone number
input 35 slip login:
#Wait 35 seconds to see the above string
display Logging in...\n
output my_slip_id\13
#Let you know that things are advancing along and then
sends in the ID
input 30 Password:
#Wait 30 seconds for the Password prompt
Password Enter your password
output \p\13
```

```
#The above causes a window to appear in which you must
#type your password. You can hard code your password
#in but it makes for lousy security.
input 15 >
output slip\13
#start the slip program on the Internet system
display Connected. Your IP address is \i.\n
#Displays your IP address
exec pingw 164.1009.201.2
#And just to make sure we're really SLIP sliding along,
#I run a ping command from my local machine to
#the gateway system to make sure that SLIP is working.
```

It's a return to the old painful ways of scripting, but after you have it down right, you'll never need to write it again. For a complete syntax of Trumpet's scripting language, see the program's documentation.

Troubleshooting a SLIP Installation

An almost limitless number of things can go wrong during a SLIP installation. Fortunately, most of the same problems—and solutions—show up again and again.

First, double-check all of the above. In most cases, it only takes one mistake for the whole thing to lock up tighter than Fort Knox. SLIP installations are extremely unforgiving of user error. Once in place, you'll be glad to know, they seldom go wrong.

Next, make sure that you and your SLIP provider are in tune on communication configurations. Trumpet supports only connections with eight data bits, no parity, and one stop bit. If your provider's modems expect seven data bits and even parity, you're out of luck. You'll need to use another program, because your version of Trumpet doesn't support that communications configuration. With other programs, you should be able to reset your communications parameters.

Tip　You might also wonder whether your POP has modems set for the other configuration. Unless you have a permanent connection, you can forget about the Internet provider changing its configuration to match yours. That's not the way the business works.

Line noise, even with error-correcting modems, can make the life of an online "SLIPper" miserable. If your connections are constantly interrupted by static or disconnections, have your local phone company check your lines. Also, if you have call waiting, deactivate it during data calls. Check your telephone directory for the commands you need to do this in your area.

After the Installation

Now that have you have SLIP, what can you do with it? Well, brace yourself. By itself, there's practically nothing you can do with SLIP. If you have a commercial program, it came with several TCP/IP applications, such as FTP and Telnet. With SLIP and these in hand, you can start exploring the Internet.

If you're doing this on the shareware route, don't abandon hope—many freeware and shareware programs are available that work with any Winsock-compliant version of SLIP. Trumpet Software has its own set of FTP, Telnet, Archie, Usenet news, and online chat clients. Other freeware/shareware programs that work with Trumpet's SLIP stack include The Gopher Book, Microelectronics and Computer Technology Corp's EINet WAIS (EIWAIS) client, and Qualcomm's Eudora mail reader.

Thanks to Winsock, you can also mix and match Internet programs from different commercial vendors. My own daily Internet software work collection includes Trumpet Winsock for the SLIP stack, plus Eudora, EIWAIS, Spry's FTP client, and NetManage's newsreader and Gopher client. Last but not least, I run NetScape Navigator for Webrunning.

Getting many of these programs can be a catch-22. To get them, you need to be online; but you need them to get online and find them in the first place. Fortunately, most of the software you'll need is on the *Inside the World Wide Web Bonus CD*. Don't have a CD-ROM drive? Try asking your friends and coworkers. Troubles and all, SLIP/PPP software is becoming amazingly popular.

Is it all worth it? That really depends on you. Putting up a SLIP connection is real work. If you're not a power user who already has, at the very least, a good understanding of data communications, don't try to do it. If you are technically inclined, however, and you already know a fair bit about the Internet, then give it a try. IP connections and programs give you the most power you'll ever have on the ever-winding road of the Internet.

Installing Web Viewers

You now have all you need to connect with the Web. To get the most from the Web, as mentioned in Chapter 2, "Introducing the Internet," you need viewer or helper applications.

Because the method of installing these programs varies from program to program and viewer to viewer, only the basics are covered here. Macintosh browsers come ready to work with particular viewers.

First, you must install the viewer program. Simply having a copy sitting on your hard disk is not enough. Normally, the process works like this: You start by moving the compressed version of the file to its own directory. Next, you decompress the file with the appropriate utility (usually PKZip for DOS/Windows and StuffIt Expander). From there, follow the program's installation instructions. After you install the viewer, make sure that it works independently. For instance, you can look at a JPEG file with LView before you hook your browser to LView.

Note   One thing to be aware of with some browsers, such as NCSA Mosaic, is that they will not use an external viewer for inline images if the browser already has an internal routine for handling the image type. As an example, Mosaic for Windows will not use LView for an inline GIF image, even if LView is your GIF viewer. Were you to open that same GIF file as a separate file, rather than as an inline part of an HTML document, LView would open the file.

That was the easy part. You now get to convince your browser that it should use these viewers. For Windows programs, that means editing the initial (INI) file (in Mosaic, the MOSAIC.INI file). This file may be in the browser's directory or in your Windows directory.

Note   Chapter 9, "Using Mosaic as a Web Client," shows you how to edit the MOSAIC.INI file to configure viewers and helper applications. At the time this book was prepared for the printer, a newer version of Mosaic was released in beta that eliminated the need to edit the MOSAIC.INI file.

With these viewers in place, you're ready to view any file you find on the Web. If you run into trouble, double-check and make sure that there are no typos in the INI file. One minor typo can prevent your browser from making sense of a file type.

Tip Before you find out the hard way—on the Web—that your browser and viewer aren't talking to each other, you can test them by trying to view an appropriate file type on your hard disk. You do this by making your browser open a local file.

Operating Systems

Finally, there's the issue of operating systems. Although most operating systems will work with one TCP/IP implementation or another, not all Web browsers can work with all versions of an operating system or environment.

Let's look at the easy ones first. Unix, Macintosh System 7.5 or higher, and OS/2 Warp will have no trouble with any browser written specifically for them. Unix users are the only ones with even a minor worry, because they must make sure that any given browser works with the GUI riding over their X-Windows networking windowing system. The most common Unix web browsers work with both the Motif and OpenLook style interfaces.

Things can get sticky with Windows and OS/2 2.1. Some browsers, notably NCSA Mosaic and Spyglass's Enhanced Mosaic, work only with versions of Windows that can handle 32-bit applications. Specifically, this means that the applications can run on Windows '95 and Windows/NT, but not on ordinary Windows. The solution to this problem is to upgrade Windows 3.1x with the Microsoft program, Win32s. The upgrade enables Windows 3.1x and Windows for Workgroups to run 32-bit, non–NT-specific Windows applications.

OS/2 2.1's problem is the same as that of ordinary Windows; unaided, it can't run 32-bit Windows applications. You cannot upgrade OS/2 2.1's Windows subsystem to run 32-bit Windows applications. Your choices here are to run an older version of NCSA Mosaic (any version earlier than Mosaic 2.0 Alpha 2); run a 16-bit Windows, such as NetScape Communications' NetScape; or upgrade to OS/2 Version 3 Warp.

In the near future, all operating systems and environments will have native TCP/IP and Web browsers. The Internet and Web rapidly are becoming part of the mainstream of all computing. In the meantime, the information in this chapter should see you clear. In the next chapter, we'll take a look at your choices in Web browsers.

Finding Web Access

F inding a connection to the Net used to be like a trip through Death Valley with no water: Some made it, most didn't. As recently as two years ago, if your school, office, or military installation couldn't get you a connection, you were out of luck. Those days are long gone. Today, you can pick from your phone company, your cable TV company, a local or national Internet provider, or an online service such as CompuServe. All these providers are called Internet Access Providers or Internet Services Providers (ISPs).

This chapter covers the following issues:

◆ How to find an Internet provider

◆ What to look for in an Internet provider

◆ How to make the right kind of connection

Finding Internet Providers

Before you can do anything on the Web, you have to find a connection. In particular, what you're looking for is an Internet provider that enables you to hook up with a network or shell connection. Online services that provide only an Internet interface, such as America Online and Delphi, cannot be used for Web purposes. This situation might change shortly. Some services, such as New York City's Pipeline, now have a graphical interface that includes Web searching capacities.

Note The online services are charging onto the Web with Web browsers of their own. America Online, CompuServe, and Prodigy all now have their own browsers. Delphi and Interchange are also moving quickly to add Web browsing features of thier own.

The first step is to learn who provides Internet connections in your area. People in suburban and urban areas have the advantage over their country cousins.

If you're in or near a city, you can find an Internet provider by looking in the business section of your local newspaper. If that doesn't work, ask around your circle of friends.

Another source of information is computer and technical magazines. Many Internet providers advertise nationally. In particular, look for copies of *BoardWatch*, *Internet World*, and *NetGuide*, all of which are reputable magazines that offer extensive coverage of the Internet and other online services.

Tip It's not easy to tell which Internet service is good and which isn't. Word of mouth usually concentrates on support, or the lack thereof. The problem with this is that almost all Internet providers these days are on the verge of being swamped. A system with good service today might have bad service tomorrow because of increased business. If a service seems to consistently have a bad reputation, then stay away; otherwise, give them the benefit of the doubt.

You should also call your local phone company or your long-distance provider to inquire about Web access. MCI's InternetMCI package, for instance, enables customers to access the Web with Netscape Communications' Netscape browser.

In some cases, all the previously mentioned resources have proved fruitless. If you find yourself faced with such a situation, you will have to resort to more drastic measures.

PDIAL and Other Information Sources

Your next stop in your search for Internet access should be Peter Kaminski's Public Dialup Internet Access List (PDIAL). This irregularly updated list contains addresses, costs, phone numbers, areas served, and services supplied by all North American Internet providers. To get the most recent copy of PDIAL, send a message to the following Internet address:

```
info-deli-server@netcom.com
```

Your message should have the subject line **Send PDIAL.** You don't have to write anything in the body of the message. If your e-mail program insists on having a message, just place a few spaces in the message's body. In a matter of minutes, if not seconds, you'll get the latest PDIAL by return post. You'll find a copy of the most recently available PDIAL in Appendix B of this book.

If you want to keep up-to-date with PDIAL, you also can subscribe to the document by sending a message to the previous address with the subject **Subscribe PDIAL.** If you want to get both the most recent copy and future editions, send both messages.

PDIAL used to be updated on a regular basis, but for many reasons this is no longer the case. The basic contact information will probably remain constant, but be forewarned that the pricing information can change rapidly. Still, caveats and all, PDIAL is an invaluable resource in finding Internet access.

Other Ways to Find Providers

If you still can't find an Internet provider, or you're not happy with the ones you've found with PDIAL, there's another way to find Internet access; read the following Usenet newsgroup:

```
alt.internet.access.wanted
```

The title of this newsgroup tells all. If no one has mentioned a service in your area, you can post your own message asking for Internet access in your area.

Stop   Whatever you do, don't post a message asking for Internet services in any other newsgroups. Because regular newsgroup readers were getting tired of always reading Internet access requests, this narrowly focused newsgroup was set up expressly for people looking for Internet access.

If you're a citizen of Australia, Great Britain, or New Zealand, you can also find FAQ files addressing your Internet access concerns. FAQs are posted in the alt.internet.services.wanted and news.answers newsgroups, as well as in the alt.internet.services.wanted directory of the `rtfm.mit.edu ftp` site.

If you have no FTP or Usenet news capacities, don't worry; you can use e-mail to get these files as well. Send a message to the following address:

`mail-server@rtfm.mit.edu`

And add the following as a message, not a subject:

`send /pub/usenet-by-group/alt.internet.access.wanted/`

This returns a message to your mailbox detailing which files are currently available in the newsgroup's directory. You would then pick the file you want by sending another message to the mail server with the appropriate file name added to the subject line. For instance, the following retrieves the current listing for Australian Internet sites:

`usenet-by-group/alt.internet.access.wanted/`
`➥Network_Access_in_Australia_FAQ`

Another valuable resource for finding Internet access is the following FTP site:

`is.internic.net/infoguide/getting-connected/`

Here, you'll find not only listings for English-speaking Net sites, but also listings for worldwide Internet points of presence. If you don't have FTP access, you can direct your access questions by e-mail to the address `refdesk@is.internic.net` and ask for the Internet Service Providers List for your country of choice.

These files are maintained by the InterNIC. The InterNIC is, in essence, the master registration and reference desk of the Internet. As an end-user, you're unlikely ever to need to call them with a question. Your Internet provider, however, will use the InterNIC to register new Internet sites and ask questions.

Of course, to reach PDIAL or the InterNIC, you'll need some type of access to the Internet. Access used to be a real catch-22 because you needed the Internet to contact PDIAL or InterNIC to get onto the Internet, but today, all online services provide at least e-mail connectivity to the Internet. These services constantly advertise "free for the first five hours" access to new subscribers. It's worth taking them up on their offer, if for no other reason than to get access to these other resources for free. Besides, you just might find that AOL, Compu-Serve, Interchange, and Prodigy have charms in their own right.

What to Look For in an Internet Provider

Once you have the names of potential Internet providers, the key factors you should look for are as follows:

- ◆ IP or shell access

- ◆ Local phone numbers

- ◆ 24-hour customer support

- ◆ 14,400 bps or faster access

The following sections cover these factors in detail.

IP or Shell Access

There are some programs—which you will take a closer look at shortly—that enable you to use a graphical Web browser (such as Mosaic) with a character-based shell account. One of these, the Internet Adapter (TIA), requires software, both on your PC and on your Internet provider's systems. If you want to use TIA and your provider doesn't support it, you're out of luck and you must look for another provider. The other shell-to-graphical-interface program, SlipKnot, works with any system.

The problem with both TIA and SlipKnot is that they can be slower than an IP connection. In most cases, though, only the most demanding user will see the difference. The problem with IP connections, as you've seen in earlier chapters, is that they can be very difficult to establish.

Stop   In your search for Internet access, you might see some services offering 800 number services. Some will go so far as to offer so-called free Internet services through their 800 phone number. The problem here is that 800 numbers often have hefty price tags attached to them. Just because a number begins with 800 doesn't mean that it's a toll-free number. It's sad but true that most companies that advertise free 800 Internet numbers are rip-off artists hoping that you will just assume that an 800 call is a free one.

Local Phone Numbers and X.25

Some companies have local phone numbers, but these numbers do not lead directly to their systems. CompuServe, SprintNet, and Tymnet all use this method. Here, you'll be using what is called an *X.25 data-link* to reach your Internet provider. An X.25 connection enables you to call a local phone number and reach a long distance Internet provider's computer without long-distance charges.

In this case, you might be facing an additional charge for using these companies' lines to access an Internet provider. Pipeline, based in New York City, uses SprintNet for nationwide service, and you must pay an hourly charge for this access. In cases such as this, you must clearly understand the pricing scheme. In particular, ask about charges for different times of the day and for high speed connections. The deal might still be affordable, but you'll need to add up all the charges before you get a good idea of what your monthly bill will be.

Another problem with X.25 hookups is that you're restricted to the speed of the modem on your end of the X.25 system. All too often, this modem will only go as fast as 9600 bps. That's barely tolerable for a Web connection. Given a choice between a nationwide service with slow modems and a small company with fast modems, you'll probably be better off with the no-name local business.

Customer Support

Full-time customer support is vital if you're going to be running on the Web after prime-time hours. You might think that the Internet and the Web will be

incidental for your work and life, but you may quickly find that you really need some information on the Web at 2 a.m., and there's a problem. That's not the moment to discover that your Internet provider has voice mail in lieu of 24-hour support.

Connection Speed

Your connection speed, more than any other factor, determines how quickly your Web sessions go. The rule of thumb is very simple: Get the fastest connection you possibly can. Remember, however, that you can only go as fast as the fastest connection in your communications chain. It doesn't do you any good to have a 14,400 bps modem if your service provider only supports 9600 bps or slower.

Besides simply looking for Internet providers with high speed modems, also look at other connection options. Integrated Services Digital Network (ISDN) is a local telephone service that offers speeds ranging from 56,000 to 128,000 bps. That's much faster than even a top-of-the-line V.34 modem.

The problem with ISDN is that telephone companies do not support the service very well. Another problem is that relatively few Internet providers—about 10 percent—support ISDN connections. You'll also pay more for an ISDN line than you would for an ordinary analog line.

The more important question, really, is whether you can get an ISDN line at all. Find out by asking your local Internet providers and telephone company.

Still, problems and all, ISDN is hard to beat for the fastest possible individual or corporate Internet service at a price that's not astronomical. The numbers vary wildly from area to area so it's difficult to make a hard and fast judgment call on pricing.

If you're interested in top Internet performance, but without the technical headaches and high prices of Frame-Relay and T-1 connections, ISDN should be your service of choice.

If you need an even higher class of speed, be ready to spend several thousand dollars. Details on how to set such connections are beyond the scope of this book. Suffice it to say, however, that you'll be working closely with your Internet provider.

How to Make the Right Kind of Connection

As mentioned earlier in this chapter, not just any connection to the Internet lets you access Web services with a graphical interface. At this time, there are five different flavors of connectivity that you can use to get to the Web:

◆ Direct TCP/IP connection

◆ Modem TCP/IP connection

◆ Shell account with the Internet Adapter

◆ Shell account with SlipKnot

◆ Proprietary interfaces

Direct Connection

The quickest way to access the Internet, a direct connection, is also the most expensive. You're unlikely to have a direct connection to the Web unless your business or school provides you with one.

Modem Connection

Perhaps the most common way of getting to the Web is by using Serial Line Internet Protocol (SLIP) or Point-to-Point Protocol (PPP) with a modem. These services work on any modem or with an ISDN adapter. You can learn more about these in Chapter 5, "What You Need to Link to the Web."

The Internet Adapter (TIA)

The Internet Adapter (TIA) and SlipKnot are a different kettle of fish. These take a very different path to providing you with Web access.

The Internet Adapter is a set of Internet access tools that enables you to use an ordinary shell account to access TCP/IP. In short, if your Internet provider supports TIA, you can use TIA to run Mosaic and other TCP/IP programs without a SLIP or PPP connection.

To get TIA to work, you need a single-user version for your PC or Macintosh, and your Internet provider must be running it on their system. TIA communicates with Web servers using your host system's IP address, then it internally redirects the TCP/IP information to your PC without requiring you to have your own IP address. The result? You get an IP-equivalent connection for a shell account price.

TIA can't do everything a normal SLIP connection can do, but it comes awfully close. The only common utility that won't run under TIA but does under normal TCP/IP hookups is ping. *Ping* is a program that enables you to check that your connection with another Internet system is working. Most end-user software, such as mail programs, Web browsers, and Gopher clients, work normally.

TIA works well. Although it puts another layer of complexity between you and the Internet, it's not really difficult to use and there's no discernible speed reduction.

You should also know that TIA emulates a SLIP, not a PPP, connection. But for almost all users, there's no practical difference.

What you can't do with TIA, however, is run IP server programs because, from the Internet's viewpoint, your system doesn't have an IP address. So if you want to run your own Web, POP mail, or FTP server, you'll still need a "normal" TCP/IP connection.

TIA is not a panacea. To use it, you'll still need a TCP/IP stack on your PC. In short, although TIA enables you to use TCP/IP programs without a true TCP/IP connection, you're not going to be spared any of the headaches of setting up a TCP/IP connection.

Cyberspace Development is the company behind TIA, but the product is marketed by InterMind. TIA is only available from online sources. Fortunately, you can get TIA from FTP sites everywhere. If you can't get a copy from a local FTP site, you can get it using the following address:

```
marketplace.com
```

When you get the program, you must obtain a free 15-day license from InterMind. After 15 days, TIA will deactivate. To keep it working, you must buy a full license. For more information, send mail to the appropriate e-mail addresses listed in table 6.1.

TABLE 6.1
TIA Information E-Mail Addresses

Service	Address
General info	`tia-info@marketplace.com`
Single User FAQ	`tia-FAQ-single@marketplace.com`
Host FAQ	`tia-FAQ-host@marketplace.com`
User Installation Instr.	`tia-install-single@marketplace.com`
Host Installation Instr.	`tia-install-host@marketplace.com`
TIA Product Brochure	`software@marketplace.com`
Dial-Up TCP/IP Help File	`tia-tcpip-info@marketplace.com`

SlipKnot

Despite its name, SlipKnot is not a SLIP program. Rather, it is a system that lets you run a Microsoft Windows graphical Web browser using an ordinary shell account.

SlipKnot manages this feat by serving as the Windows front end to either the Lynx or WWW character-based Web browsers, which gives you a graphical Web browser that will work with almost any shell account. For a glimpse of what it looks like, see figure 6.2.

To use SlipKnot, you must have a 386 or higher system running Windows 3.1*x*, Windows for WorkGroups, Windows/NT, or Windows 95. SlipKnot cannot execute under OS/2-Windows or a Mac running SoftWindows.

On the Internet provider side of using SlipKnot, you'll only need lynx version 2.2 or higher or a version of WWW. Most Internet sites have one, if not both, of these programs. To check your version of Lynx, run the following command:

```
lynx -version
```

Figure 6.1

Believe it or not, there's just an ordinary shell account hiding behind this glossy SlipKnot exterior.

Your Internet provider must also be able to transfer files to your system using any of the following data transfer protocols:

◆ Xmodem

◆ Xmodem-CRC

◆ Xmodem-1K

◆ Ymodem-Batch

SlipKnot does not support Zmodem or Kermit.

SlipKnot is a shareware program that's widely available online. If you can't find it from any other source, you can ftp it from the following directory:

```
oak.oakland.edu/SimTel/win3/internet/
```

The next chapter goes into detail about what SlipKnot's browser, SlipKnot Web, can and can't do. Suffice it to say that for an inexpensive and easy way to start browsing the Web, SlipKnot can't be beat. The program is far easier to set up than any of the IP Web browsers. The only ones that are easier to set up are the proprietary interfaces.

Proprietary Interfaces

Some online services—such as Prodigy, AOL, and Pipeline—use their own interfaces to enable you to explore the Web. With these services you have no choice but to use the proprietary interface. Usually, these services do not support other Web interfaces. Although this lack of support restricts your choice to their front-end program, it also means you get better technical support from these services because they don't need to try to be experts on half a dozen different TCP/IP programs and as many more Web interfaces.

The real advantage of these interfaces over their competitors is their ease of setup. Because these interfaces have built-in defaults about where to find things such as the DNS and the gateway system, you don't need to get your hands dirty with these details.

In the future, you can expect to see online service-specific interfaces from more major online services, such as GEnie, Delphi, and Interchange. Other Internet providers are moving toward using Pipeline's software for their own services. The next chapters cover these interfaces in more detail.

If your service doesn't support any of the aforementioned services—for example, if it has a menu system that makes it impossible to get to the shell or supplies only mail and Usenet news—you'll need to switch services. Otherwise, you'll never be able to get to the Web. Before you do this, check to make sure that your provider doesn't support either TCP/IP or shell connectivity. Chances are that they will support one or the other, if not both.

C H A P T E R

7

Examining WWW Browsers

O nce upon a time, you had one good choice for a Web browser: NCSA Mosaic. Things have changed. Today, everyone and his uncle has a Web browser they want to sell or give you. What's a Web explorer to do?

This chapter won't simply tell you to do this or that. Although it shows you specific browsers, those browsers change so quickly there's little point in making precise recommendations. What the chapter does do is tell you what features to look for in your Web browser.

This chapter looks at the following:

◆ Available browser types

◆ Features to look for in a browser

◆ A selection of browsers

Examining Browser Types

Four basic types of browsers are available. The first type requires a TCP/IP connection. Another type—America Online, Pipeline, and Prodigy are examples—work only when used with a particular online service. The tried-and-true character-based interfaces—like Lynx—offer a third type. The final browser type—for example, SlipKnot—gives you a graphical interface while working with an ordinary shell account connection.

Tip   An online service's Web access may be more expensive to use than the same access from an Internet provider. On the other hand, online service's browser connections are much easier to set up. If you don't want to get your hands dirty with DNS addresses and netmasks, an online service is the way to go.

Before shopping for any Web browser, take a look at what's already on your computer. IBM's OS/2 Warp operating system already has a browser—Web Explorer—bundled with it. Microsoft plans to include a version of the Spyglass browser with Windows 95. With both companies also offering Internet access, you might find that you don't need a Web browser.

Stop   Just because your system comes with a Web browser, don't be afraid to look for another browser if the one you have doesn't meet your needs. With a multitude of choices, there's no reason to stick with a browser you don't like.

A long chain of factors influence the speed of your connection. IP connections, because they don't have to contend with any additional system overhead, offer the quickest way to wander around the Web.

NCSA Mosaic, a TCP/IP browser, at one time was the most popular Web browser. It became the killer application that ignited the Web explosion. Thanks to its blazing success, the browser field is expanding like wildfire. NCSA Mosaic has long since ceased to be the hottest browser around. That honor now belongs to Netscape. With new and improved browsers arriving almost every week, Netscape might not always be the white-hot browser of the Web circuit.

If the gold medal for speed belongs to the TCP/IP browsers, then the ease-of-use award goes to the integrated browsers of services like America Online, CompuServe, NetCom, Pipeline, and Prodigy. In all other ways, however, no useful generalizations can be made about these proprietary browsers.

The shell browsers, such as SlipKnot, have the virtue of cheapness. Although not as fast or as easy to use as their competitors, they are often the most affordable fully graphical Web front ends.

The older character interfaces are fast, but only because they don't have to deal with a heavy load of graphics. Still, if you're in a hurry for information and don't care about its format or appearance, character-based front ends have much to offer. Also, with the right software, these interfaces enable the blind to use the Web.

You can get a browser in a number of different ways. In addition to having one bundled with your operating system, you might find that your new computer already has the front end to either an Internet provider—like NetCom—or an online service—such as Prodigy—that includes a Web browser.

Many browsers, such as Cello, NCSA Mosaic, and some versions of Netscape, are given away for free on the Internet or online services. And free doesn't necessarily mean poor quality. These free browsers are as good, if not better, than any interface for which you would pay cash. Later, this chapter shows you how to obtain some of these browsers

You can buy other browsers, such as CompuServe/SPRY's AIR Mosaic and Netmanage's WebSurfer, at a store like any other software package. Still others, such as NetCom's NetCruiser, are *shareware* (that is, you can try it for free, but to continue using the browser, you must pay for it).

Features to Look For in a Browser

So how do you find the browser that's right for you? First, as detailed in Chapter 5, "What You Need to Link to the Web," that question depends on your Internet connection type. If your only connection to the Internet is through the Interchange online service, for example, having Netscape isn't going to help you in the least. Your browser must fit your connection.

Next, your browser has to work for your system. Again, Chapter 5 discusses the issues of system and connection performance that are critical for successfully running the Web.

Tip Even if you don't have the world's most powerful system with the fastest Internet connection, you still can use the Web. The most bare-bones system—say an old KayPro CP/M computer with a 300 bps modem—can use the Web with a shell account and a character-based browser. It might not be as much fun as Netscape running on an *Integrated Services Digital Network* (ISDN) line at 128 Kbps and a 120 Mhz Pentium system, but it can be done.

The following list describes the ideal Web browser:

◆ Is easy to install

◆ Is easy to customize

◆ Enables you to navigate the Web easily

◆ Enables you to view most common Web document types

◆ Supports secure transactions

◆ Supports other Internet/Usenet tools

◆ Works quickly

Installing Your Browser

As previous chapters indicate, setting up an Internet connection can be a bear of a job. If you go with a stand-alone TCP/IP browser, such as NCSA Mosaic or Netscape, you have to wrestle that bear.

If you're not eager for hand-to-paw combat with the network, your best move is to an online service's Web service. Just install the software, and you're ready to go.

Some Microsoft Windows browsers require that Windows be upgraded with Win32s. Win32s, now up to version 1.25, is a Windows enhancement that enables Windows 3.1 and Windows for Workgroups to run some non-NT or Windows 95-specific 32-bit Windows programs.

Tip   Sometimes Win32s is bundled with your browser. More often, however, you
have to hunt it down from FTP sites. You can always find the most recent
copy of the file at the following site:

```
http://www.ncsa.uiuc.edu/SDG/Software/WinMosaic/win32s.htm
```

Customizing Your Browser

You might think that customizing a Web browser isn't that important; it is.
Customizing a browser isn't just a matter of making it look pretty; it's a matter
of configuring the browser so that it works successfully with the Web.

Although most of the Web is written in HTML and most of its graphics are in
GIF format, many documents and images are in other formats. To handle these
foreign formats, either your browser must be able to work directly with these
formats or you must be able to customize your browser so that you can use
helper applications to view the foreign formats.

Ideally, your browser would not need helper applications; but with everything
from Notes databases to Word for Windows documents appearing on the Web,
that's just a pipedream. The next best thing is to have a browser that makes it
easy to plug in helper applications to deal with new file formats.

The character-based interface browsers normally fare the worst when it comes
to helper applications. Not only are they incapable of dealing with graphics,
but they cannot cope with such non-HTML text files as those in the PostScript
or Adobe Corp's *Portable Document Format* (PDF) page description formats.

The best browsers enable you to configure helper applications by using menu
options. The ultimate browser would suggest the appropriate applications for
the foreign format document. Unfortunately, no browsers have this capability
... yet.

Navigation Advice

Getting through the Web can be as tough as trying to hack your way through
one of those nasty, sticky webs spun by monster spiders in a B-grade movie.
Your browser can be as sharp as a vorpal sword, cutting down all that stands
between you and your information goal; or it can be as useless as a dull putty
knife.

A decent Web navigator enables you to move back to previously visited sites with the click of a button. A better one enables you to decide exactly how far you want to backtrack along your route, rather than forcing you to laboriously walk back step by step.

The best Web navigator enables you to keep a permanent record of favorite destinations. This feature is invaluable if you spend any serious amount of time on the Web.

Although such Web mapping is a common feature, Web browsers have a way to go to perfect that feature. Netscape Navigator, for example, an otherwise outstanding Web browser, doesn't let you put your favorite Web sites in any order, except from first entered to last entered. A function enabling you to automatically sort the sites into alphabetical order by name would be greatly welcomed.

 Note Another nice addition to this feature would be the ability to make notes on each site, for when you're trying to remember exactly what it was that fascinated you about a particular site a month ago. Alas, no browser currently comes with an automatic search function to find a site by the notes you have added to it.

Viewing

Previously, this chapter touched on the problem of viewing foreign file formats. As the Web grows, more formats are being used to make Web documents. Consequently, sometimes even to view a page you need a browser that's up to the task.

A browser must be able to read HTML 1.0 and GIF89a—the basics. Once, those were the only capabilities it needed. Today, a browser should also be able to handle HTML 3.0 documents, and Adobe Acrobat PDF file format for text. Graphically speaking, your browser should be literate in GIF89a, GIF24, JPEG, and *Portable Network Graphics* (PNG).

The well-equipped Web explorer also has helper applications to handle QuickTime and MPEG movies, and Word for Windows and PostScript documents. For the foreseeable future, these extras are strictly optional.

Why does your browser need the capability to handle so many different formats? The answer lies in the next two sections, which briefly examine the world of text and graphic standards on the Web.

Text Wars

At one time, all text on Web pages was in HTML. Time moved on, and with it went the unity of a single hypermedia language. Today, several HTML variants and other document formats are used in Web pages.

This shift signals a change in the Web from a friendly place, where any Web browser can be used with virtually any document, to a hostile world, where not all browsers work with all Web documents.

This has always been something of a problem for Web browsers—it's the reason for viewers. In the future, this problem will only get worse. Pure HTML is no longer the only language of the land, and more file formats are being used to carry the basic textual information of the Web. Let's take a look at the players in the Web language wars.

Before HTML, there was *Standard Generalized Markup Language* (SGML). SGML is an International Standards Organization (ISO) page description standard (ISO 8879). SGML itself does not describe how to format a document. Rather, it provides a set of rules, or grammar, to create *Document Type Definitions* (DTDs). A DTD specifies how to identify structural items, such as keywords, end notes, and words in italics by specifying tags and their meanings for a class of documents. HTML is a variation from the SGML theme and can be thought of as a DTD for hypermedia documents.

Note Until recently, pure SGML was regarded as too complex for Web documents. Now, some Webweavers are exploring the use of SGML on the Web. The SGML community is also lobbying for HTML to move closer to SGML orthodoxy. They claim SGML offers readers far more sophisticated textual resources—such as the ability to bounce more easily from text to footnote to bibliography and back again—than does HTML.

The *Text Encoding Initiative* (TEI), for example, an SGML DTD for the humanities, enables authors to combine different editions of a text into a single hypertext document. You can have both the manuscript and its final published form in one document, for instance, and easily go back and forth between the two versions.

 Note SGML most likely will fade into a document format hidden behind an HTML mask. Electronic Book Technologies' DynaWeb points the way to this future. DynaWeb is a Unix Web server that automatically translates SGML documents into HTML for Web browsers. Some SGML documents will prove too complex for timely automatic translations. For these, manual translations into HTML will be their way on to the Web. Fortunately, this tedious job will be semi-automated with the use of tools like Avalanche Development Company's SGML Hammer, an SGML-to-HTML translator.

In the meantime, the mainstream of Web document designers are moving from HTML 1.0 to HTML 2.0. The first version of HTML, HTML 0.9, though still used with some documents, is now considered antique. HTML 1.0 remains the most popular Web document format. Fortunately, those with hours invested in legacy documents do not need to update these items. Any Web browser can read these documents.

HTML 2.0 gives the existing state of mainstream HTML usage the official blessing of the *Internet Engineering Task Force* (IETF). The HTML IETF, in turn, derives its authority from the *World Wide Web Consortium* (W3C). This group— led by Tim Berners-Lee, founder of the Web—guides the development of HTML and the other Web standards: *universal resource locators* (URL) and *hypertext transfer protocol* (HTTP). In the case of HTML 2.0, rules for forms and currently legal character sets are being formally made part of the standard.

Not all present-day HTML uses have been grandfathered into HTML 2.0, however, nor will they be in the next interim release of an HTML standard, HTML 2.1. In particular, several Netscape Communications changes are not included in HTML 2.0. Netscape has made both additions and extensions to HTML. The CENTER tag, for example, is a new addition that centers text. Netscape also has added to existing HTML practice with extensions to the IMG command. Netscape's IMG tag enables users to create floating graphics. Writers can create documents with graphic elements that stay in the same relative position on the virtual page. The Netscape changes give Web authors far more control over the appearance of their articles.

Note One area that might prove to be a breaking point between Netscape's HTML and the rest of the world's is the FONT tag, which controls font presentation. For now though, to Netscape's credit, their amendments to current HTML practice are designed to be compatible with mainstream HTML usage. In other words, if you use a Web browser—such as NCSA Mosaic—that cannot deal with Netscape's HTML variant, you can view Netscape HTML pages with no loss of information. Other changes, however, might not be so easily reconciled between HTML and HTML+Netscape advocates. Web might be torn between HTML and HTML+Netscape documents.

Whether HTML remains an open standard in the business world remains to be seen. Plans are in place to finalize HTML 2.1. HTML 2.1 will include up-to-the-minute HTML changes and minor tweaks. As to what those minor tweaks might be, even the IETF doesn't have a good answer. One of the changes being considered is adding *International Committee for Accessible Document Design* (ICADD)-specific tags to aid in translating HTML documents into Braille. Most of 2.1's changes will be similarly minor in that they will affect only a small percentage of the Web's population.

The IETF committee continues to press forward with incorporating Dave Raggett's HTML+ ideas into HTML 3.0. HTML 3.0 adds features to HTML rather than merely systematizing current practice. Some of these features include resizable tables, mathematical formulas, document-specific toolbars, and client-side form scripts.

HTML 3.0 is now at the demonstration stage. Test HTML 3.0 documents are not widely available on the Web and can only be viewed properly with Raggett's test Unix browser, Arena. When HTML 3.0 documents do become available, you will need to upgrade your browser to use them. HTML 3.0 will be backwards compatible—any HTML 3.0-compliant browser will be able to read earlier HTML documents.

In essence, HTML 3.0 will give authors additional ways to control the look of their documents. The way to accomplish this goal is a matter of hot debate and might yet lead to HTML splitting into incompatible variants. The IETF is discussing the use of style sheets and how to embed presentation control into HTML. For the latter, the ideas under discussion are to add new elements, to add attributes to existing HTML tags, or to use SGML processing instructions.

At this time, expanding the role of existing HTML tags is the most popular approach.

Some Webweavers, desiring absolute control over document presentation, are starting to use Adobe Acrobat's PDF. PDF enables authors to send documents with PostScript-like quality to the original but without PostScript's size and compatibility penalties. Today, with Netscape embracing PDF as a supported format, there is some interest in using PDF as an HTML replacement. For now, though, PDF is more commonly used as a viewer file type. The Internal Revenue Service (IRS), for example, uses HTML for their Web pages, but IRS forms arc kcpt in PDF (see fig. 7.1).

Figure 7.1

IRS forms are now available in PDF format.

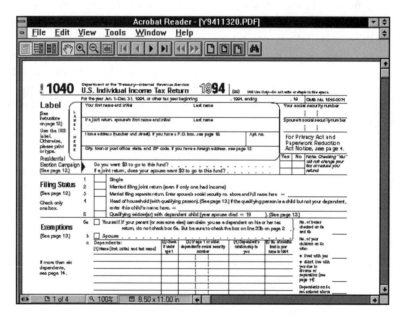

For now, although the potential for conflict exists, you can read any HTML document you find. In the future, however, HTML will not always be the only accepted Web language. As Netscape and other companies move into the Web, commercial pressure to add unique features to respective products will grow.

Stop Unfortunately, when it comes to software, uniqueness usually equals incompatibility. Nowhere is that clearer than with Microsoft's move to add Microsoft Word documents to the Web. Microsoft has two Web products.

The first, Internet Assistant for Word, combines an HTML editor with a Web browser. That's what everyone knows about Internet Assistant. What's not so well known is that Internet Assistant can also generate Web documents in Word's native format. You can create these hypermedia documents using drag-and-drop techniques that employ Microsoft's *Object Linking and Embedding* (OLE) 2.0 protocol.

With OLE connections, Microsoft makes it easy to create Web documents that include Microsoft PowerPoint graphics, Microsoft Excel spreadsheets and Microsoft Access reports. Sense a theme here? Despite Microsoft's support of the HTML open standard, the Redmond Washington giant is also pushing into the Internet with its proprietary file formats and interoperability protocol.

Microsoft's second Web program is Word Viewer, which is included on the *Inside World Wide Web* bonus disk. It is a helper program that enables users to view Microsoft's Web Word documents. One of the problems associated with this strategy is that it forces users at this point to be running Microsoft Windows. But what if you're not running Windows? Then you're out in the cold. Although a Macintosh version of Viewer might eventually be available, Viewer probably will not be ported to any other operating systems.

So what do these projected changes mean for you? They mean, sad to say, that the Web is going to be divided into incompatible sections. If there is popular support for standard HTML and open systems, you will still be able to roam over most of the Web freely. If not, expect an end to the days when you could explore the Web without restriction. Your only response will be to get a Web browser with the fullest possible support for foreign file formats.

Graphics Wars

You might not believe it, especially if you're new to the Web, but once there was no question concerning Web graphics. The Web's inline graphics were GIF. Period. End of statement. Alas, all good things must come to an end.

Today, GIF is no longer the guaranteed inline graphics format of choice. That's because Unisys, the patent owner on the *Lempel-Ziv-Welch* (LZW) data compression algorithm, began demanding licensing fees for programs using LZW. Three guesses which popular graphics format uses LZW? Yes, that's right, GIF. CompuServe, GIF's owner, then started charging fees for programs using GIF.

These charges don't affect Webweavers or users directly. You can use and view GIFs in your pages to your heart's content without payment. The changes do affect vendors that make programs that create, edit, or (and this is the important one) view GIFs—browsers.

When news of the licensing fee first came out, the graphics and online services programming communities blew up at the very notion. For years, the GIF format, though copyrighted by CompuServe, had been the free, de facto graphics standard of not only CompuServe and the Web, but for most of the online world. Graphic designers and programmers started to feel as if someone had changed the rules on them in mid-stream; they began to look for alternatives to GIF.

Browser programmers responded to GIF licensing fees by adding JPEG support to their browsers. Despite this early support, JPEG hasn't become the dominant inline image format, and it probably won't make further inroads. JPEG isn't as flexible as GIF for design purposes. JPEG is a fine format for an image to end up in (if you don't mind the loss of some resolution). It's also very hard to edit.

The immediate result of all this has been to slow down Unisys' requests for licensing fees. CompuServe, faced with outraged developers, decided to dump LZW from GIF and come up with a new GIF. This new format, GIF24, promises to be the "free, clear, and open format" for all developers that GIF was meant to be.

Meanwhile, graphics developers have been working on other alternatives to GIF. The *Portable Network Graphics* (PNG, pronounced "ping") format offers the most popular alternative. PNG designers hope PNG will replace GIF for inline images.

PNG produces smaller graphic files than GIF. It also includes 24-bit TrueColor support, and is free of all LZW licensing problems. For the down and dirty details, examine PNG's source code at the following site:

```
ftp://ftp.uu.net:/graphics/png
```

What does the preceding information mean for Web designers? First, although PNG has a great deal of freeware and shareware author support, the big-name graphics developers haven't put their support behind PNG. Aldus Photoshop, for example, has no plans right now for PNG input and output mechanisms. Consequently, some considerable time is going to pass before many top-quality PNG images become available.

More importantly (for our purposes), the Web browser designers currently are sitting on the sidelines. Will PNG get their support? Will the designers continue to support GIF? Right now, they're not talking.

Some predictions can be made. SPRY, now owned by CompuServe, will certainly support GIF24 in AIR Mosaic. Web browser vendors don't want to pay the fees, nor do they want to abandon GIF. Who can blame them? If browsers stop supporting GIF, almost every Web page on the planet will need to be changed.

Browser vendors probably will end up—reluctantly—paying fees to Unisys, while encouraging the use of other graphic formats by adding GIF24 and PNG support. It won't happen quickly. Neither GIF24 nor PNG have widespread support at the moment. Even so, eventually you will need support for one or the other—if not both—in your browser.

Supporting Secure Transactions

If you're going to log in to a subscription-only Web site, such as HotWired, or you ever plan to buy anything over the Web, your browser must support a secure transaction protocol. These protocols encrypt your private data so that no rogue spiders on the Web can intercept it.

Currently, two secure transaction formats are battling for Web domination—Terisa Systems' *Secure HTTP* (SHTTP) and Netscape's *Secure Sockets Layer* (SSL). Though they go about their work in different manners, the goal is the same: to encrypt data that moves between your browser and a Web site.

With each format, both the server and the browser must use the same security protocol. At this time, Spyglass's Enhanced Mosaic 2.0 and its many children—such as SPRY's AIR Mosaic—support SHTTP; Netscape Navigator works with SSL. Other browsers soon will be including support for one or the other.

Companies are also lining up behind the security protocols. SSL, used in Netscape's Netsite Commerce Server, has been licensed by Digital, Novell, Bank of America, and Delphi Internet Service. W3C members, including AT&T, IBM, MCI Communications, Microsoft, Netscape, Novell, and NCSA, have all come out in support of SHTTP. Notice that Digital, Novell, and Netscape support both protocols.

For Web users, this effort means that you can look forward to a time when the two competing standards will be combined and you won't have to worry about which standard, if any, your browser supports. Your browser should definitely have some form of data transfer security. Without it, you're leaving the door open for all technically astute, online criminals.

Supporting Other Internet/Usenet Tools

All Web browsers are capable of supporting some other Internet tools. You can, for example, access FTP and Gopher servers from a browser. In addition, Web browsers are adding other jobs as they move from being strictly Web browsers to all-in-one Internet front ends.

Some users, who like to pick just the right application for the job, don't care whether their browser can do anything other than roam the Web. Other users, however, like the convenience of a one-stop Internet front end.

If you prefer to use your Web browser to replace all the Internet tools, the minimal additional tools you should expect are Usenet newsgroups and e-mail. No program at this time has full e-mail support, but many of them now enable you to send messages out.

Having Usenet newsgroup support isn't enough in itself. You want your newsgroup reader to support easy newsgroup selection, message threading, and sophisticated message-reply options. With anything less, you get more annoyance than enjoyment from Usenet news. For now, the browser that makes Usenet news the most fun is Netscape.

Moving one level up, you probably want a browser that supports Telnet and its mainframe cousin, Telnet-3270. A rarer feature by far is a WAIS client. If you need WAIS access, explore Cello, the only browser with built-in WAIS support.

Work Quickly

More than anything else, your browser's speed depends on the speed of your Internet connection. Having said that, your browser can make it seem as if you arc moving much faster on the Web than you actually are.

Netscape offers this bit of magic. Netscape—and now other browsers—displays the text of a Web site first, and then takes its time bringing up the pretty graphics. It doesn't sound like much, but the overall effect makes Netscape feel much quicker. Rather than waiting for a 20 KB GIF to appear in its entirety, you can decide early as to whether you want to stick around for the whole image based on the already displayed words from a page.

Another trick in working performance wonders involves displaying information as soon as it arrives. Some browsers do this poorly, showing chunks of information in screen-blurring displays. These displays leave you rubbing your eyes and wondering whether or not you made the right decision in trading in your TV set for a Pentium and a Web hookup. The speed secret here is for the browser to smoothly show information as it appears.

The final touch, completing the illusion of speed, enables you to stop an incoming page so that you can move on to something else. There's nothing quite as frustrating as waiting for a page to appear so you can get on with another job. Many programs, like Netscape, now enable you to hit the Esc key to escape out of a boring page. Also, browsers such as Netscape cache images. If a new document you're downloading uses the same image you've already viewed elsewhere, it will call up that image from the cache.

Some true speed differences exist between browsers, normally found in how they handle graphics. Some programs, such as Mosaic, display graphics pretty slowly; others, such as Netscape, quickly paint GIFs to your screen.

Because everyone is trying to make the fastest possible browsers, don't take the comparisons above as gospel. Within a year, all contemporary browsers should be about equal in both perceived and actual speed.

A Selection of Browsers

Now that you have the basics, you're ready to take a look at browsers. Remember as you go through this section that browsers are changing on an almost weekly basis and that new ones are coming out at an even faster clip. Regard this information, therefore, as more of a general guide than specific recommendations.

AIR Mosaic

SPRY's AIR Mosaic represents the first commercial Web browser. Though it can be slow, especially when displaying large GIFs, AIR Mosaic features a Spyglass-based interface that is easy to use and to configure (as far as IP-based browsers go).

For a trial run, download a test version of the program, using FTP, from the following URL address:

```
ftp://ftp.spry.com/demo/AirMosaicDemo/
```

The commercial version is available in several packages, including SPRY's Internet in a Box, AIR Series, and Mosaic in a Box.

One of AIR Mosaic's strongest points is its ease of installation. Unlike other Windows TCP/IP browsers, you don't need to add Win32s support.

Another AIR Mosaic plus is that you can file documents into folders, which can be added to the menu bar. You can create up to 15 hotlist folders. Each of these folders can handle approximately 200 URLs. Each of these features combine to make mapping your way through the Web much simpler.

One feature unique to AIR Mosaic is its Kiosk mode (see fig. 7.2). In Kiosk mode, you see the Web page without the visual obstruction of a menu. Although this mode works well when you want to get the fullest look at a home page, it does have its limitations. In Kiosk mode, you cannot use any of the program's navigation tools; you are limited to navigating by hyperlinks.

Figure 7.2

AIR Mosaic's unique Kiosk mode gives you the big Web page picture.

If you are a CompuServe user, AIR Mosaic is the browser you are to use. Despite rumors of a single CompuServe/Web interface, like that of America Online, with CompuServe you must run AIR Mosaic as a separate application. The first versions of this model of AIR Mosaic had some serious installation problems, but they should be resolved by now.

Overall, AIR Mosaic is a good, though somewhat slow, Windows browser. For more information, contact SPRY at 800-777-9638, ext. 26; 206-447-0300; fax, 206-447-9008; e-mail, `info26@spry.com`.

America Online

When America Online (AOL) purchased BookLink Technologies, all the experts thought, "Aha, InternetWorks will become AOL's browser; just goes to show that even the pros get it wrong some days." Instead, AOL's integral Web browser has a Mosaic-like look and feel (see fig. 7.3). AOL's first stab at a browser is available only in AOL's Windows interface, but a Macintosh version will be arriving soon.

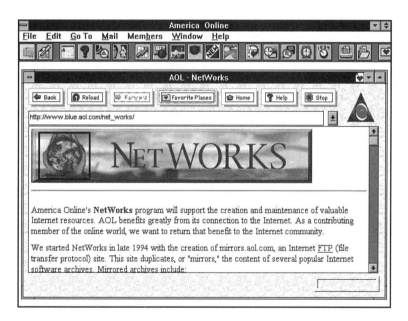

Figure 7.3

AOL's first browser is short on features, such as a history function.

The decision not to go with InternetWorks might have been a mistake. The AOL front end lacks several basic navigation tools, such as a history function revealing recently visited sites. It's not fast, it lacks features, and it has trouble with some common HTML 2.0 features, such as forms. AOL rushed this version of the browser to market in response to CompuServe's and Prodigy's arrival on the net, and every shaved second shows.

If you're already on AOL, you're stuck with it. At least AOL is easy to install. If you're not on AOL, the Web browser is no reason to consider joining AOL.

The only good thing that can be said about this browser is that AOL does work hard on its interface, so we can hope that they'll get it right sometime in 1995.

Cello

Many browsers tend to look alike, mainly because they're all chips off the Mosaic block. Netscape and AIR Mosaic, for example, both have original Mosaic designers behind them. Cello (Windows), on the other hand, is carved from its own rock (see fig. 7.4).

Figure 7.4

Cello's graphics and text rendering is crude; but otherwise, it's a fine, free browser.

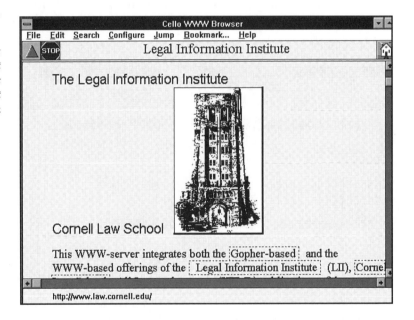

Different doesn't mean bad. Cello, an IP-based browser developed by programmers at Cornell Law School's Legal Information Institute, works more quickly than other freeware browsers. It is available over the Internet, using FTP, from the following URL:

```
ftp://ftp.law.cornell.edu/pub/LII/Cello/cello.zip
```

In addition to its speed, Cello includes several other Internet tools. You can use Cello to read Usenet news, send (but not retrieve) electronic mail, and perform WAIS searches. Cello also bundles a Telnet and a 3270 terminal emulator in its bag of goodies.

Cello does have its imperfections. The program doesn't render graphics well. Many HTML pages appear crude in Cello. Another more annoying trait is that when you resize a Window, you must reload the document before you can view it properly. Further, Cello does not support any Web security protocols.

These points are bad enough, but far more damaging to Cello's future as a Web browser is that it is no longer being updated. As the Web grows more complicated, Cello is quickly becoming an antique program. Still, if you want a freeware, all-in-one Web browser and interface, Cello has its strengths.

Lynx

If you don't care for graphics and just want your information straight from the Web, then Lynx—the premier character-based Web browser—is for you (see fig. 7.5). Because Lynx runs on VT100 terminals (or in a Telnet session), you can only see or hear multimedia items by downloading them.

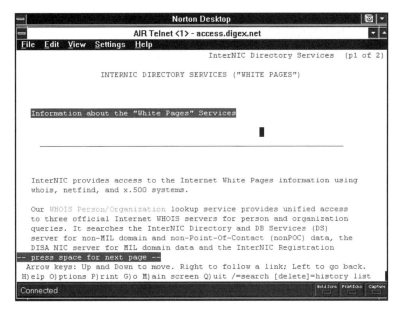

Figure 7.5

Although Lynx is not too exciting visually, you can obtain it for free on most Internet shell systems.

Lynx is not limited to ASCII text. The newest version, 2.2, supports Curses, a Unix text-based windowing system. Curses makes seeing links much easier than with other text-based interfaces.

Another plus, if you're using a dial-up shell account, is that you can download a file—with Zmodem or the like—to your local PC while your Unix system is still receiving a file from an FTP server or you're wandering the Web. It's as close to on-screen multitasking as you're going to get with a VT100-bound shell session.

The program also has the twin virtues of being cheap and free of installation. Most shell accounts already have access to a Lynx client, in which case all you have to do is type in **lynx** and you're on your way to the Web.

Furthermore, Lynx comes with a feature that not all fancy graphical browsers have: an integrated Usenet newsreader. Some features, of course, such as support for a security protocol or non-HTML text files like PDF, are beyond Lynx. If that's fine by you, then Lynx's meat-and-potatoes approach to the Web might be exactly what you need. If your Internet site doesn't have a copy of Lynx, you can download one from the following:

```
ftp2.cc.ukans.edu
```

Spyglass Enhanced Mosaic

Spyglass won the right to take NCSA Mosaic and turn it into a commercial product (see fig. 7.6). The company's first attempts at Enhanced Mosaic (Mac, Unix, Windows) have added such functionality to Mosaic as form and printing support, but the program still feels more like NCSA Mosaic with the edges smoothed off rather than a new product.

Unless you obtain Spyglass's Enhanced NCSA Mosaic through the purchase of O'Reilly and Associates' *The Mosaic Handbook,* you're unlikely to have direct contact with Enhanced Mosaic. Spyglass normally sells Enhanced Mosaic to other companies, who then modify it and bundle it with their own TCP/IP offerings. The following is a list of businesses currently marketing Enhanced Mosaic under their own name:

◆ AT&T Global Information Solutions

◆ Corel Corporation

◆ Digital Equipment Corporation

◆ Firefox Corporation

◆ FTP Software, Inc.

◆ InContext

◆ Luckman Interactive

◆ Microsoft (under the name Internet Explorer)

◆ Mortice Kern Systems

◆ Performance Systems International

◆ Quarterdeck

◆ SPRY

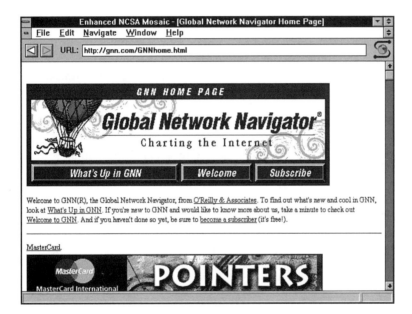

Figure 7.6

Look familiar? Enhanced Mosaic bears more than a passing resemblance to its ancestor, NCSA Mosaic.

If you're running a browser from any of the companies just listed, you're working with Enhanced Mosaic. Some, like SPRY, have heavily modified the program; others have done little with the base program.

No matter the version, Enhanced Mosaic always supports SHTTP. You shouldn't have any security worries in the commercial Web of tomorrow.

Generally, Enhanced Mosaic installs easily. The Windows version requires Win32s support. Customization was troublesome in early versions of Enhanced Mosaic. At times, in the Windows version, you even had the dubious pleasure of manually editing the INI file.

Unlike other programs, your first stop when visiting the Web with Enhanced Mosaic is not a predetermined Web site. Instead, you're presented with a home page located on your home PC. From here, a variety of useful Web sites are presented for your Web running selection. This simple trick makes Enhanced Mosaic the fastest browser at the starting gun. Once you're on the Web, however, Enhanced Mosaic slows down to typical browser speeds.

One feature Enhanced Mosaic can boast that few others can is its support for multiple browser sessions. You can connect to multiple hosts and switch between windows. It's a nice feature, but don't think about using it unless you have a 28,800 bps or faster connection.

Like Netscape, Enhanced Mosaic enables you to abort a troublesome or slow Web connection by hitting the Esc key. You might think that you won't use this feature often, but once you've been on the Web for awhile, you'll appreciate the ability to walk away from a site.

On the less satisfactory side, Enhanced Mosaic lacks some navigation tools, and it doesn't inform you of the status of ongoing downloads. When you get impatient, wondering whether or not a GIF is ever going to show up on your screen, this drawback is no small matter.

Enhanced Mosaic is being further enhanced every day. Furthermore, each seller adds its own twists to the program and to the program's add-ons. Coming up with a simple judgment, therefore, is quite difficult. All in all, Enhanced Mosaic is a good, but not spectacular, Web browser. To find out more about Enhanced Mosaic, visit its Web site at the following URL:

```
http://spyglass.www.com
```

You also can contact them at 708-505-1010; fax, 708-505-4944; or e-mail, info@spyglass.com.

InternetWorks

BookLink Technologies, now owned by America Online, puts out InternetWorks (Windows). This TCP/IP Web browser, like Cello, takes its own approach to the Web (see fig. 7.7).

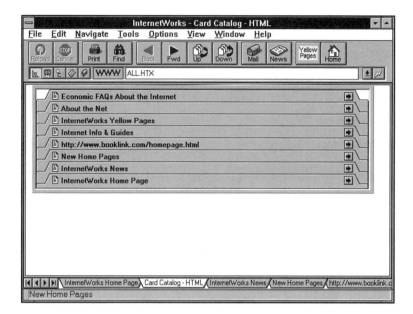

Figure 7.7

InternetWorks' card catalog is a wonderful to map your Web wanderings.

One of InternetWorks' most interesting features is its use of notebook-style divider tabs for each Web page. It takes getting used to, but is actually quite fun to use once you get the hang of the interface.

The most outstanding InternetWorks feature, however, is its card catalog. This navigation function enables you to create multiple card catalogs. You can keep and sort your favorite Web site URLs for easy searching and retrieval. InternetWorks' card catalog feature offers the best means of mapping out the Web currently available.

The program also comes with Usenet tools, such as an e-mail sender and a Usenet news client. InternetWorks' all-in-one interface enables you to use all three aspects of the program at one time: send e-mail, read a Usenet article, browse the Web.

InternetWorks also is one of the first—though hardly the last—browsers to support OLE 2.0. For the technically astute Windows user, this feature enables you to link Internet data to other OLE-aware applications, such as Microsoft Word and Excel.

InternetWorks, unfortunately, has not one but two Achilles' heels. First, the program can be painfully slow. Second—guaranteed to cause a headache—display updates can cause massive screen flickering.

The normal version of InternetWorks is a commercial program, but you can test the program using its freeware little brother—InternetWorks Lite. I-Lite is available at the following URL:

```
ftp://ftp.booklink.com/lite
```

I-Lite doesn't offer the full multitasking capabilities that its big brother does, nor does it carry OLE 2.0; but you can play with the program's look and feel.

Current versions of InternetWorks do not support either Web security protocol (SHTTP and SSL). Because the parent company AOL supports SHTTP, newer versions of InternetWorks undoubtedly will make up for this lack.

InternetWorks is not a great Web browser yet. Take a look at its newest version when you have a chance. If the program's problems have been cleaned up , InternetWorks might be the perfect browser for you.

NCSA Mosaic

NCSA Mosaic (Mac, Unix, Windows), the grandfather of all graphic browsers, might be getting a little long in the tooth, but it's still a good program (see fig. 7.8). Not so long ago, you couldn't say that. During the long alpha testing period for Mosaic 2.0, several versions of the program were downright dreadful. Things certainly have improved.

The Windows version requires the latest edition of Win32s, and all the versions can be difficult to set up. Once it's in place, however, the program is both stable and reasonably fast.

Mosaic helps you navigate the Web in several ways. You can make annotations on pages you've visited. These comments then appear at the bottom of a page the next time you visit it. The program also enables you to create a hotlist of URLs as well as cascaded menus of URLs using the Hotlist Manager.

Mosaic is also in the forefront of supporting the newest HTML standards. At this time, for example, Mosaic offers the best support—except for the test browser Arena—for HTML 3.0 pages.

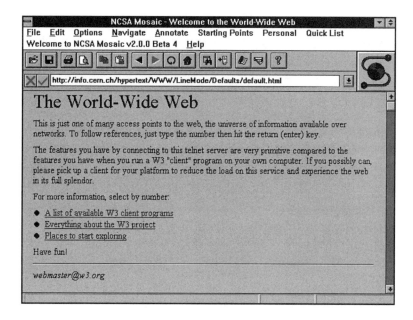

Figure 7.8

The newest version of NCSA Mosaic isn't quite as powerful as the top browsers, but it doesn't suffer by comparison either.

The newest Mosaic also includes a top-notch customization tool. Those who have wept over the pain of adjusting Mosaic by tweaking the INI file will jump for joy over this development.

The new, improved Mosaic also comes with outgoing e-mail and newsgroup support. Although the program is no Netscape, these features do set it above less sophisticated browsers.

At this time, Mosaic does not support a security protocol. Once the protocol competition is settled—which shouldn't be long—Mosaic will likely support the winning protocol.

Some other browsers might have more features or better speed, but NCSA Mosaic is solid, has great HTML support, and best of all, is free. You can check out your copy at the following URL:

```
http://www.ncsa.uiuc.edu/SDG/Software/Mosaic/
```

NetCruiser

NetCom On-Line Communication Services' NetCruiser (Windows) might eventually be a great browser, but it certainly isn't today. NetCruiser is the graphical front end to NetCom's service.

NetCruiser comes with a full array of Internet and Usenet tools. Unfortunately, few of them work quite right. The Web browser, for example, has some problems and crashes quite a bit at this point.

On the plus side, NetCruiser is one IP application that is easy to install. It's not quite "push in the disk and let her rip," but it's close.

Like any proprietary interface, of course, you're stuck with the tools that NetCom offers. With NetCruiser, for example, you won't be able to use the Eudora mail reader. The flip side is that you do get to use a single, integrated front end.

On the minus side, NetCruiser doesn't offer sophisticated Web navigation tools. Further, the program does not inherently support much more than the HTML and GIF formats. NetCom is, however, constantly working on NetCruiser. In fact, NetCruiser is probably the most rapidly updated Web browser available.

A beginner will probably be happy with NetCruiser, but a more experienced user might get frustrated with its restrictions. Still, the software is free, and at $19.95 for a month of service, you're not going to go broke from giving NetCruiser a try. You can arrange to take the browser out for a drive around the virtual block by calling NetCom at 800-501-8649, 408-983-5970; fax, 408-241-9145; or sending e-mail at `info@netcom.com`.

Netscape Navigator

Netscape Communications' Netscape Navigator (Mac, Unix, Windows, Windows 95) is, without question, the leading Web browser today. It's faster than the other browsers, loaded with features, and available in versions for more operating systems than any other browser. There's little to dislike and a great deal to love about Netscape (see fig. 7.9).

Netscape comes in two versions. The first can be obtained, using FTP, from the following site:

`ftp://ftp.mcom.com/netscape1.1/`

If you're in school, or you're working for a non-profit group, you can use this edition for free. Otherwise, you can order a copy of Netscape by sending e-mail to the following address:

`sales@netscape.com`

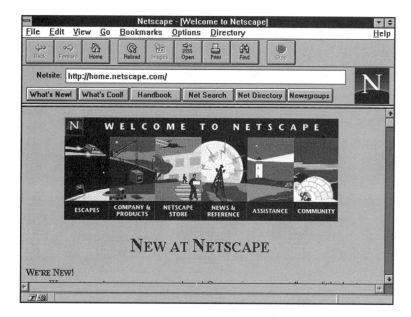

Figure 7.9

Netscape combines features, speed, and innovation for today's top browser.

Netscape is one program that scarcely lacks any features. It comes ready to work with secure servers that use the SSL protocol. Netscape also supports outgoing e-mail and has an easy-to-use and powerful Usenet newsreader. Although it has no other Internet applications, Netscape makes it easy to link up with pre-existing net programs, such as Telnet clients.

One small but delightful feature is Netscape's status bar at the bottom of the display. From this bar you can determine exactly what the browser is doing at any given moment. Although this information might not be terribly useful, it does help keep the impatient at bay, showing that something is indeed happening.

Netscape is also easy to install. You don't have to deal with INI files. Everything you might need to change is available from the Options menu. It's as easy to install as an IP program can be.

Where Netscape really kills the competition is speed. Netscape displays graphics faster than anyone else in the business. The browser uses great caching to boost your speed when you need to look back a page. The program also enables you to display and interact with text and links—before the complete graphics display arrives.

Netscape's navigation aids are also of championship quality. The View History utility, for example, enables you to create a permanent bookmark for a site long after you've left it behind. If a user could only sort the bookmark list by selected criteria, the navigation tools would be perfect.

Netscape works best with its server software, NetSite, or with pages written in HTML with Netscape enhancements. But make no mistake—Netscape gets along with any site or language. Before any other browser, for example, Netscape will be adding PDF support, and it already has JPEG support.

The program is also popular with many vendors. You can look forward to cruising over MCI's InternetMCI in a Netscape vehicle; other services are adopting Netscape as well. The future of Web browsing appears to be Netscape, and with a product this good, that's great news.

Prodigy

Believe it or not, Prodigy (Macintosh, Windows), home of the crayola-crayon interface, is not only the first online service to come out with any Web browser, the firm is the first online service to come out with a good Web browser (see fig. 7.10).

Figure 7.10

The Web browser is everything that the old-style Prodigy wasn't: quick, attractive, and well-organized.

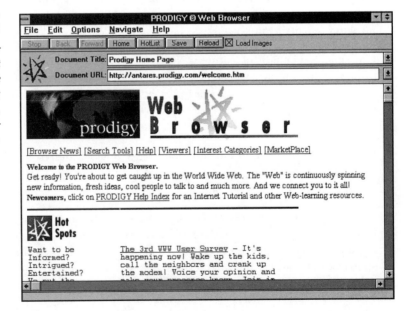

Prodigy is not hard to install, but it is difficult to customize. Setting up the program is simply a matter of loading the disks and following the instructions.

Alas, were it only that easy to add viewers to the program. To install a viewer, you not only have to figure out what application works as a viewer, you also have to determine (on your own) the appropriate MIME type and subtype for all but the most common Web file types. This can be very annoying. (See Chapter 9, "Using Mosaic as a Web Client," for more information on MIME.)

Once everything is set up and running smoothly, you should enjoy Prodigy's Web browser. The program comes with the usual navigation tools—hotlists, history, and forward and backward arrows.

Within the browser, you can send e-mail, but you need to head back to the Prodigy information service before you can read Usenet news. In the future, Prodigy will move to an entirely HTML format. When that move happens, you'll be able to access almost all Internet functions from a single Web browser/Prodigy interface.

At this time, Prodigy does not support a security protocol, a drawback to be remedied without great delay.

The Web browser is quite fast. Getting to it, however, might take you some time. The Prodigy service, which you must load and log in to before using the browser, moves as slowly as the last seconds before quitting time do.

The browser's speed comes in part from Prodigy's method of caching popular Web sites. In caching, information is kept in memory so that when you call for it, it comes immediately from your Prodigy server rather than from its location on the Web. Caching saves time because you don't have to deal with an overloaded server or the speed fluctuations of the Internet. The only problem with this service is that the cached information does not get updated with changes to the Web. Prodigy does inform you, however, when each site was cached so that you can manually tell Prodigy to go directly to the source for its information.

Another reason for Prodigy's speed is that it enables you to click on links while a document is still arriving. Unlike NetScape, however, Prodigy does not display graphics as they arrive.

Basically, Prodigy stands head and shoulders above the other service-based Web browsers. Its poor customization support aside, Prodigy's browser can stand with the best of the IP browsers.

SlipKnot

Do you want the Web's graphics without the headaches of IP connectivity? Then, you are a candidate for SlipKnot. SlipKnot (see fig. 7.11) is a shareware program that works with any Internet provider shell account that also provides either the Lynx or WWW browser.

Figure 7.11

You can't resize windows in SlipKnot; but in other ways, it's a fine browser.

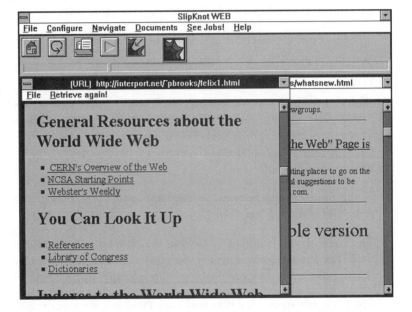

SlipKnot works by using Lynx or WWW for basic connectivity, and then translating their input into a graphical Web display. Unfortunately, SlipKnot skims on some basics. You cannot, for example, resize windows. Still, though the program's a little slow, it does give you the basics of graphical Web browsing.

SlipKnot comes with the basic set of browser tools. Don't look for anything fancy here, like a newsreader, but for walking around the Web, SlipKnot serves quite well. Because SlipKnot also comes with a terminal mode, you can always get directly to Usenet and Internet host-based character applications, like the trn. newsreader and the ELM mail front end.

As you might expect, SlipKnot comes with only minimal support for Web text and graphic formats. Further, the program does not come with any security support. By its very nature, such support would be difficult to implement.

Installation is not terribly easy. It is, however, much easier to install than any of the IP applications. You can give it a try yourself by using FTP to get it from the following URL:

```
ftp://ftp.netcom.com/pub/pbrooks/slipknot
```

Web Explorer

Web Explorer, OS/2's Warp World Wide Web browser does a grand job of making the Web accessible to OS/2 users. The browser is fast and effective (see fig. 7.12).

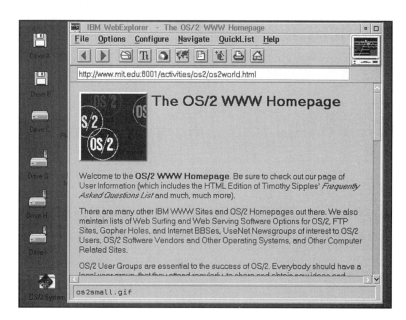

Figure 7.12

IBM's Web Explorer gives OS/2 users a first-class ticket to the Web.

This IP application can be very easy to install—*if* you connect to the Internet through IBM's own Advantis Internet system. If you elect to enter the Internet through another Internet provider, be ready to wrestle with the ordinary IP connection woes.

In addition to the usual collection of navigation tools, Web Explorer comes with a Web Map to make your Web journeys easier. Thanks to OS/2's multitasking nature, Web Explorer also makes any Web trip more productive by enabling you to run numerous Internet and local PC jobs at once.

Web Explorer's chief virtue is its ease of customization. Pull-down menus and OS/2 notebooks enable you to customize everything from font sizes and colors to the setup of file viewers. Unfortunately, no OS/2 viewers exist for some file types. The most important missing viewer is one for PDF. The latest versions of Web Explorer can use any MS-DOS or Windows viewer, however, so this disadvantage is not fatal.

Although Web Explorer does not have a security protocol at this time, it definitely will be supporting SHTTP soon.

If you're an OS/2 user, Web Explorer is the Web browser for you. Yes, you can customize Netscape—or any another 16-bit Windows browser—to work in a Win-OS/2 session, but you probably will be most pleased with Web Explorer's complete integration with OS/2.

Finding Resources
on the Web

FTP stands for *File Transfer Protocol* and is an application that facilitates the transfer of files from one computer to another. FTP allows files to be transferred regardless of how the computers are connected or what operating system they are using. If both computers understand the FTP protocol, they can exchange files. Although the nuances of the ftp commands vary slightly from one implementation to the next, the basic FTP structure remains the same.

Because files can exist in variations on different computers, the FTP protocol allows for handling these variations. This chapter discusses the nuances and conventional use of FTP to access anonymous FTP sites on the Internet.

Getting Started with FTP

To learn the basics of FTP, it is assumed that you have transfer privileges on both your local or client computer. If you are already logged on to your local machine, execute the following command:

```
ftp remote-computer-name
```

This command starts the FTP application on the local or client machine. The FTP application sends out a request to the remote machine and attempts to connect to an FTP data port of the remote machine. The FTP data port has a program monitoring this port, looking for incoming ftp access. The remote machine must be running an FTP server waiting for your incoming ftp requests.

```
ftp buhle.medicine.org
    Connected to buhle.medicine.org
    220 buhle FTP server (OSF 3.0) ready.
    Name (loren.upenn.edu:buhle): buhle
    331 Password required for buhle.
    Password:
    230 User buhle logging in.
```

Not all remote machines ask for a password upon logging in. Some machines, such as MS-DOS and Macintosh systems, do not use passwords. If your remote machines do not use passwords or you merely want to inhibit FTP access, you can prevent the FTP server process from running, thus making it impossible to service incoming ftp requests.

When you are prompted for the name of the user on the remote machine, the default user name is chosen as the user name currently in use on the local machine. Thus, if you are logged in to a local account of "buhle," for example, the default user name of the remote machine in the prompt is also buhle. If there is a valid account on the remote machine named buhle and the correct password of this remote account is entered, access will be given to the directory controlled by buhle on this remote machine. Keep in mind, the user name and password requested by the FTP process is on the remote computer's account. The privileges available for manipulating files in this remote account are the privileges defined for user "buhle" on this remote machine.

After the remote system has accepted the login with a valid user name and password, you may begin transferring files in either direction. FTP will give you the ftp> prompt to accept further ftp commands. To move a file from the local

machine to the remote machine, use the put command. To move files from the remote machine to the local machine, use the get command. These commands have the following syntax:

```
ftp> put source-file destination-file
ftp> get destination-file source-file
```

The *source-file* is the existing file to be copied; the *destination-file* is the name of the newly created copy. If the *destination-file* name is omitted, the *source-file* is used.

To transfer a file from an FTP server on buhle.medicine.org, user "buhle" first logs on to the FTP server, as shown in the following. User "buhle" then transfers the file README using the get command on the name of the file to be transferred. Note that by omitting the destination file name, user "buhle" will name the transferred file README on the client computer.

ftp buhle.medicine.org	Typed by the user to connect to a machine called ftp.medicine.org from the remote computer
`220 buhle FTP server (OSF 3.0) ready.` `Name (loren.upenn.edu:buhle): `**`buhle`**	Enter user name on the remote machine
`331 Password required for buhle.` `Password:`	Enter password for the account "buhle" on the remote machine
`230 User buhle logging in.` `ftp> `**`get README`**	Command to retrieve the file README from the remote machine
`200 PORT command successful`	Information from the remote machine

`150 ASCII data connection for README (1.2)(32 bytes)`
`32 bytes received in 0.002 seconds`
`ftp> `**`quit`**
	End the connection with the remote machine

Browsing a Remote Machine

When you access a remote machine, you should review its system directory. You might not know exactly where the file you desire is stored or you might want to browse the remote system to figure out what you want to copy. The basic commands to get a directory listing are dir and ls. These two commands have the same format, as follows:

```
ftp> dir directory-name local-file-name
ftp> ls directory-name local-file-name
```

Both commands list the files contained in the remote *directory-name* and place the directory listing in the *local-file-name*. If you neglect the *local-file-name*, the directory will be printed to the screen. If you neglect the *directory-name*, the current directory of the remote machine will be listed.

If you want to be more specific in your search for files, you might want to select all files that have the txt extension at the end of their file names. The asterisk (*) frequently is a wild card to match an unspecified number of characters. For example, the following command might generate file names such as lunatic or lunar-lander:

```
ftp> dir luna*
```

Exactly which files are listed depends on whether or not the asterisk wild card includes the period character. If the remote system uses the Unix operating system, the period "." is merely another character and file names lunatic and lunatic.txt will appear. On VMS and MS-DOS systems, the file name is composed of a file name and an extension, separated by a period. Because no extension was specified, the example would only return the file name lunatic. To obtain the same behavior on a VMS or MS-DOS system as that observed on a Unix system, the following command would have to be used:

```
ftp> dir luna*.*
```

The ls command gives a simplified listing of the directory. This command is often used for producing a list of files for input to another program. Generation of a simple list of files for internal use with the mget command will be shown later. The result of the ls appears as follows:

```
ftp> ls
150 Opening ASCII mode data connection for file list
README
```

```
file_1
file_2
subdirectory_1
wildthing
```

If the command ls filename is used, the list of files on the remote system is stored in the file called "filename" on the client's system.

On most systems the asterisk (*) is a wild card for any number of characters. On Unix systems, the question mark (?) can be used as a wild card for one character in that position, as in the following example:

```
ftp> ls l?re
lore
     lure
lyre
ftp>
```

In this example of ls, a file called README.FIRST appears in the directory. The user can retrieve this file with the get command, exit FTP, and read the file locally. Or the user can direct this file to the screen using the get command, as follows:

```
ftp> get README ˜
150 Opening ASCII mode connection for README (1230 bytes)
This is the first line of the file README
This file explains the contents and layout of this
directory and
subsequent subdirectories . . .

. . . lines deleted . . .

226 Transfer complete
1230 bytes received in 0.20 seconds (6.8 Kbytes/s)
```

Unfortunately, these command lines send the entire file to the screen, without any flow control. If the file has more lines than the screen can hold at one time, the user will watch the lines scroll by on the screen. The user can obtain the file a screen at a time using the following command:

```
ftp> get README   "¦more"
```

This command uses the pipe mechanism of Unix and pauses for the user to press Enter to request the next screen. A *pipe* connects the output of the first command (i.e. the GET) to the input of the second command (i.e. the "more" function). This ability to pipe depends on implementation of the client FTP.

Directories

The user can move between the subdirectories using the following commands:

```
ftp> lcd directory
ftp> cd directory
```

cd moves the user around on the remote directory. lcd moves the user around in his or her local directory. There are several rules for using lcd:

◆ If no directory is given, lcd moves you to the default directory of the client's account. This is the directory where clients find themselves after logging in.

◆ If the command lcd .. is used, the client moves up one directory.

◆ If the directory starts with a slash (/), lcd moves to this directory, regardless of the current location, in an absolute location of the file in the file system. Although many people like to move relative to their present location, this relative location might be different for different users. The absolute location is definitive.

◆ If the directory starts with an alphanumeric character, the client attempts to move to a subdirectory in the current directory with the same name. This is a relative motion. *Relative motion* means moving from your present location to another location, using commands like "up two levels and then down into directory A." The instructions are highly dependent on your preset location. An absolute movement is independent of your location—from wherever to a specific place.

The cd command has similar rules:

◆ If the command cd .. is used, the remote directory immediately above the current directory is selected.

◆ If the directory starts with a slash (/), cd moves to this directory, regardless of the current location, in an absolute fashion.

◆ If the directory starts with an alphanumeric character, the remote directory attempts to move to a subdirectory in the current directory with the same name, in a relative motion.

To discover your current location on the remote system, use the pwd command, as follows:

```
ftp> pwd
/pub/directory/loren
```

ASCII and Binary Transfers

The default mode of transfer for FTP is ASCII, as seen when producing a directory of the file system with dir and ls. FTP has two common modes: binary and ASCII. A *binary* transfer preserves the exact bit sequence of the file on the remote system to that client system. Keep in mind that if the bit sequence between the client and the remote system is not compatible, files that are meant to run, such as applications, might not run on the destination machine. For example, if you have a program on a PC and use the binary FTP mode to move it to a Macintosh, it will not be able to run on the Macintosh because the bit sequence is different between these two systems. If the file is copied from a PC to a Macintosh and then to another PC, all in binary mode, the file should be able to be run on the second PC because the bit sequence is the same as the first PC. Some files, such a GIF files, have a defined bit sequence and can be processed on machines with different bit sequences.

ASCII mode is really a text mode. The client side of FTP attempts to transfer the contents of the file in a readable fashion from the remote system. As taken from the previous example, the bits composing the file on the PC are meaningless on the Macintosh. In ASCII mode, the client translates the file to text to make it readable. Thus, a directory listing or the README file is translated to text on the client machine so it can be read. An example is to have the remote machine have documents in French, while the client machine only understands English. In the binary mode, the client has an exact copy and sees French. In ASCII mode, the client can attempt to make the translation from French to English to make it understandable on the client.

Binary transfer is necessary for moving pictures, spreadsheets, word processing files, programs, and any data that is not in simple ASCII text. To be safe, use binary mode. If you transfer a binary file via the ASCII mode, the file moved will be destroyed. The Macintosh "fetch" program, which performs FTP transfers, attempts to guess the mode of the data before the transfer.

FTP does not have any inherent knowledge of the content of the files being transferred. If the default mode is set, FTP will attempt to translate the requested file to ASCII. If the file was meant to be copied in binary mode (a GIF image file, for example), the client will translate it to ASCII and irreparably damage the file as it is stored on the client machine. If the file is transferred in binary mode, an exact copy is made.

The binary or image (I) mode can be set by typing **binary**. The ASCII mode can be set by typing **ascii** as follows:

```
ftp> binary
Type set to I.
ftp> get loren.gif
ftp> ascii
Type set to A.
ftp> get README
```

Most database and spreadsheet programs store their data in binary mode, even if the inherent data is text-oriented. To be safe, it is a good idea to transfer the file in binary mode.

Transferring Multiple Files

The get and put commands transfer individual files. To transfer several files at a time, the corresponding mget and mput commands move multiple files. The default mode is to prompt the user before transferring each file, which is useful if you want to transfer some, but not all of the files. This is particularly useful to prevent overwriting files with identical names, but different contents on the two different systems.

```
ftp> ls b*
```
This lists all the files starting with the letter "b."

```
200 PORT command successful
150 ASCII data connection for /bin/ls (127.0.0.1.1234)
red_file.doc
blue_bills.gif
howard_cook.doc
wilder.wp
wipple.doc
226 ASCII Transfer complete
ftp> binary
```
This changes the mode to binary transfer.

```
Type set to I.
Type set to Image
```

`ftp> ` **`mget *.doc`**	This is a multiple get for all files ending with the extension ".doc." The user is prompted before the transfer of each file.
`red_file.doc? ` **`y`** `howard_cook.doc? ` **`y`** `wipple.doc? ` **`n`**	Enter yes, to transfer. Enter no, to not transfer.

The FTP-generated comments of transfer have been omitted from this example for sake of clarity. If you dislike being prompted, you can type **prompt** to turn off the prompting per file.

Note that the following command does not mean to take the local copy of `wipple.doc` and place it on the remote machine as `howard_cook.doc`, as you would expect with the put command.

`ftp> ` **`mput wipple.doc howard_cook.doc`**

In this example, both files are moved from the local file to the remote file system. Although mput copies multiple files, it cannot be used to transfer a directory. To copy all the files in the subdirectory—from a remote file system into your local file system, for example—you need to change directories (using cd) into the appropriate directory on the remote system and then execute mget. As a word of warning, mget behavior might depend on the implementation of FTP running on the local machine. mget works by internally performing the ls command to generate an internal list of files to transfer and then performs multiple get operations based on this list.

Common Problems

One of the most common problems is to mistype the user name or the password. If you make this mistake, you will receive a `Login incorrect` message. There are two ways of handling this. You can either execute a quit command and start again, or you can execute the user command to restart the login process. You will be prompted for the password.

```
ftp buhle.medicine.org
     Connected to buhle.medicine.org
     220 buhle FTP server (OSF 3.0) ready.
     Name (loren.upenn.edu:buhle): buhle
     331 Password required for buhle.
     Password:
530 Login failed.
ftp> user buhle
331 Password required for buhle.
Password:
230 User buhle logging in.
```

Although it is confusing to receive the ftp> prompt without accomplishing a successful login, this is the FTP application's way of communicating with the user and does not infer anything about the status of the link between the local and remote machine.

Other mistakes include misspelling the name of the remote machine, misspelling the user name, or misspelling the name of the file requested. If you misspell the remote machine, requesting a non-existent machine, you will receive one of three errors: Host unreachable, Connection timed out, or Host not responding. If you misspell the user name, you will never be able to supply the correct password. If you misspell the name of the requested file, you will receive the No such file or directory error or something similar.

 Note Please keep in mind that the file name of the remote file is governed by the remote system's file name system. Thus, if the remote system is case sensitive, the file Junk.txt is very different from junk.txt. Although this might not be the case with MSDOC, VMS or NT systems, case sensitivity in the file name is important in Unix systems.

Anonymous FTP

The FTP examples cited so far presume the user has an account on the remote machine. Anonymous FTP enables a user to access a remote machine without having a password, which is useful when accessing public domain files, such as freeware or shareware. Anonymous FTP sites have restrictions: users can only retrieve files with the get command, users are restricted to where they can travel with the **cd** command, and the anonymous capability might be restricted to specific times on the remote site to minimize the load on this machine.

When anonymous FTP is enabled on a remote machine, a user logs in with the user name "anonymous" and, if asked, should use their e-mail address as their password. Users can peruse the area on the remote machine set up for anonymous users, and they should expect to use the image mode for transferring files that are not obviously text.

The FTP application may have between 70 to 100 commands and command options. Table 8.1 presents the most commonly used FTP commands.

TABLE 8.1
Common FTP Commands

FTP Command	FTP Command Summary
ascii	Enters ASCII mode for transferring files.
binary	Enters binary mode for transferring files.
cd *remote-directory*	Changes the working directory on the remote file system.
close	Terminates the local FTP session with the remote machine without terminating FTP. After using close, you can use the open command.
delete *filename*	Deletes a file on the remote system.
dir *file destination*	Generates a full directory listing of the remote directory. *file* and *destination* are optional. *file* can be an individual file or a wild-card construct. If the *destination* is present, the output from the file command is stored in this file on the local machine.
hash	Tells FTP to generate a hash symbol (#) for every block of data moving from a get or put command. The hash command is useful if you question whether the network is functioning. hash is a toggle. Typing **hash** a second time will stop its action.
help *command*	Produces documentation on the *command* on the screen.
lcd *directory*	Changes the location of the local directory to *directory*.

continues

TABLE 8.1, CONTINUED
Common FTP Commands

FTP Command	FTP Command Summary
ls *file destination*	Generates a short directory listing of the files in the directory of the remote machine. The arguments of ls are the same as for dir.
mget *file-list*	Obtains multiple files matching the *file-list* from the remote machine. The *file-list* can be a wild-card construct or a list of multiple files.
mput *file-list*	Moves multiple files matching the *file-list* from the local machine to the remote machine. The *file-list* can be a wild-card construct or a list of multiple files.
open *machine-name*	Connects to a computer designated by the *machine-name*. This command is used when FTP accesses multiple remote machines without restarting the FTP application. The converse operation of open is close.
prompt	This command is used prior to the mget and mput commands to select whether the user is queried for transfer of the files.
pwd	Prints the current directory on the remote machine.
quit	Closes any existing FTP session and terminates FTP.
user *username*	Sends the *username* (if omitted, the user will be prompted) to the remote machine for logging in to the remote system.

Understanding Gopher

Gopher is one of the original tools for surfing the Internet by selecting resources from menus. The Internet gopher works by exchanging information between the Gopher client running on your machine and the Gopher server on a remote machine. The Gopher client requests menus of information from the Gopher server. The user selects choices from the menus, resulting in submenus or the delivery of files. These files are typically text files displayed on your local computer, one screen at a time.

Gopher can be used to browse from one location on the Internet to another, focusing your attention on the information and not on the technical details of moving from one specific location to the next. Gopher users need not worry about domain names, Internet addresses, file system locations, or remembering arcane instructions for performing operations.

Gopher originated at the University of Minnesota to "go fer" or fetch information from a variety of servers, some administered by the sports department, others run by the administration, others by individual academic departments. A user of this service would see one menu of all the available university resources. Choosing a specific menu item would direct the user to another list of menus, perhaps containing information pertaining to the sport schedule for football, soccer, and so on. Selection of the football menu might result in the display of the football schedule for the year, a list of the players, historical information, and so on. The user can then browse this information, without realizing the football information might be coming from a computer run by the sports department, although the original menu came from a computer run by the administration.

How Does a Gopher Work?

A Gopher server can be specified in the following manner:

gopher *gopher.server port_number*

The *gopher.server* and the *port_number* are optional. If they are not specified, the *gopher.server* defaults to the name specified in the initialization file (sometimes this is the University of Minnesota) and uses TCP/IP port 70. Pointing gopher at OncoLink reveals the following:

gopher cancer.med.upenn.edu 80

```
                Welcome to OncoLink


       1. Advanced Search of OncoLink <?>
       2. Single Word Search of OncoLink <?>
  -->  3. A Short Paper on OncoLink
       4. What's New on OncoLink/
       5. Disease Oriented Menus/
       6. Specialty Oriented Menus/
       7. Psychosocial, Support Groups and Spirituality Info/
       8. Cancer News/
```

```
9. Other Cancer Information Resources/
      ...and others items...
Press ? for Help, q to Quit, u to go up a menu Page:1/2
```

Items are selected from the Gopher menu either by typing the number or selecting the menu item through the use of the arrow keys or a mouse. If you descend into one of the submenus of a Gopher, you can move back to a previous menu by using the *u* key. While reading a document, you can move backward to an earlier page by pressing the < key and move forward by hitting the > key. The Gopher client also has the ability to search menus for user designated words. An easy way to search for words contained in a menu is to use the / command, resulting in the following query from the Gopher client:

```
+-------------------------------------------------------+
¦                                                       ¦
¦   Search directory titles for:_____¦
¦                                                       ¦
¦                          [Cancel ^G] [Accept - Enter]¦
¦                                                       ¦
+-------------------------------------------------------+
```

You type the string you are looking for and press Enter. If the string can be found in the present menu, it positions the cursor at the location of this word in the menu. If the string cannot be found, you will get the message `Search failed`.

The line at the bottom of the Gopher screen gives instructions pertaining to the use of the specific Gopher client. You should check the Help (press ?) command to review the specific implementation of the commands on your Gopher client.

Selection of Item 3 results in text from the Short Paper on OncoLink appearing on the user's screen. The screen might look something like the following:

```
A Short Paper on OncoLink
by E. Loren Buhle, Jr. Ph.D

OncoLink was created ...
    . .. material omitted . . .


-- More -- (1%) [Press space to continue, 'q' to quit.]
```
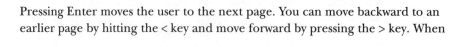

Pressing Enter moves the user to the next page. You can move backward to an earlier page by hitting the < key and move forward by pressing the > key. When you get to the end of the article by paging through the document either by hitting the spacebar or by quitting (pressing **q**), you will be asked for what to do with the document in the following prompt:

```
Press <RETURN> to continue, <m> to mail, <s> to save:
```

Pressing Enter results in your return to the earlier menu. If you press **m**, you will be asked for the e-mail address of where to send the document, as in the following example which results in the text file being sent to the specified e-mail address:

```
Mail document to: buhle@mscf.med.upenn.edu
```

You can use your conventional e-mail software to handle this message just as you would handle any other message. If you selected the s option, you will be asked for the file name of the disk file (where the client program is running) to save the document. This is only practical if you have access to disk space where the Gopher client resides.

Selection of Item 5 results in a menu of Specific Diseases. The presence of the slash (/) at the end of the title means this menu item actually is a directory of other files. In the Gopher world, menus and directories are usually synonymous.

Item 9 might select a resource on another computer, though this is transparent to the user.

Items 1 and 2 activate a searching application to find relevant text files within OncoLink. Thus, Gopher isn't limited to merely fetching menus and files for review. Selecting option 2 results in the following query:

```
+--------------Single Word Search of OncoLink-----------+
|                                                       |
| Word to search for on OncoLink:_____  |
|                                                       |
|                                                       |
|                     [Cancel ^G] [Accept - Enter]  |
|                                                       |
|                                                       |
+-------------------------------------------------------+
```

You can then enter the search word for Gopher. If you have previously performed a search, the old word appears as the default, making it easier to repeat your search without using the identical word. If you want to use a different search term, just backspace over the original word and enter something new. If Gopher finds words satisfying this word, it assembles a new menu that only contains items that match the keyword. Thus, if the word is found, a new menu is presented. Keep in mind that there are many ways of performing a search, both of local contents and of contents throughout the Internet.

Item 1 performs a Wide Area Information Search (WAIS) of the local content of OncoLink. The WAIS search engine permits the user to search for documents containing information on "tamoxifen and breast cancer," listing only those documents containing both words. Other documents on the use of tamoxifen for brain tumors and documents discussing breast cancer in general will not appear in the query result. This search function has the capability to perform phonetic spelling, thus enabling the user to imprecisely indicate the information requested.

Gopher servers exchange electronic messages with the Gopher client on your machine. The server might elect not to make certain documents available to clients outside of a certain domain. Thus, if a company's Gopher server has documents only for Gopher clients within the company, an outside user might receive the following message, or something equally cryptic:

```
Document request Refused. Client ineligible to receive

Press <RETURN> to continue, <m> to mail, or <s> to send:
```

As you begin to use Gopher searches, you may elect to follow these guidelines:

◆ Gopher search words are case insensitive. Upper- and lowercase letters are considered the same.

◆ When using a new index, keep the search simple. If the term generates too few responses, expand the scope of the term. Using the keyword "cancer" on an oncology resource would result in thousands of files.

◆ Experiment with the use of the keywords. Are the words *and, or,* and *not* permitted? These are called Boolean terms to help qualify how multiple search words can be used together.

◆ If you start a search, you might as well let it finish. Pressing a Ctrl+C will probably terminate the Gopher client completely.

Archie

There are several Internet-based services that build indexed catalogs of information to facilitate searching and retrieval. The first service provided network

access to library card catalogs. Subsequent services provide indexing of Internet-based information.

One of the earliest indexing programs was called *Archie.* Archie was designed by two graduate students at McGill University (Montreal, Quebec) as a tool for gathering, indexing, and providing information from the anonymous FTP sites around the world. Archie was named for its similarity to the word "archive" and has nothing to do with the Archie of comic book fame. The current version of Archie provides a list of file names found at more than 1,300 anonymous FTP sites around the world. Archie servers—approximately 20 public ones—gather file names during anonymous FTP visits on a monthly basis. These Archie servers distribute their findings and pass updated material to other Archie servers.

Veronica

Veronica and Jughead are named after the Archie of comic book fame. Veronica attempts to index the world of Gopher servers, much like Archie attempts to build a comprehensive index of all anonymous FTP servers. A central server periodically scans the complete menu hierarchies of Gopher servers appearing on an ever-expanding list. The resulting index is provided by the Veronica server and can be accessed by Gopher servers.

Veronica usually is a menu item on a Gopher or World Wide Web server. There might be several Veronica sites available on a given Gopher or WWW server. This variety enables a user to select a not-too-busy Veronica server. After the user selects a Veronica, Gopher asks the user for their search words. A success-ful search from the Veronica returns a new menu of Gopher items satisfying the conditions of the search.

Inside the Veronica Search

The search engine supports sophisticated search strings specifically to target the desired information. The Veronica search engine permits limited Boolean and substring searches. Boolean searches enable the user to include *and, or,* and *not,* along with a hierarchy of parentheses, to control the search. Thus, if the search were the following, all references including both smoking and drinking would be included:

```
smoking and drinking
```

If the Gopher title only had smoking or drinking, it would be excluded. If the search query were the following, all references containing both smoking and men as well as smoking and women:

```
smoking and (men or women)
```

A reference containing only the words men, women, smoking, or woman would be insufficient. A reference containing smoking and men or smoking and women would be sufficient. Note actual Boolean words *and*, *or*, and *not* are not searched.

The search of smoking and women would exclude woman, as this is spelled differently. If the search were instead the following, then both women and woman would be accessible to the search:

```
smoking and wom*
```

At this time, the wild-card character "*" can only be used at the end of the search word. The wom* search would also bring into view smoking and wombats because this qualifies in the search criteria. If the search were the following, both wombats and wombat would be excluded:

```
smoking and wom* not womba*
```

Jughead

Jughead is an index searcher of Gopher services that is rarely seen. Jughead searches particular Gopher sites. Thus, the menu item might be the following:

```
Search Gopher menus at the University of Pennsylvania
```

To the user, this appears as just another Gopher index search.

Understanding Finger

Finger is an old Unix utility to examine the user login file and learn something about the user. For one thing, you can learn if the user is logged in to the system at that very moment. If the user has configured his account for interrogation by outside users, it can also reveal the user's e-mail address and other information.

Using Finger

The command structure for finger is as follows:

finger *username@hostname*

The *username* is optional and requests specific information about a user whose first or last name matches the *username* on the *hostname* system. If you are using the user's login name, the name match is case sensitive, meaning "Joe" is different from "joe." If you are using the user's actual name (such as the GECOS file of /etc/passwd of Unix systems), the search is case insensitive. To be safe, you can use all lowercase and will find a match most of the time.

The *hostname* is the name of the computer where you are making the inquiry. If you execute only the finger command without arguments, you will make an inquiry on the system on which you are currently logged.

If user buhle had a file called .plan with world-read permission in your home directory and the corresponding home directory has world-read and execute permissions, you would see buhle's plan. If there is a file called .project present in the home directory, this file would also be displayed. If these files were located in this directory, you would see the following:

finger buhle@archive.xrt.upenn.edu
```
[archive.xrt.upenn.edu]

Login name: buhle              In real life: Loren Buhle
Directory: /usr/usrc/buhle        Shell: /bin/csh
Last Login: Sat, Feb 11, 1995 on ttya1 from xrt.upenn.edu
No Plan.
```

finger buhle@archive.xrt.upenn.edu
```
[archive.xrt.upenn.edu]

Login name: buhle              In real life: Loren Buhle
Directory: /usr/usrc/buhle        Shell: /bin/csh
Last Login: Sat, Feb 11, 1995 on ttya1 from xrt.upenn.edu
Project: Finish the chapters of this book
Plan: Generate an unbiased and freely available medical resource for
everyone.
```

Finger frequently is used to measure the system load and show the users currently logged in to the system. If the username is left off, information about the computer and the users logged into the computer will be generated.

```
finger @archive.xrt.upenn.edu
[archive.xrt.upenn.edu]
                          CPU load: 0.85 2.30 1.00
Login Name             Tty   Idle    Login         Office Home
buhle    Loren Buhle p0    0:10    Feb 10 12:23   G-Founders
buhle    Loren Buhle t1    0:02    Feb 10 12:24   G-Founders
buhle    Loren Buhle t2    2:10    Feb 10 12:24   G-Founders
curley   Robt Curley p3    2:12    Feb  9 15:32   Outland
```

In this particular example, three user processes assigned to the user name buhle are currently running. The actual user is Loren Buhle, who maintains an office in G-Founders. The three processes with rapid initial login times infer the use of an X-window terminal. The user curley has only one process running and has been logged on since February 9. This user process has not performed any CPU or input/output operations for the last two hours and twelve minutes.

The CPU load is a feature on only some finger servers. The three numbers give a rough estimate of the average load on the computer in the last five, ten, and fifteen minutes. A user load of 1.00 means the machine was 100 percent busy. A user load of more than 1.00 (2.30, for example) means the system was saturated at least two times a single CPU processor load. If there is more than one CPU in a symmetric multiprocessor system (SMP) where each CPU can work independently, a two processor system fully loaded could tolerate a load of 2.0 without becoming saturated. A load of 0.85 means a single-processor system isn't fully loaded to capacity.

Finger as a General Information Processor

Because finger displays the .plan and .project files to outside requests, this becomes a simple way to provide small bits of information useful to the public. On a purely fictitious server machine called hostname.org, a process might periodically overwrite the .plan file with the latest weather information. For example, if a program placed some text about the weather in an account called "weather," writing this to their plan file, an outside user could finger the account and read the weather information, as follows:

```
finger weather@hostname.org
```

```
finger weather@hostname.org
[hostname.org]

Login name: weather             In real life: Who knows
Directory: /usr1/weather        Shell: /bin/ksh
Plan:

Recent weather in the San Francisco Area on May 12, 1995
--------------------------------------------------------
4 pm PST--This evening, there is a chance of darkness with a small chance
of scattered light, depending on the phase of the moon and the cloud
cover. At about 5:30 am PST, the darkness will give way to increasing
amounts of light.
```

Problems with Finger

The client process sends a request for information to the finger server on the remote machine. If the server is unavailable, possibly because the machine has crashed, the network is broken, or the remote server is not running the finger server (called the finger daemon on Unix systems), the user will obtain the following message:

```
finger buhle@xrt.upenn.edu
[xrt.upenn.edu]
connect: Connection refused
```

There is insufficient information from this message to discern the status of the remote server.

Understanding Whois

Whois is several things: it is the name of a particular white pages directory, it is a general directory, and it is an application that accesses these directories.

Whois Background

The original directory, or white pages, was maintained by the Defense Data Network (DDN) at the Network Information Center (NIC) and contained approximately 70,000 entries at its peak. The original listees included anyone with responsibility for running Internet networks. Eventually, anyone who filled out a form could register into this database.

When the original network, ARPAnet, was decommissioned, the maintenance of the white pages and the registration was transferred to the InterNIC, the new Internet Information provider to maintain the Whois directory for non-military network and domain contacts. The military Whois directory is maintained at `nic.ddn.mil` and the non-military Whois directory is maintained by `ds.internic.net`

There was some controversy whether entries in the non-military white pages would be restricted to names of contacts with some authority over a portion of the Internet or opening the process to anyone who wanted to be listed. Some of the logic behind restricting the access stemmed from the limitation of the original whois to process large databases. Recently, the *Wide Area Information Service* (WAIS) searching process has been applied to this database, thus allowing the potential for maintaining a larger class of users.

Using Whois

There are several ways to access the Whois information. This chapter discusses the use of the Whois application and the Telnet process to the Whois database. The Whois application is used by placing the individual's name after whois, as follows:

```
whois buhle
Buhle, Loren (BL10)          BUHLE@MSCF.MED.UPENN.EDU
University of Pennsylvania
Department of Radiation Oncology
P.O. Box 7806
Philadelphia, PA 19101


Recorded last updated on 15-Mar-92.


The InterNIC Registration Services Host contains ONLY
Internet Information
(Networks, ASNs, Domains, POC's)
Please use the whois server of nic.ddn.mil for MILNET Information.
```

If the exact spelling is not known, the period or asterisk can be used as a wild card, as follows:

```
whois buhl.
Buhl, Steward (BS325)
Buhle, Loren (BL10)        BUHLE@MSCF.MED.UPENN.EDU
```

In this example, two matches were found using the first four letters of the name. The handle, BL10, is an identifier, known as the *unique handle*, which can be reapplied to the Whois application to obtain the complete whois record from the whois database.

If you access the user buhle by the handle, a "!" character is used:

whois !BL10   (for systems that can handle the !)
whois \!BL10   (for Unix systems that interpret the ! as a special
                        character)

This command will receive the complete database on this individual.

Some Whois applications support the capability to specify the appropriate whois directory using the -h argument, as follows:

```
whois -h nic.ddn.net buhle
whois -h ds.internic.net buhle
```

The first line searches the military whois database. The second searches the non-military database.

Whois through Telnet

If your local client does not support the whois application, you can telnet to the InterNIC, log in using whois as the user name, and start making queries. The following is a transcript of use of a remote whois server:

telnet ds.internic.net   Connect to the
                                                    remote service

```
Trying ds.internic.net...
Connected to internic.net
Escape character is `^]'
```

   . . . lines deleted . . .

[vt100] InterNIC> whois   Specifies what
                                                    service you want
                                                    to use, in this
                                                    case "whois"

```
Connecting the databases...

Whois: buhle
```
Ask for the
person in
question

```
Buhle, Loren (BL10)            BUHLE@MSCF.MED.UPENN.EDU
University of Pennsylvania
Department of Radiation Oncology
P.O. Box 7806
Philadelphia, PA 19101


Recorded last updated on 15-Mar-92.
```

You close from this service by pressing Ctrl+D twice, one to end the Whois
session and the second to close the connection to the server.

Using X.500 Directory Services

One of the shortcomings to the whois command is its inability to scale to user
directories of millions of users. The whois command was designed to handle
tens of thousands of users, not millions. The Internet now has grown to
millions of users. As an alternative to finger, looking up an individual in the
global "white pages" to find an e-mail address and location is a frequently
desired, but unfulfilled, task.

X.500 is the directory service adopted by the Organization for International
Standardization (ISO) to provide a platform for directory lookup of individuals
throughout the world. X.500 was designed to support an unlimited number of
e-mail addresses. This ability to manage large user directories makes X.500 the
directory of choice for the InterNIC, the entity that keeps track of names and
resources on the Internet.

This section discusses the philosophy of X.500 using the native protocol, then
discusses the ISO version of X.500 to be used throughout the world.

The X.500 Concept

X.500 directory service is based on a series of nested directories, with finer and
finer access as the user proceeds further into the X.500 resource. These
resources might be organized first by country, then by organizations within that

country, then by departments within that organization, and finally the individual within the organization. Using phone books as an example, there would exist a tree of shelves containing phone books. To look up the author's e-mail address, you would look for the United States shelf and locate the Pennsylvania subshelf. The Pennsylvania subshelf would contain the Philadelphia phone book, and the author's name would be contained within that Philadelphia book.

Each of the resources would be maintained by a specific local entity. Thus, Bell Atlantic maintains the Philadelphia phone books, which are then maintained within the Pennsylvanian shelf, which are maintained within the United States shelf, and so on. This distributed nature of the resources allows easier maintenance and rapid searching. The maintainer only handles the local information and can change the local resources without influencing any other resource (the Chicago phone book, for example). The distributed nature of the resource means someone searching the Pennsylvania resource does not have to go through any other country or state's resources, as they would with the whois command.

If the user doesn't exactly know where in Pennsylvania the author resides, they can use wild cards to probe for matches against the X.500 database and select from the possibilities found. Thus, if the user knows this author is in a company starting with "C" somewhere within Pennsylvania, they can enter "C*" and view the possibilities. The native syntax of X.500 is designed to be used by a computer, not a person, so such an inquiry might appear as:

```
c=US@o=C*@cn=Buhle
```

In this example, the country is delimited as "c=", the organization is delimited by "@o=", and the user name is delimited by "@cn=".

The ISO Approach to X.500

The ISO standard to X.500 directory service uses a client-server organization. X.500 clients are known as Directory User Agents (DUA). X.500 servers (the phone books) are called Directory Server Agents (DSA). To look up someone in the global "phone book," the user's DUA contacts a DSA. The DSA does the actual searching and returns the result to the DUA. If your software does not have a DUA, you can use public DUAs through Gopher, WWW, and Telnet. If you use the InterNIC's DUA, they break down the X.500 directory structure into the following four levels:

1. Person

2. Department

3. Organization

4. Country

A public DUA can be used by connecting via Telnet to ds.internic.net with the user name x500.

The X.500 Directory Service is a very ambitious project that has been ongoing for a number of years and, as of this writing, remains incomplete.

Understanding Wide Area Information Server (WAIS)

In navigating the Internet, the question "Where do I begin?" might pop into your mind. Where do you point your World Wide Web browser to start surfing? As the number of Internet WWW resources proliferates, this is becoming an increasingly important question. The Wide Area Information Server (WAIS) provides full-text indexes of information servers on the Internet. Like Veronica and Jughead, WAIS can be used to find and access information without regard to examining specific sites. Your request might take the form of "Provide me with a list of files about X." WAIS searches respond with a list of items within the precomputed WAIS index of items ranked by the frequency of their occurrence.

WAIS was developed by Thinking Machines in collaboration with Apple Computer, Dow Jones, and KPMG Peat Marwickl to develop a generalized retrieval system for accessing data around the world. WAIS works in two parts.

◆ The server side, which indexes WWW sites periodically and maintains this index for access by WAIS and WWW clients

◆ The client side, which includes WAIS clients and WWW clients

WAIS clients use natural language queries to the WAIS servers, resulting in menus of likely files. WAIS is distinct from Archie- and Veronica-class servers in

that it is used to index descriptions of the contents of the server and test-based target documents, as well as many other types of information on a WAIS server.

WAIS is a distributed information service that takes its input in a simple natural language format, offers indexed search for fast retrieval, and has a "relevance feedback" mechanism to permit the results of initial searches to bias future searches. For example, suppose your query to the WAIS client is vague, producing a long list of possible resources for further examination. You might select a subset of this list and request "something similar to these selections." WAIS servers can be used to index resources such as telephone directories, reports, catalogs, spreadsheets, graphics, and video. Using a WAIS search engine with a WWW interface, such as the target of a hypertext link, can provide a powerful, yet simple-to-use, resource.

WAIS search engines also support Boolean queries, supporting syntax such as "red and green not blue," which would get all items containing both red and green, excluding all records with only blue. Partial requests, such as "hum*" might show "hum," "hummingbird," "humid." For users who don't know how to spell their search term, WAIS can optionally use the soundex and phonix search algorithms to "guess" correct matches.

The soundex and phonix algorithms are very handy when you aren't sure how to spell what you are looking for. In reviewing the search terms for the cancer information resource, OncoLink, it was obvious that many people can't spell the medical terms for which they're seeking information. If the search engine attempts a literal match, it will only report similar misspellings as they are found in the literature. If the soundex and phonix routines are employed on the incoming search term, the desired information is found very quickly. Hopefully, the frustration level also drops significantly.

Using a WAIS Engine

To use a WAIS engine, the client (user) specifies a data source, search words, and any optional relevance feedback information. WAIS finds all documents that contain the specified search words—up to the specified document limit. In addition, the results of the inquiry are ordered or ranked based on the number of hits that are located within the document.

Both the WAIS client and server applications are readily available from a number of Internet sources, most notably wais.com. The Unix clients can be obtained by anonymous FTP (for Unix, see nic.switch.ch in the directory /pub/mirror/wais/unix). WAIS clients are available for PCs, Macs, Unix, and other systems.

The WAIS server creates the index of information by indexing material for rapid perusal by the WAIS client. The specific type of index is called an *inverted* index and is known for its rapid speed of finding matches. The typical WAIS indexer supports a number of predefined file types that include GIF, MAIL_DIGEST, TEXT, NETNEWS, and many others. File types that are not predefined are usually indexed by file name or by paragraph. The WAIS indexer does a full text review of the desired material and creates a separate indexed structure that is used by the WAIS search engine. When the WAIS client issues a query, only the index is searched, and a pointer to the associated document or image is retrieved. The titles of these documents are presented to the user for further selection. If the user wants to select the second document on the returned menu, the menu item provides instructions for obtaining the original document. If the WAIS search involves a WWW client, the selection of an item from the returned menu returns an URL. This URL is acted upon by the WWW client, and the corresponding document, as stored in the WAIS index on the WAIS server, is retrieved.

An overview of the client-server interaction of the WAIS architecture follows:

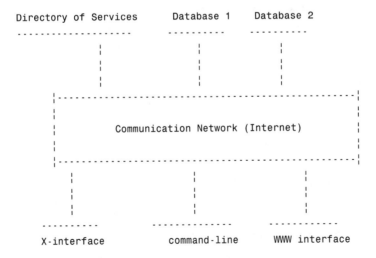

WAIS Databases

The "Directory-of-Servers" is a WAIS server containing indices of the descriptors of other servers. This "yellow page"-like service (as in the telephone book)

resides at a known address. In the US, they are `directory-of-servers:`
`quake.think.com` or `directory-of-servers:cnidr.org`.

Instead of referencing documents, these servers reference participating
databases. When a new information provider wants to join WAIS, the provider
must submit its location, description, and other relevant information to the
directory server. The WAIS Directory of Servers currently contains over 500
registered databases.

There are many WAIS servers currently on the Internet. A directory-of-servers
database is available on several sites. You can address a query to it and thus find
out what databases are available on a particular subject. You can get your
personal copy of the directory-of-servers by anonymous FTP from think.com in
the directory wais, as the file `wais-sources.tar.Z`.

WAIS Source Description Structures

A source description structure is used by the client WAIS program to contact a
WAIS database server. This structure is never seen by the normal WAIS user.
The purpose of this structure is to provide a conceptual link between the
information user and the database vendor. The structure provides a means for
the database vendor to inform the user of database-specific information, such
as how to contact the database or the cost of using the database, as well as
serving as repositories for the user's customizations. The fields in the source
description structure, such as how to contact a server, what database name to
use, and how much the server costs are required. The other fields are optional.
Some of these fields might contain suggestions on how their servers can be
useful.

The following is an example source structure, revealing the Common Lisp
printer format, chosen because of its capability to parse on many different
platforms and from many different languages.

```
(:source
    :version              3
    :ip-name              "quake.think.com"
    :ip-address           "192.31.181.1"
    :tcp-port             210
    :maintainer           "brewster@think.com"
    :database-name        "directory-of-servers"
    :cost                 0.00
    :cost-unit            :free
    :description
```

Note   The directory of servers is a white pages of servers maintained by many others.

WAIS Question Description Structures

A question descriptor structure is used by a WAIS client to pose queries to the WAIS server. While the WAIS users never see the following structure, questions are the basic way a user interacts with a WAIS server:

```
(:question
   :version     1
   :seed-words  "how do I use the WAIS system?"
   :relevant-documents ( )
   :sources
   ( (:source-id
     :filename "wais-docs" )
     (:source-id
     :filename "CMNS")
     )
     :result-documents ( )
  )
```

The question descriptor structure is a convenient way to store the current state of a particular interaction (the question) so that it can be used later, either explicitly by the user or by a smart client to submit requests to the server automatically.

The question descriptor has four basic parts (and one optional part), as follows:

◆ The search words used in the question

◆ The sources to search

◆ Some documents that might be similar to the desired results

◆ The resulting documents as returned from the sources (WAIS servers)

◆ Optional fields (how to display the question, for example)

Flow of a WAIS Operation

The WAIS client translates user queries into the WAIS protocol (currently Z39.50-92) and queries the master database, the directory of servers, to find the relevant databases. WAIS then transmits the request to a selected set of databases over the Internet or internal network. These database servers keep complete inverted indexes on stored document contents and execute full-text searches on them. In response to a query, a server returns a list of relevant object descriptors, which correspond to documents containing words specified in the user's query. The WAIS client displays the query results with a score denoting the number of occurrences of the query words in a document, the location of the words in the document, the size of the document, and other factors. This score helps to provide feedback to the users to further refine their queries.

Steps in a WAIS Search

The following steps detail the way in which you conduct a WAIS search:

1. The user selects a set of databases to be searched from either the Directory-of-Services or the available databases (stored in /usr/local/wais as the default location on Unix systems).

2. The user formulates a query by giving keywords to be used in the search.

3. When the query is run, WAIS asks for information from each selected database.

4. Headlines of documents satisfying the query are displayed. The selected documents contain the requested words and phrases. Selected documents are ranked according to the number of matches within each document.

5. To retrieve a document, simply select it from the resulting list.

6. If the response is incomplete, you can state the question differently or feed back to the system any one or more of the selected documents you find relevant.

7. When the search is run again, the results are updated to include documents which are similar to the ones selected, meaning documents sharing a large number of common words.

Using a Public WAIS Service

If you want to try an existing WAIS, two demonstration sites are available to allow you to get acquainted with WAIS. You can use telnet to login to the following addresses:

```
quake.think.com    (login as: wais)
sunsite.unc.edu    (login as swais)
```

Both demonstration sites run swais (Screen WAIS), a simple WAIS client for Unix.

The WAIS Software

Publicly available WAIS software contains software for creating the WAIS servers (WAISindex and WAISserver), communication software (Z39.50 standard and WAIS protocol software), WAIS clients, and testing software.

The WAISindex program is a simple indexer for the information retrieval engine. This program indexes every word of the input files, creating an "inverted file index" to permit keyword searching based on the whole document. Because it is written in ANSI C, it can be ported readily to many standards-compliant platforms.

The WAISserver software listens on the designated TCP port (default is 210) for questions in the form of Z39.50-88 packets and uses the appropriate index to answer the question. WAISsearch is a simple client interface to send questions to WAIS servers. These clients exist for simple terminal interfaces, X-windows using either Motif or Xaw, GNU Emac, and others. The freeWAIS implementation of WAIS also provides Mac and Microsoft Windows WAIS clients.

Part III

Using Web Clients

Using Mosaic as a Web Client

I f you've never used the World Wide Web, you're probably looking for a quick and easy way to start navigating on the Web. NCSA's Mosaic is the ideal application for anyone interested in experiencing the Web firsthand. The next several chapters take a detailed look at how to acquire, set up, use, and customize Mosaic for Windows.

Specifically, this chapter examines the following:

◆ System requirements for installing and running Mosaic

◆ Acquiring Mosaic

◆ Installing and configuring Mosaic

Looking at System Requirements

Before you get too excited about jumping on the Web and finding various hot spots, you first need to make sure that your computer system is set up to run Mosaic. As you've seen in the previous chapters, getting on the Internet and onto the Web is becoming easier and easier each day, but still requires some system-administration tasks. Some of these tasks, such as setting up a *local area network* (LAN) to be part of the Internet, can get complex. If you opt to get on the Internet by using a dial-up access provider, however, the process can be relatively painless. In either case, after you get on the Internet and the Web, most of the difficult work is done.

Are You on the Web?

First, you need to make sure you have access to the World Wide Web. In most cases, if you know you have "full" Internet access, you usually have Web access. In some cases, however, you need to be wary of access providers who promise you full access but in reality offer you everything but the Web. Some Internet access providers provide you with menu options or similar ways in which to access Internet resources. These features might not be sufficient for you to use the World Wide Web. You must, in a sense, be a *part* of the Internet to have access to the Web.

You can have full access in either of the following ways:

◆ **Local area network.** In some cases (and if you want to have a very fast connection), you are part of the Internet if your company, school, research facility, or government agency's network (LAN) is on the Internet. If you are not sure you are on a LAN, or don't know whether your LAN is hooked up to the Internet, ask your Help desk or system administrator. She or he should be able to assist you. If you are on the Internet by means of your LAN, you do not have to worry about using a modem to dial up a provider. You just need to log on to your network and gain access to the Internet. Again, you must ask your system administrator to help you get the required access privileges to the Internet.

◆ **Dial-up service.** Many of the new users on the Internet and the Web today use dial-up access. Access is accomplished by means of a common modem and a phone call to a local or national Internet provider. When you access the Web by using a dial-up service, you should use a 9600–14,400 bps modem link. Anything slower than this will probably discourage you. (In fact, 14,400 bps seems slow at times.) To get this type of

service, check your local telephone book (or refer to Chapters 5, "What You Need to Link to the Web," and 6, "Finding Web Access," for more help). When you look for an access service, you need to make sure that it offers SLIP/PPP service. You must have SLIP or PPP to get on the Web. See Chapter 5 for more information on SLIP/PPP.

Tip Two books from New Riders Publishing—*Riding the Internet Highway, Deluxe Edition* and *New Riders' Official Internet Yellow Pages*—are great resources for finding access providers and other Web information. Both books have comprehensive lists of access providers.

When you know you have access to the World Wide Web, you are ready to make sure that your computer system can handle Mosaic.

Upgrading to WIN32s

This section focuses on Mosaic Alpha 7 as it is used on the Microsoft Windows platform. Many of the procedures and navigational instructions shown here can be used for the Macintosh system; the installation instructions vary greatly, however, particularly the ones shown in this section. For specific installation procedures for the Macintosh, refer to the installation notes provided by NCSA at http://www.uiuc.edu.

Note As this chapter was being finalized for publication, NCSA released a Beta version of a new Mosaic client. This client added many new features and eliminated the need to edit INI settings. Because not every Web user has this new Beta version, the procedures discussed in this chapter are still valid for many users. Chapter 11, "Finding Out More About Mosaic," includes detailed updated information concerning this new Beta version (version 2.0 Beta 4).

The latest version of Mosaic for Windows is a 32-bit application and can run on Windows 3.1 or later versions. Because Windows 3.1 is *not* a 32-bit operating system, you must either upgrade to Windows 3.11 (or a later version) or upgrade your current copy of Windows 3.1. Although upgrading to Windows 3.11 or Windows for Workgroups is not a bad idea, you can use a set of files provided by Microsoft to upgrade Windows 3.1 to run 32-bit applications, such as Mosaic. These files, known as WIN32s, version 1.20 (or WIN32s, version 1.25, which became available at the time of this printing), are provided on many bulletin board systems (such as CompuServe), FTP and Gopher sites, and through Microsoft. For your convenience, these files also are provided on the enclosed *Inside the World Wide Web Bonus CD*.

Note The latest version of WIN32s (version 1.25) helps to address the National Language Support problems encountered by previous versions of Windows and eliminates the COMPOBJ.DLL problems experienced by some users. If you use a language other than English (American) or have problems with COMPOBJ.DLL, you should upgrade to this version. If not, you can continue to use version 1.20.

On the CD The \WIN32S directory on the enclosed *Bonus CD* contains a file named WIN32S.ZIP. To install this file on your system, copy the file into a subdirectory named WIN32S in your WINDOWS/SYSTEM subdirectory on your system hard drive. Next, use the installation instructions that follow this Note.

If you do not have access to a CD-ROM drive, you can obtain WIN32S.ZIP from the following sources:

Microsoft FTP server:

`ftp.microsoft.com/developer/devtools/win32sdk/win32s115a.zip`

NCSA FTP server:

`ftp.ncsa.uiuc.edu/mosaic/windows/win32s.zip`

Before you begin to install WIN32s on your machine (see the preceding Note for the location of the file), make sure you have about 3 MB of free disk space on your hard drive. You need this much room to decompress and install the WIN32s set of files. To unzip the file, you also need to have a copy of PKUNZIP on your system. (If you don't have a copy of PKUNZIP, copy the contents of the PKWARE directory from the *Bonus CD* to your system.) You should include PKUNZIP in your DOS PATH= statement, so that you can access it from any directory on your system. (For more information about using and registering PKUNZIP, see the enclosed help file with the program.)

Now that you have the necessary files on your system, follow these steps to install WIN32s:

1. Start a DOS session and unzip WIN32S.ZIP into two directories by typing **PKUNZIP -d WIN32S.ZIP**. The -d parameter preserves the subdirectories that are set up in the zip file. Two subdirectories, named /DISK1 and /DISK2, will appear in your /WIN32S subdirectory.

2. Return to Windows and start File Manager. Change to the directory that contains WIN32s and, from the DISK1 subdirectory, double-click on the SETUP.EXE file to execute the file. Or select **F**ile, **R**un from Program Manager and select or type the full path to this file in the **C**ommand Line field, such as **C:\WINDOWS\SYSTEM\WIN32S\DISK1\SETUP.EXE**.

3. Click on OK to start the installation process of WIN32s. This may take several minutes.

4. After WIN32s is installed on your system, you need to restart Windows for WIN32s to take effect on your system.

You're now ready to install Mosaic.

Installing Mosaic

Like other Windows applications, Mosaic for Windows adheres to standard Windows conventions and installation procedures. Because the Mosaic file you receive probably will be compressed in a ZIP file, you need to unzip it by using PKUNZIP. (If you don't have PKUNZIP, the preceding section tells you how to get it.)

You can download a free copy of Mosaic (usually called WMOS20A6R1.ZIP or something similar) from several places. On the Internet, you can obtain it by means of ftp at the following locations:

◆ ftp.ncsa.uiuc.edu/pcmosaic

◆ sunsit.unc.edu/pub/packages/infosystems/www/clients/mosaic/mosaic-ncsa/windows

◆ miriworld.its.unimelb.edu.au/pub/clients/pcmosaic

◆ ftp.luth.se/pub/infosystems/www/ncsa/windows

◆ ftp.sunet.se/pub/pc/mosaic

If you have access to CompuServe, you can obtain Mosaic for Windows in the Internet New Users forum and Internet Resources forum. Check in several library sections for the latest version of the application. America Online might also have it posted someplace in its service.

Another great source is the *National Center for Supercomputing Applications* (NCSA), which created Mosaic. You can ask for a copy of the NCSA catalog,

which offers manuals and other information, by e-mail at
`orders@ncsa.uiuc.edu`, or from the following postal address:

> NCSA Orders
> 152 Computing Applications Bldg.
> 605 East Springfield Ave.
> Champaign, IL 61820-5518

Note   As you learned in Chapter 5, "What You Need to Link to the Web," you must make sure that you have a Winsock 1.1-compliant *dynamic link library* (DLL) on your system to run Mosaic. This DLL provides the compatibility between different TCP/IP applications and your TCP/IP protocol stack. If you don't have one already, install the Trumpet Winsock provided on the *Bonus CD*. If you are on a network, ask your administrator to make sure you have the correct Winsock DLL on your system.

After Mosaic is placed on your hard drive, select **F**ile, **R**un from Program Manager. Next, fill in the **C**ommand Line field with the full path to where MOSAIC.EXE resides. If you have the Mosaic files in a subdirectory named \TEMP, for example, type **C:\TEMP\MOSAIC.EXE** in the **C**ommand Line field box. Click on OK to start the installation process. This process may take several minutes to complete.

Customizing Mosaic

Now that you have Mosaic installed on your hard drive, you are ready to start surfing the World Wide Web. Before you get too involved, however, you might want to customize Mosaic's appearance and the way it performs. Customization may reduce your initial headaches by speeding up the way Mosaic handles graphics and text.

The following configuration instructions are written on the assumption that you are comfortable editing and changing INI files. To change some of Mosaic's options, you need to change the MOSAIC.INI file. First, make a backup copy of MOSAIC.INI. This step is very important. You are going to edit several lines of the file and, if something goes wrong during the customization process, you might need to return to the original file. You'll find the MOSAIC.INI file in the \WINDOWS directory on your system.

Next, open MOSAIC.INI in a text editor, such as Notepad (see fig. 9.1). The following sections describe individual components of the file and how to customize it for your particular setup. In some cases, given your experience with other Internet tools or services you have, you may decide not to change a setting. This is fine and should not cause you any problems. This discussion is intended to help you tweak Mosaic before you get online and lose track of time and responsibilities. (It happens, believe us.)

Figure 9.1

MOSAIC.INI file loaded into Notepad for editing.

Setting Your E-Mail Address

The first line in the [Main] section is the E-mail= line, which enables you to correspond with the Mosaic developers if you send them a query. You'll find this option under the Mail to Developers option in Mosaic's Help menu. Change this line from `"user@site.domain"` to your specific email address. If, for example, your address is `rtidrow@iquest.net`, you would make the following change to the e-mail line:

`E-mail="rtidrow@iquest.net"`

Be sure to include the quotation marks ("") in the name.

Autoloading a Home Page

When you first start a Mosaic session, Mosaic (by default) loads a home page (see fig. 9.2). The Autoload Home Page= line is set to Yes (by default) in the MOSAIC.INI file and logs you in to the Mosaic for Microsoft Windows Home Page at NCSA. This is helpful for first-time users, but can get very tiresome after awhile. If you change the Autoload Home Page= line to No, Mosaic does not load a home page when you start up Mosaic. If you have a favorite starting point on the Web or if you have a local HTML file on your hard drive, set this line to read that address or path.

Figure 9.2

Autoloading a home page upon start up.

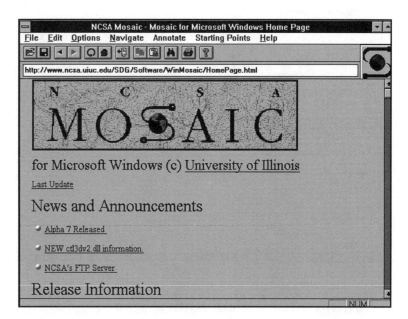

The line immediately after the Autoload Home Page= line tells Mosaic which URL address to use as the startup home page. Suppose, for example, that you visit the Microsoft Web site whenever you use Mosaic. You can make this site your first stop by making it your default home page every time you run Mosaic. To do this, type the following address in the Home Page= line:

```
Home Page=http://www.microsoft.com
```

To configure a default home page, substitute your favorite home page URL to the right of the equal sign (=) in the preceding line.

One thing you'll soon discover when you use Mosaic (or any other Web browser for that matter) is that it is relatively slow when you are using a dial-up account and modem. To make your default home page appear quickly, save the home page to your hard drive and use that file as your default home page. The file must be saved as an HTML document (the file format used by the World Wide Web). If you have an HTML document named WWW.HTM on your hard drive in the subdirectory named \NETWORK\MOSAIC\, for example, type the following address in the Home Page= line:

```
file:///c¦\NETWORK\MOSAIC\WWW.HTM
```

Notice that HTML file names have a three-character extension (.HTM) because of the character limitations imposed by DOS. Be sure to use the .HTM file extension for your local files and use the extension when you reference them.

On the CD

Several sample HTML home pages are included on the *Bonus CD*; you can place them on your hard drive and use them as default home pages. These files are located in the \HOMEPAGE subdirectory and can be copied into any directory on your hard disk. If you want to create your own home page, see Chapters 18–20 ("Writing Web Documents," "Introducing Hypertext Markup Language (HTML)," and "Writing HTML Documents") for more details about how to write HTML documents.

Help, FAQ, and Bug Lines

The following lines in the MOSAIC.INI file reference the online Help pages maintained by NCSA and can remain the same. You can, however, change them if NCSA moves these documents in the future. If so, just change these lines to point to the new URLs.

```
Help Page=
FAQ Page=
Bug list=
```

Displaying Inline Images

In addition to huge multimedia files, inline graphics on Web pages are the biggest hurdle for you to cross each time you access a site. Graphics greatly increase the time necessary to access a site, sometimes to such a degree that

Mosaic seems to come to a halt. When you have a SLIP/PPP connection, you can set the Display Inline Images= line to No to tell Mosaic not to download the graphics of each site automatically. After you get to a site, you can view the graphics by clicking on the inline image icon with the right mouse button— Mosaic will load the image for you.

The default for the Display Inline Images= line is Yes.

Dump Memory Blocks

Mosaic Alpha 7 (and later versions) do not include the Dump memory blocks= line. If you have an earlier version, keep the default setting of No.

Setting Background Color

The standard look of Mosaic is a gray background. To change Mosaic's standard gray background to a white background, modify the Grey Background=yes line, as follows:

```
Grey Background=no
```

Figures 9.3 and 9.4 contrast the two looks.

Figure 9.3

Mosaic with its standard gray background.

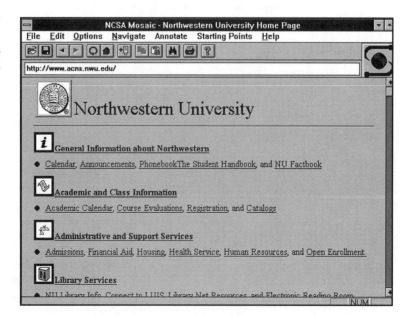

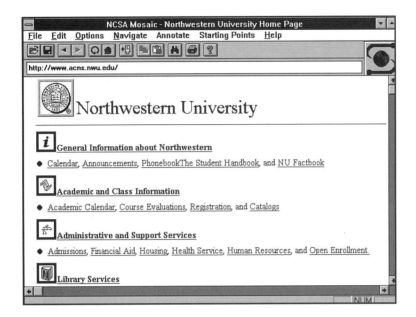

Figure 9.4

Mosaic with a white background.

Setting Page Layout Items

In the [Main] section of the INI file, you can set two options that affect the way HTML documents appear on-screen. First, the Fancy Rules= line sets the type of rule (line) displayed. If you want the more decorative rule when a document is tagged with an <hr> coding, keep the default setting of Yes. (See Part V, "Creating Web Documents," for more information on rules and HTML codes, such as <hr>.)

Second, you can change round bullets to flat lines by setting the Round List Bullets=Yes line to No. Round bullets are the dots (◆) displayed in lists in many HTML documents. By substituting flat lines for the round bullets, you can greatly reduce the time needed to access a document.

Selecting the Default Hotlist

As you will see in Chapter 11, "Finding Out More About Mosaic," Mosaic enables you to save Web sites to a hotlist by means of the Hotlist menu option. This hotlist gives you a quick and easy way to return to sites you have visited and found interesting. You use the Current Hotlist= line to set the default hotlist name. When you first load Mosaic, the hotlist named "Home Pages" is the default. After you set up your own hotlist(s), remember to come back to this line and set it to your favorite hotlist to make that hotlist the current one.

For now, leave the Current Hotlist= line set to Home Pages.

Setting Anchor Preferences

Even if you have never been on the World Wide Web, you're probably familiar with anchors in Help files or other hypertext documents. *Anchors*, or *link anchors*, are the hyperlinks that link a word, phrase, graphic, or document to another document, phrase, word, or graphic. By default, these anchors are shown in blue, which is fine when you have a color monitor. But if you are using a monochrome monitor (or a laptop computer in a poorly lighted area), you might prefer to underline the anchor. To do so, set the Anchor Underline= line to Yes.

Another option you can change is the next line in the [Main] section. The Anchor Cursor= line tells Mosaic to change the mouse cursor from an arrow to a little hand when it is placed over an hyperlink entry. To invoke this function, make sure that this line is set to Anchor Cursor=yes. (To turn it off, set it to No.)

 Tip

For information about how to change the anchors' color from blue to green or red or another color, see the "Specifying Anchor Colors" section later in this chapter.

Displaying URLs

The Show URLs=yes line tells Mosaic to display the URL in the status bar when you move the cursor over an anchor. Set this line to No to turn off this feature. The default is Yes.

Setting FTP Options

The Extended FTP= line enables you to set Mosaic to show file icons and file sizes when you access a Gopher or FTP site. To display these icons, set this option to Yes. When the line is set to No (the default setting is Yes), all that is displayed is a list of directories and files.

Tip You should keep the Extended FTP= line set to Yes so that you know the sizes of files before you access them. Large files, of course, take more time to access than smaller ones.

Setting Main Window Options

You can set three options that affect the way in which Mosaic's interface looks and displays information. The first of these options, the Toolbar= line, displays the toolbar at the top of the Mosaic window. When you set the Toolbar= line to Yes, it displays the toolbar. No shuts off the display. Unless you have a really good reason not to show the toolbar, you should keep this option set to Yes. The toolbar is very handy as you navigate the Web.

You can use another option to display the status bar in the lower left corner of the Mosaic window. This area displays transfer and file access information while you are accessing a site. Keep the Status bar= line set to Yes to keep the status bar displayed. (You can turn it off or on from the Options menu, as well.)

The third window option you can set is the Title/URL bar= line. This tells Mosaic to display the URL bar and Status Indicator (the rotating globe in the upper right corner of the window). Keep this line set to Yes to display these items. No to turn them off.

Setting 8-Bit Sound

If you don't have a 16-bit sound card installed in your system, make sure that the Use 8-bit Sound= line is set to Yes. If you have a 16-bit sound card, such as a Sound Blaster 16, change this option to Yes.

Note Later in this chapter, in the "Configuring Multimedia Components" section, you are shown how to configure multimedia devices so that you can use them with Mosaic.

Specifying Anchor Colors

The next section of MOSAIC.INI, [Settings], has a single line (Anchor Color=) that determines the color of the link anchor in the documents displayed. The default color is blue and its value is 0,0,255. To set the color to red, use the value 255,0,0; to set it to green, use the value 0,255,0; for other colors, experiment with these values until you find the color you like.

Determining Window Size and Position

The four lines that appear in the [Main Window] section of MOSAIC.INI tell Mosaic where the main window appears and how large it is. If you are comfortable with pixel heights and widths, adjust those numbers in this section. If not, return to the Mosaic main window and use your mouse to resize it. Then, from the **F**ile menu, choose Save P**r**eferences to save the current size and position of the Mosaic window.

 Tip   Be sure to select the Save Preferences option after you resize and reposition your Mosaic window. Otherwise, the next time you start Mosaic, the window's size and location will be the same as they were before you changed them. You'll wonder why your window keeps "jumping" back to its original location.

Setting E-Mail Titles

If you decide to send e-mail to the developers of Mosaic, use the [Mail] section of the MOSAIC.INI to set the mail message's default title. When you load Mosaic, the default title (which appears in the Default Title= line) is "WinMosaic auto-mail feedback." You can change this to something more personal, such as "Help with Mosaic Wanted." Clearly, you can change the title when you compose the message. But if you know that this default title line exists, and what it says, you won't wonder why this title keeps appearing in your messages.

Configuring Newsgroup and Mail Settings

In the [Services] section, you can set the NNTP_Server= and SMTP_Server= lines to make sure that you can read USENET newsgroups and receive e-mail from the Mosaic developers (if you send them a message). (For more information on newsgroups, see Chapter 14, "Accessing Newsgroups via the Web.") The NNTP Server= line should be set to your service provider's *Network News Transport Protocol* (NNTP). The default setting in MOSAIC.INI is from the University of Illinois's news.cso.uiuc.edu. Set yours to your access provider's server. The syntax for the NNTP Server= line is usually "news.*site.domain,*" in which *site* is the name of your service (such as IQuest) and *domain* is the domain name (such as .net). Be sure to enclose the address in quotation marks (""). Ask your service provider for the site and domain names if you didn't receive them when you obtained your account.

The SMTP_Server= line is the address of your local service's Simple Mail Transport Protocol (SMTP) server. The default setting for this line is NCSA's server, which is `ftp.ncsa.uiuc.edu`. Your provider's address may look something like `"smtp.iquest.net"`, or something similar. Be sure to enclose the address in quotation marks ("").

Configuring Multimedia Components

One of the most innovative features of the World Wide Web is the capability to transmit sound, graphics, and videos across great distances. Mosaic enables you to define which applications you want activated when you encounter one of these types of files during your navigations. The [Viewers] section in the MOSAIC.INI file lists the associations and directory paths to your multimedia applications. These applications (called Helper Applications) are external to Mosaic.

Table 9.1 shows the types of files Mosaic can recognize, and some of the available applications.

TABLE 9.1
Multimedia Applications and Mosaic

Media Types	File Extension	Application
Text	DOC, RTF, PS	Word for Windows
Sound	AU, WAV, MIDI	WHAM (must have sound card), WPlany (must have SPEAK.EXE loaded)
Graphic	JPG, GIF, TIF	LView, Photoshop
MPEG Movies	MPG, AVI, MOV	Movie Player (must have QuickTime for Windows)

 Tip If you need to acquire a copy of one or more of the applications in table 9.1, you can find some of them on CompuServe, America Online or various FTP sites. Some of the listed applications are commercial applications and can only be purchased from registered software vendors.

Setting MIME Types

The [Viewers] section (see fig. 9.5) lists file types in the MIME format. *MIME* (Multipurpose Internet Mail Extensions) is a format used to attach sounds, images, and other files to e-mail. In the [Viewers] section of the MOSAIC.INI file, the lines TYPE0=, TYPE1=, and so on, indicate the MIME type Mosaic recognizes, (such as "audio/wav" for sound files, "image/gif" for graphics files, and "video/mpeg" for video files").

Figure 9.5

Multimedia settings in MOSAIC.INI.

```
Notepad - MOSAIC.INI
File  Edit  Search  Help
[Viewers]
TYPE0="audio/wav"
TYPE1="application/postscript"
TYPE2="image/gif"
TYPE3="image/jpeg"
TYPE4="video/mpeg"
TYPE5="video/quicktime"
TYPE6="video/msvideo"
TYPE7="application/x-rtf"
TYPE8="audio/x-midi"
TYPE9="application/zip"
rem TYPE9="audio/basic"
application/postscript="ghostview %ls"
image/gif="c:\winapps\lview\lview31 %ls"
image/jpeg="c:\winapps\lview\lview31 %ls"
video/mpeg="c:\winapps\mpegplay\mpegplay %ls"
video/quicktime="C:\WINAPPS\QTW\bin\player.exe %ls"
video/msvideo="mplayer %ls"
audio/wav="mplayer %ls"
audio/x-midi="mplayer %ls"
application/x-rtf="write %ls"
application/zip="C:\WINDOWS\APPS\ZIPMGR\ZM400.EXE %ls"
rem audio/basic="notepad %ls"
telnet="c:\network\qvt\tnstart.exe"

[Suffixes]
application/postscript=.ps,.eps,.ai,.ps
application/zip=.zip
```

Note You can add your own MIME type in the [Viewers] section by defining a new TYPE#, specifying a viewer, and, if necessary, adding a suffix list. (See the section called "Setting Media File Extensions" later in this chapter for more details about a suffix list.)

For more information about MIME types, check out the following FTP site:

`ftp://isi.edu/in-notes/media-types/media/types`

Specifying Viewers

Immediately following the MIME TYPE#= lines is a section of lines (see fig. 9.6) in which you specify the viewer for each file type listed. Mosaic uses these INI lines to find which application to activate when a specific file type is

downloaded. To ensure that Mosaic can find and then activate the application you have associated with a given file type, you must edit these lines to reflect the path and executable name of the application.

```
                        Notepad - MOSAIC.INI
File   Edit   Search   Help
TYPE1="application/postscript"
TYPE2="image/gif"
TYPE3="image/jpeg"
TYPE4="video/mpeg"
TYPE5="video/quicktime"
TYPE6="video/msvideo"
TYPE7="application/x-rtf"
TYPE8="audio/x-midi"
TYPE9="application/zip"
rem TYPE9="audio/basic"
application/postscript="ghostview %ls"
image/gif="c:\winapps\lview\lview31 %ls"
image/jpeg="c:\winapps\lview\lview31 %ls"
video/mpeg="c:\winapps\mpegplay\mpegplay %ls"
video/quicktime="C:\WINAPPS\QTW\bin\player.exe %ls"
video/msvideo="mplayer %ls"
audio/wav="mplayer %ls"
audio/x-midi="mplayer %ls"
application/x-rtf="write %ls"
application/zip="C:\WINDOWS\APPS\ZIPMGR\ZM400.EXE %ls"
rem audio/basic="notepad %ls"
telnet="c:\network\qvt\tnstart.exe"

[Suffixes]
application/postscript=.ps,.eps,.ai,.ps
application/zip=.zip
text/html=
text/plain=
```

Figure 9.6

These lines point to the application for the specific MIME viewer.

Suppose, for example, that you want to be able to view MPEG videos with Mosaic. To do so, you need to have on your hard drive an application, such as MPEGPLAY, that plays MPG files. To set up Mosaic to play MPEG videos, you must reference your MPEG application from the INI file. In the MOSAIC.INI file, find the following line:

```
video/mpeg="c:\winapps\mpegplay\mpegplay %ls"
```

This line simply tells you that Mosaic will play MPEG (.MPG) video files by accessing the MPEGPLAY application from this path. (The "%ls" extension simply replaces the normal .exe extension of a Windows application.)

If you happen to have the MPEGPLAY application (or another MPEG-compliant application) on your system but it does not reside in the c:\winapps\mpegplay directory, change the preceding line to reflect your specific path. If, for instance, you have your MPEGPLAY application in C:\MPEG\MPEGPLAY, your line would read as follows:

```
video/mpeg="c:\mpegplay\mpegplay %ls"
```

Be sure to keep the quotation marks ("") in the line. Also, make sure you keep your backslashes and slashes going the right way. Remember, DOS systems use backslashes (\) in their names. (This can get very confusing when you start typing in HTTP addresses that use forward slashes.)

The last line in the [Viewers] section is a reference to the Telnet application on your system. Mosaic uses this line, `telnet="c:\trumpet\telw.exe"`, to connect to some servers. Be sure to update this line when you are configuring Mosaic. If, for example, you are using QVT WinNet as your telnet application and it is placed in your c:\network\qvt subdirectory, use the following syntax:

```
telnet="c:\network\qvt\tnstart.exe"
```

(Note that `tnstart.exe` is the executable file for QVN WinNet.)

Stop As you navigate the Web and encounter various types of multimedia files, you may have to edit the [Viewers] section of the INI file a great deal until everything works correctly. Another point you should keep in mind is that multimedia files are large and will slow down your navigation quite a bit, especially if you are using a SLIP/PPP account. Keep this in mind as you click on those sound clips from the latest Rolling Stones concert online.

Setting Media File Extensions

The preceding section showed you how to set your MIME TYPES and viewer applications. The next section in the MOSAIC.INI file, the [Suffixes] section, lists the various extensions for media files retrieved by FTP or from HTTP version 0.9 servers. When it encounters these files, Mosaic uses the information in the [Suffixes] section and the [Viewers] section to determine the name and path of the external viewer to launch.

Many World Wide Web servers, however, are HTTP/1.0. In these cases, the [Viewers] section lists all the information necessary for activating the external application.

Table 9.2 shows the default extensions for files in the [Suffix] section of MOSAIC.INI.

TABLE 9.2
File Extensions Listed in [Suffix]

Type of File	Extensions
application/postscript	.ps, .eps, .ai, .ps
application/x-rtf	.rtt, .wri
audio/wav	.wave, .wav, .WAV
audio/x-midi	.mid
image/gif	.gif
image/jpeg	.jpeg, .jpe, .jpg
image/x-tiff	.tiff, .tif
video/mpeg	.mpeg, .mpg
video/quicktime	.mov
video/msvideo	.avi

Note When a file of a type listed in this section is written to your hard disk, it uses the last suffix in a particular line. If the viewer requires a specific extension, list that extension last. You might, for instance, use Paintshop Pro to view JPG files. Because these files sometimes are listed as JPEG or JPE, you need to make sure that .jpg is the last extension in the image/jpeg= line. This ensures that Paintshop Pro can read the image correctly.

To add other file types, list the type of file, add an equals sign (=), and list the extensions. The extensions must be separated by commas and always have a period before the extension, such as .jpg.

Specifying Annotation Directories

Mosaic enables you to add to Web documents text messages that do not edit the document, but are displayed whenever you view that document. You might, for instance, find an interesting document about space shuttle history. You can add some notes to this document by using the Annotate option in the Annotate menu. Then, when you view that document again, you can refer to those earlier annotations and add to them. And with Mosaic for Windows, you can share these annotations with others in a workgroup environment.

The [Annotations] section of MOSAIC.INI enables you to change the directory on your local drive (Directory= line) and your Group if on a network (Group Annotation Server= line). If you share the annotations across a network, the Group Annotation Server= line must include the machine name on the network and the port number. If you do not know your machine name and port number, you will need to ask your system administrator for them. If you do not plan to share annotations, keep the Group Annotation= line set to No.

You also can set the Default Title of the annotation in the Default Title= line. You might, for instance, want to change the title to read Personal Annotation by Rob, or whatever your name is.

Setting User Menus and Hotlists

The [User Menu] and [HotList] sections of MOSAIC.INI refer to the menus and hotlists you set up while you are using Mosaic. You should not edit these sections in the INI file, because you may inadvertently damage these settings. These settings will be changed while you are actually using Mosaic while on the World Wide Web. Depending on the number of menus set up on your system, you may have several [User Menu] sections, perhaps as many as five or six.

Tip   For more information about how to create menus and hotlists, see Chapters 10, "Navigating the Web for the First Time," and 11, "Finding Out More About Mosaic." If you want to learn more about the [User Menu] and [HotList] sections of MOSAIC.INI, refer to the installation guide bundled with Mosaic.

Caching Documents

The [Document Caching] section of the MOSAIC.INI file determines the number of documents Mosaic stores in memory. When you load a document, Mosaic retains the previous document (or as many as you indicate in the [Document Caching] section) in a memory cache, so that you can return to it quickly. The default is 2. If you have a large amount of memory (RAM), you might want to increase this number, perhaps to 6. If you find that your memory resources are being used quickly, decrease this number.

If you have very little memory (such as 4 MB) on your system, you might want to change the default number to 1 or even 0. By setting it to 0 (zero), you turn off caching. Remember to turn caching on if you upgrade your memory. You can turn caching back on by adding the number of documents that you want to cache, such as 1, 2, or so on.

Selecting Fonts

Do not edit the various [Font] sections in the MOSAIC.INI file. To change fonts, use the **C**hoose Font option from the **O**ptions menu while you are using Mosaic.

Configuring Proxy Information

Some MOSAIC.INI files have a section named [Proxy Information]. A *proxy gateway* enables Mosaic to pass on a network request to an outside agent through a *firewall*, which performs the request for Mosaic. The agent then returns the information to Mosaic. The network request is in the form of an URL. This type of gateway is set up so that Mosaic clients "sealed off" from the Internet can rely on agents to access the Internet for them. A user of a Mosaic software client using a proxy gateway still thinks he or she is on the Internet, even though he or she technically is not.

Proxy gateways currently are implemented on a per access method basis, such as ftp, gopher, wais, news, and http. Each URL access method can send its requests to a different proxy. The following sample INI section adds proxy support to Mosaic for Windows:

```
[Proxy Information]
http_proxy=http://aixtest.cc.ukans.edu:911/
ftp_proxy=http://aixtest.cc.ukans.edu:911/
wais_proxy=http://aixtest.cc.ukans.edu:911/
gopher_proxy= http://aixtest.cc.ukans.edu:911/
```

 Tip   For more information about obtaining a Web server that supports proxy services, go to the following URLs:

```
http://info.cern.ch/hypertext/WWW/Daemon/Overview.html
```

```
http://www.ncsa.uiuc.edu/SDG/Software/WinMosaic/ProxyInfo.html
```

Finishing Touches

Now that you have gone through the MOSAIC.INI file, save it and close it. You may have to restart Windows for the changes you have made to take effect. The next two chapters show you other ways to configure Mosaic so that it best fits your working habits. Fortunately, these changes can be made through menus and menu options while you are running Mosaic.

Navigating the Web for the First Time

In Chapter 9, "Using Mosaic as a Web Client," you learned how to install and configure Mosaic for Windows. This chapter shows you how to use Mosaic to navigate the Web. Although this chapter has specific instructions for using NCSA Mosaic (the most popular Web browser to date), many of the commands, options, and navigational skills described here apply to other Mosaic-like applications, such as Netscape.

This chapter discusses the following topics:

- ◆ Starting Mosaic

- ◆ Locating specific URL sites

- ◆ Saving a site of interest

- ◆ Saving and printing documents

- ◆ Exiting Mosaic

Starting Mosaic for the First Time

This chapter assumes that Mosaic is already installed on your system and that you have a connection to the Internet. Depending on the type of Internet connection you have, you can start your World Wide Web exploration in a couple of different ways. (See Chapter 9 for more information about the different types of Internet connections available.)

Tip   Throughout this chapter, Netscape Tips have been added to help those users who use Netscape as their primary Web browser.

If your connection to the Internet is through a *local area network* (LAN), you can simply double-click on Mosaic in the Windows Program Manager after you've logged into your network. If you've done everything correctly, Mosaic should appear on your screen and start downloading the start-up page (see fig. 10.1). By default, this start-up page is the NCSA Mosaic home page. Now you can start navigating the Web.

Figure 10.1

Mosaic and the default NCSA start-up page.

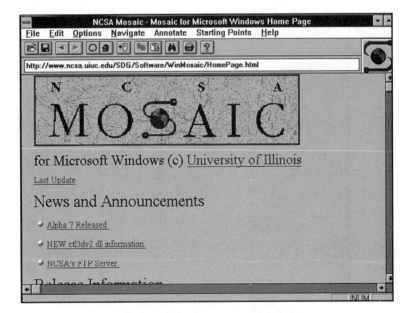

Note Talk to your network administrator if you think you have Internet access but you cannot get connected to the Web by means of Mosaic or another Web browser. Depending on your company's Internet access policy, you may or may not have full Internet access, which is necessary to access the World Wide Web.

If you have a dial-up connection to the Internet, you need to start your TCP/IP protocol stack first and make a connection with your access provider before you start Mosaic. Most stacks offer some type of automatic dialing script that enables you to dial up your provider automatically upon execution of the protocol stack. One such stack is Trumpet Winsock (see fig. 10.2).

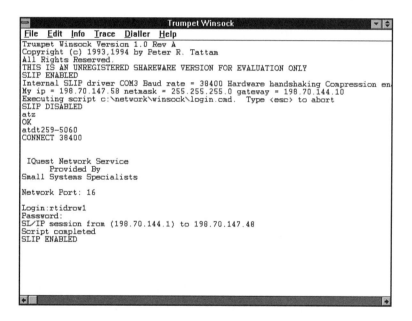

Figure 10.2

Example of a Trumpet Winsock dial-up script.

After you establish a connection with your access provider and have a SLIP/PPP connection, you are ready to activate Mosaic. Double-click on Mosaic in the Windows Program Manager. If everything goes as it should, Mosaic appears on the screen and starts downloading the start-up screen.

Note If you want to change the default start-up page, see Chapter 9, "Using Mosaic as a Web Client," for more details.

Examining Mosaic's Initial Interface

After you start Mosaic, you can begin your neverending search of sites on the Internet, including World Wide Web sites, FTP files, Gopher sites, and so on. One of the problems with Mosaic or any other Web browser, however, is that users often are not sure what to do next. Although you can do many things after you get your Web browser started, first you should get a little more familiar with the basics of the Mosaic screen. Chapter 11, "Finding Out More About Mosaic," discusses all the buttons, tools, and menus in greater detail. This chapter, however, gets you started quickly so that you can begin to enjoy the benefits of being on the WWW.

What Is the Spinning Globe?

Probably the most unusual item on the Mosaic interface is the animated globe. This globe—displayed in the upper right corner of the screen if you use Mosaic for Windows (see fig. 10.3) or the upper left corner if you use Mosaic for the Macintosh—is Mosaic's trademark. The globe spins when you instruct Mosaic to go out and access an URL. As you'll read later, the globe is not only a nice graphic image, it also serves a functional purpose.

Spinning globe

Figure 10.3

The spinning globe in Mosaic for Windows.

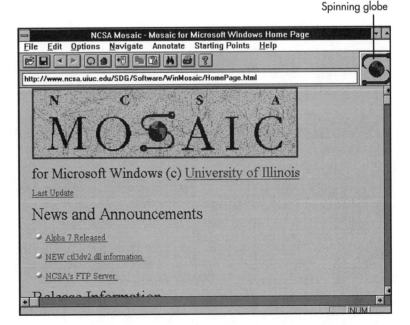

Tip   Netscape, not to be outdone, includes a pulsating "N" instead of a spinning globe (see fig. 10.4). Click on it to discontinue a download.

Pulsating "N"

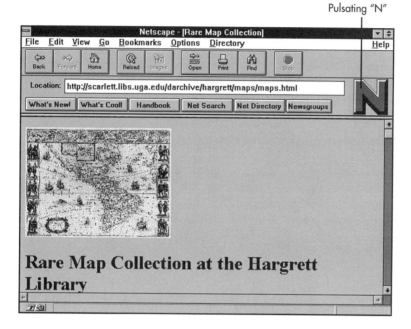

Figure 10.4

The pulsating "N" on the Netscape interface.

As you will discover when you start navigating the Web, many sites have large graphics files that take a relatively long time to download to your system. The spinning globe (and the status line at the bottom of the screen) tell you that Mosaic is still working and that you should be patient for a few moments. Frequently when you reach a site, you immediately want to link to another site by means of a hyperlink in a HTML document, or perhaps type a brand new URL. If you act while the globe is spinning, you can cause an error (you'll see an error message) or, depending on the stability of the software you're using, you can crash your system. Wait for the globe to stop spinning before you click on a hotlink or attempt to go to another URL site.

Tip   You can use the spinning globe to your advantage during an URL connection. If you want to stop a connection in progress (perhaps the connection is taking too long or you simply change your mind), click on the

continues

globe. In this way you usually can stop the URL lookup. With any beta software, not everything works perfectly, of course. Clicking on the globe usually works—but not always.

Try it, though. You just might save several minutes of downtime spent waiting for a site you may not even be interested in.

In the Macintosh version of Mosaic, another feature of the spinning globe is that it changes its look according to the type of function being performed. The globe displays one icon during an FTP download, another icon during a Gopher connection (or other similar connections), and so forth.

Examining the Main Window

Although the spinning globe is an interesting item on the Mosaic interface, the most important part of the screen is the main document window. This part of the screen displays the document to which you are connected. This document can be made up of text, graphics, hypertext links, forms, headings, lists, and multimedia file links.

In most cases, the document is in HTML format. Mosaic (and most other Web browsers) interpret this format and display the document as its author intended it to appear. What makes a Web document unique and useful is the skill with which the document's author uses different elements to convey specific ideas. Some documents, for instance, do not need fancy graphics or complicated lists or forms. In other documents, however, the use of various elements can convey to readers features such as the author's professionalism, artistic talents, and marketing skills.

Note As you navigate to different Web sites, you might encounter home pages that inform you that a page may look better using Netscape 1.1b or a similar browser. This message means that the Web page is using coding features, such as tables, centered text, and the like, that are associated with more advanced versions of HTML. As more Web authors use HTML 3.0 as their standard authoring language, more Web browsers will be upgraded to read this updated language. (At the time of this book's publication, HTML 3.0 is not yet accepted as a standard language.)

A Web document is similar to a page in a book, replete with text and illustrations. As described in earlier chapters of this book, the Web offers documents

that can "come alive" when you select specific items. These items are *hypertext* items (also known as *hotlinks*); usually, they are marked in some way so that the reader notices them. As a default, Mosaic shows these elements as blue under-lined text. In figure 10.5, for example, the phrase "About Indiana University" is a hypertext link to another source.

Figure 10.5

A hypertext link in a Web document.

Other items in HTML documents that can be hotlinked include graphics, bullets, headlines, forms, and maps. See Chapters 18, "Writing Web Docu-ments," and 19, "Introducing Hypertext Markup Language (HTML)," for more information about HTML documents and how to create them.

Clicking on Hypertext Links

Now, having seen your first Web document, what do you do with it? You have several options, depending on how the document is set up and its purpose. You can, of course, read it as you read any other document. Mosaic is designed to display documents of varying length. With Mosaic, as with any other Windows-compliant application, you use the scroll bars at the side and bottom of the screen to scroll through long documents (see fig. 10.6).

Figure 10.6

Use the scroll bars to look at the entire Web document.

Scroll Bars

Something else you can do with a Web document is click on the hypertext links and move to the resources they denote. As mentioned earlier, a hypertext link can be any of several types of elements in a Web document. The link's reference also can vary, depending on the type of information the document's author wants the reader to access. In short, any Internet resource that contains a *Uniform Resource Locator* (also known as an URL) can be linked to a hot spot.

You can, for instance, link one hotlink to another Web page by using the format `http://URLofResource`. The `URLofResource` is the complete URL of the item being referenced, such as www.eff.org. (This URL, by the way, is the home page of the Electronic Frontier Foundation.) Referencing other Web documents is the way in which many of the Web's documents are set up by referencing other Web documents. This set-up enables users to "jump" from one Web page to another, in the same document or in a completely different one. In addition, you can link a hotlink on a Web page to an FTP file, Gopher site, Telnet resource, or newsgroup.

On the Web page shown in figure 10.7, several items are "hot"; that is, several hot spots are set up on the document. If you click on an item in the numbered list, such as "Other Railroad-related Hypertext documents," Mosaic takes you to the site shown in figure 10.8). Because this site happens to be another Web

page, it is similar in appearance to the preceding Web page. From this site, you can continue reading the document, jump to another site by means of a hot spot in the document, or return to the preceding page.

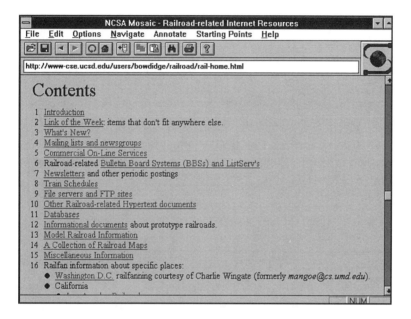

Figure 10.7

A Web document with various hot spots.

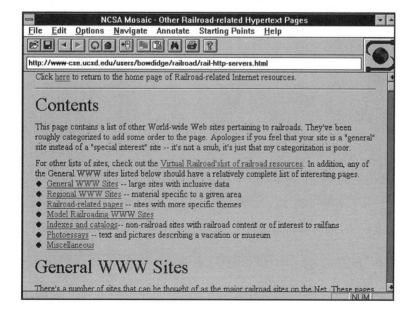

Figure 10.8

The result of clicking on a hot spot in the preceding figure.

You can return to the preceding page in any of the following ways:

◆ **Click on the left arrow.** An arrow on the Mosaic toolbar, and on the toolbars of most other browsers, enables you to return to the preceding page. In most cases, the preceding page is cached in your system's memory so that you can return immediately to that page without again downloading all the text and graphics. In Chapter 9, "Using Mosaic as a Web Client," you learned how to set the cache size of your Mosaic configuration. Refer to that chapter if you want to resize the cache.

◆ **Click on a "return to" hot spot.** Some Web pages contain hot spots that return you to the preceding page or to the home page of the site.

◆ **Use the History option.** The History option in Mosaic's Navigate menu enables you to see a complete list of the URLs you have accessed in the current session. In figure 10.9, for example, you can see the exact path taken to get to the Railroad document. To return to a particular site, just click on that URL in the History list and then click on the Load button. Mosaic will jump to that site.

Figure 10.9

The History dialog box displays a list of sites you have accessed during the current session.

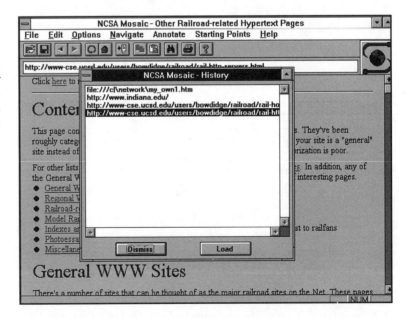

Tip If you use Netscape, you can find the most recent list of sites in the Go menu (see fig. 10.10).

New Riders Publishing
INSIDE
SERIES

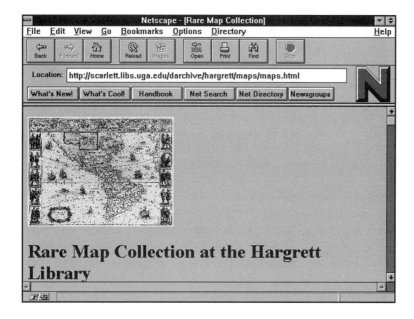

Figure 10.10

Netscape's Go menu shows a list of sites you have accessed during the current session.

With practice, you'll learn to figure out where you are and how to get back to the original document. Chapter 11, "Finding Out More About Mosaic," describes other ways to find your way back to your starting point.

Looking at Other Interface Items

As you've already seen, the URL is equivalent to a home or business address in the real world. If you want to send something to someone, you must know that person's complete address, including the name, street address (sometimes with a suite or floor number), city, and ZIP code. Similarly, to send something on the Web, you use its addressing scheme—the URL—and you need to know the location's address before you can go there.

In Mosaic, the URL box appears at the top of the screen, to the left of the spinning globe. In Mosaic 2.*x*, you can connect to a site by entering an URL in this box, and pressing Enter. One of the problems with this approach is that you can make an error when you type the URL. Unfortunately, another human is not at the other end of the connection. You do not connect to a person who can decipher the address and try to find the resource to which you want to connect (as a postal worker does with your letters and packages when you accidentally leave off the ZIP code). If you type in the wrong URL, your browser returns an error message telling you that it could not connect to the

URL you listed. (Another way to enter an URL is to use the **F**ile, **O**pen URL option.)

Tip

If you receive an error message telling you that you cannot connect to a server, don't always assume that the server is busy or down. First, make sure that the URL you typed is the correct address. You may have typed a slash (/) when the URL calls for a period (.), or vice versa. Another common error is using a backslash (\) instead of a slash (/). This is common with DOS users who are intimately familiar with backslashes. Always assume first that the error is yours. You'll be amazed at the number of times your fingers get ahead of you when you're transcribing those cryptic URLs.

Although several other items appear on the main document window, they are not described here. (See Chapter 11, "Finding Out More About Mosaic," for descriptions of each of these items and a list of the functions of the menu items.) What you've learned up to this point is enough to get you up and running with Mosaic or another similar Web browser. The following section helps you take the next step after you've navigated through a few Web sites.

Taking the Next Step

Now that you are on the Internet and have access to the Web, you probably want to explore and use the resources available to you. Because jumping from one resource to another on the Web is so easy, you may enjoy just doing that— clicking on hot spots in documents as you find them. Although this is an excellent way to find new sites and become familiar with the Web and its offerings, it is not a good way to find specific resources you might want to use for business, school, hobbies, or travel.

This section shows you how to use some additional features of Mosaic that help make your online time more productive. You can also use some of the techniques described here with other browsers, such as Netscape.

Note

See Chapter 8, "Finding Resources on the Web," for more information about using different search utilities, such as Archie, WAIS, and Veronica to locate specific items on the Internet.

Finding a Specific Site

Having looked at, read, or grown tired of the document currently on your screen, you probably want to go to another site. Several options are available to do this.

If you know the address of a site, type the URL in the URL box or select **F**ile, **O**pen URL, then type the URL and press Enter. To find the URL of a site, use the Web Scrapbook at the back of this book. You can also use a directory, such as *New Riders' Official World Wide Web Yellow Pages*, to find sites of interest. The important thing to remember is that you must type the full URL, without mistakes.

If you do not know of a site to go to, Mosaic includes a list of sites that you can connect to by means of a menu option. The Starting Points menu has a list of sites that the developers at NCSA predefined for you (see fig. 10.11). Several of the options that follow enable you to link directly to other Web resources:

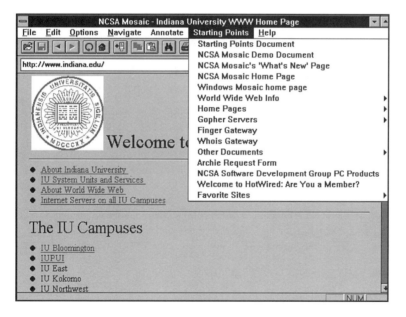

Figure 10.11

The Starting Points menu in Mosaic for Windows.

◆ **NCSA What's New Page.** Connects you to the NCSA Web page that lists news and new sites on the Web. This is a great resource that enables you to stay abreast of some of the latest happenings on the Web and the Internet.

◆ **NCSA Mosaic Home Page.** Jumps you to the NCSA home page for Mosaic.

◆ **Windows Mosaic Home Page.** Connects you to the Mosaic for Windows home page. Use this site to get information, documentation, and updates on the current version of Mosaic for Windows.

◆ **World Wide Web Info.** Lists several sites that contain information on the World Wide Web initiative. Excellent resource for finding out more about the Web itself, but probably not the ideal place to start your first Web adventure.

◆ **Home Pages.** Lists 21 university Web sites to which you can connect with a click of the mouse. You might want to see whether your alma mater is listed here and connect to its Web server to find out more about the university's online resources.

◆ **Other Documents.** Lists other Internet points that you might find interesting. Unless you have already decided to visit one of the universities listed in the Home Pages option, you might try visiting one of these sites as your first real venture into the Web.

Note The other options in this menu are discussed in detail in Chapter 11, "Finding Out More About Mosaic." Refer to that chapter if you have questions about them.

Not only can you use the Starting Points menu to go to predefined spots, you also can store favorite places that you find on the Web on this menu. For more information, see the "Saving a Site of Interest" section later in this chapter.

Tip One of the most useful starting places on the Web is Yahoo (see fig. 10.12). Yahoo is a comprehensive list of categories and subcategories that connect you to sites on the Internet. Currently, it has over 26,000 URLs listed.

To find Yahoo, type in the following URL:

`http://www.yahoo.com/`

Another useful starting place is the Internet Directory (see fig. 10.13) at the following URL:

`http://home.mcom.com/home/internet-directory.html`

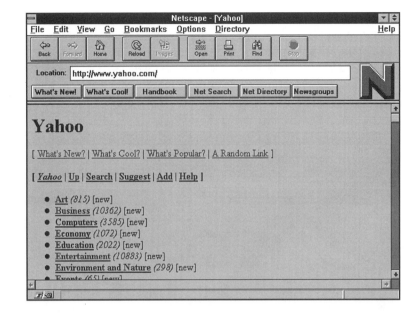

Figure 10.12

Use Yahoo as a great starting point to find new sites on the Web.

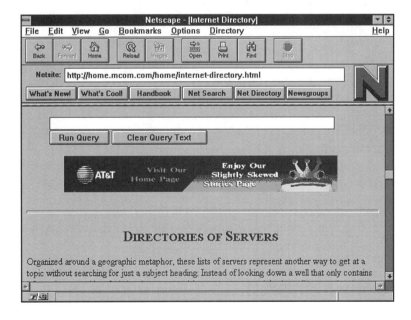

Figure 10.13

The Internet Directory is another helpful online listing of sites.

As an example, and to get you moving in cyberspace, select Starting Points, Home Pages, and click on Indiana University. This connects you to the Web server at Indiana University (see fig. 10.14). From this location you can perform any number of actions on the document, as described earlier in this chapter. For this example, click on the hot Internet Servers on all IU Campuses spot, which takes you to a site not currently listed in your menus.

Figure 10.14

The Indiana University Web home page.

If you like this site (or any others that you find while you are surfing the Web) and you think you might return to it later, you can save it as one of your menu options. You also can create brand new menus that appear at the top of the Mosaic screen—a handy feature if you want to classify sites in easy-to-understand and easy-to-find ways.

The following section shows you how to save sites to a current menu and how to create your own menu items.

Saving a Site of Interest

To save a site, you need to know its URL and have a name for it. If you are currently at a site you want to save, this information is provided when you save

the site. You do not necessarily have to give the site its official name, but you should give it a name that has meaning, so that you will be able to make sense of the name when you later return to the listing. Names such as "Site 1," "Cool Site 2," and so forth may confuse you later.

To save a site to a current menu and starting point, follow these steps:

1. From the **N**avigate menu, select Menu Editor to display the Personal Menus dialog box (see fig. 10.15).

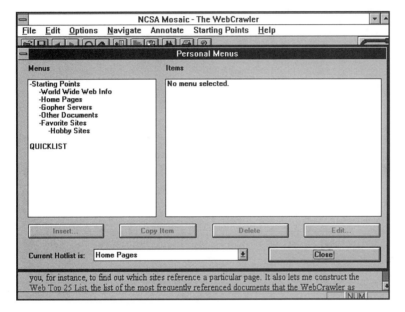

Figure 10.15

The Personal Menus dialog box.

2. In the Menus area, click on the name of the option under which you want the new site to appear. You might, for instance, want to add the site to the Other Documents option. To do so, click on that name.

3. Notice that the Insert button is highlighted, and that all the sites currently located in the Other Documents option are displayed in the Items area of the dialog box. Click on the Insert button.

4. The Add Item dialog box appears, with the current Web document's title and URL displayed in the Title and URL fields, respectively. An example of the Add Item dialog box is shown in figure 10.16.

Figure 10.16

*The Add Item
dialog box.*

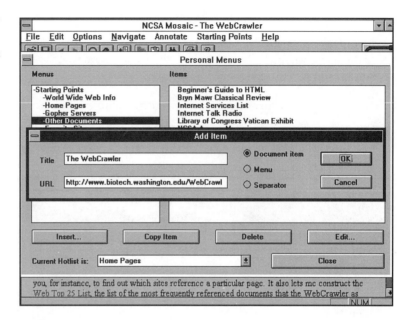

The Add Item dialog box enables you to add an item to an existing menu,
to add a new submenu, or to add a new menu to the menu bar. The
following three buttons on the Add Item dialog box enable you to do
specific tasks:

- ◆ **Document Item.** Select this button to add an item to the selected
  existing submenu.

- ◆ **Menu.** Select this button to add a new menu to the menu bar.

- ◆ **Separator.** Select this button to add a separator line to a menu.

For this example, make sure that the Document Item button is selected,
which tells Mosaic that you want to add an item to the Other Documents
submenu.

5. Make sure that the Title field contains the correct name of the site. The
   current document's name is provided here, but you can modify it as you
   see fit.

6. If an URL is not provided in the URL field, fill in the correct address for
   the name of the site you want to place on the menu. Click on OK.

The Personal Menus dialog box is displayed, with the new item (The WebCrawler) placed in the Items list (see fig. 10.16). Now you can add more items to the menus or click on the Close button to return to the main Mosaic window.

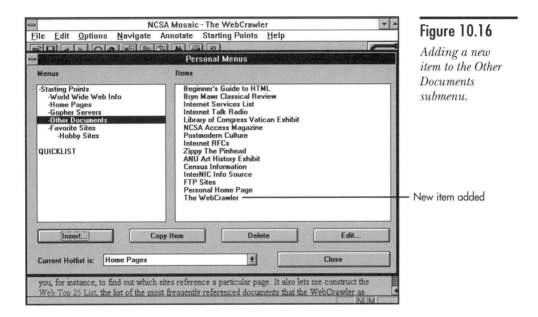

Figure 10.16

Adding a new item to the Other Documents submenu.

To add a completely new menu to Mosaic and store your favorite sites in it, follow these steps:

1. From the main Mosaic window, select **N**avigate, Menu Editor. In the Personal Menus dialog box, select the blank space directly above the QUICKLIST submenu. The instruction Click "Insert" to add a top-level menu appears in the Items box (see fig. 10.17).

2. Click on Insert to display the Add Item dialog box. Notice that Menu is the only button you can pick. The other two options are grayed out.

3. In the Title field, type a name for the new top-level menu. (The default title is Personal Home Page.)

Figure 10.17

Adding a top-level menu.

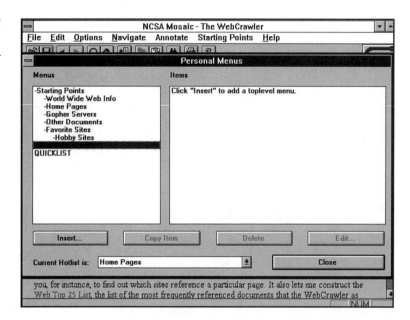

Tip

Remember that this top-level menu appears at the top of the main Mosaic window—an important consideration when you select a menu name. You might, for instance, want to make the title short—fewer than 10 characters—to keep the menu bar tidy. Most Windows applications keep menu names to one or two short words, at most.

Notice also that these new menus do not adhere totally to standard Windows applications' specifications. The new menu, for instance, does not include an accelerator key (also known as a "hot key") denotation.

4. Click on OK to display the Personal Menu dialog box. To add the menu to the menu bar, click on Close. Your new top-level menu appears on the main menu bar.

Now you need to fill the new top-level menu with submenus and specific sites. (To add new sites to this menu or to the new submenus, simply use the preceding steps on how to add new sites.) To add submenus to this menu (or to other top-level menus that already exist), follow these steps:

1. Select **N**avigate, Edit Menu. Click on the top-level menu to which you want to add submenus.

2. Click on Insert. When the Add Item dialog box appears, click on the Menu button. Just the Title field is displayed (see fig. 10.18).

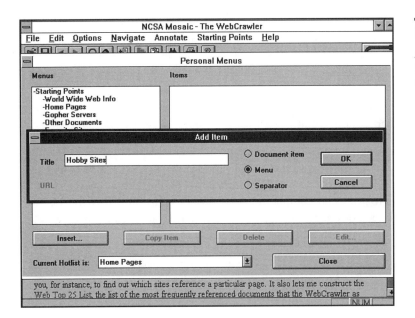

Figure 10.18

Adding submenus to top-level menus.

3. Enter the name of the new submenu, such as Hobby Sites. Click on OK.

4. The Personal Menu dialog box is displayed, with the new submenu in the Item area of the selected top-level menu.

5. Continue adding submenus, as needed.

Tip

If you need to edit a menu, submenu, or site name, select the name you want to change in the Personal Menus dialog box and click on the Edit button. In the Edit Item dialog box, you can enter a new name or modify an existing one. After you finish, click on OK to display the Personal Menus dialog box.

To delete a menu, submenu, or item, select the name you want to delete in the Personal Menus dialog box, click on the Delete button, and click on OK when the prompt appears.

This section showed you how to use some of Mosaic's built-in lists to find new Web sites and how to save sites after you've found them. The next section shows you how to save specific documents when you are connected to a site.

Saving a Document to Your Hard Drive

You read about HTML documents in Chapter 1. Later chapters show you how to create your own. After you've connected to HTML documents by means of the Web, you can save the documents to your local hard drive. You might want to save a particularly interesting page, for instance, to use as your default starting page. Or you might want to save one so that you can view a document or file when you are not connected to the Internet. Saving HTML documents also can be useful when you want to reduce connect charges or use the documents with other applications on your computer.

A document might also contain other types of resources, such as an MPEG file or WAV file, that you want to save to your hard drive. Commonly known as *multimedia* files, these files are usually fairly large. One of the best ways to use these files is to save them to disk and then play them from your hard drive. Because Mosaic does not have to store the file temporarily, play it, and then discard it, you save both time and memory resources.

One way to save a file or document to your hard drive is to use the Save As option. The Save As option in the File menu enables you to save the current document in the following three ways:

◆ **HTML format.** This option writes the file to your hard drive and retains all the HTML information, including *link anchors* (links to other documents), HTML codes, URLs, and other formatting. Use this format to store HTML documents if you plan to use them as starting points.

◆ **ASCII text format.** This option saves the current document to your hard drive as a stripped-down version of the HTML document, with all the HTML codes, URLs, and other formatting removed. Use this method if you want to read a document offline as a plain text file.

◆ **Binary format.** This format saves binary files to your hard disk. These can be sound files, graphic files, video files, archived files (such as zipped files), and other binaries.

 Stop When you save HTML documents, you do not save the inline graphics that are part of the document. These graphics remain on the remote server and are accessed by the document when you load the document from your disk into Mosaic or another Web browser. You should be aware that if you load these documents while connected to the Web, you might spend a great deal

New Riders Publishing
INSIDE
SERIES

of time waiting for the inline graphics to be loaded. To prevent inline graphics from being loaded, make sure that the **O**ptions, Display Inline Graphics option is turned off.

The other way to load files and documents to disk is to toggle on the Load to Disk option in the **O**ption's menu. You must have this feature turned on before you connect to any document you want to save to disk. If you connect to a site that you want to save to disk, select **O**ptions, Load to Disk, and click on the Reload button on the Mosaic toolbar (the fifth button from the left). In this way, you automatically reload the current document and display the Save As dialog box. In the Save As dialog box, you then can specify the name and directory to which to save the current document.

When you leave the Load to Disk option toggled on, each document you connect to is saved to your hard drive. For each document, you must specify a name and directory in the Save As dialog box.

Select **O**ptions, Load to Disk to turn off this feature when you finish saving files to your local disk.

Tip
A quick way to load a file to disk is to use the mouse. Move the cursor over the link anchor (hotlink) of the item you want to save to disk. Press Shift and click the left mouse button. When the Save As dialog box appears, you can name the file and select the directory for the file. When you use this method, you do not have to worry about turning the Load to Disk option on or off.

Printing a Document

Another feature of many Web browsers, including Mosaic, is the capability to print a hard copy of the current document. This capability is handy if you want to retain a hard copy of the document or if the document contains several pages that you want to peruse offline (or if you just like to make printouts).

Of course, when you make a hard copy of the document, you bypass the special nature of the Web—its hypertext links. You can't have these links when you go offline. If you have inline graphics turned on when you load the document into Mosaic, however, the graphics remain in the document. Remember this when you start to print large documents—several graphics may slow down and hog your printer's resources.

To print the current document, use the File, Print option from the Mosaic main window. To print the entire current Web document, click on OK in the Print dialog box (see fig. 10.19). Or click on the Printer icon on the toolbar.

Figure 10.19

Mosaic's Print dialog box.

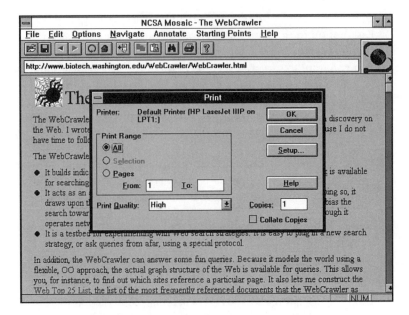

To preview the document before you print it, select File, Print Preview. A representation of the document as it will be printed is displayed.

To select the printer, type of printer, and other settings, select File, Print Setup. Configure these settings as you would in any other Windows application.

Tip

When you print a Web document that contains hotlinks (which most of them do) these hotlinks may look strange on the hard copy. Some, in fact, may not even appear on your hard copy, whereas others may appear in a very tiny font. This is due in part by the type of fonts you have configured on your system.

Scaleable versions of the fonts must be installed on your system so that you can match the fonts displayed on-screen in Mosaic with the fonts that print. In the next chapter, you see how to set up fonts in Mosaic and how to use different styles. Refer to Chapter 11 now if you are having difficulty printing a particular document.

Ending Your Web Session

Now that you've made a short visit of the World Wide Web and learned a few primary features of Mosaic, you can end your session. When you are ready to close Mosaic or any other browser you might be using, ask yourself whether you want to save the item to which you currently are connected. If so, save it as an item on one of your hotlist menus.

To end your Mosaic session, simply close it as you would any other Windows application. You can, for example, select File, Exit. Or, double-click on the Control menu in the upper left corner of the Mosaic window.

After you close Mosaic, be sure to log off your account, especially if you are using a dial-up SLIP/PPP account, so that you don't rack up useless time on your account. Simply closing Mosaic or another Web browser *does not* log you out of your account. You must log out manually through your TCP/IP software.

If you are attached to the Internet by means of a LAN, ask your administrator about, or review, your company's internal policy for staying logged on or logging out at the end of your WWW session. Each company has its own standard operating procedure for logging out from the Internet.

Finding Out More About Mosaic

One of the more intimidating aspects of the Internet and the World Wide Web is the complexity of the software used to access them. Even though the Web is intended to be easy to navigate, and applications like Mosaic are relatively easy to use on a certain level, some quirks still exist that need further explanation. This chapter is intended to cover these points.

Use this chapter as a reference and learning tool after you are comfortable with Mosaic. As in the last chapter, many of the principles in this chapter can sometimes be applied to other Mosaic-like browsers, such as Netscape. This chapter covers the following topics:

◆ Understanding Mosaic's commands and options

◆ Setting fonts

◆ Getting help

Navigating the Mosaic Interface

In the previous two chapters you learned how to install, configure, and use Mosaic. This section is designed to help round out the discussion of how to use Mosaic's commands and options. Some of the menu options are not discussed here because they are described in detail in Chapter 10, "Navigating the Web for the First Time."

Using File Menu Options

In Chapter 10 you learned how to use the Open URL option in the **F**ile menu. That chapter did not, however, describe the Open URL dialog box (see fig. 11.1) displayed when you select the Open URL option. This dialog box contains the following three fields:

Figure 11.1

Use the Open URL dialog box to navigate to different Web sites.

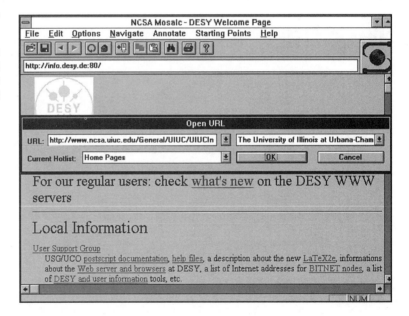

◆ **URL.** Shows the URL of the current document. To connect to a different site, you highlight this field, type the appropriate URL, and press Enter.

◆ **Current Hotlist.** Shows the name of the currently active list of items. As you saw in Chapter 10, "Navigating the Web for the First Time," you can

add or delete these lists by using the **N**avigate, Menu Editor option. To change the current hotlist from this dialog box, click on the down arrow and select a hotlist from the drop-down list.

◆ **Currently selected document.** This unlabeled field, which is the top right field in the Open URL dialog box, displays the name of the current document. If the document you want to connect to is in a hotlist, click on the down arrow and select the document from the drop-down list.

Click on OK or Cancel to close the dialog box.

To open an HTML document that you have saved on your local hard drive, you use the Open Local File option. As you saw in Chapter 10, this feature is handy when you want to open a document quickly without having to connect to it by means of the Web. You also can use this option to view an HTML document you have created to see what it looks like in Mosaic.

The **S**ave option saves the currently active document to your hard drive. For more information about saving documents and files to your hard drive, see the Using Save As portion of the "Saving a Document to Your Hard Drive" section in Chapter 10.

When you make changes to your interface by using the **O**ptions menu (see the "Using the Options Menu" section later in this chapter) or you resize the Mosaic window, you must select the Save Preferences option in the **F**ile menu. This option ensures that your changes take effect and are used the next time you start Mosaic.

Tip

One of the most frustrating features of Mosaic is related to the Save **P**references option. When Mosaic first starts up, you may not like the size and shape of the window. Go ahead and use your mouse to reshape the window, but be sure to select **F**ile, Save **P**references. Otherwise, the next time you start Mosaic, the window will revert to the size and shape it had the first time you started the application.

As you will learn in Part V, "Creating Web Documents," you can create your own Web documents by using HTML format. One of the ways to quickly learn how to code your documents is to see how experienced Webmasters do it. You can do this by selecting **F**ile, **D**ocument Source to open a window that displays the current document and its associated HTML code (see fig. 11.2).

Figure 11.2

*Viewing an
HTML document
in the Document
Source window.*

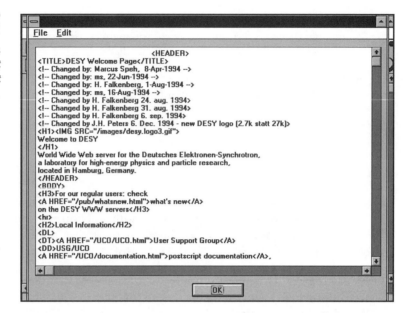

If you are unfamiliar with HTML codes, the Document Source window display may be somewhat intimidating. After you understand the codes, however, you'll want to use this feature to view several documents so that you can see how sophisticated documents are set up. In fact, you'll learn to appreciate the art and skill exhibited in some Web documents.

The following descriptions pertain to the two menus (**F**ile and **E**dit) available in the Document Source window:

◆ **File.** This menu's **S**ave option enables you to save the document to your hard drive as an HTM file. The menu's E**x**it option closes the Document Source window.

◆ **Edit.** This menu's **C**opy option enables you to copy selected text from the displayed document to the Windows Clipboard. You might use this option, for instance, to copy a sample of text from the active document to a document you are creating, thus reducing the time needed to create a document.

Tip   If you select the Document Source option and you do not see the current document, you need to close the Document Source window and reload the current document. To do this, either click on the toolbar's Reload button or

New Riders Publishing
INSIDE
SERIES

select **N**avigate, Reload. After you have reloaded the document, select **F**ile, **D**ocument Source. The reason you don't see the current document is because Mosaic does not cache the current document correctly, particularly if you have returned to the document by using the Return To arrow on the toolbar.

Using Edit Menu Options

As with most Windows applications, Mosaic has an Edit menu that contains options such as **C**opy and **F**ind. The **C**opy option is used to copy selected text from the following sources:

◆ **Data entry boxes.** When you fill out fields in Mosaic or in a form, you can use the **E**dit, **C**opy command to save that information to the Clipboard.

◆ **URL boxes.** You can copy a URL from one field to another by using the **E**dit, **C**opy option. This capability is handy when the URLs are extremely long.

◆ **Document Source window.** You can copy selected text from the Document Source window to the Clipboard so that you can reuse the text in another document.

Stop Don't confuse this **C**opy option with the **C**opy option in normal Windows applications, such as Word for Windows. You cannot use it to copy highlighted items from a Web document to the Clipboard if you're using the Windows version of Mosaic (although you can do so with the Mac version). To select text in a Web document, use the Document Source option, highlight the text you want, and select **E**dit, **C**opy. Although the text is in ASCII text version and contains HTML codes, you can at least copy and paste that text in another document. After you paste the section into another document, you can delete the HTML codes.

Similar to the Find option in a standard word processor, the **E**dit menu's **F**ind option enables you to locate specific text in a document. In the Find dialog box's Fi**n**d What field (see fig. 11.3), you place the word or phrase you are searching for. To find a word or words that exactly match the text string you place in the Fi**n**d What field, click on the Match **C**ase check box. Use the **F**ind Next button to find the next occurrence of the word or words you are searching for. (Another way to activate the Find feature is to click on the Find button on the toolbar.)

Figure 11.3

The Find dialog box.

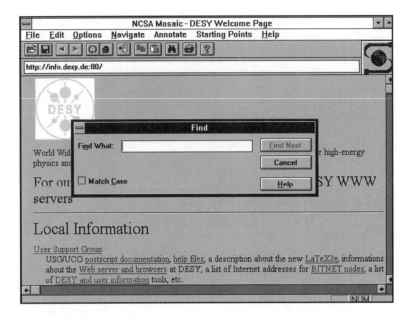

Using the Options Menu

Some of the configuration settings you set when you installed Mosaic (see Chapter 9, "Using Mosaic as a Web Client") can be set also in the **O**ptions menu (see fig. 11.4). The following settings are included:

◆ Show **T**oolbar

◆ Show **S**tatus Bar

◆ Show Current URL

◆ Show Anchor URLs

◆ Change Cursor Over Anchors

◆ Extended FTP Directory Parsing

◆ Display Inline Images

◆ Show Group Annotations

◆ **U**se 8-bit sound

Refer to Chapter 9 for more information about these items. Some of these options do not need to be changed once you set them up, but you may want to experiment with them after you've used Mosaic for several sessions.

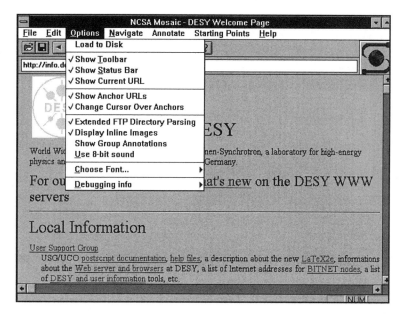

Figure 11.4

Use the Options menu to set up the way Mosaic looks and works.

Note   As you may recall, you learned how to use the Load to Disk option in Chapter 10, "Navigating the Web for the First Time." You used this option to save documents and files to your hard disk.

The Show Anchor URLs option tells Mosaic to display the URL for a link when you pass the hand cursor over that link. The URL is displayed in the status bar at the lower left corner of the main Mosaic window. This feature is helpful when you want to know what type of hotlink is set up. You might want to know, for instance, whether a hotlink is a graphics file (such as a GIF file), an FTP resource, or a Gopher list, so that you can determine whether you want to click on that hotlink.

Setting Fonts in Mosaic

As you saw in Chapter 10, having the correct fonts configured in Mosaic affects the way documents print. The **C**hoose Font option enables you to select the way in which Web documents are displayed. From the submenu displayed when you select this option, you can choose several styles that make up a Web document (see fig. 11.5). Although the Web document's author controls the basic layout of the way in which a document displays and what types of items are placed on the document, you can control the way the document appears onscreen.

Figure 11.5

The Choose Font option submenu offers many font styles.

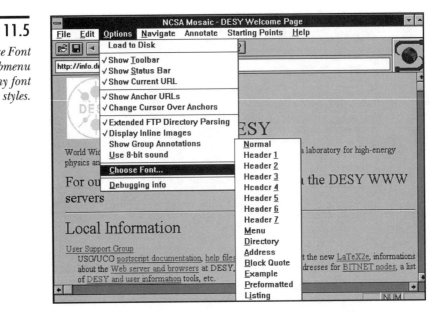

Table 11.1 lists the styles you can change by using the **C**hoose Font option.

TABLE 11.1
Document Styles

Menu Option	Description
Normal	Standard paragraph style in Web documents
Headers 1–7	Headlines displayed in a Web document (the main title on the home page usually is coded as Header 1 or Header 2)
Menu	Lists that are displayed in menu form
Directory	Lists that are displayed in directory form
Address	The document author's name and e-mail address (by default, usually italic), displayed at the bottom of the document
Blockquote	Quotations in a document
Example	Samples of code in a document

Menu Option	Description
Preformatted	Style frequently used to create tables in an HTML document; sometimes text (such as program listings) is preformatted in a monospace font, which you may want to change to another font.
Listing	Longer sample code listings than those coded as Example

To change the default styles of a Web document, you select **O**ptions, **C**hoose Font, then choose the paragraph style you want to change. If you want to change the way the main title looks, for instance, click on Header **1** and, in the Font dialog box (see fig. 11.6), change the font, font style, or size as you see fit. An example of the font appears in the Sample box at the bottom of the Font dialog box. Click on OK when the font style suits you.

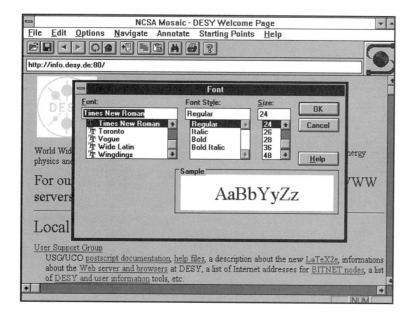

Figure 11.6

Use the Font dialog box to select and view a new font for a style.

By comparing the Web document shown in figure 11.7 with the version shown in figure 11.8, you can see how minor font changes greatly affect a document's appearance. This document, like many others on the Web, does not include all the elements listed in table 11.1. You can easily see, however, how the font changes the appearance of even a fairly simple document, such as this one.

Figure 11.7

A document with the default font (Times New Roman) used for all headings and paragraph text.

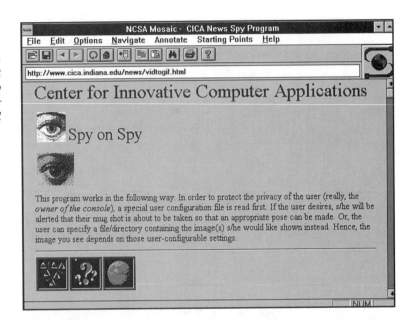

Figure 11.8

The same document, after a few changes have been made.

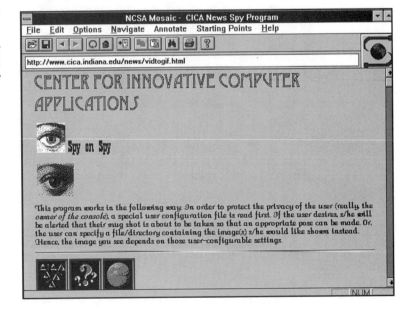

In figure 11.7, Times New Roman is the default typeface for the entire document. In figure 11.8, a few changes have been made to the headings and

paragraph style. Header 1, for instance, was changed to Desdemona; Header 2 was changed to Playbill; and the Normal style was changed to Caligula.

 Note   Not all authors adhere to identical tagging practices; thus, some elements in a document—such as code listings—might not be tagged the way you expect them to be tagged (in this case, with the Example style). You cannot change the tags, which are determined by the author. You can, however, change the document's appearance on your screen.

To change the styles back to the original, simply follow the same procedures, changing each style back to its original font, such as Times New Roman.

Debugging Information

Another option on the **O**ptions menu, **D**ebugging info, enables you to toggle on and off a series of alerts and warning messages. This option is intended for developers, not for the normal Mosaic user. Generally, you can just ignore it.

Using the Navigate Menu Options

During your Web navigation sessions, you probably will use the **N**avigate menu and its options more than any other menu. In Chapter 10, "Navigating the Web for the First Time," you saw how to set up your own menus and items by using the Menu Editor option. And you've used the History option to return to sites to which you've connected during a Web session.

The **N**avigate menu also contains the following options:

- ◆ **Back.** Enables you to return to the previous document or documents, depending on what size cache you have. You can do the same task by clicking on the Back button on the toolbar.

- ◆ **Forward.** Enables you to move forward through the document or documents that you've connected. You can do the same task by clicking on the Forward button on the toolbar.

- ◆ **Reload.** Enables you to reload the document to which you are connected. This capability is very helpful if you have inline graphics turned off and want to view a graphic in a document. If this is the case, select **O**ptions, Display Inline Images, and choose the Reload option in the **N**avigate menu. You can do the same task by clicking on the Reload button on the toolbar.

◆ **Home.** Returns you to your start-up page, which may be a local file, a Web document of your choice, or the default NCSA server home page. The Home button (which looks like a house) on the toolbar does the same task.

◆ **Add Current To Hotlist.** Enables you to save the current document immediately to your hotlist of sites. You can change the current hotlist by selecting **F**ile, **O**pen URL, then clicking on the down arrow in the Current Hotlist dialog box. Click on the hotlist you want to make current, such as Other Documents, and click on Cancel (not on OK). This causes any documents you add to be added to the new hotlist.

Annotating Documents

How many times have you seen a document on the Web about which you want to write a short note? You can do this with Mosaic by using the Annotate menu's Annotate option. When you select this option, the Annotate Window appears (see fig. 11.9), in which you can draft notes about a particular site or resource.

Figure 11.9

Use this feature to type notes about a document.

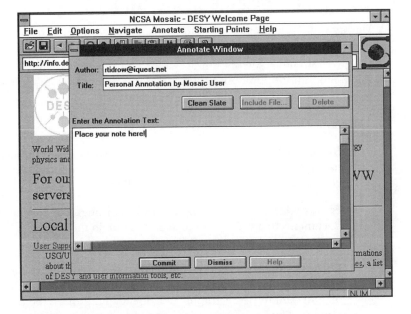

Your e-mail address appears in the Author field. You can change this address to anything you like. The Title field displays the default title you set in the MOSAIC.INI file (see Chapter 9, "Using Mosaic as a Web Client") when you

configured Mosaic. You can change this title to another one whenever you create an annotation—just highlight this field and type the new title.

In the Enter the Annotation Text box, type the note you want to make for the current document. Click on the Commit button to accept the annotation and close the window. The next time you load this document, you'll see the words "Personal Annotations," which indicate that an annotation is attached to it.

 Note You should note that the new annotation does not show up on the current document until you reload the document. Click on the Reload button on the toolbar or select **N**avigate, **R**eload to make the annotation appear immediately.

To read an annotation, select Annotate, Annotate, and read the note in the Enter the Annotation Text area. You can modify, add, or delete the information in this area. To remove the entire note, click on the Clean Slate button.

The Include File, Delete, and Help functions have yet to be implemented; they may work in a future release of Mosaic.

Examining More Starting Points Options

In Chapter 10, "Navigating the Web for the First Time," you saw how to use and add items to several of the options available in the Starting Points menu. This section discusses the rest of the options in this menu (see fig. 11.10).

These options and their functions are as follows:

◆ **Gopher Servers.** Lists eight gateways to Gopher information servers. One of the servers includes Veronica and the original Gopher site at the University of Minnesota. You also can see a list of all the Gopher sites in the world.

◆ **Finger Gateway.** Enables you to connect to the Finger Gateway at Indiana University. This Unix utility enables you to search e-mail and other information about people who are connected to the Internet on Unix-based networks.

◆ **Whois Gateway.** Enables you to search for people on the Internet.

◆ **Archie Request Form.** Enables you to access world-wide Archie servers by using a form-based gateway for the Web.

Figure 11.10

Options on the Starting Points menu.

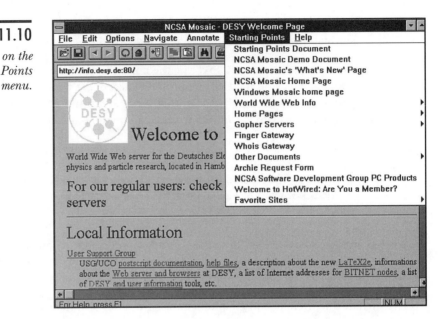

Note If you are not familiar with Gopher, Veronica, Finger, Whois, and Archie, see Chapter 8, "Finding Resources on the Web," which shows you how to use these features during your Web sessions.

Using Help Features

Living up to its promise of providing documents online, Mosaic's help options are available to you only while you are connected to the Web. These documents are not stored on your hard drive. Having the help options available online is a good way to keep documents up to date with the most current list of bugs, workarounds, and help procedures. This method also has a definite drawback when you can't gain access to the NCSA server because of heavy traffic or other problems.

Note Even though the documentation and other information are stored online, you can download these files from the NCSA FTP site. In many cases, some of these files come with the archived version of Mosaic (they usually are stored as TXT and WRI files).

The following are the **H**elp menu options:

◆ **Online Documentation.** Provides a manual for using Mosaic.

◆ **FAQ Page.** Provides you with a FAQ (*frequently asked questions*) file about Mosaic. This document is very handy if you are troubleshooting a problem in Mosaic. In it, you may find the answer to your question.

◆ **Bug List.** Lists the bugs in Mosaic.

◆ **Feature Page.** Displays a list of the features and enhancements in each version of Mosaic.

◆ **About Windows Mosaic.** Shows the version number, copyright information, names of the Mosaic developers, and the e-mail address of NCSA.

◆ **Mail to Developers.** Enables you to send an e-mail message to the developers at NCSA. This feature is intended to provide the developers a way of receiving information about bugs and troublesome features you are experiencing. Don't use this option to send "friendly" correspondence. The developers are swamped with technical e-mail messages and truly have neither the time nor the energy to deal with nontechnical issues.

Bringing You Up-To-Date

As this book was being prepared for the printer, a new version of Mosaic was available in Beta that included several key enhancements and bug fixes. Some of the release notes for Mosaic 2.0.0 Beta 4 are included in this section to help you understand some of these changes.

If you do not have this latest version, you can download it from the following anonymous FTP server:

```
ftp.ncsa.uiuc.edu
```

You also can download it from the following Web site:

```
http://www.ncsa.uiuc.edu/SDG/Software/WinMosaic/HomePage.html
```

Changes to MOSAIC.INI

As you learned in Chapter 9, the way you used to have to change many features of Mosaic was through its MOSAIC.INI settings. If you have the latest version of Mosaic, however, you no longer need to edit this file. Instead, Mosaic options can be modified using options available on the **O**ptions menu. This greatly increases the usability of Mosaic because you make changes as you navigate the Web.

Changes to the Options Menu

This section lists and briefly describes the new settings on the **O**ptions menu. All of the new options are available within the Preferences choice from the **O**ptions menu.

The following options appear in the Miscellaneous option:

◆ **Change Cursor Over Anchor.** Changes the standard arrow cursor to a hand with a pointing finger when you move the cursor over an anchor ("hyperlink").

◆ **Underlined.** Underlines each hyperlink in the Web document. This is helpful if you have a black and white monitor.

◆ **Show URL in Status Bar.** Displays in the status bar the URL of the hyperlink upon which you have placed your cursor.

◆ **Visually Age Visited Anchors.** Changes the color of a hyperlink as it "ages." When you click on a hyperlink, Mosaic changes it from blue to red or green, telling you that you have visited this site recently. Over a specified amount of time (see the following option), the color slowly returns to its unvisited color of blue.

◆ **Expired Visited Anchors: XX (days).** Enables you to set the days it takes for a visited hyperlink to return to its unvisited color (usually blue).

The following options appear in the Current Anchor Highlighting menu:

◆ **Framed.** Places a solid frame around the current hyperlink.

◆ **Button.** Displays the current hyperlink as a 3D button.

◆ **Hatched.** Places a broken frame around the current hyperlink.

◆ **None.** Displays the current hyperlink without a frame, 3D button, or hatched frame. You should note that the left and right arrow functions are disabled when you select this option.

◆ **Red: Green: Blue:.** Enables you to select the color of the frame around the current hyperlink.

◆ **Change.** Enables you to select the color of the frame around the current hyperlink by using custom colors from a color palette.

The following option appears in the Unvisited Anchor Color menu:

◆ **Red: Green: Blue:.** Displays the color value for hyperlinks that you have not visited. This option also enables you to change the color by changing the value of the color number in the respective field. To select the hyperlink color from a color palette, select the Change function.

The following options appear in the Visited Anchor Color menu:

◆ **Red: Green: Blue:.** Displays the color value for hyperlinks that you have not visited. This option also enables you to change the color by changing the value of the color number in the respective field. To select the hyperlink color from a color palette, select the Change function.

◆ **Clear.** Clears the list of all visited hyperlinks.

The following options appear in the Cached Anchor Color menu:

◆ **Red: Green: Blue:.** Displays the color value for hyperlinks that point to files that are cached on the disk. This option also enables you to change the color by changing the value of the color number in the respective field. To select the hyperlink color from a color palette, select the Change function.

◆ **On.** Tells Mosaic to display the disk-cached items with the assigned hyperlink color.

Staying Current

As with any beta product, features and procedures change rapidly. The best way in which to stay current with the most current Mosaic release is to frequently visit NCSA's Web site. At this site you can find release notes, release drafts, links to supporting sites (such as where to find the most current Win32S files), and other instructions. Unfortunately this book cannot stay current with all the rapid changes that are taking place with Mosaic and its related applications.

Navigating the Web with Netscape

N etscape Communications Netscape browser has become the premier Web browser on the World Wide Web frontier. By some estimates, Netscape has captured upwards of 70 percent of the market share of Web browsers. This chapter introduces you to some of Netscape's features and shows you how to customize the way it works and looks. This chapter also discusses some of the more advanced features of Netscape 1.1, such as security and mail handling.

Specifically, this chapter discusses the following items:

◆ Sending e-mail in Netscape

◆ Using bookmarks

◆ Using the toolbar

◆ Using the status bar

◆ Using the current URL

◆ Using extended FTP

◆ Displaying inline images

◆ Using sound

◆ Choosing fonts

Understanding Netscape's Interface

Netscapes interface is similar in a lot of ways to the Mosaic interface. If you are comfortable with Mosaic, you should feel right at home with Netscape (see fig. 12.1). Netscape also offers new features, menus, and toolbar buttons that help you make the most out of your Web travels. In many respects, Netscape is the most advanced Web browser available today.

Figure 12.1

Netscape 1.1's interface.

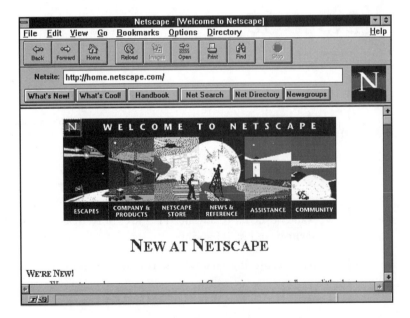

Viewing the Netscape Window

The primary area of Netscape is its main window, where you view Web documents and graphics. Figure 12.2 points out the major features of this window. See table 12.1 for descriptions of each of these features.

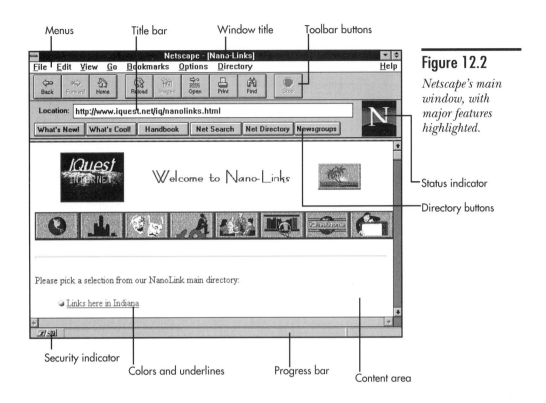

Menus   Title bar   Window title   Toolbar buttons

Figure 12.2

Netscape's main window, with major features highlighted.

Status indicator

Directory buttons

Security indicator   Colors and underlines   Progress bar   Content area

TABLE 12.1
Netscape's Interface Features

Element	Description
Menus	Use the various menus to perform numerous tasks in Netscape, such as opening files, mailing messages, changing preferences, and finding help.
Toolbar buttons	Click on toolbar buttons to perform some of the most common tasks in Netscape, such as revisiting pages, reloading pages, printing, finding text strings, and stopping transfers in progress.
Window title	This is the main title of the Web document. The title appears in brackets ([]) next to the word "Netscape."

continues

TABLE 12.1, CONTINUED
Netscape's Interface Features

Element	Description
Title bar	This bar displays the current URL. You can type in a new URL and press Enter to move to another Internet site.
Directory buttons	Click on these buttons to bring up pages that help you navigate the Internet. You can find out whats new, see some cool sites, call up the Netscape Handbook (online documentation on the Netscape browser), search the Internet, choose sites from an Internet directory, and use newsgroups.
Status indicator	This is the Netscape company logo. During a transfer, animated meteors fly across the logo to indicate that the transfer is in progress. Click on this logo to stop a transfer and to return to the Netscape home page.
Colors and underlines	These features indicate hotlinks in a document. Underlining is used only on black-and-white monitors. After you select a hotlink, your selection is highlighted and changes colors to indicate that you have clicked on it recently. You can change this color by means of the Options menu.
Content area	This is the main document area in Netscape. Scroll bars on the right and bottom of the screen help you navigate through pages that may fill up more than your screen is capable of displaying.
Progress bar	One of the handiest features, the Progress bar indicates the size of the document Netscape is transferring and the percentage of the document that has been transferred.

Element	Description
Security indicator	This feature shows you if a document is secure or not. If the indicator displays a broken key, the document is not secure. If it displays a key with two teeth, the document is considered a high-grade encrypted document. If the indicator displays one tooth, the document is considered a medium-grade encrypted document. Netscape's security feature is discussed later in this chapter.

Using Netscape's Menus

Many of the features contained in Netscape's menus are similar to those in Mosaic or are self-explanatory. This section focuses on the menu options and some newer features of Netscape, followed by a lengthy discussion on bookmarks. See the "Using Bookmarks" section for information on using the Bookmarks menu.

Sending E-Mail in Netscape

One of the shortcomings of Web browsers has been the way they handle mail messages. With Netscape 1.1, you are given a much stronger environment to send mail and post newsgroup articles. In the File menu, the Mail Document option is available. By using this option, you can create a mail message and attach Web page attachments to it to send to someone. In the Send Mail/Post News dialog box (see fig. 12.3), you can address your mail message, specify the attachment URL (if you want to attach a page to your message), and write your mail message.

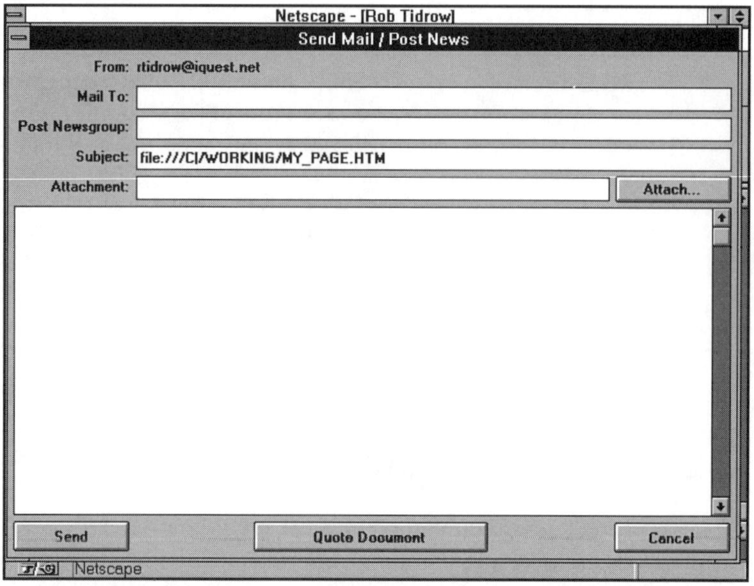

Figure 12.3

Use the Send Mail/Post News dialog box to create mail messages in Netscape.

Netscape - [Rob Tidrow]

Send Mail / Post News

From: rtidrow@iquest.net
Mail To:
Post Newsgroup:
Subject: file:///C|/WORKING/MY_PAGE.HTM
Attachment: [Attach...]

[Send]   [Quote Document]   [Cancel]

Netscape

The first time you use the **M**ail Document option, you must specify the name of your mail server (known as SMTP) and provide your e-mail address in the Mail dialog box (see fig. 12.4).

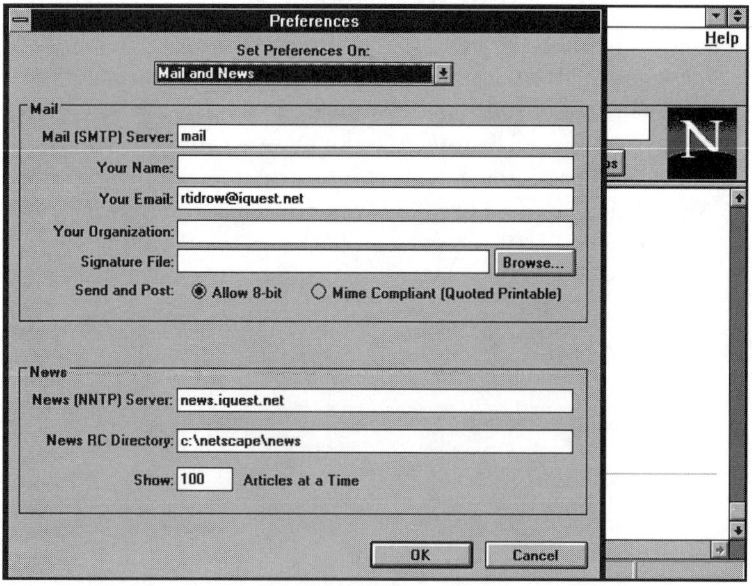

Figure 12.4

You must fill in the Mail dialog box before you send your first mail message with Netscape.

Preferences

Help

Set Preferences On:
Mail and News

Mail

Mail [SMTP] Server: mail
Your Name:
Your Email: rtidrow@iquest.net
Your Organization:
Signature File: [Browse...]
Send and Post: ⦿ Allow 8-bit   ○ Mime Compliant [Quoted Printable]

News

News [NNTP] Server: news.iquest.net
News RC Directory: c:\netscape\news
Show: 100   Articles at a Time

[OK]   [Cancel]

Tip If you do not know your SMTP server or your e-mail address, contact your Internet access provider or, if you're connected to the Internet via a local area network (LAN), ask your system administrator.

Using Bookmarks

Because information sources and methods of information retrieval vary, it's best to organize your resources by subject. Netscape not only serves as a World Wide Web browser, but it can also be used for searching other protocols such as FTP and Gopher; thus, Netscape enables you to combine the most popular resources together for access when you need it. If you are looking for information on frogs, for example, you can include sites that have searchable databases by means of WWW, photographs by means of FTP, and research papers by means of Gopher.

Different Web browsers have different ways of storing your favorite Internet sites. Netscape uses *bookmarks*. Bookmarks in Netscape are similar to bookmarks that you place in your favorite novel—they are simply references to Internet resources, such as Web pages, that you want to access quickly.

This section reviews how bookmarks work, and pays extra attention to how bookmarks can be subcategorized so that you can navigate the Internet in an organized manner.

After you access Netscape's Bookmarks feature in the **B**ookmarks menu, you will see two commands on the top of the menu, **A**dd Bookmark, and View **B**ookmarks (see fig. 12.5). When you pick Add Bookmark, Netscape adds your currently loaded document's URL into the list. The URL appears at the bottom of the menu the next time you look into it.

When you choose the View **B**ookmarks function in Netscape, the Bookmark List dialog box pops up with several options (see fig. 12.6). This dialog box serves as an editor/navigator that lets you manage your favorite Internet resources. Here, you can add your current document, jump to an Internet site that you have stored, or edit the appearance and organization of your list.

Figure 12.5

*Netscape's
Bookmark menu
options: Add
Bookmark and
View Bookmark.*

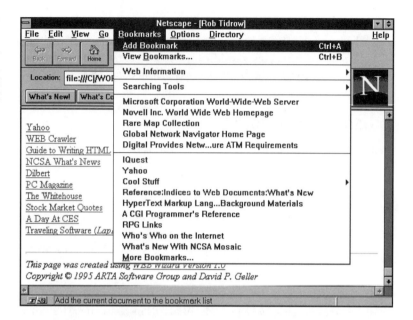

Figure 12.6

*The Bookmark
List dialog box.*

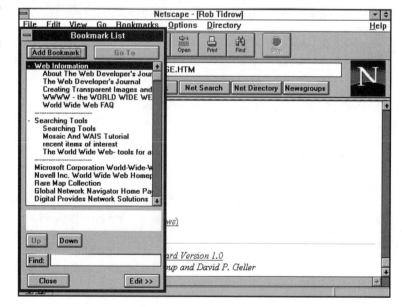

Along the top of the Bookmark List dialog box are two buttons that relate to storing and navigating the Internet. Add Bookmark adds the currently loaded document to your bookmark list. In reality, the document's URL and not the actual document is stored. This distinction is important because it enables you to store the *locations* of documents, not the actual documents themselves. The next time you access this document, you then are guaranteed that you are viewing the most recent version of that document. Features like bookmarks are optimal for frequently changing information, such as news.

The other button at the top of the Bookmark List dialog box is the Go To button. This button is dimmed until you click on one of the items in the Bookmark List, after which you can click on the Go To button to download that document to your browser

ote   Don't be surprised if you are denied access to a document that you have previously stored as a bookmark item. Sometimes Webmasters temporarily turn off their Web servers for general maintenance or other reasons. You also might have tried to access the document while it is being updated from another source. If you get a denied document error message, wait a couple of minutes and try again. If you can't access a document for a couple of days, then you know its time to take the document's URL off your bookmark list.

Editing the Bookmark List

As you learned earlier, when you add a bookmark to a document to the Bookmark List, Netscape automatically places the new bookmark at the bottom of the Bookmark menu. This might be fine when you have only a few book-marks saved, but it becomes a little annoying when your list starts to grow. At this point, you may want to do some house cleaning on your list and organize your sites.

To do this, Netscape includes two buttons on the Bookmark List dialog box that helps you manage the placement of a bookmark. The Up and Down buttons (see fig. 12.7) enable you to move a selected bookmark up the list or down the list, depending on where you want it placed in the list.

Figure 12.7

*Click on the Up
and Down
buttons to move
selected book-
marks on the
Bookmark List.*

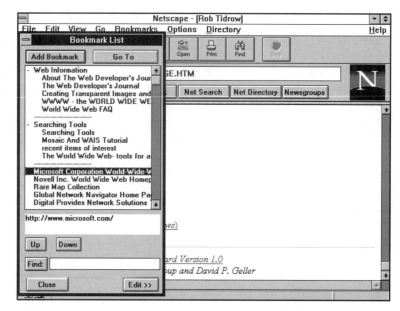

Another key feature of the Bookmark List dialog box is the Edit portion. You
can expand the dialog box by clicking on the Edit button. This displays the
complete Bookmark List dialog box (see fig. 12.8), in which you can add more
organization and control over your Bookmark menu.

Figure 12.8

*The expanded
version of the
Bookmark List
gives you more
control over
your Bookmark
dialog box.*

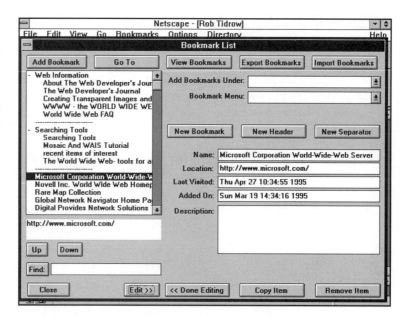

The View Bookmarks button loads a temporary document into Netscape with a listing of your sites' hyperlinked text. Although there are other utilities on the Internet that can do this for you, with Netscape you can create a document and then save it as HTML format, or access the View Source option from the View menu (see fig. 12.9).

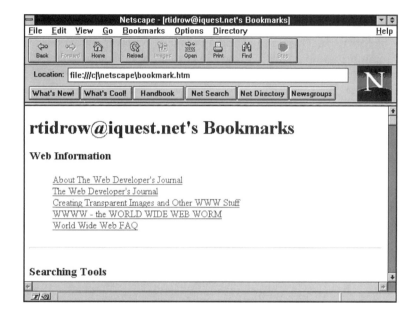

Figure 12.9

Clicking on the View Bookmarks button within the Bookmarks dialog box generates a file with a hyperlinked list of your stored URLs.

Exporting and importing bookmarks can also be done from this menu. If, for instance, you need to send people a list of URLs, the quickest and easiest way to accomplish this is to export the file and have them import it. As well as giving you a place to define a name and a URL for your document, the dialog box also has a field called Last Visited, where it notes the last time you had looked at the document. Added on tells you when you added the URL to Netscape's Bookmark function, and includes an area where you can take notes on a document. This area is important to note, since Netscape does not have an annotate function.

The buttons here are very simple in their purpose. Explanations of what each button does are listed in the following:

◆ **Two Arrows.** These buttons let you move the position of the Document name in the list of bookmarks.

◆ **Copy.** This button duplicates your selected page, where you can then edit the name or location to make changes.

◆ **Fewer Options.** This button makes the dialog box smaller, so you have more screen room to view pages while you are browsing.

◆ **Remove Item.** This button deletes your selected document from your Bookmark list.

◆ **New Bookmark.** This button adds documents to your bookmark list. This button brings up a dialog box where you can type in a document's URL and name.

◆ **New Header.** This button creates nested menus or submenus.

◆ **New Divider.** This button creates lines between sections within the Bookmark menu. This feature is great for organizing URLs that are similar in topic.

The capability to organize the menu is what makes Netscape's Bookmark menu's Bookmark function helpful. Netscape enables you to create a menu so you can organize your favorite URLs by topic. With the following steps, you can create your own submenus:

1. Select View Bookmarks from the Bookmark menu.

2. Click on the New Header Button.

3. Enter the name of the nested menu as you would like it to appear in the menu itself.

4. Click once on the name of the header on the list to the left.

5. Click on the New Bookmark button.

6. Enter in the name and location of the document that you would like to appear in the nested menu.

7. Once you click on the Done Editing button, you can check to see if it worked!

In the future you can look forward to more advanced features that address the issue of storing and retrieving your favorite Web sites. Since the World Wide Web is, in reality, still in the beginning stages, there will be an explosion of sites

as corporations, schools, and individuals realize that they have the power to publish on their own. You will need advanced features to sort, search, and store useful sites.

Using Netscape's Toolbar

The *toolbar* is the row of buttons along the top of the screen (see fig. 12.10). These buttons help you navigate between and store the documents you access while surfing the Net. With these buttons and a click of the mouse, you can apply the most popular menu commands. The toolbar buttons provide quick-and-easy access to documents while you browse.

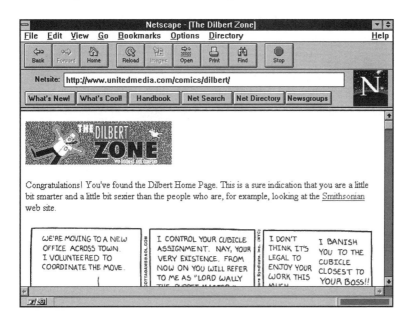

Figure 12.10

Netscape's toolbar buttons.

The following list describes the toolbar buttons (from left to right) and their functions:

◆ **Open URL.** This button has the same effect as the **F**ile menu's Open URL function. It displays a dialog box that asks for a location. You can either type in an URL directly, or select one of the entries from your saved hotlist. The field on the left hand side contains the actual URL for the document. This is where you would enter one by hand if you type it in. The field at the upper right has the title of the document to which you are referring in your hotlist. Below the URL field, you can select the hotlist to which you want to refer.

◆ **Save Document.** This button saves the currently loaded document to a file on your hard drive. Saving an HTML document from here is just like saving any other file that you are working on. The dialog box is similar to those on most word processors. Be sure to add the extension .HTM to the file name; otherwise, Netscape will not load the file and you will not be able to save the graphics to your hard drive.

 Note

Saving a document is helpful for many reasons. You can refer to a saved document as often as you want, for example. You also might want to set a document that is on your system locally for your home page. This way you will not have to wait for Netscape to retrieve the document before you can use Mosaic (or vice versa). With some programs, such as Netscape, you can interrupt a session by asking for another document, and then return to the Netscape session.

One of the best reasons for saving HTML documents is so that you can learn how to create your own HTML documents. After you save the document, you can switch to your word processor and study the commands used by the document's author. This is a good way to learn some of the complex HTML coding features.

◆ **Page Backward.** With this button, you can view the previously viewed documents, one page at a time. Click on this button to load the page that precedes the current page.

◆ **Page Forward.** This button takes you one page forward if you have used the Page Backward button. Using this button does not load the next document from the World Wide Web, but only loads the next document ahead of the one in memory. Because the document is stored temporarily on your system, using the forward and backward buttons takes less time than retrieving the documents through the Net takes.

◆ **Reload.** Use this button to retrieve again a document and all its graphics from the file server. This feature is helpful for virtual documents and programming, where reviewing constantly changing files is necessary. Virtual documents, such as a weather report from a system or an order from an online mall, usually are created instantly by the World Wide Web server or by a database linked to the server. By clicking on the Reload button, you request the document as if it had never been received before. The process takes longer to use than the Page Forward and Page Backward buttons because it has to retrieve the document again through the Net.

The best use for this button, however, is to create your own HTML documents. Because most HTML editors are not WYSIWYG (what you see is what you get), they cannot display the document as Netscape can. By keeping Netscape loaded while you create your HTML documents in a text editor, you can preview the results of your editing. Whenever you make and save a change to the HTML document, click on the Reload button to see the results.

◆ **Home Page.** Click on this button to move immediately to your home page. Because you define home pages in your preferences, you can make it a default location loaded when you launch Netscape, such as your company's home page, where consistently changing information may warrant frequent access.

◆ **Find.** Click on the Find button to do a text search in the currently loaded page. The Find button finds a string of text. This tool can be very useful for long documents, but it does not search linked documents. To search more than one document at a time you have to go to sites that have a searchable database.

◆ **Print.** This button prints the currently loaded page, including the graphics. Depending on your printer driver and settings, you may get the standard Netscape gray background on your prints.

Using Netscape's Directory Menu

To aid the user by providing a bunch of preset links, Netscape has included a menu called the directory menu. Inside this menu are Web documents that are helpful in the search for technical details on the Web or general Internet information. The following is a list of each of the functions listed in the menu and what they return:

◆ **What's New?** Brings you to a page on Netscape's Web server that lists new Web sites that the staff of Netscape Communications Co. feels are interesting.

◆ **What's Cool?** Selecting this option brings you to a page that lists sites that the staff of Netscape Communications Co. thinks are interesting and thorough.

◆ **Go to Newsgroups.** This will log onto your Usenet News server and enable you to read current articles.

Figure 12.11

The results of clicking on the What's New? menu option.

Figure 12.12

The results of clicking on the What's Cool? menu option.

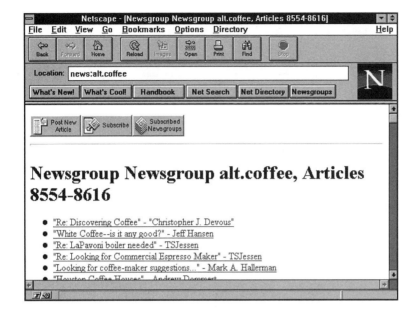

Figure 12.13

The results of clicking on the Go to Newsgroups menu option.

◆ **Netscape Galleria.** Going to the Galleria will bring you to a list of Internet Web servers that are using the Netscape Web server software.

◆ **Internet Directory.** This will bring you to a document on Netscape's server that lists and links to other servers, which will help direct you to information that you are looking for.

◆ **Internet Search.** Searching for specific information on the Internet can be a challenge—selecting this feature will present a list of databases that you can use to help you find what you are looking for.

◆ **Internet White Pages.** This will bring you to a page listing all of the services that will aid you in finding a person on the Internet. Most of the sites will return an e-mail address for the person you are looking for.

◆ **About the Internet.** If you are looking for general information on the Internet and how it works, this is the option to select.

Figure 12.14

The results of clicking on the Internet Directory menu option.

Figure 12.15

The results of clicking on the Internet Search menu option.

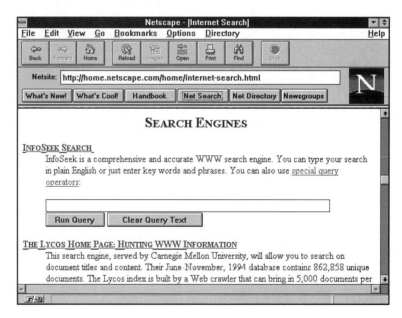

Using the Status Bar

Netscape's status bar displays the current status of a document—a handy feature, because retrieving a document can take a long time. When you move your pointer to the hypertext links in a loaded document, notice that the status bar (at the bottom of the window) displays the URL for the specific document or file linked by the text. And because the status bar also displays whatever protocol was used to retrieve information, you can see not only the HTTP URL, but also whether the hypertext link is a Gopher or FTP site.

The status bar also displays the steps being taken to acquire a document you have requested. Messages displayed include a request from a file server, a notice that the server is waiting for information, and a notice that it is receiving the information. Netscape will present a progress bar that displays the length of a download.

The status bar is for informational purposes only. You cannot do anything to or with the status bar—it just shows you what steps are being taken to retrieve a document.

Using the Current URL

A field just below the toolbar displays the URL for the currently loaded document. This field is mostly for your information, but you can edit the information (using the Cut, Copy, and Paste buttons) by clicking directly in this field. After you edit the information in the Current URL field and press Enter, Netscape tries to find the document whose URL you have entered. Although this shortcut is even faster than clicking on the Open URL button, you cannot use it to take information saved in your hotlist. To include that information, you have to remember the appropriate URL and enter it in here.

Just being able to see the location of a document is a big help. With the URL you can see not only the location of the file server that contains your document, but also the directories in which the document is located.

You can use Netscape just as easily in an FTP session. As the following section explains, by entering the FTP address you enable Netscape to display the directories and download the files for you.

Using Extended FTP

One of the benefits of using Netscape as a browsing tool is its adaptability. With this one program, you can access the World Wide Web, Gopher, WAIS, and Newsgroups. Other forms of data and information use these protocols to give users unique services, such as whois, finger, and veronica.

This section focuses on how to use Netscape to retrieve files from other Internet sites, by using the *file transfer protocol* (FTP). In the most popular FTP, referred to as *anonymous FTP*, you access files and directories on other machines without actually having an account. Files are placed so that everyone can look at them, without compromising the security of a network. In Netscape, you can use FTP by entering a URL in the Current URL field, or by selecting Open URL from the **F**ile menu.

To use Netscape for the FTP, you must log in to the FTP server as user:anonymous. Be sure to put your name and e-mail in your preferences so that Netscape can answer the FTP server correctly. Sometimes FTP servers do not let you in if your e-mail address is not entered correctly.

When you are logged on to the file server, the list you see is similar to the list displayed in Netscape's Gopher presentation. Next to the file names is an icon that represents a directory or document. *Documents*, in this case, can mean either text files, graphics files, or executable programs. Although you are able to see executable programs, keep in mind that you are using FTP and are not able to launch a program without first downloading it. Because compressed files move more quickly through the Net than uncompressed files, you might have to decompress a file after you download it. See Chapter 8, "Finding Resources on the Web," for more information about popular compression techniques and how to decompress files.

Most FTP servers give you an introduction and specific instructions for downloading files from the site you have logged on to. An introductory message might look something like this:

```
Message from FTP server:
230-Welcome to Vyne Communications' FTP server.
230-Our server is growing as fast as the rest of the I-way; Surf this way
again soon!
230-
230-We USED TO have the official release of Marvel's Generation X, but
that
230-has now been taken offline. Please, even if you have come here for
another
230-reason, send E-mail to joe@vyne.com asking for more Marvel images. We
very
230-much would like to serve such files for you, but have yet to convince
Marvel
230-that this is a good idea. Your support will help. Thanx.
230-
230-Comments, suggestions, constructive criticism:      joe@vyne.com
230-Complaints, whining, flames:                        /dev/null
230-
```

Netscape displays this message under a line that divides the list of files. At the top of the list of files, a notice alerts you to the message.

You use FTP in Netscape just as you use the Web. If you are interested in looking in a specific directory, just click on the hypertext name of that directory. When you do this, Netscape retrieves the contents of that file from the FTP server. When you click on the document name, Netscape starts downloading the file. You can monitor the downloading of the file by watching the status bar at the bottom of the window.

When Netscape downloads a file from the FTP server, it places the file in a specific directory. If you want this directory to be different from the one in which Netscape resides, you must change your temp directory in the preferences.

If you venture down a couple of layers in the directories, you might want to move back up (the equivalent of using the DOS CD command). To move up one directory, click on the hyperlinked text (called the Parent Directory) at the top of the list of FTP files.

You do not have to log out of the FTP server as you do with other FTP software. Simply quitting Netscape or opening a new document logs you out. If you need to, you can navigate back to the FTP session by using the Page Forward and Page Backward buttons at the top of the window.

Displaying Inline Images

Clicking on hypertext links and zooming from one location to another in seconds can be very exciting, especially because these documents can be located anywhere in the world. The images that people place in their documents make the experience entertaining. These images range from company logos, to photographs of events and parties, to pictures from NASA. A great way to keep people's interest is to use images in your documents. Just as the publishing industry continually improves graphics and illustrations in magazines to hold the interest of readers, the World Wide Web continues to change and improve its graphics.

The proper name for displaying an image within the Netscape document is called *inline images*. Netscape has an interesting way of displaying images. If the images are prepared a certain way, Netscape displays them first at low resolution, increasing the resolution as time passes. In this way, you can see the image quickly up front, and in more detail as you continue to download the image. Netscape can also download and display images simultaneously. Both of these features give the appearance of downloading the document faster.

To ensure that Netscape displays the images in the documents you browse through, pick Auto-Load Images in the Options menu. The next time you download a file, you'll see the images.

Some people prefer to keep the Auto-Load Images option turned off, because viewing the document takes too long when the option is on. In this case, Netscape displays an icon at the location of each image, but does not retrieve the images. When you want to look at a specific image, all you have to do is click on the icon. Netscape then downloads only the image you click on.

Using Sound

Although Netscape can download images so that you can view them in a document, it cannot single-handedly download all multimedia formats and present them to you. Netscape cannot play a sound file, for example, without some help. On the Internet, most of these files are in the Sun AU format, a UNIX format used mostly by Sun computers. Some files, however, are in Wav format for Windows, MPEG format for all platforms, or Quicktime format (for both Windows and the Mac).

Because Netscape cannot process these files, and because the file formats and technology change quickly, Netscape relies upon other software to do the work. In this way, the Netscape software remains a small and simple (and the developers can concentrate on HTML browsers and servers). Generally, a sound icon means that some audio exists to which you can listen.

To hear downloaded sounds, you must use your preferences to alert Netscape to the program you want to use. The preferences' Helper Applications include a list of file extensions, with a brief description of the file format they belong to. For each file format, you have to choose a player application and tell Netscape what directory the application is in.

When you click on the icon or hypertext link for the sound file, Netscape immediately begins to download the file, temporarily storing the data on the hard drive. After the file has been downloaded, your program of choice automatically launches and plays the file.

Choosing Fonts

Generally, publishers of everything from magazines and books to CD-ROMs design the product carefully to make it attractive to potential buyers. This creative work in graphic design is a full-time job. Artists carefully work on the placement of photographs and type, using fonts, colors, illustrations, and headlines to create an attractive product.

With, Netscape the designer cannot control many conditions, such as the size of the window and the resolution of the screen. As a designer of the document, you may not even know whether the user is viewing the graphics. With this in mind, you have to work on the document in a way that enables the end user to have as much creative input to the look of your information as you do—viewers can choose their own fonts and type sizes.

Although this might seem a disadvantage to the designer of a document, it gives you, the viewer, greater control over what you see and how you see it. When someone creates an HTML document, that person is not concerned with the fonts a viewer is using. (As a matter of fact, the designer has no control over which fonts the viewer uses—the viewer controls the fonts.) The creator of a document is concerned only with the headlines and body text. Document creators can design the images in a document and can control which text is what size. Other options, such as which text is italicized, are in the creator's hands as well.

To change your font settings, open the Options menu and choose Preferences. Here, you can pick settings for your fonts. The styles are organized in the same manner as that in which the HTML code is written. You can go through the different logical styles and pick a font for each of them.

Netscape is a powerful browsing tool with which you can tour the world. The controls discussed in this chapter are helpful in easing your search and assist you in remembering the sites you liked the best. The controls also help you make documents look the way you want them to look.

Using E-Mail on the Web

The Internet has seen much growth recently because of the graphical interface of the World Wide Web. Even so, e-mail—a large portion of the communications on the Internet today—does not utilize the World Wide Web. E-mail remains the largest, easiest, and fastest form of sending information through the Net. One benefit of e-mail that no other method of communication has at the moment, including the World Wide Web, is that it is in ASCII (plain text), a distinction that enables e-mail to be transferred among all the networks connected throughout the Internet. Commercial networks that have been known to have limits communicating with each other now can exchange e-mail with ease—because of the Internet.

As consumers move from commercial services to the Internet (or access the Internet from within commercial services), sending messages from one network to another becomes more important. One thing that we can count on happening, more so than other things, is that plain text e-mail almost always gets through. Another benefit is that e-mail is an intimate form of communication. It goes right to the desktop of whomever the message is addressed to. Because of this, e-mail is treated with the same social values and customs as phone conversations. Unless you are returning someone's phone call, for example, you better have something interesting to tell the person when you call!

What Is E-Mail?

E-mail is today's electronic equivalent to the telegraph. Most people who are using the Internet today were likely introduced to the Internet through e-mail. It is the most popular and most frequently used function.

Technically, e-mail is a text message that simply gets passed from one point to another until it arrives at its destination. Although it is intimate in nature, it is in no way considered private. E-mail can pass through as many as ten computer systems in its travels, presenting the opportunity for it to be "captured" along the way. Because there are millions of messages per day, the chance of your e-mail message being intercepted is unlikely, and, in the event that e-mail could not be delivered, you would most likely be notified that delivery was unsuccessful.

The Internet was originally created to send e-mail. Between the late sixties and the early seventies, research and government institutions used e-mail to share information and resources. It was a tremendously expensive way to communicate. Being federally funded, however, allowed large research projects to pay for this benefit by sharing important and related information so they could team up and achieve quicker results.

Back then, computer systems were very expensive because operating systems such as Windows and graphical interfaces did not really exist. Because of the expense and resources that computers took, most computers made allowances for more than one user to save resources. Out of these changes and needs, Unix was born. A specialty of Unix is multitasking, a benefit of which is that it allows multiple people to use the computer at the same time. E-mail developed out of the need for users to trade messages, whether or not the users were signed on and using the computer system at the moment. When the computer systems were connected and the Internet was formed, this messaging functionality became more popular because it allowed people who were not physically in the same location or time zone to communicate. Sending a message then was quite simple. All you had to do to send a message was to know the name of the person you were sending it to. If the person was at another location, you had to know the location as well.

E-Mail Today

Today, not much has changed with e-mail. What is different is the number of people to whom you can send e-mail. Because they are using different computer systems, their addresses might not be as consistent as they were ten years ago. What we can count on, though, is that the e-mail address will be formed in the following manner:

```
To: Name@place.domain
From: Name@place.domain
Subject: Short summary goes here
Hello. This is the body of the message. Bye!
```

Although the message above is quite simple, there are many things that get added while it is en route from one computer to another. Usually, information is added regarding where the message was handled and what time it got there. Other information is added as well, such as whether files are attached. Also added are numbers for identification and tracking. The added information is only visible to the individual who receives the message. Even members of commercial services, such as CompuServe and Prodigy, see this added information in their e-mail messages, even though the information is not standard in their internal e-mail systems. Details about addressing e-mail messages are covered later in this chapter.

So, how does e-mail apply to the World Wide Web? It is very important because the Web does not have a function for sending messages from one person to another. They simply left it out because it already exists—it's called e-mail. The latest and greatest of Web browsers today can send e-mail messages, but it does not do it through the Web. It simply communicates with an e-mail server, known as a *POP* server. The current version of POP is 3, also known as a POP3 server. Versions of POP do not change too often because of the plain text nature of e-mail. The POP server already does that job very well as it is.

Why Use E-Mail while Browsing the Web?

The Web is basically an information presentation and browsing tool. There seems to be no immediate need to send information to an individual while you are browsing—does there? Actually, there are many reasons that you might want to send a piece of information. The scenarios that follow will be discussed in this chapter:

◆ You can forward a Web location (URL) to an associate who might be interested

- ◆ You can send someone text from a Web page

- ◆ You can send comments or questions to Web site maintainers

- ◆ Web site maintainers (Webmasters) can collect data from you

- ◆ You can use a Web browser as an e-mail front end

In addition to providing a tool with which users can send standard messages, you might notice that some of the functionality in Web sites is actually with e-mail. A large amount of input from Web browsers is delivered via e-mail. This may or may not happen with your knowledge. It does not really matter if you know or not, as long as the Web site works as it was meant to. Sometimes, in visiting a Web site, you might notice that the hyperlinks are broken. Broken links occur when changes in computer systems or files have been made. Many managers of Web sites request that you let them know if you find a hyperlink on their site that is not working correctly. If you try to access a hyperlink with a broken link, you get an error message like `File not found`.

Two Different Ways E-Mail Is Integrated with WEB Sites

World Wide Web sites are a terrific way to distribute information. A huge amount of text, graphics, video, and sound can be made accessible to the public by means of the Web. Only e-mail, however, enables people who are viewing this plethora of information on the Web to communicate back to the Web site. As important as this method of communication is, the HTTP protocol (which is the unseen language upon which the Web is delivered) does not have a function for e-mail. Because of this lack, users must rely on Web browsers to handle e-mail functionality.

Most Web browsers have a function that sends mail by using the same e-mail protocol that most desktop computers on the Internet use. The browsing software only is able to *send* e-mail, however. In other words, if a Web browser is connected to the e-mail server using the POP3 protocol, the browser can send a message to anyone, as long as standard Internet addressing is used to send the message. Software developers, whose primary focus is upon the development of WWW browsers, have not concentrated upon adding functions that enable users to read e-mail, because they envision Web browsers as *browsing* tools only. It is likely that by the time that people are exploring the World Wide Web, they have already mastered the process of sending and receiving e-mail through alternative sources. Because of this, software and servers are usually set

up and are in use. If another e-mail reader were brought into the process, it might interfere with your current software.

The good news, though, is that most of the time a Web browser's e-mail functionality is compatible with your e-mail server (as long as it's a POP3 server, which is very popular), and any e-mail that you send from your browser leaves through your current Internet e-mail account. If the person who receives your message wants to reply to it, you will be able to receive and read your e-mail using the same e-mail software and techniques that you have been using before.

Although the ability to send e-mail is in today's latest and greatest Web browsers, it has not always existed. Until late 1994, e-mail functions were not popular in Web browsers. To overcome the lack of e-mail functions, many Web site maintainers allowed people to send them e-mail by creating a Web page that was a form. By sending users to this page when they click on an e-mail link, they can create the sections in which users can type their address and information that they would like to send.

Because the e-mail is not being sent from the Web server, they do not have to be concerned about whether or not they have their message addressed correctly; nor do they have to be concerned that they have their e-mail server configured correctly. The actual mail sending is done from the Web server itself, and the e-mail often is sent to another computer system, if not another computer network. Many corporations which have Web servers will have the e-mail forwarded to an individual's e-mail account, which he or she chooses. The account might even be on CompuServe or America Online.

Note   By the time you read this, almost all Web browsers will have built-in e-mail functionality. There are, however, some aspects of handling e-mail from the server side that are attractive. If e-mail is created through an online form, the Web maintainer can include graphics and other stylistic designs to entice the user to send a message. The message does not even have to look like e-mail. It can be a form with pull-down menus and radio buttons. It can be a survey with very specific questions, and, when you click the "send" button, can be e-mailed to a database that stores and analyzes the data. The positive side of handling e-mail from the server side is that information can be presented and requested from people in a specific form, making it ultimately easier for them. The downside of handling e-mail from the server side is that the user does not have much say about which format to use or where the e-mail message should be delivered.

Using the Built-In Mail Function

The built-in e-mail function acts the same across different brands of Web browsers. The e-mail command is in the **F**ile menu, with the name Mail. On some browsers, such as Netscape, it is found under the name Mail Document.

Tip   The fact that the e-mail function is often found under Mail Document implies that the Web browser builders anticipated that you might want to send the URL or the text of the document to a friend, or even to yourself! Sending e-mail to yourself is, in fact, a good way for you to remind yourself of something important. When I am at home, I e-mail URLs of Web documents to my work Internet address.

Before you can use the built-in e-mail function, you need to set your current e-mail account information in the preferences. If you do not, Mosaic will inform you that you cannot mail. There are two basic settings you can modify. The first one is your identity—the return (or "from") e-mail address that you use when you send out a message. The other important piece of information is the e-mail server that actually sends the e-mail. In Mosaic, you can change settings in the preferences option by picking **P**references from the **O**ptions menu (see fig. 13.1).

Figure 13.1

How to get into Mosaic Preferences.

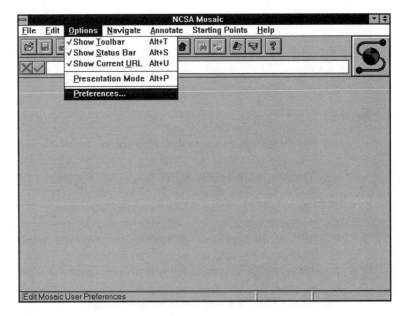

After the **P**references option is chosen, Mosaic brings up the extensive NCSA
Mosaic for Windows Preferences dialog box. In the Services section, which can
be selected by clicking on the Services tab, you can enter your e-mail settings
(see fig. 13.2).

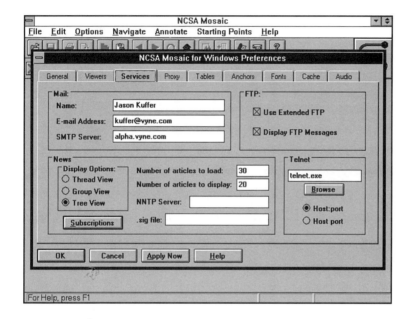

Figure 13.2

*Entering your
e-mail preferences.*

Once the Services tab is selected, you can enter your e-mail settings. You can
modify settings in the following fields:

◆ **Name.** Here is where your real name goes. An example would be John
Doe. Whatever you enter here appears in the return e-mail address.

◆ **E-mail Address.** When you send e-mail to someone and get a reply
back, that reply will have gone to the address you enter here—in other
words, this is your return address.

◆ **SMTP Server.** This is the computer through which the e-mail is sent. It
is best if you select a server you have an account in through which you
receive your e-mail.

Forwarding an URL to a Friend through E-Mail

Probably the most popular function of e-mail and the World Wide Web is to
alert people to the fact that you have found some interesting information. The
actual process of doing this is quite simple, as shown in figure 13.3.

Figure 13.3

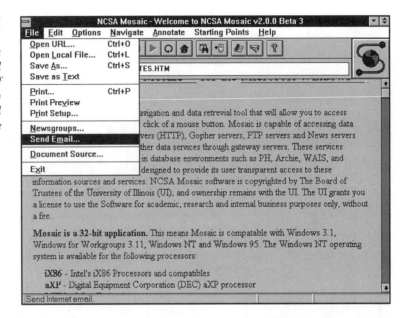

You can access the e-mail function of Mosaic by selecting Send Email from the File menu.

After the e-mail dialog box is open, sending a message to someone is as simple as filling in the e-mail address and the information you would like to send (see fig. 13.4).

Figure 13.4

The Mail dialog box in Mosaic.

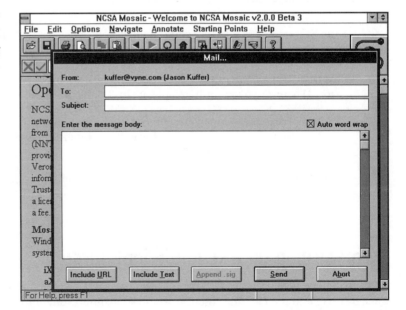

The best place to start in the Mail dialog box is the e-mail address of the person to whom you are sending the message. Important things to know in addressing e-mail are covered later in this chapter. If you do not fill in this part of the dialog box, you won't be able to send e-mail.

The Subject field, although not necessary to fill in, is important, especially since e-mail has become popular. It's not unusual for people to receive 20 to 40 messages a day, and often the only way to distinguish junk e-mail and good e-mail is to read the subject.

The message body is where the message actually resides. This is where you actually type your message. Some e-mail systems, however, have a limit to the file size of an e-mail message. If the message that you send is too long, you would not be notified that it was too long unless the person receiving the e-mail noticed that some information was missing.

To the right of the message body there is a function called Auto word wrap, which is designed to wrap words if the text extends past the margins defined by the dialog box. Usually, it is best to leave this function at its default setting, On.

If you want to send a note to a friend notifying him or her of an interesting Web site, clicking on the button labeled Include <u>U</u>RL copies the URL information into the message body (see fig. 13.5). Sending URLs has become common enough these days that if you get a piece of e-mail with nothing in the body except an URL, it is likely that the URL was sent to you because the sender (whose identity is shown in the return address field) thought of you when he or she visited the site.

If you want to add to the note, you can make room so that you can type comments below the URL. After clicking on the Include <u>U</u>RL button, you press Enter a couple of times to give some clearance between the URL information you are sending and your comments. If you don't want to send an URL to a friend, and you are more interested in just passing a note, type the entire note within the message body.

Figure 13.5

Clicking on the Include URL button copies the URL for the current page in the message body.

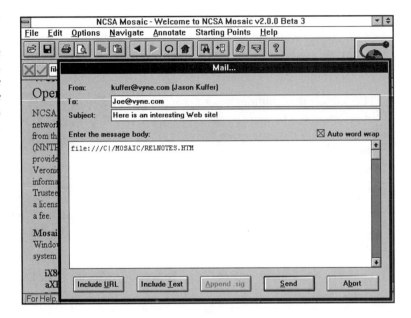

Sending Text from a Web Page to a Friend

Sending actual text from a Web page is just as easy as sending the URL. Text from a Web site will, however, take up more room in e-mail. Remember that not only does this take up disk space and lengthen the time it takes for the file to open, but the person might not want to read all the information that you are sending. This is why sending the URL is the preferable thing to do.

If you are at a Web site and want to send information of interest to a friend, click on the Include **T**ext button (see fig. 13.6). When you do so, Mosaic takes the text from the currently loaded Web page, strips it of HTML codes, and places it in the body message area of your note. If you want to add information, such as why you sent what you sent, you can type it in before or after the imported Web site text. When your remarks are placed in the body message area, a greater-than sign appears before your remarks, which enables the reader to distinguish your remarks from the text that was taken from the Web site.

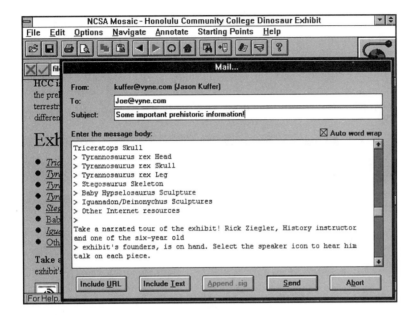

Figure 13.6

Clicking on the Include Text button imports text from the currently loaded Web page.

Using Forms on the Web

Before e-mail functions were built into Web browsers, building functionality and interactivity into a Web site was a challenge. The first step toward interactivity was building form functions into version 2.0 of Mosaic. Today, most Web browsers that use a graphical interface have forms functions (see fig. 13.7). Even so, as advanced as that was, Mosaic still lacked some e-mail functions. The forms function was the first step Web administrators used to add some functionality.

Although the lack of an e-mail function was seen as a drawback then, it certainly was not something that kept people from achieving some interesting results with the e-mail forms that they created. As a matter of fact, the limitations had a positive effect. Although it is possible to send e-mail, most forms that end up sending e-mail did not let you choose who the e-mail was going to. This would promise that e-mail was sent to a specific mailbox.

When you fill out a form and push the **S**end button, the Web server receives the information that you entered and passes it onto a script. The script, usually a *Common Gateway Interface* (CGI) script, processes the information and forwards it to whatever software is responsible for handling the data. In the case of e-mail, the most common software is Sendmail, which is the Unix program that is responsible for all mail communications on a file server.

Figure 13.7

A standard form used to send e-mail to a specific (controlled) address.

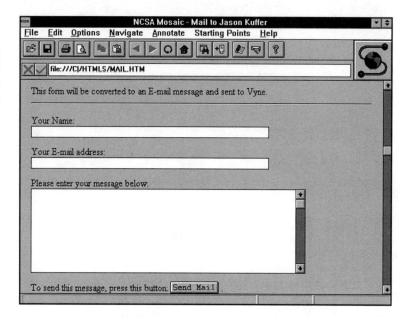

Being rigid with information is definitely a drawback, but with forms, you can be creative with the Web pag (see fig. 13.8). A Web form can have pull-down menus, check boxes, and radio boxes. The fields of the form are chosen by the creator of the Web site. Then, when a person uses the information to fill out a form, he or she cannot deviate from the idea of the form. It is also a lot easier for automatic processing software to use data when the data is consistent. The location New York, for example, can be entered in the following ways: NY, N.Y. ny, N.y. New York, NYC, New York City, Manhattan, and so on, which would be confusing to databases which store and process the information entered.

Whatever a form's purpose, keep in mind that you are only limited by what the creator of the form had in mind. The creation and use of forms can vary greatly. There are a few things, however, that you can count on as being consistent.

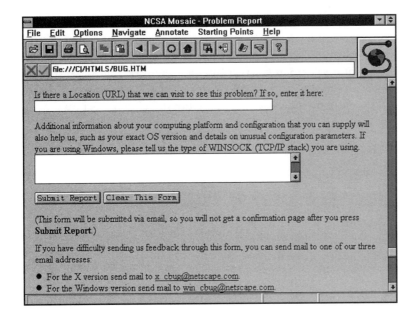

Figure 13.8

An example of a form used to collect specific data. In this case, it is a bug report form for Netscape Communications Company.

All forms contain a Submit button to send the information to the file server, but it might not always be labeled as "Submit." It can also be labeled as Send, E-mail, and so forth. Most forms also have a button labeled Reset or Start Over, which is a feature that is built into HTML that many Web site creators use. When this button is clicked, it basically deletes anything that you have entered in the form and returns the page to the way it was when you first loaded it.

Basics on Addressing E-Mail

Now that you have seen how to send e-mail with Web browsers, you should take some time to see how to address e-mail properly. If you do not know the exact e-mail address of the person you are trying to send your message to, it simply won't get there. Sending e-mail to an address that is not exact is like trying to call a person and not knowing their exact phone number. Because computers like things to be perfect, you have to put some extra effort into making sure you understand where you are sending your message.

Although you might have to work a little harder to remember these things, the good news is that e-mail addressing is quite simple. There really is not much more information you need to know other than WHO are you going to send a message to and WHERE he or she is. The most important part is the latter.

Larger corporations may have people on staff who make sure your e-mail gets to the correct user if it gets lost. Sometimes, even if you do not spell the addressee's name correctly, the message goes into a default mailbox on the network administrator's computer system (on their network, not yours). Every once in a while, the administrator might wander through this mailbox to make sure people are getting their messages (and are not trying to break into the computer system).

Earlier in this chapter, you saw the general format of how e-mail should be addressed:

To: `Name@place.domain`

This section describes this step further and discusses what is needed in each of these places to assure you that your message is going to get through. You'll need to fill the following three fields:

◆ Name

◆ Place

◆ Domain

Name

Fill in the name part of the address with the name of the person to whom you are sending the e-mail. The nice thing about the person's name is that you don't have to worry about what part of the name is upper- or lowercase. If the person's name were McGuire, for example, sending an e-mail message to "mcguire" would work just as well as sending it to "Mcguire." The most important thing about the person's name is that you spell it right! Computers are not smart enough (at least right now) to understand that you might have transposed two letters when typing the e-mail address. If you use e-mail software that includes some form of address book, you might not find it easy to remember an address because you aren't used to typing it yourself. The concept is similar to the use of single-touch dialing on a phone: When your phone is not available, you can't remember any of the numbers you call because you rarely have to dial them. As of now, there are no features in Mosaic or its beta versions that allow for address book functions so you can't rely on the computer to remember the addresses for you.

Another important thing to keep in mind is that there are some limitations as to what characters can be used in the e-mail address. No e-mail address, for example, can have a space in it. Why? Because e-mail software, in its early history, enabled you to send a message to more than one person at a time by placing a space between all the people to whom the message was being sent. Spaces might not work with Mosaic and your e-mail server. It is definitely worth a try. The other limitation is that no characters other than alphanumeric characters are allowed in the e-mail address. You can't use the following characters:

```
;    !    #    $    %    &    *
```

Only numbers and letters are allowed because Unix uses these characters to carry out functions and sort e-mail.

So keep it simple. The name of an e-mail message should look something like the following:

```
kuffer@place.domain
```

Place

The place in an address refers to the actual computer on which the person receives their e-mail, and it might not necessarily be their desktop computer. More often, it is their e-mail server which, in turn, forwards the e-mail to a computer at a place of the person's choosing. The place might be at the person's home on the weekends, or at his or her vacation home. It is not uncommon for an e-mail message to be held until the server is further notified where the person is. The conventions as to how the place should be typed are exactly the same as the name—capitalization does not matter, no spaces, and no characters other than alphanumeric characters.

The only thing in the place category that might be different from the name is that there might be more than one place—more than one computer—that receives the e-mail. Or you might be sending the e-mail to a person who has many different computers on a single network. In this case, you have to specify which computer you are sending to. Many people have more than one e-mail address. One might actually be used for correspondence and another might be used for other e-mail, such as discussion groups and commercial newsletters. When this happens, the computers are separated by typing a period between their names. So, for example, the following address sends mail to a correspondence mailbox:

```
kuffer@vyne.com
```

And the following e-mail address could be used to receive information, commercial newsletters, and discussion groups:

```
kuffer@next.vyne.com
```

With this address, the e-mail is sent to a computer named "next" on the Vyne network.

There is really no limit as to how many computers and networks deep an address can get. It can get downright silly how many periods you might see!

Domain

Every e-mail address must have a domain, unless you are sending an e-mail address to a person who shares the same e-mail server you are using. If you are not sure whether or not you should specify the domain, it is best to include it. The domain is responsible for directing the e-mail to where a computer is. It is a very general breakdown of where in cyberspace a computer resides. The domain actually does not specify what location as much as what network the computer is on. For example, major domains are as follows:

- ◆ .com is for businesses and commercial use

- ◆ .edu is for educational institutions

- ◆ .org is for not-for-profit organizations

When outside of the United States, the domain specifies what country the person is in. For example, .fr stands for France and .ca stands for Canada. Most of the time, the domain letters are obvious, but others are not so easy to figure out; for example, .za is for South Africa.

The domains use the same rules as the name and place. In addition, the domain must come at the end of the e-mail address. No exceptions.

Popular E-Mail Networks

Table 13.1 lists some popular network gateways and how to send e-mail through them. This is not, by far, a complete listing of all the networks and variations, but following this format will definitely get your message to its destination.

TABLE 13.1
Some Popular Network Gateways and Their Formats

Network	Standard Format	Sample E-Mail Address
Internet	name@place.domain	kuffer@vyne.com
CompuServe	account#@compuserve.com	70720.1053@compuserve.com
America Online	account@aol.com	kuffer@aol.com
MCI Mail	account#@mcimail.com	123456@mcimail.com
AppleLink	name@applelink.apple.com	kuffer@applelink.apple.com
eWorld	name@eworld.com	kuffer@eworld.com
GEnie	name@genie.com	kuffer@genie.com
Prodigy	account#@prodigy.com	abcd53ef@prodigy.com

Accessing Newsgroups via the Web

N etwork news is the Internet's equivalent to *bulletin board systems* (BBSs), much like the equivalent group on Compu-Serve and other private dial-up operations. Newsgroups are one of the essential areas of the Internet that impart the sense of "community" to participants interested in a particular topic. Newsgroups allow individuals to communicate in a somewhat public environment, much like at a cocktail party where many related discussions are occurring simultaneously.

What Are Newsgroups?

Network news, sometimes called Usenet News, is the name for the collection of ever-growing news archives and all related programs. The data within Network news is organized into discrete discussion sets called *newsgroups*. Each of these newsgroups can be accessed by a variety of news programs to present these discussions in an orderly way. Of the 10,000 or so existing newsgroups, the user might want to have a menu of a few hundred selections. These selections constitute a menu of the newsgroups, such as current news in Florida, developer tips on Microsoft NT, discussions on visual computing, and so on. Within each menu is a submenu of specific message threads of ongoing discussions. The individual elements within a message thread are called "news." This chapter begins by comparing listservs and newsgroups. It then discusses the different types of newsgroups and the general way of interacting with these newsgroups. The grafting of the Network news functionality and the World Wide Web also is discussed.

Listservs are one of the original methods for time-delayed communication in the public forum. Listservs, newsgroups, and e-mail all operate on the premise that interaction happens at the user's convenience. Time-delayed communication differs from real-time sessions, like the IRC-Chat or Unix's talk sessions, where the interacting parties all must be online during the interaction. With listservs and newsgroups, the "virtual community" participating in the conversation will reply at some time in the future, at each user's convenience. The delayed nature of these communications allows these conversations to occur at the convenience of the rest of the world, side-stepping issues such as datelines and busy schedules. Someone, somewhere, will reply to your message at his or her convenience. The same cannot be said for the telephone, which generally operates on the premise of real-time interaction. The value of time-delayed communication for the telephone is seen by the proliferation of "voice mail" and answering machines.

Listservs versus Newsgroups

Listservs were originally run through a program called LISTSERV, developed in the early 1980s. As evidenced by the uppercase name, the LISTSERV software evolved in an IBM-mainframe world to maintain an electronic mailing (e-mail) list. Users subscribe, unsubscribe, and perform other instructions by submitting mail to this software. The LISTSERV software evolved beyond the IBM mainframe into a software class called *listservs*. Although most listservs exist in the Unix environment, some of the more popular listserv sofware programs are Majordomo, mailserv, and almanac.

Aside from these administrative functions, the listserver software provides a central e-mail focal point. Users wanting to send e-mail to the members of specific interest groups maintained by listserv send their e-mail to a specific address. The listserv software resends this message to the members of the mailing list. If this resending of e-mail is done automatically, the list is called *unmoderated.* If the material is screened prior to its release on the e-mailing list, the listserv is *moderated* and the specific person who does the screening is called a *moderator.* The moderator also maintains the administrative aspects of the list, such as archiving the contents of listserv, culling obsolete addresses from the list, and so forth.

One of the advantages of listserv is the low user requirements. Users must be capable of sending and receiving e-mail. They do not need any additional software. Often, this functionality is within the realm of almost all systems with gateways to the Internet, such as CompuServe, GEnie, Prodigy, AOL, and so forth.

Note The moderator controls who subscribes to the listserv. Most listservs are *public*—available to all participants except for those who have violated the rules of the listserv or committed some similar transgression. Some listservs are closed, allowing only a select audience of people to submit and receive e-mail from the listserv.

One of the problems with listservs is the inability to segregate different conversations within a specific listserv. The analogy is having an open room where a speaker reads messages in the order they were received. The recipient receives all the messages and must segregate and process these messages manually. If the listserv has only a few messages per day, this is fairly trivial. However, some listservs pass hundreds of messages per day, overflowing most users. For users who currently have only e-mail access to the Internet, the listservs continue to provide a vital presence in the Internet community.

Evolution of the Newsgroup

Newsgroups evolved from the listserv experience. The newsgroup user activates their newsreader software on their computer and interacts with a local newsgroup server. This newsgroup server maintains local copies of a selection of the Usenet Newsgroups (there are about 10,000 Usenet newsgroups, and some maintainers of these central newsgroup providers elect to filter out politically sensitive newsgroups). Users of a newsgroup may elect to subscribe to a subset of the newsgroups on this local server for their daily perusal of interesting newsgroups. When they run their newsreader software (nn or tin, for example) and select a specific newsgroup (sci.med.disease.cancer, for instance), most newsreaders will see a collection of message threads. These message threads are similar to the listserv e-mail, only they are segregated by topic. This enables the user to follow certain conversations and sidestep uninteresting conversations. A user may elect to send a public message and thus continue the thread, or send private e-mail to the previous public message.

Not all newsreaders thread the messages within a specific conversation. Some of the less advanced newsreaders merely list all the news in chronological order of receipt. Even without threading of the message traffic, newsgroups still present an advantage over listservs. With listservs, the user receives e-mail for every interaction. Only the top header information of the news message is downloaded into the client's newsreader program. If the user selects a specific news message, only then is the message transferred into the user's machine. This allows the user to lessen the load on their machine.

Unlike a listserv, where the individual user must clear out all the received e-mail messages, a newsgroup will scroll off old messages from the newsgroup archive. Messages read by an individual reader are usually not represented to the user a second time, further aiding the user. This scrolling of the messages from the user's news program is a source of confusion. There are two sources of scrolling or disappearance of old messages: at the local network news archive and through the history record of the user's network newsreading program.

Like listservs, newsgroups can be either moderated or unmoderated. To my knowledge, all of the Usenet News groups are public. Although newsgroup functionality provides a greater degree of control over what arrives at a user's computer, it places requirements upon the Internet to provide repositories of news and transmission of large quantities of news, as well as requiring the user to maintain newsreaders. Some large newsgroups (usually those regarding computer software topics, such as the info-vax@sri.com listserv and the corresponding comp.os.vms newsgroup) maintain both a listserv and newsgroup, bridging the information between the software delivery systems.

How Newsgroups Are Organized

Newsgroups are organized in a hierarchy, with the broadest-reaching groups listed first, followed by an arbitrary number of subgroupings. The name of each

group is separated from its parent in the hierarchy by a period. Thus the "rec" group stands for recreational, which is followed by music, followed by rock, and so on, to arise in a newsgroup called rec.music.rock.

A sampling of some of the major categories of newsgroups follows:

◆ **alt.** This is the "alternate way of looking at things." The newsgroups in this section present a range of topics from the truly incoherent fringe to very serious material. The group include groups such as alt.sex, alt.support.cancer, alt.gopher, and a huge variety of areas. Because of the wide-ranging content of this subgroup, the alt newsgroups are sometimes omitted from the offering. Unfortunately, for people with cancer searching for "virtual community" support from people involved with cancer, this broad censorship eliminates such topics as alt.support.cancer and alt.support.cancer.prostate.

◆ **bit.** The most popular BITNET LISTSERV discussions groups are often archived in this area.

Note bitnet is a message and file retrieval network with a long heritage in the education community. bitnet consisted of its own network of phone lines, and so on, some of which still exist today. Most of the functionality of bitnet has been superseded by the Internet with its far greater capacity and reliability.

◆ **biz.** Discussions of business. This group originally involved advertisements and other marketing material that was generally deemed offensive to netiquette.

◆ **comp.** This is one of the original newsgroups. It targets computer science and related topics, such as computer hardware and software issues, operating systems, events, and topics of general interest to people involved in the computer field.

◆ **news.** This group is concerned with news of the network and newsreader software. This includes groups such as news.newsusers.questions (questions from new users) and news.announce.newusers (important information for new users).

◆ **rec.** This newsgroup focuses on hobbies, recreational activities, arts, and entertainment.

◆ **sci.** This group discusses scientific research and applications unrelated to computer science. For example, sci.med.diseases.cancer appears in this section. Other areas include many of the established scientific and engineering disciplines, including some social sciences.

◆ **soc.** This group discusses social issues, ranging from politics to socializing and everything in between.

◆ **talk.** These groups are famous for long, unresolved discussions that range over many message threads, involve lots of people, and are often unresolvable. Issues like religion, how history should be rewritten, and so forth often end up in this section.

◆ **misc.** This is the original miscellaneous group of newsgroups that did not have a home anywhere else. Groups such as misc.jobs (jobs offered and wanted) and misc.forsale ensure this group will be here for a long time.

The following list show a tiny sampling of newsgroups you can find on a wide range of topics.

alt.sport.bowling
alt.sport.pool
alt.sport.baseball.phila-philles
alt.sport.football.pro.phila-eagles
alt.startrek.creative
alt.startrek.klingon
alt.suburbs
alt.support
alt.support.divorce
alt.support.diet
alt.support.grief
alt.support.phobias
alt.support.spina-bifida

bit.listserv.confocal
bit.listserv.movie.memorabilia
bit.med.resp-care.world

comp.databases
comp.databases.informix
comp.databases.ingres
comp.databases.ms-access
comp.databases.object
comp.databases.oracle
comp.databases.paradox
comp.databases.pick
comp.databases.rdb
comp.databases.sybase

comp.databases.theory
comp.databases.xbase.fox
comp.databases.xbase.misc
comp.editors
comp.graphics
comp.graphics.algorithms
comp.graphics.animation

misc.consumers
misc.consumers.house
misc.education
misc.education.adult
misc.education.language.english
misc.education.multimedia
misc.fitness
misc.forsale
misc.jobs.contract
misc.jobs.offered
misc.jobs.offered.entry
misc.jobs.resumes
misc.kids
misc.kids.computer
misc.kids.vacation
misc.legal
misc.wanted

news.announce.important
news.announce.newsgroups
news.announce.newusers
news.answers
news.groups
news.groups.questions
news.groups.reviews
news.lists
news.newsites

rec.answers
rec.aquaria
rec.arts.cinema
rec.arts.startrek.current
rec.arts.theater
rec.autos.tech
rec.aviation.owning

sci.chem
sci.cognitive
sci.cryonics
sci.econ
sci.econ.research
sci.edu
sci.electronics
sci.med
sci.med.aids
sci.med.dentistry
sci.med.nursing
sci.med.nutrition

soc.answers
soc.college
soc.couples
soc.couples.intercultural
soc.culture.afghanistan
soc.culture.african
soc.culture.african.american
soc.culture.feminism
soc.culture.japan
soc.culture.jewish
soc.religion.quaker
soc.singles
soc.veterans
soc.women

talk.abortion
talk.environment
talk.politics.china
talk.politics.medicine

Some newsgroups are created for local use only, such as a company-wide or university-wide newsgroup. These newsgroups generally are of interest to the local community only, such as the newsgroup for Business 101 at Wharton or discussion of the local social events, and so on. Local newsgroups are named and run by the local newsgroup administrator who only needs to ensure there is no name conflict with any other Internet newsgroup with international distribution.

The administrators of these newsgroups also decide what subset of newsgroups will be received from their Internet provider's centralized network news archive. The daily news feed might provide 3,000 newsgroups with a machine

load of 60 to 100 MB of new material per day. The news administrator may decide not to carry certain newsgroups because of the content of the newsgroup, or the activity of a particular newsgroup might be too active for the computer and its limited disk space. Indeed, a very active group consumes computer cycles and disk space.

Note   A very active newsgroup also tends to limit the lifetime of a message within a newsgroup before it scrolls off. The scrolling of messages from a newsgroup appears to happen in two ways. After a user reads a specific message within a news thread, it does not appear in any subsequent news session. This focuses the user on incoming news. Users can, however, override the default conditions of their newsreader software and reread previous messages. Ultimately, the messages, read or unread, will scroll out of the newsserver completely. The amount of time any article remains on the computer system depends entirely on how long the administrator allows these items to be stored. This may vary from days to months and also depends on the volume of traffic within a specific newsgroup.

Newsreader Programs

There are many newsreader programs from which to choose. Within the Unix world, the programs rn, trn, nn, and tin, described in the following list, are the most common programs. Many of the newsreader programs becoming available in the personal computer world have evolved from these Unix-based programs and share many of the same features.

◆ **rn** is one of the original newsreader programs, crafted when there was not much news traffic and few features were even known to be desirable.

◆ **trn** evolved from rn to be the first newsreader to support threaded messaging. *Threaded messaging* allows the segregation of messages by special topics, much like individual clusters of people talking at a party.

◆ **nn** was designed to support a busy news system and support many of the features developed for trn. The nn program is often used by experienced Unix users. It is somewhat complicated to use, and has a manual of more than 50 pages.

◆ **tin** is a relatively new newsreader, fashioned after nn but very simple to use. The tin program is often used by newcomers to the Unix world.

The next section introduces some of these newsreaders and discusses some of the general features of interacting with a newsgroup.

General Newsreader Operations

The operation of a newsreader depends largely on the specific operations allowed by a newsreader. Sometimes, the newsreader is incorporated into a World Wide Web browser, using the "news:" portion of an URL. At the very least, the newsreader software will permit the user to select from a menu of newsgroups. The user may elect to subscribe to certain newsgroups and unsubscribe from other newsgroups. This subscription process only selects the names of the newsgroups that will appear in future menus. This subscription process does not imply automatic receipt of any of the contents of the specified newsgroup. Thus, subscribing and unsubscribing allows users to pare down the list of newsgroups they choose to follow.

After a user selects a newsgroup, he or she will see the message threads (or all of the messages) that are unread by the user. If this menu has a "+4" in one of the columns, the user is seeing the number of unread messages within a message thread. In this example, there are four unread messages pertaining to this specific "conversation" or message thread. If there is only one message, a "+" will appear. When a message within this thread is read, the unread message count will decrease or the "+" will go away. If the user exits the newsreader and then goes back to the same newsgroup, the previously read news messages will not be present. This default feature keeps the user from wading through previously read messages. All newsreaders have the capability to reread previous messages until they have permanently scrolled off the local newsserver. In many cases, the newsserver contents are archived offsite if you need to read a message that has left the newsserver.

After reading a specific message, the user might want to reply to an individual message. The reply usually is a personal e-mail message to the person who wrote (posted) the previous message. Personal e-mail will not appear on the newsgroup. Some newsreaders allow the user to include some of the earlier message in the reply, which is a good idea in order to enable the recipient of the reply to recall the context of the original message. If the original poster has several hundred e-mail postings in the course of one week, having a reply with some of the original material present helps him or her remember what was happening. Receiving a reply containing only the message "I disagree with items one and two, but agree with number three" is useless unless the context of the earlier message is included.

If the user wants to contribute to a public message thread, the "f", or follow, command allows the user to tack on another message to the message thread. This new piece of news is first posted to the local news server, then propagates to the rest of the news servers around the world. The original poster of the news message is usually the only person authorized to delete a specific news item.

News Reading Inside the World Wide Web

Network news can be accessed within the World Wide Web using the URL `news://<netwrk.newsrc.net>` where `netwrk.newsrc.net` is the Internet name of the local news archive. This should be defined by your local network administrator. In many cases, the news source is defined as one of the setup resources for the WWW browser. Figure 14.1 shows the newsgroups subscribed by the owner of this Netscape WWW client. Note the form bar at the bottom of the figure allowing the user to pick and choose from the available newsgroups made available by the local network news administrator. The number of unread message is in the left column of the listing.

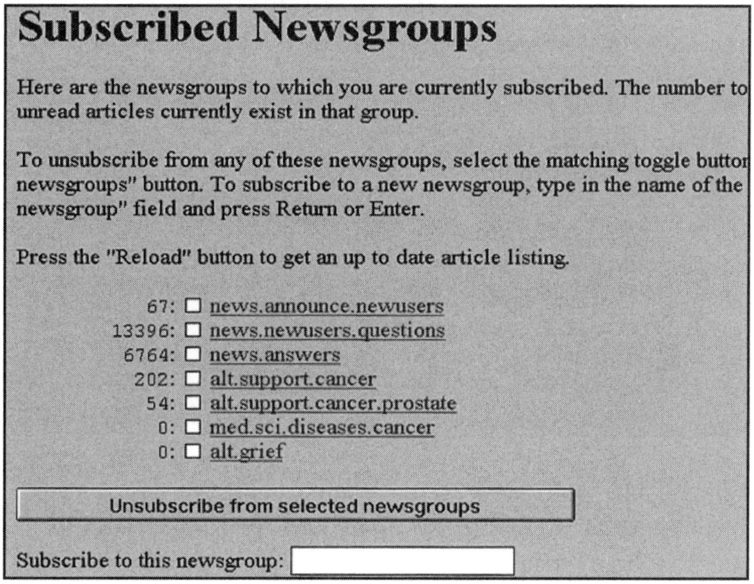

Subscribed Newsgroups

Here are the newsgroups to which you are currently subscribed. The number to unread articles currently exist in that group.

To unsubscribe from any of these newsgroups, select the matching toggle button newsgroups" button. To subscribe to a new newsgroup, type in the name of the newsgroup" field and press Return or Enter.

Press the "Reload" button to get an up to date article listing.

```
   67: ☐ news.announce.newusers
13396: ☐ news.newusers.questions
 6764: ☐ news.answers
  202: ☐ alt.support.cancer
   54: ☐ alt.support.cancer.prostate
    0: ☐ med.sci.diseases.cancer
    0: ☐ alt.grief
```

    Unsubscribe from selected newsgroups

Subscribe to this newsgroup: _____

Figure 14.1

A list of newsgroups the user is subscribed to on this Netscape client.

Figure 14.2 shows some of the message thread captions from the newsgroup alt.support.cancer. The toolbar at the top of this figure shows a variety of functions. The right-most function is used to post a message. This starts a new message thread within this newsgroup. The second option is a "catchup" option, which screens the local news archive and presents only the most current messages. This is particularly helpful when returning from an absence of reading your news. Instead of wading through potentially thousands of messages, the user's news pointer can be brought up to date and only the most recent messages are presented. The converse operation, to show all the articles, rolls back the user's pointer to allow all the messages in the local archive pertaining to this newsgroup to be shown. The second to left button is an "unsubscribe," which deletes the user's pointers to their position within the local newsgroup archive and disengages updating messages from this news-group. The right-most button goes to other message groups.

Figure 14.2

Message thread captions from alt.support.cancer.

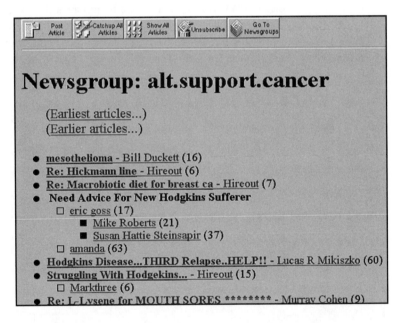

Examination of the first message thread within figure 14.2 shows the topic "mesothelioma," initiated by Bill Duckett, has 16 messages in the thread. Selection of this message thread allows the user to go through each message in chronological order. The user may choose to reply privately to the sender, or publicly by appending a message to the thread.

Figure 14.3 shows an individual message within a newsgroup thread. This is a reply to an original posting, as evident by the partial quote (that is, the presence of the ">" character in the left column denotes the original message).

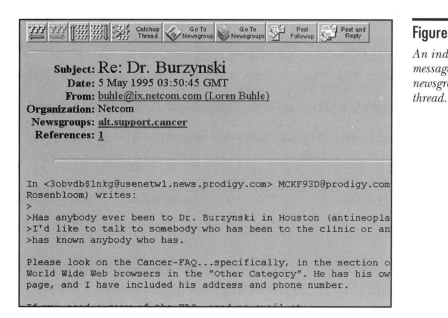

Figure 14.3

An individual message in a newsgroup thread.

If the user clicks on the address to the right of From:, in this case buhle@ix.netcom.com, an e-mail form will be generated by the Netscape WWW client and a private e-mail message can be sent to the last person contributing to the message thread. The toolbar at the top of the figure shows other options, such as contributing another message to the thread and thus furthering the public conversation. Other options include skipping to the next message within the thread, skipping to other message threads within the newsgroup, and skipping to another newsgroup. Additional features in this presentation include the newsgroup used, in this case alt.support.cancer, and the number of messages within this thread, in this case one.

Some messages might be of interest to multiple newsgroups. Although a simple approach would be to publicly post the message on a related newsgroup as a separate message, this is frowned upon, especially by users who read these related newsgroups and will run into multiple copies of the message. It is much better to crosspost the message to the various newsgroups. If a user reads the message in one newsgroup, the message is marked "READ" in all other newsgroups accessed by this user, cutting down on the number of redundant messages.

Figures 1 through 3 came from the Netscape browser, but similar functionality exists on other modern WWW browsers, such as Netcom's Netscape news-reader. Early generation WWW browsers could only read the newsgroups. No replies back to the newsgroups were possible within the WWW. Only Lynx, the text-based WWW client, was capable of replying to message thread through e-mail generated by the user. The need to exchange messages on the news-group from a single platform, such as Netscape's Netcom, makes integration of these Internet features relatively painless, once they are correctly configured.

Part IV

Becoming a Web Site

Putting Up a Web Server

Now that you have looked at various WWW sites and discovered the variety of information available, you may be thinking about setting up your own Web server. In this chapter, the basics of set-up, system requirements, and some helpful hints are discussed.

Before setting up a site, look at the pros and cons of doing so. If you are receiving service through an established Internet provider, setting up your own site may not be necessary as most major providers have sites set up which users are free to use. Similarly, if you are setting up information that is only to be used on your own site (that is, which will not be accessible to the rest of the world), there is no need to set up a server; the files can be accessed locally without any further work.

If, however, you want to have your information available to users off system, setting up a Web server is the best option.

Defining a Web Server

Simply put, a Web server is a software package that processes HTML documents for viewing by other sites. The server enables users on other sites to access documents that you have chosen to make available to them.

Hardware Requirements

Web servers can be run from any hardware platform. There are servers that are specifically designed for Macintoshes, PCs, and various other platforms, including the Amiga.

As would be expected, the more powerful the machine running the server, and the faster its connection to the Internet, the better it will run.

While having a high-power machine like a Sun might be advantageous when creating Web documents, it really doesn't matter much for the server, since the machine's main purpose is to house documents that will be accessed by users on other outside systems. Therefore, a multiprocessing machine might be nice to use, but anyone accessing the server from outside will not notice the difference in speed.

The main hardware issue, therefore, is how much memory is available on the machine. The amount of memory needed depends on what is going to be made available. If only a few pages of text without graphics are going to be kept, very little memory is needed. On the other hand, if you plan to use graphics, sound files, or large documents (such as online versions of product manuals), a greater amount of memory is needed.

When deciding how much memory, it's better to err on the side of too much rather than too little. After you have been on the Web for a while, you might decide that your server needs to have more documents available, and that will mean more memory. It's better to start with the greater amount of memory now, and avoid having to upgrade within the next year.

Given a basic machine of any type, plus memory, the only other hardware requirements are network connection materials. These will, in most cases, consist of a network interface card and the wiring to attach the machine to the network.

Software Requirements

The most important software is the Web server itself. Just as it can be run under a number of hardware platforms, it can also run under several operating systems, including MS Windows, Windows NT, UNIX, and VAX VMS. Sites from which the server software can be obtained are described in the following sections.

Connection Requirements

A serious Web site would want at least a 56 Kbps connection. The site must be on the Internet.

If your company already has a full-time Internet connection, you simply need to have the server connected to the local network.

If, however, the company is not already on the Internet, the process of connecting the server is more complex. The first question to be answered is "how fast should this connection be?"

In truth, there is no such thing as a fast enough connection. The minimum speed that is acceptable for Web servers is a 56 Kbps connection. Anything slower than this will crawl along at a rate that will immediately discourage users from accessing the site.

Faster connections are also available, such as the T-1 line. The faster the connection, however, the more expensive it is. Finding the balance between speed and company budget is an important issue at this point. Remember, however, that if the server proves to be popular and an extremely useful tool, a faster server might be wanted in the next year. It's far less expensive to get the faster connection now than to upgrade later.

Another factor to consider is the service provider. A service provider is a company that provides Internet connections for other businesses and users. The provider does much of the work, which makes the transition from non-Internet connected to being on the Net an easier move.

There are hundreds of service providers available now, ranging from national companies such as Netcom to more local providers such as Clark Internet

Services in Maryland. Important considerations when talking to a service provider include the following:

◆ What is the cost of service? Not all providers charge the same amount. Also, be sure to check to see if there are special rates for paying quarterly or yearly. Are extra fees added for technical support and other such services?

◆ What is provided? Will the provider do all necessary set-up work? Will they provide technical support? Are there any courses that company members can take to help teach how to maintain the site?

◆ How reliable is the service? Check to see how long the service has been in operation, and what sort of clients they are used to assisting. If possible, find out what other clients think of the service provided.

Finding Web Server Software

The following sites have Web servers available. They are all accessible through either URL or anonymous FTP.

TABLE 15.1
Web Server Sites

Server	Site	Description
NCSA httpd	FTP to `ftp.ncsa.uiuc.edu` directory `Web/ncsa_httpd`	NCSAs server for UNIX. One of the most used servers.
CERN httpd for UNIX	anonymous FTP from `info.cern.ch`	CERNs server
Gn HTTP/ Gopher for UNIX	URL `http:// hopf.math.nwu.edu/`	GNs server can be used for both WWW and Gopher clients. This is the recommended server for sites which are migrating from Gopher to WWW.

Server	Site	Description
Perl for UNIX	URL http://bsdi.com /server/doc/ plexus.html	A server written in the PERL scripting language.
MacHTTP	URL http:// www.uth.tmc.edu /mac_info /machttp_info.html	The only recommended server for Macintosh.
HTTPS for Windows NT	anonymous FTP from emwac.ed.ac.uk directory pub/https	For Windows NT systems on either Intel or Alpha platforms.
NCSA httpd for MS Windows	anonymous FTP from ftp.ncsa.uiuc.edu directory Web/ncsa_httpd/version. contrib	NCSAs httpd ported to MS Windows. Almost identical to the UNIX
SerWeb for MS Windows	anonymous FTP from winftp.cica. indiana.edu	A very basic server.
OS2HTTPD for OS/2	anonymous FTP from ftp.netcom.com directory pub/kfan	A basic server for OS/2 written and maintained by Frankie Fan.
KA9Q NOS for DOS	anonymous FTP from inorganic5.chem.ufl. edu	A DOS-based server for both HTTP and Gopher. It is recommended for sites that are in the process of transferring from Gopher to Web sites.
CERN HTTP for VMS	URL httpd:// delonline.cern.ch /disk$user/duns/doc/	A port of CERN HTTP to VMS.
NCSA Amiga	URL http:// insti.physics.sunysb. edu/AMosiac/home.html	UNIX version of NCSA's server ported to the Amiga. It is packaged with the Amosiac browser.

Setting Up a Server for MS Windows

Before choosing to spend large amounts of money on new hardware to run a Web server, it is a good idea to see how a server works under MS Windows, a common platform that is available in many companies. The sample installation here is of WinHTTPD, a freely available program. This is also one of the most straightforward and easy to complete installations and setups, so it will allow users to immediately see how a Web server will look and operate once complete.

To begin, make sure there is a Web browser installed on the machine where the server will be set up. Connect to URL `http://www.city.net/win-httpd/`. This site contains information about many Web server packages for both MS Windows and Windows NT. To get information on the package that will be installed in this example, select the text "Downloading the Server Package."

 Note   The file extension whtp13p1.zip will change as newer versions of the program become available. The next version, for instance, will probably be called either whtp14p1.zip or whtp20p1.zip.

When the download is complete, the file must be unzipped. This is done using the command `pkunzip -d whtp13p1.zip`, which should be entered at the DOS prompt. This will unzip the file into its component parts while maintaining the directory structure that was used before the files were originally compressed. This file structure is imperative to the proper execution of the program; if the structure is not in place, files might not be found when needed.

If a copy of pkunzip is not already in place on the server machine, it can be downloaded from `http://somcru.med.unc.edu:70/1/ftp`. The file pkunzip.exe is a self-extracting file; typing `pkunzip` will cause it to unpack and be ready to run.

Step one, downloading the software, is already complete, so click on the highlighted text that reads "Set up the software to move on to the next part of the installation" (see figure 15.1).

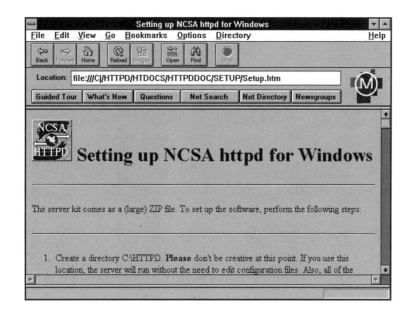

Figure 15.1

Setting up the server.

Follow the instructions to set up the correct time zone for the system.

Before the server will run properly, you must confirm that the time zone variable, TZ, has been set. TZ is used to tell httpd the time zone to which the computer's local clock is set, since the Common Log Format requires that times be recorded by Greenwich Mean Time (GMT). TZ is set within the AUTOEXEC.BAT file. The following line should be added to this file in order to set the variable:

```
SET TZ=zzznddd
```

zzz is the three letter abbreviation for the local time zone. EST for Eastern Standard Time, for example, or PST for Pacific Standard Time.

n is the number of hours difference between local time and GMT. For the EST zone, this number would be 5.

ddd is the local Daylight Savings Time code, assuming that Daylight Savings Time is observed locally. This would be EDT for Eastern Daylight Time.

Putting all of these numbers together, a user on the East Coast would set his TZ variable as follows:

```
TZ=EST5EDT
```

Now, go back to the Web server where the initial Installation screen is still displayed, and proceed to the Configure the Server screen (figure 15.2) by clicking on the highlighted text.

Figure 15.2

The Server Configuration Screen.

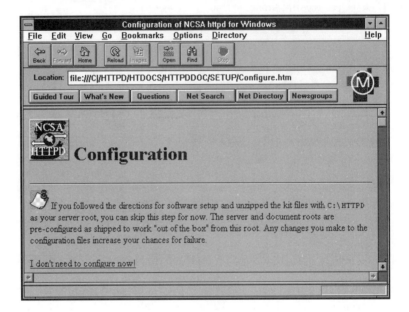

As stated in this document, the server is pre-configured to automatically run on the system where it is installed. For now, continue with the pre-existing setup, in order to avoid making mistakes. Hints for changes you may want to make later are included at the end of this chapter.

With the server at least minimally configured at this point, it's time to start it. For information on doing this, go to the Start Up page (figure 15.3). This is done by clicking on the highlighted Start Up text.

First install the HTTPD.EXE icon on your desktop. The best place to put it would be in the same folder with your Web viewing program (figure 15.4).

Before it can be used, the server must be installed on the desktop. Go to the Windows screen, and from the File menu, select New to add a new item. The address of this item is `C:\httpd\httpd.exe`. Once this item has been added, its icon should appear on screen. Figure 15.6 shows this icon in the Internet folder; it is the last icon in the folder.

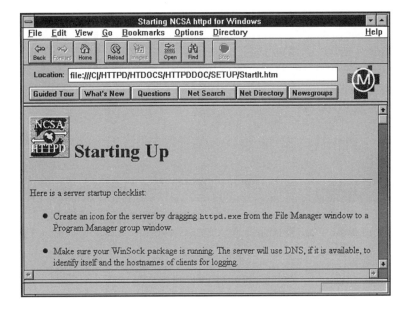

Figure 15.3

The Starting Up page.

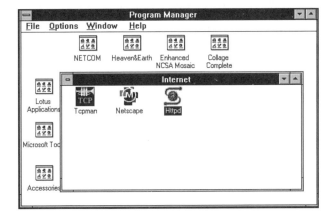

Figure 15.4

The Httpd icon.

Once the icon is installed, it should be ready to run. To test whether the server software is actually configured and running properly, double-click on the Httpd icon shown in figure 15.4. When the icon appears in minimized form at the base of the screen, the server is up and running. To test it, use your Web viewer to load a document from the local system (information about creating documents can be found in Part V of this book). If the document loads correctly, the server is installed and ready to use.

If the file does not load, first check to be certain that the path you have specified is correct. Then make sure you are actually connected to the Internet, and that HTTPD is running. If there are still problems, it is probably because one of the configuration parameters is incorrect, or the directory structure of the various httpd files is not maintained when unzipping the initial file. Recheck these, and if there are still problems, try to re-install.

If the server still does not work, you may have encountered one of its bugs. Either contact its creator or try installing a different server.

Specializing Your Server Configuration

Now that the basic set-up is complete, you may want to change some of the parameters for how your server is running. To do so, go to the Configure.htm page again (shown in figure 15.2), then to the setup overview page (shown in figure 15.5) to see the various options that can be changed. The major ones are discussed here; continue browsing the various htm pages to see others that can be changed.

General Hints for Configuration Changes

The following hints are useful when changing scripting for all servers:

◆ All comment lines begin with the pound sign (#). Any line beginning with a pound sign is ignored.

◆ HTTP setup files are not case sensitive; it does not matter whether you use upper-, lower-case characters, or a mixed set.

◆ All extra white space is ignored.

◆ Commands are formatted as follows where *directive* is a command which HTTP understands, and *data* is the information on which this command should be executed.

```
directive data
```

◆ Only one directive can be given per line in the configuration file.

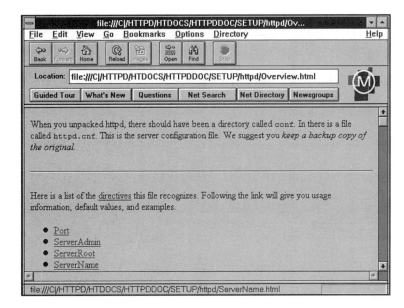

Figure 15.5

The Setup Overview page.

What Changes Can Be Made

There are four configuration files for HTTPD. They are the server configuration file, the server resource map, the access configuration file, and the mime types configuration file. They are described in detail in the following sections.

The Server Configuration File

The server configuration file, located in directory conf, is called httpd.cnf. Be sure to make a backup copy of this file before making any changes! This is an important precaution to take in case the newer version of the httpd.cnf file causes system problems; if the error cannot be tracked down, the old version can always be reinstalled.

The main information screen for the Server Configuration File is shown in figure 15.6 below.

Figure 15.6

The Server Configuration File.

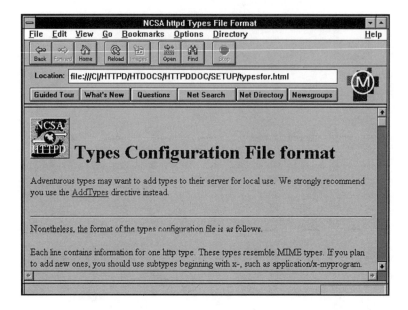

For details about setting any of these options, go to the information screen for that directive.

The one directive that you probably want to set immediately is ServerAdmin. This is used to send mail to the server administrator if there is a problem. The format is as follows where *address* is the address to which error reports will be sent:

```
ServerAdmin address
```

The system automatically defaults to having no address set. Because receiving notice when errors occur is useful, setting this address is recommended. In this way, the user will always be notified when an error occurs and he will not need to rely on his memory to check the error log for this information.

To keep track of the errors that are encountered by the server, use the ErrorLog directive. This sets the file to which HTTPD will log the errors it encounters. The following error conditions are logged:

◆ Clients that time out

◆ Scripts with no output

◆ Server bugs that cause either a segmentation violation or a bus error

◆ User authentication problems

◆ Any haccess.cnf files that try to override parameters which they are not allowed to change.

The format for this directive follows where *file* is the file (and path) that connects to the error log file. The default for this is logs/error.log.

```
errorlog file
```

To keep track of user access to your server, use the logfile command. It is formatted in a manner similar to errorlog:

```
logfile file
```

Again, *file* is the file to which access information will be stored. The default is logs/access.log.

The format of entries in this log is as follows where *remote-host* is the hostname or IP address of the client. [date] is the date of access, and *request* is the HTTP request sent to your server:

```
remote-host [date] request
```

The Server Resource Map

Directives in this file enable you to change such options as the directory from which files will be sent, indexing options, aliasing, and the type of icons that are set for various documents. The main Server Resource Map information document is shown in figure 15.7. This file is not changed as often as the Configuration file, and does not affect the way a server is run to as great an extent.

Figure 15.7

*The Server
Resource Map
information file.*

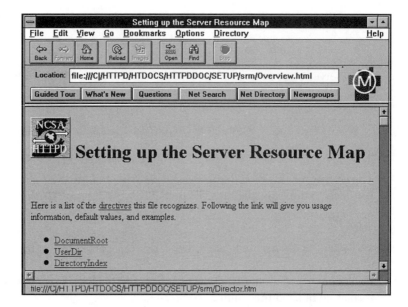

The Access Configuration File

Access configuration is used to determine who is and is not allowed to use certain parts of your server. This information is covered further in the discussion of server security. The main Access Configuration page is shown in figure 15.8.

Restricting access to certain areas of the server is an important security measure. While all on-site users might be given unlimited access to all files found on the machine, it is not wise to give this access to all off-site users. If the server hosts not only Web documents, for example, but also internal memos, only the former should be made available to users from outside the system.

Another circumstance where restricted access is important is in the transfering of FTP files. If the site is available for FTP use, take extra care to select which files can and cannot be accessed from off-system. Otherwise, the company's financial reports might suddenly be appearing across the Internet.

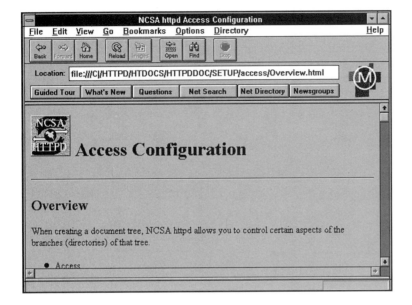

Figure 15.8

The Access Configuration page.

Putting a Business on a Web Server

N ow that so many people are using the Internet as their main source for gathering information, it is becoming increasingly beneficial for companies to have their product information online. The Web is an excellent place to do this, because users can not only see textual descriptions, but can also see pictures and even animated images, as well as learn information about the product or company.

Deciding to put a business on the Web is not an easy task because there are many things to consider. Not the least of these are cost and manpower. A Web site, depending on its complexity and how often it is used, can be extremely expensive, not only in initial set-up costs (hardware, telephone costs), but in maintenance. There are ways to get around some of these costs, which are discussed in this chapter.

The major items to be discussed in this chapter are as follow:

◆ Why set up a Web site?

◆ Using Web providers

◆ Pros and cons of maintaining a site alone

◆ Important qualifications for site maintainers

Why Become a Web Site?

Many companies are hesitant to become Web sites due to the costs involved for equipment and labor. What they are not taking into consideration, however, is the immense benefit of being on the Web. Although not all businesses and organizations will benefit from a Web site, many will be able to expand their marketing and user base simply by creating a single page on the Web, such as those shown in figures 16.1 and 16.2. The following are some of the many benefits that a company can realize with a Web site:

◆ Wider marketing base

◆ Easy access for customers

◆ One-time set-up of information

◆ Information can be changed instantly

Using the Web Site as a Sales Tool

To help illustrate the way in which a company can benefit from the Web, the following is an example scenario of a business that sells T-shirts. Many of the same principles and dynamics encountered by this company may relate to the way you do business.

You are the Sales Manager for a company that produces and distributes T-shirts. Your main market is clubs and organizations that need team shirts or something printed for a special event. One day, you receive a phone call from representatives of a local computer company. They are planning to appear at a major trade show and need T-shirts advertising their newest product. The company is soliciting price quotes and information about available colors from local T-shirt printers.

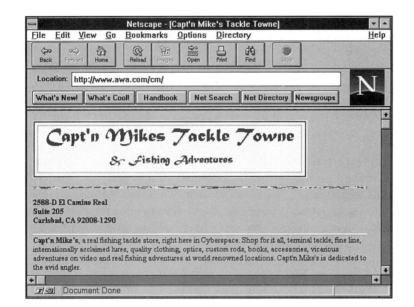

Figure 16.1

A business home page.

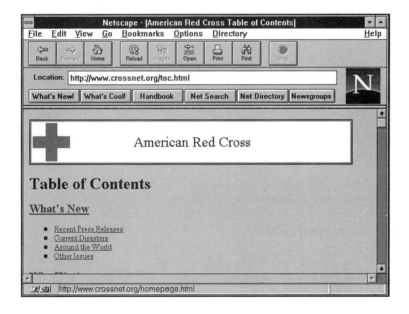

Figure 16.2

The American Red Cross home page.

In the past, you might have just quoted the numbers and colors to them over the phone, or perhaps faxed them a sheet listing pertinent information.

Today, however, you can suggest that they access your company's Web page. There, they can find not only all of your pricing and color information, but they can also find actual samples of the colors. Your Web page can also display pictures of shirts you have designed, or information about the graphic artist with whom you are consulting to help customers with design problems.

The computer company representative is interested and passes along information about his new product. You pass this information to the graphic artist, who comes up with several designs, which you immediately add to the Web site and make available to your potential customer. She reviews the designs, chooses the one she likes best, and places an order. She can do all this without ever having to leave her office and come by the shop.

You might think creating a Web page is an excessive advertising and marketing move for a small promotional clothing items company. Consider how it would be, however, if you were a computer store manager. Your immediate market is people who know about (or at least need to know about) computers. Advertising by means of computer seems a reasonable option, therefore you set up a Web site.

When potential customers first access your site, they see a short summary of information about your store, including your telephone number and address. Next, they can go to another page, depending on the sort of purchase they are considering. If they are considering the purchase of a new desktop publishing package, for example, they would go to the Software page, and then to the Desktop Publishing page.

Your Desktop Publishing page displays a summary of the major products that your company sells. After looking at short descriptions of each product, a potential customer can choose to get further information about a specific product of yours, called PublishMe.

Your PublishMe page shows the way the product works, its history, its compatibility with other products, and displays some screen shots of the program itself.

The customers then go back and compare this information with information about a few other packages or other advertising, narrowing down their

possibilities. By the time they are in your store, they already know a lot about the products available and can save time by looking only at the ones that suit their needs.

If, by viewing the information available over the Web, the customer determines that this is the package he definitely wants, he can simply order it over the Web. Order information is transferred directly to your store, and you can ship the program to him the same day. If, however, he wants to look at several packages and see them actually running, he will go into your store. Even this trip to the store has benefits, however: the customer will be saving some of both his and your time by already having background on the available packages and knowing which of them he wants to examine further.

There are numerous other possibilities of how a business can benefit from being on the Web, but one thing is clear: having a Web site for your company is gaining increasing importance. As people rely more and more on computers for information, and look online for whatever knowledge they need, companies that have their information available quickly and in a pleasing manner will be the ones that get the business.

You have various options for how you use the Web in your business. These options depend upon how much information you want to disseminate over the Internet. You can either take advantage of the resources of other companies that offer advertising space to other companies through their Web sites, or you can set up your own Web site. The first option is discussed in the following section.

Some companies, however, would be better served by having their own Web site. A major consideration in making the decision to set up a private site versus using a provider is the size of a company. Although a small business might only want to display a limited amount of advertising information—perhaps only store hours, major items sold, and prices—a larger company might also want to provide customer support information, product upgrades, and many other services. At that point, using a Web provider would not be cost effective because the amount of information being stored and the frequency with which it would need to be accessed and modified would make it expensive to maintain. Instead, setting up a private server, with one or more full-time employees making the necessary changes and providing maintenance, would cost far less in the long run.

Microsoft, for instance, would not be well served using a provider. They have far too much information to make available on the Web. Simply printing a list of all available products would take up an immense amount of space. So instead, they have set up their own site, `http://www.microsoft.com` (see fig. 16.3). Here they show not only advertising literature for various products, but also bug fixes that can be transferred directly to your computer. In addition, there are other customer support functions available, as well as many useful add-ons to their commercial products.

Figure 16.3

Microsoft, a company best served by having its own Web site.

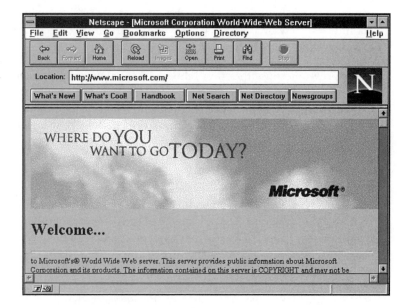

Using a Web Provider

A Web *provider* is a company that has created a Web site that is made available to other companies and individuals to display their information. The provider charges a fee to each company, and in return offers assistance in creating and maintaining Web pages, as well as the space and Internet connection to make the page available to end users. The provider is basically a library that carries a "book" for each company that subscribes to the service.

Provider services are becoming very popular. Many small providers are springing up across the United States and abroad. There are also larger companies

offering Web services, including MecklerWeb and CommerceNet. The following sections discuss these two large providers, as well as several smaller provider companies.

About MecklerWeb

MecklerWeb is a product of Mecklermedia Corporation, located in Westport, Connecticut. MecklerWeb is a Web site dedicated to distributing information about media companies to users throughout the Internet. According to their executive summary, MecklerWeb is designed to be the "users' first stop on the Internet." This is an apt description because the information made available there includes the latest Internet news, "how-to" tips, product reviews, and numerous pointers to available resources (see fig. 16.4).

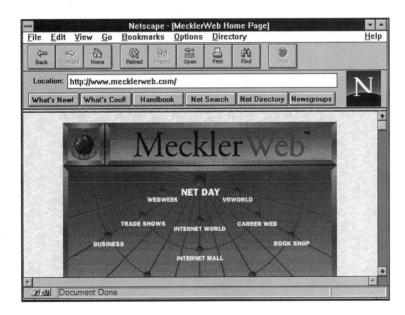

Figure 16.4

The Mecklermedia home page.

 Note   MecklerWeb contains information on numerous technological advances, including the latest information on CD-ROMs, virtual reality, and multimedia. This information is compiled from both Mecklermedia's magazines and books, as well as its Virtual Reality Expositions, which are held annually in New York and San Jose.

MecklerWeb obtains funding from numerous sponsors and advertisers (see fig. 16.5). These are companies or organizations that display their corporate logo or product icons in visible areas of MecklerWeb's lead pages for each content area. If you click on one of these icons, you see information about the products, services, or company that sponsored the icon. This investment is very cost-effective because no matter what part of MecklerWeb the user is examining, your company's logo is displayed.

Figure 16.5

Meckler's sponsor list.

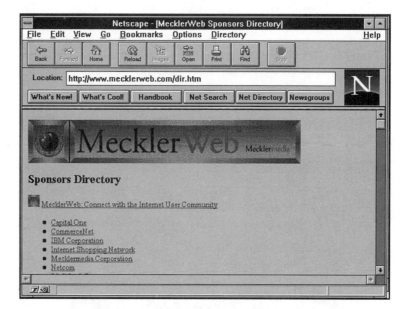

Getting Further Information

For further information about MecklerWeb, including pricing, either send e-mail to `info@mecklermedia.com` or visit their Web site, `http://www.mecklerweb.com`.

About CommerceNet

CommerceNet is a collection of companies and organizations that has as its goal the creation and maintenance of an electronic marketplace in which all business is transacted by means of the Internet. CommerceNet enables users to stop dealing with piles of paper: eliminating printed catalogs, paper order forms, or piles of bids for contracts. Instead, all information is available at the click of a button and is printable when needed (see fig. 16.6).

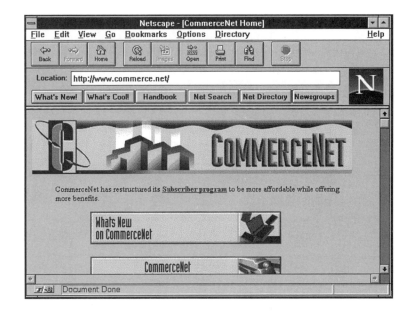

Figure 16.6

CommerceNet's home screen.

Among the services that CommerceNet plans to include are credit reporting, broker referrals, network notarization, and financial and transportation services. The benefits of this service, in their opinion, include faster distribution of information, as well as a major cut in operating costs.

Funded by both consortium members and a six-million-dollar cooperative agreement from the *Technology Reinvestment Project* (TRP), CommerceNet enables users to join on one of several levels. General users can access CommerceNet information by means of the Web, while consortium members can be sponsors, associates, or subscribers, depending upon the amount of involvement and financial support they are willing to give; the more money invested, the greater the return. The following list briefly describes the differences between the membership levels:

◆ *Sponsors* are listed in CommerceNet's directories. They are able to participate in work groups, join in marketing projects with CommerceNet, access starter kits, and take training courses offered by CommerceNet.

◆ *Associates* are similar to providers, but without voting privileges for CommerceNet organizational meetings. They are also listed in all directories and have their logos displayed prominently.

◆ *Subscribers* receive all the benefits of sponsors, except they are not able to join in marketing projects. This is an ideal place for small businesses because cost and time commitment are low, but the visibility is great.

Figure 16.7

The CommerceNet home page used to subscribe to their service.

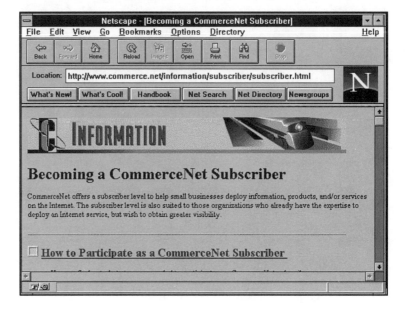

Users are the people targeted by the advertising of the sponsors, associates, and subscribers. Users must subscribe to CommerceNet, the way they would subscribe to a magazine. In return for their subscription, they can view all the information available on the CommerceNet Web pages.

Getting More Information

To get more information about CommerceNet, either send e-mail to info@commerce.net or look at their Web page, http://www.commerce.net/.

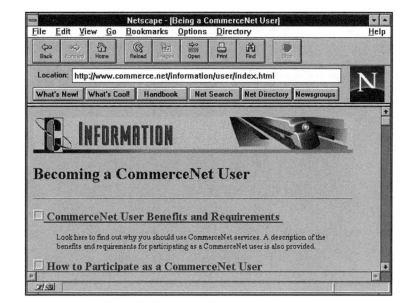

Figure 16.8

The CommerceNet User Information home page.

Other Web Service Providers

Although the above two companies are the major Web providers currently in operation, there are many other services available. Following are just a few of the available services.

Internet Media Services

Internet Media Services (see fig. 16.9), located in Palo Alto, California, offers Web page production and maintenance to businesses of all sizes. They design the Web page, link it to other pertinent sites, and maintain it. Their main focus is creating pages that reside on the user's home system, so some work will still have to be done in-house by your company.

Figure 16.9

The Internet Media Services (IMS) home page.

IMSs home page can be found at `http://netmedia.com/`.

The Sage's Pages

The Sage's Pages (see fig. 16.10) are a service provided by Sage Internet Services of New Brunswick, New Jersey. They design and maintain Web pages for companies and public service organizations on their machine. All pages are viewed from their main Sage Page, `http://www.sic.com`. Among the services offered is their "Faxability" program. With this, users enter the information needed to order a product on the Web page. This information is queued at the SIC offices and then faxed directly to the company so the order can be filled.

Further information about SIC's services can be found at `http://www.sic.com/`.

BBN Planet

BBN Planet, located in Massachusetts, offers a wide range of Web services for commercial, educational, and government organizations (see fig. 16.11). They can either provide services by setting up a system at the user's site, or by placing information directly on their system. BBN Planet helps with the development and design of Web pages for their clients, as well as with training so the clients can do this work themselves.

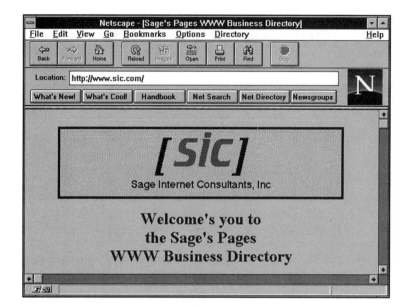

Figure 16.10

The Sage's Pages screen.

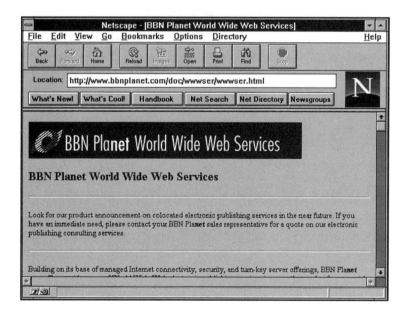

Figure 16.11

BBN Planet's Web Services.

For further information, see BBN Planets home page at http://
www.bbnplanet.com.

Providing Your Own Web Site

What should you do if neither of these services is quite what your company needs or wants? You should consider creating your own Web site. One benefit of creating your own site is that none of your competitors will have information available on the same site. Another benefit is that you can have complete control over the information you disseminate and can change that information at will.

On the negative side, you will not have someone to run to if there is a problem. People on your site will be responsible for all areas of the product, from the Internet connection to maintaining the site.

If you create your own site, you should take extra caution in dealing with security issues. An example of a possible security issue is making sure that users who access your Web site are not also able to look at any nonpublic company information that resides on the same system. Someone must also ensure that all information is released at the proper time. New product release notices, for example, should not be released before the product is ready.

Note For specific information about security issues, please see Chapter 17, "Commerce on the Web." For more information about setting up the server, see Chapter 15, "Putting Up a Web Server."

Choosing a WebMaster

When you are running your own Web site, the most important person on your team is the WebMaster. He or she is the person who keeps the server running, makes sure information is accessible, and keeps the system's security at an acceptable level. Choosing such a person is a difficult task, but the following suggestions should help.

The first thing you must consider, obviously, is how much knowledge the person has about the Web in general. Does this person know where to find general information on a subject or how to do a search on a specific idea or term? Does he or she understand the general setup of the Web and how links work?

Next, look at your nominee's technical knowledge about running the server itself. Can your intended WebMaster install and maintain the server? Does he or she know how to set the various options to specialize the system to your needs? What does your nominee know about security?

Finally, and equally important, does your candidate know how to create Web documents? Having a working server is not terribly useful if there is no information available. Ask about his or her ability to add graphics, sound, and animation.

One of the best ways to examine a potential WebMaster's skills is to look at other sites he has maintained or at least created documents on. If they seem to be in order, and the work is similar to what you need, you may have found the person you want.

What About Credentials?

Although there are courses available to train WebMasters, graduates of these courses do not necessarily make the best WebMasters. Some of the best people in the field are those who have spent their time looking through the Web and who have picked up the information on their own. These users generally understand the creation and maintenance of Web sites because they have had a desire to gain this knowledge, rather than because they have been "forced" to do so as part of a course.

The down side of this is that some crucial piece of knowledge can be missing, as you might discover at an inconvenient time. A person who is used to searching the Web for solutions to problems, however, is likely to be able to solve the problem more quickly than someone with lots of credentials, but little actual experience.

Creating Exciting Web Sites

Now that you have a site (or service provider, if you chose that route), the next important thing to do is make sure the information you are distributing is something people will want to look at. The following hints will help you to create a more interesting and useful Web site that users will want to access repeatedly.

Accurate Information

First and foremost, make sure the information you are presenting is accurate. If a user discovers that your information is extremely incorrect or outdated, he is unlikely to consider you a useful source in the future.

Presentation

The Web gives you the ability to make a document look visually appealing based on how it is formed; use it. Crowded straight-text files do not appeal to the user, no matter how much information they contain. The following hints, however, are always useful:

◆ Use space to your advantage. Leaving extra space around text selections makes them easier to read.

◆ Make use of graphics. They always catch people's eye. Don't overuse them, however.

◆ Keep the screen from looking too busy. Trying to cram in several lines of text and three pictures will distract the reader too much.

◆ Color is available. Use it to get the browser's attention.

For more information about creating documents, see Chapter 20, "Writing HTML Documents."

Designing Links

Make sure your document links are useful. If a user chooses to click on an option to get further information, make sure the information is of the sort he or she expects to find there.

Similarly, make sure links are well described. The user should have an idea of what is on the next page before she gets there. Being able to go back to a previous level of a document hierarchy is useful; however, it should be obvious that returning to a previous level is what a specific link does, or you might confuse the user.

A useful link might use the following pattern:

1. The home page, or starting point, gives an overview of the company. From here, it is possible to get information about specific parts of the company: user support, new products, or product orders.

2. The User Support page would link back to the home page or forward to specific bug fix pages.

3. The Bug Fix pages would link back to User Support and the home page.

4. New Products would link back to the home page or forward to the Product Orders page.

A less useful variant of this model would force the user to go from the New Products page back to the home page before being allowed to access the Product Orders page.

Commerce on the Web

The possibilities for commerce on the World Wide Web are both wondrous and agonizingly abstract at this time. The market demographics, especially with the rapid influx of new users each month, also is unclear. Who is using the Internet? Will these users spend money buying goods and services via the Internet? Do the benefits of taking business to the Internet offset its risks and offer value beyond the current catalog or storefront business? Can a company afford *not* to be on the Internet, ceding visibility to competitors willing to take the risk? This chapter explores some of the implications of commerce on the Internet. It concludes with views on where Internet commerce might be in the next few years and what it will take to get there.

Having a business presence on the Internet implies different things to different people. Having a World Wide Web home page on the Internet gives name recognition to marketers and, if they choose, their product line. Many commercial WWW sites are focusing on marketing and public relations, with support of order entry slated for sometime in the future. These organizations may maintain a simple home page in an electronic "mall," showing off a few premium-line products. Other organizations might dabble with virtual trade shows or online catalogs of goods and services. One commercial site has gone so far as to discuss the philosophy of their company and feature the environmental and human rights focus of their organization without featuring their main product line. Some organizations are contemplating the extension of their existing interactive help-line services into targeted product-specific user communities. For example, some of the software support services traditionally operating through services such as CompuServe are contemplating support via the Internet.

This unfocused approach to the Internet is partially due to difficulty in establishing the market demographics, especially with the rapid influx of new users from non-traditional sources, such as America Online, Prodigy, and other marketers of services. Earlier demographics showed most of the WWW users were of the college age set, with little disposable income. As Internet access becomes common, either by penetration of local Internet providers or the proliferation of Internet access from traditional online services, the market demographics will continue to change. If Web shopping follows the market trends of catalog shopping, most of the purchasing will occur from the home. Currently, the majority of home computers lack the muscle and high bandwidth connections needed for comfortable WWW access. Some marketers argue the WWW store interfaces are neither simple nor attractive enough to put most consumers in a buying mood. Thus, the goals of many business for a presence on the Internet is unclear. They can't afford not to be present, but many don't know the exact message they wish to broadcast. Some businesses are diving in to see what works, whereas others are holding back with a "wait-and-see" approach.

The different business uses of the Internet at this time are as follows:

◆ **Promotion.** Provides name recognition for the company and can dovetail with existing promotions.

◆ **Advertisement Support.** Complements existing advertisements or provides new advertisements. A coupon is occasionally mailed to the user if a WWW Form has been filled out.

◆ **Service of Existing Goods and Services.** Provides new information about existing products, answers to user questions, and information about upcoming products and education classes.

◆ **Transactions.** Offers order processing of goods and services from a company.

◆ **Subscription Based Use.** Follows the magazine and newspaper trade, usually providing a blanket rate covering issues within a defined time-frame. This simplifies the correlation between use and billing for the use, and produces a steady cash stream.

◆ **Internal WWW sites.** Provide an opportunity to drive new management approaches to match the information flow. Management can appreciate the value of the WWW by their use with existing proprietary data. The WWW provides a tremendous ability to surf and research complex multimedia information. One of the best uses is to surf and mine the existing corporate data.

◆ **Customer/Technical Service.** Maintaining an online help desk enables businesses to provide information about product distribution, future products, and so forth.

◆ **Sponsorship of Events.** Promoting theaters and nonprofit fund-raising events on the commercial sponsor's home page shows a sense of community spirit and goodwill.

Evolution from Traditional Transfers

One of the oldest models for conducting commerce over the Internet is the *Electronic Data Interchange* (EDI). The EDI standard has traditionally required special one-to-one arrangements between trading partners, exchanging electronic business forms such as invoices and purchase orders. The *Internet Engineering Task Force* (IETF) is in the process of releasing a standard way for safely sending business documents over the Internet. The IETF EDI Working Group is finishing work in the EDI X.12 and Editfact standard document using the *Multipurpose Internet Mail Extension* (MIME) extension to electronic mail. MIME is a standard for placing mail attachments, such as word-processing and spreadsheet documents in an RFC 822-type e-mail message. More importantly, MIME contains security provisions, including encryption. X.12 is the U.S. Standard for EDI document formats, whereas Edifact is the United Nations standard.

As companies embrace the Internet for visibility in front of their customers and shareholders, some of the following concerns might arise:

◆ Security

◆ Reliability

◆ Need to keep the costs of the transaction low (especially if it involves verification)

◆ Accountability

Security

Many network managers are loath to entrust their business to a network that historically has been a hacker's playground. Frequent stories of unauthorized access to account records, credit card records, and other privileged information by hackers on the Internet have sensitized both network managers and customers interested in purchasing goods and services on the Internet. Security issues involve at least two areas: securing the company from attack from marauders on the Internet and securing individual transactions.

When any corporation connects to the Internet, the connection provides an opportunity for hackers to explore. This fact should be accepted and security measures be instituted to audit and protect internal networks and company assets. The general solution is to construct a firewall segregating the corporate network and the Internet. This firewall can be instituted by combinations of hardware and software that focuses on protocols, types of traffic traversing the firewall, frequency of both successful and unsuccessful attempts to pass through the firewall, and other methods of assessing Internet traffic. In all cases, a secured audit trail is an essential part of any firewall installation.

As you go from the company's connection to the Internet, you come upon the problem of the unsecured routing of information along the Information Highway. One of the problems of using the Internet is the way data travels through the multiple "hops" along the way. When you send a message along the Internet, you don't know nor can you specify the particular path your message will take. Although this ambiguity can be seen as a feature to maintain a high degree of availability for a virtual connection, it says nothing about the security of the information along this pathway. It would be fairly easy for a savvy user to download messages with a specific e-mail address and read its

unencrypted contents. Once a pathway is opened, it is a safe bet that most of the subsequent traffic for a given transaction will track through this pathway.

Although many of the messages currently on the Internet are open and available to anyone wishing to read them, messages containing sensitive information traversing the Internet should be encrypted and their origins authenticated. If the company's business is multinational, the certain encryption mechanisms, such as the Federal government's *Data Encryption Standard* (DES), must comply with Federal export regulations. In the case of the DES code, exporting an implementation of this encryption algorithm is the legal equivalent of exporting munitions, with commensurate penalties.

Background on Encryption

Two encryption schemes—*secret-key* and *public-key*—are currently in use in the World Wide Web client-server environment. The secret-key encryption cryptography requires both the sender and receiver of a message to know and use the same secret key. The sender uses the key to encrypt the message and the receiver uses the same secret key to decrypt the message. DES is an example of one of these secret-key encryptions.

The generation, transmission, and storage of these keys is called *key management*. Key management is a core element in maintaining the security of this type of cryptosystem because compromising the key will result in the compromise of all the existing encrypted data. If the key is transmitted along with the message, it is fairly easy to decrypt the message. Thus, keys are often transmitted by some other mechanism unrelated to the Internet. In the related world of *Automatic Teller Machines* (ATM), the *Personal Identification Number* (PIN) is the secret-key known by both the user and the bank. You would never dream of writing the PIN number on your ATM card or related receipts for fear that when the ATM card is stolen, the PIN number's effectiveness will be compromised.

Public-key cryptosystems solve the transmission part of key management. Keys are generated in pairs, with a public key and a private key. The user's public key is published, but the private key remains secret. Neither the sender nor receiver need to worry about transmission of the secret key, because all communication involves only the public key. Thus, the security of the communications channel is unimportant. Anyone can send a confidential message using the public key, but the message can only be decrypted by the person knowing the private key.

Public-key encryption is a patented technology that is freely available for non-commercial use. Commerical users of this technology must obtain a license from RSA Data Security, Inc. *RSA* is the name of one of the types of public-key encryption algorithms licensed by this company. Other algorithms employing similar concepts include *Pretty Good Privacy* (PGP) and *Privacy Enhanced Mail* (PEM).

Public-key encryption is used for authenticating digital signatures. Authenticated digital signatures are being investigated by lawmakers in Utah, California, and Washington for recognizing digital signatures as legally binding. The recognition of legally binding signatures is vital for acceptance of contracts and other legal documents between customers and other outside parties. The proposed Utah law also establishes the legal requirements for registering the public keys with an organization located in the state of Utah. Whether this organization will be the U.S. Postal system, banks, or computer security companies remains to be seen.

Security and the World Wide Web

Any company performing transactions on the Internet must provide a secure pipeline for financial transactions between companies selling goods and services on the Internet and the many millions of potential Internet customers. Most of the present schemes translate traditional purchases into the realm of the Internet by encrypting channels for consumers to transmit credit card numbers to merchants and for the merchants to verify transactions with financial institutions.

The secure and authenticated channel connecting the vendor and the consumer provides new opportunities for business, such as the automatic downloading of software updates directly to registered users.

Reliability

Who is responsible for network outages where there is no centralized management or authority? Will the Internet provider take care of connections extending from the marketer's internal network? Who will resolve a network outage that is not controlled by the user's Internet provider, such as to the customer's front door?

The Internet in its present form does not have a central authority to arbitrate and investigate problems. This lack of centralized authority reflects the history

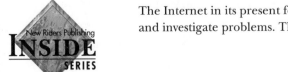

of the Internet and its collegial development environment. Unfortunately, this lack of a central authority has made troubleshooting arising problems potentially difficult to identify, arbitrate, and solve. This lack of a central authority leaves Internet buyers and marketers feeling insecure. A national authority for Internet traffic, such as an agency of the U.S. government, is insufficient to attack this problem. The Internet is an international entity and future problems will be international in scope. Any central Internet organization must have international authority to investigate and resolve international problems. At present, this problem is unresolved.

Paying Up

To truly close a business deal on the Internet, money must be exchanged. Money exchange requires formal arrangements with financial settlement firms, as well as banks. At present, there is no precedent for formal and structured use of the Internet for financial and contractual activities. The ensuing paragraphs explore different methods of money exchange through the World Wide Web. At the time of this writing, most of the schemes are tentative and have not stood the test of time.

Some companies sidestep the issue of money transactions completely by using the Internet only to advertise their wares, establish a corporate image, and possibly test-market a shortened version of their conventional print catalog. Customers can browse an electronic catalog and call an 800-number to place a conventional order. The value of the online catalog could involve up-to-date pricing and special Internet specials, as well as additional marketing of the catalog's contents by multimedia. The traditional order placement enables the company to follow established business practices while exploring the market penetration and demographics of Internet commerce.

Most of the transactions are predicting that commerce on the Internet will occur by encrypting portions of the WWW form containing sensitive account information between the WWW client and the WWW server. This encryption might use the Secure Hypertext Transport Protocol (S-HTTP) or the Secure Sockets Layer (SSL) to discourage the review or tampering of transactions. CommerceNet was the first official foray into business completely on the Internet. This Menlo Park, California operation is an alliance of big-name vendor and user organizations ranging from Apple Computer to Bank of America. One of their central goals is to make the Internet secure for doing business. CommerceNet follows the model of using a secure server so that a customer's credit card and order information is encrypted when he or she is paying for goods and services. A credit card number could then be passed directly to the payment processor over the Internet.

The use of a secure server presumes the customer and marketer are both running WWW clients and servers capable of supporting whatever encryption is used in the transaction. Because a credit card is involved in the transaction, the transaction must be validated prior to its completion, which might raise the cost of the transaction 30–60 cents per transaction. In addition, the customer's identity and the items purchased are recorded by both the merchant and the financial institution processing the order. Although this is no different from traditional practices, some users of the Internet feel this encroaches on the traditional anonymity of the Internet.

Nonetheless, online encryption and validation of credit transactions has been advanced by Microsoft in their announcements with VISA, as well as with Netscape Communications' agreements with MasterCard, Bank of America, and First Data Corporation. Encryption of the financial transaction is only one of the methods proposed. Other methods, such as those proposed by CyberCash and DigiCash, employ the use of tokens of commerce, much like the purchase of postage stamps or traveler's checks.

Alternatives to Credit Card Transactions

One of the methods advanced by CyberCash, of Reston, Virginia, is the use of cryptographic "tokens" to represent currency. These tokens are then used to purchase items on the Internet. The vendor redeems these tokens with CyberCash's server. This model is analogous to traveler's check transactions and might offer more anonymity to the consumer than credit card transactions.

DigiCash, a company based in Amsterdam, also is following the traveler's check model with their "E-cash." Consumers purchase E-cash from banks or automatic teller machines. *E-cash* is encrypted e-mail containing a list of 64-bit numbers. Like the numbers of a traveler's check, each number corresponds to a record at the issuing bank, crediting the consumer with a certain amount of money. A user wishing to purchase an item sends a copy of the E-cash to the merchant, who then forwards the E-cash to the bank for payment. The bank debits the consumer's E-cash balance and pays the merchant. DigiCash's system is anonymous in that the merchant doesn't know the identity of the consumer from the E-cash record, merely that the E-cash is good. This method also has a low per-transaction processing cost. Because there is no verification involved,

DigiCash should cost less than a penny per transaction, compared with 30–60 cents per transaction for conventional credit card transfers.

Accountability

Purchasing items on the Internet is an anonymous business. Although it might be more palatable when the marketer is a known entity, with a familiar physical appearance, there is a potential hesitancy for consumers to do business with a vendor when they cannot validate the vendor's identity or integrity. Consumers might have qualms about handing any negotiable token, encrypted or not, over to a merchant the buyer has never heard of before, who might have been in business for only a short time, and whose physical location might be anywhere on the planet. What recourse does the consumer have if the business transaction goes awry? In other business models, such as answering a classified advertisement where similar questions of vendor identity and integrity might arise, the customer has several avenues of recourse. What recourse is there on the Internet? At present, this problem is unresolved.

Commercial Sites Already on the Web

This section highlights some commercial sites that are on the Web today. As you will see, many diverse businesses want to or have found a need to post their products or product information on the Web. For a more comprehensive list of business sites, see Chapter 29, "Looking at the Best Commercial Sites."

At the heart of the Internet is the physical layer of wires that attach all the computers and networks together. Many telecommunications companies, including MCI, SPRINT, and AT&T, either support these lines now or want to have a major influence on them in the near future. The next few sites illustrate their plans.

AT&T Home Page

OK, you're probably getting tired of hearing Tom Selleck's voice telling you all about the future of "global" communications. Take a look at AT&T's Web page (see fig. 17.1) and discover what "You Will" be doing...someday.

http://www.att.com

Figure 17.1

See what AT&T is promising "You Will" be doing in the future.

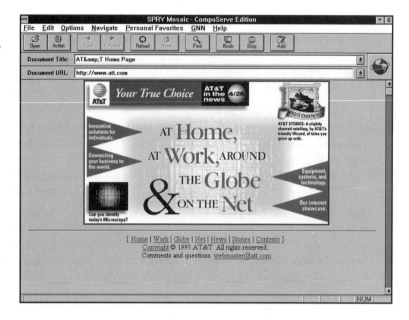

Nippon Telephone and Telegraph Corporation (NTT)

NTT is the largest corporation in the world (see fig. 17.2). See what it can offer you, if anything. This site presents information on doing business in Japan and has a multimedia map of that country.

```
http://www.ntt.jp
```

Pacific Bell Home Page

You can find information about Pacific Bell (see fig. 17.3) and an overview on the Education First program that will interconnect California school and library systems through the Information Highway.

```
http://www.pacbell.com/
```

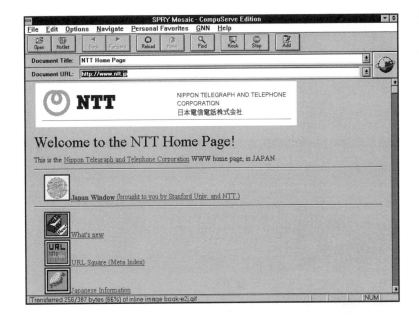

Figure 17.2

Nippon Telephone and Telegraph has huge influence over the way the Information Superhighway is developed.

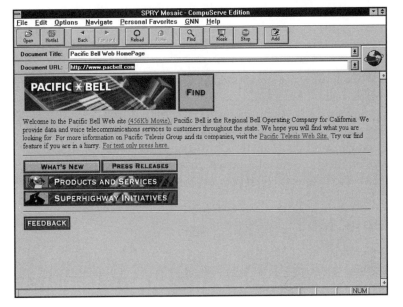

Figure 17.3

Pacific Bell is helping to lead the way to connect school systems to the I-way.

Southwestern Bell Telephone's Digital Drive-In

For something really cool, check out the Southwestern Bell Telephone (St. Louis, MO) Web site (see fig. 17.4). The Digital Drive-In helps educate you about emerging topics in telecommunications technology.

```
http://www.sbc.com/
```

Figure 17.4

Pull into the Digital Drive In for the latest releases on the telecommunications frontier.

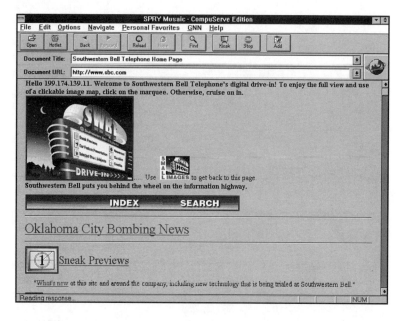

Have you ever turned on those shopping networks on your TV and wondered who actually bought stuff that way? If so, turn your browser to one of the many shopping sites on the Web and ask yourself the same question. These next few sites are intended to help you spend your money ("electronic cash").

The Internet Mall

The Internet Mall (see fig. 17.5), which is a commercial Net enterprise, has dozens of virtual storefronts selling media items, personal items, computer wares, books, and various services.

```
http://www.mecklerweb.com/imall
```

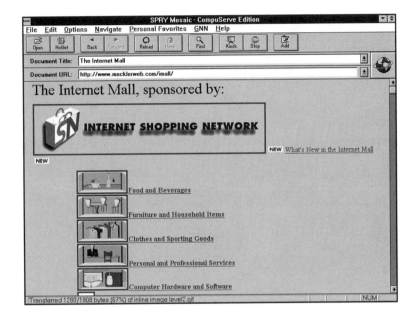

Figure 17.5

Get out your credit card and go shopping.

Internet Shopping Network

So you thought you could escape the Home Shopping Network? Not quite. This site is a subsidiary of the Home Shopping Network and membership is required (see fig. 17.6). If you're inclined to become a member, just call the toll-free number listed to become a member or fax a membership application that can be downloaded to your computer. Why fight the traffic when you can have everything delivered right to your door?

```
http://www.internet.net:80/
```

Downtown Anywhere

Finally, a real cybertown to visit and get the true feeling of being in the "big city" (see fig. 17.7), but without the smog, crime (that you can see), and traffic jams. And without people to bother you. Downtown Anywhere has newsstands, museums, and, of course, shopping. You also can visit a library. Open up some credit here and go have fun. At least no one will notice what you're wearing.

```
http://www.awa.com/
```

Figure 17.6

Become a member and start ordering.

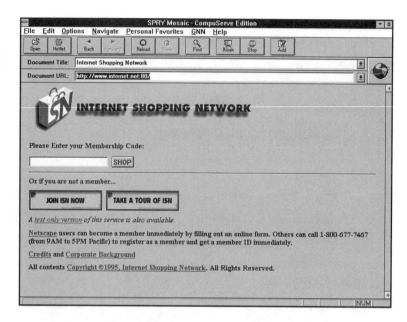

Figure 17.7

Downtown Anywhere is designed to simulate life in a city in cyberspace.

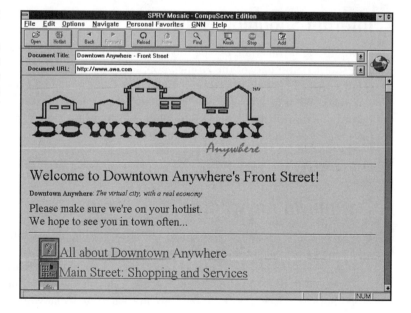

Netropolis

Here's another "city of the future" that has shopping, games, and other niceties to enjoy. I certainly hope you're not a "people-person."

http://www.dash.com

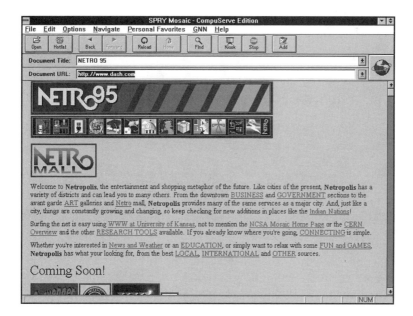

Figure 17.8

Netropolis is another friendly place to visit.

Shopping in Singapore

If your boss doesn't send you to Singapore on a business trip, how are you ever going to get a nice jade carving? Visit the Shopping in Singapore site (see fig. 17.9). That's how. This site enables you to order cameras, oriental art, electronic goods, and other items. You also can see images of the shopping district in case you do get an opportunity to travel there.

http://www.ncb.gov.sg/sog/6.shop.html

Figure 17.9

Shopping in Singapore is just like being there...sort of.

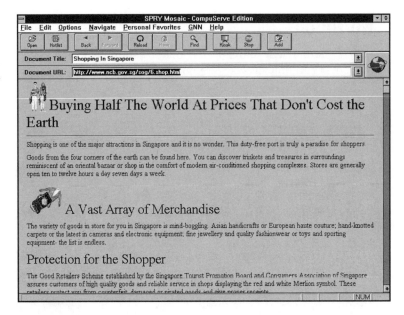

Spencer Gifts

Need a gift for your boss? How about a lava lamp? Spencer Gifts provides you with a catalog for electronic shopping (see fig. 17.10). Now you won't have to be self-conscious looking at all those wacky gifts on the middle aisle.

```
http://www.btg.com/spencers
```

For a more comprehensive list of commercial sites on the Web, see Chapter 29. Also, you might want to pick up a copy of *New Riders' Official World Wide Web Yellow Pages*, which has over 4,500 listings of general Web sites, including commercial sites.

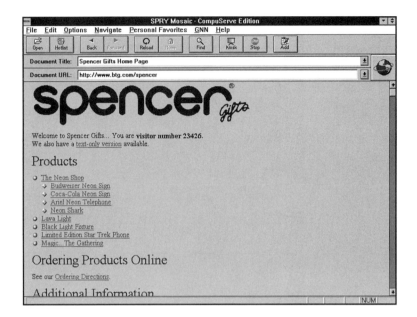

Figure 17.10

Spencer Gifts offers a catalog so that you can order that whoopie cushion or lava lamp from the luxury of your home.

Where Next?

For commerce to occur on the Internet, the customer base must be defined and a degree of trust must be built between the marketer and the customer. Some interactions, such as marketing and public relations, require a low degree of trust. We are already bombarded by unsolicited catalogs and promotional literature. If commercial WWW sites can offer value beyond the traditional catalog, such as information on availability, pricing, multimedia enhancement, and rapid search indexes to find merchandise rapidly, this will go a long way to building trust. Online order entry is a natural extension, but it draws upon the vagaries of the Internet with the issues of security, reliability, and accountability. These issues must be resolved for the Internet market to mature.

Part V

Creating Web Documents

Writing Web Documents

After your server is set up and ready for use, you can create some documents for viewing. As discussed in previous chapters, you can connect to several types of documents through the Web. All types of documents can be accessed using Mosaic, and the information contained in the documents is transferable from one system to another.

The type of document being accessed can be determined by the *Uniform Resource Locator* (URL) that is associated with it. The URL is the address that must be used to access a particular document, and is an important indicator of what sort of information can be found on that page. An explanation of URLs and how they are formatted is provided in the following sections.

Understanding WWW Addressing

Before you create a document, take a look at how Web document addresses are formatted. The following URL, for example, is the address to NCSA's Beginner's Guide to HTML document:

```
http://www.ncsa.uiuc.edu/General/Internet/WWW/HTMLPrimer.html
```

The first part of the URL is called the transfer format. Addresses that begin with `http`, are immediately identifiable as Web documents. `http` means that the document is linked to other documents using the *Hypertext Transmission Protocol.* Other types of documents have different transfer formats, and are explained later in this chapter.

The colon and double slash (://) are standard formatting features and are immediately followed by the name of the machine where the document resides (in this case, `www.ncsa.uiuc.edu`). Following the next slash is the site's directory path (/General/Internet/WWW/). Finally, `HTMLPrimer.html`, is the name of the document itself. The .html extension on the filename indicates that the document uses *Hypertext Markup Language* (see Chapter 1, "Introducing the Web"). In Windows, this extension name is shortened to `htm`.

You address FTP or Gopher sites in much the same way as you do an HTTP site; the only difference is in the initial part of the name and the file name. An FTP site, for instance, might be addressed as follows:

```
ftp://ftp.ncsa.uiuc.edu/Web/ncsa_httpd
```

If the file is a local file on your PC, its address can look like the following example:

```
file:///C:/WWW/HTML/HOME.HTM
```

This file, `HOME.HTM`, is found on the C:\ drive, in the directory `HTML\HOME`.

Exploring Different Connections

What are the differences between HTTP, FTP, Gopher, and other document connections? Quite simply, they are a matter of how a site is set up, and what type of documents are housed at the site.

Many transfer formats are available over the Web. http is the most common, as it is the language of the Web. Several of the other commonly used formats are discussed in the following sections.

HTTP Connections

An HTTP connection, such as that found at http://www.ncsa.uiuc.edu/, is a connection to a site that contains mainly documents set up specifically for the World Wide Web (see figure 18.1). Such a site can contain simple text documents, or more likely, multi-media documents with pictures, sound bites, and animation. HTTP documents often contain direct links to other HTTP documents, both on the same and different sites.

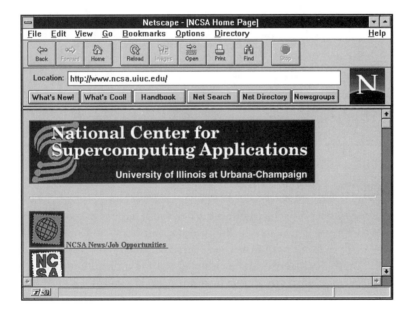

Figure 18.1
An HTTP site.

FTP Connections

An FTP site, such as ftp://ftp.ncsa.uiuc.edu/ (see figure 18.2), is one that contains files that can be downloaded to your local machine by means of the File Transfer Protocol (FTP). An FTP site is a useful source of information because it contains either programs or textual information that are of use on your home machine. Most FTP sites are plain text, with no special formatting or pictures. The sites house files that can be used on your machine, either as executable programs, or documents to be viewed and printed.

Figure 18.2

An FTP site.

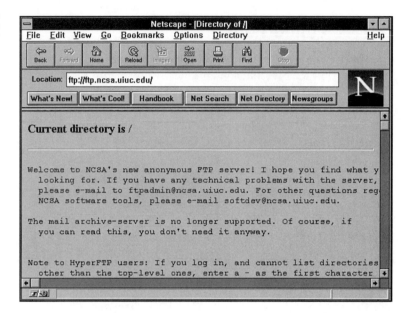

Gopher Connections

A Gopher site, such as gopher://gopher.ncsa.uiuc.edu/ (figure 18.3), contains documents set up for use and search by the Internet Gopher. The Gopher is a program that will go out on the Internet and search for information that fits certain criteria. These documents can be either straight text or multi-media, and can be either viewed through Mosaic or downloaded to your local machine.

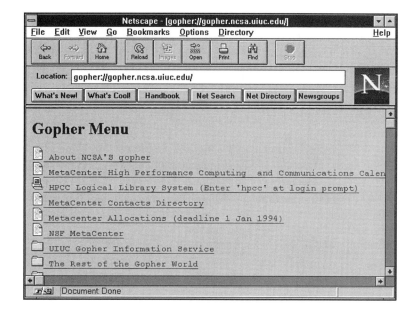

Figure 18.3

A Gopher Site.

What Difference Does It Make?

Since these three types of connections are similar, it might appear that there's no reason for choosing one type over the others. There are, however, pros and cons to each type of site.

You can most easily access an FTP site, because it does not require a high-speed connection or special viewing abilities. Instead, documents have to be brought back to the user's local site for viewing and processing. This is time-consuming, especially when you do not know exactly what information you are looking for. Also, documents at FTP sites are not linked to other documents that might contain similar information or further details.

Gopher sites are more complex than FTP sites because they can be searched for specific subjects and can be linked to other related information. Gopher is a slow, plodding tool, however, and the time-consuming nature of a Gopher search makes the process much less appealing than doing the same search in Mosaic. Another strike against Gopher is that Gopher documents may not always be viewable at once because the documents first have to be downloaded to the local site.

Documents at HTTP sites are immediately accessible to the user and can be viewed before being downloaded. Links to other documents are provided, and it's simple to move from one subject to a different, related one without spending a tedious amount of time finding the exact search term needed. Connections are reasonably quick.

Therefore, in setting up a new site, clearly the way to go is an HTTP connection.

Designing Good Web Pages

Now that you have decided that you indeed want an HTTP site, you can begin creating a document. To do so, you use the Hypertext Markup Language (HTML), which was created specifically for the design of WWW documents. The basic syntax of HTML will be explained in Chapter 19, "Introducing Hypertext Markup Language (HTML)."

The remainder of this chapter is devoted to style points you should keep in mind when designing the page. A good Web page is far more than simply the formatting of text. Reading the following formatting and style hints before starting to design your own page is strongly recommended.

There are many criteria that should be taken into account when designing a Web page. First you must consider what information you want to include on your page, and where you want your page to appear. When those decisions have been made, the next consideration is how you want the information to be presented—do you want to use just text? What about graphics and sound files?

In the following sections, several questions will be answered:

◆ What information should be included?

◆ How much information is too much?

◆ How your information should be formatted?

◆ Should graphics be used?

◆ Should sound bites be used?

◆ How often should the information be changed?

◆ How do you get people to notice your page?

◆ What makes one page better than another?

What Information Should Be Included?

The first decision you encounter regarding the creation of your Web page deals with what information to include. Most people's first inclination is to include all possible information on the chance that someone might want to read it. While this might seem like a good idea, trying to put too much information on one page makes it difficult to navigate, and discourages people from reading.

The best idea is to start with general information, and work toward specific. Information that should be on the home (or starting) page of any Web site or group of pages includes the following:

◆ A reason for this page—what the page is about. It can be a short company statement or an explanation of why you are writing about a particular subject.

◆ The person or company responsible for the page—whose page it is.

◆ A direct link to a mailing screen, or the e-mail address of the maintainer—how to contact the page maintainer. If the page is a company page, including a street address and voice phone lines is a good idea.

◆ The most recent update to a page—last update. Keeping track of this is important for both page maintainers and users. The maintainers need this information in order to determine if the page is out of date. Users need it to determine whether the page's content has changed since they last accessed it.

◆ An outline of other areas that can be accessed from this page—where to go next. Be sure that the descriptions are concise but understandable; if the user doesn't know where you are pointing him, he probably will not go.

How Much Information Is Too Much?

As described previously, the amount of information on a Web page is a good indicator of how well-organized a page (or group of pages) really is. The structure described previously, where each page presents a further level of information than the previous page, is the best one to use.

One important thing to remember about the Web is that you can make several pages link together. By doing so you can cover as much information as you want, without overpowering the user. In a similar vein, don't make any page too long; if the user has to scroll down too many times to view the page, there might be too much information. Try splitting the page into several pieces.

A good rule of thumb for determining whether or not these is too much information of the page, is to look at the amount of white space (space without text or a graphic) that appears on screen. If it is less than 30 percent of the screen, you might have too much information displayed to the viewer at once.

The following are hints on creating good white space:

◆ Use many short paragraphs, rather than one long paragraph. A good guideline is to not let a paragraph run more than three or four lines on screen.

◆ Use headers between subjects. They are larger and have more space around them than paragraphs.

◆ Center graphics on the screen, rather than setting them to one side. When everything is aligned to the left (or right), a page can begin to look off-balance, as if it's tilted to one side.

How Should Your Information Be Formatted?

Two important formatting questions that you should ask yourself are: "What sort of page connecting structure should I use?"; and "what type of text and graphics should I be using?" The first question ties in with the suggestions given about what information to include. The second question includes decisions about white space and the amount of information you want to display to the viewer at one time.

The way pages are interconnected is an integral part of their design. If users cannot move easily from one page to another, they will quickly grow tired of your Web site and go searching for information elsewhere.

Pages should start with general information, and connect to further pages with more information. As an example, let's look at a popular entertainment site, "The Moose's Guide to Northern Exposure" (figure 18.4). On the main screen there is a menu of possible questions the user might have on reaching this screen. Each question links to a new page, with further information on that particular subject. At the end of the main page, shown in figure 18.5, there is information about the list maintainer and when the information was last updated.

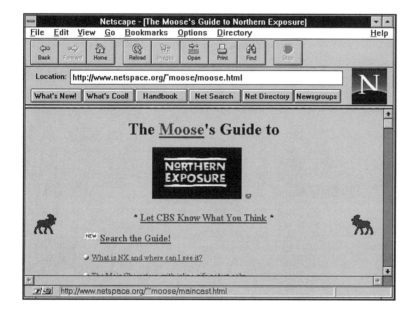

Figure 18.4

The Moose's Guide to Northern Exposure, top of page.

Because this is a page relating to a television series, one obvious link would be to a list of episodes. Looking through the main page, there is indeed an option for an "Episode Listing." Clicking on this item brings us to the page shown in figure 18.6.

This is a further level of detail than was given on the initial screen, but it is still not overpowering. The episode titles and numbers are listed, but not information about each show's content. To get this, you must choose an episode title and click on it. This brings you to the synopsis of that particular episode, as seen in figure 18.7.

This screen is the first screen where an immense amount of detail can be seen. Such a format of increasing depth of information is the best way to organize a group of Web pages, because it allows the users to get as much information as they really want.

Figure 18.5

The Moose's Guide to Northern Exposure, bottom of page.

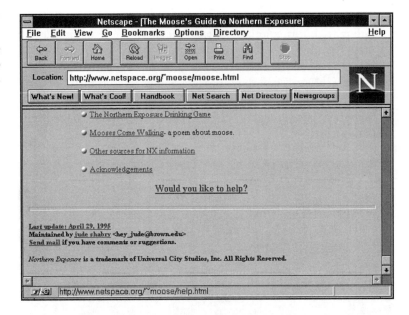

Figure 18.6

A listing of Northern Exposure episodes.

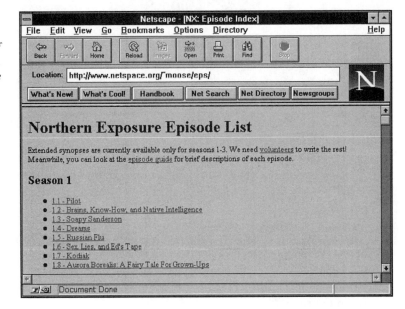

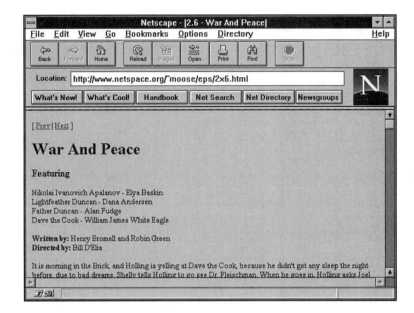

Figure 18.7

The synopsis of a particular episode.

Another feature you should consider, and that is on this set-up, is a list of "related pages." This list, shown in figure 18.8, gives brief descriptions of pages on the Web that are known to relate to the subject of "moose." The user can click on any one of the page references and go to that page to find more moose-related information. While not all of the pages are of highly-useful content (as shown in figure 18.9), they do relate to the subject, and would most likely be of interest to someone who really likes the moose.

What Type of Text and Graphics Should Be Used?

When using a graphically-based display like Netscape, the look of text is almost as important as the actual content of a page. Making a page visually appealing is an important part of the design process. The commands needed to do the formatting are described in Chapter 19, "Introducing Hypertext Markup Language (HTML)." The following are some hints to make a page appealing:

♦ **Color:** This can be found not only in graphics, but by choosing different colors for text.

♦ **White space:** The importance of leaving space around text cannot be emphasized enough. The easier the page is on the eye, the more likely someone will take the time to read it.

Figure 18.8

*A list of moose-
related pages.*

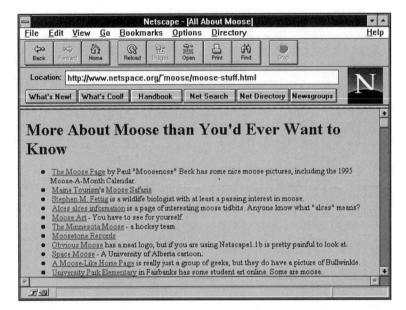

Figure 18.9

*One of the moose
pages, a drawing
by a first grade
student.*

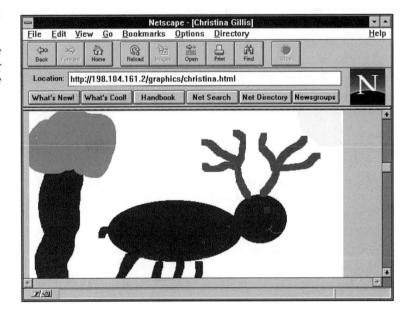

◆ **Graphics:** Graphics can add to your page when used properly. Or they can completely overpower it when used poorly. See the following section for an in-depth discussion of graphics on Web pages.

◆ **Graduated text sizes:** HTML is designed with different sizes of text for different item types. Take advantage of these when designing your page because they make it easier to find information. A larger heading, followed by smaller items, is a good way to split up information.

Should Graphics Be Used?

Graphics can be either the savior or the downfall of a Web page, depending on their use. With an interface such as Mosaic or Netscape, the temptation is to use as many pictures as possible in order to show off the capabilities of the Web. This is not always a good idea. Graphics files are very large, taking up lots of server space that might be needed for other files. More importantly, however, is the fact that graphics files take a long time to load. If a user is working with a low-speed modem (or even a high-speed connection, sometimes), the delay while graphics are being loaded onto the system can be bothersome. If you do plan to use graphics, follow these simple rules:

◆ Only use graphics if they have a reason for being on the page. A picture might be nice, but it might not have anything to do with the information being presented.

◆ Keep the number of pictures used to a minimum. One or two pictures on a page are generally enough.

◆ If possible, create two versions of your page: one with graphics, the other without. This gives the users the option of taking time to view it with graphics, or simply seeing the text if they are working with a slower Internet connection and do not want to spend the time waiting for files to transfer.

Should Sound Bites Be Used?

Sound bites are a nice touch to a page. Hearing the text can often have an effect that simply reading it does not give. Remember, however, that not all users can load sound files. To avoid loss of information, make sure the message in the sound file is also available in textual format.

Sound files also can take up large amounts of disk space, making them tedious to load.

How Often Should a Web Page Be Updated?

The question of how often a Web page should be updated has no concrete answer. Updates depend on the content of the page. A page that describes seminar offerings at a university, for instance (figure 18.10), would need updates once each semester. A page discussing local events might need constant updates as new events are scheduled and added to the calendar (figure 18.11).

Looking at the information once a month is never a bad idea; as often as not, you can discover something that should be changed.

Whatever time frame is used to update the page, be sure to record the most recent update. Being able to look back and see when the page was changed makes it much easier to keep track of how information is being distributed.

Figure 18.10

A seminar schedule for the Johns Hopkins University. This is an item which would be updated once each semester.

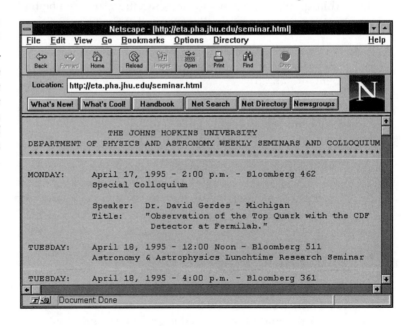

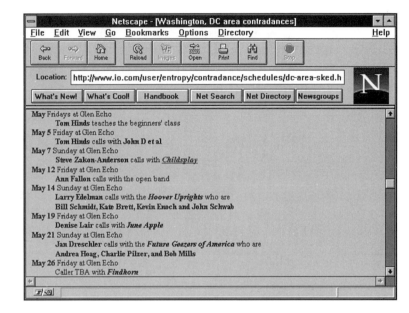

Figure 18.11

A dance schedule. This is an item which would be updated regularly.

How Do You Get People to Notice Your Page?

Even with the best designed page, it is not easy to get people to take a look. The key to getting the page noticed is to let people know it exists. Tell friends about the page, and ask them to provide links on their page that will bring people to yours. If the page is related to a specific subject, mention it on mailing lists and newsgroups about that subject.

Once people know your page is there, they will begin to access it. If the information is interesting or useful, they will tell others about the page, and more people will begin to add it to their hot list.

If your page is really well designed, it may get recognition from one of the many people who keep lists of interesting pages. One such list is the "Cool Site of the Day," shown in figure 18.12. Maintained by Glenn Davis, this site is updated daily with the name and URL of an interesting site. A list of all previous Cool Sites is also kept. Any of these make an excellent place to look for ideas on how to make your own page more appealing.

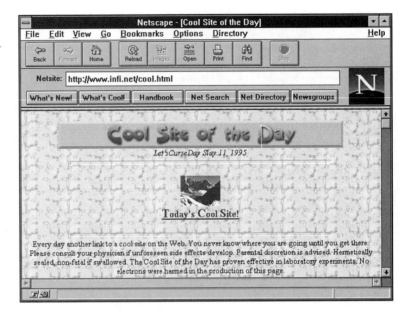

Another place to look for good Web pages that might inspire you is the Whole
Internet Catalog Top 25 list (figure 18.13). Updated weekly, this is a list of the
sites that were accessed most often in the previous seven days.

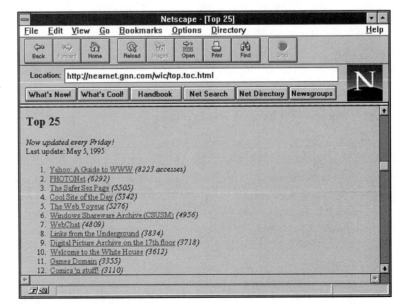

What Makes One Page Better Than Another?

When it comes to Web pages, the term "good" is difficult to define. To some users, it means, "fun to look at." To others, it means, "lots of useful information."

The best pages are a combination of these ideals. Useful information presented in a fun or interesting way is the best way to have a page that will be appreciated and used by others.

A good eye for design is important when creating a Web page. If you aren't certain that your page looks good, ask someone else to take a look.

Above all, don't give up. It may take several tries to make that "perfect" page. Constant rearranging of information is not a bad thing; if nothing else, it will ensure that the people who do look at your site will keep checking to see what has happened.

Introducing Hypertext Markup Language (HTML)

The most common method for creating Web documents is through the use of *Hypertext Markup Language* (HTML). HTML is based on the *Standard Generalized Markup Language* (SGML). Designed as a standard for formatting text documents, mainly in desktop publishing, SGML was approved by the *International Standards Organization* (ISO).

Due to its complexity, SGML was of limited use. The easiest way to use it in document formatting was with commercial products, many of which are quite costly. As a result, users decided that a new language was needed.

Researchers at CERN began working on a new version of SGML. They looked to take SGML's ability to be used on multiple platforms, and to make the language less complex. As a result, they created a language that could use hypertext linking codes in order to format documents. This came to be known as HTML.

HTML was created specifically for use in Web documents. Simply put, HTML is a set of formatting codes added to plain ASCII text in order to set fonts, justifications, and links to other documents.

Basic Format of HTML Commands

HTML is a very complex language with many available commands. Most commands are easy to use, as long as you can remember the correct format. Due to the number of available formatting options, however, not all of HTML will be discussed in this chapter. We will cover enough information to get you started on developing Web pages, but keep in mind that there are many more options that can be followed.

Before you begin to dissect HTML, take a look at what a coded page looks like. Figure 19.1 shows a standard HTML page as viewed with a text editor. Look closely; the actual text is visible between cryptic terms such as <HEAD> and </HEAD>.

Figure 19.1

An HTML page as viewed with a standard text editor.

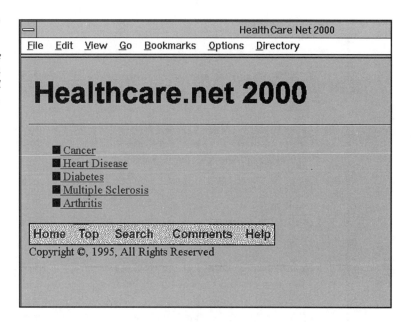

Now take a look at figure 19.2. It's the same page, but viewed through Netscape. The mysterious commands are gone. Instead, there are different size text items, as well as graphics.

Test Form

File	Edit	View	Go	Bookmarks	Options	Directory

Text Fields:
Basic input type: [ ] with default: [This is the default]
Input type: [Text for 20 characte] Password Entry field [ ]
Text Areas:
[ ]
Checkboxes: ☐ Apples ☒ Oranges ☐ Pears
Radioboxes: ◉ Choice 1 ○ Choice 2 ○ Choice 3

One-of-many Option menus... [Third Option ▼] or [First Option ▼]
Submit button (mandantory): [Submit Form] [Reset]

Figure 19.2

The same page, as viewed in Netscape.

If you would like to access some sample HTML pages, refer to the README.TXT file on the *Inside the World Wide Web Bonus CD.*

On the CD

Types of Pages

Before you look at HTML elements, take a look at some of the types of pages that are commonly found on the Web. The most common is a standard, no-frills page such as the one shown in figure 19.2. It contains text, graphics, and links to other Web pages.

The other common document type is a "form" (figure 19.3). As implied by its name, this is a document that allows the user to enter information in specified fields. The information is then transferred to whatever search function or mail program the page designer has specified. Forms are an excellent way to get feedback on the design of a Web site.

Figure 19.3

New Riders WWW Yellow Pages, which uses forms.

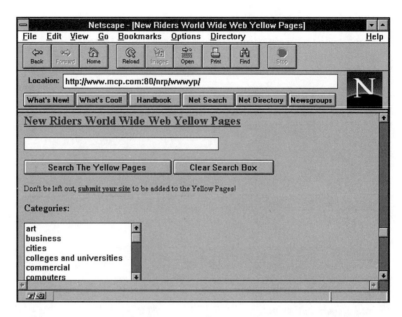

The basic format for an HTML command is open caret, command, close caret. To start an HTML document, for instance, the following is the first line of the document:

<HTML>

The command continues to function until it is closed, or canceled. This is done by negating the command by adding a forward slash before the command name. At the end of the document, the following final line appears:

</HTML>

Figure 19.4 shows the document as viewed with a text editor. It has only a start and end point; there is no text to display with the Web browser.

The previous format is used for all HTML commands, with some minor variations. Some commands, for instance, have specific parameters that need to be declared as part of the command. The general command is <command *parameter* = *value*> where *parameter* is the specific parameter that is being set, and *value* is what that parameter is being set to.

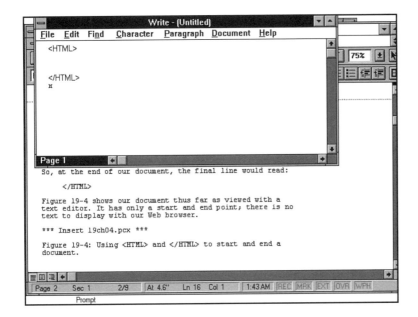

Figure 19.4

*Using <HTML>
and </HTML>
to start and end
a document.*

To end the use of a command with a parameter, only the command needs to be canceled. The syntax is as follows:

</command>

HTML is generally not case sensitive; therefore, the commands <HTML> and <html> are interpreted identically. The only time that case sensitivity is an issue occurs when you use a parameter such as the TYPE parameter for lists. These are described in detail in a later section of this chapter.

Basic Character Formatting

Basic formatting of text, including italics, boldface, and underlining, can be done using the following commands.

◆ **Italics.** To set italics on a word or phrase, use the command <I>.

The text, "The last word in this sentence appears in <I> italics. </I> Now text appears normal again" appears as "The last word in this sentence appears in *italics*. Now text appears normal again."

◆ **Bold Face.** To put a word or phrase in bold face, use the <B> command.

The text, "You can emphasize a word or phrase using <B> bold face </B> characters" appears as "You can emphasize a word or phrase using **bold face** characters."

◆ **Underlined Characters:** To underline characters, use the command <U>.

The text, "<U> This sentence is underlined. </U> This one is not" appears as "<u>This sentence is underlined</u>. This one is not."

Any of the previous formats can be combined, creating text that is in bold face italics, underlined bold face, or any other combination of the three.

The following sections examine how these commands work. Going back to the text editor, you will add commands to make bold, italics, and underlined text, as shown in figure 19.5. When viewed with a Web browser, the code will display as shown in figure 19.6.

Figure 19.5

Using bold, italics, and underline markers.

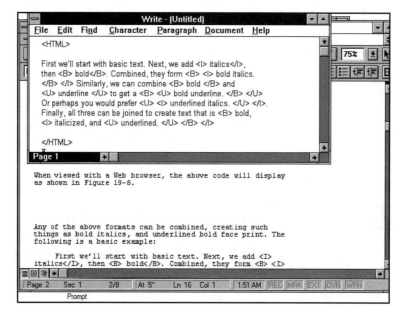

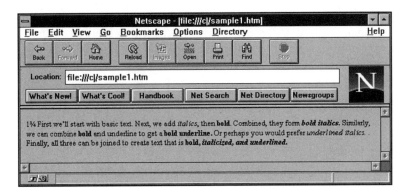

Figure 19.6

*Code viewed
through a
Web browser.*

The Elements of a Web Page

Now that you have the basic text formatting commands, take a look at the commands used to actually format the page. These commands include such information as headings, font sizes, connections to other pages, and actual paragraph types.

Headings

Headings are commands that contain information about a document. This includes the document's title, index functions, and link information.

A document's heading information is found at the beginning of the document, and is set apart by the commands <HEAD> and </HEAD>. The following list explains the parts of the heading in greater detail:

◆ **Index markers:** Index markers are used when a document can be searched using the reader's Web browser. If the document can be read in this manner, the command element <ISINDEX> is used.

◆ **Titles:** The document's title is the text that appears at the top of the browser, in the title bar. The title is denoted by the <TITLE> and </TITLE> commands.

◆ **Base HREF:** An HREF is a header that references a specific URL. The BASE HREF is used to specify the name of the file in which the document is stored. The command is formatted as follows:

<BASE HREF = *URL*>

URL is the full address of the document. This is a useful command when the document is going to be calling other documents, especially if the linked documents are referenced as being at locations relative to the main one. The BASE HREF does not display on-screen; it is merely a place marker.

◆ **Section Headings:** A section heading is the title that appears at the start of a specific division of the text. To divide a document into separate sections, headings of various levels are used. There are six levels of headings, denoted by the use of the tag <H*n*>, where *n* is a number from 1 to 6. All text between headings will appear as a single paragraph, no matter what white space is included, unless specific paragraph breaks are imbedded in the text. Section headings can also appear in the text area of the document.

Take a moment to put together the headings you are now able to use. In the text editor, continue working on your document. This time, however, add a title, several levels of headings, and an HREF linking to another page. The complete code is shown in figure 19.7.

Figure 19.7

Adding Titles, Headings, and HREFs to the document.

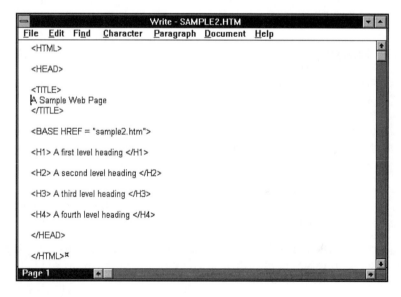

When viewed through Netscape, the previous text displays as shown in figure 19.8.

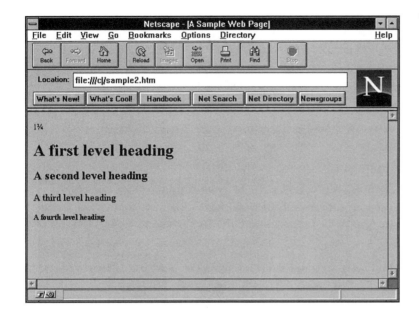

Figure 19.8

Titles, Headings, and HREFs in Netscape.

Body Sections

The body of an HTML document is the main text. This includes all paragraphs, any lists of information, definitions, and forms. The body is where most information resides. This is also where graphics and sound files can be placed.

Paragraphs

To divide paragraphs within a document, use the <P> command. When a <P> is displayed, a paragraph break will appear. The paragraph element is not affected by white space or carriage returns. The following provides an example:

```
The information in this document will be divided into

several paragraphs.

The paragraphs will not break where there is white

space in the original HTML document, but instead,

where a paragraph marker is used. <P> Here we begin a

second paragraph.
```

The previous text would display as follows:

```
The information in this document will be divided into several
paragraphs. The paragraphs will not break where there is white space in
the original HTML document, but instead, where a paragraph marker is
used.

Here we begin a second paragraph.
```

Lists

There are several types of lists that can be created using HTML commands. To create a list, start with one of the following list element commands. Each item on the list should be preceded with the command <LI>, which stands for list item.

◆ **Ordered List:** An ordered list is one that is numbered. The command used is <OL>. An ordered list would be coded as follows:

```
<OL>
<LI> Element One
<LI> Element Two
<LI> Element Three
</OL>
```

◆ **Unnumbered List:** An unnumbered list is not numbered; instead, each item is preceded by a bullet. The command to start an unnumbered list is <UL>. An unnumbered list would be coded as follows:

```
<UL>
<LI> Element One
<LI> Element Two
<LI> Element Three
</UL>
```

◆ **Descriptive List:** A descriptive list, signified by the command <DL>, is based on using a title followed by an indented description or explanation of the item(s) on the list. The title is specified by the tag <DT>, and the description by <DD>.

```
<DL>
<DT> Creating Lists
<DD> To create a list using HTML, there are several options.
```

<DT> Descriptive Lists
<DD> The first type we will discuss is the
Descriptive List.

</DL>

Take these list types, and add them to the HTML document. Each list will be displayed below a heading explaining what type of list is shown. Each list is also preceded by a paragraph describing it, formatted using the <P> element. The code to do this is shown in figure 19.9.

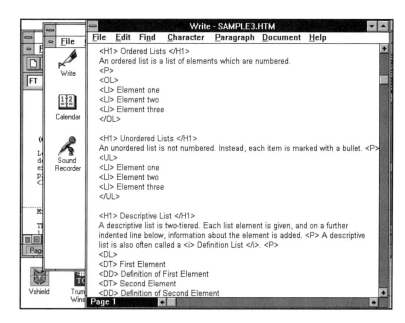

Figure 19.9

HTML code for lists.

The formatted text is shown in the following two screens. Figure 19.10 shows the ordered and unordered lists, and figure 19.11 shows the descriptive list.

Special Text Formatting

There are many ways to format text beyond these initial samples. Following are several of the more commonly used elements.

Figure 19.10

The Ordered and Unordered lists.

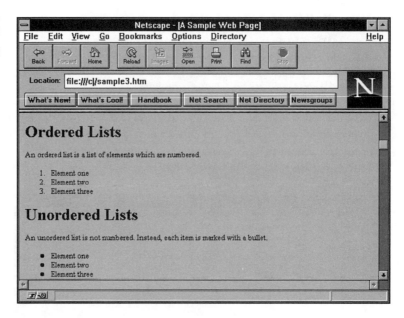

Figure 19.11

The Descriptive list.

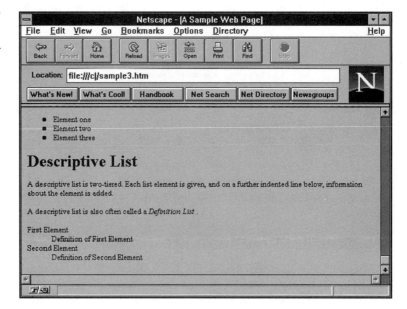

◆ **Preformatted Text (PRE):** Preformatted text has been imported directly from another program, and should be displayed exactly as shown in the editor. This is done using the commands <PRE> and </PRE>. Preformatted text can include embedded tags, such as links to other documents.

◆ **<XMP>:** <XMP> is another tag used for preformatted text. It is more limited than <PRE>, however, because it does not allow embedded tags.

◆ **Quotes:** When quoting a piece of text from another document, set it apart using the <BLOCKQUOTE> command.

◆ **Adding comments:** When writing an HTML document, it is often useful to put in comments, or reminders, that tell you what you did, or when you made a change. Often, these commands do not actually want to be seen by the user. To place text in your HTML document that you can later view while editing the document, but which will not be seen by the user, use the following format:

<! *mycomment* >

where *mycomment* is the note to yourself.

◆ **Address:** The <ADDRESS> command formats the text that follows it into italics. It is especially useful for e-mail addresses and physical addresses. Text beginning with <ADDRESS> and ending with </ADDRESS> will be set apart on a separate line.

◆ **Samples:** To display samples in a monospaced font in the exact format it is typed on the HTML page (that is, end of lines where they were placed in the original document), use the command <SAMP>. This is useful for displaying code segments.

◆ **Drawing lines across the page:** <HR> allows the user to draw a horizontal line across a page. This can be used to separate sections of a document, or to set off a specific area of the document.

Creating Links to Other Documents

Now that you can do the basic formatting for your Web page, look at how to connect it to other pages, or to move users directly to other parts of the document. This is done using links, or anchors. An anchor is denoted by the element <A>.

Linking to Another Document

A link to another document is created using the following syntax:

>   <A HREF=*URL*>*anchorpoint*</A>

where *URL* is the address of the document, and *anchorpoint* is the text that displays on-screen. The text will display on-screen, and, if the user clicks on it, lead to another Web page.

Links within a Document

Sometimes, if a document is long, it is useful to have links that move the user to a specified part of the document. This is done using the following command set:

>   <A NAME=*anchor_name*>*anchorpoint*</A>

>   <A HREF=*anchor_name*>*anchorpoint*</A>

The NAME variable is used to define the target location, and HREF is the link that connects to that particular location. *anchor_name* is the exact location that will be reached, and *anchorpoint* is the on screen text that, when clicked, will send the user to that point in the document.

Linking to a Target Point in Another Document

It is possible to combine the two previos actions and send the user to a specified point in another document. This is done using the following command:

>   <A HREF=*URL#anchor_name*>*anchorpoint*</A>

URL is the address of the new document, and *anchor_point* is the exact spot in the document that is accessed. *Anchorpoint* is the text that displays on screen.

Anchors and Links in Action

Go back to the HTML document and implement some of these links. First, create a link that simply takes you back to the List document, shown in

figure 19.10. The second link will take you directly to the Descriptive list, as shown in figure 19.11.

The code used to create these links is shown in figure 19.12. The screen as it will appear to the viewer is shown in figure 19.13. As can be seen, the links are highlighted in a different text color, as well as underlined. Pointing at one of them causes the URL to which it is linked to display in the lower left corner of the screen. Clicking on the anchor will move you to that document, or, in the latter case, to that particular place in the document.

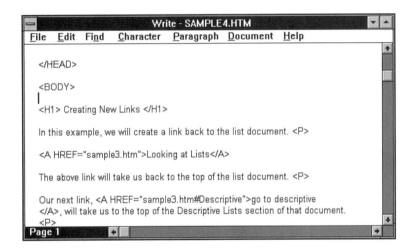

Figure 19.12

HTML code used to create links.

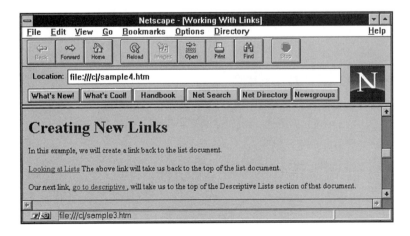

Figure 19.13

Viewing HTML links with Netscape.

Using Forms

Forms allow the user to enter information directly on a Web page, and then have it transmitted to a server. This server will process the information and forward it either to the page owner or, in the case of a search engine, to the search mechanism.

Starting a Form

A form is denoted by the element <form>. A document can have several forms within it, and each can perform different tasks or ask for different information.

The <form> element has two qualifiers, action and method. Action is the URL of the program that will process the completed form. Forms are generally processed by programs written with CGI, the Common Gateway Interface. If the form should be sent to a registration site to register the user, for instance, action would be the address of the registration program.

Method is the way in which the information will be moved from the client to the program that will process it. The options are get or post. Post is recommended, since it is accepted by more applications.

Using these qualifiers, a <form> descriptor would be as follows:

```
<form action=cgistuff\format method=post>
```

In this case, the form will be posted to a program called format, located in the cgistuff directory.

Inputting the Information

Once the form is defined, input fields can be added. These fields allow the user to enter information which is then assigned to a specified variable name. This is done using the <input> element.

<input> has the following options: type, name, and size.

Type

Several types of data can be used for the variable. They are shown as follows:

- ◆ **type="text"** is characters entered on the screen. They will display as the user enters them.

- ◆ **type="password"** is also a character string. However, it will not display
  on screen.

- ◆ **type="checkbox"** is a box that can be selected. It translates to a yes or no when the information is formatted, depending on whether the box was selected or not.

- ◆ **type="radio"** allows the user to select one of several radio fields. A radio field is one that is associated with a small button. Only one button can be selected at a time.

- ◆ **type="reset"** will, when selected, reset the entire form to its default values.

- ◆ **type="submit"** is a button that causes the form to be submitted to the server for processing.

Name

The name qualifier is a string of text that identifies the input associated with a specific type. This is for identification purposes during processing, and does not appear on screen.

Size

The size qualifier determines the maximum size allowed for text or password input.

Selecting from a Field

One way that a user can enter information on a form is by selecting an item from a list. This is done using the <select> element. This command works in conjunction with the <option> element.

<select> has several arguments:

- ◆ **name="textstring"** is the identifier used to keep track of the selected option.

- **size=n** is the number of <option> items which will display at one time.

- **multiple** is an option which, when present, allows the user to select more than one item from the list.

The <option> tag is used to list the items available in a selection list. One option can be specified as the default selection, using the <option selected> tag.

A list of options would be coded as shown below:

```
<select>

<option> choice a

<option> choice b

<option> choice c

<option selected> choice d

</select>
```

In this example, four items would be listed. By default, choice d would be highlighted.

Entering a Text Area

The tag <textarea> allows the user to enter text freely within a certain area of the screen. This can be used to get user comments on your page. The <textarea> field has three qualifiers:

- **name="textstring"** is the variable name associated with the entered text.

- **rows=n** specifies how many rows of text the user will be allowed to enter.

- **cols=n** specifies how many characters can be entered per line.

Building a Form

Now that you have several data entry formats, you can create a form. In your form, you will ask users to enter their account name and password, in order to access another computer. They will also have to choose which computer to

access. When this information has been entered, the user will be able to either submit it for processing, or reset the screen to its default setting, canceling the process.

The code used to do this is shown in figure 19.14. Because it is complex, however, you will be walked through it here.

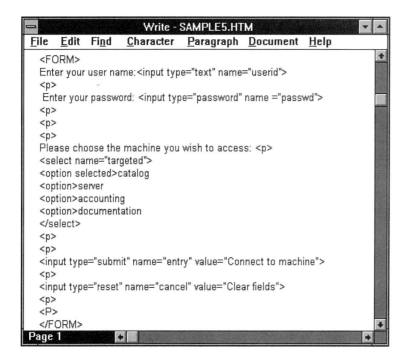

Figure 19.14

Using HTML code to create a form.

First, ask for the user name and password. This is done with the following two commands:

    Enter your user name:<input type=text name=userid>

    <p>

    Enter your password: <input type=password name=passwd>

    <p>

By using the password type on the second entry, you increase the user's security, since his password will not display on-screen.

Now, ask the user to choose a machine. This will be done using the <select> fields, with each possible target machine as an <option>.

Please choose the machine you wish to access: <p>

<select name="targeted">

<option selected>catalog

<option>server

<option>accounting

<option>documentation

</select>

By default, the user will go to the machine named catalog; however, clicking on any of the other options will change this and allow him to go to that machine instead.

Finally, you need buttons that allow the user to either submit this login request or clear the screen entirely:

<input type="submit" name="entry" value="Connect to machine">

<p>

<input type="reset" name="cancel" value="Clear fields">

Now you're ready. The formatted screen will display as shown in figure 19.15.

Figure 19.15

A form to access another computer.

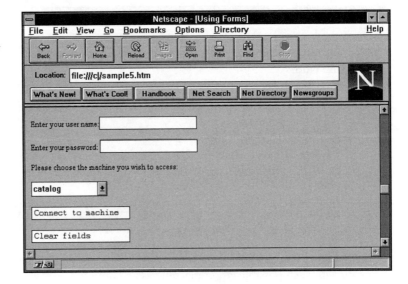

Beyond Basic Text Formats

HTML allows more than just basic text formatting. Other commands are available that are used to link pages together, as well as to include graphics, audio, and video links to a document. See Chapter 20, "Writing HTML Documents," for more information on creating an HTML document.

Beyond HTML: The Netscape Extensions

As the Web becomes more complex, and more formatting options are needed, various groups create additions to the HTML language. The Netscape extensions are among the most established and easiest to use. They include both new commands and additional qualifiers that can be used on the basic HTML commands described previously.

The Netscape extensions will only work with the Netscape viewer. They are item tags and qualifiers that can be used with basic HTML commands such as those listed previously, in order to add extra touches that personalize a page and make it more interesting.

When the page is viewed with Netscape, the tags will add these new text formats. If the page is viewed with a different browser, however, the user will only see the standardized version of the graphic.

Drawing Lines Across a Page

<HR>, a basic tag for HTML, enables the user to draw a horizontal line across a page. This can be used to separate sections of a document, or to set off a specific area of the document. To this command, Netscape has added four new tags that can be used to change the way this line is displayed.

Use the SIZE modifier to change the thickness of the line.

There are several reasons for using different width lines. They can be used to set off certain areas of a document, for instance. Lines of different widths are shown in figure 19.16.

Figure 19.16

*Different line
widths as viewed
in Netscape.*

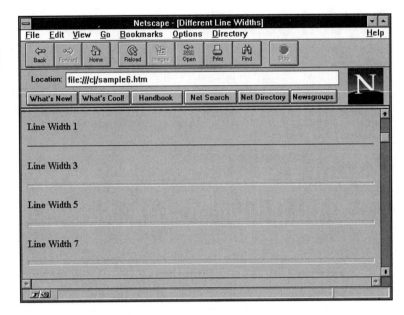

<HR SIZE=*number*>

Number is used to describe how thick the line should be.

By default, a horizontal line is as wide as the page. To change this, the WIDTH
parameter has been added. Users can declare the width of a line either in
number of pixels, or as a relative width, based on the width of the entire page
(see fig. 19.17).

<HR WIDTH=*number/percent*>

Number is a number of pixels, or *percent* is the percent of the entire width of
the page.

Netscape has added the ALIGN command, which enables users to decide
whether the line will align with the right side, left side, or center of the page.

<HR ALIGN=left/right/center>

Finally, the shading of the line can now be changed. Normally it is gray, but it
can be changed to a solid black line.

<HR NOSHADE>

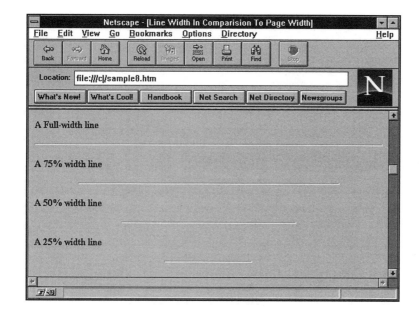

Figure 19.17

Relative widths as viewed in Netscape.

Changing Bullets on a List

By default, a bulleted list uses a solid disc for its marker. It is possible to change this marker to either a circle or a square. This is done using the type parameter.

<UL TYPE=disc/circle/square>

Disc, circle, and square are the possible shapes for the bullet (see fig. 19.18).

Formatted Numbers on a Numbered List

In a numbered list, numbers are generally done in Arabic. Using the Netscape extensions, however, you can have a list that uses various TYPE tags to order using Roman numerals or alphabetical letters, in either capital or lower case.

- ◆ **<TYPE=A>** gives the list ordered with capital letters (A, B, C, and so on).

- ◆ **<TYPE=a>** gives the list ordered with lower case letters (a, b, c, and so on).

Figure 19.18

*Different bullet
types in Netscape.*

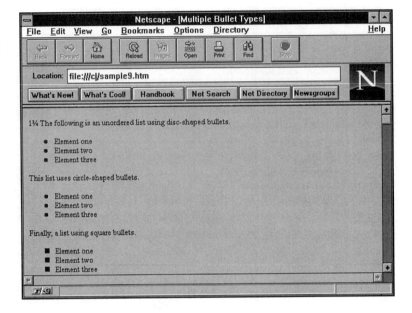

◆ **<TYPE=I>** will give the list in upper case Roman numerals (I, II, III, IV,
and so on).

◆ **<TYPE=i>** will give the list in lower case Roman numerals (i, ii, iii, iv,
and so on).

◆ **<TYPE=1>** will default back to Arabic numerals.

To start a list with other than item one, the START tag has been added. It is
formatted as <START=*n*> where *n* is the number that the list will start with.
START should always be defined using an Arabic number; however, any TYPE
tags will be applied when the list is actually printed. So if <TYPE=i> has already
been set, and you declare <START=6>, the first item on the list will be numbered vi. This is shown in figure 19.19.

New Elements

New elements are constantly being added as people discover formatting
styles that they would like to be able to use. These elements only work
under Netscape currently, but may be added to a future standard (non-
platform specific) version of HTML. As with other Netscape-specific elements and element qualifiers, these commands will be ignored by any viewer
but Netscape.

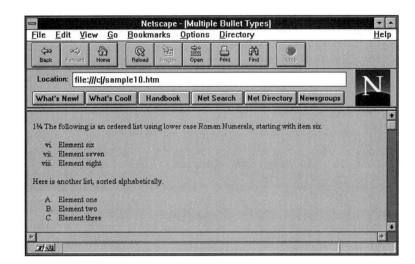

Figure 19.19

*Changing the
number types in
an ordered list.*

The following sections describe these new elements.

No Breaks

To force a word to stay on one line, without any sort of hyphenation and break, use the no break option. This is set using the command <NOBR>. It is especially useful when specifying, for instance, the address for a site, where any misplaced hyphens could make the address invalid.

Word Breaks

If, within a NOBR section, there is a specific place where you want to allow a word to break, use the <WBR> command. Note that <WBR> does not force a word break to occur; it only gives Netscape the knowledge that if a break is needed there, it can be made. Figure 19.20 shows code using <NOBR> and <WBR>. Figure 19.21 shows the code as it is viewed with Netscape.

Changing Font Sizes

With the Netscape extensions, it is now possible to change both the basic size for all text on a page, and the size of specific characters.

Font sizes are set with values ranging from 1 to 7. The default size is 3. To set the default font size for a page, use the following command

<BASEFONT SIZE=*value*>

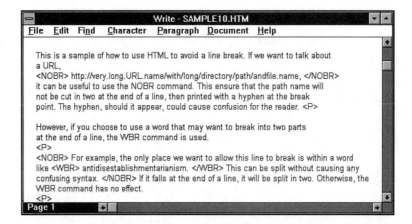

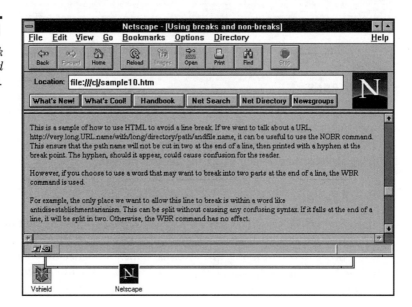

To change the font size for a specific area of a document, use the following command

<FONT SIZE=*value*>

When changing the font size, not only can a specific value be used (the value between 1 and 7, as described), but a font size can also be changed in relation to the baseline size, using a plus or minus sign before the value. For example, if

the baseline font size is 3, you can specify <FONT SIZE=+2> to increase the font size to 5, or two above the baseline level.

Changing the size of a font is useful for many reasons. Making certain words in a sentence larger in relation to the rest of the sentence will make them more noticeable to the reader. This could be done, for instance, with a link name in order to be certain the user notices it.

Another time that using relative sizing could be useful is when giving information on a subject. The more important paragraph could be done in a larger size than the less important one.

In figure 19.22, the HTML commands to change font size within a document are being used to alter the sizes of certain words and phrases. Figure 19.23 shows this text as viewed through Netscape.

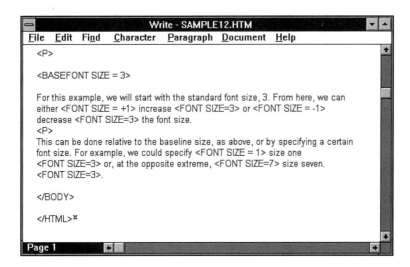

Figure 19.22

HTML code to alter font sizes.

Centering Text

The <CENTER> command enables you to center text between the left and right margins of the page, rather than left align it. All lines of text between <CENTER> and </CENTER> will be formatted in this manner.

The <CENTER> command is to text what <HR ALIGN=CENTER> is to lines. Figure 19.24 shows examples of both lines and text in different alignments.

Figure 19.23

Variable font sizes as viewed with Netscape.

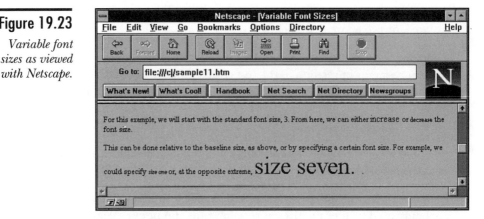

Figure 19.24

Aligning text and lines to the left, right, and center.

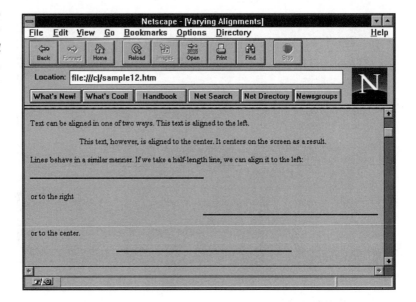

Writing HTML Documents

World Wide Web documents are plain ASCII text files with embedded ASCII formatting instructions in a language called Hypertext Markup Language (HTML). HTML is the common language for interchange of hypertext between the World Wide Web (WWW) client and server. Much of the fabric of the WWW is contructed from HTML. As opposed to other languages, markup languages are run through an interpreter to produce the desired output. A "regular" language often is compiled, which is altogether different.

Typically, a WWW client requests a file from the WWW server, interprets the received HTML, and displays the material on the user's desktop. HTML can represent hypertext news, mail, documentation, hypermedia, menus of options, database results, structured documents with inline graphics, and hypertext views of existing bodies of information. HTML is a non-proprietary document tagging language based on the International Standard 8879:1986 Standard Generalized Markup Language (SGML). HTML is portable from one computer platform to another and is designed to be simple enough to be easily produced by people and programs, but also adheres to the larger SGML standard. With the appropriate "DTD" flag set for HTML, this SGML subset can be parsed by an SGML parser.

Understanding HTML

Although HTML is usually associated with the WWW server, HTML does not have to be used with one. HTML can be used in hypertext e-mail (as a format for MIME mail), news, and anywhere basic hypertext is needed. HTML includes simple structure elements, including several levels of headings, bulleted and numbered lists, menus and hypertext links. This chapter focuses on HTML in the WWW client-server environment.

HTML is currently undergoing revision to HTML+. This newer standard includes features for more sophisticated online documentation, form templates for the entry of data by users, tables, and mathematical formulas.

Note Several WWW clients support HTML constructs that are proprietary to the vendor. The Netscape browser, for example, supports the <center>... </center> construct for entering text. When on a WWW client that does not support this construct finds this syntax, it is ignored. Thus, the behavior of HTML documents using the proprietary elements becomes dependent on the browser in use.

Although HTML is expected to be a language of communication flowing over the network, there is no requirement that the files actually be stored in HTML. Servers may store files in other formats, or in variations of HTML that include extra information of local interest only, and then generate HTML on the fly for each request. Some of these other formats are Acrobat's PDF format, Microsoft Word format, WordPerfect, and so forth. In the case of Acrobat and MS Word, free viewers are available to act as helper programs to the WWW clients.

Simple Markup and Interpretation

HTML is a simple markup language for ASCII text for interpretation by WWW clients. HTML describes both the structure and organization of a document. Although it suggests an appropriate presentation of the document, the WWW

client ultimately resolves the appearance of the document when it interprets the HTML document for the user's screen. In HTML documents, tags define the start and end of headings, lists, character highlighting, links, and many other elements. Most HTML elements are defined by a start tag, giving the element name and attributes, followed by the content, followed by an end tag. Start tags are defined by the < and > symbols, and end tags are defined by </ and >. Different tags can be embedded to combine type styles. Some common HTML tags are listed in table 20.2 at the end of the chapter. The tags are case-independent, though placing the tag in all capitals makes them easier to find when casually browsing the HTML-marked text.

Although special toolkits for creating HTML are evolving, HTML can be created using any text editor. A simple HTML document might appear as follows:

```
<HEAD>
<TITLE>This is the title of this document</TITLE></HEAD>
<BODY>
<H1>This is the first header message</H1>
This is the first paragraph of this document<P>
We will now generate an ordered list:<OL>
        <LI>Item one
        <LI>Item two
</OL><BR>
And now an unordered list:<UL>
      <LI>First item which has an <i>italics</i> item
      <LI>Second item
</UL><p>
This is an offset list:<DL>
        <DD>This is the first offset item
        <DD>This is the second offset item
        <DL>This is not offset, but is still an item
        <DD>This is the third <b>boldface</b> offset item<OL>
              <LI>This is doubly indented item one
              <LI>This is the second item
        </OL>
</DL>
This is the less-than sign: &lt; and this is the &gt; sign. You can put
up fractions, such as 3/4 with &#178;, asterisks with &#42; and even
superscripts, like area squared&#178;.
```

```
The copyright marker appears as follows: &#169;.
</BODY>

This is the first header message
This is the first paragraph of this document

We will now generate an ordered list:
        1. Item one
        2. Item two
And now an unordered list:
        ·  First item which has an italics item
        ·  Second item

This is an offset list:
        This is the first offset item
        This is the second offset item
This is not offset, but is still an item
        This is the third boldface offset item
                1. This is doubly indented item one
                2. This is the second item


This is the less-than sign: < and this is the > sign. You can put up
fractions, such as 3/4 with ³/₄ , asterisks with * and even superscripts,
like area squared².

The copyright marker appears as follows: ©.
```

The HTML document is divided into two pieces: a HEAD segment and a BODY segment. The HEAD segment contains information that identifies the file to the WWW client and may be used for indexing the document on the WWW server. The contents of the <TITLE>…</TITLE> tags may appear at the top of the WWW client window. The <BODY>…</BODY> portion of the document contains the bulk of the HTML that will be interpreted and formatted by the WWW client for the user's screen.

Reviewing this example, the first line on the user's screen will be This is the first header message in large, boldfaced letters. The <H1> tag refers to the largest header tag. This large header line is followed by a sentence and ends with a <P> or a linebreak. A blank line appears. Although most HTML tags come in pairs, beginning and ending some special behavior, tags such as <P>,

, and <HR> are singular.

The next line brings you to lists. The first list is an ordered list, started by the <OL>. The WWW client interprets the list items preceded by numbers. The list is concluded with the closing tag </OL>. The unordered list follows in much the same fashion, starting with <UL>, placing the list items with <LI>, and finishing the list with </UL>. The use of the definition list follows in the same fashion, except the <LI> used in the lists is replaced with either a <DD> or a <DL>. The <DD> is useful for indenting elements without assigning a number (for <OL>...</OL>) or a bullet item (for <UL>...</UL>). The <DL> item is similar to <DD>, but is not offset. In this example, another ordered list is started inside the <DL>...</DL> construct, demonstrating the hierarchy of HTML tags.

Tip

> Because it is a frequent mistake for the beginning HTML author to neglect the trailing tag (for example, </DL>), it is often worthwhile to offset nested HTML tags with tabs. The HTML author can troubleshoot by drawing brackets connecting the start of the tag (<UL>) with the end tag (</UL>). This is particularly useful when there are several nested tags extending over many lines of HTML.

Italics and boldface features are used in this example. Text-based WWW clients can use underlining to handle HTML elements they do not support. On WWW clients that are not capable of rendering certain features, such as italics for the Lynx WWW client, these features are usually rendered with underlining.

The end of this example demonstrates the ability to display numeric and special graphic entities. Just as the ability to render italics isn't certain on all WWW clients, not all WWW clients can handle numeric and special graphic entities. Special designations for the < and > symbols are required because the WWW client will attempt to interpret these characters as an HTML tag. Many of the accent marks follow the paradigm of &, followed by an intelligible comment, such as &atilde stands for the tilde character (~), &ccedil stands for a cedilla (ç), and so on. The ISO 8859/1 8-bit single-byte coded graphic character set is also used for other items, using the structure &# followed by a number. In the example, the fraction 3/4, an asterisk, a superscript number two, and the copyright symbol are shown.

A simple way to learn some of the tricks of HTML is to use the WWW client

(Netscape, Mosaic, and so forth) to browse other WWW sites on the Internet. When you stumble across an intriguing HTML page, activate the VIEW SOURCE function of your WWW client to look directly at the remote HTML. You might be able to download the remote HTML for further study.

Although the majority of HTML tags are commands for text formatting, the exceptions include hypertext links, insertion of image graphics within text or inline graphics, and forms. We begin by examining the hypertext links.

Hypertext Links

Hypertext links point to other resources, either within the same document, to external documents, or to other resources. Every hypertext link has a reference (HREF) and an anchor. A hypertext link comes in two pieces: the pointer itself and the element of the hypertext key that appears to the user. The entire hypertext link is bounded by the "<A...>" and </A>" characters. For example:

```
This is a
<A HREF="http://www.cancercare.org/lb-cr.html">
picture of Loren Buhle</A>.
```

This would appear on the client as:

```
This is a picture of Loren Buhle.
```

Where the italicized phrase above will probably be offset in blue on the client screen, denoting the hypertext key. In the HTML, the <A HREF=...>...</A> is the pointer. When the user activates the hypertext key ("picture of Loren Buhle"), the WWW client follows the URL specified.

This URL might point within the WWW server, in which case the http://.../ is not necessary, or might point to some other location on the Internet. For purposes of portability, it is a good idea to state the absolute URL address. Certainly the relative address is shorter and simpler, whether pointing within the same directory or pointing to another directory in the same server (for example, using the ~ character for a relative indication of the file position), but this is particularly dangerous when the directory structure changes over time. What was once a pointer to an HTML file in the neighboring directory will break when the directory structure is rearranged. Avoiding relative pointers whenever possible is useful in the long run when attempting to maintain thousands of "old" HTML files.

Hypertext links can point to specific locations within an HTML document. A table of contents at the top of document, for example, will point to anchors within the same document. In another example, a lead document might point to a specific location in a second document—the second document, for example, might be a glossary of terms. If there is no internal anchor (or the internal anchor cannot be found), the link may point to the top of the second document. If the internal anchor within the second document is found, the WWW client positions the text at the location of the embedded anchor.

Internal links can be demonstrated using a simple Table of Contents example, like the following:

```
<H3>Table of Contents</H3><OL>
    <LI><A HREF="#intro">Introduction</A>
    <LI><A HREF="#chap_1">Chapter 1</A>
    <LI>This chapter is missing
    <LI><A HREF="otherbook.html#chap_2">Chapter 2</A>
</OL>


<A NAME="intro"><H4>Introduction</H4></A>
...some text....
<A NAME="chap_1"><H4>Chapter 1 - Title of Whatever</H4></A>
```

The WWW client would interpret this HTML as follows, where the italicized terms would be the hypertext, which usually appears to the user as blue text:

```
Table of Contents

    1. Introduction
    2. Chapter 1
    3. This chapter is missing
    4. Chapter 2

Introduction
...some text...
Chapter 1 - Title of Whatever
```

This example shows a level 3 header, followed by an ordered list. The first item of the list is the Introduction. The '<A HREF="#...">', with nothing to the left of the #, means this is an internal link. If this key is activated, it will seek the anchor "intro" somewhere within the document. This anchor is shown by the <A NAME="intro">...</A> farther down in the example. The WWW client will position the word Introduction at the top of the user's screen. The same behavior occurs with the link to Chapter 1. The choice of the anchor word, either "intro" and "chap_1," is at the HTML author's discretion, but should be unique within the document. It is a good idea to standardize the names of the anchors. The hypertext key shown to the user, "Chapter 1," should be similar to the title of the anchoring target, but need not be exact.

Uniform Resource Locators (URLs)

As you've learned in previous chapters of this book, Uniform Resource Locators (URLs) are used to specify the location and method of interacting with any Internet resource. The URL was introduced earlier in the discussion of the absolute hypertext pointer. The exact form of the URL depends upon whether the remote resource is a WWW server, FTP, Telnet, Gopher or other resource. WWW clients can handle all these types of remote resources. For WWW clients, an URL begins with the name of the server you want to access: http://www.cancercare.org/ followed by the location within the resource within this resource: faq/cancer_faq.hml to form the following address:

```
http://www.cancercare.org/faq/cancer_faq.html
```

Because any URL can be used, HTML has the flexibility to reference many types of data. A URL can point to more hypertext, an image, a sound file, an MPEG animation sequence, an Adobe PDF file, or even a Microsoft Word document. Table 20.1 shows some of the conventional types data encountered on the WWW. Remember that not every browser will be able to handle all these file types. Although a PC or Macintosh WWW client might be able to handle a Microsoft Word document, a Unix or VMS workstation running an X-windows-based WWW client cannot handle this document. Likewise, a computer without sound capacity will not be able to handle a sound file.

TABLE 20.1
Defining Resource Data Types

Extension	Congruous Application
HTML	Hypertext markup file
HTM	Hypertext markup file for DOS
XBM	Bitmapped graphics
AU	Audio (raw) format

Extension	Congruous Application
JPEG	Graphics format
MPEG	Animation/movie format
AIFF	Audio format
PDF	Adobe PDF format

An URL can also specify one of many types of protocols. To create a link to download a file instead of viewing it, for instance, use an URL specifying the file transfer protocol (FTP) instead of Hypertext Transport Protocol (HTTP), like in the following example:

```
ftp://www.cancercare.org/lb_cv.html
```

Pointing the URL to a developing HTML file on your local disk is a simple way to develop your own HTML without a WWW server. Aiming your WWW client at the following will allow the user to work on this file on their local computer:

```
file:///c:\onco\file1.htm
```

Images

Images are displayed within an HTML document using the following construct:

```
<IMG ALT="picture of a tree" ALIGN=MIDDLE SRC="tree.gif">
```

The <IMG...> construct is one of the few HTML tags that does not require an end tag. The two optional arguments are [ALT=] and [ALIGN]. [ALT=] is an alternate text label, and is handy for WWW clients that cannot display images (Lynx, for example). If you want to hide the image completely from the text-based WWW client, use ALT="", which is useful when the image is purely decorative. [ALIGN=] positions the text immediately following the image, with possibilities of TOP, MIDDLE, and BOTTOM.

Images can serve as hypertext links to other documents or other images. In the first example, the link points to another document. In the second example, the link points to a sound file. The third example shows a link pointing to a larger version of the GIF file.

```
<A HREF="tree_document.html">
        <IMG ALT="tree icon" SRC="tree.gif"></A>
```

```
<A HREF="dog_bark.au"><IMG ALT="dog barking" SRC="dog.gif"></A>

<A HREF="large_image.gif"><IMG SRC="small_image.gif"></A>
```

The purpose behind having a small postage-stamp version of the image is to minimize the time a user takes to download a page. Large graphics demand a lot of the network's bandwidth and take time. If the user's interest is piqued by the small image, they can activate the hypertext link and see the larger image.

Transparent Background Images

Icons on an HTML page often look better if their background color matches the browser window, making them appear to float in the document. Because it is impossible to determine the color of the WWW client window offhand for an exact match, one method is to convert the standard GIF87 image to GIF89a format and set the background color to transparent. With a transparent background, WWW clients that support transparency will show throught the browser's background. This task can be performed using either of the following steps.

1. Take the image and convert it to a GIF image. If the image does not have a single background color, take a painting or photo-retouching package and make the background one color level. The goal is to make the background of the image a single value that does not occur anywhere else in the image. If this value also appears elsewhere in the picture, these points will disappear when displayed on a transparency-supporting WWW client. Determine what this colormap entry is and set this entry to a light gray (Red=207, Green=207, Blue=207) to support WWW clients that cannot handle transparency. This is merely a guess, presuming the user has not changed the default background of many of the early WWW clients.

2. If the image is not in GIF89a format, it needs to be converted. Most GIF pictures are in GIF87a, which does not support transparency. A C program called *giftrans* (available from: http://ftp.rz.uni-karlsruhe.de/pub/net/www/tools/giftrans.c, as well as MS-DOS versions) converts GIF87a images to GIF89a, letting the user specify which entry in the colormap is to be set transparent. If this colormap entry is called *index,* and the input GIF87a file is called pict.gif, use the following command:

   ```
   giftrans -t index  pict.gif > pict1.gif
   ```

The file pict1.gif is a GIF89a and would have the transparent bit set for the *index* colormap value. Keep in mind many programs do not explicity support GIF89a and will strip the transparency bit off when processing the file. Thus,

the last step of image production should be setting the transparency option. It is not a good idea to make the transparent GIF file a hypertext key because the blue hypertext coding will outline the now invisible outline of the icon, appearing quite strange!

Image Maps

Hypertext links can also be portions of images. Using a mouse-based WWW client such as Mosaic or Netscape, the user clicks on different parts of a mapped image to activate different hypertext links. An image map is indicated in an HTML document by using the following reference:

```
<A HREF="http://www.domain.com/cgi-bin/imagemap/picture">
        <IMG SRC="picture.gif" ISMAP></A>
```

Note the addition of the ISMAP keyword to the <IMG...> construct and the slight difference in the HREF portion. This hypertext reference executes a common gateway interface (CGI) program called *imagemap* with an argument 'picture'. This presumes the WWW server is called www.domain.com and has a directory of executables in a directory cgi-bin. This imagemap program returns the URL corresponding to the x,y-coordinates of the point where the GIF image was clicked, based on the map file reference by the argument 'picture'.

Image maps with icons or buttons for certain subjects or departments are a nice touch to HTML pages. Zooming can be added by linking an area of an existing image with a separate file containing a small area with greater detail.

Using Forms and CGI Scripts

Forms offer the WWW client the ability to send information back to the user. Forms open up the possibility for user interaction, such as filling out a survey or ordering a pizza. A number of gadgets are available to build a form. A user can enter text, select items from a prespecified list, check boxes, then submit the information to the server. A program on the server interprets the data and acts upon it appropriately, either by returning information in hypertext form, downloading a file, interacting with legacy software and serving the output of legacy software in HTML format, or electronically communicating your number and credit card numbers to a business for next-day delivery. All forms begin with the following construct:

```
<FORM METHOD=POST ACTION="cgi-bin/program">...</FORM>
```

> Remember that the information exchanged in the forms often is in plain, open text—readable by anyone. Credit card information should be encrypted, as discussed in the chapter on commerce on the WWW.

The ACTION is an URL pointing to a program to process the order once the SUBMIT button is pressed. Although the default action was METHOD=GET, this should always be replaced with METHOD=POST, especially when large amounts of data will be transferred.

The following example demonstrates how the <INPUT…>, <TEXTAREA…>, and <SELECT…> tags and their attributes are used to create a form. It is important always to have the <INPUT…> attribute in all forms as follows:

```
<INPUT TYPE=SUBMIT VALUE="Continue">
```

This button causes data entered into the form to be transmitted to the server program specified by the <FORM ACTION…> attribute. The VALUE attribute merely defines the label of the button, such as Continue, Submit, or OK.

The form inputs an undesignated length of the input string. The first input string is blank and the second has a presupplied default (in the HTML). The second line of input shows text input limited to twenty characters. The Password Entry field, although not hiding the characters as the user types them in, does permit the FORM to accept only certain characters. Thus, a password might be required to contain at least five characters and less than nine characters. The third line is a freeform text box for open-ended text submission. The check boxes and radio boxes are prearranged menus, currently having preset defaults of "oranges" and "Choice 1." The One-of-many Option menus presents two slightly different types of pull-down menus. The first menu has two simultaneous default entries, while the second only uses one default. The form concludes with the required Submit Form button and the Reset button. The Submit Form button sends the output to the CGI program for further processing. The Reset button clears all the fields. The source code for this form appears in Table 27.3.

Common Gateway Interface (CGI)

When the form is submitted, the data contained in the form must be decoded.

Just like the x,y coordinates from image maps are passed to the imagemap program, the data from the FORM is passed to a program for processing. Programs that use data submitted from an HTML form must conform to the Common Gateway Interface (CGI) specification. These programs can be written in C/C++, Perl, sh, ksh, or csh. The CGI specification is stated in `http://hoohoo.ncsa.uiuc.edu/cgi/interface.html`.

On a Unix-based WWW server, the CGI program will receive the FORM through the standard input *(stdin)*, presuming the METHOD=POST attribute is used. The output produced by the CGI program goes to the standard output *(stdout)* to be sent back to the WWW client. If the METHOD=GET is used, all the data is encoded in the environmental variable QUERY_STRING. Environmental variables have a limited length, making them unsuitable for large strings of data.

Integration with Legacy Software

The discussion of FORMs and the CGI interface mentioned the use of HTML and the WWW to interact with legacy systems. The FORM can be viewed as the point of data entry. The CGI interface parses the incoming data and can resubmit the FORM if there is insufficient information present. If the CGI program determines sufficient and internally consistent information is present, the CGI program can construct an input script for existing legacy software. The FORM, for example, can provide input to the corporate database software. Perhaps the input is received by the database as an SQL query produced by the CGI program. The database retrieves the requested information and can output this information through an HTML report writer to the standard output (*stdout* for Unix systems). The WWW client conveys this HTML output directly to the user's screen. The critical components of this strategy are the ability to script the input to the legacy software and the ability to produce HTML, either directly with an HTML report writer or by a subsequent program to convert the output text file to HTML.

HTML can leverage both the existing legacy systems and the portable, graphical-user interface of the WWW clients (Netscape and Mosaic, for example) to rapidly generate a high quality corporate interface to existing systems!

Good Practices

After generating and reading thousands of HTML pages, some general practices become clear. In this section, these general concepts are divided into two sections: logistical planning to manage a large WWW server, and safe-to-produce, easily navigated HTML documents. These practices will aid in the evolution of the WWW server, making it easy to manage and grow in the future.

Good Practices: Document Management

Any resource containing a multitude of interlinked documents of different origins and vintages must have a management system. This management system ranges from the realm of managing the document's pedigree, obsolescence, and revision history, copyright issues, author, reviewers and review status, as well as establishing a standardized look and feel of all documents on the resource. One way of coding the author is to include the following in the <TITLE>...</TITLE> portion of each document:

Note

```
<HEAD>
<TITLE>This is the Title of the Document</TITLE>
<LINK REV="made" HREF="mailto:buhle@www.healthcare.net">
</HEAD>
```

> *Vintage* refers to the version of the document—how old it is. *Pedigree* refers to the origin of the document—who wrote it. *Review status* gives one indication of where and when it was reviewed. Also, the author may give more information beyond the source, such as who wrote the document from the EPA.

As part of good document management, it is important to avoid merely replicating the conventional wall of books in a library in an electronic form. You need to organize the HTML documents so information can be found rapidly. If you look at the conventional library, a user seeking information from a library often spends a substantial portion of time leafing through promising books, searching for just the right knowledge. The WWW brings powerful tools of both casual browsing and focused research to the electronic library, allowing the user to rapidly traverse resources throughout the Internet. If the user must leaf through one menu after another, however, haven't you just replicated the shelves of library books? The answer is somewhere on these shelves, all he or she has to do is find it! In other words, in an analogy of menus being shelves of books, a user confronted with many menus is just as lost as looking at a wall of shelves; looking at the titles of the books (or shelf entries) isn't very helpful.

Neither are extensive menus. Although a fascinating problem, the resolution to this problem is beyond the scope of this chapter.

In addition, HTML documents are often read out of sequence, sometimes called a nonlinear fashion. The user might be reading one document, then activate a hypertext link that places them into the middle of another document. The user never saw the beginning of this second document and thus never saw its Introduction. The author of the second document must take this into account. Indeed, in the author's OncoLink experience, most readers preferred to have large files (approximately 30 printed pages) subdivided into small modules. Because the order the modules were read was unclear, each module has to be designed to be self-standing. Hypertext links tie together each module with its neighbor to provide a cohesive train of thought.

At the technical level of maintaining a resource of thousands of HTML files, a system for verifying the integrity of all the hypertext links—internal links within a document, internal links to all of the documents in a particular WWW server, as well as the integrity of the hypertexts links to resources throughout the Internet—must be maintained. Even as simple an action as moving HTML files from one directory to another can invalidate hypertext links pointing to these document throughout the Internet. Methodology for verifying and correcting these links when changes occur must be at hand.

Good Practices: Device Independence

HTML is meant to produce portable documents. Conventional HTML language does not contain information about the fonts or paragraph shapes and spacing as it is displayed on the screen. It is a fantastic advantage to know the document will be rendered successfully on whatever platform is used for viewing, including a plain text terminal. It is also important to realize that although the general appearance of HTML files is similar on WWW clients, different WWW clients use different spacing and fonts. It is important to use the structuring elements, such as headers and lists, in the way they were intended. If the rendering isn't exactly right on a particular client, don't try to fix it by using inappropriate elements or forcing extra spaces with empty elements. Doing so could be interpreted differently by other WWW clients and look very strange. To establish a uniform client appearance, the WWW client often can be tailored. Consider the following rules of thumb concerning device independence:

◆ Use the heading levels in order, starting with level 1 at the top of the document, followed by level 2 headings, followed by groups of level 3 headings within level 2 headings, and so on.

◆ Don't pad with extra spaces or lines in HTML text. These extra spaces are generally ignored unless they are within the <PRE>...</PRE> context.

Stop Don't make references within the body of your HTML text to aspects of particular browsers. Don't say "click here" because this will not make much sense if the WWW client doesn't have a mouse. Likewise, don't depend on use of an ISMAP as the sole method for picking menu choices when the client might be a line-oriented browser.

HTML has no way of knowing whether the WWW client's window is sufficiently wide to display two inline images with intervening image captions. Indeed, the caption to the second image might be wrapped around to reside next to an image on the subsequent line and cause the user to read the wrong caption with the wrong image.

Common Mistakes

Errors in HTML result in documents that are either unreadable or may be readable, but are not WWW client or device independent. The behavior of error handling in HTML is undefined, so certain WWW clients may perform something close to what is intended, while other browsers might dump the text following the mistake and result in a truncated document. There is no guarantee what a WWW client will do when encountering an HTML error.

Common Mistakes: Paragraph Breaks

The misuse of the <P> is one of the most prevalent causes of ugly HTML renderings. Although the <P> tag is singular, it is often used to signal an end-of-paragraph, rather than a paragraph break. In most cases, this is not important because a paragraph break and an end-of-paragraph marker are very similar. The <P> should not, however, be placed before or after the headings <H1>...</H1>, horizontal lines <HR>, or immediately before or after a list element (<LI>, <DT>, <DL>) of any type. These elements already imply paragraph breaks. Often the additional <P> is added to force whitespace between the bodies of text. This behavior is only supported on some WWW clients.

Common Mistakes: Character and Reference Errors

A character reference and an entity reference are ways to represent information that might be interpreted as an HTML tag. To print the <P> character in HTML, it is necessary to write `&lt;P&gt;` in raw HTML. There are other examples of this functionality at the beginning of this chapter. The most common error in the use of references is to forget the trailing semicolon. No additional spaces are needed before or after the entity/character reference.

Common Mistakes: Directory Reference Errors

It is possible to generate an URL that requests an index of all the HTML files in a WWW server directory. This directory might be in the pregenerated index file, such as the index.html file in the referenced directory, but if not must construct an HTML document containing all the documents in the directory. To specifically request such an index, it is important to include the trailing slash in the URL. Thus, to obtain an index of the heart-disease directory, use the following URL:

```
http://www.healthcare.net/heart-disease/
```

Common Mistakes: Incomplete Domain Names

HTML documents are sometimes coded within the perspective of the local network environment. Shortcuts and local names might appear in the URL to ease the effort of stating the official Internet name of the resource. Thus, the local name *www* might be used because everyone within the HTML authoring group knows this refers to an specific machine. Outside users, however, cannot resolve the name *www* to a specific name. The local aliases are not defined on the Internet. If the fully qualified name had been used, for example *www.healthcare.net* (presuming this name exists in the domain nameserver or DNS), anyone can access this resource.

Common Mistakes: Missing Quotes in the Tags

With fairly long URLs, it is common to forget the starting or ending quotation mark. For example, the following URL:

```
<A HREF="www.cancercare.org/faq/cancer_faq.html">
```

would sometimes come out as such, where the ending quotation mark is forgotten:

```
<A HREF="http://www.cancercare.org/faq/cancer_faq.html>
```

The behavior of WWW clients varies. Some display the proper link but don't allow the user to follow it; other WWW clients attempt to find the next quote mark in the HTML (in this example, text beyond cancer_faq.html>) and swallow up large portions of the subsequent HTML.

Common Mistakes: Missing End Tags

This is the most common error of both novice and experienced HTML authors. All HTML elements, except the elements such as <P> and <HR>, have beginning and ending tags. This is shown in table 20.2, part b. There is a start tag, some content which might be text or other nested HTML elements, and an end tag. The end tag always has a slash </...> in it. A common mistake is either to forget the end tag completely or forget the slash in the end tag. Forgetting an end tag results in undefined behavior by the WWW client.

TABLE 20.2
Common HTML Tags
(a) Header Tags

<H1>...</H1>	Most prominent header
<H2>...</H2>	Second level header
<H3>...</H3>	Third level header
<H4>...</H4>	Fourth level header
<H5>...</H5>	Fifth level header
<H6>...</H6>	Least prominent header

(b) General Formatting

<TITLE>...</TITLE>	Specify document title

(b) General Formatting

<HEAD>...</HEAD>	Header of HTML document
<BODY>...</BODY>	Contents of HTML document
<p>	Force a new paragraph
 	Forces a line break
<HR>	Horizontal line
<PRE>...</PRE>	Preformatted text
<LISTING>...</LISTING>	Example computer listing
<BLOCKQUOTE>...</BLOCKQUOTE>	Quoted text

(c) Logical Styles

<EM>...</EM>	Emphasis, often rendered in italics
<STRONG>...</STRONG>	Stronger emphasis, often boldface
<CODE>...</CODE>	Display an HTML directive, usually monospaced
<SAMP>...</SAMP>	Include sample output, monospaced
<KDB>...</KDB>	Display a keyboard key
<VAR>...</VAR>	Define a variable, often italics
<DFN>...</DFN>	Display a definition
<CITE>...</CITE>	Display a citation

(d) Physical Styles

<B>...</B>	Bold font
<I>...</I>	Italics

TABLE 20.2, CONTINUED
Common HTML Tags

<U>...</U>	Underline
<TT>...</TT>	Typewrite font
<STRIKE>...</STRIKE>	Strikethrough

(e) Lists

<UL>...</UL>	Unordered list
<OL>...</OL>	Ordered list
<MENU>...</MENU>	Menu list
<DIR>...</DIR>	Directory list
<LI>	Item on a list
<DL>...</DL>	Definition list/glossary
<DT>	Term to be defined (not indented)
<DD>	Definition of term (indented)

(f) Miscellaneous

<! — TEXT ——>	Comment in the HTML source
<LINK HREF="URL",[REV=],[REL=]>	Define a relationship between documents
<ADDRESS>...</ADDRESS>	Address information
<ISINDEX>	Specify index file
<NEXTID>	Set a variable value
<BASE>	Path of a current file

(g) Hyperlinks or Anchors

<A NAME="target">...</A>	Defines a target for a jump
<A HREF="#...>...</A>	Link to a target in the same file
<A HREF="URL">...</A>	Link to a target in separate file

(h) Graphics

<IMG SRC="URL",ALT="text",[ALIGN=][SMAP=]>	Include a graphic image

(i) Forms

<FORM [ACTION=][METHOD=>...</FORM>	Define a form
<INPUT [TYPE=text|password|checkbox|radio|submit|reset], [NAME=],[VALUE=],[CHECKED],[SIZE=],[MAXLENGTH=]	Create a gadget
<SELECT [NAME=],[SIZE=],[MUTIPLE]>...</SELECT>	Define a list of objects
<OPTION [SELECTED]> Define values within a <SELECT> <TEXTAREA NAME="...",[ROWS=],[COLS=]>...</TEXTAREA>	Define a text area

(j) Obsolete Features

<HP>...</HP>	Highlighted Phrase
<PLAINTEXT>	Everything after this tag is treated as plaintext
<XMP>...</XMP>	Example listing
<LISTING>...</LISTING>	Listing element

Note

These tags might not be implemented on all WWW clients.

The following is the source code for the FORM.

```
<HEAD>
<TITLE>Test Form</TITLE>
</HEAD><BODY>
<FORM ACTION="http://hoohoo.ncsa.uiuc.edu/htbin-post/post-query"
METHOD="POST"><HR>
Text Fields: <BR>
Basic input type: <INPUT TYPE="text" NAME="Entry1" VALUE="">
with default:
<INPUT TYPE="text" NAME="Entry2" VALUE="This is the default
text...."><BR>
Input type: <INPUT TYPE="text" NAME="Entry3" SIZE=20
VALUE="Text for 20 characters">
Password Entry field
<INPUT TYPE="password" NAME="password" SIZE=8 MAXLENGTH=5 VALUE=""><BR>
Text Areas:<BR><TEXTAREA NAME="textarea" COLS=60 ROWS=3></TEXTAREA>
<BR>
Checkboxes:
<INPUT TYPE="checkbox" NAME="Checkbox1" VALUE="TRUE" > Apples
<INPUT TYPE="checkbox" NAME="Checkbox2" VALUE="TRUE" CHECKED> Oranges
<INPUT TYPE="checkbox" NAME="Checkbox3" VALUE="FALSE" > Pears<BR>
Radioboxes:
<INPUT TYPE="radio" NAME="radio1" VALUE="TRUE" CHECKED> Choice 1
<INPUT TYPE="radio" NAME="radio2" VALUE="TRUE" > Choice 2
<INPUT TYPE="radio" NAME="radio3" VALUE="TRUE" > Choice 3
<p>
One-of-many Option menus...
<SELECT NAME="First-name">
<OPTION>First Option</OPTION>
<OPTION>Second Option</OPTION>
<OPTION SELECTED>Third Option</OPTION>
<OPTION>Fourth Option</OPTION>
<OPTION>Fifth Option</OPTION>
</SELECT>
 or
<SELECT NAME="Last-name">
<OPTION SELECTED>First Option</OPTION>
<OPTION>Second Option</OPTION>
<OPTION SELECTED>Third Option</OPTION>
<OPTION>Fourth Option</OPTION>
<OPTION>Fifth Option</OPTION>
</SELECT>
<BR>
Submit button (mandantory): <INPUT TYPE="submit" VALUE="Submit Form">
<INPUT TYPE="reset" VALUES="Clear Values">
</FORM>
</BODY>
```

Using Adobe Acrobat on the Web

The World Wide Web is attractive to us because it lets us communicate electronically, and enables us to include graphics, photographs, and different font sizes. What makes the Web successful is that it enables you to view and exchange this information no matter what computer system you use, and no matter what configuration you have. The Web was born and evolved into what it is today because of user demand. Not many pieces of software out there today can claim as much participation and contribution from their users.

While the World Wide Web was being formed and becoming popular, the software company Adobe was working hard on a product that would provide the same benefits as the Web. Adobe was a single company using its existing technology to move into the paperless world. Since Adobe was the company that created PostScript, the main technology behind most document publishing today, no one knew better than they how to create file formats and documents that retained large amounts of graphical information. Most of today's magazines, books, and newspapers are created with PostScript.

Influences of Adobe on the PC Industry

An interesting challenge that Adobe addressed is transferring these documents from computer system to computer system. Simply moving a file from one PC to another is easy. Moving files from PCs to Macs, Unix, or mainframe computers, however, is challenging due to the computers' inability to understand various file formats. And the challenge gets even greater when different networks are used and different computer platforms are hooked up to the same computer equipment. If a file does not consist of text alone, computers simply cannot understand it without translation. Also, most laser printers and some fax machines, which are computers too, have PostScript built into them.

Realizing these challenges, Adobe based PostScript on the simplest form of computer communications—a language that all computers, networks, and printers understand—plain text. Translating graphics-rich documents into simple text made moving documents from one computer platform to another problem-free.

Because of this simplicity, the PostScript document format became one of the more popular document formats on the Internet. PostScript enabled people to create technical papers including illustrations, designs for network topologies, software and hardware manuals, even photographs, and distribute them with no concern about who would retrieve these documents. If you can download a PostScript document, you certainly can send it to your local laser printer and print it out.

Most documents these days have the PS extension. They also might have the EPS extension for computers that might require three letters. Creating your own documents enables you to have columns, different font sizes, and illustrations within your documents. It is the answer for any document requiring more than simple text presentation.

 Note   With the introduction of TrueType fonts from Microsoft with Windows 3.1, however, many users have access to "nice-looking" documents without the expense of PostScript.

The problem in using PostScript was that although people could find and transfer documents without being concerned about technical issues, they still had to print them in order to read their contents. This obviously could be a waste of time and money. Internet users would rather communicate completely online. If it's on paper, it's offline.

This was a concern not only to Internet users, but also to many people in the industry. The question was, how do we create documents that have the portability of PostScript and the ease of use of a single document format that anyone can open and view onscreen? For Adobe, the question was answered rather simply. They created Adobe Acrobat. *Adobe Acrobat* is a piece of software that not only helps us read documents, it helps us create documents that can be read by anyone. And to top it off, Acrobat files can be read onscreen. Adobe took Acrobat one step further by enabling users to print Acrobat documents with the same degree of quality with which they were created.

Acrobat is based on PostScript. Some might say that it is the next version of PostScript—one that is not dependent on paper. Therefore, Acrobat is an effective aid to information exchange among Internet users.

Acrobat files are plain text like those of its predecessor, PostScript. They are basically void of anything that would make transferring a document from one computer system to another a hard job. Just as impressive is that you can use whatever tools you want to create Acrobat files. Any program that you have been using to create pages for print would be able to create files that can be distributed and read with Acrobat. Adobe has included tools for creating and reading Acrobat files on PC, Mac, and Unix computer systems. This is what is appealing about Acrobat to most people on the Internet.

When documents are graphics-intensive, they tend to take up a huge amount of room. This also was taken into consideration when Acrobat was created. All text and graphics within an Acrobat file are compressed, so most Acrobat files tend to be small. The average size is about 50 KB to 1 MB. Uncompressed these files would range from 100 KB to 10 MG. One of the greater challenges of using the Internet to transfer documents is keeping the documents small enough to enable people who have modems to download files without trouble. Acrobat files do this very well.

Finding Acrobat

Acrobat has several different applications. Acrobat Reader is the most popular application. Acrobat Reader is available online, and sometimes included in software products like Adobe Photoshop. Other pieces of Acrobat software are Acrobat Exchange, which enables an Acrobat file to be edited, and Acrobat Distiller, which simply converts Postscript files into Acrobat files.

Working with Acrobat files is easy. As a matter of fact, Adobe provides Acrobat Reader free of charge. Acrobat Reader opens and reads Acrobat files. Acrobat Reader can be found on CompuServe, America Online, and many other places on the Internet. The following is Adobe's FTP site address:

`ftp.adobe.com`

Note   The *Inside the World Wide Web* bonus disc contains a copy of the Acrobat Reader 2.0. See the Appendix, "Using the Inside the World Wide Web CD-ROM," for information on installing the Reader on your system. For updated information and files, be sure to visit Adobe's FTP and Web site frequently.

Not only does Adobe's FTP site have the free Acrobat Reader but it also has plenty of Acrobat files that you can download as well.

Adobe's Web site:

`http://www.adobe.com/`

has a whole section on Acrobat, with other software and links to sites that use Acrobat to distribute information.

Adobe has been very generous with Acrobat since version 2.0, when they decided to offer the Reader for free. Prior to version 2.0, Adobe charged about $25 per reader. Then the Internet community put pressure on Adobe to allow free access to the software. Adobe was able to do this eventually because Acrobat Reader is a part of the Acrobat package. It is basically a viewer. If you want other software like Acrobat Exchange, Acrobat Distiller, and PDF Writer (a printer driver), you have to buy a package from Adobe. Acrobat Exchange and Acrobat Distiller enable you to create Acrobat files, and even code in hyperlinks.

The commercial version of Acrobat can be purchased from many stores and software catalogs.

Using Hyperlinks with Acrobat

When Acrobat was made, Adobe wanted to do more than build an electronic version of paper. They added some functions that enable you to do things like copy text from a file, and program hyperlinks. The commercial version of

Acrobat can create hyperlinks within the document itself. You can create a document in Microsoft Word, for example, create a Portable Document Format (PDF) file, open the file in Acrobat Exchange, and program in hyperlinks. Most likely these hyperlinks will be from a table of contents to the appropriate chapters. When this document is opened, the hyperlinks work like they do in Web browsers. The only difference is that Acrobat provides no telltale sign of where a link is, unlike Web browsers that use color and underlining to indicate the location of links.

Acrobat users often create "buttons" that can be clicked on, however. The buttons are actually button-like graphics coded with hyperlinks. Clicking on a button leads you to another page. To create hyperlinks you need to buy the commercial version of Acrobat, and use Exchange for the hyperlink functions. You can use the Acrobat Reader or Acrobat Exchange to view the hyperlinks.

Note   The section "Linking Acrobat" that comes later in the chapter discusses a new partnership between Adobe and Netscape whereby Acrobat and the Netscape Web browser will work together seamlessly. This arrangement allows for hyperlinks not only within an Acrobat file but also outside of Acrobat to Web sites.

Version 2.0 of Acrobat includes a searching feature available to all users. Although this feature doesn't enable you to edit text within an Acrobat file, it recognizes text as text and therefore makes searches possible.

Using Acrobat with the Internet

Acrobat can work with the Internet in two ways. The first way is retrieving Acrobat files from the Internet, which is much like downloading any other file off the Internet. The second way is linking from Acrobat to the Internet, whereby clicking on a hyperlink from Acrobat would locate additional information on the Web.

Linking Acrobat

Using a way that we are already familiar with—file transfer—a Web browser can link to an Acrobat file and automatically retrieve it. Using either FTP, or simply placing the file in a directory of HTML files and linking to it, enables us to download the file with our Web browsers. When the file is downloaded through a Web browser (with an HTTP link, not an FTP link), the Web browser launches Acrobat and opens the file. This method requires a special configuration, which is discussed later in this chapter. Otherwise your Web browser might just download the file without opening it.

You can use the same process with other file formats you find on the Web. With a graphics format you either see the file in the Web browser or launch the appropriate application that can read the graphic format of your downloaded file. Files are opened by *viewers*. Viewers are responsible for opening downloaded files. This is done to keep down the size of the Web browser, which means faster performance and continuous software upgrades through the developers of the viewer software, which is usually shareware. Even sound and video files are displayed through viewer applications. A viewer application is not necessary to access the Web, but it certainly makes going online a more enjoyable experience. The section "Configuring Your Web Browser for Acrobat Files" reviews the steps to alert both NCSA Mosaic and Netscape on how to determine that Acrobat is the viewer application for PDF files.

The other way Acrobat files can work with the Internet is by linking users to Web sites from Acrobat files. This is a new and interesting way to send people to a source of information. You can link graphics-intensive documents, with features and formatting not possible with the Web (such as specific fonts), to sites where more information can be found. The best example is a living bibliography whereby not only are the sources of information given, but also the links to the full information itself and the Internet sites that hold it.

There are many uses beyond a bibliography for linking to Web sites from Acrobat files. This is a rather new idea at the time of the writing of this book, so it will take about a year before we see creative applications. As this book is being written, the agreement between Adobe and Netscape is still being defined in detail. Their press releases state, however, that in the future they intend to build Acrobat into the Netscape reader, which would enable Netscape to directly open and display Acrobat files. As this is a rather ambitious project, it could take a long time to come to fruition. In the meantime, however, Adobe has come out with an additional piece of software called *Weblink* that will handle the links between the two programs. Weblink is an extension of Acrobat. Netscape and other Web browsers already have the function of handing off files and launching the appropriate programs to open them. The big news is the Weblink function from Adobe, which allows Acrobat to literally send a URL to Netscape to open and display. Weblink will launch Netscape even if it is not running. Most likely other Web browsers in the future will have similar features when a standard application communication for URLs is devised.

As of the writing of this book, Weblink is popular but still in beta. Adobe has released the beta software to the public. Such a position is unusual for commercial manufacturers, but popular in Internet culture. You can find the software at this URL:

```
http://www.adobe.com/
```

In the Acrobat section of the Adobe Web site are links to the Weblink software for both the PC and the Mac. There are also PDF documents with instructions on how to use the Weblink software. The Weblink file for the PC is named wwwlink.api. You download it and then place in the PLUG_INS directory of your Acrobat software. When Acrobat is launched, it automatically recognizes the presence of this software and acquires the new feature. You still have to configure it to tell it which directory your Web browser is in, so it knows what application to launch when you click on a Web link inside an Acrobat file.

Configuring Your Web Browser for Acrobat Files

Because Acrobat and the PDF file format are new in the industry, Web browsers are not shipped with the link between Acrobat and the Web browser set up. These settings are where the viewer preferences are set, with instructions on which software is to be launched for each file format. We'll take a look at how to accomplish this for both NCSA Mosaic and Netscape.

Follow these steps to set up NCSA Mosaic to load Acrobat when a PDF file is downloaded:

1. Make sure Mosaic is running.

2. Select **P**references from the **O**ptions menu (see fig. 21.1).

3. Click on the Viewers tab (see fig. 21.2).

4. Click on the Associate Mime Type of menu and look for a listing with either Acrobat or PDF defined. If the listing appears in this list the settings have already been set.

5. Click on the Add button at the bottom of the window.

6. Enter the extension and program location information (see fig. 21.3).

Figure 21.1

Viewer settings
can be accessed
through the
Preferences option
in Mosaic.

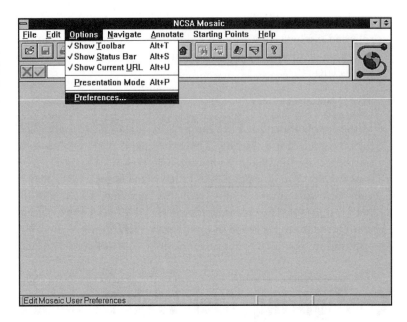

Figure 21.2

Clicking on the
Viewers tab
displays the
settings in
Mosaic.

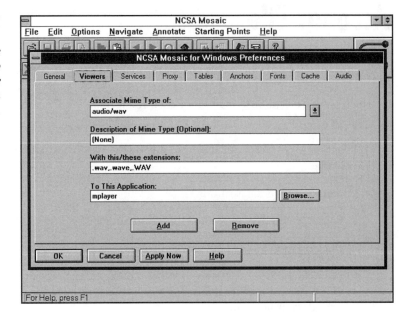

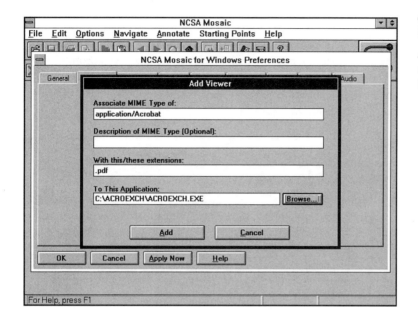

Figure 21.3

Entering the viewer settings in Mosaic.

7. In the Associate MIME Type of field type **application/Acrobat**.

8. In the With this/these extensions field type **.pdf**.

9. In the To This Application field enter the location of your Acrobat software. It is easiest to use the Browse function and locate the Acrobat application on your hard disk drive.

10. Click on the Add button.

11. Click on the OK button.

Now Mosaic is ready to retrieve PDF files and launch Acrobat when the files are downloaded. You can try downloading an Acrobat file by going to the Adobe Web site mentioned earlier in this chapter. If the settings are correct, Acrobat will launch and open the downloaded file.

Tip   You can find an updated list of sites that contain PDF files at the following Adobe URL:

```
http://www.adobe.com/Acrobat/PDFsites.html
```

Netscape uses an easier way to recognize files and pick viewer applications. Basically, whenever Netscape runs across a file format that it does not recognize, it asks you to locate the appropriate viewer application. To accomplish this you have to go to the Adobe Web site mentioned earlier in this chapter; there you are guaranteed to find Acrobat files. When you download a PDF file, you are prompted as shown in figure 21.4.

Figure 21.4

Netscape has launched Acrobat and opened this file.

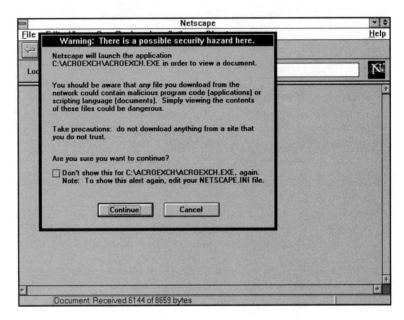

This message indicates that you are about to download a file that your system does not recognize and that might be dangerous to it. This is merely a warning against the potential harm to your system of a file containing a virus. Be sure to download files from reputable sites only.

You can click on the check box stating Do not show this warning again to prevent your system from prompting you with this message again. Some choose to turn off this prompt because it is not necessary to download the file.

After you click on the Continue button, Netscape launches your Acrobat application. If Netscape does not know where the application is located, it prompts you to locate it. After you tell Netscape the location of your Acrobat application, it retains the information.

Figure 21.5

Retrieving an unknown document with Netscape.

If you do not have a copy of Acrobat, you can still download files and save them for use after you acquire Acrobat. Web browsers usually prompt you whether you would like to save a file to your hard disk drive if it (or you) cannot find the viewer application. With the Adobe/Netscape agreement, version 1.1 of Netscape seems to recognize a PDF even though the settings have not been made in the Helper applications settings within your Preferences.

Note Retrieving PDF files and other file formats works exactly the same way. If new versions of software and file formats are released, the procedure for downloading and viewing applications probably will be the same (see fig. 21.5).

Configuring Acrobat with Weblink

Working with links built into Acrobat files is rather simple. If the link exists, click on it. If the link is to a Web site, then Acrobat launches Netscape and connects to the Web document that has been programmed into the Acrobat file.

ote Weblink is in the beta stage at the time of the writing of this book. It is available to the public at no charge, however. Because of this, name of the software could change when it is officially released.

To configure Acrobat to know that you have Netscape and where it is located, follow these steps:

1. Make sure that you have either Acrobat Reader or Acrobat Exchange launched.

2. Select Pre**f**erences from the **E**dit menu.

3. Select **W**WW Link from the Pre**f**erences menu (see fig. 21.6).

Figure 21.6

WWW Link can be accessed through the Preferences option in the Edit menu in Acrobat Exchange.

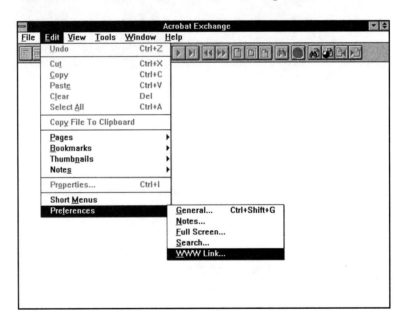

4. Click on the **B**rowse button in the WWW Link Preferences dialog box (see fig. 21.7).

5. Locate the Acrobat application on your hard disk drive.

6. Click on the OK button to finish your location of the Acrobat application.

7. Click on the OK button to finalize your settings.

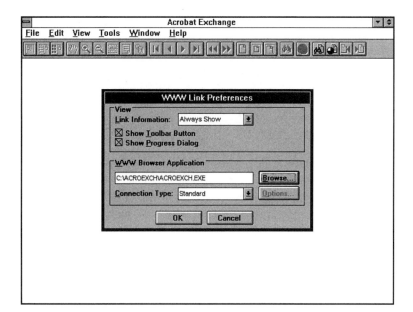

Figure 21.7

Weblink settings are changed in the WWW Link Preferences dialog box.

Now the settings are set so that whenever you click on a Web link from within Acrobat, Netscape is automatically launched and the Web site is accessed.

Part VI

Emerging Technologies on the Web

New Riders Publishing
INSIDE SERIES

Looking Toward the Web's Future

The invention of new technology often raises many questions: "Will this last? What use will this knowledge be to me in 10 years? Will anyone even know what this was in 10 years?" For many innovations, the answer is that in 10 years, the technology will be obsolete. People might remember it, but they already will have moved on to bigger and better things, and to systems that work better.

With the Web, however, this situation is not likely to be the case. Because of its dynamic nature and growth, the Web is a technology to invest in now, for it will be around for a long time. It might not look the same in 10 years, but the basics will remain the same, and people will still be using it as a major source of information on the Internet.

Although the Web has existed for only a short time, it is already being used in numerous areas by both public and private institutions. Multiple government agencies are now accessible through the

Web, and more are added each day. As discussed previously, businesses are just starting to discover how beneficial advertising and performing transactions on the Web can be. Educational institutions are making more information available on the Web, and students are discovering that they can get increasingly more research done by searching Web pages rather than library books.

The Web and the Government

The White House has its own Web site (http:\\www.whitehouse.gov) where you can find press releases and texts of speeches. The main screen of the White House Web site is shown in figure 22.1. You can also find Web pages for numerous other federal government agencies, as well as various state governments.

Figure 22.1

The White House home page.

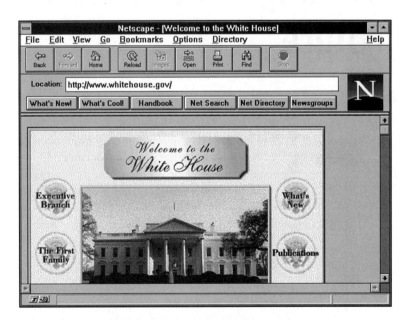

Numerous other federal government agencies can also be found, as well as various state governments. For instance, The Central Intelligence Agency can be found at http://www.ic.gov (see fig. 22.2). This site has information about the history of the CIA, as well as information on other government security agencies.

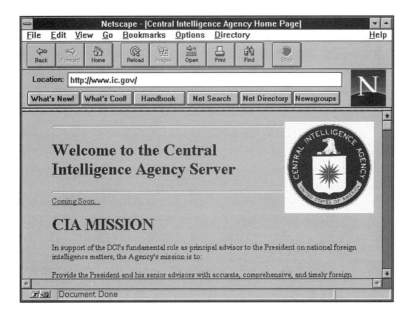

Figure 22.2

The CIA's home page.

Want to view the newest stamps? Try visiting the U.S. Postal Service at http://www.usps.gov. As shown in figure 22.3, this site offers information about the Post Office and how it is run, as well as stamp designs. In the future, it might even allow users to order stamps over the Internet.

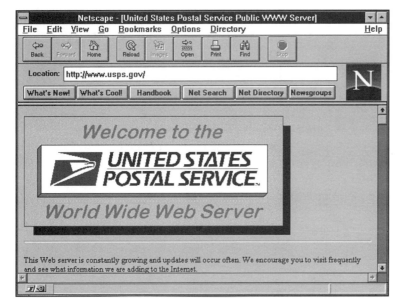

Figure 22.3

The United States Postal Service home page.

Local governments also are starting to be added to the Web. Before long, minutes from local town meetings will be available, as well as any important proposals that school boards will be discussing each month. Rather than having to wait for local newspapers to publish school board proposals, you will be able to look at the proposal—as well as any opinions that have been appended to the proposal—almost as soon as the proposal is first presented.

The city of Boulder, Colorado, has already started working on this technology. As seen on a visit to `http://bcn.boulder.co.us/government/boulder_city/center.html`, there is information about the city council's members and meeting agendas, as well as calendars of local activities (see fig. 22.4).

Figure 22.4

Boulder, Colorado's home page.

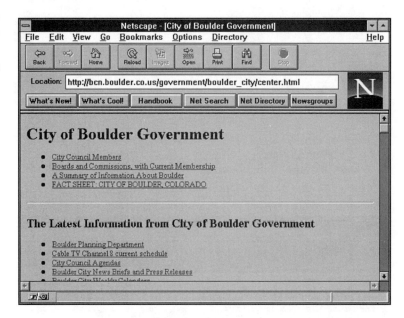

Similarly, the city of Chicago, Illinois can be found at `http://reagan.eecs.uic.edu` (see fig. 22.5). This is part of a new experimental City Information System which is under development at the University of Illinois at Chicago. Included at this site is a sound bite welcome from city Mayor Daley, as well as information about transportation, events, and weather.

As technology becomes available, you might even be able to view the actual town or school board meetings on the Web. Rather than finding time in your schedule to go to the actual meeting, or checking to see when a videotape of the meeting might be shown on the local public-access cable channel, you will be able to go to a Web document that shows a videotape of the meeting. You will be able to fast forward over the sections that are not important to you and replay interesting information to be certain you have all the pertinent facts on the subject.

Similarly, videotaped presidential press conferences likely will be available, as will important international meetings and peace conferences. Consider being able to watch CNN, but having the ability to pick and choose which of the news reports you want to watch. That's what the Web will enable you to do.

The Web and Business

Individual companies already have set up advertisements on the Web, whether as part of their own sites, or through MecklerWeb or a similar technology.

Before long, it will be almost unprofitable for any major company—especially one that deals in new technologies—to exist without its own site to show advertisements and product information. As discussed earlier, it is far easier to take a look at a new product by going to a business's Web page than by physically going to the store to look for a product or searching advertisements in the newspaper. In addition to finding advertisements on the Web, consumers might soon be able to do their shopping on the Web as well.

Do you want to actually purchase an item that you've been viewing? Step into the Mall! Already in the process of being created, the Internet Mall allows users to place orders for items that can then be shipped to their homes or businesses. Holiday shopping couldn't be easier! No longer will you have to stand in lines at stores or wait on hold for the attendant at the mail-order company to take your order. Instead, you can find the item you want and enter your credit information in order to have it shipped right away.

Take a walk through the Mall to find a birthday gift. First, go to `http://www/mecklerweb.com/imall` (see fig. 22.6). Looking at the directory, there are several areas which could be explored, including music, books, services, and many types of clothing.

Figure 22.6

The Internet Mall lets your fingers do the shopping.

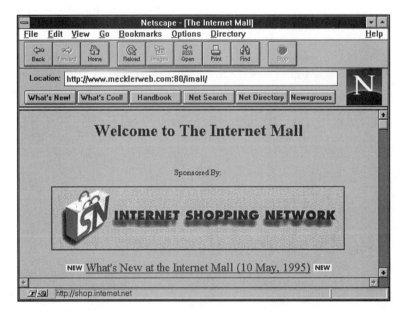

A personal item seems like the best option to start exploring, so select the Personal Items icon (see fig. 22.7). Another set of options is available now; choose to go to Gifts (see fig. 22.8).

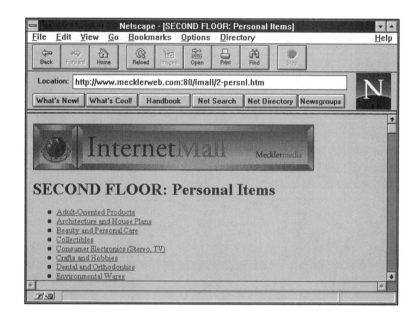

Figure 22.7

Personal items at the Internet Mall.

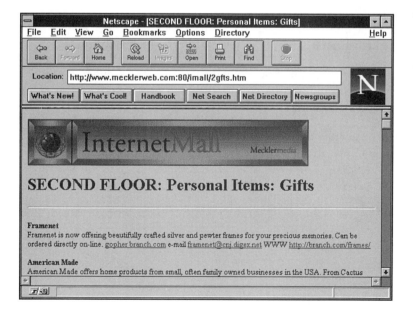

Figure 22.8

Gift shops at the Internet Mall.

After looking at the shop listings, it's time to visit an actual "store." The Egg's Nest sounds interesting, so click on that option. In the store, there are several eggs on display (see fig. 22.9). After looking around, the perfect gift is found and can be ordered and shipped directly to the lucky recipient.

Figure 22.9

The Egg's Nest, one of many shops at the Internet Mall.

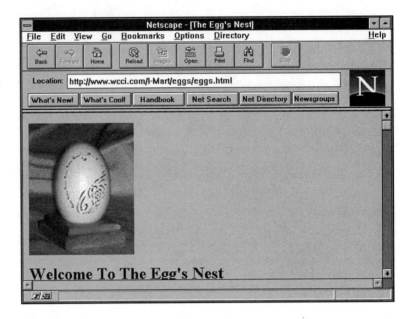

The Mall isn't the only shopping site on the Web. One very popular site is Book Stacks Unlimited, located at `http://www.books.com` (see fig. 22.10).

Here, visitors have the option of browsing through the stacks, either at random or by category specifications. Alternatively, there is a search engine available to assist in finding specific books.

Today, the book needed is a mystery by Ellis Peters. Choosing the "Start Search" option brings up the screen shown in figure 22.11. Information about searching for books is found here; to enter search criteria, go to the Search Information Screen (see fig. 22.12). Here, enter the author's name (Ellis Peters).

Figure 22.10

Book Stacks Unlimited, Inc., an online bookstore.

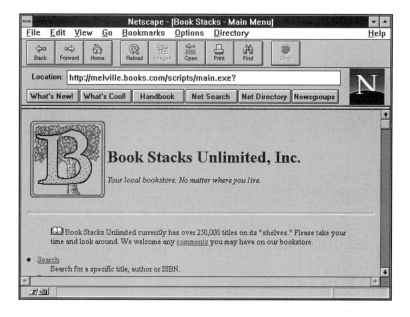

Figure 22.11

Starting a book search.

Figure 22.12

Entering search information.

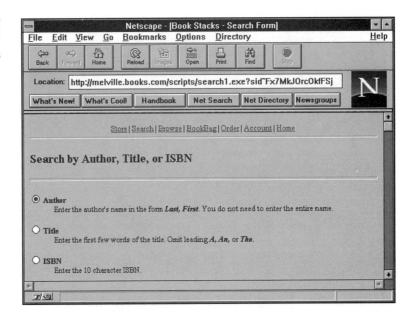

After this information has been entered, the bookstore is searched for any books by Peters. All books found in the search are displayed, as shown in figure 22.13. From this list, the desired book can be selected.

Figure 22.13

The book search results.

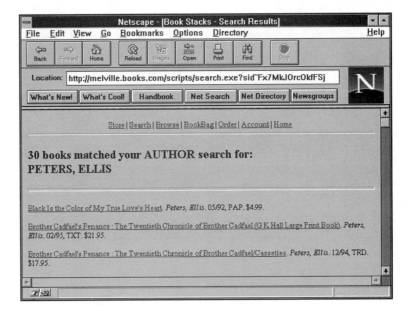

If there is still time to browse, the selected book can be put in a "bookbag" and held for a later order. Bookbags are held between visits and can be reviewed at any time.

Today, however, there is no time to keep browsing, so place an order for this book. The Order Screen, shown in figure 22.14, appears, requesting information about shipping and payment methods. After this is entered, the book purchase is recorded at the store. In a few days, the book will arrive.

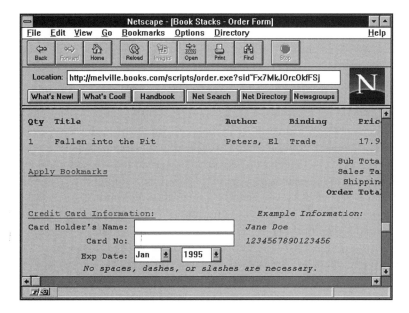

Figure 22.14

Ordering a book.

Still more stores are available. Users can order almost anything from the Web: chocolate, books, games, clothing, music, or anything else they might desire. A good starting point for shopping is *New Riders' Official WWW Yellow Pages*, which contains listings for numerous stores and shopping centers.

In the future, you will not need to be concerned about the safety of using your credit card on the Net. Security will ensure that no one other than the site to which your order is directed will be able to view the actual number you used.

Today, however, transactions are not that secure. Any information sent across the Internet is in danger of a possible interception. This includes passwords and credit card information. Although encryption helps to lessen the risk of this information being used by others, there is still a chance that it might happen. The exact level of risk is questionable, so use caution when transferring information.

Individuals are not the only ones who will be using the Web to perform transactions. As services such as CommerceNet become more popular, major companies will begin performing most of their major negotiations through the Net. International conferences can take place in real time through video conferencing from one Web site to another (see Chapter 23 for more information). Companies will be able to exchange information more quickly. Checking stock reports will be easier as all the up-to-date information is made available.

Education and the Web

Many educational resources already are available through the Web. Libraries are adding their catalogs, and universities are posting information about degree programs (see fig. 22.15). You can also find research documents containing information about almost any subject. Before long, travelling to a library to find this information will become a near obsolete venture. Instead, students will be able to find any information sources they need without leaving their desks. Need a copy of the most recently published analysis of the *Aeneid*? There will be several sites providing information about it. The publisher probably will already have the book itself available (for a fee, of course), and you will be able to either download it or view the pages you need directly on-screen.

Many university libraries already have their catalogs available for perusal through the Web. Johns Hopkins University, located in Baltimore, Maryland, has already added several of its libraries to the Web. In the Library Information page, shown in figure 22.16, users can see which collections are currently available. Each can be perused for a specific title, author, or subject entry. With this information in hand, users can either visit the library themselves and go directly to the book needed, or ask their local university to special-order the book.

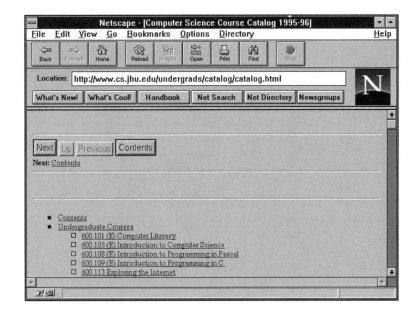

Figure 22.15

Johns Hopkins University's Computer Science Program.

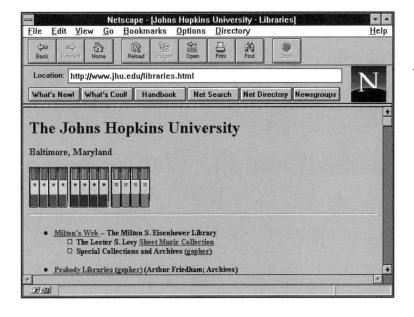

Figure 22.16

Libraries at the Johns Hopkins University site.

What about that college class you always wanted to take, but was never offered at a convenient time? The local continuing education program also will be available through the Web, and you'll be able to follow each lecture when it is convenient for you. Post questions to the teacher; an answer will be available seconds after he or she sees the query. Assignments can be left on your own site, and the professor can view it there, making any changes in a document that automatically will be attached next time you look at your original paper.

The possibilities are amazing. Even elementary school students will be using the Web to access information and pass along news to other students. Exchange students will be able to communicate with their classmates-to-be long before they actually arrive at their new school. Students will be able to take language classes that are actually taught in the country where the language is spoken.

The SchoolWeb project is currently working to get grades K through 12 on the Web. This project matches corporate sponsors with schools that need equipment, then finds local professionals who can help set up the site. Still in its infancy, this project will allow students across the United States to view the Web and show their own school to others, as well.

Several schools are already on the Web as a result of this endeavor, including Highland Middle School. Students and teachers work together to decide what information should be included on the site, and to prepare it for publication. By doing this, not only do they make more information available to the community, but students gain useful knowledge of new technologies and their use.

Entertainment and the Web

Not only will work and education be easier when you use the Web, but you also will be able to find entertainment more easily. Say, for example, that several new movies are opening this weekend, and you don't know which one to see. By looking at the Web sites owned by their production companies, you can preview each movie. Then, if you're curious, you also can read any reviews the critics have published. After you've decided which movies you are interested in seeing, you can check the schedules for local theaters to find the show time

that is most convenient, and possibly even pre-order tickets. If you're curious about how the movie was made, there might even be a "backstage video" of the show available on the production company site.

Travel and the Web

Planning a vacation? Take a look at the Traveller's Guide site. The first question you'll be asked is what sort of vacation you want—one for yourself, one for the whole family, or perhaps a romantic getaway. Once this, as well as the number of people in your party, is established, you'll be asked when you want to take the trip so the TravelWeb will know whether to quote on-season or off-season prices.

Now, where would you like to go? For your first trip, perhaps you want to take the entire family to Florida for two weeks. Looking up Florida, the Traveller's Guide immediately offers several of the top tourist attractions for your perusal: Walt Disney World, Sea World, Palm Springs, and Cape Canaveral. You can look at the attractions and admission prices available at each place.

After consulting with the family, you decide to go to Disney World, with a day trip to Cape Canaveral. Where will you be staying? Numerous hotels are available at Disney World itself, as well as a number of local hotels. On the one hand, staying outside the park area is likely to be less expensive than staying in the park. On the other hand, if you stay in the park, there's the convenience of being at the park already and being able to go back to your room whenever you need to rest or change before dinner.

To decide which hotel to use, go to the already active TravelWeb page (see fig. 22.17). Hotels for each area of the country are shown, as well as rate and facility information. After looking through the list, you can find the most convenient and economical choice for your trip. This is far easier than calling each hotel or working with a travel agent.

Now that you've made your decision, it's time to start looking at airfares. TravelWeb posts the most recent prices available, as well as information about any specials being offered and how long they will last. You can book the passages now or ask the TravelWeb server to store the information while you reconsult your bank account before actually making the trip "official."

Figure 22.17

TravelWeb, a new way to make hotel reservations.

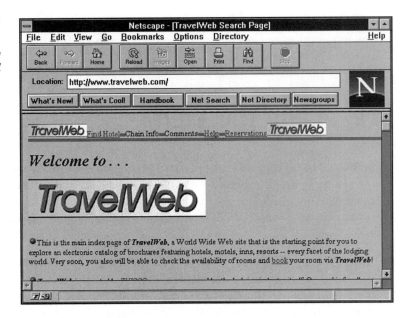

The trip is all planned, and your tickets and confirmation will arrive in the mail soon. Before you leave the TravelWeb program, however, you decide to plan a surprise trip for yourself and your spouse. You choose a weekend close to the date of your anniversary and inform the TravelWeb server that you want to take a four-day trip somewhere romantic within the United States. TravelWeb suggests a number of sites, through which you can search and view the possible options. To your surprise, there are other suggestions besides the usual ideas of Las Vegas and the Poconos. After perusing the options, you choose a trip to Seattle, knowing your spouse has always wanted to go there. Noticing that his or her favorite musical is on tour and will be in the city while the two of you are there, you make ticket reservations for that as well.

With TravelWeb, you planned two trips without leaving your house or dealing with a travel agent who might have tried to convince you to spend more than you had intended. These factors alone show the benefits of using the Web to facilitate your travel arrangements.

Going Beyond

The previously discussed categories represent only a few Web possibilities that will be available in the future. None are certain, but all are likely. The Web

basically will be a jumping point for any new network technologies that become available; what we see here will be dependent upon what other new things become available. The possibilities are endless; the only limitation will be the speed at which people come up with new ideas.

Technological Additions to the Web

As more activities and services become available on the Web, the technologies used to create Web pages must evolve as well. A new version of HTML is in the works and will be available in the next year, offering many new formatting options. One offshoot of HTML which is already in the works, and which will be an extremely interesting addition, is VRML, the Virtual Reality Modeling Language.

Virtual reality has always captured people's attention, and brings up images of high-tech headgear and hand controls which make it possible to be "inside" a video game or dream scenario. VRML works on a similar theory: Users will be "inside" the Web, navigating between sites without the use of URLs or search engines. Work on this project is taking place at several sites (see fig. 22.18). However, only very high-powered machines, such as Sun workstations, currently can view the results of this new language.

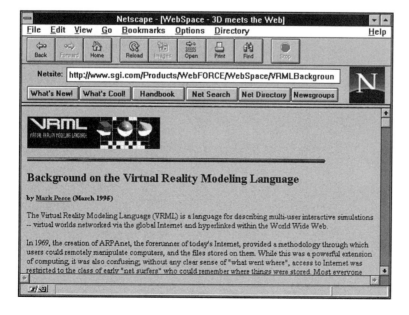

Figure 22.18

VRML, a new way to navigate the Web.

Interactivity on the Web

O ne of the attractive features of the Internet is the creation of the "virtual community" of individuals brought together by their mutual interests. This virtual community has evolved alongside the development of Internet utilities, embracing e-mail, listservs, newsgroups, and many other network-related utilities. Interactivity started as e-mail from one individual to another individual, growing to e-mail from one individual to many individuals, and proceeding further into the world of listservs and then newsgroups. Along the way, the method of interactivity, including the realtime talk, chat, and video communities, also grew. Though the methods have their own inherent benefits and flaws, what remains constant is the need to interact and communicate our findings. This chapter will review the following:

◆ Interactivity on the Internet

◆ The integration of interactivity and the World Wide Web

◆ The reasons why our social needs for interactivity will make the Internet become as integral as the telephone in our social fabric

◆ Information overload

◆ Wasting time on the Internet

For purposes of illustration, an example of a cocktail party will be used throughout this chapter.

Electronic Mail

In the beginning, there was simple electronic mail (e-mail), that linked individuals from point to point and was analogous to passing paper messages from one individual to another at a party. Messages relevant to one user continue to follow this point-to-point conveyance, with some effort being made to bring additional features to the content and handling of the message. The text-based e-mail message has been extended from pure ASCII text to include multimedia through the proposed Multipurpose Internet Mail Extensions (MIME) extensions. Users can now include word-processing files, sounds, images, and so forth in the body of the e-mail message. At present, most of the interaction on the Internet is text-based, which probably reflects the computer capability of both the sending and receiving parties. Text-based messaging is smaller than the transmission of images, sound, or video and therefore can be transmitted more efficiently. Because social interactivity also involves more than just reading text, interaction will eventually evolve to encompass other modalities in the future.

One of the problems of sending e-mail is knowing whether the e-mail was ever received and, if received, was read by the intended party. The receipt acknowledgment of e-mail messages is starting to be addressed in a variety of proprietary message systems, but has not yet been standardized. Person-to-person e-mail will continue to be a significant method of selective interaction.

E-Mail Aliases

The need to share e-mail with a variety of individuals gave way to one individual sending e-mail to an alias containing a group of e-mail addresses. For example, a user sending e-mail to members of his softball club might define an alias called "ball_team" to be joe@mail.com, howard@mail.com, sue@mail.com, and so on. Mail sent to ball_team by the user would automatically be forwarded to Joe, Howard, and Sue. The analogue to the cocktail party would make the alias to be guest list. The host sends invitations to everyone on his guest list, which usually remains private.

Listservs

Access and management of an e-mail alias on a large scale gave rise to listservers. *Listservers* are programs that automatically manage dissemination of e-mail to the members whose e-mail addresses are maintained by the listserv program. In a sense, listservs are automatic versions of the simple alias. A user can subscribe, unsubscribe, ask questions, and obtain certain information directly from the listserv program without troubling any of the people manging the service. The analogue to the party would make the greeter the listserver. Anything passed on to the greeter would be announced to all members of the party, whether they cared to hear it or not.

Listservs can also be filtered by a moderator to check the content of the e-mail before it is propogated to other members of the group. Moderation of an e-mail list is usually done by a set of rules known to participants of the group. These rules, or local *netiquette*, are intended to define acceptable and unacceptable behavior. Adherence to known rules keeps the interactions within bounds of the purpose of the listserv, prevents exploitation of the membership (such as bombardment by unsolicited advertising), excludes inappropriate postings, and so forth. While this can be viewed as censorship, management of a "flame war" or high-volume messaging between a few members can put off other members of the listserv who are not interested in the specific issue under discussion. This is particularly a problem with listservers, where essentially all of the e-mail is received by all the members, desired or not.

One of the problems of very active listservs is information overflow. Imagine the cocktail party with a constant barrage of announcements to all parties. Although it is possible to respond to almost all the announcements, the segregation of relevant information from irrelevant information lies in the discretion of the parties involved in the discussion. The number of active participants to passive participants varies enormously within each list. This ratio depends on factors including the topic, the amount of time the participants want to devote to the listserv, and other factors.

Replies to e-mail traffic on the listserv can be either public or private. Public replies are shared by everyone. Private replies, especially if they are significant to only one party, can be done privately through e-mail to the individual. Knowing when to reply privately and when to reply publicly isn't always clear. If the question contains information that would unlikely to be of use to anyone else, post it privately. On the other hand, if many other people are curious as well, a private e-mail reply is lost to the rest of the listserv audience. Going back to the party analogy, a participant might inquire of the host "Where is the bathroom?" While this is a private request, it is very likely that other participants of the party are also interested in this same question (hopefully, not simultaneously). The host can answer this question over and over again, or announce it publicly for all to hear. On listservs, it is very common for certain questions to be asked over and over again. Sharing this information publicly with the listserv audience is a more efficient use of everyone's time.

Newsgroups

Management of the enormous amount of message traffic generated by listservs is one of the reasons why the newsgroups are popular. Like listservs, newsgroups are segregated by topic. Unlike listservs, the information contained with newsgroups can be segregated by specific subjects into *threads*, which are analogous to different conversations at a cocktail party all occuring in the same room. A participant may go from one conversation or message thread to the next, participating in one while merely listening to another. Yet another conversation might be of no interest to the participant, and is bypassed completely. The messages or message threads are presented to the user in a menu. If they elect to participate in a discussion, they download only those messages pertinent to this specific discussion. Downloading messages is a more efficient use of Internet resources and, more importantly, the user's time. Because the identification of the message contents is contained in the subject label, the use of a misleading or empty subject label may cause potentially interested users to miss this message.

All these methods, the person-to-person e-mail, the listservs, and the newsgroups, work in a time-delayed fashion. The information travels to another location where it is read at a later time. This is particularly important when working on an international scale, where an individual's work time might be another person's rest time. Delayed response means messages are handled at the recipient's convenience. Some users prefer to receive their office correspondance by e-mail so they are not continually interrupted. They can respond at their convenience, with the detail and degree of audit required. Although this might make the recipient very happy, it does not work well for time-critical information where the sender needs an immediate answer. Time-delayed transmission is part of the heritage of the Internet, which started when the resources of communication were expected to be unreliable. Connections between different nodes on the Internet were slow and might only be in place for a few minutes per day (UUCP dial-up connections between computers, for example). As the speed and duration of connectivity increased, direct communication in virtual real-time became possible.

Interactive Communication

There are a variety of direct communication programs working in real time on the Internet, including the Unix talk program, the VMS phone program, and chats. The talk and phone programs are analogous to e-mail in that all three forms of communication involve two parties that agree to communicate in real time. Imagine Howard, working from computer first.company.com, is talking to Joe, working on computer third.company.com. Howard might type the following:

```
talk  joe@third.company.com
```

If Joe is logged into third.company.com, he will see the following:

```
Message from Talk_Daemon@first.company.com
talk: Connection requested by howard@first.company.com
talk: respond with:  talk howard@first.company.com
```

Joe's terminal will then beep several times to bring his attention to his screen. If Joe chooses to respond, he would type **talk howard@first.company.com**, and a connection will be made. Each user's screen clears and a horizontal line appears in the middle. Each user will see the other person's text on the top of their screen. Anything the user types will appear at the bottom of their screen. Thus, if Joe types (at the bottom of his screen), his screen will appear as follows:

```
Thanks a lot Joe, I really need the encouragement....Howard.


_ _ _ _ _ _ _ _ _ _ _ _ _ _ _ _ _ _ _ _ _ _ _ _ _ _
           Nice job last night, Howard...next time bring the superglue
for your glove so you don't drop as many balls!
```

Howard's screen would show:

```
Nice job last night, Howard...next time bring the superglue for your
glove so you don't drop as many balls!


_ _ _ _ _ _ _ _ _ _ _ _ _ _ _ _ _ _ _ _ _ _ _ _ _ _
Thanks a lot Joe, I really need the encouragement....Howard.
```

The immediacy of this method is obvious as some programs display every key as it is typed. Editing only occurs on the existing line and, if you type badly, every keystroke is seen by the other party. Any insults or snide remarks, even if they are only temporary, are seen by the other party. Other implementations only transmit after the user has hit Enter.

Chats

While the talk program was a point-to-point communication between explicitly defined parties (Joe and Howard), chats involve several people at once. Often the people involved in the chat are anonymous and if they are quiet, their presence might not be realized by the other parties. The electronic chat is the closest to the cocktail party in that response from users is usually immediate, impromptu, and can be heard by an undefined audience. The largest party of chat users is the Internet Relay Chat or IRC-Chat. This is sometimes described as the "anarchy that works." IRC-Chat often involves inpromptu conversations with thousands of users coming and going at any given point in time.

Real-Time Video

Direct communication tools, such as IRC-Chat and talk, are all text-based and thus consume fairly few resources on the Internet. If packets of information between parties are slightly delayed, the conversation can be awkward, but it does continue. Tools for communicating by audio (phoning) and by video over the Internet do exist, but they reveal the design limitations of today's Internet. All the packets on the Internet are expected to arrive at some time in the future, without specific prioritization. Interactive video and audio transmission over the Internet presume a guaranteed time for delivery of the packets in a certain timeframe. If the packets are delayed due to excessive collisions, the video and audio will break up, be bursty, and otherwise render the transmission unintelligible.

The Internet obtains its cost benefits by sharing communication lines. Whenever there is sharing of communication resources, the probability of these resources being busy is always present. When the Internet gets busy, the network slows down. Following the standards employed on the Internet today, each packet of information is treated with equal priority. This is tolerable for delayed communication, but for direct communication requiring real-time

performance, such as delivery of a certain number of video frames per second, this is intolerable. Video goes into slow motion, becomes jerky and sometimes stops on or between frames. Audio transmission also becomes shaky and the sound can break up, rendering the transmission unintelligible. Today, real-time video and audio can be accomplished on the Internet because the paths taken during the transmission are not busy. As more people interact with voice and video, the demands on the Internet will increase rapidly. Two methods to handle this load have been proposed: resource reservation and multicasting.

Resource Reservation

Savvy users might propose to do interactive video during "quiet times" on the Internet when there is less contention for resources. If all the users are within a specific network locale, a quiet period might be attainable. Users needing guaranteed access at their own convenience can agree to pay their Internet provider for a dedicated piece of the Internet for a period of time. This might work as long as all the parties involved exist within the Internet provider's portion of the Internet. If the parties are spread throughout the world, the messages are subject to traffic along the paths taken outside the control of the Internet provider and thus are subject to resource contention. As use of the Internet continues to increase, "quiet times" on the Internet will become less and less.

Multicast Backbone (Mbone)

The Multicast Backbone (Mbone) protocol and transmission process was formulated to offer live, worldwide audio and visual feeds across the Internet. Mbone is a virtual network existing as a layer on top of the physical Internet to support routing of IP (Internet Protocol) packets. The network is composed of nodes that directly support IP multicast LANs like Ethernet, connected by virtual point-to-point links called *tunnels*. The connecting points of these tunnels are usually workstation class computers running the multicast routing daemon and capable of supporting IP multicast transmission. Multicast packets encapsulate the multicast packets with the traditional datagrams to pass between the intervening routers and subnets composing the Internet. When the encapsulated packets reach the other point on the tunnel, the packets are unencapsulated and the multicast packets are reassembled into the desired message. The Mbone is fairly new and not widely used. It is a standardized approach to using multicast messages to deliver time-sensitive packets across the Internet.

The Evolution of Interaction on the Web

So far, we have discussed the evolution of interaction on the Internet. There are two general methods of communication: time-delayed and real-time. The time-delayed methods evolved from a network limited in computer resources. From these limitations, a culture of Internet interaction evolved, ranging from person-to-person e-mail, to mailing lists run at either a personal level or by programs called listservs to orchestrated messages centers, called newsgroups. The culture of interaction fit nicely with contention for people's time. E-mail could be handled at a user's convenience, when there was no contention for the *user's* resources. While many communications fell into this time delayed area, some messages needed to be delivered with some degree of immediacy. Presuming the destination party was online and receptive to interruption, programs like talk, phone, and chat made direct communication possible. There are many problems encountered along the way.

One of the problems associated with time-delayed communication is that messages traversing the Internet do not support prioritization. Message from the nuclear reactor saying a meltdown is imminent get the same priority as a chat session about last night's TV show.

Another problem, especially with regard to time-delayed communication, is the preservation of the integrity of the message. All of the interaction discussed above presumes the contents are completely public. Indeed, messages traversing the Internet can be picked off by anyone with appropriate software and read, modified, and resent without any knowledge of the sender or recipient.

Security Problems

The security of the messages exchanged becomes increasingly important as interaction through the Internet (e-mail, listservs, newsgroups, IRC-Chat, and so forth) becomes a significant part of our lives. We can use encryption methods to make reading the contents of the message difficult, keeping in mind the encryption method employed must be in compliance with Federal regulations of international export. Of course, the e-mail's destination address is not encoded, because the programs handling the e-mail must understand the address in order to deliver the message. A savvy user could screen for specific e-mail destinations, intercepting only those messages destined for specific addresses and attempt to decode the encrypted part at his leisure.

Another problem is verifying the user reported to be sending the message really is the person who "signed" his name and used the return e-mail address. A digital signature could be added to each outgoing message to authenticate the message, though this does not provide any guarantees. Indeed, it is very difficult to prove who actually composed a text-based message coming from a particular computer. Even with this level of authentication, it is very difficult to prove a specific individual sat at a given computer, then composed and sent a specific message. The legality of a digital signature is discussed in greater length in Chapter 17, "Commerce on the Web."

Information Overload Problems

One of the problems discussed earlier is information overload of an individual. With all the message traffic, delayed or real-time, it is difficult to remember what has happened, who said what to whom, repeat issues addressed exhaustively a short time ago, and so on. There is so much going on, it is hard to get much real work done. One approach is to have a library of information available for reference during the interactions. Thus, if a topic had just been discussed ad nauseum a short time ago, members of the listserv or newsgroup could refer this user to the relevant on-line archives. *Frequently Asked Questions* (FAQs) are often used to preempt repeat questions. Couching discussions along with a bulletin board system has made Lotus Notes a popular commercial package.

A nonproprietary way of handling this problem is to integrate the World Wide Web with multithreaded discussion groups. The Web offers hypermedia navigation through information throughout the world. This capability permits users to bring powerful search and navigation tools to explore the many libraries of information throughout the world. However, libraries are often cast as read only resources. Remember the stern looks from the librarian? One does not talk in libraries—they are a place to read. Wouldn't it be great to carry on discussions in a virtual library, referring to resources contained within the virtual library of the World Wide Web? The WWW is a natural place to store the archive of past discussions of listservs and newsgroups, facilitating their access by powerful hypertext (and ultimately hypermedia) access. Thus a user could afford to take some time off from a discussion group without fear of losing the context of the discussion and its referenced documents. Information discussed in a different context could be referenced using the WAIS indexing tools for referencing in current discussion.

Working or Wasting Time on the Web

The World Wide Web has made the Internet much easier to use. WWW browsers are great for surfing through the myriad of resources as well as intensive scouring of Internet for information. No matter how obscure or arcane, there is probably a resource, or mention of information pertaining to your search on the archive of a listserv or newsgroup. With such powerful and simple-to-use tools, the WWW becomes almost a narcotic with an addictive draw to find out what is new on the Internet. This presents an interesting dilemma to the employer regarding the use of an employee's time. An employee might be furiously working away at her workstation, but unbeknownst to her employer, she is participating in an IRC-Chat session about politics. Before the employee knows it, two hours have passed.

On the other hand, if the employee is working in a politician's office and is monitoring the concerns of the constituents, this may be her job. Indeed, the Internet is a great source of intelligence pertaining to company-related traffic. If a bug or perceived problem is found in a software program, it will often appear first on the Internet. An employee monitoring this traffic could pick up this discussion and alert his management.

Information and conversation is addictive. This is well known, and keeps many social clubs in business. While the Internet is more detached than a social club (it is a virtual social club), it is easier to use and is just as addicting. If the Internet is used on company time, policies and procedures similar to those implemented for use of telephones should be considered.

Part VII

Exploring Web Sites: A Scrapbook

24

Looking at the Best General Sites

One of the most extraordinary features of the World Wide Web and the Internet is its wealth of information guides and resources. This chapter lists and briefly describes some of the best guides, directories, search utilities, and catalogs available on the Web. This chapter also provides a directory of Internet access providers.

Internet Resources

If you are looking for a specific topic on the World Wide Web, you can use Chapters 24–29 of this book. Or, you can locate one of the following guides and directories to help you search for a topic or particular site.

Agricultural Guide

http://sunsite.unc.edu/pub/docs/about-the-net/libsoft/agguide.dos

This specialized guide is entitled "Not Just Cows." The purpose of the guide is to direct the user to resources (in agriculture and related science) available on the INTERNET or BITNET.

ALIWEB

http://web.nexor.co.uk/public/aliweb/aliweb.html

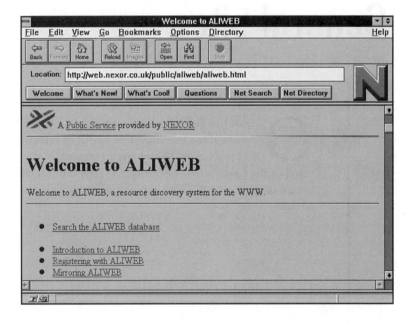

Another good searching tool for the growing number of Web resources.

Archie

http://web-co.uk

Archie, an electronic directory service on the Internet, can help you find files anywhere on the Net.

ArchiePlexForm

http://www.lerc.nasa.gov/Doc/archieplex-httpd.html

This is a form-based version of ArchiePlex, an Archie gateway for the Web. With this resource, you can use keywords to search for resources on the Web.

Artificial Life

http://alife.santafe.edu

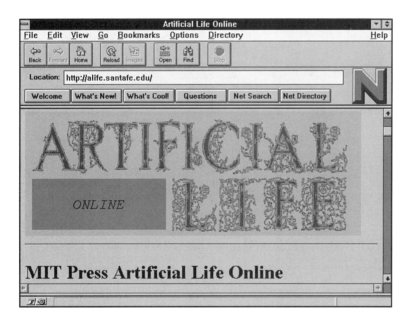

This site serves as a forum for information about all aspects of the Artificial Life enterprise. Services provided here include an FTP site containing preprints and software, a bibliographic database on artificial life, and links to various Usenet services.

AskERIC Virtual Library

http://eryx.syr.edu/COWSHome.html

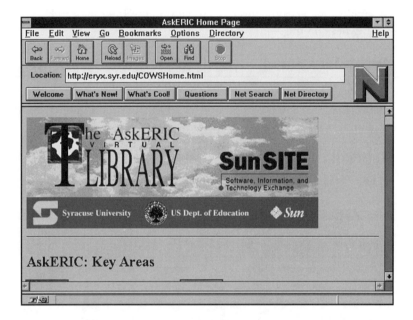

This server provides access to ERIC (Educational Resource Information Center), a federally funded national information system that has access to many education-related resources in the Internet. Included are an online dictionary, electronic books (through project Gutenberg), an acronym dictionary, and the CIA World Fact Book.

Astronomical Publications Resources (APR)

http://stsci.edu/net-publications.html

This Web site, which has pointers to many astronomical resources on the Internet, is a useful starting point to most of the online astronomical publications.

Astronomical Software Resources (ASR)

http://stsci.edu/net-software.html

The ASR site is a useful starting point to find most of the astronomical resources available on the Web. It is conveniently divided by type of access

(WWW, WAIS, Gopher, Telnet, FTP). As of January, 1994, resources include: Astrophysics Preprints—SISSA; ADC Documents, NOAO News, NRAO Preprint Database; STECF Newsletter; STELAR Apj, ApJS, AJ, PASP, A&A, A&AS, MNRAS, and JGR Abstracts; STSci Preprint Database; IAU Circulars Astronomical Union; CfA Index of ApJ, AJ, PASP; DIRA2 Database; and the Electronic Journal of Astronomical Society of the Atlantic.

The Best of the Web '94 Recipients

http://wings.buffalo.edu/contest/awards/index.html

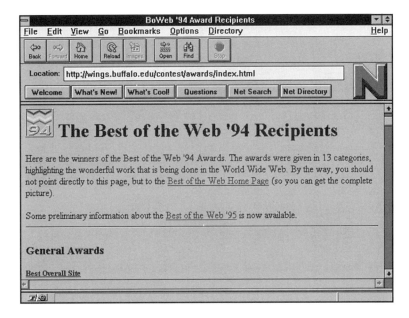

Here is where to find the Best of the Web. This site highlights the winners of the Best of the Web '94 Awards (all 13 categories). Visit this page for more information about the awards and the winners.

Cello

http://fatty.law.cornell.edu

This DOS-based Internet browser incorporates the World Wide Web, Gopher, FTP, Telnet, and Usenet.

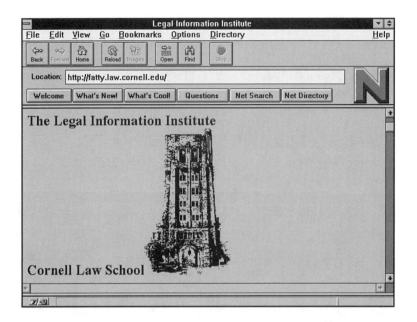

Cello FAQ

http://www.law.cornell.edu/cello/cellofaq.html

This site contains common questions and answers about Cello, a multi-purpose Internet browser similar to Mosaic. Cello provides friendly access to the Internet's myriad information resources. It supports World Wide Web, Gopher, FTP, CSO/pf/qi, and Usenet News retrievals natively, as well as other protocols.

Centre Universitaire d'Informatique World Wide Web Catalog

http://cuiwww.unige.ch/w3catalog

This resource, also known as the *CUI W3 catalog* (University of Geneva, Switzerland), searches through directories of other Web documents.

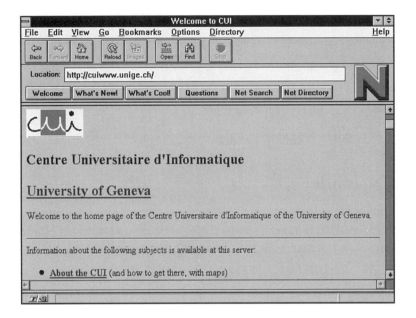

Cognitive and Psychological Sciences on the Internet

http://matia.stanford.edu/cogsci.html

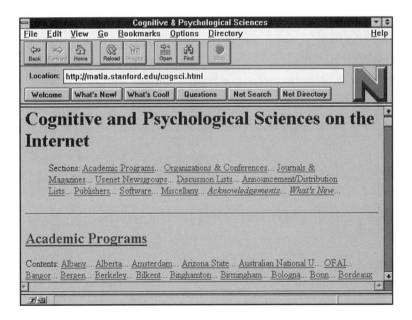

This resource contains links to academic programs, organizations and conference lists, journals and magazines, Usenet newsgroups, discussion lists, and other general information regarding cognitive science.

CUSI

http://web.nexor.co.uk/public/cusi/cusi.html

From this Web resource you can search the Web by using keywords in several directories and catalogs.

EarthLink Network

http://www.earthlink.net/

EarthLink Network is an Internet provider based in Southern California. Their server provides a great source of links to business customers, as well as to other selected Web sites.

EUnet Slovakia

http://www.eunet.sk/

As a regional Internet provider, EUnet Slovakia has links to other European Web sites. Among the expected, you can get updates on the latest book from Stephen King!

Felipe's Bilingual WWW Pages

http://edb518ea.edb.utexas.edu

This interactive Web site contains Gopher and Web links to various Latin American resources. Information is in both English and Spanish.

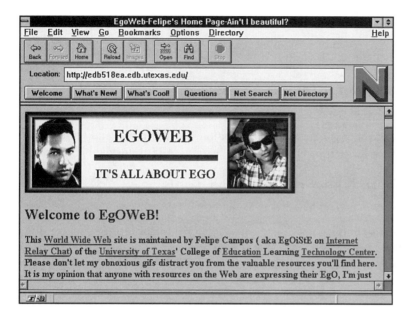

FUNET Information Services

http://www.funet.fi/funet/FUNET-english.html

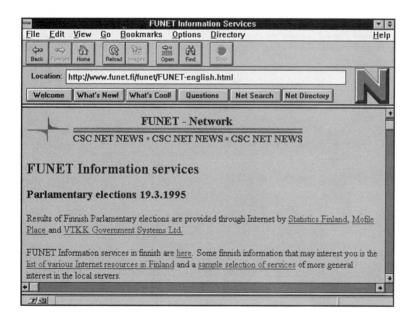

The first stop in your search for Finnish Internet resources. Use the mouse-sensitive map here for links to other sites in Finland, as well as for general information about this Scandinavian country.

GIS-L and comp.infosystems.gis FAQ

http://www.cencus.gov/geo/gis/faqindex.html

This server provides geographical information, data, software, and pointers to other Internet Geographical Information Systems (GIS) information sources.

The Guide to Network Resource Tools

http://www.earn.net/gnrt/notice.html

Here's where to find a good introduction to all the major Internet networking tools (WAIS, Gopher, NetNews, X.500, Hytelnet, and Telnet). Here you can find out where to find them, how to use them, and where to go for more information.

HNSource

http://history.cc.ukans.edu/history/WWW_history_main.html

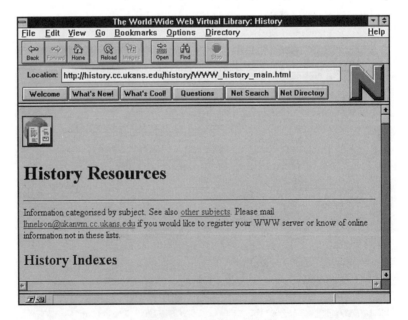

This site provides information, announcements, guides, and references, about (and to) various Internet resources. It also includes links to FTP sites, WAIS sites, OPACs, and Gophers.

HTML FAQ

http://www.umcc.umich.edu/~ec/www/html_faq.html

This resource maintains a FAQ of common questions and answers about Hypertext Markup Language (HTML). The FAQ covers the creation and transformation of documents into the Web format.

Hydra Information Technologies

http://www.hydra.com/Hydra.html

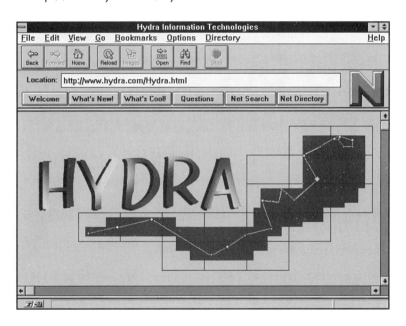

Hydra Information Technologies is a New York-based Internet consultant and developer. This resource includes information about the company and the services they provide. You'll also find connections to several good Web resources from this site.

Hypertext USENET FAQs

http://www.cis.ohio-state.edu/hypertext/faq/usenet/FAQ-List.html

This site contains a hypertext database of FAQs about the Internet.

Images from Various Sources

http://info.alaska.edu:70

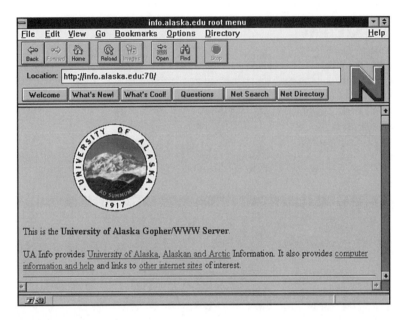

This site links to 35 image archives throughout the world. A variety of images are available; many are of weather, geological, and biological collections from government and private sources.

Index to Publishers Online

http://www.bookport.com/source/9505.html

This page maintains an extensive list, indexed alphabetically, of publishers with a presence on the Internet.

Internet Browsers

http://life.anu.edu.au/links/syslib.html

This is a resource for Internet browsers and navigators, such as Mosaic and Cello. These browsers are available for various platforms, such as Windows, X-Windows, and Apple computers.

Internet Search

http://home.mcom.com/home/internet-search.html

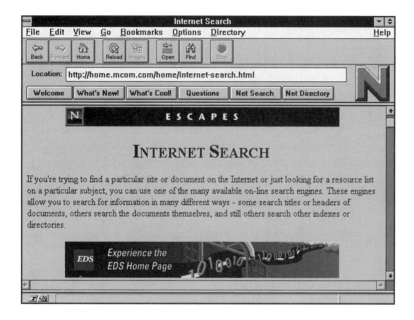

This is a great place to start your search of the Net, with links to just about every search engine out there.

The InterNIC Directory and Database Services

http://www.internic.net/

This site, provided by AT&T, offers a directory of services from AT&T and a registration service by Network Solutions, Inc. You can find an online Directory of Directories, Internet Documention, RFCs, and The Scout Report.

InterNIC Directory Services (White Pages)

http://ds.internic.net/ds/dspgwp.html

At this Web resource you find free access to X.500, WHOIS, and the Netfind white pages on the Internet.

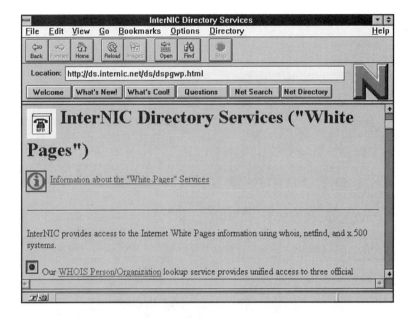

Ireland-Related Online Resources

http://http.hq.eso.org/~fmurtagh/ireland-resources.html

This list of network-accessible online resources about Ireland includes some bulletin board services, some commercial information systems (such as CompuServe), and some commercial bibliographic services.

The JumpStation

http://www.stir.ac.uk/jsbin/js

This Internet resource helps you search for specific Web sites by using keywords.

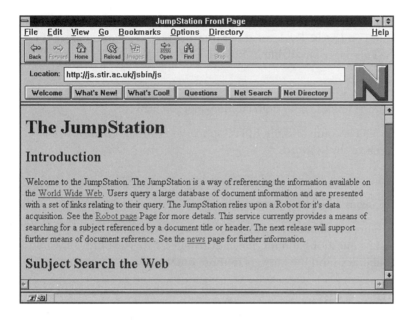

Latvia OnLine

http://www.vernet.lv/

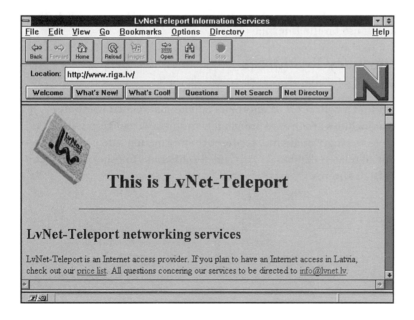

A good source of news, general information, history, and business and commercial updates on Latvia. Find out about Internet providers and import/export news. This page is available in Russian also.

LISTGopher

http://ericmorgan.lib.ncsu.edu/staff/morgan/morgan.html

Using your e-mail account and the LISTGopher, you can search library-related LISTSERV archives by keyword.

Lynx FAQ

http://ftp2.cc.ukans.edu/about_lynx

This Lynx resource contains the Lynx FAQ. Here you can find the most commonly asked questions about Cello, a distributed hypertext browser with full Web capabilities (and the answers to those questions).

Mosaic Home Page

http://www.ncsa.uiuc.edu/SDG/Software/Mosaic/MCSAMosaicHome.html

This is the Web server for the National Center for Supercomputing Applications (NCSA), which features the Mosaic application. Mosaic, one of the best tools for Web surfers, provides a network-distributed hypermedia system for information discovery. Internet-based, Mosaic is free for academic, research, and commercial use on the Internet.

NetVet Veterinary Resources

http://netvet.wustl.edu

Here you can find a collection of veterinary and animal-related computer resources that includes archives of animal legislation and regulation, listings for colleges of veterinary medicine, conference information, the Electronic Zoo, and animal-related databases. This site also has links to other animal- and veterinary-related systems.

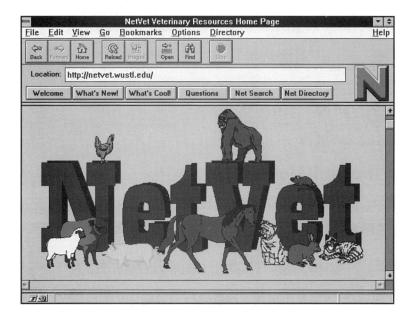

NIKOS WWW Search

http://www.rns.com/cgi-bin/nomad

NIKOS is a fast and friendly Internet Resource Locator. This Internet search resource will search about 1 million Web pages, using keywords.

Open Government Project (Canada)

http://debra.dgbt.doc.ca/ogp.html

This bilingual (French/English) site has detailed information about members of the Canadian Senate and House of Commons, as well as Supreme Court rulings and biographies of the justices. It features several pictures, maps, and links to other Canadian information servers.

Oxford University Computing Laboratory Archive Service

http://www.comlab.ox.ac.uk/archive/

This site offers a large variety of resources, links, and information available on the Web. Archived here are extensive resource materials including image archives, software programs, sound archives, museums, and art galleries, as well as a plethora of other information.

Publishers' Catalogs Home Page

http://www.lights.com/publisher

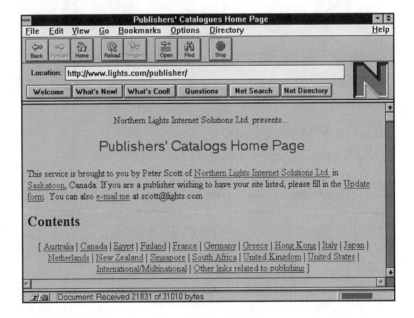

Users can link to many of the most popular publishers from throughout the world, here arranged geographically (by country). Among the U.S. publishers available are City Lights Publishers and Booksellers, Harvard University Press, and New Riders Publishing.

Quantum Physics/High-Energy Physics

http://www.cern.ch/Physics/HAP.html

This server contains extensive international links to academic and research institutions specializing in high-energy physics. Journals, abstracts, and conference information are all available from this site.

Query Interface to the WWW Home Pages Harvest Broker

http://www.town.hall.org/brokers/www-home-pages/query.html

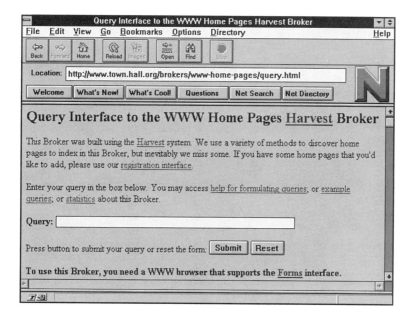

This page maintains an index of more than 17,000 Web home pages.

Recreational Pharmacology Server

http://stein1.u.washington.edu:2012/pharm/pharm.html

This site has an exhaustive collection of drug FAQs, data sheets, articles, resources, and electronic books about drugs that are frequently used for recreational purposes. The site also contains a large list of Internet links to drug-related sites.

Search Today's Usenet News

http://ibd.ar.com/News/About.html

This site provides a search engine with which to look (by keyword) for specific articles in that day's Usenet group.

Servidor WWW da RNP

http://www.rnp.br

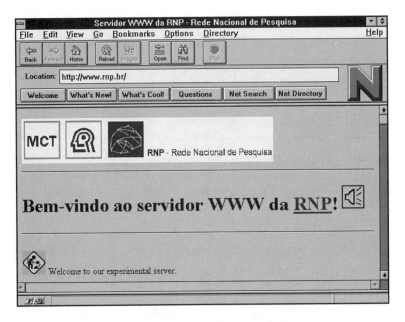

This central Web server for the Brazilian Research Network includes information about the Web and Internet in general in Brazil, and has links to most other Web, Gopher, and FTP servers in Brazil. At present, the information is provided in Portuguese only; English versions will be added in the future.

Special Internet Connections

http://www.uwm.edu/Mirror/inet.services.html

This is an Internet *list of links*, that is, a document that lists the addresses of interesting, useful resources on the Internet. Topics include art, astronomy, news servers and journals, games, chat, physics, business/financial, law, literature, history, Gopher sites, space, and so on.

Thailand: The Big Picture

http://www.nectec.or.th

This Web site contains an extensive list of Internet servers about (and located in) Thailand. In addition to general information about Thailand, this server contains links to many Thai academic institutions.

UNINETT

http://aun.uninett.no/

A nice graphical representation of Internet resources in Norway, with links to corporations, schools and universities, and cultural centers such as museums.

University of Michigan Library

http://www.lib.umich.edu/

General information about the University of Michigan library system, including special programs and services, is available here, as are CD-ROM guides and newspaper indexes. This site also provides an Internet resource guide, arranged by subject.

Vermont/New Hampshire WWW Resources

http://www.destek.net/Maps/VT-NH.html

This site's interactive map provides pointers to Web sites in these two New England states. The map highlights colleges, universities, shopping outlets, and more.

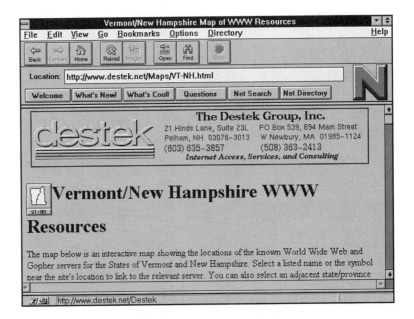

W3 Search Engines

http://cui_www.unige.ch/meta-index.html

This is another Internet search tool. Tools found at this site enable you to search the Web by using broad categories, such as news, people, and software.

WAIS

http://server.wais

WAIS, the acronym for *Wide Area Information Server*, is a search and retrieval tool that scans for resources by searching indexes of databases.

Internet Services

Many companies have popped up all over the world providing on-ramps to the Internet. This section lists and briefly describes some of the Internet service sites that are available by the Web.

Actrix Home Page

http://actrix.gen.nz/

This is the Web site for Actrix, an Internet provider. Actrix provides Internet support and service in New Zealand.

Advantis

http://www.ibm.net/adv/

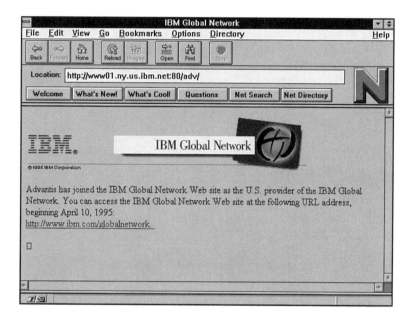

Advantis is the U.S. provider of the IBM Global Network. In addition to company information, this server provides information about the IBM Global Network, a quarterly newsletter, announcements, and services, as well as a link to the IBM home page.

Alpha.net

http://teknetix.com/ALPHAhome.html

This Internet provider for the Midwestern United States supports T1 connections.

AlterNet

http://www.alter.net/

This national Internet provider can support T1 connections.

ANS CO+RE Systems

http://www.ans.net/

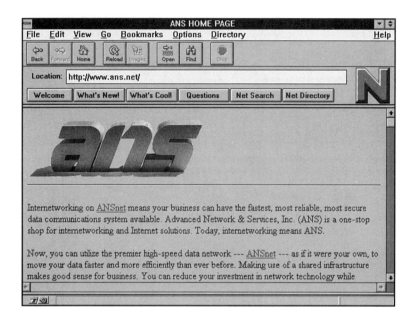

This is the site for ANS CO+RE Systems, a national Internet provider that supports T1 connections.

ARInternet

http://www.clark.net/pub/ari/

This Landover, Maryland, Internet provider specializes in services for science, engineering, medicine, and educational professions.

auroraNET

http://www.aurora.net/

This Internet provider, which serves Canada, also provides T1 connections.

BARRNet

http://www.bbn.com/barrnet.html

BARRNet, which supports T1 connectivity, provides connections and support for using the Internet.

Barrnett

http://www.barrnet.net/

This San Francisco area Internet provider provides service to the West Coast.

BBN Internet Services

http://www.near.net/

BBN Internet Services provides connections and support for using the Internet. This New England Internet provider supports T1 connections.

BINCnet

http://www.binc.net/

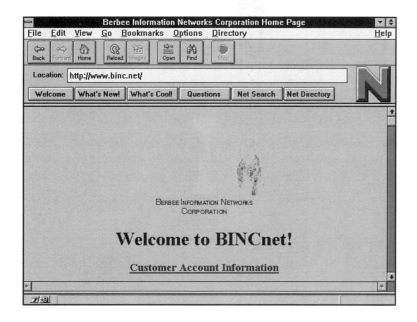

This is the home page of BINCnet, an Internet provider that serves the Wisconsin area.

CA*net

http://www.canet.ca/canet/index.html

CA*net, an Internet provider that serves Canada, provides connections and support for using the Internet.

CalvaNet

http://www.calvacom.fr/

This French Internet provider is based in Velizy, France.

CERFnet

http://www.cerf.net/

CERFnet provides connections and support for using the Internet. This west coast Internet provider can support ISDN connections.

CompuServe

http://www.compuserve.com/

This is the home page of the international online service. Find out about CompuServe and its services, including its Internet forum.

Concentric Research Corporation

http://www.cris.com/

This home page for Concentric Research Corporation provides information about the company's products and services. The Concentric Network provides the communications for the wide variety of information and entertainment services available in the market at affordable rates. This information service company provides flat-rate Internet access.

connect.com.au

http://www.connect.com.au/

This is one of Australia's Internet providers. When you set up an account, you get access, connections, and network support to the Internet.

Contributed Software GbR

http://www.contrib.de/e-Contrib/Contrib_Home.html

This Internet services provider is located in Berlin, Germany. In addition to product and server information, their server contains free software.

CRL

http://www.crl.com/CRL-info/Basic.Services.Info

CRL provides connections and support for using the Internet. This national Internet provider can support T1 connections.

Crocker Communications

http://www.crocker.com/

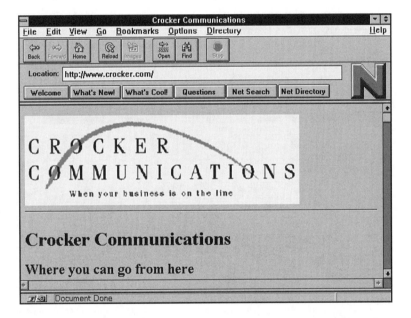

Crocker Communications provides connections and support for accessing the Internet. This Internet provider serves the Massachusetts area.

CyberGate, Inc.

http://www.gate.net/

This Internet provider serves the Florida region. Check their URL Roulette and the other interesting items and links on their home page.

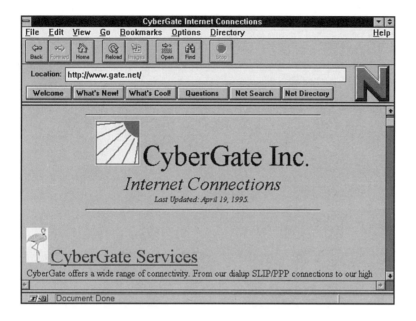

Cyberstore Systems

http://www.cyberstore.net/

Cyberstore Systems provides Internet services and support. This Canadian Internet provider can support T1 connections.

DATABANK

http://www.databank.com/

This is the server for DATABANK. Here you can find information about DATABANK's products and services, including Internet access. This Internet provider and Web developer serves the state of Kansas.

Dayton Network Access

http://www.dnaco.net/

This is the site for Dayton Network Access, an Ohio-based Internet provider and Web developer that serves the state of Ohio and surrounding areas. Here you can find information about Dayton Network Access' products and services, including Internet access.

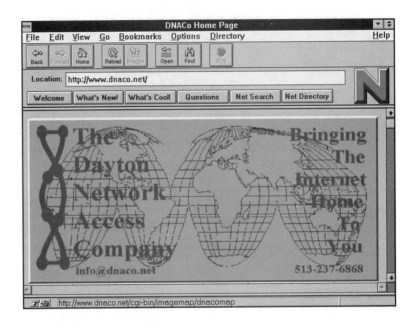

Demon Internet

http://www.demon.co.uk/

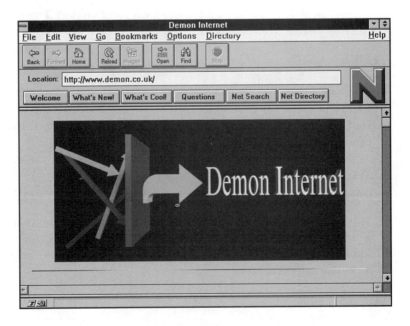

This is the site for Demon Internet, an Internet provider that serves the United Kingdom. Here you can find information about Demon Internet's services, including Internet access.

The Destek Group

http://www.destek.net/

This New England Internet provider has good links to state information and other points of interest in the northeast. Here's where to find information about The Destek Group's services, including Internet access.

Digital Express Group

http://www.digex.net

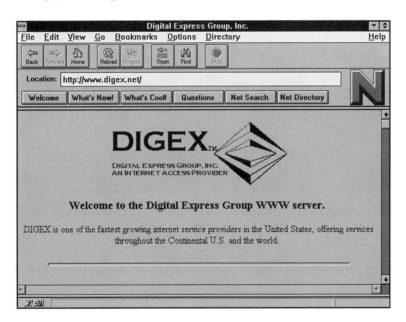

Here you can find information about the Digital Express Group's services. This Internet provider serves the east coast, and can support a T1 connection.

Digital.Net

http://digital.net/

This Internet provider serves the Central Florida area. The Digital Decisions home page includes interesting information, such as a local Web guide, Web overview, and local hotlists.

E-Znet

http://www.eznet.net/

This New York Internet provider services and supports the Rochester area
server. E-Znet supports ISDN connections.

EarthLink Network

http://www.earthlink.net/

EarthLink Network is an Internet provider based in Southern California. Their
server provides a great source of links to business customers, as well as to other
selected Web sites.

The Eden Matrix

http://www.eden.com/

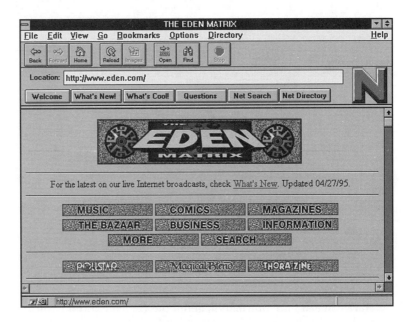

The Eden Matrix is an Austin, Texas, Internet provider (and home of the live
Internet concert broadcast by the same name). Users will find information
about alternative music, 'zines, comics, and more.

Electric Chicago

http://www.echi.com/

Chicagoland's Internet provider and developer, with a growing list of links to clients and other places of interest.

ElectriCiti

http://www.electriciti.com/

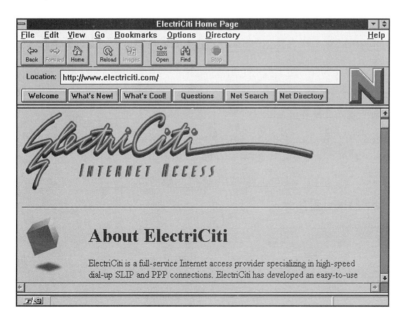

ElectriCiti, which provides connections and support for the Internet, serves the San Diego area. Links are available to local businesses and other points of interest.

Electronic Systems of Richmond

http://www.I2020.net/

This Internet provider, based in Richmond, Virginia, supports the eastern United States.

EMi Communications

http://www.emi.com/EMIhome.html

At this site for EMi Communications you can find information about EMi Communications' services and Internet access. This Internet provider serves the state of New York.

The EmiNet Domain

http://www.emi.net/

This full-service Internet provider, based in Palm Beach County, supports the south Florida region. Their home page has information about the company's services and products, including fascinating Web sites, generous FTP sites, the stock market, and online stores.

Eris Systems

http://erisys.org/

This Internet provider and consultant serves the Ypsilanti and Ann Arbor, Michigan, area. Eris Systems specializes in helping medium and small businesses set up and establish Internet-based information servers.

EUnet

http://www.EU.net/

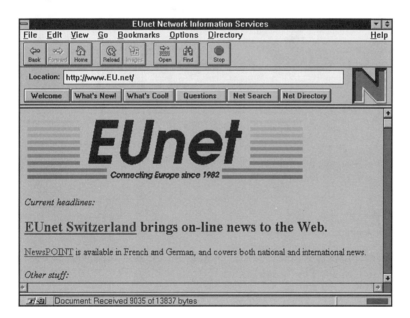

This European Internet provider and developer has links to Web points of interest all over the continent and the Isles. These pages are provided in several languages.

EuroNet Internet

http://www.euro.net/

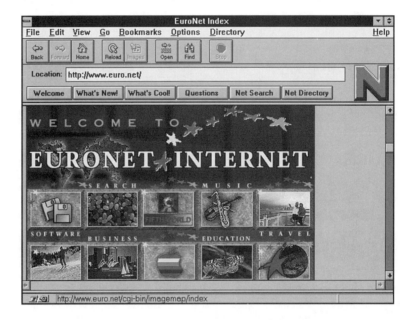

In this nicely done home page for EuroNet Internet, a European Internet provider and developer, links are available to many Europe-related travel, recreation, business, education, and news sites.

Fry Multimedia

http://www.frymulti.com/

This Internet provider and developer, located in Ann Arbor, Michigan, is the technical division of Fry Communications.

Fujitsu

http://www.fujitsu.co.jp/

This Internet provider supports the Japanese online community. The home page is in Japanese.

gofast.net

http://gofast.net/

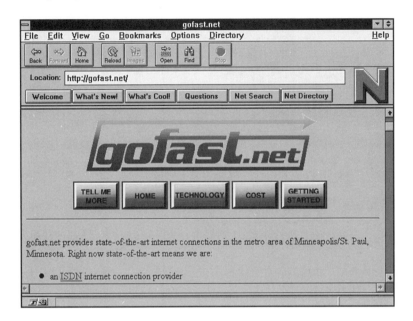

This is the site for gofast.net, which provides a one-stop-shopping Internet connection. The home page has information about gofast.net's services, support, and products. This Minnesota Internet provider supports ISDN connections.

The Great Lakes Area Commercial Internet

http://www.glaci.com/Welcome.html

Check out the home page of the Wisconsin-based Internet provider. Find out about their services and how to link to regional points of interest.

The Gulf Coast Internet Company

http://www.gulf.net/

This is the Web page for Gulf Coast Internet. This Pensacola-based Internet provider serves the Gulf Coast of Florida and provides a full range of Internet services, from individual access to high-speed business network access. Stop here and take the visitors' tour of Pensacola.

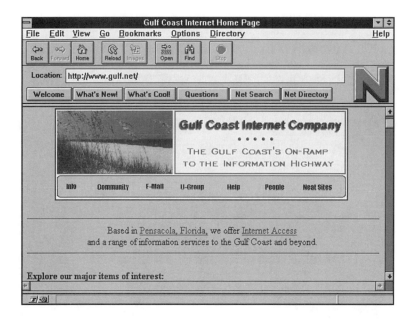

Hong Kong Supernet

http://www.hk.super.net/

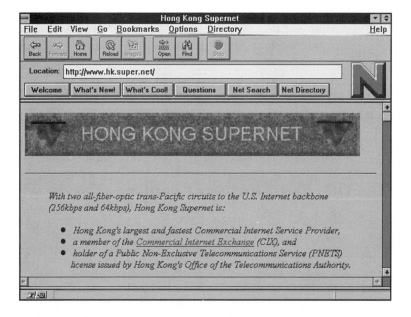

This major Hong Kong Internet provider has two circuits to the U.S. Internet backbone.

Hybrid Networks

http://hybrid.com/HybridHomePage.html

Hybrid is an Internet service provider. Their home page provides corporate information, including help wanted opportunities, product information, and announcements.

I-2000

http://i-2000.com/

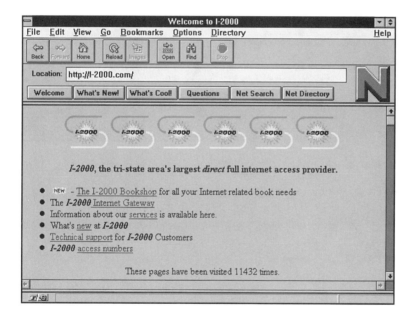

This is the site for I-2000, an Internet provider that serves the New York City metropolitan area. Here you can find information about I-2000's services and Internet access.

IDS World Network

http://www.ids.net/

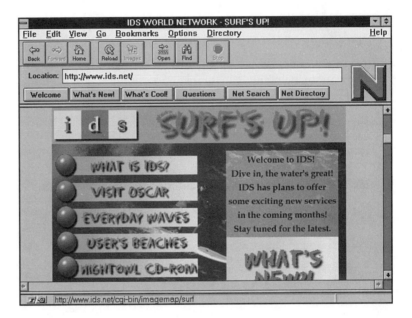

This home page for IDS World Network, an Internet provider that serves certain markets on the East Coast, provides information about the company's products and services. The page includes interesting information from around the globe.

IIA Home Page

http://www.iia.org/

This is the site for International Internet Association, a free Internet provider based in Washington, D.C. On this page you can find information about the company's services and Internet access.

Infonaut Communication Services

http://www.infonaut.com/

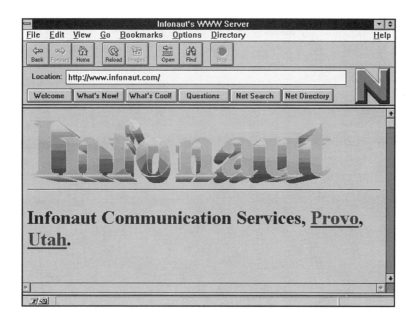

This is the site for Infonaut Communication Services. Their home page has information about Infonaut's services and Internet access. This Internet provider serves the Provo, Utah area and supports all standard Internet services.

Information Discovery, Inc.

http://www.i-discover.com/

This is the site for Information Discovery, Inc., an Internet consulting firm. Check out their "Resource Toolbox," with links to many Web searching tools and services.

INS Info Services

http://www.infonet.net/

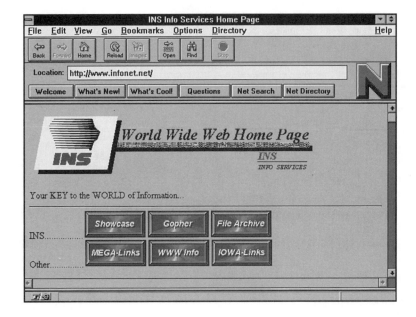

This Internet provider serves the state of Iowa and the Midwest.

INSINC

http://www.insinc.net/

This is the site for INSINC, a Canadian Internet provider that serves Canada and the United States. Here you can find information about INSINC's services and Internet access.

INTAC Access Corporation

http://www.intac.com/

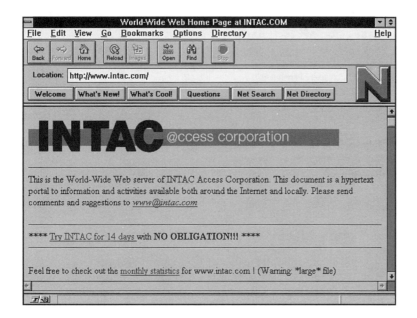

At this site, you can find information about INTAC Access Corporations' services and Internet access. This Internet provider for the Northeast supports T1 connections.

Intelligence Network Online, Inc.

http://www.intnet.net

This Web page is produced by Intelligence Network Online, Inc. Their home page has information about the company's services and products. Intelligence Network Online is a full-service Internet provider that serves Florida's Tampa Bay area and supports high-speed T1 connections.

InterMind

http://www.intermind.net/

This Internet provider supports the Nevada online community and also has links to Las Vegas information.

Internet Atlanta, Inc.

http://www.com/atlanta/index.html

The Southeast is served by this Internet provider, which can support T1 connections.

Internet Initiative Japan

http://www.iij.ad.jp/

The home page of this Japanese Internet provider is available in both English and Japanese.

Internet Public Access Corporation

http://www.ipac.net/

This Internet provider serves the San Jose, California area.

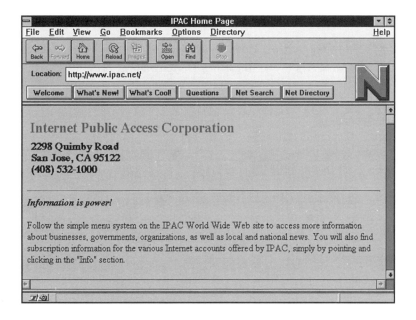

InternetU

http://iu.net/

This Internet provider serves Florida's Brevard County area. Their home page has information about the company's services.

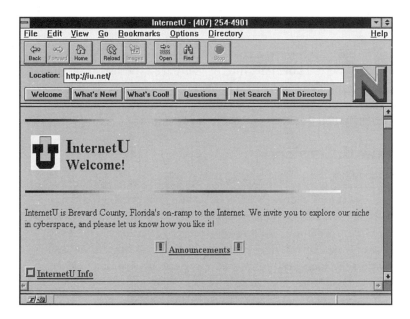

Interpath

http://www.interpath.net/

This Internet provider serves the southeastern United States.

Interse

http://www.interse.com/

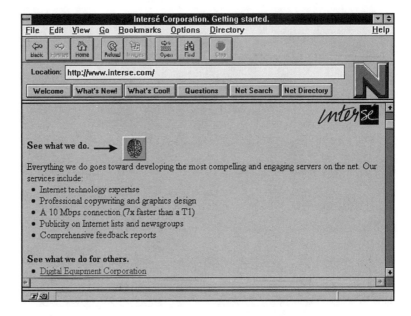

This is the home page for Interse, a company that writes World Wide Web server home pages. Services include: Internet software expertise, professional copywriting and graphics design, marketing and sales expertise, a 10 Mbps connection (seven times faster than a T1), publicity on Internet lists and newsgroups, detailed feedback reports, and ongoing information maintenance.

IQuest Network Services

http://www.iquest.net/

The home page of IQuest Network Services, an Internet provider and developer whose services include custom Web pages, form remailing, virtual shopping systems, and information about how to get your own Internet account and how to create your own HTML pages. Also located on this page is the Galaxy Mall, which offers the latest in Internet shopping and professional services, including opening your own store front.

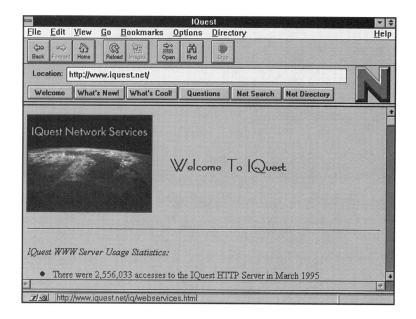

IT Solutions

http://www.its.com/

This is the site for IT Solutions, an Internet provider based in the Rocky Mountain region. Here you can get information about IT Solutions' services and Internet access.

Jax Gateway to the World

http://jax.gttw.com/Jax-GTTW/index.html

This Internet provider serves the state of Florida.

Lanka Internet Services

http://www.lanka.net/

At this site you can find information about services, including Internet access, offered by Lanka Internet Services, the first and only Internet provider in Sri Lanka. Other services provided by the company include Internet and store-and-forward fax services.

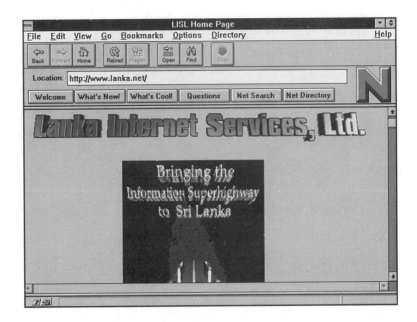

LvNet-Teleport

http://www.riga.lv/

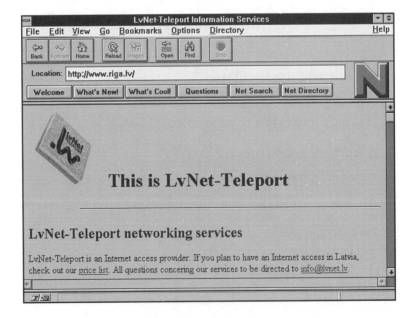

LvNet-Teleport provides Internet service in Latvia. The home page has information about LvNet-Teleport's services.

MGL Systems

http://www.mgl.ca/

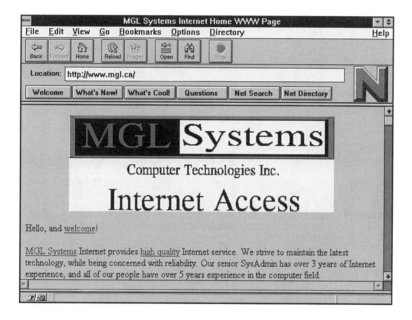

This Canadian Internet provider supports and services Toronto and surrounding areas.

MicroSystems Internet Services

http://www.comnet.com/

This is the home page of Utah Wired, provided by MicroSystems Internet Services. The simple home page has information about Utah and local business and maintains links to many useful Web sites.

MISNet Internet

http://andromeda.mis.net/

This Internet provider serves the state of Kentucky. This page also includes the Bluegrass cafe.

MV Communications, Inc.

http://www.mv.com/

MV Communications, Inc., provides connections and support for the Internet. This Internet provider serves the New Hampshire area.

NederNet

http://www.nedernet.nl/

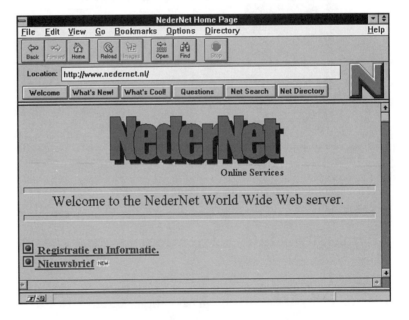

This Dutch Internet provider is based in Rotterdam.

NetPoint Communications, Inc.

http://www.netpoint.net/

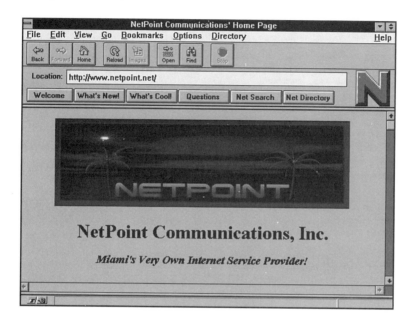

This home page for NetPoint Communications, Inc., provides information about the company's products, consulting, and marketing services. NetPoint, which serves Florida's Miami and Ft. Lauderdale metropolitan area, also offers services in both English and Spanish.

NORDUnet—Nordic Backbone Network

http://info.nordu.net/

This Internet provider serves Denmark, Finland, Iceland, Norway, and Sweden. Look here to find servers in Scandinavia and a clickable map of the Nordic countries.

North Shore Access

http://www.shore.net/

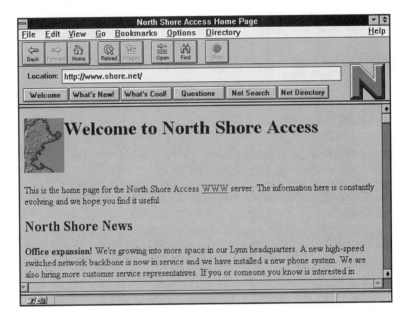

This Internet provider serves the metropolitan Boston area. The home page has information about North Shore Access's services and products, including online classes. North Shore also has links to local government and other interesting sites on the Web.

One World Telecommunications

http://www.owt.com/

This page, the site for One World Telecommunications, has information about One World Telecommunications' services. This Internet provider serves Washington state's online community. The interesting home page includes what's new on the net and links to good starting points.

ONRAMP Network Services

http://www.onramp.ca/

This Internet provider serves the Toronto, Canada region.

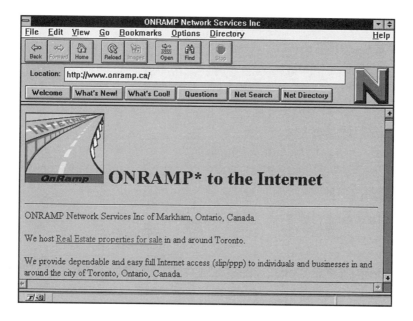

PacketWorks

http://www.packet.net/

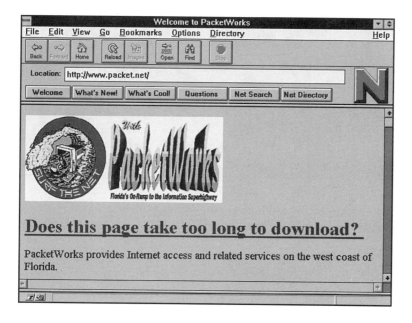

This Internet provider serves the west coast of Florida.

PEM

http://www.pem.com/english_index.html

This provider supports Internet service in the Stuttgart, Germany region.

PFM

http://www.PFM-Mainz.DE/

This home page for PFM, the Internet provider that serves Germany's Mainz/ Wiesbaden area, is written in German. This page provides information about the company's products and services.

Pilot Network Services

http://www.pilot.net/

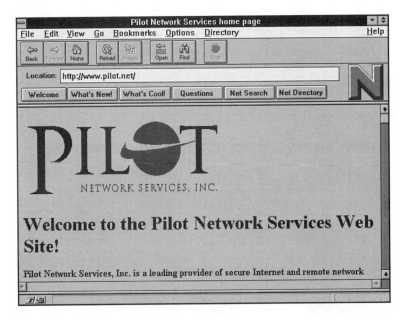

Pilot Network Services provides connections and support for using the Internet. This Internet provider supports California's San Francisco Bay area.

Portal Information Network

http://www.portal.com/

This Internet provider, serving the San Francisco Bay area, supports T1 connections.

QNSnet

http://www.qns.com/

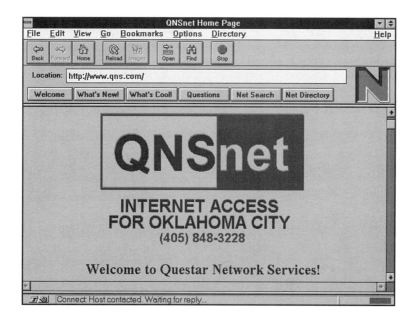

This Internet provider serves Oklahoma's Oklahoma City area. QNSnet, a full-service Internet provider, specializes in setting up and maintaining Internet service.

SatelNET Communications

http://www.satelnet.org

This Internet provider and developer is based in southeast Florida. Their server contains links to their clients, as well as links to general Web resources.

Singapore Telecom

http://www.singnet.com.sg/

Singapore Telecom provides connections and support for the Internet. This Internet provider serves Singapore.

Sprint Communications

http://www.sprintlink.net/

This is the server for Sprint Communications. Here you can find information about Sprint's communications products and services, including Internet access and networking.

Supernet

http://www.supernet.net/

This is the Web page for Supernet. Their Surfer's Paradise claims to have the fastest routes to the best sites and much more, including the Super Mall. This Internet provider serves Tallahassee and supports T1 connections.

SURAnet

http://www.sura.net/

Started by the Southeastern Universities Research Association, Inc., a nonprofit research consortium, this Internet provider primarily serves academic, government, and nonprofit institutions in the southeastern United States, the Caribbean Basin, and South America.

SWITCH

http://www.switch.ch/

This Internet provider serves Switzerland and supports ISDN connections.

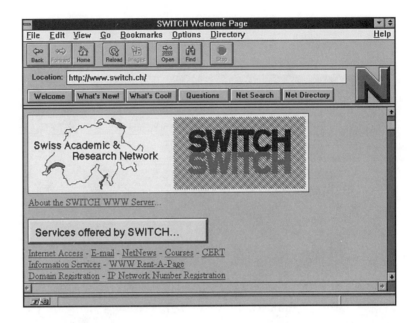

Synergy Communications

http://www.synergy.net/synergy/synergy.html

This company provides national Internet service in the United States.

Tachyon Communications Corp.

http://www.tach.net/

Tachyon Communications Corp. provides connections and support for the Internet. This provider serves the state of Florida.

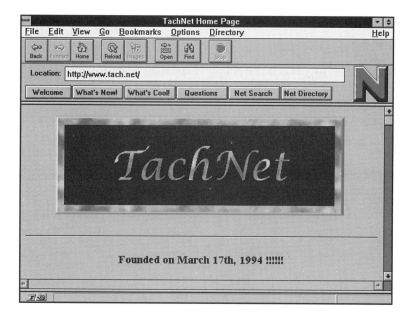

Technet

http://www.technet.sg/

This is the site for Technet, an Internet provider that serves Singapore. Here you can find information about Technet's products and services, including Internet access.

TFSnet Online Information Service

http://www.fileshop/com/

This home page for TFSnet Online Information Service provides information about the company's products and services. This Internet provider serves the Midwestern states.

thenet.ch

http://www.thenet.ch/thenet.ch/

This Internet provider supports ISDN connections to the Swiss Internet community.

ThoughtPort Authority

http://www.thoughtport.com/

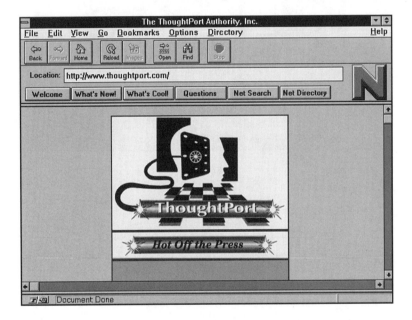

This is the site for ThoughtPort Authority. Here you can find information about the company's products and services, including Internet access. This national Internet provider can support T1 connections.

Tyrell Online Services

http://www.tyrell.net/

This home page for Tyrell Online Services provides information about the company's products and services. This Internet provider serves the central portion of the United States. Included on its pages are Worldspan, a worldwide travel service, and other links to the world.

US Internet, Inc.

http://www.usit.net/

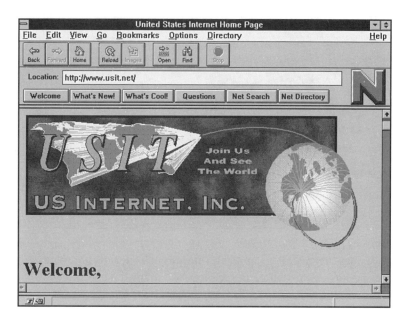

This Internet provider serves Knoxville and eastern Tennessee, and supports T1 connections.

U-NET

http://www.u-net.com/

This home page for U-NET provides information about the company's products and services. This Internet provider serves northwest England.

WAIS, Inc.

http://server.wais.com/

WAIS, Inc., provides online publishing systems and services to organizations that want to distribute information through the Internet.

Wimsey Information Services

http://www.wimsey.com/

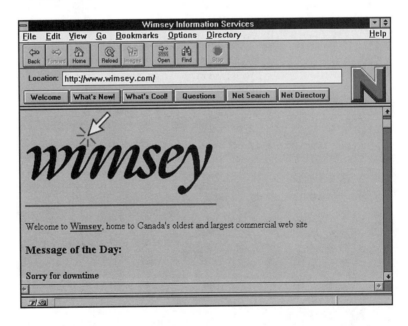

Wimsey Information Services is a Canadian Internet provider. Its home page includes information on the company's services and many links to ski-related Web sites.

Wis.com

http://heather.wis.com/

This Internet provider serves central Wisconsin. This is a good starting point for information about local sites.

wyoming.com

http://www.wyoming.com/

This is the site for Wyoming.com. Here you can find information about the company's products and services, including local Internet access. This Internet provider supports the state of Wyoming.

xs4all

http://www.xs4all.nl/

The home page of a Holland Internet provider. Currently, this page is available only in Dutch.

Web Resources

The beginning of this chapter listed and described Internet resources. This section describes Web-specific resources, including directories, Archie servers, and Best of the Web sites.

Ammar's Little Hut

http://civlab0.civil.mtu.edu:3770/hutgate.html

An interesting collection of pages and links to other Kuwaiti Web sites, including sounds, pieces of wisdom, and humor.

Arachnophilia: Florida Institute of Technology's WWW Server

http://sci-ed.fit.edu

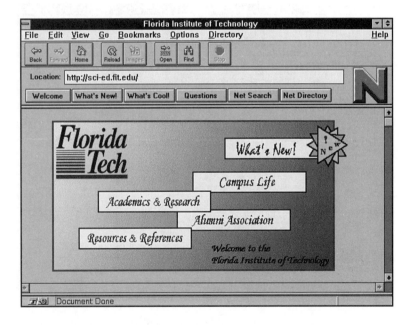

This site, specifically for educators and researchers, provides pointers to information resources and search tools around the Web.

Archie Hypertext Servers

http://webb.nexor.co.uk.archie.html

Here you can find a list of Archie servers around the world.

Association of Internet Resources (AIR), Hong Kong

http://http://www.air.org/

AIR is a Hong Kong server with many interesting international links to data, including a selection of starting points to understand the Internet, the NCSA Mosaic Demo Document, the NCSA Mosaic's "What's New" page, InterNIC Info Source, White House papers, postmodern culture, and the Zippy The Pinhead's page.

The Australian Graduate School of Management (AGSM)

http://www.agsm.unsw.edu.au/Welcome.html

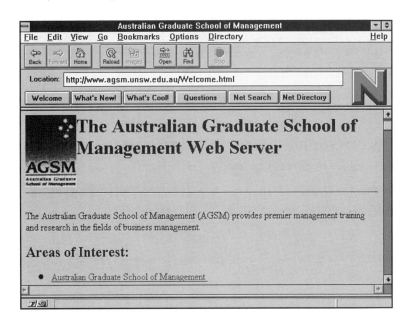

This server provides overview information about the School of Management, including MBA programs, research centers, working papers, and faculty information. Included at this site are the AGSM Gopher server, an FTP service area where AGSM working papers and information are stored, a library catalog, Australian company information, and a list of Australian Web servers.

Australian World Wide Web servers

http://www.csu.edu.au/links/ozweb.html

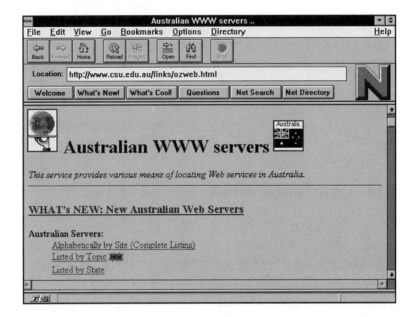

This resource has an interactive map of Australian Web sites, as well as recent additions and indexes arranged alphabetically and by type of service.

Belgian WWW/Gopher resource map

http://info1.vub.ac.be:8080/Belgium_map/index.html

This site has a mouse-sensitive map that lists Belgian Web sites and includes information on academic, government, and commercial resources.

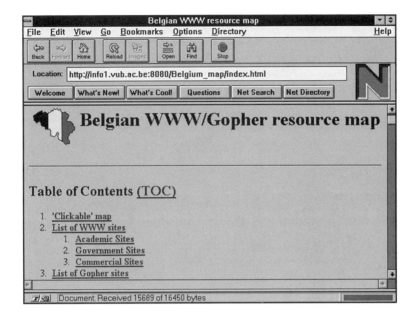

Best of the Web '94

http://wings.buffalo.edu/contest

To find the best of the Web, visit this site. Found here are highlights of the places judged as the best sites on the World Wide Web. The selections were based on the criteria of quality, versatility, and power.

California World Wide Web Servers

http://www.llnl.gov/ptools/california.servers.html

Arranged by topic or type of information, this is an in-depth index of all Web sites in and about the state of California, including government, education, commercial, and other sites.

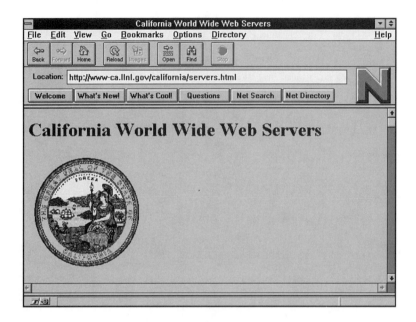

Canadian Geographical World Wide Web Index

http://www.sal.ists.ca/services/w3_can/maps.html

Updated weekly, this sensitive, clickable map points to Web sites all around Canada. The map is divided into provinces.

Central Index of Canadian World Wide Web Servers

http://www.csr.ists.ca/w3can/Welcome.html

At this site you can get a list of Web servers in Canada. (To get the list, from the Web server's directory, click on North America—Canada.) A colorful map of Canada is accessible, along with textual lists of educational, commercial, and other servers. For provinces (and subdivisions, like "Southern Ontario"), other maps are available. Most of the servers shown are for institutions of higher learning, holding the usual information about administration, course offerings, and activities. There are many servers for areas of culture, science, tourism, and provincial governments. Both French and English versions of many listings are available.

New Riders Publishing
INSIDE
SERIES

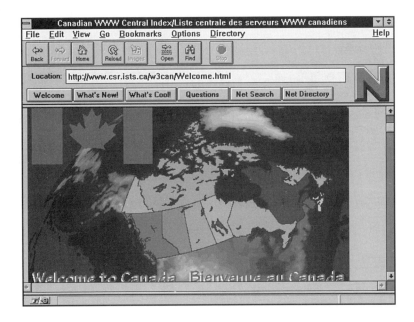

Chile

http://www.doc.uchile.cl/servers.html

This site, the Web home page for Chile, focuses primarily upon academic institutions in Chile, although information about the Web and Internet is included. A hypertext map is also provided.

China Home Page

http://utkvx1.utk.edu/~xurs/china.html

This page, supported by the Institute of High Energy Physics, contains links to China's largest scientific, technical, and business-related Web sites. A Chinese music site also is listed here.

Colombia

http:www.univalle.edu.co/

This site provides links to most other Web servers in Colombia. The primary focus is on academic institutions.

Danish Information Servers

http://info.denet.dk/dk-infoservers.html

This index lists many Danish Web sites. Here you can find information about DKnet, the Danish part of EUnet.

ELVIS+, Co.

http://www.elvis.msk.su/

Come to this Russian site to find exchange rates, a Russian-English dictionary, fax service to Moscow, advertisements, and an index of other Russian Web sites. Use the search engine to search on keywords.

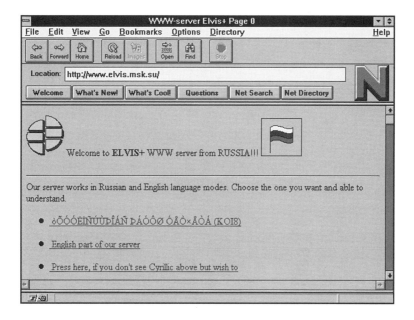

The ETEXT Archives

http://www.etext.org/

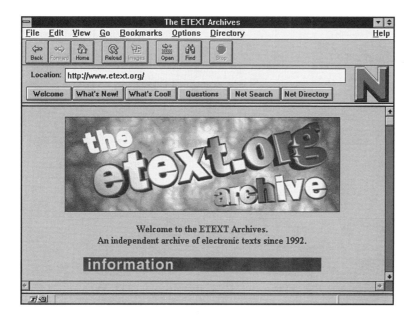

A massive collection of electronic texts is available from this archive. Some of the links include electronic books, magazines, Net literature, computer-related materials, political archives, underground digest archives, and many others.

Felipe's Bilingual WWW Pages

http://edb518ea.edb.utexas.edu

This interactive Web site contains Gopher and Web links to various Latin American resources. Information is in both English and Spanish.

Full List of Information Servers in Israel

http://www.ac.il

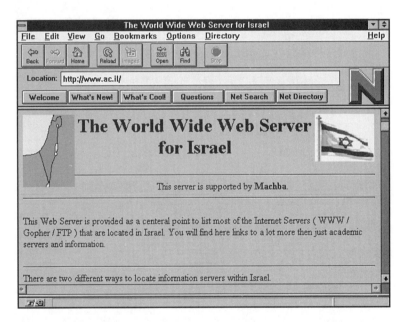

Link with various Web sites in Israel from here. This list, arranged by city, contains mostly educational and research servers.

German Map of Servers

http://www.leo.org/demap/

This is Germany's very full clickable map of Web sites. Improvements are being made to include even more sites.

GNN Digital Drive-In

http://gnn.interpath.net/gnn/special/drivein/index.html

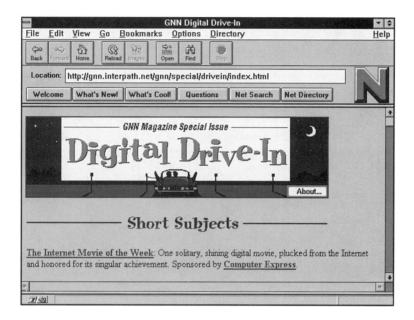

This is a good site for individuals interested in developing their own multimedia projects for the Web. It contains information on new tools, access to digital movie newsgroup discussions, and a weekly example of outstanding digital movies available on the Net.

Home Page for the Netherlands

http://www.eeb.ele.tue.nl/map/netherlands.html

Here you will find an interactive map showing Holland's Web sites. Also included is a hotlinked listing of these sites, as well as additional information about the Netherlands.

HTML FAQ

http://www.umcc.umich.edu/~ec/www/html_faq.html

This resource maintains a FAQ of common questions and answers about Hypertext Markup Language. The FAQ covers the creation and transformation of documents into the Web format.

Hungarian Home Page

http://www.fsz.bme.hu/hungary/homepage.html

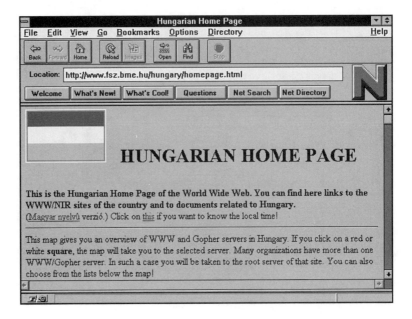

This mouse-sensitive, clickable map of Hungary provides links to local Web sites. Also included is a hypertext listing of sites, arranged by city, as well as information about Hungarian culture, history, geography, and cuisine.

Icelandic World Wide Web Servers

http://www.rfisk.is/english/sites.html

This site presents an interactive map of Iceland, with pointers to its educational and commercial Web sites.

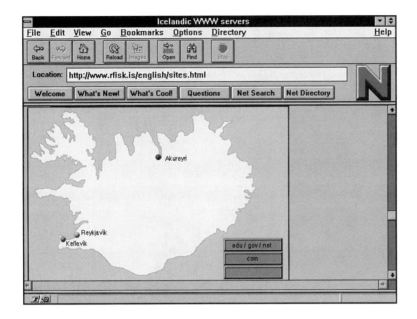

Information about Austria

http://www.ifs.univie.ac.at/austria/austria_info.html

This is a source of quick information about Austria and its economy, culture, history, geography, defense, labor, communications, and government.

Information Society

http://phoenix.creighton.edu/~duke/

This song directory includes record company information, audio clips, and photos. Also included here are a screen saver and links to discographies.

Information Systems in Austria

http://www.ifs.univie.ac.at/austria.html

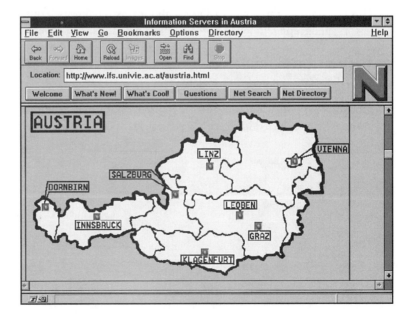

Visit this resource and use its interactive map to get more information about the Web sites in Austria.

Internet Directory

http://home.mcom.com/home/internet-directory.html

From this page you can go anywhere on the Web. This a directory of directories. If you dare, you can get the full list of servers—an enormous list.

Internet Resources for Macintosh

http://www.uwtc.washington.edu/Computing/Internet/MacintoshResources.html

To find Macintosh resources on the Internet, look to this site from the University of Washington. Links include e-mail lists and newsreaders. Also look up Mac communication software reviews.

Internet Services in Turkey

http://www.metu.edu.tr:80/Turkey/inet-turkey.html

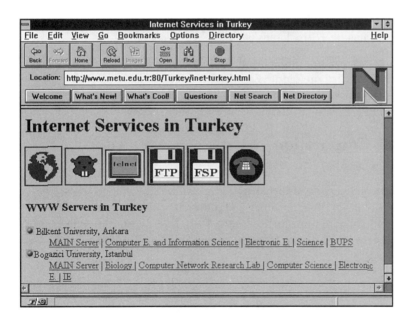

Here you can find a list of Web and other sites in Turkey; most are universities and other organizations.

The InterNIC Directory and Database Services

http://www.internic.net

For a comprehensive look at a service that brings you information about getting started on the Internet, visit this online guide. It provides Scout reports, Internet resources, and Web picks.

Ireland's Web Servers

http://itdsrv1.ul.ie/Information/ServerMapIreland.html

A mouse-sensitive, clickable map of Ireland provides links to more than 50 Irish Web sites, including companies and institutions of learning.

ISnet—The Icelandic Internet

http://www.isnet.is/

Stop here to get access to more than 70 Web sites in Iceland. You can also search for people and specific subjects contained within ISnet.

Israel Sensitive Map

http://shum.cc.huji.ac.il/israel_sens.html

At this Web server you can find a list of Web servers in Israel. From the Web server's directory, click on Middle East, Israel. A map of Israel shows server locations by city. By clicking on the map's background, you can find the complete list of educational, commercial, and other servers.

J.M. Huber Corporation

http://www.huber.com/

In addition to an overview of the corporation and an explanation of its divisions and subsidiaries, this consumer and industrial company offers many Web resources, including an introduction to the Web, Internet starting points, information searches, Internet Indexes, commercial site directories, and a link to CommerceNet.

Kuwait Info Page

http://www.cs.cmu.edu:8001/Web/People/anwar/kuwait.html

Here you can find details on Kuwaiti history, culture, cuisine, and literature, with links to other Middle Eastern Web sites.

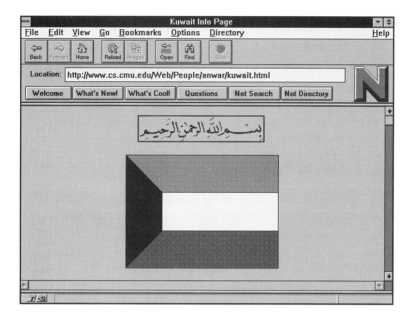

Links from the Underground

http://www.links.net/

This is a collection of weird and unusual places to visit on the Web. You can find almost 500 links from this page!

List of Latvian Information Resources

http://www.vernet.lv/Latvia/sites-list.html

This Web page contains information about resources in Latvia. Included are links to Latvian universities and research departments, a map of Riga, the capital, and links to Latvian Gopher servers. The site also contains a link to Latvia On-Line, which provides general information about Latvia, including its constitution, travel and business information, and more.

List of Russian World Wide Web Servers

http://www.ac.msk.su/map_list.html

This is a good starting place to visit Russian Web sites. Many sites are in English.

List of Multimedia Servers in Poland

http://info.fuw.edu.pl/pl/servers-list.html

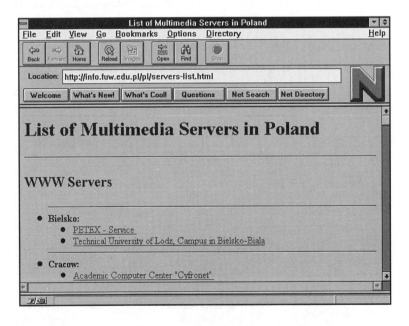

Here you can find a list of about 100 Web sites in Poland, arranged by city. Most are education and research institutions, with a few government sites in Warsaw.

List of W3 Servers in France

http://www.urec.fr/cgi-bin/list

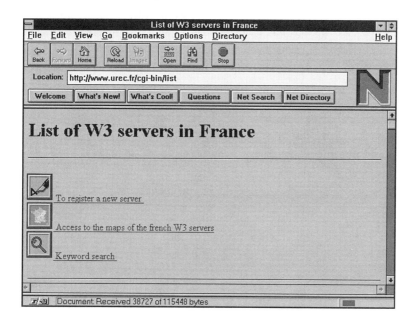

Exactly what it says. This server provides information (in French) and links to dozens of Web sites in France. The emphasis is primarily on academic and research institutions, although some government agencies are listed as well.

Lynx FAQ

http://ftp2.cc.ukans.edu/about_lynx

This Lynx resource contains the Lynx FAQ. Here's where to find the most common questions and answers about Cello, a distributed hypertext browser with full Web capabilities.

Map of Alabama

http://www.eng.auburn.edu/alabama/map.html

This mouse-sensitive, clickable map of Alabama provides links to the state's Web sites, including education, commercial, and military institutions. The NASA Spacelink can also be found here.

Massachusetts Map of WWW Resources

http://donald.phast.umass.edu/misc/mass.html

This virtual map will guide you to commercial and educational Web sites in Massachusetts. It also includes detailed maps of Amherst and Boston.

Master Index of Taiwan World Wide Web Servers

http://peacock.tnjc.edu.tw/ROC_sites.html

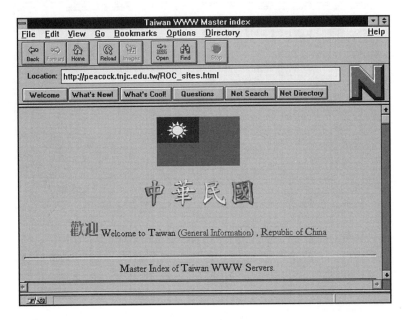

You can search this resource on Taiwan to find information about and the location of Web sites and organizations, or other information of local and Internet interest.

The Ministry of Foreign Affairs of Argentina

http://www.ar:70

This Web site provides links to Gopher and Web servers in Argentina. The bulk of the servers are in Spanish only.

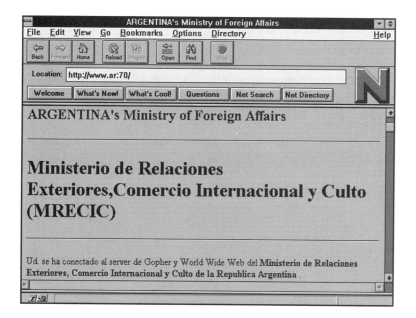

The MIT World Wide Web Consortium (MIT W3C)

http://nfo.cern.ch/hypertext/WWW/Organization/Consortium/
W3OSignature.html

This is the home page for the World Wide Web Consortium, CERN and MIT. They set the standards for Web interoperability and provide help, direction, subject searching capabilities, and software and online documentation. If you are interested in how and why, this is the site to investigate.

NCSA Mosaic FAQ

http://www.ncsa.uiuc.edu/SDG/Software/MacMosaic/FAQ/FAQ-mac.html

This resource hosts a FAQ file for the Macintosh version of NCSA Mosaic.

New Jersey World Wide Web Sites

http://www.stevens-tech.edu/nj.html

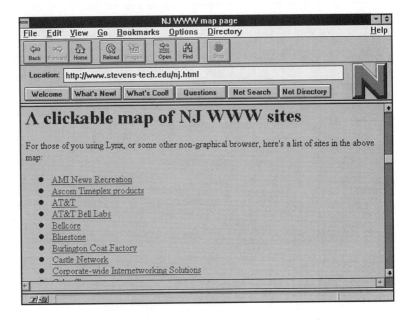

On this page is a clickable map that highlights the state of New Jersey, including Web sites and educational and research institutions.

New York World Wide Web Servers

http://www.rpi.edu/NewYork/List.html

This New York server provides a list, organized by service sector, of Web sites in the state.

New York World Wide Web Sites

http://wings.buffalo.edu/world/nywww.html

This site has a mouse-sensitive map of the state of New York, with links to colleges, universities, military bases, and other interesting sites.

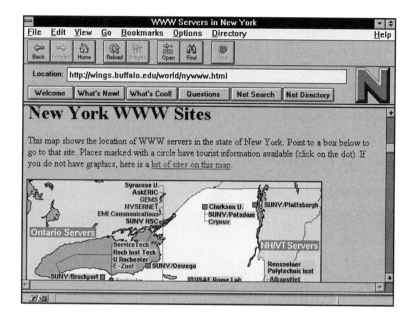

Nightingale

http://nightingale.con.utk.edu:70/0/homepage.html

This is a comprehensive guide to nursing-related Web sites, put out by the College of Nursing at the University of Tennessee at Knoxville. The guide contains information about the outlook for national health care, nursing programs offered at other colleges, professional publications available on the Net, and so on.

NIR List in Greece

http://www.forthnet.gr/hellas/nir-list.html

This site contains a list (in English) of Web servers in Greece. Emphasis is placed on academic and research institutions. In addition, links to university libraries are provided.

Northeast Asia World Wide Web Servers

http://www.ntt.jp/AP/asia-NE.html

This mouse-sensitive map has information about Web sites in China, Hong Kong, India, Japan, Korea, and Taiwan.

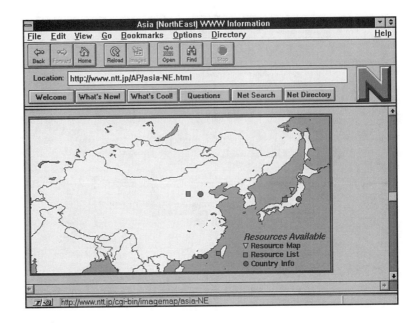

Oxford University Computing Laboratory Archive Service

http://www.comlab.ox.ac.uk/archive/

This site offers a large variety of resources, links, and information available on the Web. Archived here are extensive resource materials, including image archives, software programs, sound archives, museums, and art galleries, as well as a plethora of other information.

Poland World Wide Web Sites

http://info.fuw.edu.pl/pl/PolandResourceMap.html

A small but growing list of Polish Web sites can be found on this mouse-sensitive map.

Portugal Home Page

http://s700.uminho.pt/homepage-pt.html

A very nice clickable map summarizing Web and other sites in Portugal. From here, you can access general and tourist information as well as details about cultural events.

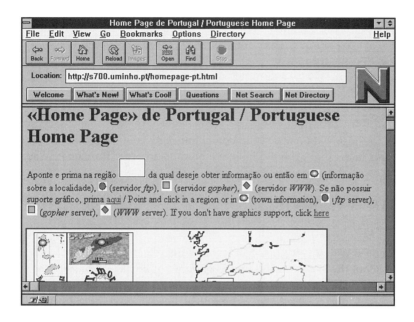

RESTENA

http://www.restena.lu/

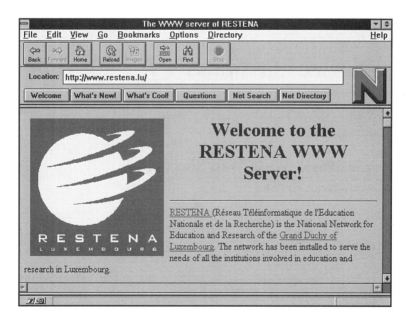

This is the server for the National Network for Education and Research of the Grand Duchy of Luxembourg. Here you can find links to other Web sites in this Northern European country.

Romania

http://info.cs.pub.ro/

Visit this site for information about the Politechnic University of Bucharest and about Romania in general. Also available are pointers to other Romanian Web sites.

Servidor WWW da RNP

http://www.rnp.br

This is the central Web server for the Brazilian Research Network. It includes information about the Web and Internet in general in Brazil, and has links to most other Web, Gopher, and FTP servers in Brazil. At present, the information is provided in Portuguese only; in the future, English versions will be added.

South African WWW servers

http://www.is.co.za/www-za.html

Here you can find links to commercial, educational, and other interesting Web sites in South Africa. This resource has a mouse-sensitive map of these sites.

Southeast Asia World Wide Web Servers

http://www.ntt.jp/AP/asia-SE.html

This mouse-sensitive map contains links to Web servers in Indonesia, Malaysia, Singapore, and Thailand.

Southwest Asia World Wide Web Servers

http://www.ntt.jp/AP/asia-SW.html

Check out this mouse-sensitive map for Web resources in Afghanistan, Bangladesh, India, Iran, Israel, Kuwait, Nepal, Pakistan, Saudi Arabia, Sri Lanka, and Turkey.

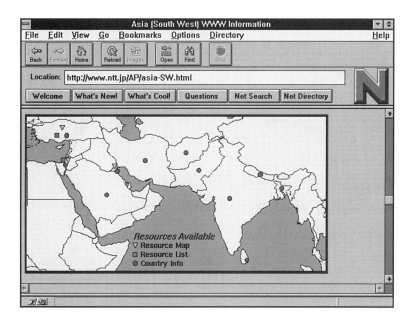

Spain Internet Resources

http://www.uji.es/spain_www.html

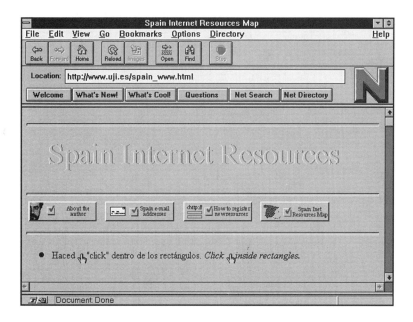

This uniquely designed mouse-sensitive, clickable map links you with Web sites throughout Spain.

(Spider's Web) Writing

http://gagme.wwa.com/~boba/primer.html

Sooner or later Web surfers are going to come to the conclusion, "Hey, I can do that," and get involved in creating their own Web sites. This page contains lots of resources and guides to start the aspiring Web master on his or her way.

Switzerland-Based WWW Servers

http:///www.math.ethz.ch/~zari/admin/chw3.html

From the home of the Web itself, this list contains information about, and links to, dozens and dozens of Web servers in Switzerland, including "the" World Wide Web server, the main server for the Web initiative itself. The emphasis of this list is academic- and research-oriented, but servers oriented toward more general interest are included also.

Thailand World Wide Web Information-Map

http://www.chiangmai.ac.th/thmap.html

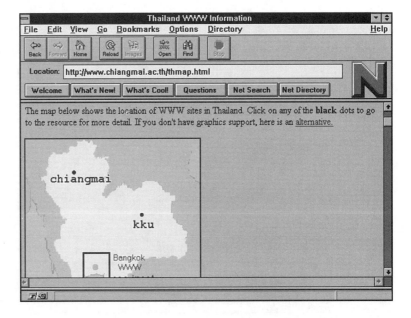

This resource maintains access to Thailand's educational, commercial, and technical Web sites. Also, a mouse-sensitive map can help you locate Thailand's Web servers.

UK Sensitive Map

http://scitsc.wlv.ac.uk/ukinfo/uk.map.html

From here you can access two interactive maps: one with cultural and research Web servers, the other with commercial Web servers. You can also point to a tourist map.

United Kingdom-Based WWW Servers

http://src.doc.ic.ac.uk/all-uk.html

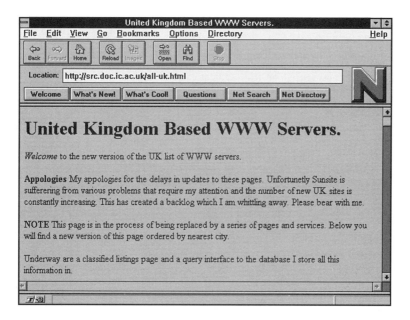

At this site you can get a list of Web servers and other useful information about the United Kingdom. A tourist map also is available by clickable link.

U.S. Department of the Interior

http://info.er.usgs.gov/doi/doi.html

In addition to general information about the United States Department of the Interior, this server contains links to the Bureau of Indian Affairs, Bureau of Land Management, Bureau of Reclamation, National Biological Survey, National Park Service, and the United States Fish and Wildlife Service.

Virtual Book Shop

http://www.virtual.bookshop.com/

From this site you can search for and buy rare, first edition, antiquarian, and collectible books from booksellers all over the world. The search function available from this site includes keywords and authors.

W3 Servers

http://www11.w3.org/hypertext/DataSources/WWW/Servers.html

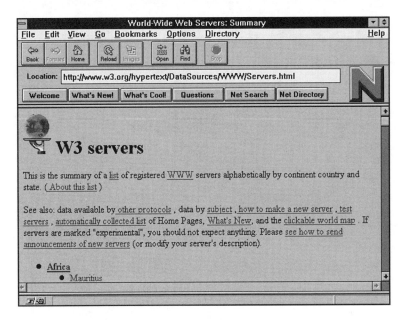

All registered World Wide Web servers are accessible from this page, which is accessible through the top Web page, "Overview of the Web." You can click on items according to continent or country. Usually, at the "country" level, a

clickable "sensitive" map leads to other maps, lists of servers, and/or specific servers. Many maps are quite large, colorful, and detailed.

Web Servers in Norway

http://www.ii.uib.no/~magnus/norway.html

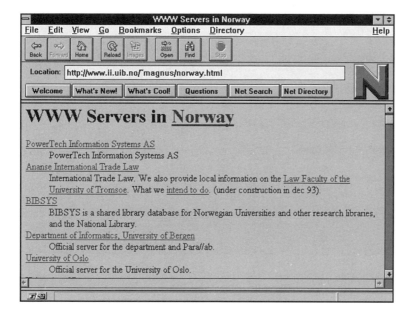

Most of the Web sites in this list are for academic institutions; however, business, commercial, governmental, and "fun" sites are included as well.

Web Servers (Spain)

http://www.gae.unican.es/general/es-servers.html

This site contains information about and links to academic and research Web servers in Spain. The information here is mixed (Spanish and English).

WebCrawler

http://www.biotech.washington.edu/WebCrawler/WebQuery.html

The WebCrawler is a program that runs through the Web visiting as many sites as it can to create a master index of what is on the Web. After the user enters a keyword, the WebCrawler brings up sites pertaining to this word.

Welcome to Lithuania

http://neris.mii.lt/

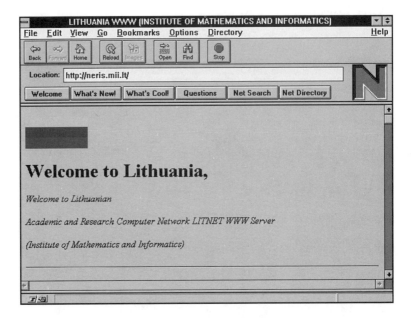

A good source of information about Lithuanian news, history, academic resources, art and culture, and a listing of other Web sites. Also a good place to find tourist information.

What's Hot and Cool on the Web

http://kzsu.stanford.edu/uwi/reviews.html

As the site name suggests, this server contains links to many of the hot and cool servers all over the Web. Users can find lists and reviews of more than 150 selected sites, such as the popular Dr. Fun's page, exhibitions of stellar art, and directories to e-zines.

The Whole Internet Catalog

http://www.digital.com/gnn/wic/index.html

You can search this multicategory catalog by choosing from different subjects and areas of interest. Many interesting topics are highlighted here.

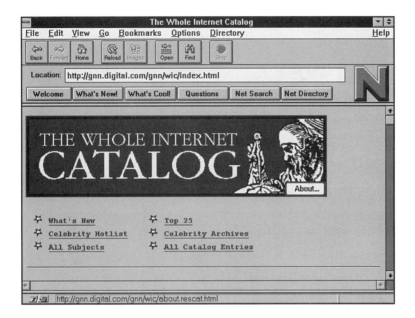

World Wide Web Servers in Japan

http://www.ntt.jp/SQUARE/www-in-JP.html

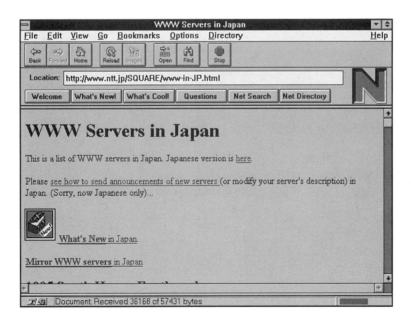

This is a comprehensive list of Web sites in Japan, including universities, companies, and other items of general interest.

World Wide Web FAQ

http://sunsite.unc.edu/boutell/faq/www_faq.html

This site maintains a FAQ containing common questions and answers about the Web.

World Wide Web Servers in Germany

http://www.chemie.fu-berlin.de/outerspace/www-german.html

This site contains an extremely detailed list of Web sites all over Germany, divided by locality and city. Sites include commercial, educational, and general interest areas.

World Wide Web Servers in Iceland

http://www.isnet.is/WWW/servers.html

This is a short but growing list of Web sites in Iceland, including the University of Iceland and the Icelandic Fire Authority.

World Wide Web Servers in Korea

http://www.dongguk.ac.kr/

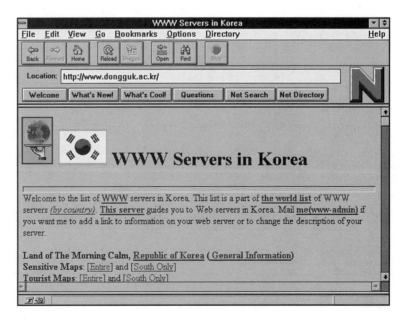

Organized by city and location, this is where to find the Web sites in North and South Korea, including universities, corporations, and others.

World Wide Web Servers in Slovakia

http://nic.uakom.sk/hypertext/homepage.html

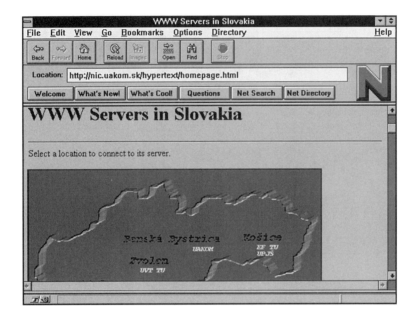

This is a short but growing list of Web servers in the new republic of Slovakia.

World Wide Web Servers in Turkey

http://www.metu.edu.tr:80/Turkey/

This mouse-sensitive map of Turkey's Web sites includes some basic historical and geographical information about Turkey.

World Wide Web Servers—Italy

http://www.mi.cnr.it/NIR-IT/NIR-map.html

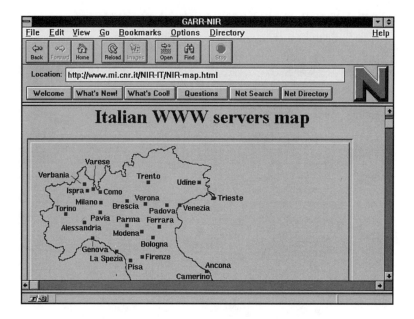

This interactive map with links to Italian Web sites is also a good place to get general information about the country and its attractions.

World Wide Web Servers—Massachusetts

http://sturtevant.com/wwwlist/mas.html

This Web site maintains hundreds of links to Bay State colleges and universities.

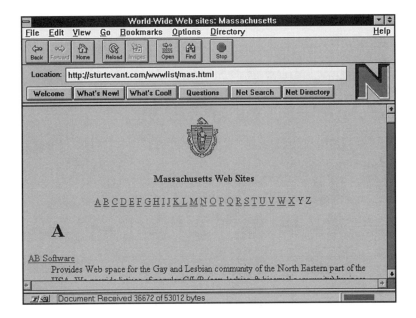

World Wide Web Servers—Switzerland

http://www.math.ethz.ch/~zari/admin/chw3.html

A listing of Web sites in Switzerland, including many CERN-related entries. Commercial, educational, and research institutions are represented.

World Wide Web: The Project

http://info.cern.ch/hypertext/WWW/TheProject

This is the home page for the World Wide Web Project. It has all sorts of information about the Web and links to everywhere. If you want to know about the Web, this is the place to start.

World Wide Web Home Page

http://www.w3.org/

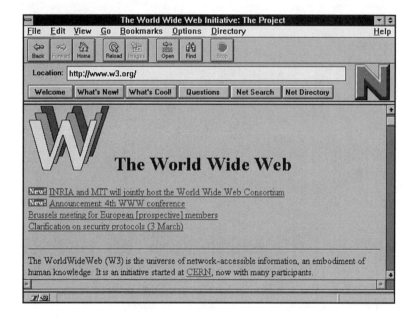

This is the top-level server location for the World Wide Web, and is the address for the "official" home page. This is the official center of the Web. For details, please refer to "World Wide Web: The Project."

Wow, It's Big!

http://www.netgen.com/cgi/comprehensive

This site contains an enormous database of more than 10,000 Web sites around the world. With customizable search queries, users can easily access the sites they might want to visit.

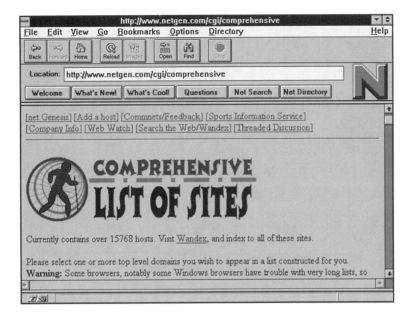

WWW Biological Science Servers

http://info.er.usgs.gov/network/science/biology/index.html

This Web site contains Internet links to many Gopher servers and other Web sites about bioscience.

WWW Servers in Kuwait

http://civlab0.civil.mtu.edu:3770/kuwait.html

At this site you can get a list of Web servers in Kuwait.

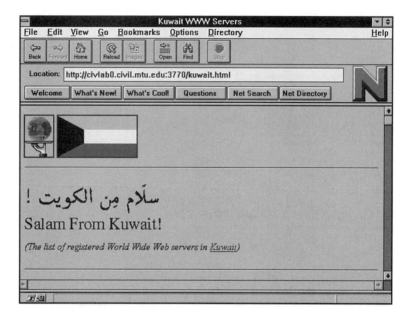

WWW Servers in Mexico

http://info.pue.udlap.mx/mexico-geo.html

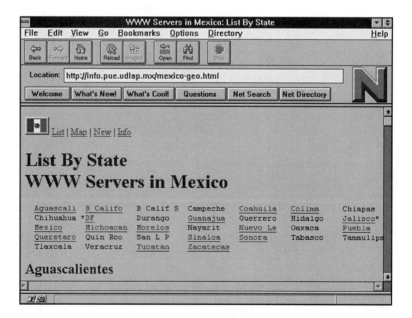

At this site you can get a list of Web servers in Mexico. From the Web server's directory, click on North America, Mexico. A colorful cities/servers map of Mexico is displayed, along with textual lists of educational, commercial, and other servers. The Virtual Tourist service and the "What's New" item also are clickable. Most of the servers are for institutions of higher learning, and point the way to the usual information about administration, course offerings, and activities.

WWW Servers in Thailand

http://www.chiangmai.ac.th/Servers-th.html

This resource maintains access to a list of Thailand's educational, commercial, and technical Web sites.

Yahoo

http://www.yahoo.com/

Yahoo is a searchable guide to the Web. With more than 26,000 sites divided into 19 separate subjects areas (alphabetized from Art to Society and Culture), this server is an invaluable starting place for any Web journey. In addition to subject area and keyword searches, the Yahoo server also provides other search engines such as WebCrawler, Lycos, EINet Galaxy, Aliweb, and CUSI search engines.

Looking at the Best
Technical Sites

I t's a foregone conclusion that if you're on the World Wide
Web, you have a computer. This chapter looks at some of the
newest sites (as of this writing) that contain information for
computer users. The chapter also lists some research and science
resources you can find on the Web.

Before You Get Too Involved

To help start you on your way, the Macmillan SuperLibrary Web site (see fig. 25.1) is full of computer resources. You can find it at the following URL:

```
http://www.mcp.com
```

Figure 25.1

Visit the Macmillan SuperLibrary for a comprehensive source of computer books and general reference material.

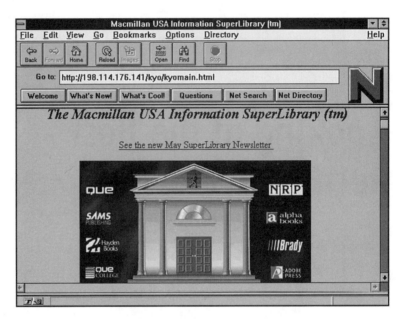

Another interesting Web site to browse is the Silicon Graphics (SGI) Home page shown in figure 25.2 (a good example of a nicely done home page). This Web server houses press releases, educational information, and other technical documents.

Set your browser to the following URL for the SGI Web page:

```
http://www.sgi.com
```

Several other major computer companies have home pages on the Web. Table 25.1 lists some of these companies and their URLs.

Figure 25.2

SGI's home page is full of graphics and cool stuff.

TABLE 25.1
Computer Companies on the Web

Company Name	URL
Apple Computer	http://www.apple.com
Digital Equipment Corp.	http://www.digital.com
Hewlett-Packard	http://www.hp.com
Hitachi	http://www.hitachi.co.jp
IBM	http://www.ibm.com
Intel	http://www.intel.com
Microsoft	http://www.microsoft.com
Motorola	http://www.mot.com
Novell	http://www.novell.com
Sony Computer Science Laboratory	http://www.csl.sony.co.jp

continues

TABLE 25.1, CONTINUED
Computer Companies on the Web

Company Name	URL
Sun Microsystems	http://www.sun.com
Taligent	http://www.taligent.com
Xerox	http://www.xerox.com

Computer Sites

A Day at COMDEX

http://www.halcyon.com/comdex/welcome.html

A virtual tour of the largest computer show in the world, attended by more than 200,000 people each year. This server also includes an index to the participating computer companies.

Access HP

http://www.hp.com/home.html

Here you can find information on Hewlett-Packard, its products, and services. Customers can even ask questions.

Alabama Supercomputer Network

http://sgisrvr.asc.edu/index.html

This server, from the Alabama Supercomputer Network, opens the door to information about high-performance computers. This site has links to other, related servers on the Web.

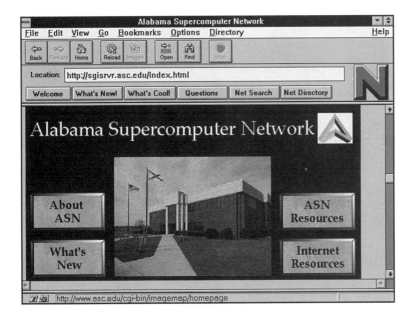

Aladdin Systems

http://www.internex.com/DTP/Aladdin.html

The Aladdin Systems server offers not only information about the company, but also details about their software products, including StuffIt Macintosh Utilities, StuffIt Deluxe 3.0, and StuffIt Space Saver.

Astrophysics Data System (ADS)

http://adswww.colorado.edu/adswww/adshomepg.html

The ADS is a suite of information-management, manipulation, visualization, and access tools that help you select and access data in a distributed environment. This data can be imported to or exported from analysis systems through the use of the ASCII and FITS I/O standards. ADS also provides direct access to the HEASARC Browse tool, NSSDC's Online Data and Information Service, the NASA/IPAC Extragalactic Database, and SIMBAD (Set of Identifications, Measurements, and Bibliography for Astronomical Data). You can get to this information by means of a simple-to-use graphical user interface (GUI).

Bioinformatics

http://bioinformatics.weizman.act.il

This Gopher server provides data and software related to bioinformatics, including public-domain software for biology and mirror storage for the main databases of the Human Genome Project and Molecular Biology.

Borland Simplify

http://www.human.com/simplify/index.html

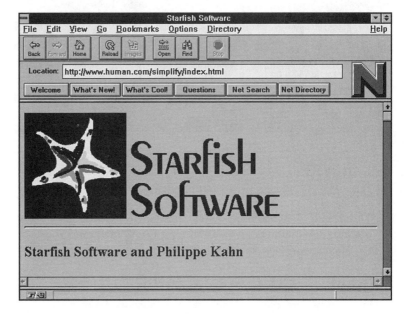

The Borland server provides not only company and product information, but also demos of their products and links to other relevant sites.

CADC (Canadian Astronomy Data Center) Home Page

http://ucluelet.dao.nrc.ca

The CADC maintains archives of scientific data from the Hubble Space Telescope and the Canada France Hawaii Telescope. It also serves as a distribution point for various astronomy-related software packages.

Center for Advanced Computing Research

http://www.ccsf.caltech.edu/ccsf.html

Formerly known as CalTech Concurrent Supercomputing Facilities, the CACR provides information about its organization and its supercomputing and parallel computing research.

The Center for Innovative Computer Applications (CICA)

http://www.cica.indiana.edu/cica

CICA's home page contains information on high-performance computing, visualization, sonification, graphics, and so on. The place to go for information on cutting-edge computer technologies and applications.

ClarisWeb

http://www.claris.com/

Claris develops several popular Mac and Windows software applications. In addition to general information about the company, this server provides product information, technical support, update releases, templates, and related articles.

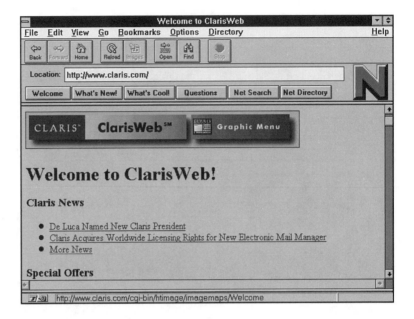

CommunicationsWeek

http://www.wais.com:80/cwk/

Get the latest information from this enterprise networking magazine, a publication of CMP Publications. Reviews, past issues, and industry news are available here.

Compaq Worldwide Web Server

http://www.compaq.com

This site highlights the product information, service and support, corporate overview, and just about everything else you want to know about the Compaq Computer Corporation.

Compton's NewMedia

http://www.comptons.com/

Compton's NewMedia is best known for its electronic encyclopedia. This site provides not only information about the company, but also details and descriptions of all its interactive, multimedia software.

Computer Retail Week

http://www.wais.com:80/crw/

The latest industry news is available from this online version of *Computer Retail Week*. You can also take part in the magazine's online poll.

Computer Security

http://mls.saic.com

This server, from the Wateridge facility of Science Applications International (SAIC), is concerned with security issues. The server offers many resources of information on the Web, as well as newsgroups.

Computer-Mediated Marketing Environments

http://colette.ogsm.vanderbilt.edu

This resource is devoted to research about the ways in which *computer-mediated marketing environments* (CMEs), especially the Internet, are revolutionizing the way firms conduct business.

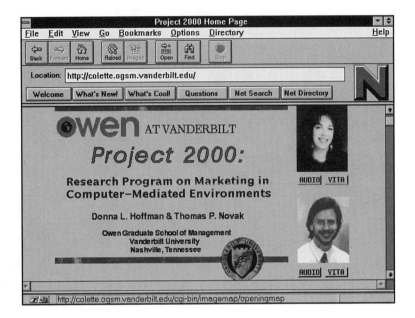

Cornell Theory Center Overview

http://www.tc.cornell.edu/ctcIntro.html

At this site, learn about research projects that encompass parallel computing and visualization. The server is maintained by Cornell University's Cornell Theory Center, which is supported by the National Science Foundation.

Creative Labs

http://www.creaf.com/

Creative Labs, Inc., based in Milpitas, California, develops and sells PC sound, video, and CD-ROM multimedia products. Their product, Sound Blaster, has set the industry standard for sound on PC-based platforms. From this site, the company provides information on its multimedia kits for entertainment, education, and productivity markets.

Cryptography, PGP, and Your Privacy

http://draco.centerline.com:8080/~franl/crypto.html

How private is your computer? This voluminous server can tell you. You can also learn ways to increase your computer protection.

Curious Pictures

http://found.cs.nyu.edu/CAT/affiliates/curious

Curious Picture is an animation company. Their server contains samplings of their special effects, graphics, and animation work.

Current Weather Maps/Movies

http://rs560.cl.msu.edu/weather

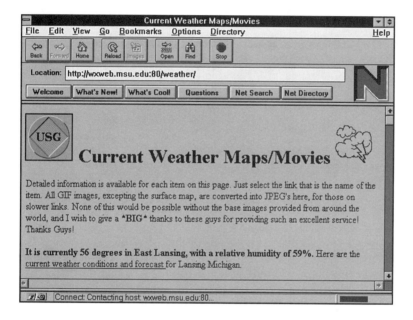

This Web site, which is updated hourly, provides links to downloadable software sites that are helpful when you use interactive weather browsers. International information is available, as are satellite-supplied visual and infrared maps.

Cyberkind

http://sunsite.unc.edu/shannon/ckind/title.html

Cyberkind, a publication about the Internet and World Wide Web, features art, fiction, nonfiction, and poetry. The only stipulation is that submissions contain some link to computers, networks, or cyberspace. To see your name in lights (those of a monitor), send submissions to shannon@sunsite.unc.edu.

Digital Equipment WWW Information Server

http://www.service.digital.com/home.html

In addition to Digital Equipment product and service information, this server contains archives to public-domain software. The site also includes an online catalog from which you can purchase products from Digital Equipment.

DIVE—Distributed Interactive Virtual Environment

http://www.sics.se/dce/dive/dive.html

Despite its name, this is a very interesting site. Located in Sweden, this site provides downloadable software you can use to create 3D interactive virtual reality projects.

The Dragon Wing

http://www.cs.ubc.ca//nest/imager/contribution/forsey/dragon/top.html

Interested in hierarchical b-spline surfaces, or perhaps multivertex editing techniques? This site provides material on these topics, as well as demonstrations of computer modeling and animation of human bodies and faces.

Entertainment and Media Professional

http://www.cenco.com/emp/

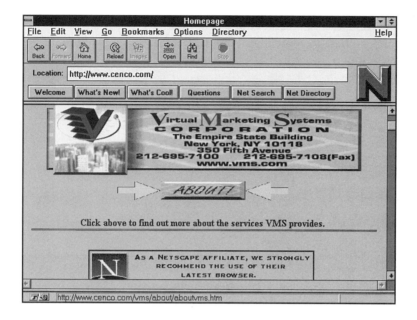

This information resource for multimedia producers and developers provides details about distribution and publication channels.

Florida State University Supercomputing

http://www.scri.fsu.edu

This Web site contains a bibliography and many abstracts related to supercomputing. The Supercomputer Computations Research Institute (SCRI) also offers descriptions of software they developed, and general information about the Institute.

Imperial College Department of Computing

http://src.doc.ic.ac.uk

This is the home of the Department of Computing, Imperial College, United Kingdom, as well as the UKUUG (UK UNIX Users Group) Archive and the DoC Information Service.

InformationWeek Interactive

http://www.wais.com:80/iwk/

This Web resource is host to *InformationWeek*. You can browse current and past issues, reviews, career advice, industry updates and news, and gossip in this online business and technology weekly.

Insight Knowledge Network

http://memec.com/

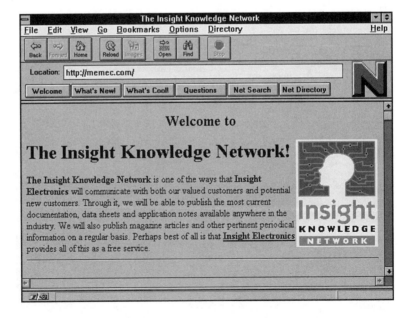

Here is where to find the latest documentation, data sheets, and application notes on the electronics and semiconductor industry. This site is provided by Insight Electronics, a semiconductor specialist and distributor.

Institute for Molecular Virology

http://www.bocklabs.wisc.edu/Welcome.html

A unique virology resource for students, scientists, computer visualization experts, and the general public.

InteliQuest

http://voyager.enet.net/iquest/index.html

At this site you can order audio-, video-, and multimedia-based educational programs from InteliQuest's online catalog.

InteractiveAge

http://www.wais.com:80/ia/

Browse *InteractiveAge*, an online publication, for the latest on the information highway.

IRCAM DSP and Musical Software

http://www.ircam.fr

This site offers a variety of computer music resources. Included are a list and brief description of IRCAM software (digital signal processing, voice and sound synthesis, music composition, wind instrument making, and other programs), as well as calendars of the IRCAM-EIC concerts and tours, and links to various other music servers.

ISSI (International Software Systems Incorporated)

http://www.issi.com/issi/issi-home_page.html

International Software Systems Incorporated offers services such as software reengineering and other jargon-filled process engineering products. An online journal and access to employee home pages can also be found here.

Loughborough University of Technology Computer-Human Interaction (LUTCHI) Research Centre

http://pipkin.lut.ac.uk

This server contains general information about computer-human interaction. Contains information about LUTCHI research projects, official LUTCHI publicity releases, as well as documents, images, and movies associated with those projects.

Macintosh Index

http://ici.proper.com/1/mac

This site indexes Macintosh-related information on the Internet. The information resources listed here include newsgroups, a great place to look for current information, and e-mail lists.

Macintosh Information

http://www.engr.scarolina.edu/

This Web site, the server of the University of South Carolina's College of Engineering, offers Macintosh information and links to other Mac Web sites.

Macmillan Computer Publishing

http://www.mcp.com/

Macmillan is a large publisher of computer-related materials. This Web site offers a catalog of available titles and enables you order them directly. Look at samples from new and current titles from Sams, Hayden, New Riders Publishing, and Que.

MacZone Interactive

http://www.geo.net:8240/

This site offers MacZone's online catalog, which contains information on Power Macintosh products and Software Toolworks CD-ROMs.

Mediamatic Online

http://mmol.mediamatic.nl:/Default.html

The home page of the group that explores the cultural implications of new media, and its role in society. Read their quarterly magazine and stop by the "Doors of Perception," a look at interactivity and design at the Netherlands Design Institute in Amsterdam.

Meiko

http://www.meiko.com:80/welcome.html

Meiko specializes in "open, scalable parallel computing." The server provides product information, announcements, reviews, and a company overview. Information on the rock group Yes, including an archive of newsletters, is also here.

Miller Freeman

http://www.mfi.com/HomePage.html

Miller Freeman, Inc. (MFI) produces trade shows and publishes books, business magazines, special-interest consumer magazines, and CD-ROMs. Their home page provides an overview of the company and a list of MFI's current products and services.

MIRALab Computer Animation Research Lab

http://cuisg13.unige.ch:8199/HomePage.html

The MIRALab at the University of Geneva, Switzerland, is a leader in the development of computer graphics, computer animation, and virtual reality technology. This site provides information on those fields, as well as tips and links to help users find other sources.

MIT Demonstrations

http://www.lcs.mit.edu/

This server offers an index and demonstrations from research groups at the Massachusetts Institute of Technology Laboratory for Computer Science.

NCSA (National Center for Supercomputing Applications)

http://www.ncsa.uiuc.edu/General/NCSAHome.html

The site for NCSA (National Center for Supercomputing Applications), a high-performance computing, communications, and research center serving the science and engineering community.

NEC

http://www.nec.com/

This site offers loads of information about NEC, its history, and current projects. This page is available in both English and Japanese.

Network Computing Devices

http://www.ncd.com/

NCD's home page contains background information on the company and its three major projects: Z-mail, X-terminals, and PC-Xware. A catalog of third-party software compatible with the XWindows system is here also.

Network Computing Online

http://www.wais.com:80/nwc/

The client/server community is the target of this electronic magazine. You'll find ISDN reviews, the latest in technology, and the beta-test column here.

Nihon Sun Microsystems

http://www.sun.co.jp

This site provides a directory for Sun Microsystems in Japan, and includes the Rolling Stones Official Web Server site (with access to Rolling Stones music, merchandise, and information). Also provides multimedia links to the Science University of Tokyo and other Asia-Pacific resources.

Open Systems Today

http://www.wais.com:80/ost/

This online version of *Open Systems Today*, a CMP publication, serves the open distributed computing industry. Check out the hitchhiker's guide to other sites!

PC Index

http://ici.proper.com/1/pc

From this server you can jump to the best, most action-packed PC-related FTP, Gopher, and Web sites. Issues of several of the best online magazines can be downloaded. You can also connect to the American Computer Exchange to get the latest prices on used PCs and related equipment.

PERL (Practical Extraction and Report Language)

http://www.cs.cmu.edu/Web/People/rgs/perl.html

An HTML-formatted and highly indexed PERL programming reference document.

Piedmont Supercomputing Center

http://services.csp.it/welcome.html

The server for the Centro Supercalcolo Piemonte, a computer center in Turin, Italy, that provides computational support for scientific and research institutes.

PowerPC News

http://power.globalnews.com/

PowerPC News, an independently published biweekly publication, offers information about the microprocessor systems used by Apple and IBM.

San Diego Supercomputer Center

http://www.sdsc.edu/

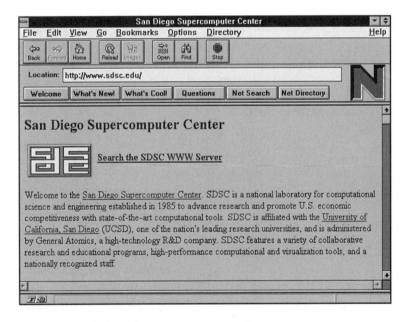

This site provides information about the Center's education programs, tools for high-performance computation and visualization, and research projects. The San Diego Supercomputer Center, in conjunction with UCSD, promotes economic competitiveness and research in the high-performance computing industry.

Social Issues and Cyberspace

http://www.ics.uci.edu/~ejw/csr/cyber.html

Public radio has come to the Web, in the shape of The Cyberspace Report from KUCI (88.9 FM) in Irvine, California. The program features reports on Internet communities and electronic mail—anything that combines aspects of society and computers. The server is offered through UC Irvine.

Technical Reports Archive

http://www.cs.indiana.edu/cstr/search

At this Indiana University Web server, you find the Unified Computer Science Technical Report Index. For people who need fairly heavy technical information, this represents a nice compilation of reports that you can scan.

University of Michigan College of Engineering

http://www.engin.umich.edu/college

This Web server contains the Computer-Aided Engineering Network. From the University of Michigan's College of Engineering, the site offers network services.

University of Missouri

http://www.cstp.umkc.edu/

This Computer Science Telecommunications Program at the University of Missouri provides research information and general computer information.

University of Washington—Image Processing

http://www.cs.washington.edu/research/metip/metip.html

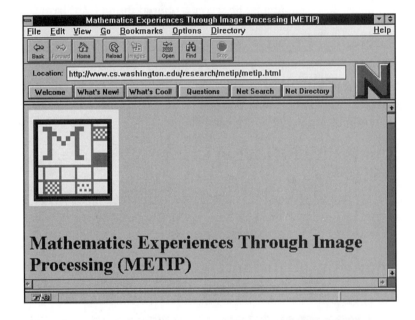

This server, Mathematics Experiences Through Image Processing (METIP), uses image processing to create learning activities for middle schools. Sponsored by the Department of Computer Science and Engineering at the University of Washington.

University of Wisconsin Computer Sciences Department

http://www.cs.wisc.edu/~upluse/

The home page of the Undergraduate Projects Laboratory (UPL) of the University of Wisconsin Computer Sciences Department highlights the projects

and people of the UPL. The UPL is one of the only laboratories of its kind that allows undergraduates from multiple disciplines to have access to Unix workstations for personal independent programming projects and computer research.

UTIRC (University of Toronto Instructional and Research Computing)

http://www.utirc.utoronto.ca/HTMLdocs/NewHTML/intro.html

This site provides information concerning instructional technology and applications, support for multimedia and visualization techniques, as well as access to and support for high-performance computing.

The Well-Connected Mac

http://rever.nmsu.edu/~elharo/faq/Macintosh.html

Whether you want shareware, freeware, or mailing lists, this is a great place to look. Links lead to commercial sites, hardware/software reviews, and even electronic bulletin boards.

Windows Magazine

http://www.wais.com:80/win/

At this site you'll find the latest in news, updates, shareware, and profiles of people involved in the Microsoft Windows world.

The Whole Frog Project

http://george.lbl.gov/ITG.hm.pg.docs/Whole Frog/Whole.Frog.html

Contains computer models and reconstructions of frogs, which can be rotated and made transparent. Interesting example of computer imaging.

Worldwide Collaborative Multimedia Magazine

http://www.trincoll.edu/homepage.html

This weekly magazine is published by students at Trinity College in Hartford, Connecticut. Submissions come from all over the world.

The XFree 86 Project

http://www.xfree86.org/

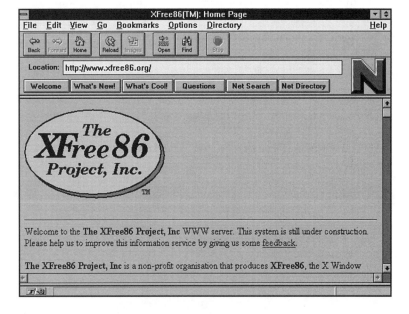

The home page for this nonprofit corporation provides news and updates on publicly available implementations of the X11 Window System for i386-, i486-, and Pentium-based hosts.

Yahoo—Computer

http://akebono.stanford.edu/yahoo/Computers/

The Yahoo Computer directory contains links to more than 2,850 sites. This directory is divided into such categories as art, communication, computer science, databases, software, supercomputing and parallel computing, telecommunications, and many others. You can search by keywords from the Yahoo search feature or use other search engines.

Research Sites

If you have to put together a research paper or find out more about a specific topic in one of the sciences, visit some of these sites.

Arachnophilia: Florida Institute of Technology's WWW Server

http://sci-ed.fit.edu

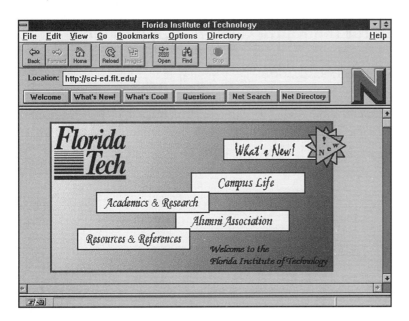

This site, specifically for educators and researchers, provides pointers to information resources and search tools around the Web.

Australian Environmental Resources Information Network (ERIN)

http://kaos.erin.gov.au/erin.html

This resource has facts about biodiversity, protected areas, terrestrial and marine environments, environmental protection and legislation, international agreements, and general information about ERIN.

Carnegie Mellon University—Computer Vision

http://www.cs.cmu.edu:8001/afs/cs/project/cil/ftp/html/vision.html

This department of Carnegie Mellon University offers information about their computer vision research program. The site also references other research sites and collections of images.

Center for Advanced Computing Research

http://www.ccsf.caltech.edu/ccsf.html

Formerly known as *CalTech Concurrent Supercomputing Facilities,* the CACR provides information about its organization and its supercomputing and parallel-computing research.

The Center for Innovative Computer Applications (CICA)

http://www.cica.indiana.edu/cica

CICA's home page contains information on high-performance computing, visualization, sonification, graphics, and so on. The place to go for information about cutting-edge computer technologies and applications.

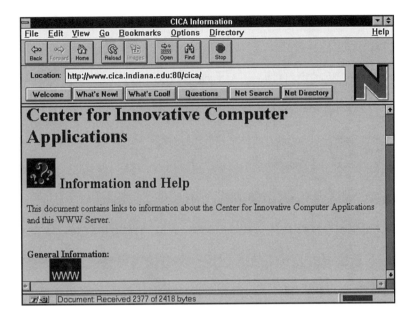

CERT, France

http://www.cert.fr/

CERT is a French scientific research center active in the areas of aeronautics, space, and defense. This site provides general information about the Center and its many divisions and departments (including optics, microwaves, and automation).

Columbia University

http://www.ctr.columbia.edu/

This Web server is maintained by Columbia University's Center for Tele-communications Research. The site has project information, as well as references to other resources at Columbia.

Computer-Mediated Communication Studies Center

http://www.rpi.edu/~decemj/cmc/center.html

This home page carries an overview of the Computer-Mediated Communication Studies Center. The Center has information of interest to researchers and students. The site links to the CMC magazine and other resources.

COOMBSQUEST Social Sciences and Humanities Information Facility

http://coombs.anu.edu.au./CoombsHome.html

COOMBSQUEST is the worldwide Social Sciences and Humanities Information Service of the Coombs Computing Unit, Research Schools of Social Sciences and Pacific Studies, Australian National University, Canberra, Australia. This resource provides direct access to the world's major electronic repository of social science and humanities papers, and other high-grade research material that deals with the culture and religions of Australia and the Pacific Rim.

Cornell Theory Center Overview

http://www.tc.cornell.edu/ctcIntro.html

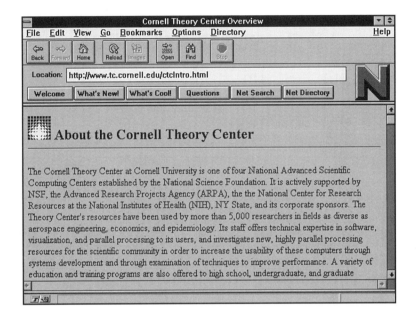

At this site, learn about research projects that encompass parallel computing and visualization. The server is maintained by the Cornell University's Cornell Theory Center, which is supported by the National Science Foundation.

Electric Propulsion

http://cougarxp.princeton.edu:2112/afosr.html

This site contains information about research into alternate forms of propulsion, including plasma rockets. In addition, the site provides information about the Princeton laboratory, its staff, and current research.

ELSNET (European Network in Language and Speech)

http://www.cogsci.ed.ac.uk/elsnet/home.html

This site addresses the development of language technology in Europe and other countries by helping to coordinate progress on both scientific and technological fronts.

Florida State University Supercomputing

http://www.scri.fsu.edu

This Web site contains a bibliography and many abstracts that relate to supercomputing. The Supercomputer Computations Research Institute (SCRI) also offers descriptions of software they developed, as well as general information about the Institute.

Geoscience at Texas A&M University

http://ageninfo.tamu.edu/geoscience.html

This server contains many links to Geographical Information Systems (GIS) and remote sensing servers. Catalogs and directories, maps, data sources, earth science labs and research team information, weather resources, and other relevant information can all be found here.

ITRE Home Page

http://itre.uncecs.edu/

Information about transportation research and Geographical Information Systems can be found on this server. This site also features examples of image mapping.

Journal of Computer-Mediated Communication (JCMC)

http://www.huji.ac.il/www_jcmc/jcmc.html

Published by the Annenberg School for Communication at the University of Southern California and the Information Systems Division of the School of Business Administration at the Hebrew University of Jerusalem, the *Journal of Computer-Mediated Communication* (JCMC) provides scholarly information about information and communication.

The Laboratory for Perceptual Robotics

http://piglet.cs.umass.edu:4321/

This server provides the laboratory's mission statement, faculty biographies, and information about current research, as well as movies of current work.

LBL Imaging and Distributed Computing Group

http://george.lbl.gov/ITG.html

One focus of the Lawrence Berkeley Laboratory is the application of scientific imaging to educational endeavors. The "Whole Frog" project is explored at this site, with movies, images, and data on three-dimensional frog anatomy.

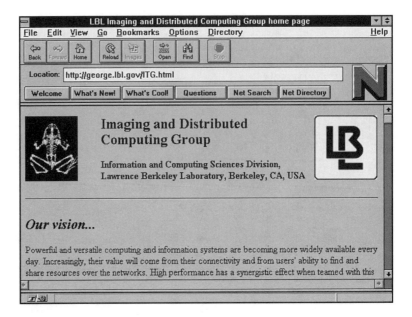

Lockheed Missiles & Space Company

http://www.lmsc.lockheed.com

New Riders Publishing

INSIDE
SERIES

The Lockheed Missiles and Space Company sponsors this site and provides company information and press releases.

Loughborough University of Technology Computer-Human Interaction (LUTCHI) Research Centre

http://pipkin.lut.ac.uk

This server contains general information on computer-human interaction. Contains information about LUTCHI research projects, official LUTCHI publicity releases, as well as documents, images, and movies associated with those projects.

Martin Marietta Energy Systems Gopher

http://www.ornl.gov/mmes.html

Martin Marietta's server contains information on their energy projects and technologies for both government and commercial applications.

MIRALab Computer Animation Research Lab

http://cuisg13.unige.ch:8199/HomePage.html

The MIRALab at the University of Geneva, Switzerland, is a leader in the development of computer graphics, computer animation, and virtual reality technology. This site provides information on those fields, as well as tips and links to help users find other sources.

MIT—Artificial Intelligence Laboratory

http://www.ai.mit.edu/

The world of artificial intelligence moves from fiction to fact within the walls of this MIT laboratory. Research projects range from computer-based learning to the development of robotics.

National Technology Transfer Center (NTTC)

http://iridium.nttc.edu/nttc.hmtl

This resource features state-by-state listings of agencies designed to simplify the adaptation of new technologies to industry. It also provides updates on conferences, and a current list of Department of Defense projects soliciting private assistance from small businesses.

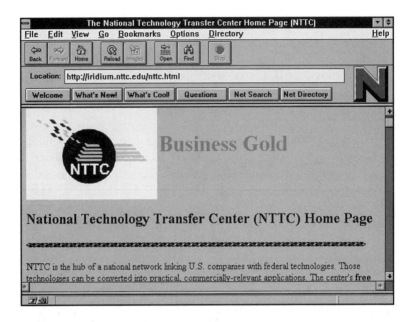

NCSA (National Center for Supercomputing Applications)

http://www.ncsa.uiuc.edu/General/NCSAHome.html

This site provides information about the National Center for Supercomputing Applications, a high-performance computing and communications facility and research center designed to serve the U.S. computational science and engineering community.

Neurosciences Internet Resource Guide

http://http2.sils.umich.edu/Public/nirg/nirg1.html

This comprehensive Internet resource addresses biological, chemical, medical, engineering, and computer science aspects of neurobiology.

Northwestern University Astronomy

http://www.astro.nwu.edu/home.html

This site contains a faculty directory and information on graduate and undergraduate programs of astronomy research. A gallery of gamma-ray bursts can also be found here.

Pacific Forestry Center

http://www.pfc.forestry.ca/

Learn about current research activities and programs developed by the Pacific
Forestry Center, located in Victoria, British Columbia, Canada. The home page
offers an introduction to the Center, a contact list, profiles of the staff, and
recent publications.

Piedmont Supercomputing Center

http://services.csp.it/welcome.html

This is the server for the Centro Supercalcolo Piemonte, a computer center in
Turin, Italy, that provides computational support for scientific and research
institutes.

Pollution Research Group

http://www.und.ac.za/prg/prg.html

The Pollution Research Group (PRG) is a group in the Chemistry Department
of the University of Natal. The PRG focuses on water and wastewater management, with emphasis on closed-loop recycling and clean technologies. This site
contains information on the PRG and their efforts, as well as links to other
waste-treatment-related Web sites.

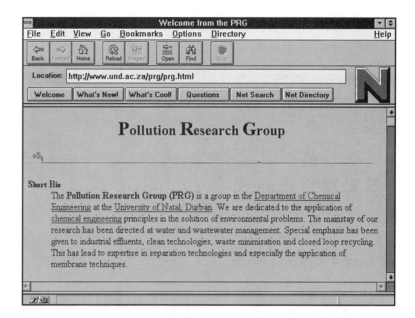

Research Libraries Group (RLG)

http://www-rlg.stanford.edu/welcome.html

The RLG is a nonprofit organization that provides support for libraries and other research facilities. This page describes the group's search system, article citation system, and bibliographic database. Online exhibits by group members can also be found here.

San Diego Supercomputer Center

http://www.sdsc.edu/

This site provides information about the Center's education programs, as well as its high-performance computation tools and visualization and research projects. The San Diego Supercomputer Center, in conjunction with UCSD, promotes economic competitiveness and research in the high-performance computing industry.

Servidor WWW da RNP

http://www.rnp.br

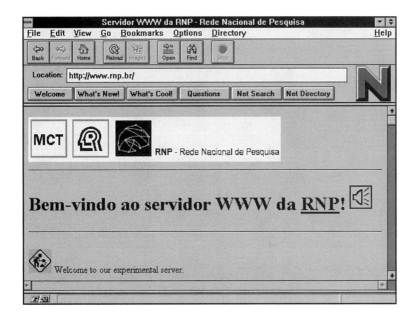

The central Web server for the Brazilian Research Network. It includes information about the Web (and Internet in general) in Brazil, and has links to most other Web, Gopher, and FTP servers in Brazil. At present, the information is provided in Portuguese only; in the future, English versions will be added.

SIRIM

http://www.sirim.my

The Standards and Industrial Research Institute of Malaysia (SIRIM) is a governmental department responsible for conducting industrial research and establishing standards in Malaysia. This site provides contact information with SIRIM; in the future, it will include direct e-mail connections.

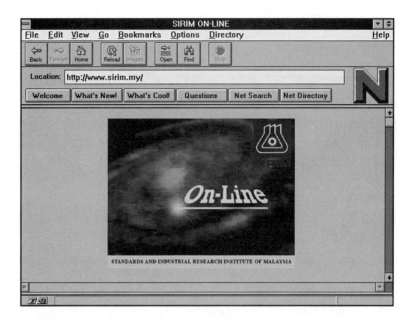

Southampton High Performance Computing Center

http://cs1.soton.ac.uk/

This server provides background about the Center, as well as access to information about current research. Keyword searches of the server make finding information about a specific topic quite easy.

Technical Reports Archive

http://www.cs.indiana.edu/cstr/search

At this Indiana University Web server, you find the Unified Computer Science Technical Report Index. For people who need fairly heavy technical information, this index represents a nice compilation of reports that you can scan.

Telecommunications Research

http://www-atp.llnl.gov/atp/

The Advanced Telecommunications Program at the Lawrence Livermore National Labs. The site offers significant information about research in this field.

The University of California Search for Extraterrestrial Civilizations

http://sereninfo.ssl.berkeley.edu

This site contains information about the UC Berkeley SETI Program, SERENDIP (Search for Extraterrestrial Radio Emissions from Nearby Developed Intelligent Populations), an ongoing scientific research effort aimed at detecting radio signals from extraterrestrial civilizations. Details about the program and updates on current research activities are also accessible.

The University of Minnesota Remote Sensing Lab

http://walleye.forestry.umn.edu/0/www/main.html

The University of Minnesota Remote Sensing Lab server contains information about all aspects of image processing and GIS, as well as general information about remote sensing. This server also features a GIS Jobs Clearinghouse, archives, and so on.

University of Missouri

http://www.cstp.umkc.edu/

This Computer Science Telecommunications Program at the University of Missouri provides research information and general computer information.

University of Wisconsin Computer Sciences Department

http://www.cs.wisc.edu/~upluse/

The Undergraduate Projects Laboratory (UPL) of the University of Wisconsin Computer Sciences Department has a home page that highlights the projects and people of the UPL. The UPL is one of the only laboratories of its kind that allows undergraduates from multiple disciplines to have access to Unix workstations for personal independent programming projects and computer research.

USC Information Sciences Institute (ISI)

http://www.isi.edu/isi.html

ISI does research in fields such as information processing and communications. This page provides technical reports and details on current ISI projects.

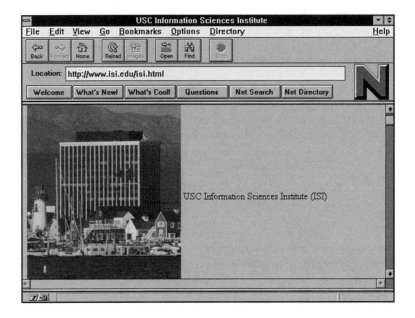

Weizmann Institute of Science

http://wissgi.weizmann.ac.il/

This home page gives you access to the Institute's departments and libraries, with updates on various research projects.

Science Sites

The following sites contain information and resources pertaining to various science disciplines. Some of the topics included here are biotechnology, telecommunications, and artificial life.

ANU (Australian National University) Asian-Settlements Database

http://coombs.anu.edu.au/WWWVL-AsianStudies.html

This searchable database contains abstracts of theses and research studies (provided by the Asian Institute of Technology) about issues of demography and social geography in Asia.

Artificial Life

http://alife.santafe.edu

This site serves as a forum for information about all aspects of the Artificial Life enterprise. Services provided here include an FTP site containing pre-prints and software, a bibliographic database on artificial life, and links to various Usenet services.

Astronomical Software Resources (ASR)

http://stsci.edu/net-software.html

The ASR site is a useful starting point for finding most of the astronomical resources available on the Web. It is conveniently divided by type of access (WWW, WAIS, Gopher, Telnet, FTP). As of January, 1994, resources include the following: Astrophysics Preprints—SISSA; ADC Documents, NOAO News, NRAO Preprint Database; STECF Newsletter; STELAR Apj, ApJS, AJ, PASP, A&A, A&AS, MNRAS, and JGR Abstracts; STSci Preprint Database; IAU Circulars Astronomical Union; CfA Index of ApJ, AJ, PASP; DIRA2 Database; and Electronic Journal of Astronomical Society of the Atlantic.

Astrophysics Data System (ADS)

http://adswww.colorado.edu/adswww/adshomepg.html

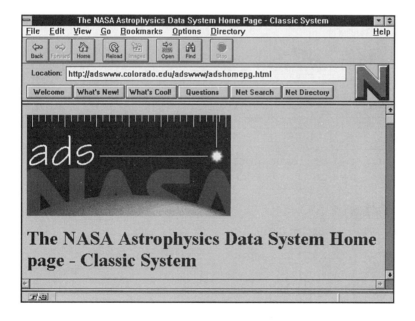

The ADS is a suite of information-management, manipulation, visualization, and access tools that help you select, and access, data in a distributed environment. These data can be imported to or exported from analysis systems through the use of the ASCII and FITS I/O standards. ADS also provides direct access to the HEASARC Browse tool, NSSDC's Online Data and Information Service, the NASA/IPAC Extragalactic Database, and SIMBAD (Set of Identifications, Measurements, and Bibliography for Astronomical Data). You can get to this information via a simple-to-use graphical user interface (GUI).

AT&T Bell Laboratories WWW Information Page

http://www.research.att.com

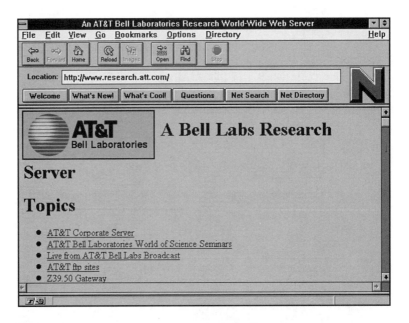

This page from AT&T Bell Laboratories provides information about the lab and about current research and development projects.

Bioinformatics

http://bioinformatics.weizman.act.il

This Gopher server provides data and software related to bioinformatics, including public-domain software for biology and mirror storage for the main databases of the Human Genome Project and Molecular Biology.

Bradford Robotic Telescope

http://www.eie.brad.ac.uk/rti/intro.html

England's Bradford University has developed a robotic telescope that can be controlled through the Web. Users place "job" listings and check back for results. This is a good site for children interested in science and technology, astronomy buffs, and so on.

CADC (Canadian Astronomy Data Center) Home Page

http://cadcwww.dao.nrc.ca/

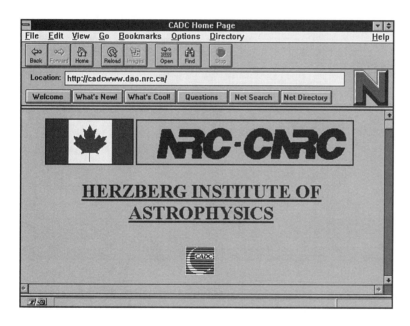

The CADC maintains archives of scientific data from the Hubble Space Telescope and the Canada France Hawaii Telescope. It also serves as a distribution point for various astronomy-related software packages.

Cambridge Astronomy

http://cast0.ast.cam.ac.uk/

In addition to information about the Cambridge astronomy department and general news, this server contains interesting astronomical data. The latest Hubble Telescope photos, Solaris FAQs (*frequently asked questions*), documentation for software packages, as well as links to other related data are accessible from this site.

Canadian Geographical WWW Index Travel

http://www.unamitoba.ca

This site provides weekly weather information.

Center for Complex Systems Research

http://www.ccsr.uiuc.edu/

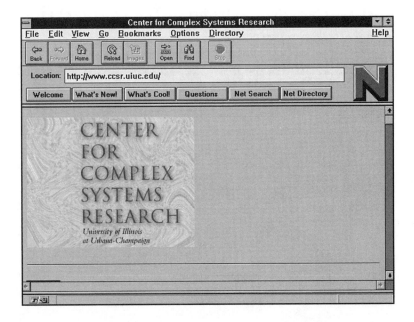

This server offers a variety of papers and technical reports in different areas of biology, physics, and mathematics. Of particular interest is a paper on a chaos-based system for producing music.

Center for Extreme Ultraviolet Astrophysics

http://cea-ftp.cea.berkeley.edu

The Center for Extreme Ultraviolet Astrophysics, a department of the University of California at Berkeley, is devoted to research in extreme ultraviolet astronomy. The Center is the ground base of EUVE (the Extreme Ultraviolet Explorer), a NASA satellite launched in 1992. This site has details about the EUVE Guest Observer (EGO) Center, the Public Archive of Mission Data and Information, and satellite operation information.

Chemistry Department at Stony Brook

http://sbchm1.sunysb.edu/

This site contains a directory of the staff, as well as information about the graduate and undergraduate programs (including current research and online projects). You can also tour the campus from this site.

Cognitive and Psychological Sciences on the Internet

http://matia.stanford.edu/cogsci.html

This resource contains links to academic programs, organizations and conference lists, journals and magazines, Usenet newsgroups, discussion lists, and other general information about cognitive science.

CSU Entomology WWW Site

http://www.colostate.edu/Depts/Entomology/ent.html

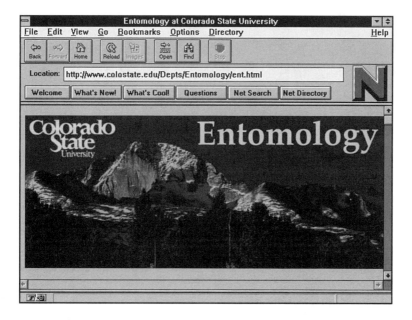

This site contains online photos of insects, entomology educational programs, and extensive Internet entomology links.

The Curiosity Club

http://nisus.sfusd.k12.ca.us/curiosity_club/bridge1.html

This Web site offers young scientists an exploration of astrophysics as well as a play space.

Current Weather Maps/Movies

http://clunix.cl.msu.edu:80/weather

This site contains moving imagery, including visible and infrared spectra, from weather satellites covering the entire globe.

Decavitator Home Page

http://lancet.mit.edu/decavitator

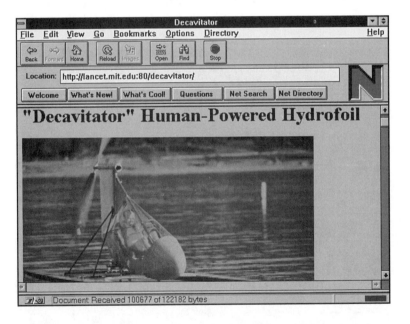

The Decavitator, a human-powered hydrofoil built by MIT students, holds the world speed record for this type of craft. This site provides information about the Decavitator and other human-powered vehicles, as well as still and video images of the vehicle. See also the International Human-Powered Vehicle WWW Server.

Elsevier Science

http://www.elsevier.nl/

At this Web site, this publisher of over 1,100 scientific journals has plenty of information about its online publications.

ELSNET (European Network in Language and Speech)

http://www.cogsci.ed.ac.uk/elsnet/home.html

This site addresses the development of language technology in Europe and elsewhere by helping to coordinate progress on both scientific and technological fronts.

EMBnet (European Molecular Biology Network)

http://biomaster.uio.no/embnet-www.html

A group of European Internet sites that provide computational molecular biology services to international researchers.

European Space Agency

http://www.esrin.esa.it

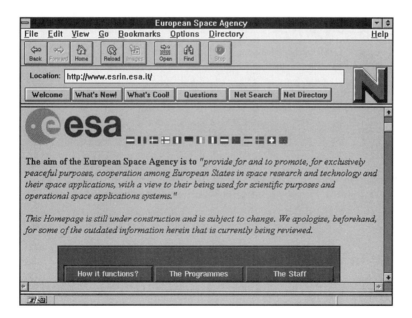

The home page of the European Space Agency includes information about ESA's mission, specific ESA programs (Science, Manned Spaceflight and Microgravity, Earth Observation, Telecommunications, Launchers), and issues related to the space and aeronautics industry.

F-16XL High Lift Project Home Page

http://dval-www.larc.nasa.gov/F16XL/index.html

Aviation buffs will want to visit this site for its movies and tech reports on an experimental version of the General Dynamics F-16 fighter.

Fermi National Accelerator Laboratory

http://fnnews.fnal.gov/

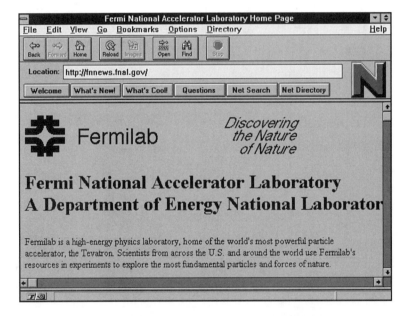

The Fermi high-energy physics lab provides this online tour of the facilities. A photography exhibit, employment opportunities, and software tools are available, as are several primers on the laboratory and associated areas of research.

Geographic Information and Analysis Laboratory (GIAL)

http://zia.geog.buffalo.edu/

This server maintains information and links to geographic information and Geographic Information Systems (GIS).

Geography-Project GeoSim (Geography Education Software)

http://geosim.cs.vt.edu/index.html

The topics and issues concerning human population are explored here. Multimedia and simulation programs offer interactive insight into population trends and effects. Links to Migration Modeling and Mental Maps provide interesting learning experiences in the field of geography.

Geography-USGS Education

http://info.er.usgs.gov/education/index.html

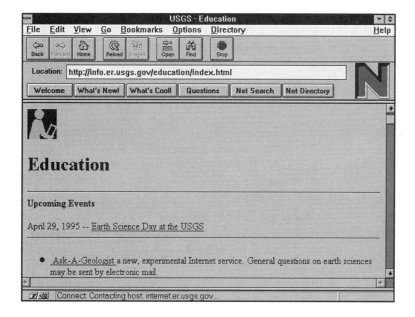

Provides access to links to the U.S. Geological Survey National Center Tour Information, the GeoMedia, What's Under Your Feet, Fact Sheets, and Dinosaurs at the Museum of Paleontology. Research your favorite geography topic through the USGS Library System link.

The Geometry Center

http://www.geom.umn.edu

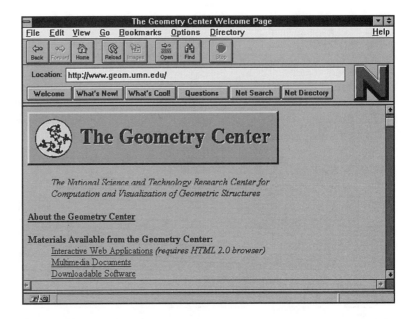

The Geometry Center at the University of Minnesota is a National Science Foundation Science and Technology Research Center. The Center is involved in the development of computational tools for visualizing geometrical structures, and in assisting mathematicians to communicate with the public. With the downloadable software available here, you can graph geometrical structures with your computer. This site also contains images and movies.

Geoscience at Texas A&M University

http://ageninfo.tamu.edu/geoscience.html

This server contains many links to Geographic Information Systems (GIS) and remote sensing servers. Catalogs and directories, maps, data sources, earth science labs and research team information, weather resources, and other relevant information can all be found here.

Harvard Biosciences Online Journals

http://golgi.harvard.edu/journals.html

Here you can access selected online journals and periodicals about biology and medicine. Included here are peer-reviewed e-journals, journal indexes, and databases.

The Hub

http://hub.terc.edu/

In the realm of math and science education, this server offers resources that aid in report creation, project completion, proposals, and curriculum development.

ICTP (International Centre for Theoretical Physics)

http://gopher.ictp.trieste.it

This site has information about the scientific activities at ICTP (Trieste, Italy). You can also find information about scientific publications, courses, and other services offered by the International Centre for Science and High Technology, and the Third World Academy of Sciences at Trieste.

Illinois Mathematics and Science Academy

http://www.imsa.edu/

The focus of this institution is education for students with special talents in math and science. Its three-year residential program is unique to the nation. The Academy also houses the Illinois research and development lab for K–12 science and math education.

Images from Various Sources

http://info.alaska.edu:70

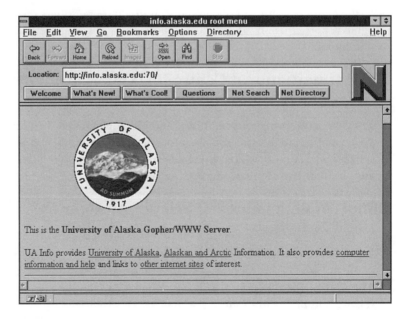

This site links to 35 image archives throughout the world. A variety of images are available; many are of weather, geological, and biological collections from government and private sources.

India's Inter-University Centre for Astronomy & Astrophysics (IUCAA)

http://iucaa.iucaa.ernet.in/welcome.html

This server provides details about the Centre, as well as information on academic activity, including their research interests, recent publications, the academic calendar, and details about their science popularization program in India. Users will also find information about the astronomical Image Processing and Data Center, as well as links to other astronomy and astrophysics servers on the Web.

Institute for Molecular Virology

http://www.bocklabs.wisc.edu/Welcome.html

A unique virology resource for students, scientists, computer visualization experts, and the general public.

Institute of Geophysics and Planetary Physics

http://igpp.ucsd.edu/

This server contains background information about the Institute, which is located in California, and its research projects on marine seismology and acoustic measurements. Plenty of maps and images related to geology and seismology can be found here.

The Interactive Frog Dissection

http://curry.edschool.Virginia.EDU:80/~insttech/frog/

Operate without getting your hands dirty, thanks to the University of Virginia's Curry School of Education. This site, designed for high school biology classes, uses pictures and animation to teach (and show) you all about frog dissection.

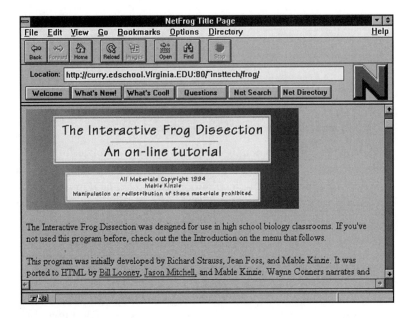

Interactive Genetic Art

http://robocop.modmath.cs.cmu.edu:8001/

This unusual Carnegie Mellon computer science project presents images and movies to be voted on by users. After 10 votes, a new "generation" of images is generated based on voting results. The images might take a while to load, but the results are well worth the wait.

The International Human-Powered Vehicle WWW Server

http://www.ihpva.org

The International Human-Powered Vehicle Association (IHPVA) is dedicated to promoting the development and improvement of human-powered vehicles. This site provides information about the organization, its current projects, and its past successes. The site also contains links to cycling Web pages. See also the Decavitator Home Page.

International Ultraviolet Explorer Satellite

http://iuesn1.gsfc.nasa.gov/iue/iuedac_homepage.html

In addition to information about the Ultraviolet Explorer Satellite project, this server contains software, a hypertext newsletter, and archived data. Users will also find many publications on topics ranging from robotics to astronomy.

Internet Resources for Geographic Information and GIS

http://abacus.bates.edu/~nsmith/General/Resources-GIS.html

This server is host to a document with complete information on Geographical Information Systems.

IUCAA (Inter-University Centre for Astronomy and Astrophysics)

http://iucaa.iucaa.ernet.in/welcome.html

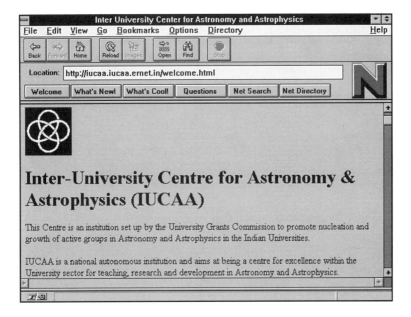

This server highlights information about the IUCAA. The IUCAA was set up to promote the growth of groups in astronomy and astrophysics in India. The Centre runs vigorous visitor programs involving short and long-term visits of scientists from India and abroad.

Lockheed Missiles & Space Company

http://www.lmsc.lockheed.com

This Web site contains information about the Lockheed Missile and Space Company, a major aerospace and defense company that specializes in the development of space systems, missiles, and other high-technology products. This page includes company information and press releases.

MGD (Mouse Genome Database)

http://www.informatics.jax.org/mgd.html

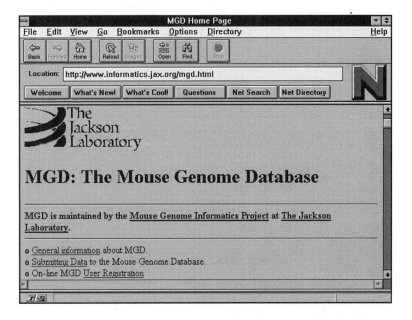

This site provides a comprehensive database of genetic information about laboratory mice.

The Mining Channel

http://www.wimsey.com/Magnet/mc/index.html

Look here for information about mining and emerging mineral exploration companies, as well as industry newsletters, ads, and other sites.

NASA Astrophysics Data System

http://adswww.harvard.edu/

This service provides access to abstracts and some full-text articles in the fields of astronomy and astrophysics. Data collected from NASA space missions can also be accessed here.

NASA/Kennedy Space Center

http://www.ksc.nasa.gov/ksc.html

Learn about the American space program and its participants, read about different missions, view pictures—all at the Space Center. This site also has good links worldwide to other space-related servers.

National Geophysical Data Center

http://www.ngdc.noaa.gov/

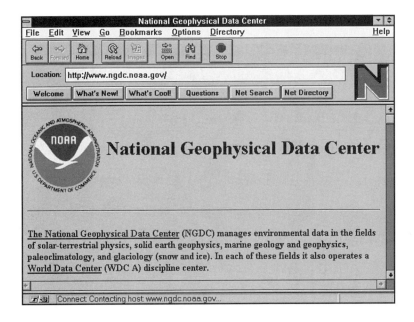

Available here are reams of data about solar-terrestrial physics, solid earth geophysics, marine geology and geophysics, paleoclimatology, and glaciology. Cyclone, tornado, and hurricane reports are all updated frequently.

Natural Resources Canada (NRCan) Gopher

http://www.emr.ca/

At this site you can find information from the Canadian government about forests, energy, mining, and geomatics. Also available are reports from the Geological Survey of Canada and an overview of NRCan statutes, organization, and personnel. This site provides links to other Canadian environmental and government Gophers.

Neurosciences Internet Resource Guide

http://http2.sils.umich.edu/Public/nirg/nirg1.html

This comprehensive Internet resource addresses biological, chemical, medical, engineering, and computer science aspects of neurobiology.

NMSU Astronomy

http://charon.nmsu.edu/

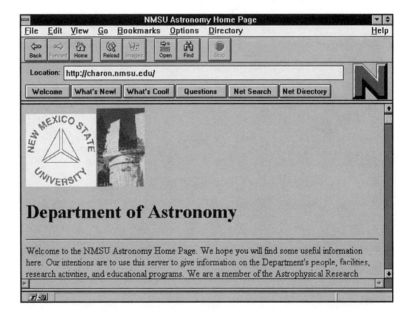

The people, research, facilities, and educational activities of the New Mexico State University Department of Astronomy are provided at this site. View images of planets, moons, and the collision of comet Shoemaker-Levy 9 with Jupiter.

The Northern Lights Planetarium

http://www.uit.no/npt/homepage-npt.en.html

Maintained by Norway's Northern Lights Planetarium, which is dedicated to understanding and experiencing the Aurora Borealis. This site contains images of the Northern Lights, information about the planetarium and its scheduled shows, and a link to the Norwegian Home Page.

Northwestern University Astronomy

http://www.astro.nwu.edu/home.html

This site contains a faculty directory and information about graduate and undergraduate programs of astronomy research. A gallery of gamma-ray bursts can also be found here.

Quantum Physics/High-Energy Physics

http://www.cern.ch/physics/hep.html

This server contains extensive international links to academic and research institutions specializing in high-energy physics. Journals, abstracts, and conference information are all available from this site.

The Safari Splash Home Page

http://oberon.educ.sfu.ca/splash.htm

In 1994, the Royal British Columbia Museum explored Barkeley Sound. This site contains photos, movies, and sound clips documenting the expedition.

The Space Telescope Electronic Information Service

http://marvel.stsci.edu/top.html

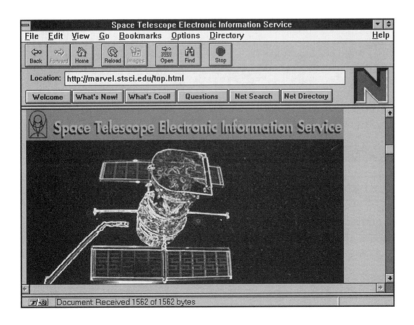

Operated by the Space Telescope Science Institute WWW Server, this site provides access to data and images acquired by the Hubble Telescope during its operation. The site contains information and tools researchers can use to search Hubble archives, as well as still and moving images in a variety of formats suitable for the general public.

Tulane Medical Center

http://www.mcl.tulane.edu/

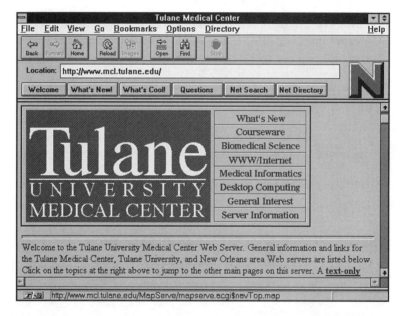

This server provides information about the Center and its activities. Texts and educational software on medicine and biomedical science are available also.

UC Berkeley Museum of Paleontology and the WWW Subway

http://ucmp1.berkeley.edu/subway.html

Here is where to find multimedia museum displays from UC Berkeley's Museum of Paleontology. Also featured is an interactive subway, a tool linking users to other museums and Web sites around the world.

The University of California Search for Extraterrestrial Civilizations

http://sereninfo.ssl.berkley.edu

This resource contains information about UC Berkeley's SETI and SERENDIP (Search for Extraterrestrial Radio Emissions from Nearby Developed Intelligent Populations) programs. This ongoing scientific research effort is aimed at detecting radio signals from extraterrestrial civilizations. Details about the program and updates on current research activities are also accessible.

The University of Minnesota Remote Sensing Lab

http://walleye.forestry.umn.edu/0/www/main.html

The University of Minnesota Remote Sensing Lab server contains information about all aspects of image processing and GIS, as well as general information about remote sensing. This server also features a GIS Jobs Clearinghouse, archives, and so on.

Virtual Frog Dissection Kit

http://george.lbl.gov/ITG.hm.pg.docs/dissect/info.html

Come here to control the dissection of a virtual frog, using a form-based protocol. Updated images are generated based on your instructions. This site is available also in Spanish, French, German, and Dutch.

Weizmann Institute of Science

http://wissgi.weizmann.ac.il/

This home page gives you access to the Institute's departments and libraries, with updates on various research projects.

Woods Hole Oceanographic Institute

http://www.whoi.edu/

This home page for Massachusetts' Woods Hole Oceanographic Institute provides information about their latest research and about classes offered at the Institute.

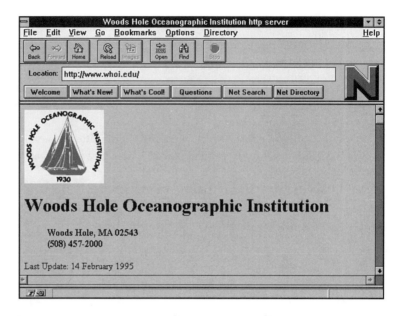

WWW Biological Science Servers

http://info.er.usgs.gov/network/science/biology/index.html

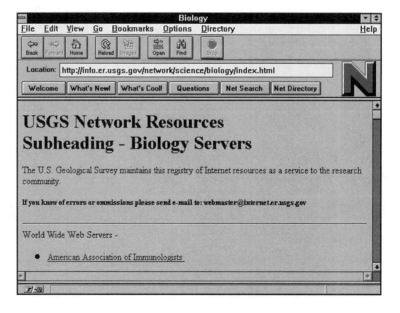

This Web site contains Internet links to many Gopher servers and other Web sites about bioscience.

CHAPTER 26

Looking at the Best Arts and Humanities Sites

When you get a little burned out looking at commercial sites or technical sites, go to a museum or a library. This chapter focuses on art, history, museums, and other sites related to the arts and humanities.

Places to Start

If you've never had the opportunity to travel to Paris and visit the Louvre, point your browser at the following URL and visit the Le WebLouvre (see fig. 26.1):

```
http://sunsite.unc.edu/louvre
```

Figure 26.1

Check out public-domain art at this site.

Here you can find computer versions of public-domain art. Unlike the pay-per-view "real" Louvre, this one is free, and aims for broad dissemination. Featured are "Famous Paintings" and a medieval art exhibit.

Local art museums also find their way onto the Web sooner, rather than later. One example is the Los Angeles County Museum of Art (see fig. 26.2). The exhibits here are well-described in narrative form, but there are no graphics yet. Recent exhibits include "B. Kitaj: A Retrospective," Mayan ceramics, and "20th-Century Drawings."

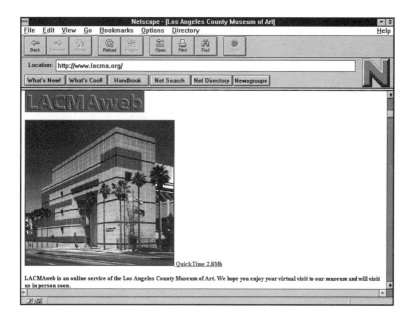

Figure 26.2

Visit the Los Angeles County Museum without leaving home.

To find this site, point your browser at the following URL:

http:///www.lacma.org/

Sometimes you just feel like sitting back and enjoying a good book. Visit one of the many libraries with holdings online. The University of Michigan Library (see fig. 26.3) is one of these libraries. It also has an Internet resource guide by subject. The URL for this site is as follows:

http://www.lib.umich.edu/

Figure 26.3

The University of Michigan is on the Web.

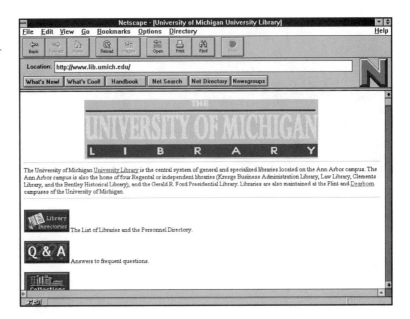

Another way to enjoy a book is to visit one of the sites that provides books online. One of these sites, On-line Books (see fig. 26.4), is located at the following URL:

```
http://www.cs.cmu.edu/Web/books.html
```

Figure 26.4

Check out Shakespeare and other electronic books at this site.

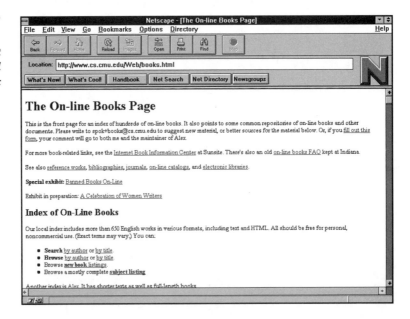

Art

This section lists and briefly describes some of the numerous art-specific Web servers. For a larger, online directory, point your browser at the *New Riders' Electronic World Wide Web Yellow Pages*: http://www.mcp.com/

African Art Exhibit and Tutorial

http://www.lib.virginia.edu

For those interested in African art and culture, this Web site provides images of African art and an overview of African aesthetics.

Amsterdam Valley

http://valley.interact.nl/av/int/home.html

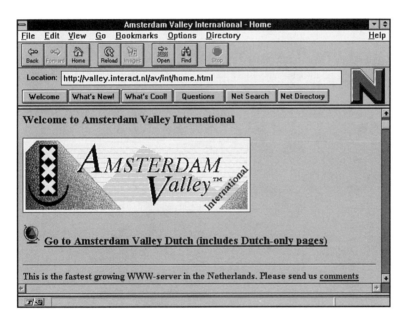

This site, which opened in early 1995, is the home of a collection of off-beat journals and technology-based businesses. In this area you can also find an art gallery and a musicians' hang-out. The area is also available in Dutch.

Art: Exhibits

http://akebono.stanford.edu/yahoo/Art/Exhibits/

This site concentrates on electronic art, dreams, reviews, graffiti, and "guerrilla art." Both online and "real" art exhibits are accessible from this site. Of particular interest are online exhibits of private collections, as well as the Census Bureau Art Gallery. There is a strong presence of commercial galleries, with close to 50 listed as of early 1995. Critiques are offered, in addition to collective art projects called *hyperart*.

AusArts

http://ausart.anu.edu.au/ITAAusArts/index.html

The AusArts site, maintained by the Australian National University, contains links to the Institute of the Arts Library Server, Canberra University, and the Electronic Library. This is a good site for individuals looking for information about the arts and higher education in Australia.

The Bog (Board for Online Graffiti)

http://www.ncb.gov.sg/BOG

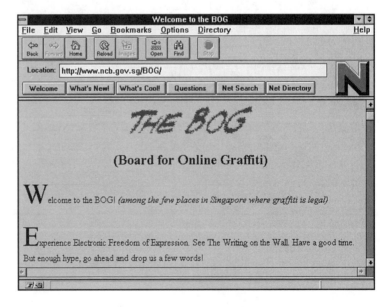

Singapore is not renowned for its tolerance of graffiti; in fact, this is probably the only place in Singapore graffiti *is* tolerated. Surf over and leave your own artwork on the walls provided.

CinemaSpace

http://remarque.berkeley.edu:80/cinemaspace

This resource, from the Film Studies Program at UC Berkeley, is devoted to all aspects of cinema and new media. Projects for CinemaSpace include academic papers on film and new media, film theory and critique, multimedia lectures, sources of film clips, and references to other sites.

Grotesque in Art

http://www.ugcs.caltech.edu/~werdna/grotesque/grotesque.html

This online gallery of horrors contains images of mankind's worst nightmares. Topics range from fear and madness to torture and death.

The Heard Museum

http://hanksville.phast.umass.edu/defs/independent/Heard/Heard.html

The Heard Museum, a private museum in Phoenix, Arizona, concentrates on the cultures of native peoples, particularly Native Americans. In addition to historical information about Native Americans, this server has information about current exhibitions at the museum, lecture schedules, lists of events, and other museum-related information.

HypArt

http://rzsun01.rrz.uni-hamburg.de/cgi-bin/HypArt.sh

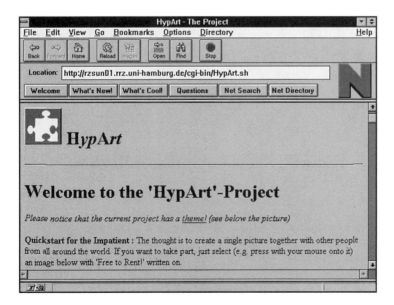

This site houses a collaborative art project. The space is presented here for you to create a picture with other people from around the world.

Le Ministère de la Culture: Direction des Musées de France

http://dmf.culture.fr/

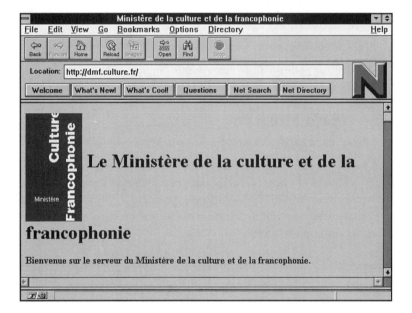

The French Ministry of Culture provides this online exhibit, called "The Age of Enlightenment in the Paintings of France's National Museums."

Lectro-Art

http://www.artnet.org/iamfree/IAMFREE/html/elecart.html

Users can obtain free underground art here.

MIT Center for Educational Computing Initiatives Virtual Museum

http://abelard.mit.edu/cgi-bin/museum-entrance/

This exhibit features the ultra-high-speed scientific photography of Harold E. Edgerton, who made famous such pictures as apples being split by bullets, the first microsecond of an atom bomb blast, or hummingbirds frozen in flight.

Musée des arts et métiers—le web (Museum of Arts and Crafts)

http://www.cnam.fr/museum/

This server maintains exhibits about crafts, professions, and technology. Topics include an exhibit about robots and a history of (mostly French) inventions. So far, all text is in French, with no English translation.

Museum Web

http://www2.primenet.com/art-rom/museumweb/

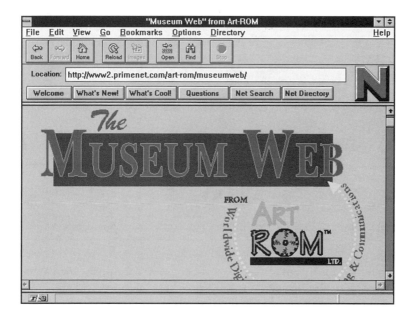

A must-see for museum lovers! This page has links to the best museum Web sites, galleries, antique collections, zoos, gardens, planetariums, and historical sites.

NYAL (New York Art Line)

http://gopher.panix.com/nyart/Kpage/kg

The primary focus of this site is visual art, particularly in the New York City area. There's online access to selected galleries, image archives, and New York City art groups. In addition to visual art, you can find information about dance, music, and techno art. There is a special section on Internet art. When you finish browsing this page, you can link to various electronic journals, museums, and schools.

Rosen Sculpture Exhibition

http://www.acs.appstate.edu/art

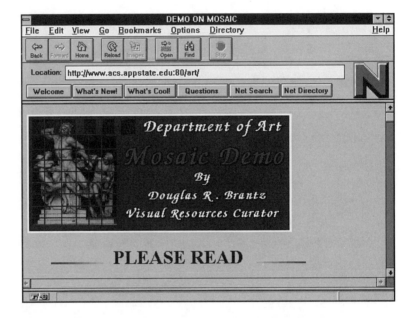

This Web site is the home page for the Department of Art at Appalachian State University, Boone, North Carolina. Currently on display are an art exhibit containing images from different periods in sculpture, an online exhibit, and the Rosen sculpture exhibition. Of course there are links to other art sources on the Internet.

Sonoma State University Alumni Art Exhibition

http://www.sonoma.edu/exhibits/alumni/

The works of 16 former students at Sonoma State University, California are represented at this site. This is the first in a planned series of such exhibitions.

UNC Virtual Museum

http://sunsite.unc.edu/exhibits/vmuseum/vmuseumhome.html

The exhibits on this page are compiled from archives at the University of North Carolina. New exhibits will be added on an on-going basis. Two recent exhibits on display include the Soviet Archive Exhibit and the Mathematical Art Gallery.

WWW Paris

http://meteora.ucsd.edu/~norman/paris

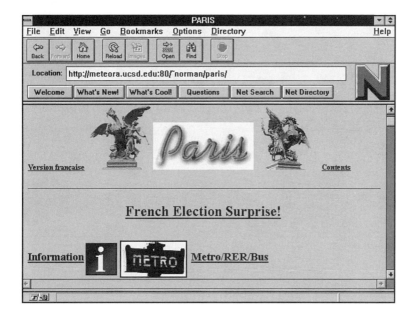

You can take a visual tour of Paris from this site which has a collection of the major monuments and museums of Paris. There are maps of the Metro, calendars of events and current expositions, and promotional images and text about local department stores. There is also a visitor's section with up-to-date tourist information on hotels, restaurants, telephones, airport schedules, a basic Paris glossary, and the latest weather images.

History

Several history-related sites are available through the Web. This section lists a handful of them.

Armadillo's World Wide Web Page

http://chico.rice.edu/armadillo

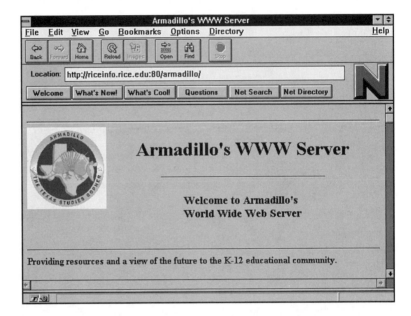

This site provides resources and instructional material for an interdisciplinary course in Texan culture.

ArtServe

http://rubens.anu.edu.au/

This resource has more than 8,000 images of prints from the 18th through the 19th centuries, classical architecture, architectural sculpture, and classical European sculpture. Highlights include: Vatican exhibit, Soviet archive exhibit, 1492 exhibit, Dead Sea Scrolls exhibit, and a paleontology exhibit.

The Heard Museum

http://hanksville.phast.umass.edu/defs/independent/Heard/Heard.html

The Heard Museum, a private museum in Phoenix, Arizona, concentrates on the cultures of native peoples, particularly Native Americans. In addition to historical information about Native Americans, this server has information about the museum's current exhibitions, lecture schedules, lists of events, and other museum-related information.

Michael C. Carlos Museum, Emory University, Atlanta, Georgia

http://www.cc.emory.edu/CARLOS/carlos.html

This online museum represents a collection that spans time from prehistory to today. The museum itself occupies a building of 45,000 square feet, a fact reflected in this Web page. Visit the "Ancient Americas," "Ancient Egypt," "Ancient Near East," "Artworks on Paper," "Asia," "Greece and Rome," "Sub-Saharan Africa," and other exhibits from this site.

The University of Memphis Institute of Egyptian Art and Archaeology

http://www.memst.edu/egypt/main.html

In addition to general information about the Institute of Egyptian Art and Archaeology, this server has a link to the exhibit of Egyptian artifacts at the University of Memphis, as well as a "short color tour of Egypt."

U.S. Civil War Reading List

http://www.cis.chio-state.edu/hypertext/faq/usenet/civil-war-usa/reading-list/faq.html

This Web resource provides access to a broad range of library catalogs, databases, and servers, including a major directory on abolitionism. Also cataloged here are an extensive reading list, an 11-hour documentary film, and a CD of songs of the Civil War era. You can find material in the following categories: General Histories of the War, Causes of the War, Slavery and Southern Society, Reconstruction, Biographies, and others.

Humanities

You either love the humanities or you hate them. This section lists and describes several humanities-related sites available on the Web.

COOMBSQUEST Social Sciences and Humanities Information Facility

http://coombs.anu.edu.au./CoombsHome.html

This is the worldwide Social Sciences and Humanities Information Service of the Coombs Computing Unit, Research Schools of Social Sciences and Pacific

Studies, Australian National University, Canberra, Australia. This resource
provides direct access to the world's major electronic repository of social
science and humanities papers, and other high-grade research material dealing
with culture and religions of Australia and the Pacific Rim.

Faculty of Arts, Gutenborg University

http://www.hum.gu.se/

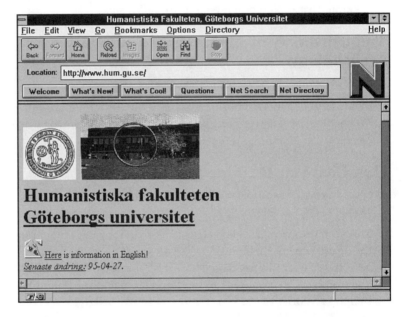

This Swedish server, devoted to the arts and humanities, offers information
from each of the university's departments, including such publications as the
Journal on Theory of Science.

The Human Languages Page

http://www.willamette.edu/~tjones/Language-Page.html

This is a resource for world languages. The languages found here include
everything from Esperanto to Kanji. In addition to dictionaries, tutorials, and
audio samples, you'll also find links to other research sites.

InforM Women's Studies Database

http://www.inform.umd.edu

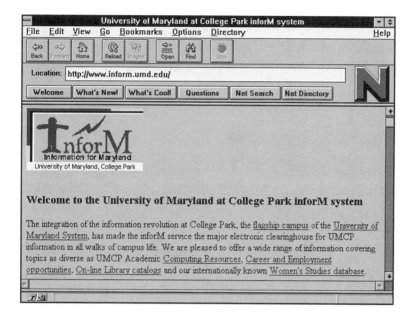

This server contains many resources pertaining to women's studies and women's issues. You can find information about health care, political issues, gender issues in the workplace and in education, reproductive rights, sex discrimination, sexual harassment, violence, work and family, women and computers, feminist film reviews, and poetry, as well as employment opportunities.

International Student Festival in Trondheim

http://www.idt.unit.no:80/~isfit/

In the past, more than 500 students have gathered at this festival in Trondheim, Norway to discuss human rights. Details on the '94 festival are available here, in addition to volunteer information for the '96 festival.

Mexican Culture FAQ

http://www.cis.ohio-state.edu/hptertext/faq/usenet/mexican-faq/faq.html

This is the FAQ from the soc.culture.mexican news group. Extensive information about Mexican culture, history, society, language, and tourism can be found here.

The PSYCGRAD Project WWW Pages

http://www.cc.utexas.edu/psycgrad/psycgrad.html

Primarily an international forum for graduate students in psychology, this site includes a student-run scientific journal, digests, and critiques.

Sociology

http://galaxy.einet.net/galaxy/Social-Sciences/Sociology.html

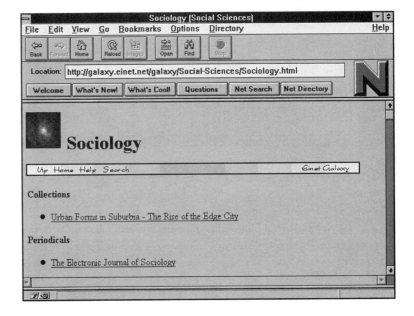

This is a gateway to sociology information on the Web. Some of the links available here include the Electronic Journal of Sociology, sociological directories, listservs for social work and sociology, the Swedish social science data service, the sociological collection at the Berkeley library, and academic organizations, as well as many other related links.

Libraries

Remember when libraries were full of old, smelly books? Well, they still are, but you can find online versions of many of the top libraries and their resources. This section lists a handful of these Web sites.

Brown University Library

http://stanley.cis.brown.edu/university-library

The Brown libraries contain approximately 1.5 million volumes, including historical archives of early American imprints, and biomedical engineering holdings.

LISTGopher

http://ericmorgan.lib.ncsu.edu/staff/morgan/morgan.html

You can use your e-mail account and the LISTGopher to search (by keyword) library-related LISTSERV archives.

Literature—Electronic Text Center

http://www.lib.virginia.edu/etext/ETC.html

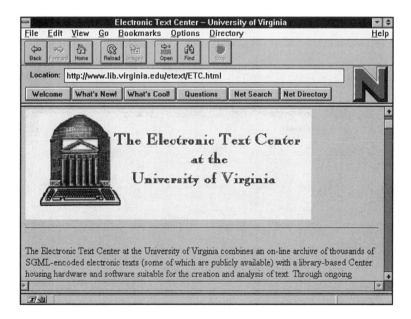

Read to your heart's content through this University of Virginia electronic library. Thousands of great works of literature are available from the home page. Through one link, you can access a collection of Early Modern English texts, the King James and Revised standard versions of the Bible, and a variety of Middle English texts.

The MIT Press Online Catalogs

http://www-mitpress.mit.edu

This Web resource maintains a searchable index of books published in the years 1993 to 1994, as well as current journals covering computational and cognitive sciences, architecture, photography, art and literary theory, economics, environmental science, and linguistics.

Research Libraries Group (RLG)

http://www-rlg.stanford.edu/welcome.html

The RLG is a nonprofit organization that provides support for libraries and other research facilities. This page describes the group's search system, article citation system, and bibliographic database. Online exhibits by group members also can be found here.

SUNET

http://www.sunet.se/

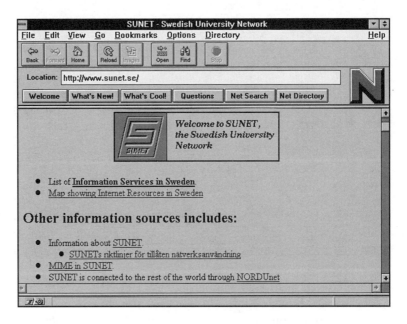

The Swedish University Network maintains this good introductory page to Web sites in Sweden. Also available is a clickable map of the country and information about Nordic libraries.

University of Colorado at Boulder Library

http://culine.colorado.edu

The server for the University of Colorado at Boulder Library contains information about the library and its many significant collections.

University of Northern Iowa Library

http://iscssun.uni.edu:80/library

This server of the University of Northern Iowa Library highlights the library's large, wide-ranging collection, which includes significant collections in many fields.

University of Toledo Library

http://www.utoledo.edu

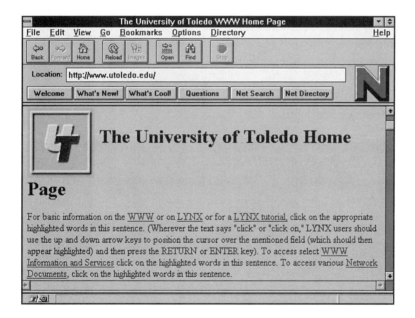

The server for the University of Toledo Library provides information about the library and its collections.

Museums

This section lists and breifly describes several museums that have Web sites.

Art.Online

http://www.terra.net/artonline/index.html

This virtual online art gallery presents original paintings, prints, and posters. You can view the collection by category, or link to galleries and museums around the world.

The Heard Museum

http://hanksville.phast.umass.edu/defs/independent/Heard/Heard.html

The Heard Museum, a private museum in Phoenix, Arizona, concentrates on the cultures of native peoples, particularly Native Americans. In addition to historical information about Native Americans, this server has information about exhibitions currently at the museum, lecture schedules, lists of events, and other museum-related information.

Huntsville Museum of Art

http://www.traveller.com/hma/

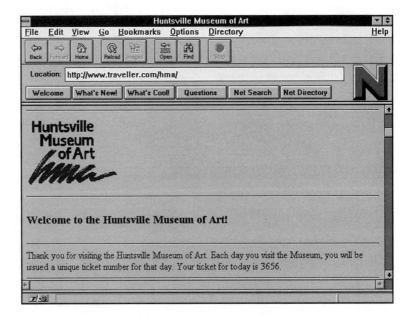

Of mostly local interest, this page for the art museum in Huntsville, Alabama, serves primarily as a forum for local museum events, exhibitions, tours, workshops, calls for volunteers, and the like.

Le Ministère de la Culture: Direction des Musées de France

http://dmf.culture.fr/

The French Ministry of Culture provides this online exhibit, called "The Age of Enlightenment in the Paintings of France's National Museums."

Los Angeles County Museum of Art

http://www.lacma.org/

The exhibits here are well-described in narrative form, but there are no graphics yet. Recent exhibits include "B. Kitaj: A Retrospective," Mayan ceramics, "20th-Century Drawings," art of the Jains (India), textiles, photographs, and "Italian Panel Painting of the Early Renaissance." Users will also find a long list of museum holdings, including paintings, drawings, sculpture, furniture, wedding dresses, and many other items.

Luxembourg National Museum of Art

http://www.men.lu/~fumanti/LuxMusee.html

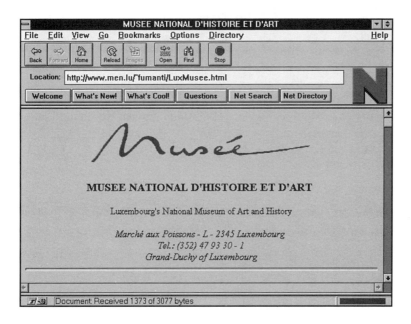

Artists of Luxembourg are well-represented in several exhibits. Recent exhibits include French artist M.R. Magritte's (1898-1967) "Le Modele Vivant." A link to the Luxembourg Ministry of Education is also available from this site.

MIT Center for Educational Computing Initiatives Virtual Museum

http://abelard.mit.edu/cgi-bin/museum-entrance/

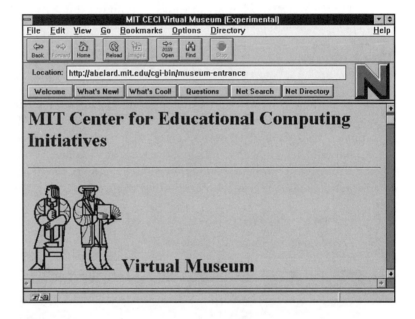

This exhibit features the ultra-high-speed scientific photography of Harold E. Edgerton, who made famous such pictures as apples being split by bullets, the first microsecond of an atom bomb blast, and hummingbirds frozen in flight.

Musée des arts et métiers—le web (Museum of Arts and Crafts)

http://web.cnam.fr/museum/

This server maintains exhibits about crafts, professions, and technology. Topics include an exhibit about robots and a history of (mostly French) inventions. So far, all text is in French, with no English translation.

Museum of New Zealand—Te Papa Tongarewa

http://hyperg.tu-graz.ac.at:80/B404BE8C/CNew_Zealand

The Museum of New Zealand offers exhibits about the Maori and about New Zealand's natural environment and history. Included also are some graphics for art objects in the museum's collection. Some graphics have a "zoom" feature.

Museum of Physics Department's Early Scientific Instruments Exhibit

http://hp133.na.infin.it/Museum/Museum.html

Winning honorable mention in the Education category at the '94 Best of the Web competition, this site is an online exhibit of physics instruments used at the University of Naples from 1645 to 1900. The exhibit includes hundreds of images and lots of descriptive text.

Museums in Holland (Netherlands)

http://www.xxlink.nl/nbt/museums/

This server contains a searchable guide to Holland's museums. Users can search by an alphabetical index or by place name. All text is in English, except for proper names of museums and places. There are no graphics yet, but this is a very comprehensive guide and well worth perusing.

The Natural History Museum of Great Britain

http://www.nhm.ac.uk

This museum is one of the most highly regarded of its kind in the world. Visitors to this site will find information about the museum, its charter, its exhibits, and access to its library. In addition, this site provides access to other natural history and general-research sites on the Web.

The Safari Splash Home Page

http://oberon.educ.sfu.ca/splash.htm

In 1994, the Royal British Columbia Museum explored Barkeley Sound. This site contains photos, movies, and sound clips documenting the expedition.

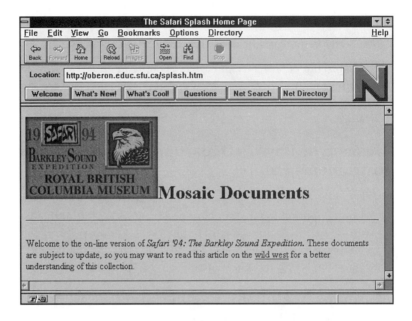

Sonoma State University Alumni Art Exhibition

http://www.sonoma.edu/exhibits/alumni/

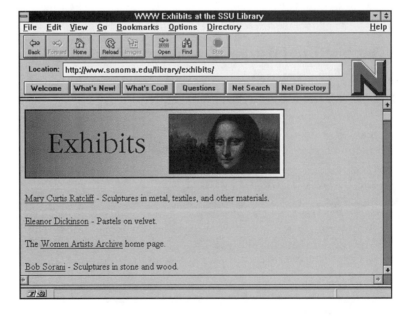

The works of 16 former students at Sonoma State University, California are represented at this site. This is the first in a planned series of such exhibitions.

UNC Virtual Museum

http://sunsite.unc.edu/exhibits/vmuseum/vmuseumhome.html

The exhibits on this page are compiled from archives at the University of North Carolina. New exhibits will be added on an on-going basis. Two recent exhibits on display include the Soviet Archive Exhibit and the Mathematical Art Gallery.

The University of California Museum of Paleontology

http://ucmp1.berkeley.edu/noinline.html

Runner-up in the Best of the Web '94 competition in the Education category, this online version of the California Museum of Paleontology provides visitors with an interactive visit to a virtual museum. Explore the online exhibits, learn about the history of the museum, and more; this site also includes links to other related sites.

The University of Memphis Institute of Egyptian Art and Archaeology

http://www.memst.edu/egypt/main.html

In addition to general information about the Institute of Egyptian Art and Archaeology, this server has a link to the exhibit of Egyptian artifacts at the University of Memphis, as well as a "short color tour of Egypt."

Whitney Museum Information

http://www.uky.edu/Artsource/whitneyhome.html

The page for the Whitney Museum of American Art in New York City has a schedule of exhibitions (from 1931 to 1997) and a chronology of events and performances. Traveling exhibits are covered also. All exhibits are described in text (no graphics).

Publications

You can find many periodicals, books, and other publications through the Web. This section lists several sites related to various publications.

Amsterdam Valley

http://valley.interact.nl/av/int/home.html

This site, which opened at the beginning of January, is the home of a collection of off-beat journals and technology-based businesses. The area includes an art gallery and a musicians' hang-out, and also is available in Dutch.

Artificial Life

http://alife.santafe.edu

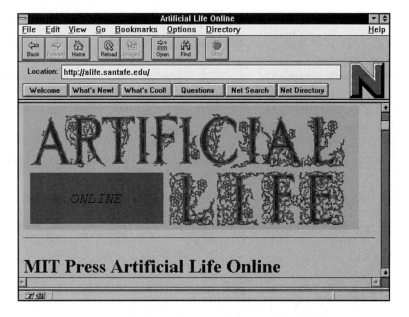

This site serves as a forum for information about all aspects of the Artificial Life enterprise. Services provided here include an FTP site containing preprints and software, a bibliographic database on artificial life, and links to various Usenet services.

Book Stacks Unlimited

http://www.books.com/

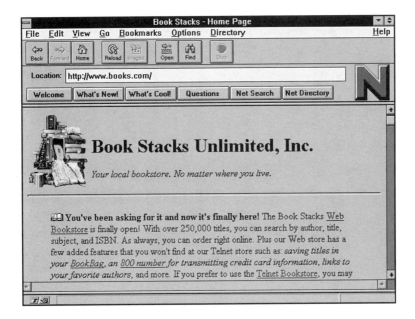

Books. Books. Books. Here you can browse for (and buy online) more than 240,000 books. With the Book Stacks server, you can search by author, title, subject, keyword, or ISBN.

Books Online

http://www.cs.cmu.edu/Web/books.html

This Web site contains hundreds of full-text online books, including many classics such as *Anna Karenina* and *The Complete Works of William Shakespeare*. It also has links to other book resources and has a searchable index.

Britannica Online

http://www.eb.com

This site provides an information service for Encyclopedia Britannica, Inc. Its database, which you can search by keyword, includes experimental articles.

British National Register of Archives

http://coombs.anu.edu.au/CoombsHome.html

This is a multivolume electronic guide to accessing a wide variety of archival materials and repositories in the United Kingdom.

Colloquium

http://www.hydra.com/wertheim/colloquium.html

Colloquium is a newsletter about managing investments. The service is free for the first two months.

CommunicationsWeek

http://www.wais.com:80/cwk/

Get the latest information from *Communications Week*, a publication of CMP Publications. Reviews, past issues, and industry news are available here.

Computer Retail Week

http://www.wais.com:80/crw/

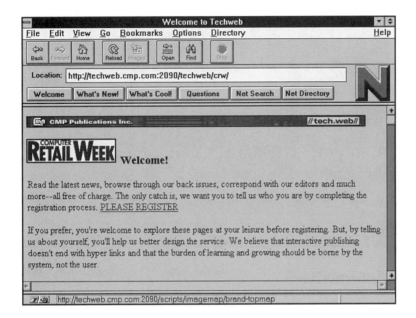

The latest industry news is available from this online version of *Computer Retail Week*. You can also take part in the magazine's online poll.

Computer Shopper

http://www.shopper.ziff.com/~cshopper/

Visit this site to get the latest online issue of the *Computer Shopper*, complete with hardware and software articles, a bulletin board, and archived issues.

Computer-Mediated Communication Magazine

http://www.rpi.edu/~decemj/cmc/mag/current/toc.html

Here it is, a paperless magazine. This is the home of *Computer-Mediated Communication Magazine*, offered by the Computer-Mediated Studies Center.

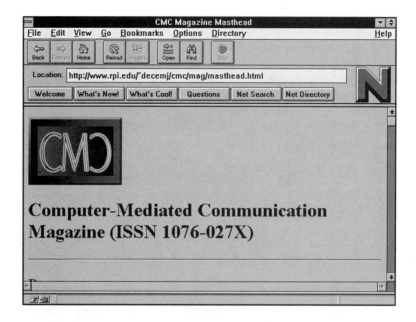

EE Times Interactive

http://www.wais.com:80/eet/

Browse the latest issues and search for past articles in this online version of CMP Publications' *Electronic Engineering*.

The electronic Gourmet Guide

http://www.deltanet.com:80/2way/egg

The eGG bills itself as an "e-zine devoted to food and cooking." The site contains lots of information about Chinese and other global cuisines.

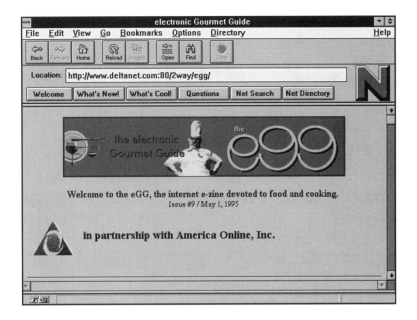

Electronic Journal of Combinatorics

http://ejc.math.gatech.edu:8080/

A current issue of this journal, about 50 pages of text, is available from this site, as are archives of past issues. Papers on such interesting topics as "Dense Packings of Equal Disks in an Equilateral Triangle" are published here.

Electronic Journal of Sociology

http://gpu.srv.ualberta.ca:8010/home1.htm

This site, sponsored by the University of Alberta, Canada, provides the electronic version of the peer-reviewed academic *Journal of Sociology*. The journal received the "1994 Best Networked Information Resources" award. Author's guidelines are included.

Elsevier Science

http://www.elsevier.nl/

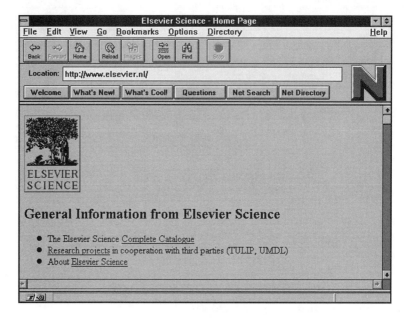

This publisher of more than 1,100 scientific journals has, at this Web site, plenty of information about its online publications.

The English Server

http://english-server.hss.cmu.edu

The English Server has archives of humanities materials, such as historical documents and classic books in electronic form, and also offers unusual and hard-to-find resources, particularly in the field of popular culture and media.

Entertainment Weekly

http://www.timeinc.com/ew/

Entertainment Weekly offers an online version of its magazine from this site. Movie reviews, multimedia reviews, and an *Entertainment Weekly* hot list of Web links are included here. Users can also search back issues for articles and reviews, or they can discuss with other surfers their views of the fine points of entertainment today.

The ETEXT Archives

http://www.etext.org/

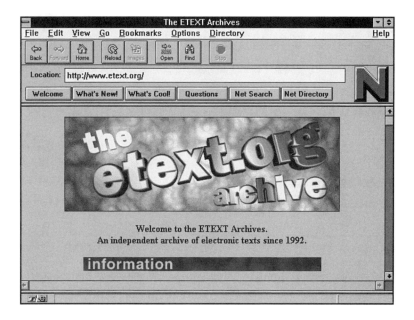

A massive collection of electronic texts is available from this archive. Some of the links include electronic books, magazines, Net literature, computer-related materials, political archives, underground digest archives, and many other archives.

GlasNews

http://solar.rtd.utk.edu/friends/news/glasnews/master.html

This quarterly publication reports on communications between cultures of the west and of the east. The server is published by Art Pattison Communications Exchange Program. Topics include advertising, public relations, and telecommunications.

Harvard Biosciences Online Journals

http://golgi.harvard.edu/journals.html

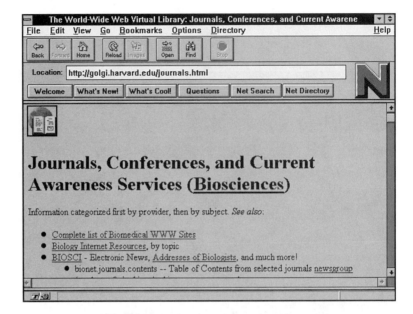

Here you can access selected online journals and periodicals about biology and medicine. Included are peer-reviewed e-journals, journal indexes, and databases.

HomePC

http://www.wais.com:80/hpc/

This site hosts the electronic version of *HomePC* computer magazine. This resource, published by CMP Publications, provides news, tips, reviews, and analysis of computer products.

INFOMART Magazine

http://www.onramp.net/infomart/infomart.html

This electronic magazine from Dallas, Texas, includes industry-related articles about information systems. A directory available from the home page lists the tenants of this technology mall.

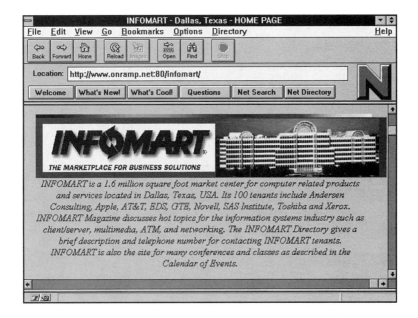

Information Week Interactive

http://www.wais.com:80/iwk/

This Web resource is host to *InformationWeek*. You can browse current and past issues, reviews, career advice, industry updates and news, and gossip in this online business and technology weekly.

Informatiques Magazine

http://www.wais.com:80/techweb/corporate/international/informatique.html

This Paris-based, French-language magazine is aimed at the MIS manager. This resource will soon be available in English.

InteractiveAge

http://www.wais.com:80/ia/

Browse *InteractiveAge*, an online publication, for the latest on the information highway.

Internet Business Report

http://www.wais.com:80/ibr/

At this site you can find the latest news about the growing area of online commerce. This online magazine is published by CMP Publications.

Internet World

http://www.mecklerweb.com/mags/iw/iwhome.htm

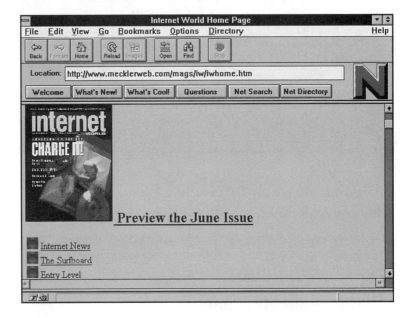

Preview the current issue of this monthly magazine, or check previous issues and columns in the online version of the magazine, published by Mecklermedia.

Investing Online

http://risc.cpbx.net/IOL/about.html

Investing Online is a monthly newsletter for people who want to use their home computer to get financial and trading information. Investors will want to check out this site, where they can look at a sample issue and find links to other related services.

Journal of Computer-Mediated Communication

http://www.huji.ac.il/www_jcmc/jcmc.html

Published by the Annenberg School for Communication at the University of Southern California, and the Information Systems Division of the School of Business Administration at the Hebrew University of Jerusalem, the *Journal of Computer-Mediated Communication* (JCMC) provides scholarly information about information and communication.

Knowledge One

http://KnowOne_WWW.sonoma.edu/

Knowledge One is an information service. You select topics you are interested in, and researchers provide a weekly summary of events on that subject.

Kyosaku Home Page

http://198.114.176.141/kyo/kyomain.html

Kyosaku is an online magazine devoted to anarchy, absurdity, humor, and the meaning of life. This page includes the Kyosaku manifesto, several issues of the magazine, and articles on such topics as Neil Armstrong, masturbation, and Lurch (of the "Addams' Family").

Macmillan Information SuperLibrary

http://www.mcp.com

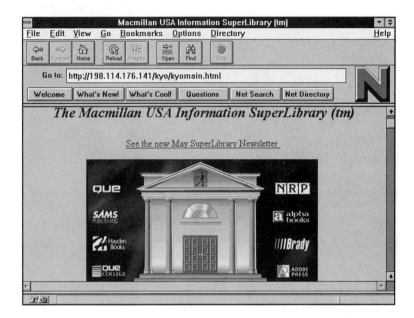

At this site, you can find a complete online catalog, as well as sample book chapters and tables of contents. The world's largest computer book publisher provides a comprehensive repository of online books and references. You also can communicate to publishers (online) or send in a good book proposal. (If you have an Internet or networking suggestion, send it to the following e-mail address: jlevalley@newriders.mcp.com.)

Miller Freeman

http://www.mfi.com/HomePage.html

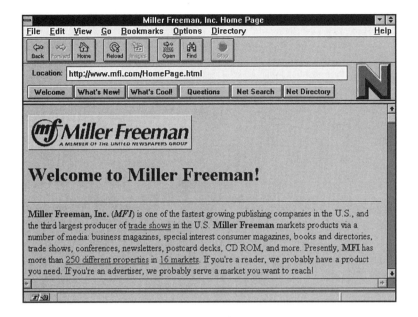

Miller Freeman, Inc. (MFI), produces trade shows and publishes books, business magazines, special-interest consumer magazines, and CD-ROMs. Their home page provides an overview of the company and a list of MFI's current products and services.

Network Computing Online

http://www.wais.com:80/nwc/

The client/server community is the target of this electronic magazine. Here you'll find ISDN reviews, the latest in technology, and the beta-test column.

New Ways to Noise

http://www.maires.co.uk:80/nw2n/

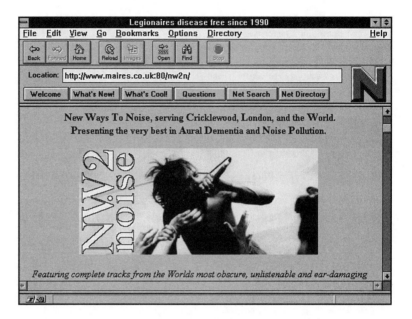

This online magazine covers the Japanese scene and other well-known underground noisemakers, including Yamatsuka Eye and Free Kitten. Audio samples and text for current hip "noise" bands are available here.

NYAL (New York Art Line)

http://gopher.panix.com/nyart/Kpage/kg

The primary focus of this site is visual art, particularly in the New York City metropolitan area. You get online access to selected galleries, image archives, and New York City art groups. This page also includes information about dance, music, and techno art, with a special section on Internet art. When you finish browsing this page, you can link to various electronic journals, museums, and schools.

Open Systems Today

http://www.wais.com:80/ost/

This online version of *Open Systems Today*, a CMP publication, serves the open distributed computing industry. Check out the hitchhiker's guide to other sites!

PC Week

http://zcias3.ziff.com/%7Epcweek/

The current issue, as well as past ones, can be found here. Find out about rumors, product reviews, and other interesting Web sites.

PowerPC News

http://power.globalnews.com/

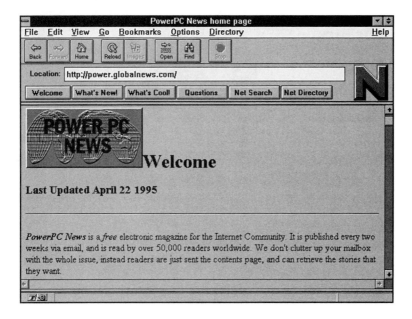

PowerPC News, an independently published biweekly publication, offers information about the microprocessor systems used by Apple and IBM.

Publisher's Catalogue Home Page

http://duke.usask.ca/~scottp/publish.html

From this home page, arranged geographically by country, users can link to many popular publishers throughout the world. A small sampling of the U.S. publishers available includes City Lights Publishers and Booksellers, Harvard University Press, and New Riders Publishing.

Strange Ways

http://www.pitt.edu/~zucker/strange-ways.html

Strange Ways is an online magazine for KISS fanatics. This site contains current and back issues of the magazine, as well as audio clips and information about rare KISS items.

TechWeb

http://www.wais.com:80/techweb/

The home page for CMP Publications, Inc., highlights this company's publishing, trade show organizing, and information marketing business. Use their search feature to find articles on a specific subject from more than 15 magazines.

Telecom Archives

http://lcs.mit.edu/telecom-archives

This is the home of the archives of *Telecom Digest*. Many back issues are on file here, along with online articles and resources related to the telecommunications industry.

Time Warner Electronic Publishing

http://www.timeinc.com/twep/

Each week this page highlights the new releases of books and electronic titles from Time Warner Electronic Publishing. Some recent excerpts include suggestions on how to drive your woman mad in bed, an illustrated screen play by Harlan Ellison, and the work of best-selling author James Patterson.

Virtual Book Shop

http://www.virtual.bookshop.com/

From this site users can search for and buy rare, first edition, antiquarian, and collectible books from booksellers all over the world. You can search by keyword or author.

VR World

http://www.mecklerweb.com/vr.htm

Check out the home page for this magazine about virtual reality. Look at past and current issues, and review books about virtual reality.

Windows Magazine

http://www.wais.com:80/win/

At this site you'll find the latest in news, updates, shareware, and profiles of people involved in the Microsoft Windows world.

Worldwide Collaborative Multimedia Magazine

http://www.trincoll.edu/homepage.html

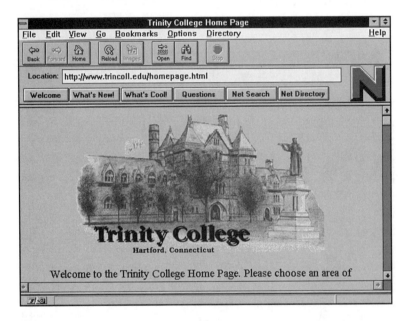

This weekly magazine, published by students at Trinity College, Hartford, Connecticut, contains submissions from all over the world.

ZiffNet/Mac

http://zcias3.ziff.com/%7Ezmac/

You can find information here about this online publishing service, also known as *ZMac*. News, software, and more are available to members.

CHAPTER

27

Looking at the Best Recreation Sites

Sometimes you just need to relax. The World Wide Web has thousands of sites dedicated to entertainment, sports, and music. Some of the most popular rock and roll groups are putting up Web pages to announce concert dates, show promotions, and even to distribute sound bites.

Other Web sites, dedicated to museums and art exhibits, enable you to sit in the comfort of your home and look at world-renowned art from around the world. You can, for instance, travel to Le Louvre in Paris and then point your browser to the Smithsonian Institution in Washington, D.C. This type of Web "experience" does not replace visiting these museums in person, but you can find out more about the museums and their holdings without spending hours and money traveling there.

Selected Sites

If you enjoy listening to cutting-edge music and like to stay informed of the independent music scene, then you must visit the Internet Underground Music Archive (see fig. 27.1). You can find videos, song clips, and band information at this site. You can find this site at the following URL:

```
http://sunsite.unc.edu/ianc/index.html
```

Figure 27.1

The Internet Underground Music Archive is one of the best sites on the Web for the latest information about emerging bands.

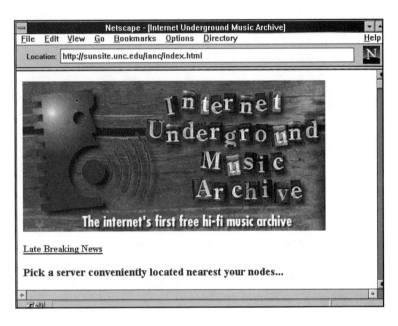

The Rolling Stones also have a presence on the Web (see fig. 27.2). At their site you can find tour announcements, photos, news, and concert merchandise. To find this site, point your Web browser at the following URL:

```
http://www.stones.com
```

One of my favorite bands is Rush. You can find lyrics, transcripts of interviews, photos, and concert announcements at several sites devoted to this power trio from Canada (see fig. 27.3). Point your browser at the following URL to find out more about Rush:

```
http://syrinx.umd.edu/rush.html
```

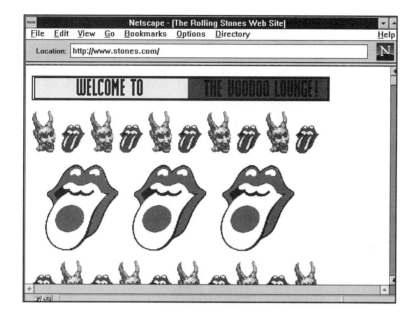

Figure 27.2

Check out the Rolling Stones on the Web.

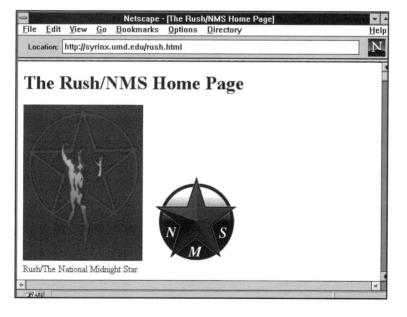

Figure 27.3

Rush fans should check out this site on the Web.

If you're into Irish rock and roll, and you like the Cranberries (see fig. 27.4), you can find their "Unofficial" Web page at the following URL:

```
http://www.nada.kth.se/~d90-fgi/Cranberries/cranberries.html
```

Figure 27.4

Visit the Official Cranberries Unofficial Home Page for pictures, sound clips, and tour info.

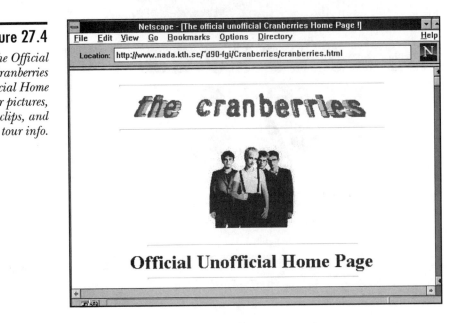

Sit back and relax and listen to the soothing sounds of Windham Hill. Or check out their home page (see fig. 27.5). In the Listening Room, you can listen to sound samples from different artists. You can find biographies, tour dates, and an open forum for discussion. Point your Web server at the following URL:

```
http://www.windham.com
```

If music isn't what you're looking for, you can find a number of entertainment sites that might interest you. One site, Time Warner (see fig. 27.6), is an excellent site for movie fans and readers of *Time* and *Entertainment Weekly*. Its URL is as follows:

```
http://pathfinder.com
```

Figure 27.5

Windham Hill is best known for their "Fresh Air" albums and CDs.

Figure 27.6

The Time Warner site is relatively new and graphics-intensive.

If you're a *Star Trek* fan, check out the Star Trek Generations Web site (see fig. 27.7) at the following URL:

```
http://generations.paramount.com
```

Figure 27.7

Have plenty of time when you visit this site—it's loaded with graphics.

Here you can find behind-the-scenes information, graphics, sound, and video clips.

Did you think you could get away from the O.J. Simpson trial? Hopefully it will be over by the time this book hits the stores, but just in case you want more information about it, see the O.J. Simpson Trial Web site (see fig. 27.8). You can even find links to other O.J. sites. You can find this site at the following URL:

```
http://sfgate.com/examiner/ojindex.html
```

If sports is your fancy, check out the Sports Server Web site (see fig. 27.9) for coverage of basketball, football, and baseball. You can get injury reports, daily scores, and division standings. Point your browser at the following URL:

```
http://www.nando.net/sptsserv.html
```

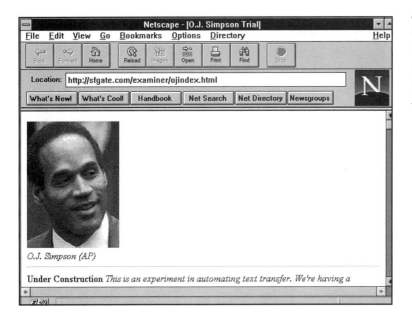

Figure 27.8

Turn off your TV and watch the O.J. trial from your computer.

Figure 27.9

Find the latest about your favorite sports team—professional or minor league.

Entertainment

This section highlights some additional entertainment sites that you might want to check out. If you have other sites that you would like to list here, send your suggestions (they might appear in the next edition of this book) to the following e-mail address:

`rtidrow@iquest.net`

Ameba

http://www.thoughtport.com/com/ameba/index.html

Visit the Dream Page—a collection of very funky art pictures. Some of these are available in the shopping area.

Art.Online

http://www.terra.net/artonline/index.html

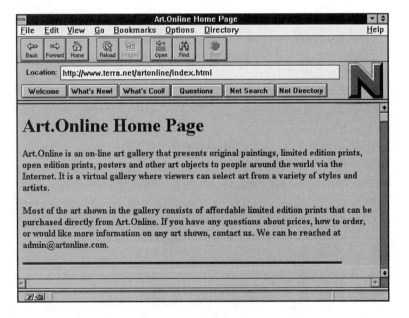

This virtual online art gallery presents original paintings, prints, and posters. You can view the collection by category, or link to galleries and museums around the world.

ArtWorld

http://www.wimsey.com:80/anima/ARTWORLDhome.html

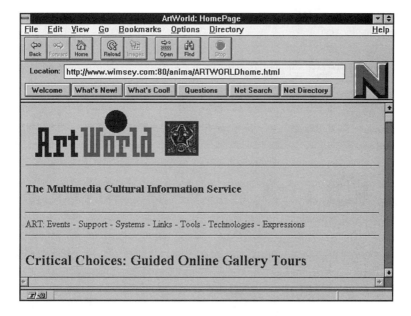

ArtWorld is a multimedia cultural and information service to art-related sites for all media and genre: visual, mass media, literature, video, performance, and design. This site has many good links to the world art scene.

Blues Brothers FAQ

http://www.cs.monash.edu.au/~pringle/bluesbros/faq.html

This site contains information about the Dan Ackroyd/John Belushi movie, *Blues Brothers*. It includes an incomplete transcription of the film, lyrics, audio clips, and fan club information.

Books Online

http://www.cs.cmu.edu/Web/books.html

This Web site contains hundreds of full-text online books, including many classics, such as *Anna Karenina* and the complete works of William Shakespeare. It also has a searchable index and links to other book resources.

Buena Vista Movieplex

http://www.disney.com/

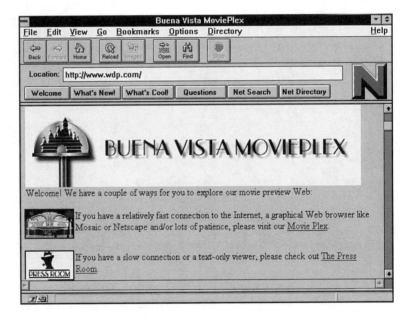

In addition to general information about the company, this server provides movie clips from the latest Buena Vista releases, as well as other interesting movie facts.

Bundyland, Home of Married...With Children

http://www.eia.brad.ac.uk/mwc/index.html

The Web promises to provide places where visitors can experience some of the most moving works of art and high culture humanity has created. This is not one of them. Dedicated to the television program *Married...With Children*, this site provides images, sounds, and clips from the show. Also includes FAQs and an episode guide.

CinemaSpace

http://remarque.berkeley.edu/~xcohen

This resource from the Film Studies Program at UC Berkeley is devoted to all aspects of cinema and new media. Projects for CinemaSpace include academic papers on film and new media, film theory and critique, multimedia lectures, sources of film clips, and references to other sites.

Condom Country

http://www.ag.com/condom/country

Safe sex on the Web! This is the place to browse and order from an online catalog of condoms and other sexual aids and devices. Check out the history of our latex friends and find out how your favorite condom rates.

Curious Pictures

http://found.cs.nyu.edu/CAT/affiliates/curious/curioushp.html

Curious Pictures is an animation company. Their server contains samplings of their special effects, graphics, and animation work.

The Eden Matrix

http://www.eden.com

The Eden Matrix is an Austin, Texas, Internet provider and the home of the live Internet concert broadcast by the same name. Users will find information about alternative music, 'zines, comics, and more.

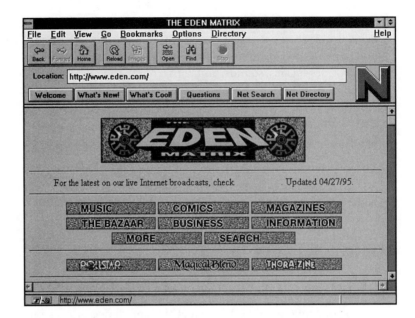

Hangman at COMMA in Cardiff

http://www.cm.cf.ac.uk/htbin/RobH/Hangman?afgvstrut|2|daerlow|

Just like the childhood game and a lot like *Wheel of Fortune*. Visitors get a limited number of chances to guess which letters belong in an unknown word. Fail…and it's the gallows!

The Howard Stern Home Page

http://force.stwing.upenn.edu:8001/~jruspini/stern/stern.html

Here is where to find everything you ever (or never) wanted to know about this radio talk-show host, including news, general information, articles, sounds, and images.

Hyperion

http://www.hyperion.com

This service includes an online guide to the television show *Babylon 5* and a guide to the San Francisco area. Also available are a used software exchange marketplace and information on other popular television shows.

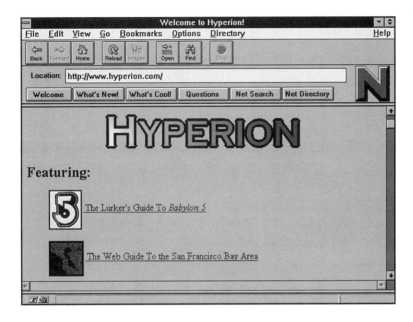

Lego Information

http://legowww.itek.norut.no

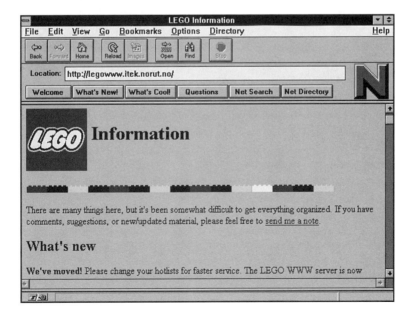

This Web site contains pictures, sets, and instructions for building with Legos. Also discussed here are various ideas, activities, and history pertaining to Legos, as well as information about clubs for Lego enthusiasts.

MCA/Universal Cyberwalk

http://www.mca.com

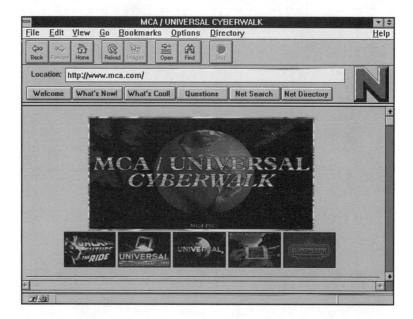

The home page for this entertainment and media giant provides information and samplings of its latest projects. The Universal Channel is a "behind-the-scenes" look at TV shows such as *SeaQuest DSV*, *Earth 2*, *Law & Order*, *Dream On*, *Vanishing Son*, and *Hercules—The Legendary Journeys* (to name a few). Users will also find an interactive game show, as well as other entertainment-related material from this site.

MGM: The Lion's Den

http://www.earthlink.net/MGM

This server provides great promos of upcoming MGM releases. Other useful links include a music library, a Cyber Vault, The Lab, a general store, and an area in which to leave comments and suggestions.

MGM/StarGate

http://www.digiplanet.com/STARGATE/index.html

This server contains previews and behind-the-scenes looks at upcoming motion picture releases.

The Mother of All Humor Archives

http://www.tc.cornell.edu/~ckline/humor/maillist.html

The name says it all. Blonde jokes, Steven Wright, Deep Thoughts—it's all here.

Museum Web

http://www.primenet.com/art-rom/museumweb

A must for museum lovers! This page has links to the best museum Web sites and to galleries, antique collections, zoos, gardens, planetariums, and historical sites.

National Public Radio

http://www.npr.org/

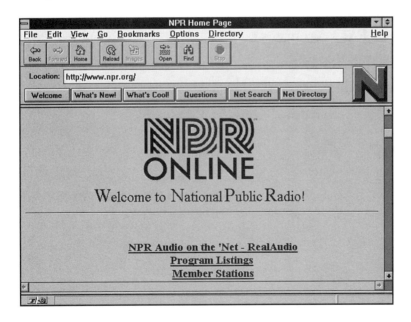

The home page of commercial-free radio. Read all about NPR, visit member stations, and download sound bites from various shows.

The Official Marathon World Wide Web Site

http://www.netweb.com/mall/marathon

Fans of this game can download graphics, screen shots, and sounds from this popular Mac-based game. Also presented here are details about its story, cast, weapons, and so on.

Online Bookstore

http://marketplace.com/0/obs

The Online Bookstore, started in 1992, offers a variety of full-text titles and is one of the best places on the Web to begin a literary prowl. A variety of electronic formats are available, some free and some for a fee. The Bookstore also offers expert consulting, seminars, and training sessions for those interested in Internet publishing.

Pablov International

http://www.twics.com/~TOKUMARU/home.html

This server contains information for those interested in Japanese cinema and Japanese perspectives on international cinema and media culture.

Railroads, Ships, and Aircraft Home Page (and the Tom Clancy FAQ Archives)

http://www.wpi.edu/~elmer

Trains and ships and aircraft, oh my! The title is a pretty good description of this site—a good place for information about, and links to, other resources concerning these types of transportation.

Sega Web

http://www.segaoa.com/

Check out this game giant's home page. Read about updates and new releases, get a look at sneak previews, and browse the library of hints, descriptions, screen shots, box cover images, and audio/video clips. Also, fill out a survey and cruise the mall.

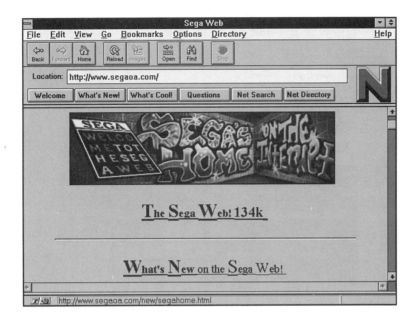

SkyBox Online

http://www2.interpath.net/interweb/skybox

From this server you can view and order trading cards online. Some of the trading cards available include the *Star Trek* and Harley-Davidson series.

Sony Online

http://www.music.sony.com

If you want to know what's new in the large world of Sony entertainment, this Web site is where to look. Sony covers every aspect of entertainment: artists, music, movies and television, and publishing. There are even audio clips of recent releases.

Star Trek Resources on the Internet

http://www.cosy.sbg.ac.at/rec/startrek/star_trek_resources.html

Star Trek fans will find this resource a useful place to begin their quest for information about the series. This comprehensive resource has information about mailing lists, archives, and other resources.

The Star Wars Home Page

http://force.stwing.upenn.edu:8001/~jruspini/starwars.html

This is the *Star Wars* Web source. Its home page has been accessed more than 1,000,000 times. For information about news, files, and merchandise, this is where to look. It's all here.

Star Wars Multimedia WWW Archive

http://bantha.pc.cc.cmu.edu:1138/SW_HOME.html

This resource is for fans of *Star Wars*. Find out about the books, movies, music, and other related information. Also, get information about the father of it all—George Lucas.

Tarot

http://cad.ucla.edu/repository/useful/tarot.html

Tarot—the ancient and mystical art of providing cocktail party entertainment. Now this prophetic art of prognosticative portents is available via the Web. Surf over for an individualized reading, and find what the cards augur.

TV Tonite

http://metaverse.com/vibe/tvtonite/tonite.html

Sponsored by OnRamp Inc. and Metaverse, this page provides an evening television guide for both broadcast and cable shows. ABC, CBS, NBC, HBO, FOX, PBS, Discovery, E!, Lifetime, MTV, Nickelodeon, TBS, TNT, USA, VH1, CNN, BET, A&E, ESPN, Cinemax, Showtime, the Movie Channel, and Disney are just a few of the channels included at this site.

Universal Studios

http://univstudios.com

This server contains information about Universal Studios cartoon shows and other shows, including *Dream On.* [Editor's note: this site, new as this book is being written, most likely will grow to include information about many Universal Studios movies and TV shows of interest.]

Vegas.COM

http://www.vegas.com

This Web site contains travel and tourist information about Las Vegas and its businesses.

VIBE online

http://www.timeinc.com/vibe

VIBE online includes features about urban music and the American youth culture. Reviews, clips, shopping, and chats are available from this server. Many additional youth-related links also are available.

Welcome to the North Pole!

http://north.pole.org

Even if it isn't Christmas, this site can fill a visitor with good cheer. Visit any time of the year to chat with Santa, the elves, and Rudolph.

World-Wide Collector's Digest

http://www.wwcd.com

This server is a gateway to information and links about collectibles of all kinds. Users will find dealers and display ads for trading cards, comic books, memorabilia, and pog manufacturers. ("Pogs," in case you don't know, are milk caps.) Also available from this site are links to professional sports schedules and archives, sports standings, product releases, professional team listings, Hall of Fame listings, and much more.

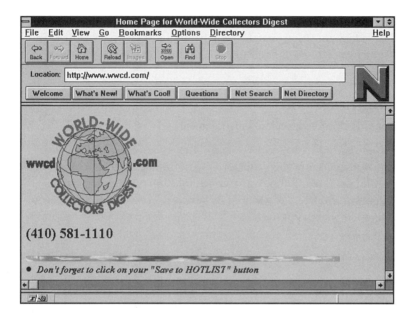

The X-Files

http://www.rutgers.edu/x-files.html

This Web site contains sounds bites and images from the FOX TV show by the same name. In addition, visitors can browse through FAQ lists, participate in surveys, and voice (well, e-mail) their opinions about individual episodes and cast members.

Yahoo—Entertainment

http://akebono.stanford.edu/yahoo/Entertainment

The Yahoo Entertainment directory contains links to more than 6,900 sites. This directory is divided into such categories as amusement parks, automobiles, drugs, eating and drinking, hobbies and crafts, multimedia, music, virtual reality, and many more. Users can search by keywords from the Yahoo search feature or use other search engines.

Food

Got the munchies? Check out some of these sites dedicated to food and drink.

The Beer Page

http://guraldi.itn.med.umich.edu:80/Beer

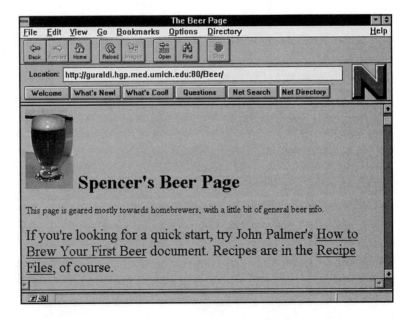

For home brewers, or just beer lovers in general, this site offers recipes, articles, and frequently asked questions. Beer label information and other indexes are also available.

The electronic Gourmet Guide

http://www.deltanet.com:80/2way/egg

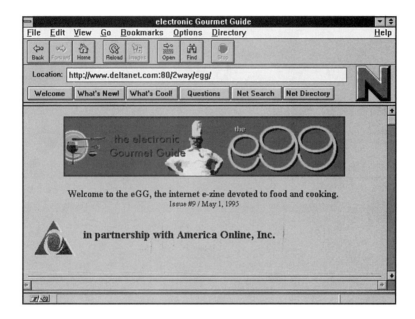

The eGG bills itself as an "e-zine devoted to food and cooking." The site contains lots of information about Chinese and other global cuisines.

Godiva Online

http://www.godiva.com

This site, dedicated to chocolate lovers, includes recipes, news, and the online catalog of the Belgian chocolatier.

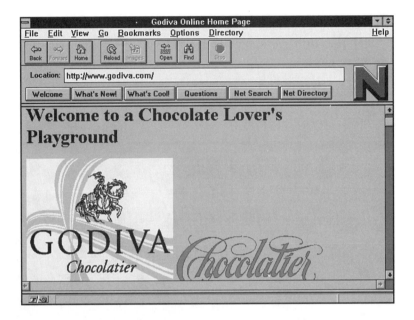

The Internet Wine Rack

http://www.clark.net/pub/wine/home.html

This site offers an online catalog of wine, beer, and other drinks. You can order from the nice selection found here, as well as find wine- and beer-related reviews and history.

Krema Nut Company

http://www.infinet.com/~schapman/mwow.cmh/krema/homepage.html

This is a site for nut nuts. View the company's online brochure and place an order.

Los Gatos Coffee Roasting Company

http://www.los-gatos.scruznet.com/los_gatos/businesses/los_gatos_coffee/storefront.html

Here you can learn all about roasting coffee, then order online from a variety of beans and strengths.

A Malt Whiskey Tour

http://www.dcs.ed.ac.uk/staff/jhb/whiskey

All you ever wanted to know about malt whiskey. This site contains information, and links to information sources, about malt whiskey, its classification, manufacture, history, and more. Includes hypertext maps and imagery of Scotland.

The Real Beer Page

http://and.com/realbeer/rbp.html

Dedicated to microbreweries and home brewers everywhere, the Real Beer Page is just the thing after a hot day's work. Includes an e-mail subscription to a listserv dedicated to beer, its brewing, and, of course, its drinking.

Triple Rock Brewing Company

http://and.com/3rock/3rock.html

In addition to historical information about beers and the brewing process, the Triple Rock Brewing Company in Berkeley, California, offers general information about itself and offers users an opportunity to receive a monthly e-newsletter.

Whole Foods Market

http://www.wholefoods.com/wf.html

This national food chain gives product information, store listings, recipes, nutritional guides, and financial reports. Try out its list of hotlinks to other health-oriented Web sites.

Wines on the Internet

http://www.wines.com

In this online guide to wines and wineries you can find news, articles, reviews, and a list of wine-related events.

Zima.com

http://www.zima.com

Join "Club Zima," find out about the beverage, and chat with like-minded Z-heads.

Music

This section lists more than 100 Web sites dedicated to music or music groups. If you're looking for the Debbie Gibson Web page, I didn't include it. Sorry.

461 Ocean Boulevard

http://http.bsd.uchicago.edu/~d-hillman/welcome.html

This site contains information about the new Eric Clapton release, *From The Cradle*. Tour information, audio clips, and images from this and other albums are available also.

Acid Jazz

http://www.cmd.uu.se/AcidJazz

This Web server provides information about the musical fusion of funky hip-hop and jazz. The site includes primers on Acid Jazz, examples of records and clubs that fit the category, and magazines. Mailing list information is available also.

Alice in Chains Home Page (Unofficial)

http://www.csos.orst.edu/~mikec/aic.html

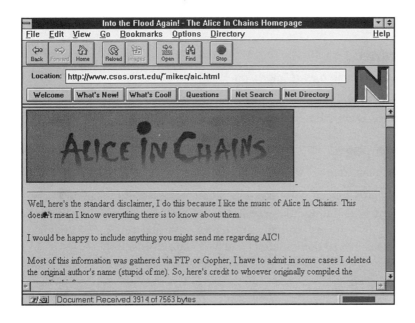

This site contains information about Alice in Chains albums, including pictures of the album covers, song lyrics, fan club information, some guitar tablature, and a history of the band. Users can also subscribe to an Alice in Chains mailing list from this site.

Amsterdam Valley

http://valley.interact.nl/av/int/home.html

This site, which opened at the beginning of January 1995, is the home of a collection of offbeat journals and technology-based businesses. You can also find an art gallery and a musicians' hang-out. This area is also available in Dutch.

Amy Grant Archive

http://www.ipc.uni-tuebingen.de/art

Fans of Amy Grant will find discography, videography, lyrics, reviews, audio clips, fan club information, and tour dates. The site is also an archive of the Amy Grant news group.

And Through the Wire—Peter Gabriel

http://www.cs.clemson.edu/~junderw/pg.html

Fans of Peter Gabriel will find discographies, mailing list information, reviews, and interviews, as well as extensive links to other Peter Gabriel-related sites.

Ani De Franco

http://www.cc.columbia.edu/~marg/ani

In addition to biography information, quotations, articles, and interviews with the performer, users will find descriptions and song titles from all albums.

atom home page!

http://www.atom.co.jp

This server contains an archive of independent, Japanese music labels. Users will find eight new albums online, including 9 Lazy 9-Brothers Of The Red, and Blue Bongos. This site also contains an archive of Virtual MACLIFE, a virtual art gallery, and links to both Sublime and Trigram records.

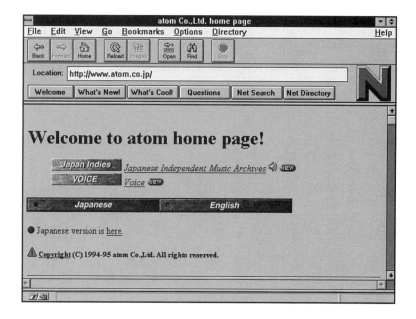

Australian Music Guide

http://www.st.nepean.uws.edu.au/~ezsigri/ausmusic/index.html

This page offers links to discographies and lyrics for more than 100 Australian bands. Club, gig, and tour information for many bands also is available.

Bad Religion

http://nebuleuse.enst-bretagne.fr:80/~lepoulti/BAD.RELIGION

This well-organized site contains information about the punk band Bad Religion. Lyrics, photos, and even some guitar tablature from the band's ten albums are available here.

Beastie Boys

http://www.nando.net/music/gm/BeastieBoys

The Beastie's home page features news about recent releases, tour information, solo projects, product information, movies, photos, and sound clips galore. Three large articles, a discography, and answers to frequently asked questions complete the offering.

Billy Joel

http://www-usacs.rutgers.edu/~rotton/billy-joel.html

Tour and album information, plus frequently asked questions about Billy Joel are featured on this server. You can also find lyrics and several album covers here.

Bjork Mainpage

http://www.math.uio.no/~srk/bjork.html

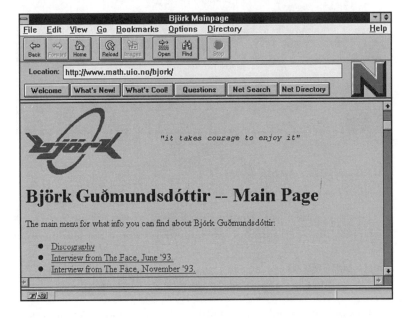

At this site, fans of the pop singer Bjork will find several text interviews, a discography, and links to ordering information.

Blues Brothers FAQ

http://www.cs.monash.edu.au/~pringle/bluesbros/faq.html

This site contains information about the Dan Ackroyd/John Belushi movie *Blues Brothers*. Users will find an incomplete transcription of the film, lyrics, audio clips, and fan club information.

BMG/Columbia House

http://biogopher.wustl.edu:70/1/audio/bmg

Here you can search online the catalogs of these two mail-order CD companies. Information about compact disc club policies and membership is available also.

Boingo Homepage

http://rhino.harvard.edu/dan/boingo/boingo.html

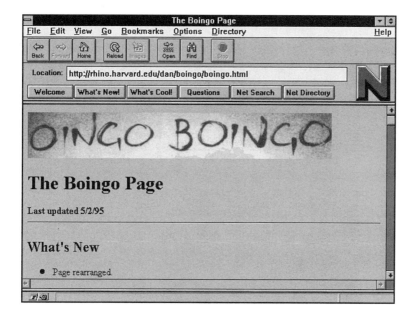

This site is dedicated to Danny Elfman's Oingo Boingo project. Tour dates, interviews with Elfman, lyrics, and track listings are available here, as is an electronic newsletter about the band.

Brian Eno

http://www.acns.nwu.edu/eno-l

This site contains extensive information about this influential experimental/ambient musician. A biography, liner notes for several albums, a bibliography of related materials, and information about several of the musician's other projects are just a few of the items found here.

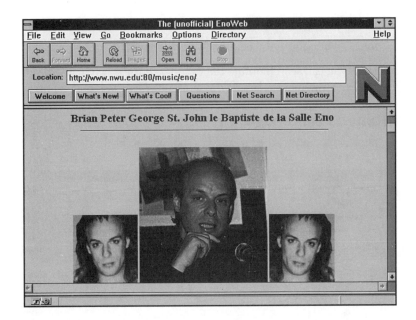

Buzzcocks

http://www.cityscape.co.uk/users/ac46/indbuzz.htm

This group forever changed the face of both pop and punk. Album covers and lyrics from the complete discography can be found at this site.

Captain Beefheart

http://www.catalog.com/mrm/beefheart.html

Discographies, product information, and a fanzine for this legend are available at this site, as is information about what may be the last recording he will ever release.

Christian Death Home Page

http://christian-death.acc.brad.ac.uk:

This page is a must for all those dark and dangerous gothics out there. Included at this site are a complete discography of the band Christian Death, information about the British gothic scene, and a list of projects the band members have been involved with. The link to the Cleopatra Records catalog provides a complete listing of the band's releases.

The Classical Guitar Home Page

http://www.teleport.com/~jdimick/cg.html

This server contains arrangements, MIDI files, articles, and frequently asked questions related to classical guitar. Users will also find reviews and information about composers Paul Copeland and Astor Piazzola.

Classical Music Reviews

http://www.ncsa.uiuc.edu/SDG/People/marca/music-reviews.html

This server contains a wonderful selection of reviews of baroque, classical, orchestral, romantic, and modern keyboard music. Giants such as Haydn, Bach, and Mozart are represented here.

Cocteau Twins WWW Page

http://garnet.berkeley.edu:8080/

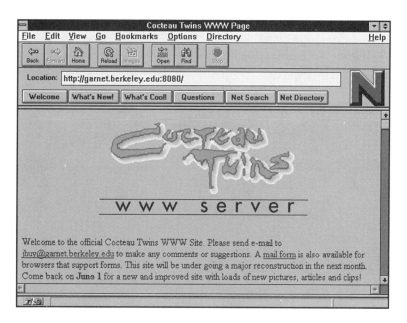

In addition to historical information about the Cocteau Twins, its members, and lyrics, this site contains video and audio clips, a discography, and photos. Users can leave feedback and will find other people's opinions about the band here.

Dead Can Dance

http://www.nets.com/dcd

Information about this unusual duo's new movie, *Toward the Within*, can be found here. Biographical information and a discography, complete with audio clips of most songs, round out the site.

Deep Purple

http://www.tecc.co.uk/public/purple/Purple.html

Deep Purple fans will find guitar tablature, lyrics, and frequently asked questions, as well as graphic images of the band.

Def Leppard

http://www.cco.caltech.edu/~witelski/deflep.html

This page contains album covers and lyrics from the band's discography. A biography of the band is available also.

Depeche Mode

http://www.cis.ufl.edu/~sag/dm

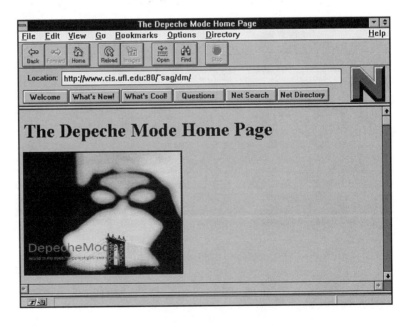

Frequently asked questions, a discography, and lyrics make this a great site for techno/pop fanatics to visit. Also available are mailing list information and links to other sites of interest to Depeche Mode fans.

Deth Specula Homepage

http://www.echo.com/specula/index.html

At this server you can find contact information, upcoming gigs dates, a video-clip performance, products for sale, as well as other information. This site also contains links to songs and lyrics from the *Internet Underground Music Archive* (IUMA).

Drive Like Jehu Home Page

http://nyx10.cs.du.edu:8001/~gsherwin/jehu.html

Here you find personal information, lyrics, reviews, and a discography from the band, as well as tour information. And you can add your name to their mailing list.

Elvis Costello

http://east.isx.com/~schnitzi/elvis.html

Frequently asked questions about the performer, lyrics, articles, and guitar tablature can be found here, as can customer service information, a discography, and interviews.

Enya

http://www.bath.ac.uk/~ccsdra/enya/home.html

This page (although unofficial) contains a great deal of information, including guitar arrangements, a discography, and translations of many songs. Many papers and articles about Enya also are available here.

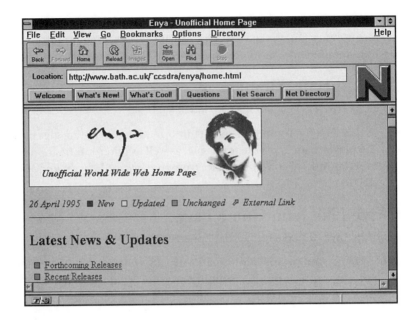

Erasure Home Page

http://www.cec.wustl.edu/~ccons/erasure

A history of the band, related images, and mailing list information can be found at this site. Well-organized links to album material and lyrics for most of the band's work are the main attractions here.

Fan-supported Black Crowes Home Page

http://rock.net:80/fan-supported/black-crowes

Run by fans, not by a "large company which keeps a cadre of lawyers handy," this site provides the typical song lists, tour date information, and lyrics. Reviews and discographies of CDs are available also.

For Squirrels WWW Site

http://www.anest.ufl.edu/~chris/ForSquirrels.html

This site includes plenty of band photos, historical information, tour dates, upcoming concert information, and lyrics, as well as audio clips and press releases.

Front 242

http://www.ifi.uio.no/~terjesa/front242/main.html

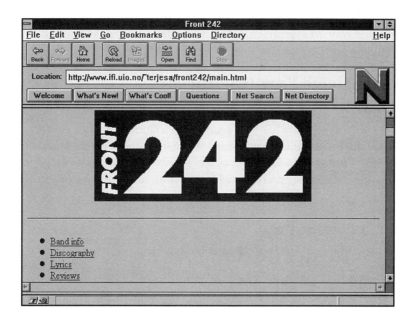

The Front 242 server includes band information, lyrics, reviews, interviews, discography, photos, and audio clips. Also, an online marketplace for selling and buying band-related material is here.

Genesis

http://www.brad.ac.uk/~agcatchp/gen_home.html

This site contains photo, album cover, and lyric information for the progressive rock band Genesis. Other features include fan club information, frequently asked questions, and the latest news about the band. Information about individual members, including Phil Collins, also can be found here.

The Grateful Dead

http://www.cs.cmu.edu:8001/afs/cs.cmu.edu/user/mleone/web/dead.html

In addition to graphics, frequently asked questions, and song lyrics, users will find set lists from several of the Dead's tours, Macintosh Grateful Dead icons, and a "dancing bear" screen saver.

Green Day Homepage

http://www.cs.caltech.edu/~adam/greenday.html

The Green Day Homepage includes fan club information, articles, pictures, album covers, and concert information. Also available are a practical how-to guide for would-be punk rockers, as well as lists of cool bands.

Guns 'n Roses Home Page (Unofficial)

http://www.teleport.com/~boerio/gnr.html

Fans of the band Guns 'n Roses will find pointers to a Guns 'n Roses FTP site, an Internet mailing list about the band, and information about group members. Some GIFs of the group and album covers are available, as are a complete list of songs, some guitar tabs, interviews with the band, tour information, and a discography.

Hammered Dulcimer Page

http://tfnet.ils.unc.edu/~gotwals/hd/dulcimer.html

This page contains an introduction to this unusual musical instrument, including a brief history, and sound and picture files. Links to information on Celtic music in general and to related mailing lists also can be found here.

Indigo Girls

http://www.mcs.net/~gumby/HTML/IG/ig-page.html

Mailing list information and the current tour schedule for this duo are online here. A three-part, unedited discography is another feature.

Industrial Music and Related Information

http://www.eecs.nwu.edu:80/~smishra/Industrial

Lovers of grinding, electronic, angst-ridden noise will delight in this page, which offers plenty of graphics and discographies from bands such as Front 242 and NIN. Links to almost all industrial information on the Web can be found here as well.

Information Society

http://phoenix.creighton.edu/~duke

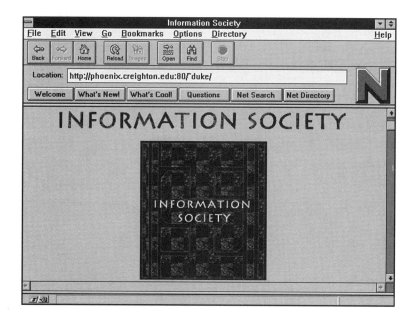

This song directory includes record company information, audio clips, and photos. Also included here are a screen saver and links to discographies.

Inter-music

http://www.ozonline.com.au:80/TotalNode/AIMC

Australian underground bands are featured on this site. Video, audio, and text from several Australian bands can be found here, as can links to other Australian music pages.

IRCAM (Institut de Recherche et Coordination Acoustique/Musique)

http://www.ircam.fr

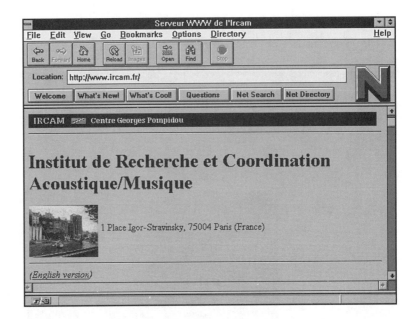

This site offers a variety of computer music resources. There's a list and brief description of IRCAM software (digital signal processing, voice and sound synthesis, music composition, wind instrument making, and other programs), as well as calendars of the IRCAM-EIC concerts and tours, and links to various other music servers.

Iron Maiden Page

http://www.cs.tufts.edu/~stratton/maiden/maiden.html

In addition to general information about the band, users will find opinions about the band and their albums. Also available at this server are covers from every album and a few audio clips.

James Taylor Home Page

http://romulus.housing.fsu.edu/~jrisberg/JT.html

This site contains lyrics and tablature from Taylor's recordings, frequently asked questions about the artist, and information about mailing lists. Online pictures and audio clips also are available from this site.

Jammin Reggae Archives

http://jammin.nosc.mil/jammin.html

This site offers a reggae dictionary, catalog lists, mail order information, and tour schedules. Photos and sound clips also are available here.

Janet's Home Page

http://www.mit.edu:8001/people/agoyo1/janet.html

This page contains information about Janet Jackson, and her music album covers, lyrics, and sound bites (even complete songs) for her entire discography are featured here.

Jazz Butcher Conspiracy Home Page

http://purgatory.ecn.purdue.edu:20002/JBC/jbc.html

From this site, Jazz Butcher Conspiracy fans will find an opportunity to fill out an online survey and peruse a detailed history of the band. Mailing list information, audio clips, reviews, upcoming tours, and lyrics also are available at this server.

Jethro Tull

http://remus.rutgers.edu:80/JethroTull

The Jethro Tull home page contains a discography, lyrics, and frequently asked questions about the band. Back issues of the newsletter and other mailing list info are available also.

Jimi Hendrix Server

http://www.parks.tas.gov.au/jimi/jimi.html

From this server, fans of Jimi Hendrix will find photos, a discography, and lyrics, as well as a summary of available video information, guitar tablature, and audio clips.

Jimi Hendrix's Electric Ladyland

http://www.univ-pau.fr/~minfo002/Www/Jimi/jimi.html

This server contains lots of poetic work about Hendrix, as well as photos and audio clips. Users will also find biographical material, album data, and lyrics.

Joe's Aerosmith Tribute Home Page

http://coos.dartmouth.edu/~joeh

This site includes images and sound files relating to the rock band Aerosmith. Users will find lyrics, a discography, band information, and so on. Hot news about Aerosmith, and current information, including tour dates, also are available here.

John Hiatt Mailing List Archives

http://www.unicom.com/john-hiatt

This server contains information about the artist's mailing list, along with updated selections from the list and reference material about the performer. Fans can also find interviews, a complete discography, pictures, reviews, and news from this server.

John Mellencamp

http://www.cs.cmu.edu:8001/afs/andrew/usr/da2x/mosaic

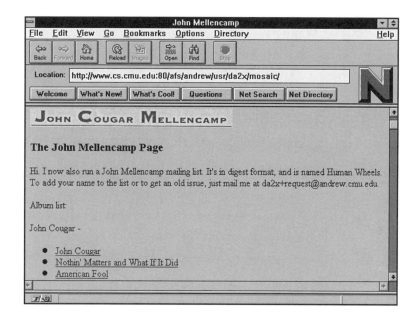

Lyrics for many of Mellencamp's albums can be found here, along with guitar tablature and pointers to other Mellencamp-related sites.

Kansas

http://www.traveller.com/~rew/kansas.html

This collection of information from the Kansas mailing list includes discographies, lyrics, and photos. Transcriptions of several interviews with the band are available also.

Kate Bush

http://actor.cs.vt.edu/~wentz/index.html

Many audio clips, including several full songs and an interview, are available. Frequently asked questions about the artist are featured also. Other performers' songs, including tracks by Elvis Costello and Enigma, are provided in the form of sound bites and songs.

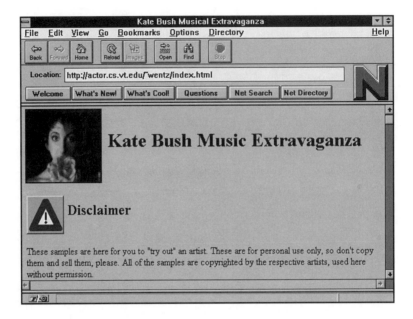

KISS

http://www.galcit.caltech.edu/~aure/strwys.html

This unofficial KISS site has album cover photos, lyrics, guitar tablature, and information about the band and band members. Related news updates and information about the KISS Army mailing list also are here. An archive of audio clips and a discography of albums round out this site.

Kitaro

http://www.mindspring.com/~shadow/kitaro/kitaro.html

Information about this Japanese new age performer, including a biography and complete discography, is available here, as is fan club information.

Kraftwerk

http://wwwtdb.cs.umu.se/~dvlawm/kraftwerk.html

The Kraftwerk server contains a discography, lyrics, photos, audio and video clips, and interviews. Users will also find mailing list information and an online forum for trading band material.

Kronos Quartet

http://m-net.arbornet.org/~stephens/kronos/kronos.html

Kronos Quartet fans will find not only an introduction to the band and its members, but also a discography, information about works performed but not recorded, opinions on albums/tracks, and articles. This is an excellent resource for one of the most challenging and interesting performing groups in any genre today.

Led Zeppelin

http://uvacs.cs.virginia.edu/~jsw2y/zeppelin/zeppelin.html

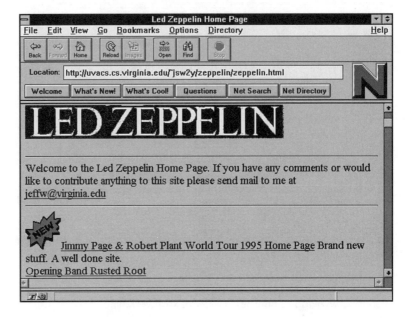

Lyrics, digitized songs, pictures, a discography, and mailing list information can all be found here. Guitar tablature and background info on the band are other features of this site.

Mariah Carey

http://biodec.wustl.edu:70/0h/audio/mariah

Fan club information, album covers, and lyrics from Mariah Carey are featured here. Archives of the Mariah Carey mailing list and many photos are available also.

Mike Markowski's Beatles Home Page

http://www.eecis.udel.edu/~markowsk/beatles

This site contains a surprisingly in-depth discography of the band. Also available at this server are photos, biographies of the famous four, and information about how to order rare Beatles memorabilia.

Misfits Central

http://watt.seas.Virginia.EDU:80/~msk4m

This server is a fan-run page dedicated to Glenn Danzig's Misfits. Users will find fan club information, songs, lyrics, chord charts, pictures, and audio clips.

Moxy Fruvous

http://wwwcsc.cornell-iowa.edu/~jcragun/fruvous.html

In addition to information about the band, this server contains a discography, tablature, lyrics, and fan club information, as well as artwork and album release information.

MusicBase

http://www.musicbase.co.uk/music

UK bands such as Terrorvision, Pop Will Eat Itself, and the Stone Roses are the focus of this site. Audio and video clips, lyrics, and interviews are available for these and other bands.

Neil Young

http://www.uta.fi/~trkisa/hyperrust.html

This site offers fans of Neil Young tons of details about the performer. This server contains personal characteristics of the artist, lyrics, guitar tablature, and much more.

New Ways to Noise

http://www.maires.co.uk:80/nw2n

This online magazine covers the Japanese scene and such well-known underground noisemakers as Yamatsuka Eye and Free Kitten. Audio samples and text for current hip "noise" bands are available here.

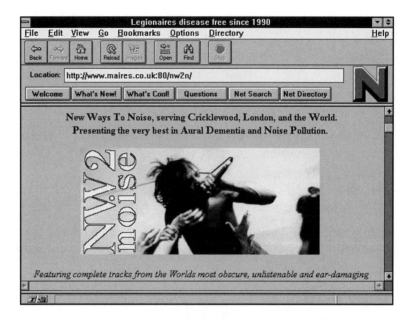

Pearl Jam

http://www.engin.umich.edu/~galvin/pearljam.html

This unofficial Pearl Jam site contains updates, pictures, audio and video clips, lyrics, and reviews. Users will also find a discography, tour information, and guitar tablature.

Pop Will Eat Itself

http://www.musicbase.co.uk/music/pwei

This server contains a discography, band information, tour news, sound and video clips, pictures, and merchandise information. Fans of Pop Will Eat Itself will also find mailing list information and a contest.

Primus

http://iris3.carb.nist.gov:8000/pub/ram/music/primus/primus.html

This trio, including bass-pounding front man Les Claypool, is the focus of this page. Guitar tablature, lyrics, plenty of photos, articles, and sound bites make this site worth checking out.

The Queensryche Page

http://www.cs.cmu.edu:8001/afs/cs/user/nkramer/ryche/ryche.html

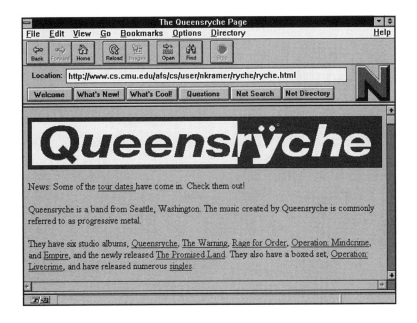

This site contains historical information about the band, discography with lyrics for nearly every song, tablature, interviews, reviews, and articles. The online magazine, *Screaming in Digital,* also is here.

Quick Fix Music Review Page

http://www-leland.stanford.edu/~witness/qfmrl/qfmrl.html

This page offers an indexed list of reviews for today's hottest bands. The reviews are short and sweet and cover mostly rock bands.

R.E.M. Home Page

http://www.halcyon.com/rem/index.html

This archive of R.E.M.-related information comes from mailing lists and news groups. Fans can find lyrics, tablature, photos, and articles about the band, as well as links to many R.E.M.-related sites.

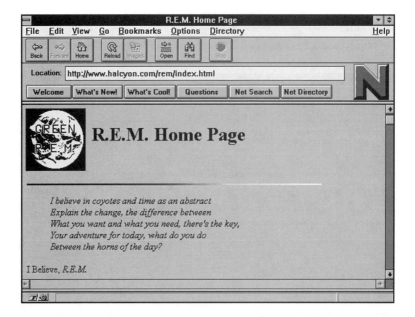

Robert Fripp

http://www.cs.man.ac.uk/aig/staff/toby/discipline.html

This page serves as a starting point for those interested in the Robert Fripp/
King Crimson mailing list. Recent back issues, a discography, and links to much
more information about this guitar wizard are available here.

Rock Net

http://www.rock.net:80

The Rock Net has a fan-supported mailing list, tour dates, and photo info for
several bands. Current bands include the Black Crowes, Zero, and Blues
Traveler.

Rush

http://www.cerf.net/~jlang/rushfan.html

The Rush server includes information about the band, tour dates, articles, and
interviews, as well as information about the National Midnight Star, a mailing
list devoted to the band.

Salzburg Information Center

http://hirsch.cosy.sbg.ac.at

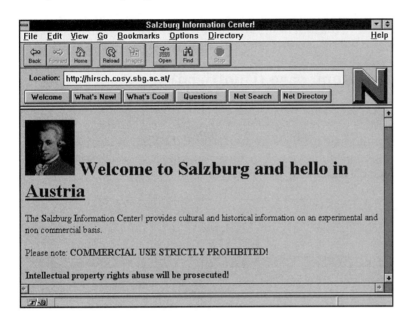

This server provides information about cultural events in Salzburg and all of Austria. The Salzburger Festspiele is covered in detail, and an archive of Austrian videos is in the works.

Schoolkid's Records

http://www.schoolkids.com/skr

This online record store offers details about the Schoolkid record label as well as selections from its best classical, jazz, and pop offerings. For hipsters, the site also caters to "foetal toejam type stuff."

Sisters of Mercy Home Page

http://www.cm.cf.ac.uk:/Sisters.Of.Mercy

This Web page contains the latest news about the Sisters of Mercy, including band member backgrounds and biographies, a discography, and plenty of lyrics. Other items of interest include a gallery of artwork by or related to the band.

SKA!

http://phoenix.aps.muohio.edu/users/dabrown/html/ska.html

In addition to frequently asked questions about the reggae spinoff known as ska, this site offers a brief list of shows, lyrics for some classic ska tunes, and a bit of humor.

Soundgarden Homepage (Unofficial)

http://web.mit.edu/afs/athena/user/s/a/saperl/www/somms/
soundgarden.html

Lyrics, album information, and a discography for the band and its associated side projects can be found here. A mailing list archive of Soundgarden information is available also, along with users' contributions.

Southern Studios

http://www.southern.com/Southern/bands.html

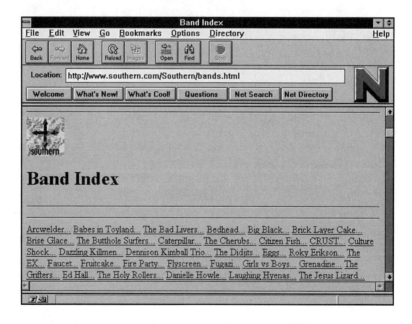

This site indexes information about bands under the Southern Studio label. You can find information about the latest releases, discographies, and tour information for bands such as Shellac, Slint, and Arcwelder.

St. Alphonzo's Pancake Homepage

http://www.fwi.uva.nl/~heederik/zappa

Frank Zappa fans will delight in this page, which offers text by and about Zappa, guitar tablature, and lyrics. In addition to a huge discography, this server contains a collection of album cover photos, video images, and notable quotes.

Stanford Symphony Orchestra

http://www-leland.stanford.edu:80/group/sso

This server contains information about the orchestra and its current activities, including an upcoming tour to China. Background about the conductor, rates for hiring string quartets, and issues of the orchestra's newsletter also are here.

Strange Ways

http://www.pitt.edu/~zucker/strange-ways.html

Strange Ways is an online magazine for KISS fanatics. This site contains current and back issues of the magazine, as well as audio clips and information about rare KISS items.

Thigpen's TECHNO Music Page

http://www.ccs.neu.edu/home/thigpen/html/music.html

This site covers the rave/techno scene, with audio clips from various artists. Music styles included on this page are breakbeat, house, and German hardcore.

Tool

http://www.rpi.edu/~pier1/music/music.html

This is a well-crafted unofficial site about the heavy metal band Tool. Lyrics, guitar tablature, and general information about the band are only the half of it. This site also contains audio clips of all the notable phrases and hooks from the band's three albums.

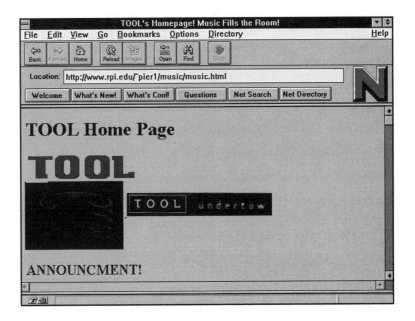

The Tori Amos Home Page

http://www.mit.edu:8001/people/nocturne/tori.html

This server contains almost everything anyone could possibly want to know about singer/pianist Tori Amos. Pictures, movies, lyrics, poetic musings about the quality of her voice, and more are available from this site.

U2

http://www2.ecst.csuchico.edu/~edge/u2.html

The unofficial U2 home page contains information about each band member, lyrics and covers for each album, and frequently asked questions about the band. Audio clips and text of many interviews and articles make this site noteworthy.

UK Indie Music

http://www.crg.cs.nott.ac.uk/~mjr/Music

Such stalwart British bands as Bastard Kestrel are featured in this compendium of Indie music. Tour, festival, and nightclub information is available, in addition to audio clips and press releases for many bands.

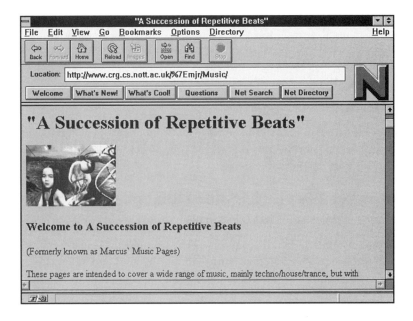

Van Halen Page

http://fallon.com/mattj/vh/vhpage.html

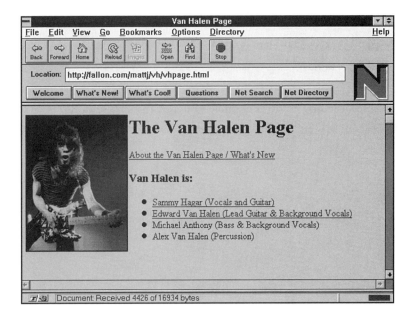

This unofficial page contains notes, lyrics, and tablature for many of Halen's albums. Also available here are photos, a discography, interviews, and mailing list information.

Vangelis Home Page

http://bau2.uibk.ac.at/perki/Vangelis.html

This site offers information about collaborative and solo efforts by Vangelis, the composer responsible for the *Bladerunner* movie soundtrack. Audio, video, and text related to his work are available here.

Verse Chorus Verse—The Nirvana Homepage

http://www2.ecst.csuchico.edu/~jedi/nirvana.html

This server contains interviews, a discography, pictures, soundbytes, and lyrics. Users will also find frequently asked questions about the band and a description of Kurt Cobain's equipment preferences.

VIBE online

http://www.timeinc.com/vibe

VIBE online includes features about urban music and the American youth culture. Reviews, clips, shopping, and chats are available from this server. Many additional youth-related links also are available.

Virginia Tech Music Department

http://server.music.vt.edu

Virginia Tech's server offers information about the department's Music and Technology and Music Education programs. Also available are an online gallery and collection of student work.

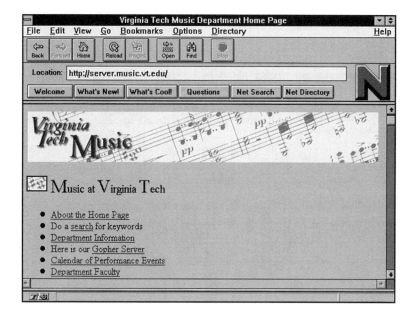

Virtual Audio

http://www.xmission.com:80/~len/va

At this site you can browse various record releases, listen to samples of music, and then order the recording online. Styles of music represented include jazz, electronic, and classical.

Vocalist Homepage

http://phoenix.oulu.fi/~mhotti/vocalist.html

This is an online forum for the discussion of singing. Back issues of the *Vocalist Digest* are available, as are tips on topics such as voice care.

Warner Bros. Records

http://www.iuma.com/Warner

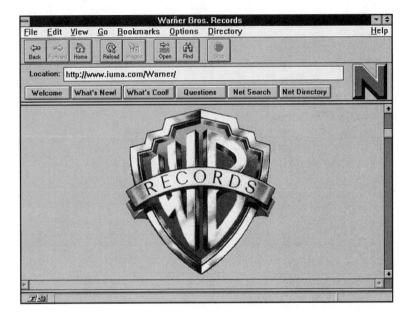

This site contains information about artists under the Warner Brothers label, including R.E.M., Madonna, Prince, Dinosaur, Jr., Eric Clapton, Tom Petty, and Neil Young. The artist's page shows album covers for all the groups and contains some nice graphics and links to information about the artists. Each artist entry includes a discography, biography, tour dates, and a description of the most recent album.

Warworld Web

http://www.uplex.net/warworld

Warworld is a Seattle-based band with plenty of attitude. This site bristles with death and testosterone. Information about the band, upcoming releases, and audio clips ("noise") are available.

WNUR-FM Jazz Information Server

http://www.acns.nwu.edu/WNUR/jazzbase

This huge jazz resource offers discographies, listings of musicians by instrument, and a primer on improvisation. Live performance updates, top 10 lists, and other media information are available also. This server enables users to search the entire Jazz Web by title and content.

Yes Home Page

http://www.cen.uiuc.edu/~ea10735/yes.html

This unofficial page is devoted to the band Yes. Currently, the page contains album cover pictures and lyrics for every Yes album.

ZZ Top

http://www.cen.uiuc.edu/~pz3900/zztop.html

This site contains plenty of lyrics, photos, and audio clips of these bearded boys from Texas. A decent discography and biography are available, as are press releases and other articles.

News Media

The best way to stay in touch with the news is to create it. If you can't do that, point your Web browser to some of these sites and stay in touch with the world.

Commercial News Services on the WWW

http://www.jou.ufl.edu/commres/webjou.htm

This is where to keep up with which newspapers are currently online. The University of Florida lists these publications, with links to select the publications of your choice.

The Electronic Guide to Santa Cruz County and Beyond

http://www.cruzio.com/index.html

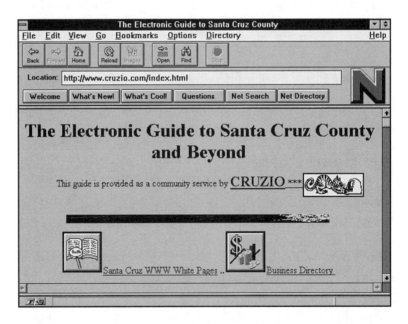

Local news and events in Santa Cruz County, California, can be found at this Web site, which includes information about entertainment, community groups, government agencies, art, and business in the county. Links to other interesting sites are available also.

Global Electronic Marketing Service

http://www.gems.com/about/index.html

Global Electronic Marketing Service (GEMS) provides online information similar to that found in the special sections of the Sunday newspaper. From this server, GEMS provides guides on business, travel, real estate, and community affairs.

InfoWeb

http://infoweb.net

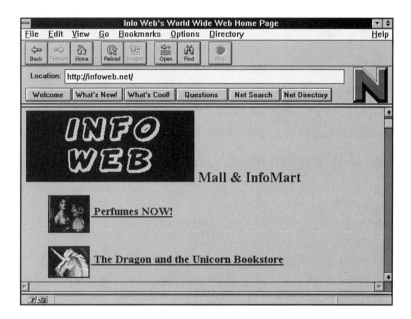

InfoWeb is a virtual mall where users not only can shop online, but also find a source of news, classified ads, help-wanted ads, and links to other Web sites.

Pathfinder

http://www.timeinc.com/pathfinder

Pathfinder is a service of Time Warner. In addition to company highlights, this page provides information about the magazines the company publishes, current updates of late-breaking news events, online chat areas, search functions, and shopping.

Social Issues and Cyberspace

http://www.ics.uci.edu/~ejw/csr/cyber.html

Public radio has come to the Web, in the shape of The Cyberspace Report from KUCI (88.9 FM) in Irvine, California. The program features reports about Internet communities and electronic mail, anything that combines aspects of society and computers. The server is offered through UC Irvine.

Recreation

Sometimes you just need to unwind and take a walk or do some hang gliding. If you feel this way, you can find more information about these recreational activities at these sites.

Hang Gliding WWW Server Home Page

http://cougar.stanford.edu:7878/HGMPSHomePage.html

Images, movies, pilot directories, links to weather services—this site is a one-stop Web page for hang gliders.

Juggling Movie Theater

http://www.hal.com/services/juggle/animations

This site is dedicated to the art, the skill, and the science that is juggling. As the name suggests, it contains video clips of jugglers and juggling. Included are great jugglers of the past, great performances, and a demonstration of different juggling techniques.

MIT Soaring Association

http://adswww.harvard.edu/MITSA/mitsa_homepg.html

This server offers background information on this student organization and details about topics such as gliding, aerobatics, and aviation. Weather information and a large archive of pictures related to flying also can be found here.

Photopia

http://www.solutionsrc.com/PHOTOPIA

The Photopia server contains stock photos users can browse and order online. You can search its database, and products are delivered to your home on a Syquest disk.

SkyBox Online

http://www2.interpath.net/interweb/skybox

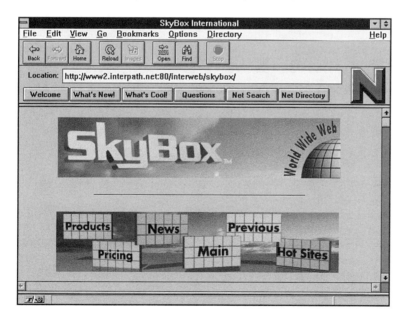

From this server users can view and order trading cards online. Some of the trading cards available include the *Star Trek* and Harley-Davidson series.

The TIME LIFE Complete Gardener Encyclopedia

http://www.timeinc.com/vg/TimeLife/CG/vg-search.html

Gardeners can use this helpful database to find the best plants, trees, and shrubs to grow in their area. The Time Life system searches a database of more than 2,000 species to match plants with the most suitable geographical areas in the United States.

TravelWeb

http://www.travelweb.com

Contains the hotel industry's first interactive color catalog, and showcases the Hyatt Hotels Corporation's 16 resorts and 87 other hotels in the U.S. and the Caribbean. TravelWeb provides detailed room, recreation, special services, and destination information for each hotel, complete with color photographs.

The Wilderness Society

http://town.hall.org/environment/wild_soc/wilderness.html

This Web resource supports a collection of fact sheets about America's national parks, Bureau of Land Management lands, forests, wildlife refuges, and other natural resources. The fact sheets cover many related subjects: below-cost timber sales, the California deserts, endangered species, the General Mining Law of 1872, grazing on public lands, and national park concessions.

Windsurfing Resources on the WWW

http://www.dsg.cs.tcd.ie:/dsg_people/afcondon/windsurf/windsufr_home.html

This site contains guides to various windsurfing locations, archived discussions of windsurfing from rec.windsurfing, as well as still and moving imagery of windsurfing.

WWW Paris

http://meteora.ucsd.edu/~norman/paris

You can take a visual tour of Paris from this site. The site has a collection of the major monuments and museums of Paris. There are maps of the Metro and the RER, calendars of events and current expositions, and promotional images and text about local department stores. There is also a visitor's section with up-to-date tourist information on hotels, restaurants, telephones, airport schedules, a basic Paris glossary, and the latest weather images. And, of course, there are links to other resources about Paris and France.

Sports

Are you interested in golf, skating, baseball, or cricket? If so, check out these Web sites. You're sure to find something that you enjoy. There's even a Tonya Harding Web page.

Figure Skating Home Page

http://www.cs.yale.edu/HTML/YALE/CS/HyPlans/lossemore-sandra/skate.html

Figure skating—grace, beauty, incredible athletic talent. This is what the Olympics are all about. This site has information about tours, competition, the '94 and '98 Winter Olympics, and, of course, a Nancy Kerrigan page. The site also includes information on speed skating.

Golf Courses of British Columbia

http://interchange.idc.uvic.ca/~golf/golfbc.html

Pros, amateurs, even duffers who enjoy walking the links will enjoy this site. This Web page provides links to more than 100 golf courses, as well as other golf-related Web servers.

Home Plate

http://www.mariners.org

This is the official Web site of the Seattle Mariners baseball team. Trivia, merchandise, history, stats, schedules—you will find it all here!

The Sheffield Collegiate Cricket Club

http://www2.shef.ac.uk/chemistry/collegiat/collegiate-home.html

Cricket fans, this one's for you. The Sheffield Collegiate Cricket Club page covers the Club's games and activities and also provides links to other cricket resources on the Internet, as well as other general sports information.

The SNowPage

http://rmd-www.mr.ic.ac.uk/snow/snowpage.html

The SNowPage server contains information about winter sports and resorts. Users will find weather reports as well as information about skiing, snowboarding, resorts, trail maps, and even a picture gallery.

Southeast Asian Games 1995

http://www.chiangmai.ac.th/sg/sg/95.html

The Southeast Asian Games, to be held 9–17 December 1995, are a counterpart to the Olympics. This site, located in Thailand, contains information about the sports included, mascots, participants, and updates on the planning for the games.

The Tonya Harding Fan Club Page

http://orange-room.cc.nd.edu/toybox/WrittenWord/Harding.html

Contains information about Tonya Harding, as well as a link to the Tonya Harding Opponent Neutralization Center.

VeloNews Experimental Tour de France Web Page

http://www.velonews.com/VeloNews

This Web site provides background information about the Tour de France, including press coverage from this year's race.

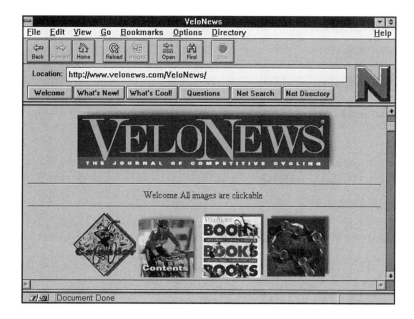

World Cup

http://www.sprintlink.net/public/http/world.html

This is the place to get information about World Cup events in the U.S., U.K., Norway, and Japan.

World Cycling Championship 1994

http://www-worldbike.iunet.it

This Web site contains information about events surrounding the 1994 World Cycling Championship.

Travel

If you are headed on a vacation or a business trip, you can plan more effectively by visiting some of these sites. Many of these Web sites offer maps, "virtual tours," and restaurant guides.

The Alaskan Center

http://www.alaskan.com

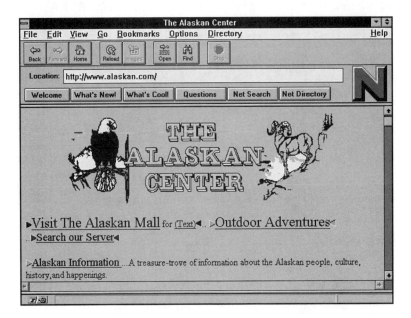

Visit this site to learn all about the largest state of the Union. Read about Alaska's people, culture, and history. Tourist information about outdoor activities such as kayaking and mountain climbing is available, as are details about towns and communities, and information about bed-and-breakfast accommodations. This site is a great resource for anyone planning to visit Alaska.

Arctic Adventours, Inc.

http://www.oslonett.no/data/adv/AA/AA.html

This Norwegian tour company has a library of more than 3,000 breathtaking pictures from the Arctic region.

Arizona Home Page

http://arizonaweb.org/index.html

Arizona's home page is a mouse-sensitive map that provides details about the state's major cities and Web sites.

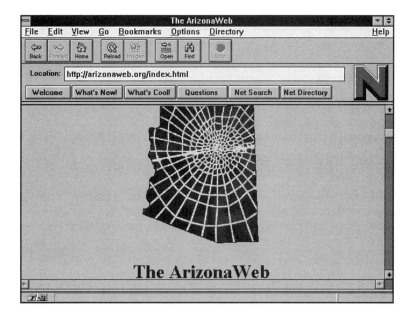

AU System Weather Report

http://www.ausys.se/weather/weather.htm

This Swedish data communications company installed a video camera pointing onto their Stockholm street. Temperature updates also are here.

Boston Area Map of WWW Resources

http://donald.phast.umass.edu/misc/boston.html

This is a good place to find information about commercial and educational Web servers in and around Boston. Here you will find links to tourist-related information.

Boston Online

http://www.std.com/NE/boston.html

This is another good starting point for information about Boston. Find out about history, entertainment, recreation and sports, government, education, transportation, and weather. If you are planning a trip to Boston or New England, this should be your first destination.

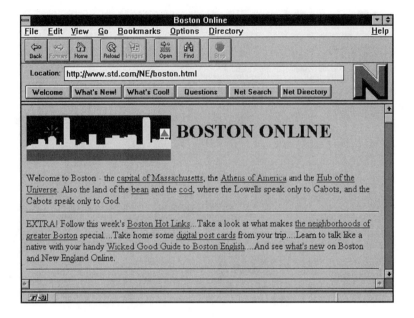

Canadian Geographical WWW Index Travel

http://www.unamitoba.ca

The University of Manitoba, located in Winnipeg, Canada, sponsors this site and provides general information about the university, including student activities, departments, a campus-wide telephone directory, and more. Other information contained here includes the *Winnipeg Free Press* headlines and Southern Manitoba weather forecasts.

The Caribbean Connection

http://mrlxp2.mrl.uiuc.edu/~stuart/caribbean.html

This page offers information about the islands for would-be tourists and people interested in Caribbean culture. Plenty of links are provided here, ranging from weather and travel information to news groups and the Central Intelligence Agency's *World Factbook*.

City.Net

http://www.city.net

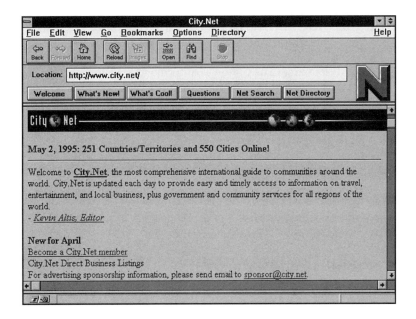

You can browse this database of travel, entertainment, local business, government, and community information for cities and communities worldwide.

The Complete Guide to Galway

http://wombatix.physics.ucg.ie/galway/galway.html

Galway is located on the western coast of Ireland. Its server is an extremely detailed guide of past and present information, including tourist sites, industry, local transportation, folklore, history, entertainment, drinking, and dining. This Web site includes maps, photographs, and illustrations.

The Connecticut Guide

http://www.atlantic.com/ct/intro.html

This is a colorful resource for learning about business and commerce, government and law, and education in the state of Connecticut. Potential visitors will find this site very useful. You can also access a list of Web sites arranged alphabetically and by category.

The Electronic Guide to Santa Cruz County and Beyond

http://www.cruzio.com/index.html

Local news and events in Santa Cruz County, California, can be found at this Web site. Users will find information about entertainment, community groups, government agencies, art, and businesses in the county. Links to other interesting sites are available also.

Embassy Suites

http://www.promus.com/embassy.html

This is the Web site for Embassy Suites hotels. From here you can check the online directory and updates on new openings. When their reservation system goes online, you can make reservations from your desk.

Florida's Computer Yellow Pages

http://infoguide.com

This guide can help you select from restaurants, hotels, and clubs in South Florida. Download pictures and satellite maps, get updated weather information, check out menus, and be sure to use plenty of sunscreen.

Guide to Rochester, NY

http://www.eznet.net/rochester

The online guide to this upstate city provides details and links to local businesses and schools, including the Rochester Institute of Technology and the University of Rochester.

Hawaii OnLine

http://www.aloha.net

This nicely designed interface introduces you to the 50th state. It includes all you need to plan a business or pleasure trip to Hawaii.

ITRE Home Page

http://itre.uncecs.edu

Information about transportation research and Geographical Information Systems can be found on this server. This site also features examples of image mapping.

Japanese Information

http://www.ntt.jp/japan/index.html

This Web server maintains extensive information about the geography, culture, law, and tourism of Japan. Archived Japanese news group information and FAQs are available also.

Los Gatos, The Town

http://www.los-gatos.scruznet.com/los_gatos/los_gatos.html

This online information kiosk for the California town of Los Gatos has information for visitors as well as residents and businesses.

Mexican Culture FAQ

http://www.cis.ohio-state.edu/hptertext/faq/usenet/mexican-faq/faq.html

This is the FAQ from the soc.culture.mexican news group. Extensive information about Mexican culture, history, society, language, and tourism can be found here.

Republic of Korea Tourist Information

http://cair-archive.kaist.ac.kr/korea/index.html

This resource, produced by the Korea National Tourism Corporation, has in-depth information about Korea, including sightseeing highlights, history, and other important facts.

San Francisco Reservations

http://www.hotelres.com

At this site you can make reservations for Bay Area hotels. This free service enables you to search the database by location, type, or keyword.

A Small Tour of Iceland

http://www.rfisk.is/english/iceland/rest_of_iceland.html

Come here for a virtual tour of this northern European island country. A good place for anyone interested in visiting.

University of Vaasa

http://www.uwasa.fi

In addition to general information about the city of Vaasa, Finland, this server provides information about the University of Vaasa, including the departments of business administration, accounting, industrial management, humanities, and the Western-Finland Center for Economic Research. Users will also find links to various multimedia sources.

vegas.com

http://www.vegas.com

This Web site contains travel and tourist information about Las Vegas and its businesses.

Virtual Tourist—California

http:/http://www.research.digital.com/SRC/virtual-tourist/California.html

This index provides comprehensive information about the state of California: government, entertainment, recreation, education, history, and a list of other California-related servers. A must for planning a trip to the Golden State.

The Washington DC City Pages

http://dcpages.ari.net

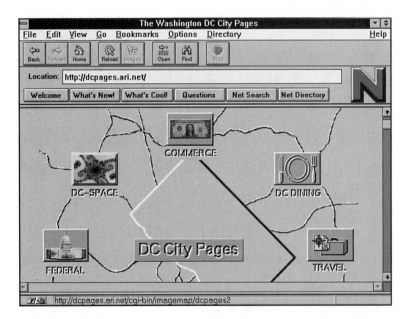

This well-done virtual guide to the capital scene includes local news, entertainment, commerce, government, and weather. A must for anyone planning to visit Washington. Make sure to take a virtual tour of the Metro!

World Wide Web Servers—Hawaii

http://info.cern.ch/hypertext/DataSources/WWW/haw.html

This site is a good first stop in your search for online information about this Pacific paradise. Links to tourist-, educational-, and technology-related sites in Hawaii are available.

WWW Paris

http://meteora.ucsd.edu/~norman/paris

You can take a visual tour of Paris from here. This site has a collection of the major monuments and museums of Paris. There are maps of the Metro and the RER, calendars of events and current expositions, and promotional images and text about local department stores. There is also a visitor's section with up-to-date tourist information on hotels, restaurants, telephones, airport schedules, a basic Paris glossary, and the latest weather images. And, of course, there are links to other resources about Paris and France.

Your Traveling Companion—Japan

http://www.ntt.jp:80/japan/TCJ/TC.html

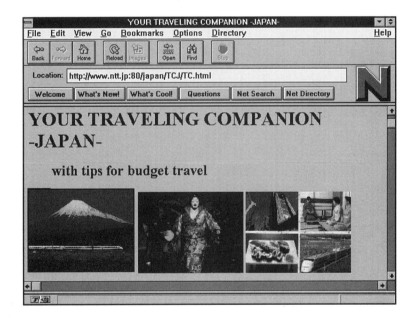

Provided by the Japan National Tourist Organization, this site provides all the information you need to plan a pleasure or business trip to this island nation. There are links to tourist information for major Japanese cities.

Looking at the Best Professional and Government Sites

T his chapter presents more than 300 sites devoted to the government or professional aspects of life. In this chapter you'll find topics on cities, countries, education, professional organizations, health care, and colleges.

Cities

By means of the World Wide Web, you can now find out information about various cities that was formerly only available through tourist agencies or a city's local chamber of commerce. Discover facts about government, dining, places of interest, upcoming events, and more!

Charleston Information

http://www.palmetto.com/places.sc/cities/chs/index.html

Individuals planning a visit to Charleston, South Carolina should consider visiting this site, the home page for the Charleston Information Center. This site includes tips and information about the art, lodging, restaurants, and cultural activities available in Charleston.

Environmental Recycling Hotline

http://www.primenet.com/erh.html

This database contains useful information about recycling programs around the country. Users can locate and learn more about the programs offered in their area from this server. General information about recycling is also provided.

The Jerusalem Mosaic

http://www1.huji.ac.il/jeru/jerusalem.html

Shalom, and welcome to the Holy City. The Jerusalem Mosaic contains information about Jerusalem and its history. The site contains pictures and paintings of the city, as well as audio clips and travel information.

List of Servers-District of Columbia

http://www.fie.com/www/district.htm

This Web site has good listing of capital-related information, covering everything from government to entertainment.

NYAL (New York Art Line)

http://gopher.panix.com/nyart/Kpage/kg

The primary focus of this site is visual art, particularly in the New York City area. There's online access to selected galleries, image archives, and New York City art groups. In addition to visual art, the site includes information about dance, music, and techno art, and a special section on Internet art. When you finish browsing this page, you can link to various electronic journals, museums, and schools.

Travel Information

http://galaxy.einet.net/GJ/travel.html

This is a one-stop shop to some of the best travel information found on the Web. Airline information, FAQs about tourism, specific information about countries and cities around the world, travel guides, and newsletters can be found here.

WWW Paris

http://meteora.ucsd.edu/-norman/paris

You can take a visual tour of Paris from this site. In addition to a collection of the major monuments and museums of Paris, the site includes maps of the Metro and the RER, calendars of events and current expositions, and promotional images and text about local department stores. A visitor's section has up-to-date tourist information about hotels, restaurants, telephones, airport schedules, a basic Parisian glossary, and the latest weather images. Also included are links to other resources about Paris and France.

Colleges and Universities

There are many college and university Web sites that provide general and departmental information, as well as reports about various scientific projects. A comprehensive list of college and university URLs can be found in *New Riders' Official World Wide Web Yellow Pages*.

Academia Sinica WWW Service

http://www.sinica.edu.tw

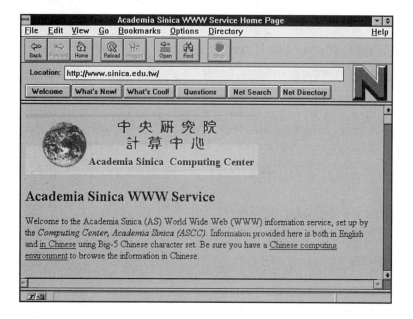

The Academia Sinica is the most prestigious institute of higher learning in Taiwan. This Web site provides general information about the Academy, as well as specific information on research conducted there.

Arizona State University-Infrared Subnode

http://esther.la.asu.edu/asu_tes/

The Infrared Imaging subnode is maintained by the Geoscience Node of NASA's Planetary Data System. The site is located at the Thermal Emission Spectroscopy Lab at Arizona State University.

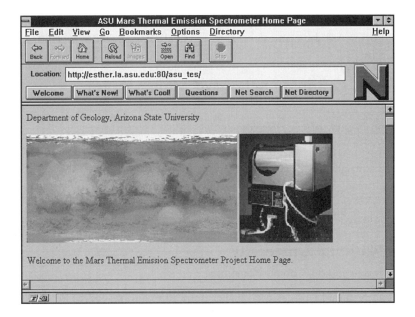

Astronomical Institute, University of Münster

http://aquila.uni-muenster.de/

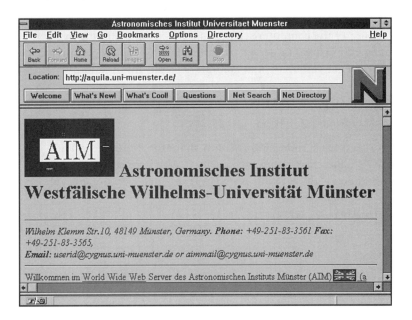

This server provides an overview of current projects at the university, including work on measuring red shifts and flare stars. Publications and staff information are available also.

The Australian Graduate School of Management (AGSM)

http://www.agsm.unsw.edu.au/Welcome.html

This server provides overview information about the School of Management, including MBA programs, research centers, working papers, and faculty information. Included at this site are the AGSM Gopher server, an FTP service area where AGSM working papers and information are stored, a library catalog, Australian company information, and a list of Australian Web servers.

Australian National University

http://coombs.anu.edu.au/CoombsHome.html

The Australian National University collects information and resources in the areas of social sciences, Asian studies, and humanities. The site, called Coombsweb, also offers links to other education-related Web home pages.

Brigham Young University Computer Science

http://www.cs.byu.edu/homepage.html

Take a virtual tour of the computer science building from the home page of Brigham Young University. The server also offers faculty listings, class schedules, computer science resources, and laboratory facility information.

Brown High-Energy Physics

http://www.het.brown.edu/

This server contains background information about the department, and details on the staff and current research projects. Also here is information about a collaboration with Fermilab as well as Hunger Net, an organization devoted to ending malnutrition.

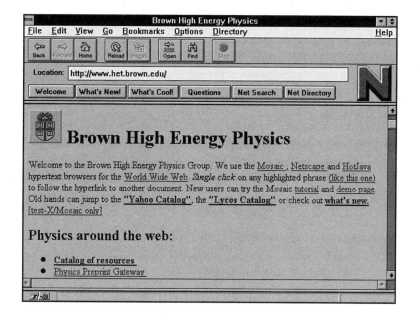

Brussels University

http://www.iihe.ac.be/

If you're considering Brussels University, in Belgium, you'll want to take a look at this home page. Academics and library information are available, in addition to a link to the Belgian Multimedia Integrated Conferencing for European Researchers.

Caltech Concurrent Supercomputing Facilities

http://www.ccsf.caltech.edu/ccsf.html

This research facility is located on the campus of the California Institute of Technology (Caltech). Research conducted here involves a variety of parallel supercomputers for the Concurrent Supercomputing Consortium.

Carnegie Mellon University: The English Server

http://english-server.hss.cmu.edu/

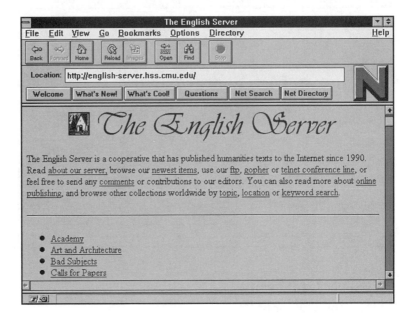

At Carnegie Mellon University, an organization of students publishes humanities texts electronically. This Web server presents a list of these online publications.

Carnegie Mellon University—Computer Vision

http://www.cs.cmu.edu:8001/afs/cs/project/cil/ftp/html/vision.html

This department of Carnegie Mellon University offers information about its computer vision research program. The site also references other research sites and collections of images.

Center for Advanced Studies

http://www.crs4.it/HTML/homecrs4.html

The Center for Advanced Studies, Research and Development, in Sardinia, Italy operates this home page. Local resources, information about Italy, selections of Italian literature, and links to other resources on the Web are offered here.

Center for Complex Systems Research

http://www.ccsr.uiuc.edu/

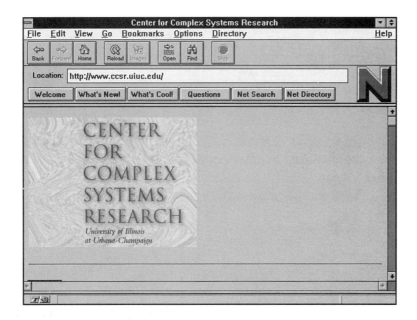

This server offers a variety of papers and technical reports in various areas of biology, physics, and mathematics. Of particular interest is a paper on a chaotic system for producing music.

Chinook College Funding Service

http://www.indirect.com/user/chinook2/

For anyone needing additional funding for their college education, this server is an excellent source of information about various government programs and scholarships.

Clemson University Computational Science and Engineering Resources

http://diogenes.cs.clemson.edu/CSE/homepage.html

In the fields of computational science and engineering, this Clemson University Web server has many resources. It offers links to servers such as Netlib, relevant newsgroups, academic contacts, and mailing lists.

Columbia University

http://www.ctr.columbia.edu/

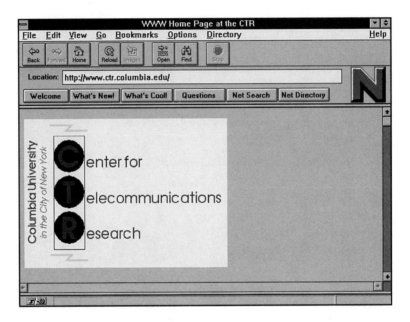

This Web server is maintained by Columbia University's Center for Telecommunications Research. The site has project information, as well as references to other resources.

Cornell

http://helpdesk-www.cit.cornell.edu/CITSHDHome.html

From this Web server, you can learn all about Cornell University. The help desk has information about computers and computer applications, a link to the Free On-Line Dictionary of Computing, and a link with information about desktop publishing.

Cornell University's Engineering Library

http://www.englib.cornell.edu

The Engineering Library at Cornell University offers information about electronic library projects, links to Internet Connections for Engineering, a guide to science and engineering journals, and Internet resources for technology, general science, and geology topics.

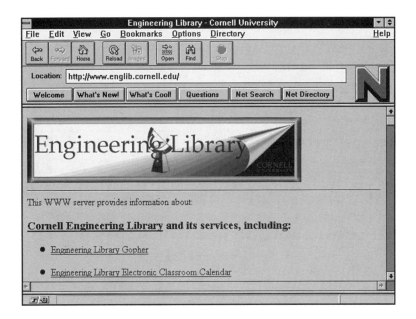

Departamento de Ciencias de la Computacion

http://www.dcc.uchile.cl/

The University of Chile is represented here. Find out what university life would be like in Chile! Browse through general information about the campus and academic programs.

Department of Process Control, Technical University of Budapest

http://www.fsz.bme.hu/

This server offers information about the department, a calendar of events, and the local time in Hungary. Opera fans will enjoy the database of opera show times.

Duke University

http://www.duke.edu/

This site has pointers to many of Duke's academic departments, Alumni Affairs, and student government associations. Also included here are job openings, course lists, a campus directory, and the library catalog. Worthy of note is a list of student Web pages.

Eindhoven University, Mathematics and Computing Science

http://www.win.tue.nl/

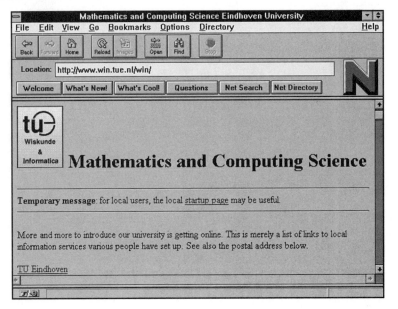

In addition to information about the university's math and computer science departments, this server offers details about computer facilities and experimental software. Of interest to music lovers is a selection of exercises on the harpsichord.

Electric Propulsion

http://cougarxp.princeton.edu:2112/afosr.html

This site contains information about research into alternate forms of propulsion, including plasma rockets. This site also provides information about the Princeton laboratory, its staff, and current research.

Harvard University Graduate School of Education

http://golgi.harvard.edu/hugse

This Harvard server offers information about the school, the academics, the staff, student life, and links to other education-related sites.

The Hebrew University of Jerusalem Campus Information System

http://www1.huji.ac.il/www_dir/hdbl.html

This site is a hypertext listing in Hebrew and English of information about the Hebrew University of Jerusalem.

Ikeda Lab Home Page

http://www.hike.te.chiba-u.ac.jp/

In addition to information about the department, which specializes in electrical engineering, this site offers plenty of technical documents and specifications. Music fans will enjoy the pictures and audio clips of renaissance instruments and early electronic music.

Indiana University

http://www.indiana.edu

Indiana University is one of the largest universities in the United States. Comprising a residential campus in Bloomington and seven other campuses across Indiana, it currently serves 94,000 students. A wide range of information is offered here, including degree programs, campus directories, departmental information, newsletters, and research services.

Indiana University Computer Science Department

http://cs.indiana.edu/home-page.html

Take a look at the course schedule for computer science majors at Indiana University. You can browse through research projects that utilize computer science applications. The robotics lab and high-performance computing are two areas of current research.

James Cook University

http://coral.cs.jcu.edu.au/

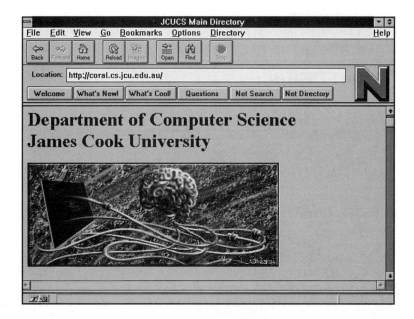

Students worldwide can link to the Department of Computer Science at James Cook University, Australia. A technical seminar series and the Australian Computer Science Academics Database are both good resources for education in the field of computer science. A list of electronic libraries and a departmental handbook are offered.

Laboratory for Pen-based Computing

http://schiller.wustl.edu/

This site, a service of Washington University, provides information about the laboratory's current projects, including visual programming languages and graphical editors using Pen technology. An online database is also available.

Latrobe University

http://www.latrobe.edu.au/

This Australian university's server offers information about faculty, research, and courses for many departments. University publications and a campus directory are also featured here.

Mathematics and Computer Science, Georgia State

http://www.cs.gsu.edu/

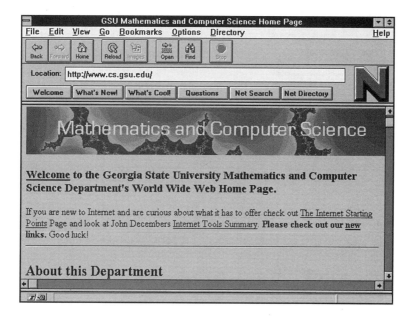

The Mathematics and Computer Science Department at Georgia State offers information about undergraduate courses, university resources, math and computer science resources, Internet resources, information about Atlanta, and research facilities located on campus.

Ministry of Education

http://www.moe.ac.sg/

Learn about the education system in Singapore from the resources offered at this Web site. The Ministry of Education offers links to worldwide educational resources, grouped by subject.

MIT Demonstrations

http://www.lcs.mit.edu/

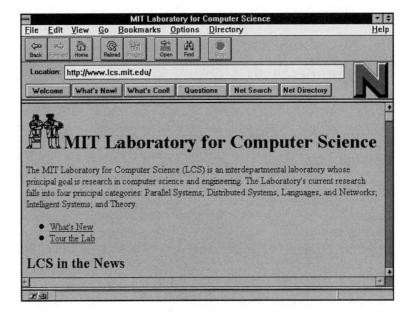

This server offers an index and demonstrations from research groups at the Massachusetts Institute of Technology Laboratory for Computer Science.

Mount Allison University

http://ollc.mta.ca/tenb.html

General information about Mount Allison University, the community college, and educational programs is presented for users in the area of the province of New Brunswick. The TeleEducation New Brunswick Network is utilized from Sackville, New Brunswick, Canada.

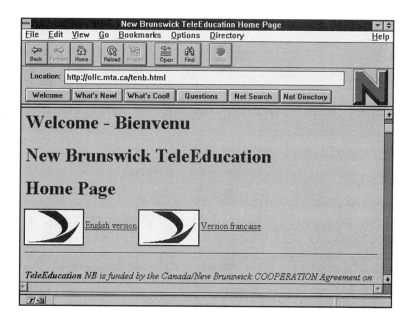

The National University of Singapore (NUS) Home Page

http://nuscc.nus.sg

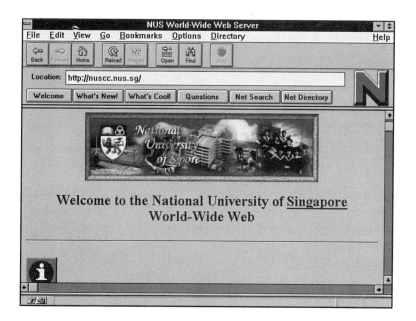

This site contains information about the NUS, including staff, an interactive map, campus publications, the history of NUS, and more. In addition, it contains information about the nation of Singapore, and links to other Web resources.

North Carolina State University College of Engineering

http://www.eos.ncsu.edu/coe/coe.html

Undergraduate and graduate programs, research, staffing, student activities, and extension services are a few of the categories offered at this home page. Links are available to other departments on campus.

North Carolina State's Webbed Library Without Walls

http://dewey.lib.ncsu.edu

The faculty, staff, and student body of North Carolina State University are served well through this electronic library. Research and educational information is organized and categorized into accessible databases, catalogs, and electronic text files.

Northwestern University

http://www.covis.nwu.edu/

This server offers research information about the advancement of education in schools today through the use of advanced networking technologies, collaborative software, and visualization tools. The effort is sponsored by the National Science Foundation and various industry leaders.

Nuclear Physics, Moscow State

http://www.npi.msu.su/

Information about the Skobeltsyn Institute of Nuclear Physics, including current work in high-energy physics and microelectronics, is available here. All information about the server is searchable, using forms.

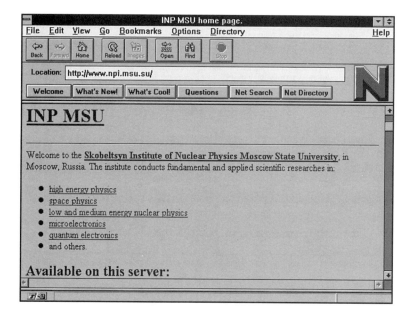

Office of Technology Transfer

http://ott22.engin.umich.edu/

This University of Michigan-based server contains several seminars and information about economic development as it relates to technology. The Center for Display Technology and Manufacturing, which is working on flat-panel display systems, is also located here.

Oklahoma State

http://www.okstate.edu/

An overview of the campus, similar to a college brochure, is available here, in addition to online library catalogs, announcements, and computer science reference information. Descriptions of and publications by each of the departments and colleges can also be found here.

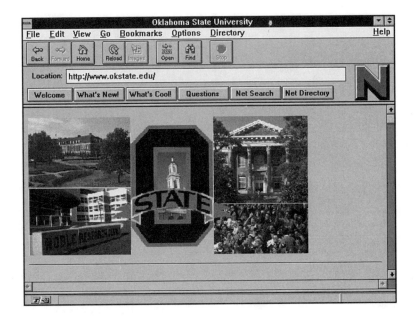

Oklahoma State University

http://a.cs.okstate.edu/welcome.html

If you want to know all about the Computer Science Department at Oklahoma State University, this Web site is your source. Inspect the departmental resources, campus information, academic schedules, and links to other educational resources on the Internet.

Old Dominion University Department of Computer Science

http://www.cs.odu.edu/index.html

This site gives students an overview of the Department of Computer Science. General education requirements, lab information, and schedules of classes are provided.

The Remarque.Berkeley.EDU Home Page

http://remarque.berkeley.edu:8001/

This server contains various student and faculty home pages. Items of interest include a minor league baseball home page, a Cinema Space, and a journal of film and media.

Stanford University

http://kanpai.stanford.edu/epgy/pamph/pamph.html

Stanford University offers a variety of special educational programs. The Stanford Continuing Studies Program and the Education Program for Gifted Youth are two such programs. Computer-based courses in math and mathematical sciences classes for bright young students are the focus.

Switzerland Home Page

http://www-swiss.ai.mit.edu/

Information about MIT's project on mathematics and computation, including a bibliography and individual home pages, can be found here. Also available are photos of Switzerland and information about its people.

TechInfo Main Menu (MIT—Massachusetts Institute of Technology)

http://web.mit.edu:1962/tiserve.mit.edu/9000/0

The TechInfo main menu is the functional home page for the administration at the Massachusetts Institute of Technology. A wealth of information is accessible about the administration, school policies, offices and services, news, course schedules, student organizations, publications, and much more.

The University of Aarhus

http://www.daimi.aau.dk/

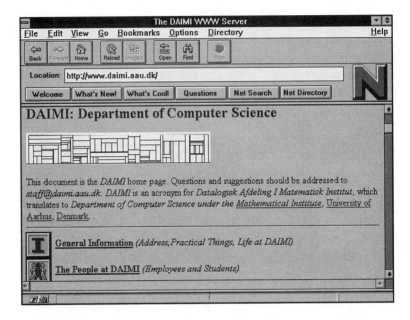

This server provides information about research activities, staff and faculty, and general information about the University of Aarhus, Denmark.

University of British Columbia, Computer Science

http://www.cs.ubc.ca/home

In addition to the standard topics of academic coursework, degree plans, and campus information, this home page for the University of British Columbia, Computer Science, contains an electronics dictionary and thesaurus.

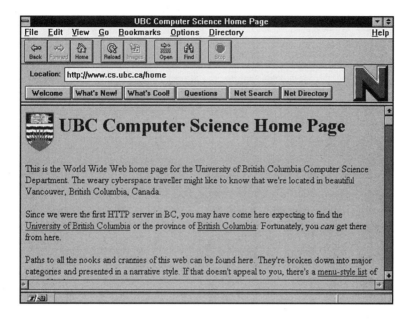

University of California

http://ucrengr.ucr.edu/

Based in Riverside, California, this site offers course information, faculty listings, academic information, and research center locations. Research plays a large role in the UC educational system. The VIS Lab and the Systems Clinic are two centers that carry out research in the areas of visualization and image processing, and industry/university partnerships.

University of Chicago

http://spirit.lib.uconn.edu/archnet/near_east.html

The Oriental Institute of the University of Chicago provides archaeological data and materials from Egypt, the Far East, and other regions. The server contains newsletters and announcements from the American Schools of Oriental Research.

University of Florida

http://www.cis.ufl.edu/

In addition to providing links to University of Florida educational departments, this site offers campus activities, student organizations, and gateways to an assortment of Web sites.

University of Geneva

http://www.unige.ch/

In addition to an online map of the campus and the normal information about the university (much of it in French), this server offers plenty of information about crystallography. Abstracts and publications are available, in addition to information about local library services.

University of Georgia Libraries

http://scarlett.libs.uga.edu/1h/www/darchive/hargrett/wpa.html

In addition to large catalogs and indexes, this server offers a collection of photographs that chronicle the various Work Progress Administration (WPA) projects built in Georgia, including streets, airports, schools and recreation facilities, flood control, and fine arts projects.

University of Iowa

http://www.cs.uiowa.edu/

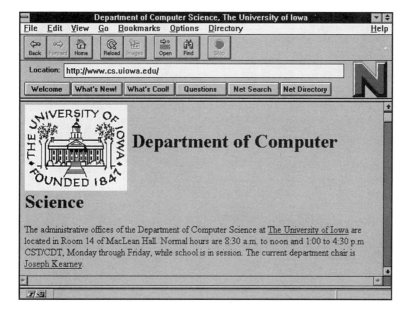

This server offers a variety of information about the University of Iowa and its Department of Computer Science. Course offerings, faculty listings, and student organizations are presented, in addition to an informative, fun link called the "Iowa Virtual Tourist."

University of Kaiserslautern

http://www.uni-kl.de/

Most of the text here is presented in German. This University of Kaiserslautern server offers links to each department, general data, and other servers.

University of Kansas

http://kuhttp.cc.ukans.edu/

This site provides details about the Lynx Web browser, in addition to the standard campus, faculty, and student information. Reference publications, a telephone book, student projects, and class schedules are available also.

University of Ljubljana

http://www.fagg.uni-lj.si/index.html

This is the server for the University's Faculty of Architecture, Civil Engineering, and Geodesy. Information about the faculty and papers on current research can be found here.

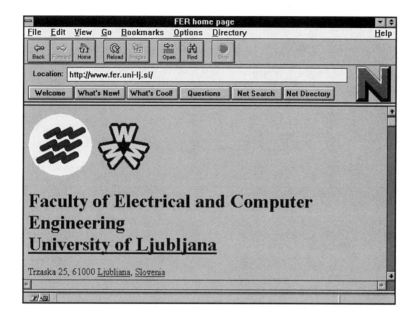

University of Maryland Advanced Computer Studies

http://www.umiacs.umd.edu/

The goal of the Institute for Advanced Computer Studies is to strengthen support for computing research within the University system. The site offers information about departments, staff, faculty, and research.

University of Maryland Student Radio

http://w3eax.umd.edu/

Users will find information and updates from this student-operated radio station. The Spartan packet radio experiment, involving the global positioning system, a NASA mission, and packet radio, is also described here.

University of Massachusetts

http://webserver.cogsci.umassd.edu/welcome.html

Users are provided access to Dartmouth research activities and reports, as well as its academic programs. The Computer and Information Science Department also offers links to other Web servers.

University of Michigan College of Engineering

http://www.engin.umich.edu/college

This Web server contains the Computer-Aided Engineering Network. Out of the University of Michigan's College of Engineering, the site offers network services.

University of Nijmegen

http://www.sci.kun.nl/

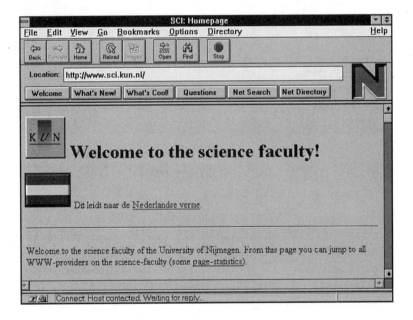

The science faculty of this Dutch university maintains this server. Information about the university's high-energy physics, mathematics, and computer science programs can be found here. The student chemistry association also provides extensive information about chemical research.

University of North Carolina at Chapel Hill

http://sunsite.unc.edu/unchome.html

Information about all the SunSITE sites, Sun Archives, and newsgroups is available here. The Office of Technology also provides Cisco Inc. archive

information, the publication called "The Packet," and the Cisco Educational Archive and Resources Catalog link.

University of Northern Iowa Library

http://iscssun.uni.edu:80/library

This server of the University of Northern Iowa Library highlights the library's large, wide-ranging collection, which contains significant collections in many fields.

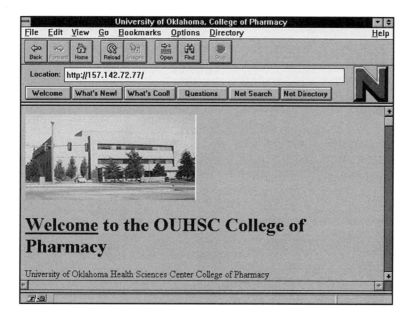

University of Oklahoma College of Pharmacy

http://157.142.72.77/

In addition to information about the College, this server provides city zoo information, as well as a searchable index of pharmacokinetic resources.

University of Ottawa Computer Science

http://www.csi.uottawa.ca/

Information about the algorithms laboratory and information science group at the University can be found here. A discussion of hypertext is especially interesting.

University of Pennsylvania

http://www.upenn.edu/

Welcome to the home page for the University of Pennsylvania. From here, you can review the academic schedules of engineering, physics, math, economics, medicine, and other departments. Link to other Penn State Web servers and check out campus entertainment and events.

University of Pisa Department of Radiology

http://www.rad.unipi.it:7080/IRMosaicHome.html

Presentations on several of the department's current projects on imaging technology are available online. In addition to the graphics, images, and text, announcements and general information about the department can also be found here.

University of Rochester

http://www.cs.rochester.edu/

This server of the Department of Computer Science, at the University of Rochester, presents categories of interest about university information, departmental brochures, technical reports, and a department subway map.

University of Salzburg

http://www.cosy.sbg.ac.at/welcome.html

From the University of Salzburg, this site brings information (in English and in German) about the University. Check out the hyperlink map of Europe.

University of Saskatchewan

http://www.usask.ca/

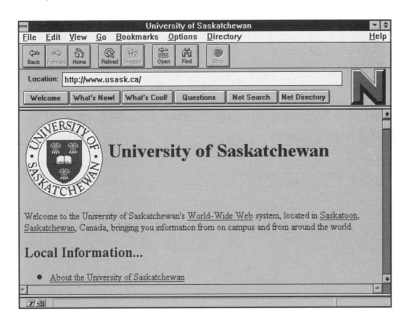

This server provides campus and departmental information, and library services. All publications about the server are searchable, using forms—a nice touch. Links to information about Canadian government, history, and other Web servers located in Canada are offered.

The University of South Africa (UNISA)

http://www.unisa.ac.za

This Web site provides information about UNISA, as well as links to other Web servers in South Africa and throughout the world. It also includes a clickable hypertext map.

The University of Tennessee

http://loki.ur.utk.edu/

This server provides alumnus information, graduate and undergraduate catalogs, and background material about the campus and surrounding areas. Topics covered in detail include science publications by university students, and football updates.

University of Texas—ARLUT

http://www.arlut.utexas.edu/home.html

From this University of Texas server, users may link to a large variety of Web resources. The Internet Resources Meta-Index, available here, is especially useful for keyword searches.

University of the Witwatersrand Computer Science Department Home Page

http://www.cs.wits.ac.za

Maintained by the Witwatersrand computer science department, this site contains information about the University, as well as FAQs about South Africa and South African wines.

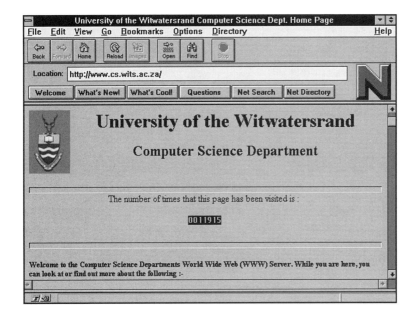

University of Toronto

http://www.utoronto.ca/uoft.html

A quick introduction to the University is available before you jump into details about the departments and colleges. Each department, along with faculty and research information, is accessible from this page.

University of Turku

http://www.funet.fi/resources/map.html

The University of Turku is the second largest educational institution in south-western Finland. This Web server displays a map of the area and information about the University.

University of Virginia—Instructional Technology

http://curry.edschool.Virginia.EDU:80/~insttech/ITpgm/

Find out all about the University of Virginia's Curry School of Education and its graduate degree programs. Meet the faculty and students, and browse the different programs available.

University of Washington Computer Science & Engineering

http://www.cs.washington.edu/

The University of Washington, located in Seattle, created this home page to bring you links to campus servers, course listings, departmental links, and information about the Puget Sound area. Explore topics about the various research fields in which the University is involved.

University of Washington Home Page

http://www.cac.washington.edu:1180/

News, announcements, course schedules, campus information, and online library catalogs for the University are available here. Information from the various colleges, including their high-energy physics and seismology laboratories, is available also.

University of Wisconsin Computer Sciences

http://www.cs.wisc.edu/

Welcome to the University of Wisconsin Computer Science Department! This site offers admissions information, research opportunities, course descriptions, and much more.

Uppsala Computer Science Department

http://www.csd.uu.se/

A map of the campus and general information about the faculty, staff, and campus are available here, as is information about publications and current projects. Updates on Swedish hacking activity and a mailed art project are also available.

Virginia Tech

http://borg.lib.vt.edu

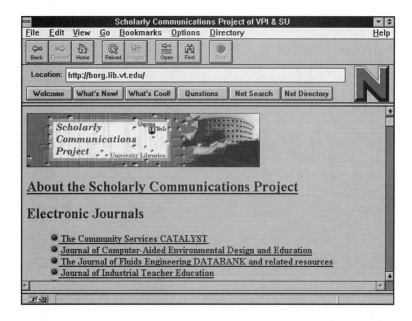

This Web site, maintained by the Scholarly Communications Project of University Libraries, provides a large variety of online journals. Some of the titles offered include the *Journal of Technology Education, Journal of the International Academy of Hospitality Research, Journal of Veterinary Medical Education*, and *Journal of Counseling and Development*.

Warsaw University Astronomical Observatory

http://www.astrouw.edu.pl/

This server offers information about the Warsaw University staff and their computer network. Information about the observatory's big project, the Optical Gravitational Lensing project, is also available.

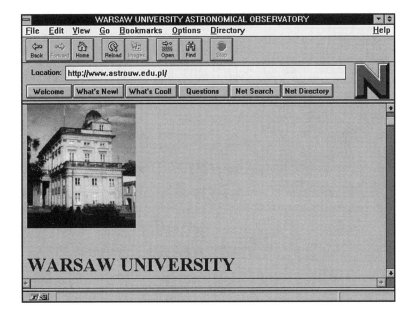

Washington University Department of Radiology

http://www.rad.washington.edu/

Online textbooks, case studies, and an image-analysis software package are available at the department's server. Openings for staff members and current research projects also are described.

Wesleyan University Department of Mathematics and Computer Science

http://www.cs.wesleyan.edu/

The Wesleyan University Department of Mathematics and Computer Science offers an overview of degree requirements, local news, computer science topics, Web resources, and information about staff and students.

Yahoo—Education

http://akebono.stanford.edu/yahoo/Education/

The Yahoo Education directory contains links to more than 1,650 sites. This directory is divided into such categories as community colleges, companies, courses, databases, financial aid, grants, journals, languages, and many others. Users can search by keywords from the Yahoo search feature or use other search engines.

Computer Science Department Overview

http://www.yale.edu/HTML/YaleCS-Info.html

This home page, from Yale University, contains links to general information about the University, student activities and organizations, the Linda Group, and research groups.

Conferences

The World Wide Web also provides information about national and international conferences of various interest groups. The following Web sites are an example of the many different kinds of conferences that you can find on the Web.

apngowid.meet

http://www.igc.apc.org/igc/www.women.html

This resource—maintained by the staff, interns, and volunteers of the Institute for Global Communications—has news and information concerning women around the world, such as the UN Fourth World Conference on Women: Action for Equality, Development and Peace in Beijing, in September, 1995.

Linkages Home Page

http://www.mbnet.mb.ca:80/linkages

Maintained by the International Institute for Sustainable Development (IISD), this site functions as a distribution point for information about environment- or development-related meetings and conferences.

Meetings Calendar (Geosciences)

http://www.met.fu-berlin.de/konferenzen/index.html

This server contains data about meetings and conferences in the geosciences, with an emphasis on meteorology. Entries are sorted by date, and some links contain calls for papers.

Countries

Use the World Wide Web as your embarkation point on your virtual travels round the world! The following sites represent the diversity of travel experiences that are available to you by means of the Web.

Academia Sinica WWW Service

http://www.sinica.edu.tw

The Academia Sinica is the most prestigious institute of higher learning in Taiwan; this Web site provides general information about the Academy, as well as specific information on research conducted there.

African Art Exhibit and Tutorial

http://www.lib.virginia.edu

For those interested in African art and culture, this Web site provides images of African art and an overview of African aesthetics.

Ammar's Little Hut

http://civlab0.civil.mtu.edu:3770/hutgate.html

An interesting collection of pages and links to other Kuwaiti Web sites, including sounds, pieces of wisdom, and humor.

ANU (Australian National University) Asian-Settlements Database

http://coombs.anu.edu.au/WWWVL-AsianStudies.html

This searchable database contains abstracts of theses and research studies, provided by the Asian Institute of Technology, relating to issues of demography and social geography in Asia.

apngowid.meet

http://www.igc.apc.org/igc/www.women.html

This resource—maintained by the staff, interns, and volunteers of the Institute for Global Communications—has news and information concerning women around the world, such as the UN Fourth World Conference on Women: Action for Equality, Development and Peace in Beijing, in September, 1995.

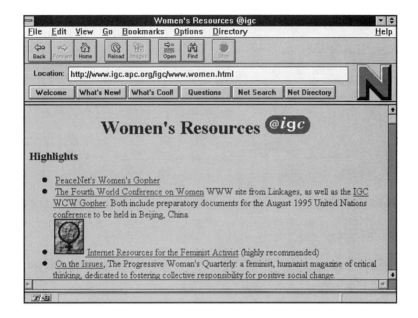

ArtMap

http://wimsey.com/anima/ARTWORLDonline.html

ArtMap is a multimedia cultural and information service to art-related sites for all media and genres: visual, mass media, literature, video, performance, and design. This site has many good links to the world art scene.

Association of Internet Resources (AIR), Hong Kong

http://www.air.org/

AIR is a Hong Kong server with many interesting international links to data, including a selection of starting points for understanding the Internet, the NCSA Mosaic Demo Document, the NCSA Mosaic's "What's New" page, InterNIC Info Source, White House papers, postmodern culture, and the Zippy The Pinhead's page.

atom home page!

http://www.atom.co.jp/

This server contains an archive of Japanese independent music labels. Users will find eight new albums online, including 9 Lazy 9—Brothers Of The Red, and Blue Bongos. This site also contains an archive of Virtual MACLIFE, a virtual art gallery, and links to both Sublime and Trigram records.

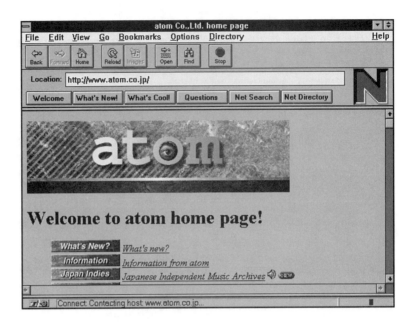

Australian Environmental Resources Information Network (ERIN)

http://kaos.erin.gov.au/erin.html

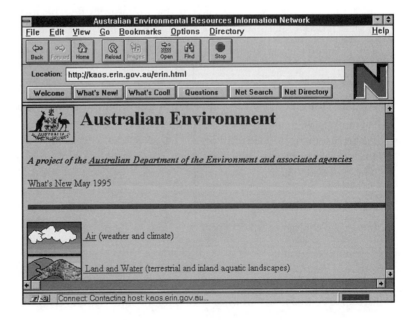

This resource has facts about biodiversity, protected areas, terrestrial and marine environments, environmental protection and legislation, international agreements, and general information about ERIN.

The Australian Graduate School of Management (AGSM)

http://www.agsm.unsw.edu.au/Welcome.html

This server provides overview information about the School of Management, including MBA programs, research centers, working papers, and faculty information. Included at this site are the AGSM Gopher server, an FTP service area where AGSM working papers and information are stored, a library catalog, Australian company information, and a list of Australian Web servers.

Australian Music Guide

http://www.st.nepean.uws.edu.au/~ezsigri/ausmusic/index.html

This page offers links to discographies and lyrics for more than 100 Australian bands. Club, gig, and tour information for many bands is also available.

Australian World Wide Web Servers

http://www.csu.edu.au/links/ozweb.html

This resource has an interactive map of Australian Web sites, as well as recent additions and indexes arranged alphabetically and by type of service.

Belgian WWW/Gopher resource map

http://info1.vub.ac.be:8080/Belgium_map/index.html

This site has a mouse-sensitive map that lists Belgian Web sites and includes information about academic, government, and commercial resources.

Bilkent University Home Page

http://www.bilkent.edu.tr/turkiye.html

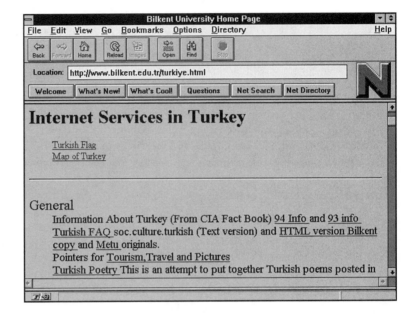

This site contains a basic collection of information about Turkey, including the flag, tourist information, poetry, library services, and telephone books.

British National Register of Archives

http://coombs.anu.edu.au/CoombsHome.html

This is a multivolume electronic guide to accessing a wide variety of archival materials and repositories in the United Kingdom.

Cambridge Astronomy

http://cast0.ast.cam.ac.uk/

In addition to information about the Cambridge astronomy departments and general news, this server contains interesting astronomical data. The latest

Hubble Telescope photos, Solaris FAQs (frequently asked questions), documentation for software packages, as well as links to other related data are accessible from this site.

Campus Info Innsbrück

http://info.uibk.ac.at:80/

This server provides information about the Innsbrück University campus, including an index to Internet servers and links to other Austrian sites. Text is in German, but an English version is in the works.

Canadian Geographical World Wide Web Index

http://www.sal.ists.ca/services/w3_can/maps.html

Updated weekly, this mouse-sensitive, clickable map points to Web sites all around Canada. The map is divided into provinces.

Central Index of Canadian World Wide Web Servers

http://www.sal.ists.ca/services/w3_can/www_index.html

At this site you can get a list of Web servers in Canada by clicking on North America—Canada, from the Web server's directory. A colorful map of Canada is accessible, along with textual lists of educational, commercial, and other servers. Other maps are available for provinces (and subdivisions, such as "Southern Ontario"). Most of the servers shown are for institutions of higher learning; they hold the usual information about administration, course offerings, and activities. Many servers are for areas of culture, science, tourism, and provincial governments. Many listings have both French and English versions.

CERT, France

http://www.cert.fr/

CERT is a French scientific research center active in the areas of aeronautics, space, and defense. Users will find general information about the Center as well as its many divisions and departments, including optics, microwaves, and automation.

Chile

http://www.doc.uchile.cl/servers.html

This site, the Web home page for Chile, focuses primarily on academic institutions in Chile, although information about the Web and Internet is included. A hypertext map is also provided.

China Home Page

http://utkvx1.utk.edu/~xurs/china.html

This page, supported by the Institute of High-Energy Physics, contains links to China's largest scientific, technical, and business-related Web sites. A Chinese music site also is listed here.

City.Net Switzerland

http://www.city.net/countries/switzerland/

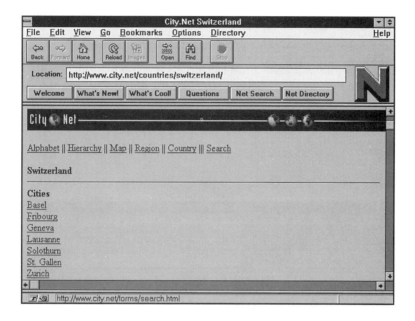

A good index of assorted tourist information about Switzerland and its cities, including maps.

Colombia

http:www.univalle.edu.co/Colombia.html

This site provides links to most other Web servers in Colombia. The primary focus is on academic institutions.

Commonwealth Government Activity on the Net

http://snazzy.edu.au/gov/augov/commonwealth.html

This site is still under construction. At present, although the commonwealth government of Australia maintains a fair number of Gopher servers, most governmental bureaus and agencies do not provide Web access. This site lists and provides links to the Gopher and Web sites that do exist, and provides updates on the plans and progress of the government to increase Web access.

The Complete Guide to Galway

http://wombatix.physics.ucg.ie/galway/galway.html

Galway is located on the western coast of Ireland. Its server is a detailed guide of past and present information, including tourist sites, industry, local transportation, folklore, history, entertainment, and drinking and dining. This Web site includes maps, photographs, and illustrations.

CompuNet

http://www.cnb.compunet.de/

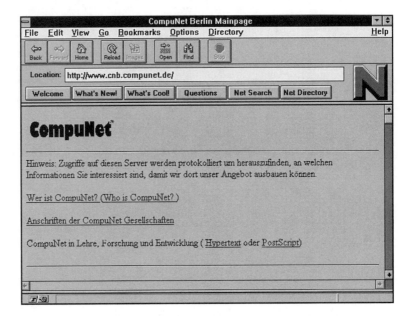

CompuNet is a German networking provider with more than 20 offices throughout Germany. In addition to financial and company information, this server provides details about all their services, including system engineering, project management, software support, technical customer service, and Unix/PC Integration.

Contributed Software GbR

http://www.contrib.de/e-Contrib/Contrib_Home.html

Contributed Software GbR is an Internet services provider located in Berlin, Germany. In addition to product and server information, its server contains free software.

The CTI Centre for Psychology Information Server

http://ctipsych.york.ac.uk/ctipsych.html

The CTI Centre, located at the University of York, is a UK gateway for computer-supported educational activities in psychology. In addition to information about the Centre, its events, projects, and staff, this server contains psychology directories, reviews, abstracts, and downloadable software.

Current Weather Maps and Movies

http://rs560.cl.msu.edu/weather

This Web site is updated hourly and provides links to downloadable software sites instrumental in using interactive weather browsers. International information is available, and visual and infrared maps are supplied from satellites.

Denmark Information

http://info.denet.dk/denmark.html

This site is just like a brief encyclopedia entry about Denmark, including geography, climate, size, type of government, and so on. Also included is a link to a FAQ (in Danish) for Danes traveling abroad.

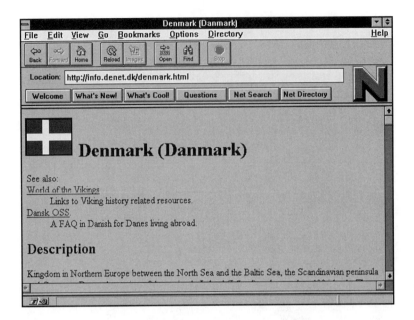

Department of Process Control, Technical University of Budapest

http://www.fsz.bme.hu/

This server offers information about the department, a calendar of events, and the local time in Hungary. Opera fans will enjoy the database of opera show times.

ELSNET (European Network in Language and Speech)

http://www.cogsci.ed.ac.uk/elsnet/home.html

This site addresses the development of language technology in Europe and abroad by helping to coordinate progress on both scientific and technological fronts.

ELVIS+, Co.

http://www.elvis.msk.su/

Come to this Russian site to find exchange rates, a Russian-English dictionary, fax service to Moscow, advertisements, and an index of other Russian Web sites. Use the search engine to search on keywords.

EMBnet (European Molecular Biology Network)

http://biomaster.uio.no/embnet-www.html

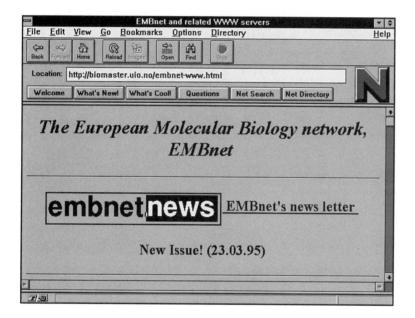

This is a group of European Internet sites that provides computational molecular biology services to international researchers.

Faculty of Arts, Göteborg University

http://www.hum.gu.se/

This Swedish server is devoted to the arts and humanities. Users will find information from each of the University's departments.

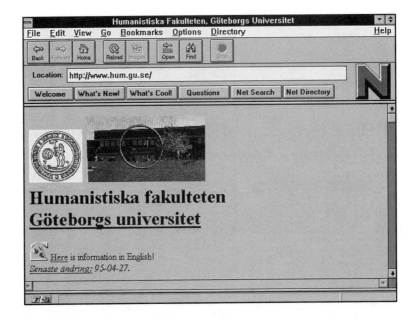

Felipe's Bilingual WWW Pages

http://edb518ea.edb.utexas.edu

This interactive Web site contains Gopher and Web links to various Latin American resources. Information is in both English and Spanish.

FUNET Information Services

http://www.funet.fi/funet/FUNET-english.html

The first stop in your search for Finnish Internet resources. Use the mouse-sensitive map here for links to other sites in Finland, as well as general information about this Scandinavian country.

Germany

http://www.chemie.fu-berlin.de/adressen/brd.html

This is Germany's home page, with great information about the country's geography, people, economy, history, government, language, and communications. Included are the World Fact Book and a list of German news services. A first stop for anyone planning a trip to Germany.

The Hebrew University of Jerusalem Campus Information System

http://www1.huji.ac.il/www_dir/hdbl.html

This site is a hypertext listing, in Hebrew and English, of information about the Hebrew University of Jerusalem.

Home Page for Luxembourg

http://www.restena.lu/luxembourg/lux_welcome.html

Check out tourist sites, Web sites, and general information about Belgium, whose capital city, Luxembourg, is the 1995 Cultural City of Europe.

Hungarian Home Page

http://www.fsz.bme.hu/hungary/homepage.html

This mouse-sensitive, clickable map of Hungary provides links to local Web sites. Also available are a hypertext listing of sites, arranged by city, as well as information about Hungarian culture, history, geography, and cuisine.

Hungary

http://www.fsz.bme.hu/hungary/intro.html

This nicely done page brings together all kinds of interesting and useful information about Hungary and her people, with a great quote by physicist Enrico Fermi.

ICTP (International Centre for Theoretical Physics)

http://gopher.ictp.trieste.it

This site has information about the scientific activities at ICTP (Trieste, Italy). You can also find information about scientific publications, courses, and other services offered by International Centre for Science and High Technology and the Third World Academy of Sciences at Trieste.

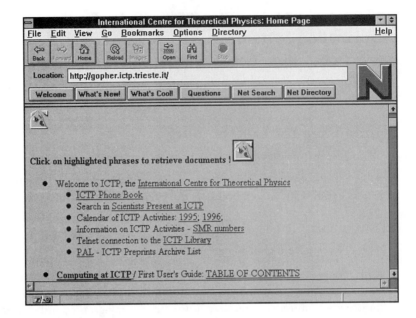

Imperial College Department of Computing

http://src.doc.ic.ac.uk

This is the home of the department of Computing, Imperial College, United Kingdom, the UKUUG (UK Unix Users Group) Archive, and the DoC Information Service.

India's Inter-University Centre for Astronomy & Astrophysics (IUCAA)

http://iucaa.iucaa.ernet.in/welcome.html

In addition to details about the Center, this server provides information about academic activity, including their research interests, recent publications, the academic calendar, and details about their science popularization program in India. Here also is information about the astronomical Image Processing and Data Center, as well as links to other astronomy and astrophysics servers on the Web.

Information about Austria

http://www.ifs.univie.ac.at/austria/austria_info.html

This is a source of quick information about Austria and its economy, culture, history, geography, defense, labor, communications, and government.

Information about Hellas (Greece)

http://www.forthnet.gr/hellas/about_hellas.html

This page has detailed information about Greece, including history, culture, language, currency, and even a link to the U.S. State Department.

Information on India Home Page

http://spiderman.bu.edu:80/misc/india

This Web site contains information about the culture, history, and people of India. It also contains imagery of India, as well as information about tourism and links to related Web sites.

Information Systems in Austria

http://www.ifs.univie.ac.at/austria.html

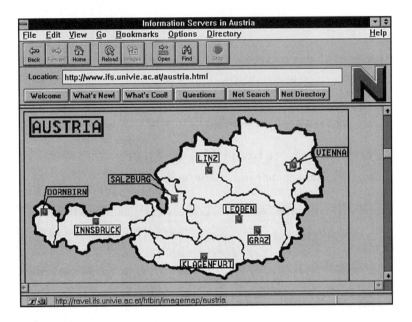

Visit this resource and use its interactive map to get more information about the various Web sites in Austria.

Informatiques Magazine

http://www.wais.com:80/techweb/corporate/international/informatique.html

This Paris-based, French-language magazine is aimed at the MIS manager. This resource will be available in French and English.

Inter-music

http://www.ozonline.com.au:80/TotalNode/AIMC/

Australian underground bands are featured on this site. Video, audio, and text from several Australian bands, as well as links to other Australian music pages, can be found here.

Ireland Online Resources

http://wombatix.physics.ucg.ie/irlnet

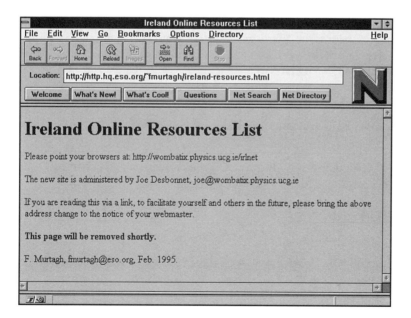

This is a list of network-accessible online resources of Irish-specific interest. Coverage includes some Bulletin Board Services, some commercial information systems (such as CompuServe), and commercial bibliographic services.

IUCAA (Inter-University Centre for Astronomy & Astrophysics)

http://iucaa.iucaa.ernet.in/welcome.html

This server highlights information about the IUCAA. The IUCAA was set up to promote the growth of groups in astronomy and astrophysics in India. The Centre runs vigorous visitor programs that involve short- and long-term visits of scientists from India and abroad.

Japanese Information

http://www.ntt.jp/japan/index.html

This Web server maintains extensive information about the geography, culture, law, and tourism of Japan. Archived Japanese newsgroup information and FAQs are also available.

Japanese Information

http://www.ntt.jp:80/cgi-bin/imagemap/www-in-JP?229,275

The name says it all: history, government, law, culture, music, publications and communications, education, language, and tourist information. Links to other Japanese servers are here also. If you want information about Japan, definitely stop here.

The Jerusalem Mosaic

http://www1.huji.ac.il/jeru/jerusalem.html

Shalom, and welcome to the Holy City. The Jerusalem Mosaic contains information about Jerusalem and its history. The site contains pictures and paintings of the city, as well as audio clips and travel information.

Kuwait Info Page

http://www.cs.cmu.edu:8001/Web/People/anwar/kuwait.html

Here you can find details about Kuwaiti history, culture, cuisine, and literature, with links to other Middle Eastern Web sites.

Latrobe University

http://www.latrobe.edu.au/

This Australian university's server offers information about faculty, research, and courses for many departments. University publications and a campus directory also are featured here.

Latvia OnLine

http://www.vernet.lv/

A good source of news, general information, history, and business and commercial updates on Latvia. Find out about Internet providers and import/export news. This page is also available in Russian.

Le WebLouvre, Paris

http://sunsite.unc.edu/louvre

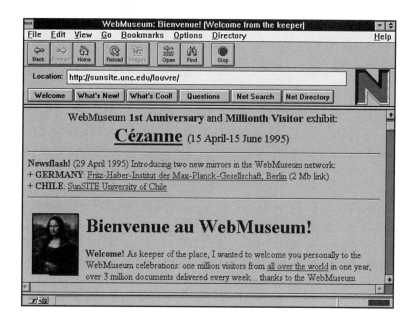

This site contains computer versions of public-domain art. Unlike the pay-per-view "real" Louvre, this one is free, and aims for broad dissemination. Featured are "Famous Paintings" and a medieval art exhibit. The Internet BEST of Web '94 contest gave Le WebLouvre the Best Use of Multiple Media Award. Obviously, its multimedia features are outstanding.

List of Latvian Information Resources

http://www.vernet.lv/Latvia/sites-list.html

This Web page contains information about resources in Latvia. Included are links to Latvian universities and research departments, a map of Riga, the capital, and links to Latvian Gopher servers. The site also contains a link to Latvia OnLine, which provides general information about Latvia, including its constitution, travel and business information, and more.

Luxembourg National Museum of Art

http://www.men.lu/~fumanti/LuxMusee.html

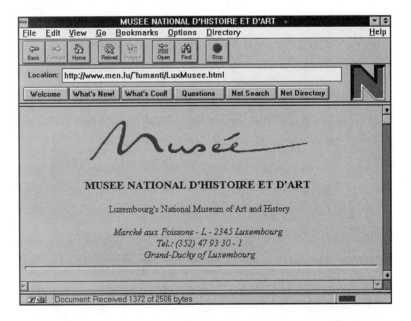

Artists of Luxembourg are well represented in several exhibits. Recent exhibits include one about the French artist M. R. Magritte (1898–1967), called "Le Modele Vivant." A link to the Luxembourg Ministry of Education is also available from this site.

Map of Denmark

http://info.denet.dk/dkmap.html

This clickable map of the Scandinavian country will provide a list of Web sites around Denmark. Commercial, educational, and general interest sites are represented.

Map of Greece

http://www.forthnet.gr/hellas/hellas.html

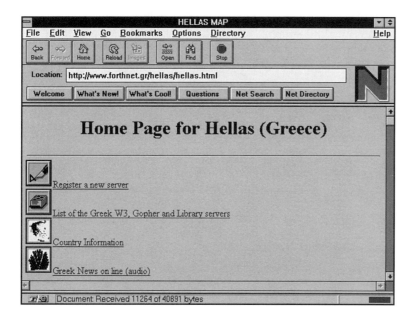

This clickable map of Greece is beautiful. Here you will find links to many Greek Web sites, including businesses and schools. Download Greek fonts and the latest news in Greek and English (audio). You will also find national sports updates and lyrics to Greek songs.

Master Index of Taiwan World Wide Web Servers

http://peacock.tnjc.edu.tw/ROC_sites.html

Search this resource about Taiwan for information about and the location of Web sites and organizations, or other information of local and Internet interest.

Mexican Culture FAQ

http://www.cis.ohio-state.edu/hptertext/faq/usenet/mexican-faq/faq.html

This is the FAQ from the soc.culture.mexican newsgroup. Extensive information about Mexican culture, history, society, language, and tourism can be found here.

Museum of New Zealand—Te Papa Tongarewa

http://hyperg.tu-graz.ac.at:80/B404BE8C/CNew_Zealand

The Museum of New Zealand offers exhibits about the Maori and about New Zealand's natural environment and history. Included also are some graphics for art objects in the museum's collection. Some graphics have a "zoom" feature.

Museums in Holland (Netherlands)

http://www.xxlink.nl/nbt/museums/

This server contains a searchable guide to Holland's museums. You can search by an alphabetical index or by place name. All text is in English, except for proper names of museums and places. There are no graphics yet, but this comprehensive guide is well worth perusing.

MusicBase

http://www.musicbase.co.uk/music/

UK bands such as Terrorvision, Pop Will Eat Itself, and the Stone Roses are the focus of this site. Audio and video clips, lyrics, and interviews are available for these and other bands.

The Natural History Museum of Great Britain

http://www.nhm.ac.uk

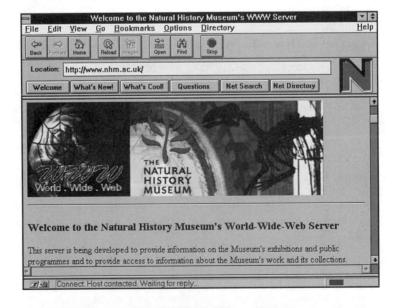

This museum is one of the most highly regarded of its kind in the world. Visitors to this site will find information about the museum, its charter, its exhibits, and access to its library. In addition, this site provides access to other natural history and general research sites on the Web.

Natural Resources Canada (NRCan) Gopher

http://www.emr.ca/

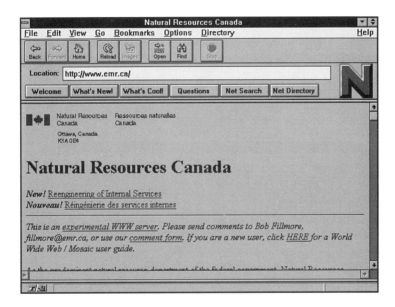

At this site you can find information from the Canadian government about forests, energy, mining, and geomatics. The site also has reports from the Geological Survey of Canada, and an overview of NRCan statutes, organization, and personnel. This site provides links to other Canadian environmental and government Gophers.

Nihon Sun Microsystems

http://www.sun.co.jp

This site provides a directory for Sun Microsystems in Japan. It includes the Rolling Stones Official Server Web site, with access to Rolling Stones music, merchandise, and information. Also provides multimedia links to the Science University of Tokyo, and other Asia-Pacific resources.

Northeast Asia World Wide Web Servers

http://www.ntt.jp/AP/asia-NE.html

This mouse-sensitive map has information about Web sites in the following countries: China, Hong Kong, India, Japan, Korea, and Taiwan.

Nuclear Physics, Moscow State

http://www.npi.msu.su/

Information about the Skobeltsyn Institute of Nuclear Physics, including current work in high-energy physics and microelectronics, is available here. All information on the server is searchable, using forms.

Open Government Pilot

http://info.ic.ca.gov

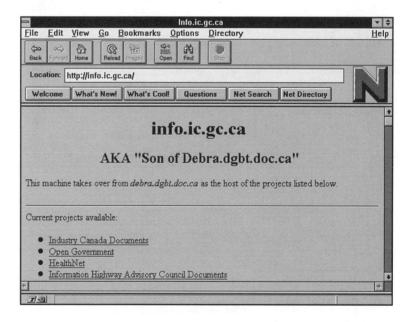

This site provides information about the Canadian government's infrastructure, industry, communications, provinces, and parliament.

Polish Home Page

http://info.fuw.edu.pl/pl/PolandHome.html

Government, geography, travel information, economy, culture, history, and Internet connectivity are all included here. Visit this site to learn about Poland and its people.

Portugal

http://s700.uminho.pt/Portugal/portugal.html

This is the place to learn about Portugal. Find history, communication, sports, culture and art, education, and European Community-related information here. Also, you can download the national anthem and scanned images.

Portugal Home Page

http://s700.uminho.pt/homepage-pt.html

A very nice clickable map summarizing Web and other sites in Portugal. From here, you can access general and tourist information, as well as details about cultural events.

Puerto Rico

http://hpprdk01.prd.hp.com/

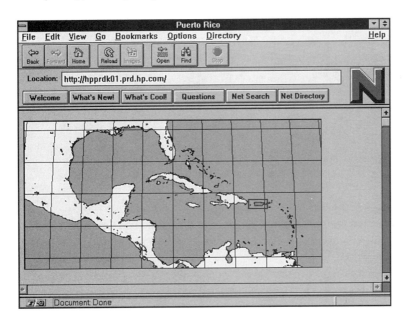

A good source of information about Puerto Rico, with hotlinks to other sites of interest in the tropics. There is a great recipe for piña coladas.

REIFF II MUSEUM

http://www.informatik.rwth-aachen.de/Reiff2/index.eng.html

Visit this site for an extraordinary tour of electronic art, photography, and quality digital renderings of conventional art. This electronic museum was created by the Institute of Art History, the Center of Computing, and the Department of Computer Science at the Rheinisch-Westfälische Technische Hochschule Aachen (Germany). Text is in German, but the pictures are well worth the visit.

Republic of Croatia Map

http://tjev.tel.etf.hr/hrvatska/HR.html

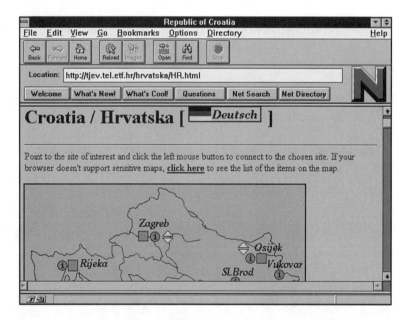

This resource has practically everything you want to know about Croatia. Included here is a compendium of old and recent history on Croatia, information about music, museums, galleries, language, pictures, and updates on the war.

Republic of Korea Tourist Information

http://cair-archive.kaist.ac.kr/korea/index.html

This resource, produced by the Korea National Tourism Corporation, has in-depth information about Korea, including sightseeing highlights, history, and other important facts.

Romania

http://info.cs.pub.ro/

Visit this site for information about the Politechnic University of Bucharest and about Romania in general. Also available are pointers to other Romanian Web sites.

SAHEL-NAFR

http://sun1.cr.usgs.gov/glis/hyper/guide/sahel_nafr

This site includes information and images about satellite images of the SAHEL and North Africa. One purpose of the images is to monitor the grasshopper and locust population in West Africa. This site provides West African countries with data about agricultural, meteorological, and hydrological conditions.

Singapore InfoWEB

http://www.technet.sg/InfoWEB

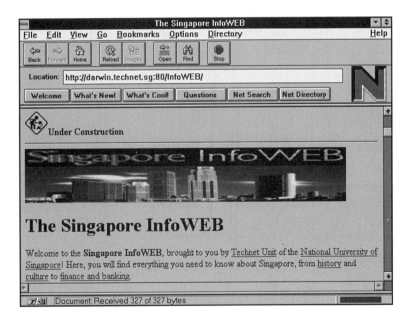

This is the best site for general information about Singapore. Included are interactive maps, the history of Singapore, its culture, defense and security, international relations, and more. This is a good site for tourists, businessmen, diplomats, or anyone with an interest in Singapore.

Slovakia Document Store

http://www.eunet.sk/slovakia/slovakia.html

Available here is nicely organized information about Slovakia, including history, culture, and language. Tourist information is also included.

A Small Tour of Iceland

http://www.rfisk.is/english/iceland/rest_of_iceland.html

Come here for a virtual tour of this Northern European island country. A good place for anyone interested in visiting Iceland.

South Africa

http://osprey.unisa.ac.za/0/docs/south-africa.html

This home page for South Africa includes information about the country's regions, major cities, weather conditions, vital statistics, and about the University of South Africa.

South African WWW servers

http://www.is.co.za/www-za.html

Here is where to find links to commercial, educational, and other interesting Web sites in South Africa. This resource has a mouse-sensitive map of these sites.

Southeast Asia World Wide Web Servers

http://www.ntt.jp/AP/asia-SE.html

This mouse-sensitive map contains links to Web servers in the following countries: Indonesia, Malaysia, Singapore, and Thailand.

Southwest Asia World Wide Web Servers

http://www.ntt.jp/AP/asia-SW.html

Check out this mouse-sensitive map for Web resources in Afghanistan, Bangladesh, India, Iran, Israel, Kuwait, Nepal, Pakistan, Saudi Arabia, Sri Lanka, and Turkey.

SUNET

http://www.sunet.se/

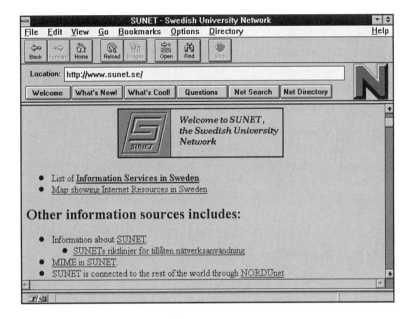

The Swedish University Network maintains this good introductory page to Web sites in Sweden. Also available is a clickable map of the country, as well as information about Nordic libraries.

Switzerland Home Page

http://heiwww.unige.ch/switzerland/

A good first stop in your search for information about Switzerland. Here you will find an interactive map of Swiss Web sites, links to the Swiss telephone book, and general tourist information.

Switzerland (Project Mac) Home Page

http://www-swiss.ai.mit.edu/

Information about MIT's project on mathematics and computation, including a bibliography and individual home pages, can be found here. Photos of Switzerland and information about its people are also available.

Switzerland-Based WWW Servers

http://www.math.ethz.ch/~zari/admin/chw3.html

From the home of the Web itself. This list contains information about and links to dozens and dozens of Web servers in Switzerland, including "the" World

Wide Web server, the main server for the Web initiative itself. The emphasis of
this list is academic and research-oriented, but servers oriented toward topics of
more general interest are here also.

Taiwan—General Information

http://peacock.tnjc.edu.tw/ROC_info.html

This server is a one-stop center for a general but wide-ranging body of information about Taiwan. Included are pages about the history of Taiwan, climate and
current forecast, travel in Taiwan, currency, business hours, and even the
protocols of tipping! This is a good bet for business people, tourists, or anyone
planning a visit.

Thailand

http://www.nectec.or.th/WWW-VL-Thailand.html

This site is part of the World Wide Web Virtual Library—Asian Studies Web
server. It contains information about Thailand, including daily news (in Thai)
from the national Thai News Agency, tourism information by region, and the
Scientific American Supplement on Thailand. It also includes images of
Thailand, and links to Web servers in Thailand.

Thailand: The Big Picture

http://www.nectec.or.th

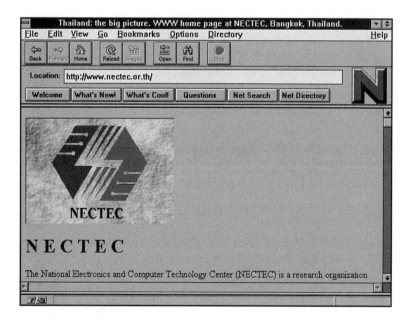

This Web site contains an extensive list of Internet servers pertaining to and located in Thailand. In addition to general information about Thailand, this server contains links to many Thai academic institutions.

Thailand World Wide Web Information—Map

http://www.chiangmai.ac.th/thmap.html

This resource maintains access to Thailand's educational, commercial, and technical Web sites. Also available is a mouse-sensitive map to help you locate Thailand's Web servers.

Travel Information

http://galaxy.einet.net/GJ/travel.html

This is a one-stop shop to some of the best travel information on the Web. Airline information, FAQs about tourism, specific information about countries and cities around the world, travel guides, and newsletters can be found here.

Tung Nan Junior College of Technology

http://peacock.tnjc.edu.tw//NEW/WELCOME.HTML

This is the Tung Nan Junior College of Technology server in Taiwan. They welcome foreign Web visitors with a quotation from Confucius: "When friends visit from afar, is this not indeed a pleasure?" Users will find general information about the campus, as well as links to other Taiwan servers.

UK Guide

http://www.cs.ucl.ac.uk/misc/uk/intro.html

A good source of tourist and other general information about the UK and Ireland. An interactive map, as well as pointers to recreational and governmental points of interest, make this a good place to start browsing for UK-related material on the Web.

UK Sensitive Map

http://scitsc.wlv.ac.uk/ukinfo/uk.map.html

From here you can access two interactive maps: one with cultural and research Web servers, one with commercial Web servers. You can also point to a tourist map.

UNINETT

http://aun.uninett.no/

A nice graphical representation of Internet resources in Norway, with links to corporations, schools and universities, and cultural centers, such as museums.

University of Copenhagen

http://gopher.ku.dk/

Here you can find general information about the University, including information about the departments of theology, law, social science, medicine, natural sciences, and the humanities. Also available are links to the Royal Library of Denmark, as well as other Danish information servers.

University of Manitoba

http://www.umanitoba.ca

The University of Manitoba, located in Winnipeg, Canada, sponsors this site and provides general information about the University, including student activities, departments, a campus-wide telephone directory, and more. Also included here are *Winnipeg Free Press* headlines and Southern Manitoba weather forecasts.

University of Vaasa

http://www.uwasa.fi/

In addition to general information about the city of Vaasa, in Finland, this
server provides information about the University of Vaasa, including the
departments of business administration, accounting, industrial management,
humanities, and the Western-Finland Center for Economic Research. Users will
also find links to various multimedia sources.

Warsaw University Astronomical Observatory

http://www.astrouw.edu.pl/

Information about the Warsaw University staff and their computer network is
available from this server. Also available is information about the observatory's
big project, the Optical Gravitational Lensing project.

Welcome to Lithuania

http://neris.mii.lt/

Here is a good source of information about Lithuanian news, history, academic
resources, art and culture, and a list of other Web sites. This is also a good
place to find tourist information.

World Wide Web Servers in Japan

http://www.ntt.jp/SQUARE/www-in-JP.html

This comprehensive list of Web sites in Japan includes universities, companies,
and other items of general interest.

World Wide Web Servers in Korea

http://www.dongguk.ac.kr/

Organized by city and location, this is where to find the Web sites in North and
South Korea, including universities, corporations, and others.

World Wide Web Servers in Turkey

http://www.metu.edu.tr:80/Turkey/

This mouse-sensitive map of Turkey's Web sites includes some basic historical
and geographical information about Turkey.

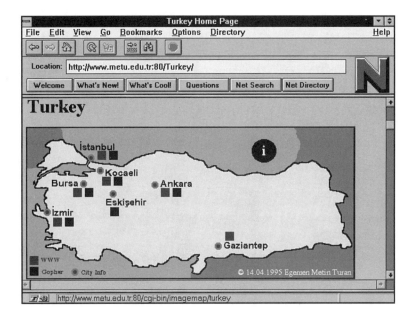

World Wide Web Servers—Italy

http://www.mi.cnr.it/NIR-IT/NIR-map.html

This interactive map with links to Italian Web sites is also a good place to get general information about the country and its attractions.

WWW Servers in Thailand

http://www.chiangmai.ac.th/Servers-th.html

This resource maintains access to a list of Thailand's educational, commercial, and technical Web sites.

Your Traveling Companion—Japan

http://www.ntt.jp:80/japan/TCJ/TC.html

Provided by the Japan National Tourist Organization, this site offers all the information you need to plan a pleasure or business trip to this island nation. There are links to tourist information for major Japanese cities.

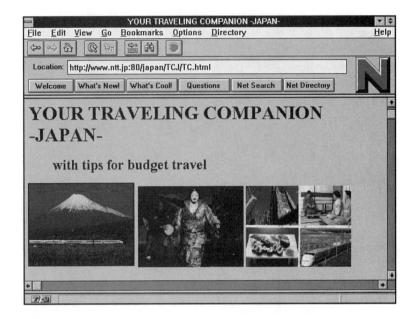

Education

The following section illustrates the diversity of educational topics you can find on the Web.

Academia Latinoamericana de Espanol

http://www.comnet.com/ecuador/learnSpanish.html

Learn to speak Spanish in Quito, Ecuador. This site has information about the Academia Latinoamericana's program, which is specifically designed for those interested in an intensive learning experience.

All My Life

http://www.tc.cornell.edu/Edu/SQ/Gibson/

In 1994, the essay "Networks: Where Have You Been All My Life?" won first place in a contest sponsored by U.S. Department of Education's National Center for Education Statistics, the National Science Foundation, and the National Aeronautics and Space Administration. The essay is presented here for your review.

An NREN That Includes Everyone

http://nearnet.gnn.com/mag/articles/oram/bio.grundner.html

The information in this resource was published by community networker, Tom Grundner (founder of Free-Net). Tom advocates a National Community Network that treats patients looking for health care information as researchers. He advocates expanding our definition of educational access to include people of all ages—senior citizens as well as kindergartners.

Arachnophilia: Florida Institute of Technology's WWW Server

http://sci-ed.fit.edu

This site, specifically for educators and researchers, provides pointers to information resources and search tools around the Web.

Britannica Online

http://www.eb.com/

Tired of carrying those large volumes of *Encyclopedia Britannica* from one room to another? This full-text version of the 15th Edition, not yet checked by the editors, offers a prospective site for alternative research.

CAF Archive

http://www.eff.org/CAF/cafhome.html

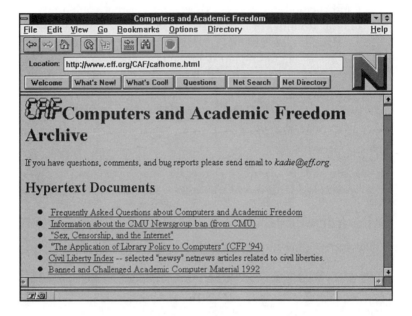

This resource is a repository for information relating to Computers and Academic Freedom (CAF). On this page you can find: *Sex, Censorship, and the Internet, Banned and Challenged Academic Computer Material,* articles related to civil liberties, FAQs about Computers and Academic Freedom, and more.

CEA Education Outreach Page

http://cea-ftp.cea.berkeley.edu/Education/

This site is a great place for educators to start exploring the educational opportunities available on the Web. From the home page, you can locate links to such categories as undergraduate outreach, K–12 outreach, distance learning, public outreach, and other Web educational sites.

Chinook College Funding Service

http://www.indirect.com/user/chinook2/

For anyone needing additional funding for their college education, this server is an excellent source of information about various government programs and scholarships.

College Pro

http://www.netweb.com/mall/collegepro/

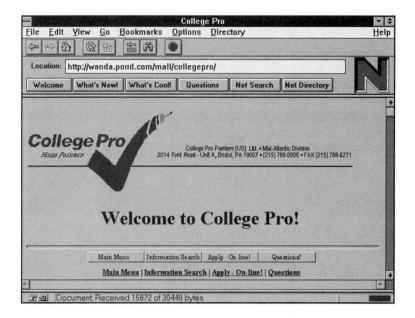

This Web site has information about a summer program for college students that affords them the opportunity to run their own businesses during summer break. The students get valuable business experience, personal growth, and an opportunity to earn great money and learn about the business world while painting houses.

CSU Entomology WWW Site

http://www.colostate.edu/Depts/Entomology/ent.html

This site contains online photos of insects, entomology educational programs, and extensive Internet entomology links.

The Curiosity Club

http://nisus.sfusd.k12.ca.us/curiosity_club/bridge1.html

This Web site offers both an astrophysics exploration and a play space for young scientists.

The Explorer

http://unite.tisl.ukans.edu/xmintro.html

The Explorer gives educators a wide range of information about lesson plans and teaching events. The newsletter, produced several times a month, delivers extensive resources in the topics of math and natural science.

Genes

http://mickey.utmem.edu/front.htm

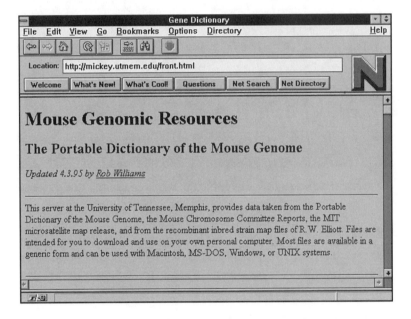

From this home page, users are offered an electronic dictionary with data about genes and anonymous DNA segments. If you are interested in the science of genetics, this is a valuable resource.

Glenview District 34 Schools

http://www.ncook.k12.il.us/dist34_home_page.html

This server, which represents a number of schools in Glenview, Illinois, includes links to the district's primary libraries and to education-related topics.

Hillside Elementary School

http://hillside.coled.umn.edu/

Sixth graders at Hillside Elementary School not only look at the Internet, but actively participate in the world of communication technology. Students, in conjunction with the University of Minnesota, contribute to the maintenance of this Web site and provide information about their curriculum and elementary school education.

HungerWeb Home Page

http://www.hunger.brown.edu/hungerweb/

HungerWeb's focus is to offer education and research about the topic of hunger. Politics, the environment, ethics, research, and clinical studies are categories of discussion. An interactive Hunger Quiz and a link to send e-mail to the President have recently been added.

Icelandic Educational Network

http://www.ismennt.is/ismennt/grunn_uk.html

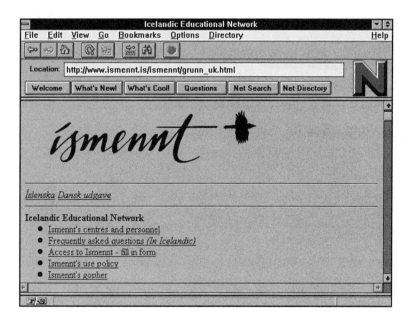

This site contains information about schools and other educational institutions in Iceland. "Kidlink" and the "World of the Vikings Project" are two of the more interesting sights to see.

Illinois Mathematics and Science Academy

http://www.imsa.edu/

The focus of this institution is education for students with special talents in math and science. Its three-year residential program is unique to the nation. The Academy also houses the Illinois research and development lab for K–12 science and math education.

InfoVid Outlet: The Educational & How-To Video Warehouse

http://branch.com:1080/infovid/c100.html

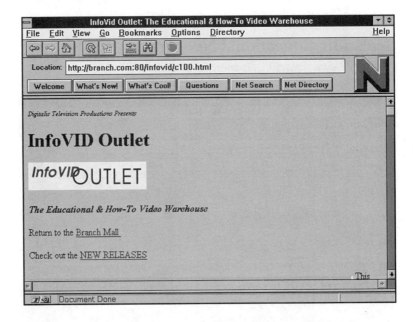

Looking for new ways to be an effective educator? This server offers thousands of videos about education and teaching.

The Interactive Frog Dissection

http://curry.edschool.Virginia.EDU:80/~insttech/frog/

Operate without getting your hands dirty, thanks to the University of Virginia's Curry School of Education. This site, designed for high school biology classes, uses pictures and animation to teach and show you all about frog dissection.

International Student Festival in Trondheim

http://www.idt.unit.no:80/~isfit/

In the past more than 500 students have gathered at this festival in Trondheim, Norway to discuss human rights. Details about the '94 festival are available here, in addition to volunteer information for the '96 festival.

Ithaca, New York Kids on Campus

http://www.tc.cornell.edu/Kids.on.Campus/KOC94/

Ithaca's third, fourth, and fifth graders benefit from this program, which strives to increase interest in computers and science interest through the use of multimedia programs, videos, and participatory activities. This site links to a large number of information resources.

Janice's K–12 Cyberspace OUTPOST

http://k12.cnidr.org/janice_k12/k12menu.html

Teachers of grades K through 12 will want to check this out. Educational tools and materials are cataloged in electronic libraries for quick retrieval. Projects, maps, and other "fun" stuff for learning are offered.

JASON Project Voyage

http://seawifs.gsfc.nasa.gov/JASON/JASON.html

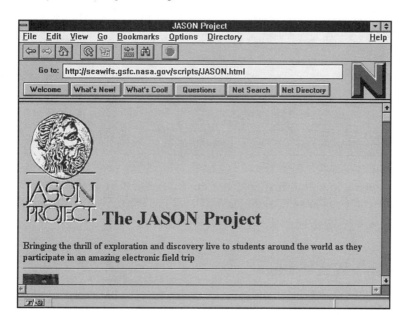

Load all your students onto the bus for this Web trip. Your students can look into the mouth of a volcano or explore other fascinating environmental phenomena. Educators find this site an innovative and effective teaching tool.

Journey North

http://ics.soe.umich.edu

This educational experiment enables students to follow the reports and activities of various scientific projects or explorations and then add their own observations. In one project, students follow the migration of wildlife on a series of maps in the World School's Journey North.

Language Bank of Swedish

http://logos.svenska.gu.se/lbeng.html

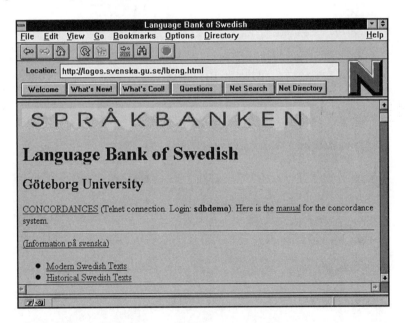

This server is devoted to information about the Language Bank of Swedish. A catalog of machine-readable texts and lexical data, the Language Bank Concordance System, Scandinavian text archives, and English/Swedish texts are offered.

Liz Brigman's WWW Page

http://is.rice.edu:80/~liz

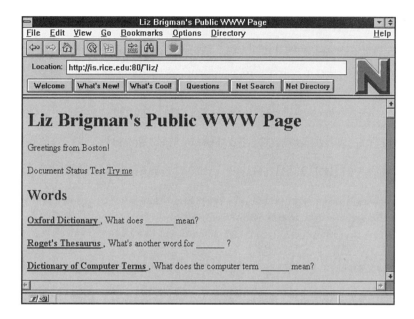

A well-presented assortment of reference materials and sources is the focus here. Use *Roget's Thesaurus* to find a synonym, utilize the *Dictionary of Computer Terms,* or search the online *Oxford Dictionary* to find the definition of a word.

Mars Surveyor MENU

http://esther.la.asu.edu/asu_tes/TES_Editor/MsurveyorMENU.html

For the latest about NASA's Mars Surveyor Program, users can access information provided by the Arizona Mars K–12 Education Program. The launch of Mars Global Surveyor is set for November, 1996, and additional orbiters and landers are slated for launch every 26 months, from 1996 to 2006. Keep up with the "latest" in the exploration of Mars.

Math and Science—The Hub

http://hub.terc.edu/

In the realm of math and science education, this server offers resources that aid in report creation, project completion, proposals, and curriculum development.

Monta Vista High School

http://www.mvhs.edu/newsmenu.html

This high school, located in Cupertino, California, is developing programs to participate in the Internet community.

Mosaic Tutorial

http://curry.edschool.virginia.edu/murray/tutorial/Tutorial.html

Teachers use this Web server to learn how to use Mosaic for the Macintosh. Two categories help you understand the basics of Mosaic and how to create documents. An online search feature is helpful for locating information about networks and general information about computers.

Murray Elementary School

http://pen1.pen.K12.va.us:80/Anthology/Div/Albemarle/Schools/MurrayElem

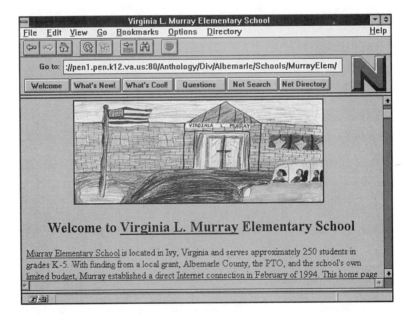

This home page offers an assortment of educational resources. The creation of this site is a joint effort of the Curry School of Education at the University of Virginia and Murray Elementary School. A Macintosh Mosaic Tutorial is included for K–12 educators.

Museum of Physics Department's Early Scientific Instruments Exhibit

http://hp133.na.infin.it/Museum/Museum.html

Winning honorable mention in the Education category at the '94 Best of the Web competition, this site is an online exhibit of physics instruments used at the University of Naples from 1645 to 1900. The exhibit includes hundreds of images, with lots of text to accompany them.

NASA Langley HPCC

http://k12mac.larc.nasa.gov/hpcck12home.html

The High-Performance Computing and Communications K–12 Program is an outreach project that involves five high schools in the Tidewater area of Virginia. The goal of the program is to integrate the investigation and development of computational sciences into the K–12 curricula.

NASA/Kennedy Space Center

http://www.ksc.nasa.gov/ksc.html

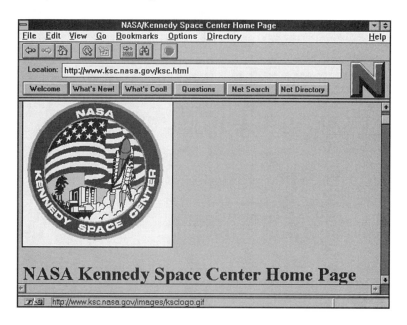

Learn about the American space program and its participants, read about the different missions, view pictures—all at the Space Center. This site also has good links worldwide to other space-related servers.

National Agricultural Library

http://probe.nalusda.gov:8000/index.html

From this home page, individuals have access to a variety of agriculture topics. The U.S. Department of Agriculture offers information about plants, animals, other biology servers, research projects, and the National Agriculture Library telephone list.

Pacific Forestry Center

http://www.pfc.forestry.ca/

Learn about current research activities and programs developed by the Pacific Forestry Center, located in Victoria, British Columbia. The home page offers an introduction to the Center, a contact list, profiles of the staff, and recent publications.

Patch American High School

http://192.253.114.31/Home.html

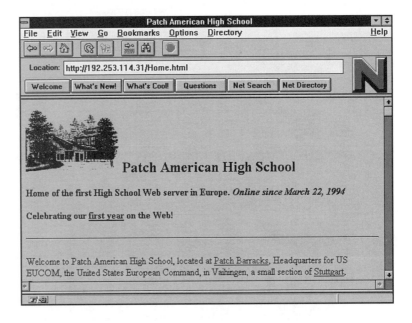

This Web site offers a glimpse into the workings of Patch American High School, located in Stuttgart, Germany. Users can browse through multimedia exhibitions, the "What's New" section, interactive communications courses, entertainment, and artwork produced by the students.

PCLT Exit Ramp

http://pclt.cis.yale.edu/pclt/default.htm

PCLT offers tutorials and education about computer-related topics. Explore
introductions to PC Hardware, TCP/IP, SNA, and review discussions about PC
serial communication and other technical subjects. The developer hopes to
add an accessible package of shareware tools.

Princeton High Schools

http://www.prs.k12.nj.us

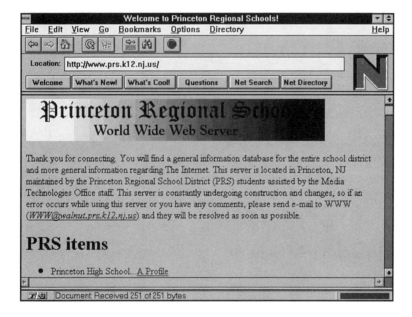

This Web site is maintained by the students at New Jersey's Princeton High
School. Reference materials and a student online newspaper are two of the
offerings here.

The Princeton Review Online

http://www.review.com/

This resource offers details about all of the College Board's standardized tests,
as well as school guides, career advice, undergraduate admissions and financial
aid information, and links to other educational resources.

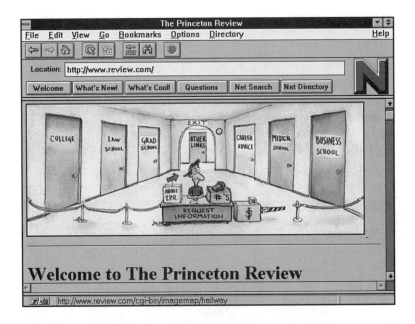

Ralph Bunche Elementary School

http://mac94.ralphbunche.rbs.edu/

Ralph Bunche Elementary School is represented here. The school newspaper, examples of student work, and a pointer to the school's Gopher are offered.

Smoky Mountain Field School

http://www.ce.utk.edu/smoky.html

From this home page you can explore the program schedules and wilderness adventures available at the Smoky Mountain Field School. Created by The University of Tennessee Division of Continuing Education, this site provides information about the supervised wilderness adventures available to people of all ages and levels of experience.

The Teacher Education Internet Server

http://curry.edschool.virginia.edu/teis

This Web site is maintained through a combined effort of the University of Virginia, the University of Houston, and the Society for Technology and Teacher Education. The goal is to provide educators with access to reading resources, networking information, international education, grant-preparation training, and other subjects.

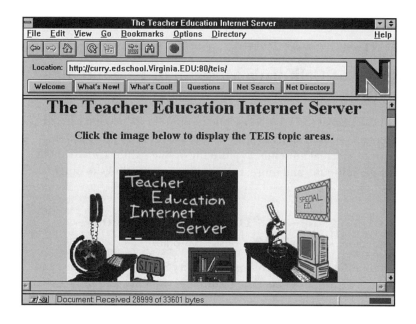

Teacher Web

http://www.stolaf.edu/network/iecc

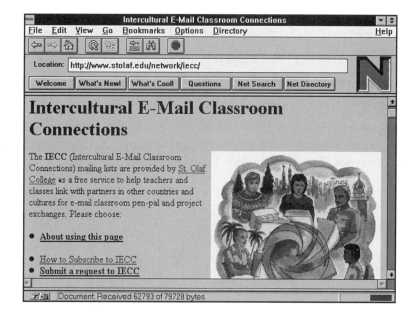

Teachers can use this Web site to locate partner classrooms for international and cultural electronic mail exchanges.

The University of California Museum of Paleontology

http://ucmp1.berkeley.edu/noinline.html

Runner-up in the Best of the Web '94 competition in the Education category, this online version of the California Museum of Paleontology provides an interactive visit to a virtual museum. Explore the online exhibits, learn about the history of the museum, and more; this site also includes links to other related sites.

University of Virginia—Instructional Technology

http://curry.edschool.Virginia.EDU:80/~insttech/ITpgm/

Find out all about the University of Virginia's Curry School of Education and its graduate degree programs. Meet the faculty and students, and browse the different programs available.

University of Washington—Image Processing

http://www.cs.washington.edu/research/metip/metip.html

This server, Mathematics Experiences Through Image Processing (METIP), uses image processing to create learning activities for middle schools. Sponsored by the Department of Computer Science and Engineering at the University of Washington.

U.S. Department of Education

http://www.ed.gov/

The USDOE maintains this Web site to provide information about their goals and activities. They offer links to the Goals 2000 online library, fact sheets, and information about the National Education Goals Act.

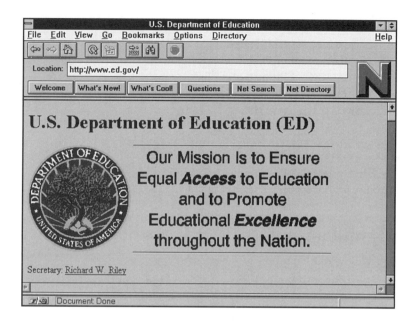

USGS—Education

http://info.er.usgs.gov/education/index.html

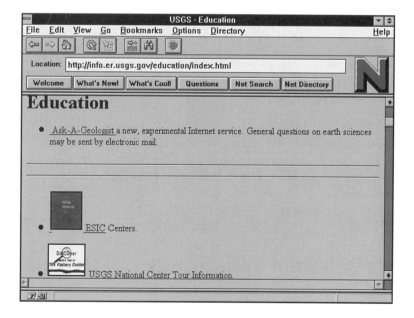

Users are provided access to links to the U.S. Geological Survey National Center Tour Information, the GeoMedia, What's Under Your Feet, fact sheets, and Dinosaurs at the Museum of Paleontology. Research your favorite geography topic through the USGS Library System link.

Virginia L. Murray Elementary School

http://curry.edschool.Virginia.EDU:80/murray/

This home page was created by graduate students of the Curry School of Education as a division of the Technology Infusion Project within the Albemarle County school system. The site represents the elementary school, which educates about 250 students.

Virtual Frog Dissection Kit

http://george.lbl.gov/ITG.hm.pg.docs/dissect/info.html

Come here to control the dissection of a virtual frog, using a form-based protocol. Updated images are generated, based on your instructions. This site is also available in Spanish, French, German, and Dutch.

What Do Maps Show?

http://info.er.usgs.gov/education/teacher/what-do-maps-show/index.html

This Web server has all you'll ever need to know about maps. Relief maps, road maps, topographical maps, aerial photographs, and 3D maps are covered. For those who teach upper elementary school and junior high school, this site offers lesson plans, teaching tips, map legends, and reproducible activity sheets.

Xerox PARC PubWeb Server

http://pubweb.parc.xerox.com/

Step through the doors of the Xerox Palo Alto Research Center at this Web site. Explore corridors to bitmap and color photo labs, the map center, PARC Research-related Digital Libraries, and the lab that collects data about Southern California earthquakes.

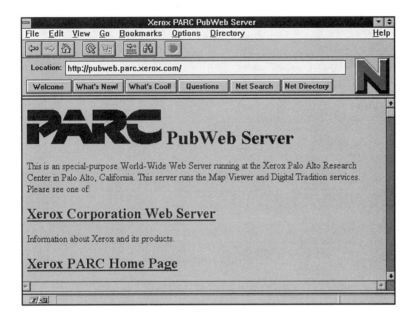

Government

The Web is home to many local, state, and national government-related sites. A broad range of topics is covered, as presented in the section that follows.

American Memory

http://rs6.loc.gov/amhome.html

Here you can find interesting material about American history. This resource, presented by the National Library of Congress, has a Civil War time line, photographs, images of photographs from the World War II era, and more.

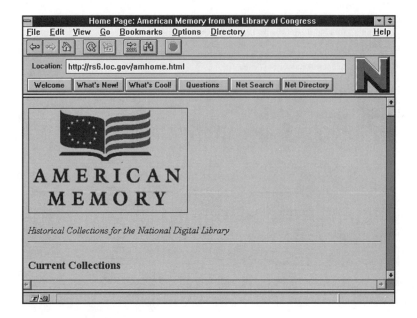

BUSREF (Business Reference)

http://nex.meaddata.com

The BUSREF library contains company directories, reference publications, information about business opportunities, and biographical information about political candidates, Congressional members, celebrities, and international decision makers.

Center for Seismic Studies

http://www.css.gov/

Here you can find the latest seismic readings from around the country. Although still under development, this site looks promising.

Central Intelligence Agency Home Page

http://www.ic.gov

Unfortunately, you have to have clearance to see the really good stuff (what did you expect?), but this site does provide the CIA mission statement and access to two unclassified publications by the CIA: *World Factbook 1994* and *Factbook on Intelligence*.

Commonwealth Government Activity on the Net

http://snazzy.edu.au/gov/augov/commonwealth.html

This site is still under construction. Although the Commonwealth of Australia maintains a fair number of Gopher servers, most governmental bureaus and agencies do not provide Web access at present. This site lists and provides links to the Gopher and Web sites that do exist, and provides updates on the plans and progress of the government to increase Web access.

The Constitution of the United States of America

http://www.law.cornell.edu/constitution/constitution.overview.html

This interesting Web site provides a hypertext version of the United States Constitution.

Environmental Recycling Hotline

http://www.primenet.com/erh.html

This database contains useful information about recycling programs around the country. From this server, users can locate and learn more about the programs offered in their area. General information about recycling is also provided.

Federal, State, and Local Government Organizations in California

http://www.llnl.gov/ptools/california.servers.html#ca.government

This Web site maintains an index of all branches of government in California, organized by level and agency.

Florida WWW Servers

http://www.cis.ufl.edu/home-page/fl-servers/

This site is a good source of commercial, educational, government, and other servers in and relating to the state of Florida. Look here to find the Internet providers in the state.

HM Treasury Server

http://www.hm-treasury.gov.uk

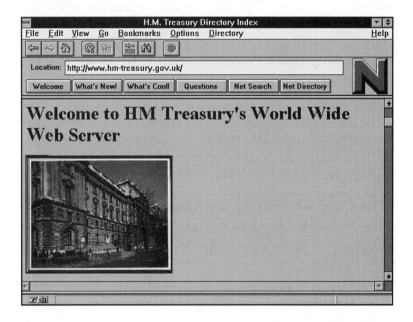

This site, Her Majesty's Treasury Web page, contains information about the budget of the United Kingdom, as well as an index of other Treasury Web sites.

Information Infrastructure Task Force

http://iitf.doc.gov/

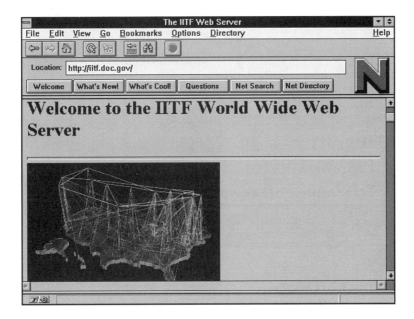

This site contains volumes of information about the IITF, including press releases, legislation, news and updates, a calendar of public events, and contact information about committees and working groups.

List of Servers—District of Columbia

http://www.fie.com/www/district.htm

This Web site has a good list of capital-related information, covering everything from government to entertainment.

Ministry of Posts and Telecommunications, Japan

http://www.mpt.go.jp/

At this site the Japanese Ministry of Posts and Telecommunications presents reports, white papers, news, and updates on telecommunications and related subjects.

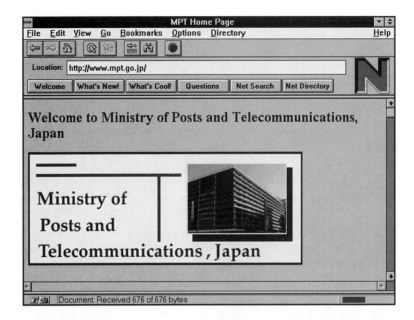

National Export Strategy

http://sunny.stat-usa.gov

This site provides the complete text of a report presented to Congress by the Trade Promotion Coordinating Committee, describing ways to develop U.S. export promotion efforts.

National Geophysical Data Center

http://www.ngdc.noaa.gov/

Reams of data are available about solar-terrestrial physics, solid earth geophysics, marine geology and geophysics, paleoclimatology, and glaciology. Cyclone, tornado, and hurricane reports are all updated frequently.

The National Performance Review

http://www.npr.gov/

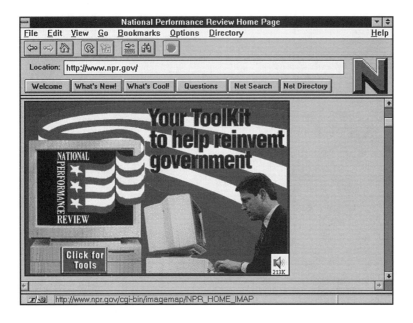

This resource starts with an audio message from Vice President Al Gore. You can then read all about the National Performance Review's directive of "reinventing government."

National Technology Transfer Center (NTTC)

http://iridium.nttc.edu/nttc.hmtl

This resource features state-by-state listings of agencies designed to simplify the adaptation of new technologies to industry. It also provides updates on conferences, and a current list of Department of Defense projects soliciting private assistance from small businesses.

NavyOnLine Home Page

http://www.ncts.navy.mil

The be-all, end-all of Web servers concerning the United States Navy, this site contains links to dozens of other Navy-related Web pages, from sites on the Blue Angels to Navy Psychiatry. Naval buffs and old sea dogs, this site's for you.

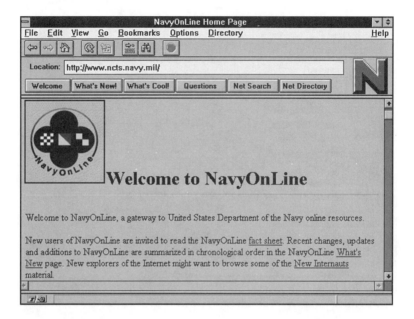

NOAA Geosciences Laboratory

http://www.grdl.noaa.gov/

This server offers information about the laboratory and its three branches: Advanced Technology, Geodynamics, and Satellite Dynamics.

Open Government Project (Canada)

http://debra.dgbt.doc.ca/ogp.html

This bilingual (French/English) site has detailed information about members of the Canadian Senate and House of Commons, as well as Supreme Court rulings and biographies of the justices. It features several pictures, maps, and links to other Canadian information servers.

SAHEL-NAFR

http://sun1.cr.usgs.gov/glis/hyper/guide/sahel_nafr

This site includes information and images about satellite images of the SAHEL and North Africa. One purpose of the images is to monitor the grasshopper and locust population in West Africa. This site provides West African countries with data about agricultural, meteorological, and hydrological conditions.

Southern California Traffic Report

http://www.scubed.com:8001/caltrans/transnet.html

This site represents another imaginative application of the Web. Users can access semi-real-time traffic reports for San Diego, Los Angeles, and Orange County. The site also provides weather reports and links to other government Net resources.

State of Texas—Government Information

http://www.texas.gov/index.html

Organized by subject and government agency, this is a great source of information about the state of Texas. Here you can find news or information about technology projects, Texas-ONE (a resource for small- to medium-sized businesses), and more.

Systems and Software

http://nemo.ncsl.nist.gov/

The National Institute for Standards in Technology provides this server, which contains announcements, publications, and notification of upcoming events. A virtual reality project is also described online, with sample video clips.

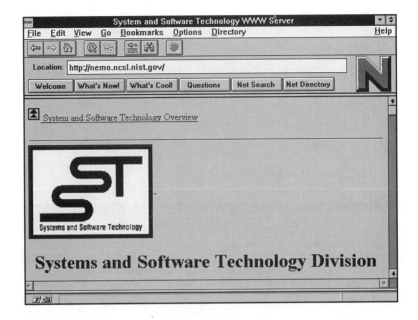

Texas Window on State Government

http://www.window.texas.gov/window-on-state-gov.html

Sponsored by the Office of the Comptroller of Public Accounts, this unique site brings together much information about Texas government, from state expenditures to lottery results.

United States Air Force Home Page

http://white.nosc.mil/air-force.html

The official home page of the USAF, this site contains dozens of links to other Air Force-related Web pages, as well as links to other aviation- and military-related sites. Aviation enthusiasts, take note—this site should be on your hotlist!

United States Census Bureau

http://www.census.gov/

This is a terrific repository of information about the population of the United States. Make sure to visit the "PopClock," which shows the population at the exact moment you entered that page.

US Army Corps of Engineers

http://www.usace.mil/usace.html

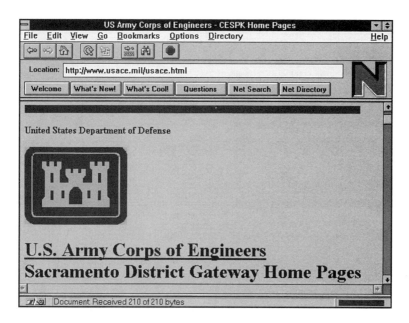

In addition to general information about the U. S. Army Corps of Engineers, users can find news updates, as well as information about its programs, facilities, and activities.

US Department of the Interior

http://info.er.usgs.gov/doi/doi.html

In addition to general information about the U.S. Department of the Interior, this server contains links to the Bureau of Indian Affairs, Bureau of Land Management, Bureau of Reclamation, National Biological Survey, National Park Service, and the U.S. Fish and Wildlife Service.

Health Care

Many aspects of health care are represented on the World Wide Web, as evidenced by the following sites.

AIDS/HIV Information

http://vector.casti.com/QRD/.html/AIDS.html

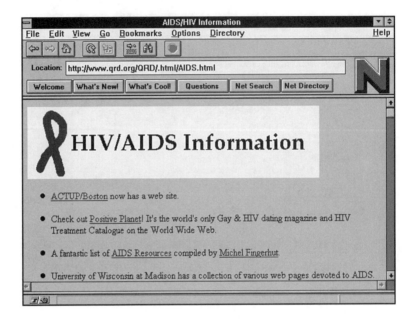

This site serves as a clearinghouse for AIDS- and HIV-related information, and provides connections to other Internet, Web, and Gopher servers. This site also maintains archives of FAQs and AIDS treatment news.

An NREN That Includes Everyone

http://nearnet.gnn.com/mag/articles/oram/bio.grundner.html

This resource contains information published by community networker Tom Grundner (founder of Free-Net). Tom advocates a National Community Network that treats patients looking for health care information as researchers. He advocates expanding our definition of educational access to include people of all ages; senior citizens as well as kindergartners.

Neurosciences Internet Resource Guide

http://http2.sils.umich.edu/Public/nirg/nirg1.html

This comprehensive Internet resource addresses biological, chemical, medical, engineering, and computer science aspects of neurobiology.

Recreational Pharmacology Server

http://stein1.u.washington.edu:2012/pharm/pharm.html

This site contains an exhaustive collection of drug FAQs, data sheets, articles, resources, and electronic books about drugs frequently used for recreational purposes. The site also contains a large list of Internet links to drug-related sites.

The World Health Organization

http://www.who.dk/

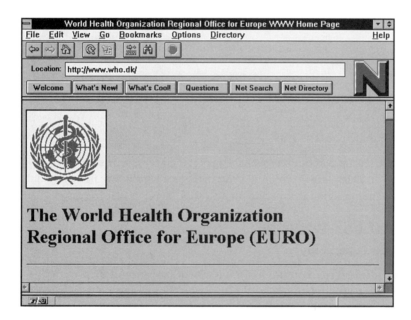

This site is the home page of WHO's Regional Office for Europe (EURO). Here you will find various health- and region-related information.

World Health Organization (WHO) WWW Home Page

http://www.who.ch

This site contains information about WHO, including previous and current projects, press releases and newsletters, and vaccination requirements for travel to different countries.

Yahoo—Health

http://akebono.stanford.edu/yahoo/Health/

The Yahoo Health directory contains links to more than 400 sites. This directory is divided into such categories as alternative medicine, companies, computer health hazards, environmental health, fitness, general health, and many others. Users can search by keywords from the Yahoo search feature, or use other search engines.

Law

Many Web sites address legal issues or present information of interest to those in the legal profession.

Australian Environmental Resources Information Network (ERIN)

http://kaos.erin.gov.au/erin.html

This resource has facts about biodiversity, protected areas, terrestrial and marine environments, environmental protection and legislation, international agreements, and general information about ERIN.

THE SEAMLESS WEBsite

http://starbase.ingress.com/tsw/

This site is dedicated to information for and about lawyers and their trade. Highlighted here are updates on legal issues, precedents, and news, as well as an online advertising forum.

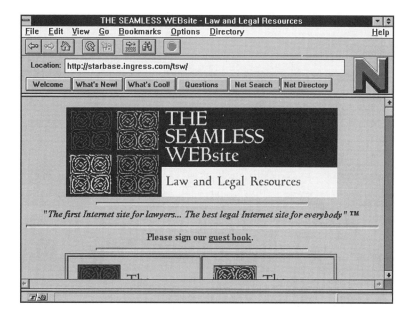

Organizations

All types of organizations are represented on the World Wide Web. The following sites are but a small portion of the wide range of interests you can find on the Web.

Abortion and Reproductive Rights

http://gopher.well.sf.ca.us

This site, a primary source for information about abortion and reproductive rights, also includes connections to many related catalogs, databases, and servers.

AdoptioNetwork Home Page

http://www.infi.net:80/adopt

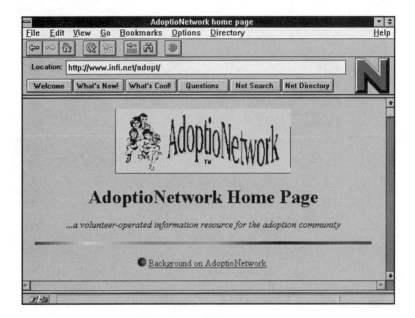

The site connects users to the AdoptioNetwork. As its name implies, the organization is dedicated to helping adoptive parents and couples who wish to adopt by providing them with support and information. In addition, the organization provides information for health care and social service professionals.

Amnesty International

http://www/human.rights/amnesty.international/ai.html

This site contains information about Amnesty International, an organization focused on human rights issues around the world.

Current Middle Ages Web Server

http://www2.ecst.csuchico.edu/~rodmur/sca

The Society for Creative Anachronism (SCA) consists of otherwise normal individuals who, on occasion, dress up in replicas of medieval armor and bash each other about with (padded) weapons. Others dress up as scullery maids,

knaves, harlots, and so on. This Web site contains information about the SCA, their rules, customs, and kingdoms. It also contains information about the Middle Ages, their arts and sciences, and subscription links to the SCA newsletter.

The Dorsai Embassy

http://www.dorsai.org

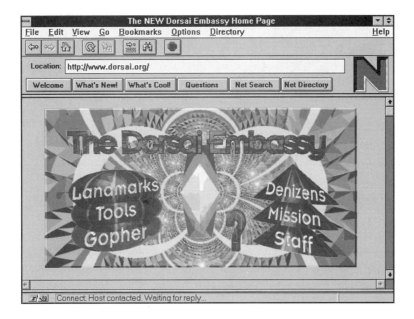

The Dorsai Embassy is a charitable, nonprofit organization dedicated to providing computer resources to low-income and disabled individuals, as well as to other charitable organizations. The group provides hardware, software, training, and, for a nominal fee, Web and Internet access.

ECSEL Coalition

http://echo.umd.edu/

The National Science Foundation supports the Engineering Coalition of Schools in its efforts to revitalize the undergraduate engineering education system. From this home page you can review information about research projects and other engineering education coalitions.

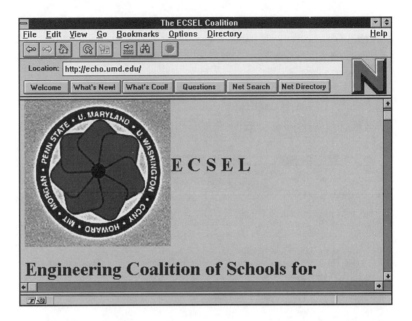

FINS-Fish INformation Service

http://www.actwin.com/fish/index.html

FINS provides information about…fish! Users with an interest in fresh- and saltwater aquaria will find this a useful site. In addition, there are movies of an aquarium with "live" fish…well…swimming…and sort of just floating there.

Greenpeace World Wide Web International

http://www.greenpeace.org/

Find information, news, press releases, and updates from and about this international environmental group. View pictures, browse the library, and connect with other environmental Web sites.

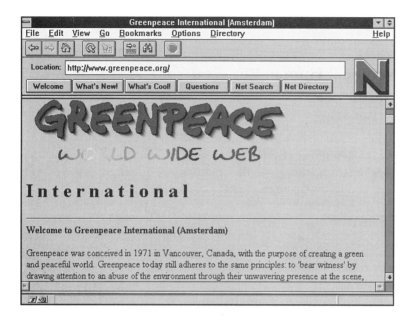

HungerWeb

http://www.hunger.brown.edu/hungerweb

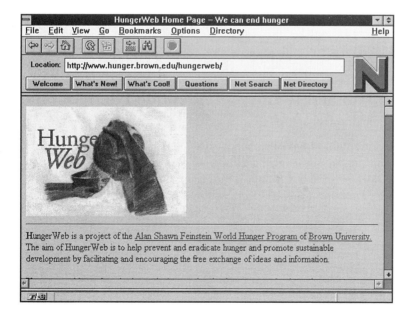

This Web site focuses on the political, economic, agricultural, and ethical implications of world hunger.

The International Human-Powered Vehicle WWW Server

http://www.ihpva.org

The International Human-Powered Vehicle Association (IHPVA) is dedicated to promoting the development and improvement of human-powered vehicles. This site provides information about the organization, its current projects, and past successes. The site also contains links to cycling Web pages.

Linkages Home Page

http://www.mbnet.mb.ca:80/linkages

Maintained by the International Institute for Sustainable Development (IISD), this site functions as a distribution point for information about environment- or development-related meetings and conferences.

Natural Resources Canada (NRCan) Gopher

http://www.emr.ca/

At this site you can find information from the Canadian government about forests, energy, mining, and geomatics. The site also has reports from the Geological Survey of Canada, and an overview of NRCan statutes, organization, and personnel. This site provides links to other Canadian environmental and government Gophers.

Precious in HIS Sight—Internet Adoption Photolisting

http://www.gems.com/adoption

The Internet Adoption Photolisting is dedicated to providing information about, and finding parents for, children available for international adoption. It includes information about adoption, and its organizers hope to enlist the several hundred adoption agencies in the United States in this project.

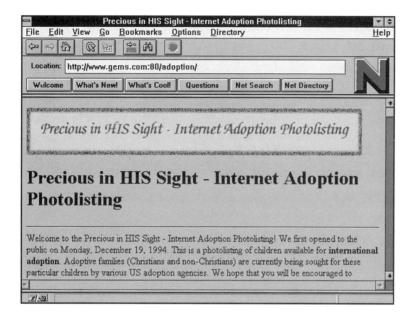

Sociology

http://galaxy.einet.net/galaxy/Social-Sciences/Sociology.html

This is a gateway to sociology information on the Web. Some of the links available here include the Electronic Journal of Sociology, sociological directories, listservs for social work and sociology, the Swedish social science data service, the sociological collection at the Berkeley library, and academic organizations, as well as many other related links.

World Health Organization (WHO) WWW Home Page

http://www.who.ch

This site contains information about WHO, including previous and current projects, press releases and newsletters, and vaccination requirements for travel to different countries.

The World-Wide Web Virtual Library: United Nations Information Services

http://www.undcp.or.at/unlinks.html

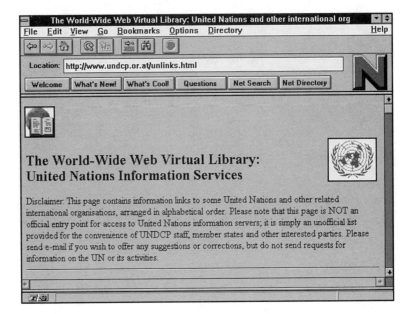

Start at this site to find information about the United Nations, its agencies, and other international organizations. This server links to other agencies and related sites.

C H A P T E R

29

Looking at the Best Commercial Sites

This chapter expands on the Chapter 17, "Commerce on the Web," discussion of commercialization on the World Wide Web. You can find dozens of businesses and commercial sites in this chapter.

Business

Many businesses have found it advantageous to disseminate information about their products on the Web. Here is a sampling of some of the most interesting and informative business Web sites that we have found.

Ameritech

http://www.aads.net

Ameritech is one of the world's largest telecommunications companies, with more than 13 million customers. Their server provides a wide array of company information, including details about the development of their new information, entertainment, and interactive services for homes, businesses, and governments.

Broadway & Seymour

http://www.bsis.com

Broadway & Seymour provides information technology to the financial services market. In addition to company information, this server also has links to other relevant Web sites.

BTG Technology Systems

http://www.btg.com/techsys

Stop at this site to browse this catalog of more than 15,000 hardware and software items. BTG Technology Systems usually sells to the government and its agencies, and represents more than 200 companies.

Buena Vista Movieplex

http://www.disney.com

In addition to general information about the company, this server provides movie clips from the latest Buena Vista releases, along with other interesting movie facts.

Business News—Singapore

http://gopher.cic.net

This Gopher site focuses on business in Singapore.

BUSREF (Business Reference)

http://nex.meaddata.com

The BUSREF library contains company directories, reference publications, information about business opportunities, and biographical information on political candidates, Congressional members, celebrities, and international decision makers.

Capella Networking

http://storefront.xor.com/capella/index.html

Capella Networking is a Boulder, Colorado company at whose Web site you can find information about the diverse inventory of products and services they provide for client to client solutions for end-users, remote sites, and telecommuters nationwide.

ClarisWeb

http://www.claris.com

Claris is a software developer of popular Mac and Windows applications. In addition to general information about the company, this server provides product information, technical support, update releases, templates, and related articles.

College Pro

http://www.netweb.com/mall/collegepro

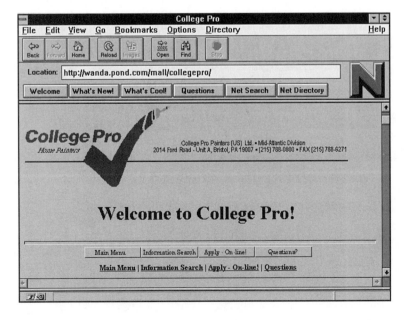

This Web site has information about a summer program for college students that affords them the opportunity to run their own businesses during summer break. The students get valuable business experience, personal growth, and an opportunity to earn great money and learn about the business world while painting houses.

Colloquium

http://www.hydra.com/wertheim/colloquium.html

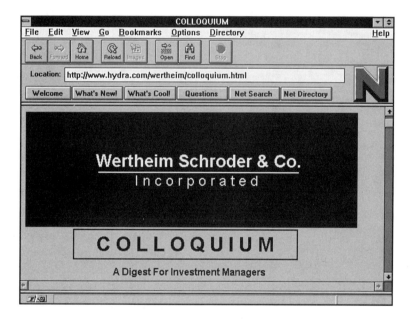

Colloquium is a newsletter on managing your investments. This service is free for the first two months.

Compaq Worldwide Web Server

http://www.compaq.com/hohttp://www.digital.com/
home.htmlmepage.graphic.html

This site highlights the product information, service and support, corporate overview, and just about everything else you want to know about the Compaq computer company.

Compton's NewMedia

http://www.comptons.com

Compton's NewMedia is best known for their electronic encyclopedia. In addition to company information, users will find details and descriptions about all their interactive, multimedia software.

Cygnus Support

http://www.cygnus.com

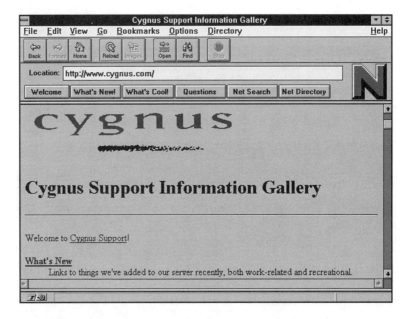

This server contains press releases, product information, and other publications from Cygnus, a developer of GNU tools. A patch to fix the bug in early Pentium chips is available also.

Dataquest

http://www.dataquest.com

Dataquest is a global information technology market research company. Their server includes general product and service information, as well as analysis and results of recent surveys and studies they have conducted.

Delmarva Power

http://www.delmarva.com

In addition to general information about this Delaware-Maryland-Virginia utility, this server has some interesting maps and facts about running a power utility.

Digital Equipment WWW Information Server

http://www.service.digital.com/home.html

In addition to Digital Equipment product and service information, this server contains archives to public domain software. Users will find an online catalog for purchasing products from Digital Equipment.

Entertainment and Media Professional

http://www.cenco.com/emp

This information resource for multimedia producers and developers provides details about distribution and publication channels.

Ericsson, Inc.

http://www.ericsson.nl

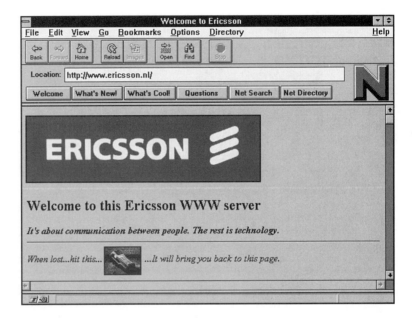

This server is offered by Ericsson, Inc., a supplier of telecommunications technology. The publications carry both technical information and general articles.

First Interstate Bank

http://www.hexadecimal.com/fi

The First Interstate Bank server provides a catalog of consumer and business banking services and products, as well as a list of bank branches.

Florida WWW Servers

http://www.cis.ufl.edu/home-page/fl-servers

This site is a good source of commercial, educational, government, and other servers in and relating to the state of Florida. Look here to find the Internet providers in the state.

General Electric

http://www.ge.com

This is the home page for General Electric. It offers product and technical information from all GE divisions.

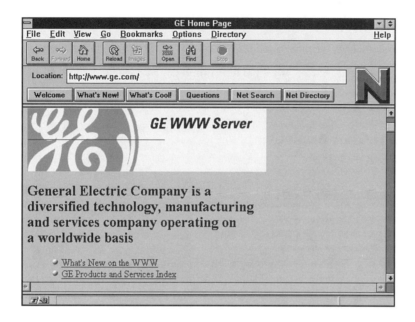

helpwanted.com

http://www.helpwanted.com

Job hunters can use this valuable resource tool to find work. With this service you can do keyword searches to find job listings in specific fields and locations.

HomeBuyer's Fair

http://www.homefair.com

At this site you can check out the real estate market in the Washington, D.C., area and find out about mortgages and other services.

HomeNet

http://www.intertel.com

HomeNet is a resource of residential and commercial real estate for the New York and New Jersey area. It includes full-color pictures of offerings, agent profiles, U.S. census data, and a mortgage calculator. This site plans to offer nationwide listings in the future.

Hybrid Networks

http://hybrid.com/HybridHomePage.html

Hybrid is an Internet service provider. Their home page provides corporate information, including help wanted opportunities, product information, and announcements.

Intelligent Market Analytics

http://www.marketmind.com

This site offers news and information about the products of Intelligent Market Analytics, as well as links to other investing and analysis sites.

Internet Business Report

http://www.wais.com:80/ibr

At this site you can find the latest news about the growing area of online commerce. This online magazine is published by CMP Publications.

Internet Credit Bureau, Inc.

http://www.satelnet.org/credit

Some of the valuable financial services offered from this site include credit information about U.S. companies, as well as matching individuals with their Social Security numbers.

ISSI

http://www.issi.com/issi/issi-home_page.html

International Software Systems Incorporated offers services such as software reengineering and other jargon-filled process engineering products. An online journal and access to employee home pages can also be found here.

J.M. Huber Corporation

http://www.huber.com

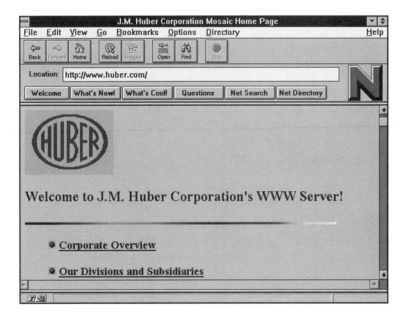

In addition to the corporate overview and an explanation of its divisions and subsidiaries, this consumer and industrial company offers many Web resources, including an introduction to the Web, Internet starting points, information searches, Internet indexes, commercial site directories, and a link to CommerceNet.

Knowledge One

http://KnowOne_WWW.sonoma.edu

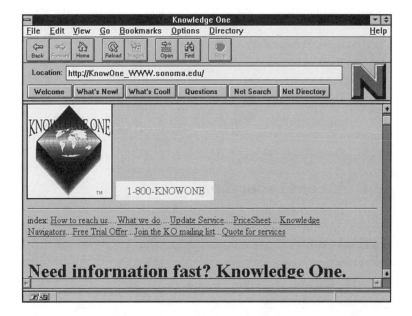

Knowledge One is an information service. Users select topics they are interested in; researchers will provide a weekly summary of events in the specified subject. This page provides sample reports and details about the company's services and how to order them.

Martin Marietta Energy Systems Gopher

http://www.ornl.gov/mmes.html

Martin Marietta's server contains information about their energy projects and technologies for both government and commercial applications.

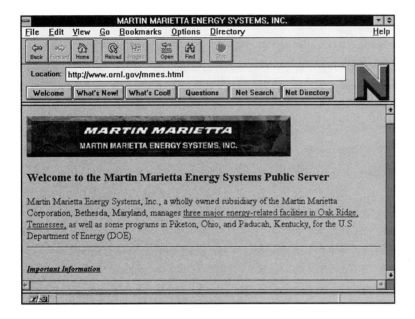

MCA/Universal Cyberwalk

http://www.mca.com

The home page for this entertainment and media giant provides information and samplings of their latest projects. The Universal Channel is a "behind the scenes" look at TV shows such as *SeaQuest DSV*, *Earth 2*, *Law & Order*, *Dream On*, *Vanishing Son*, and *Hercules—The Legendary Journeys*, to name a few. From this site, users can also find an interactive game show, as well as other entertainment-related material.

Medium for Global Access

http://www.mgainc.com

This Internet consulting firm also maintains Access Art. It's a place where artists and collectors meet.

Meiko

http://www.meiko.com:80/welcome.html

Meiko specializes in "open, scalable parallel computing." Their server provides product information, announcements, reviews, and a company overview. Information about the rock group Yes, including an archive of newsletters, is also here.

The Mining Channel

http://www.wimsey.com/Magnet/mc/index.html

Look here for information about mining and emerging mineral exploration companies, as well as industry newsletters, ads, and other sites.

NAARS (National Automated Accounting Research System)

http://www.meaddata.com

The NAARS library contains annual reports of public corporations, accounting literature, and other publications for the accounting professional. The reports are annotated with descriptive terms assigned by the AICPA. You can search these annotated reports for footnotes that illustrate one or more recognized accounting practices.

National Export Strategy

http://sunny.stat-usa.gov

This site provides the complete text of a report, presented to Congress by the Trade Promotion Coordinating Committee, that describes ways to develop U.S. export promotion efforts.

National Technology Transfer Center (NTTC)

http://iridium.nttc.edu/nttc.hmtl

This resource features state-by-state lists of agencies designed to simplify the adaptation of new technologies to industry. It also provides updates on conferences, and a current list of Department of Defense projects soliciting private assistance from small businesses.

NEC

http://www.nec.com

Here you can find loads of information about NEC, its history, and current projects. This page is available in both English and Japanese.

Network Computing Devices

http://www.ncd.com

NCD's home page contains background information about the company and its three major projects: Z-mail, X-terminals, and PC-Xware. A catalog of third-party software compatible with the XWindows system is also here.

NETworth (The Internet Resource for Individual Investors)

http://networth.galt.com/www/home/start.html

NETworth features free, in-depth information about mutual funds. This server provides information direct from the mutual fund companies, including prospectus and performance figures. The Morningstar database supplies performance figures on more than 5,000 mutual funds. Users will also find a large sampling of financial newsletters, weekly market outlooks, and interactive question-and-answer forums with market experts.

Nihon Sun Microsystems

http://www.sun.co.jp

This site provides a directory for Sun Microsystems in Japan, and includes the Rolling Stones Official Server Web site, with access to Rolling Stones music, merchandise, and information. It also provides multimedia links to the Science University of Tokyo, and other Asia-Pacific resources.

Open Government Pilot

http://debra.dgbt.doc.ca/opengov

This site provides information about the Canadian government's infrastructure, industry, communications, provinces, and parliament.

PAWWS

http://pawws.secapl.com

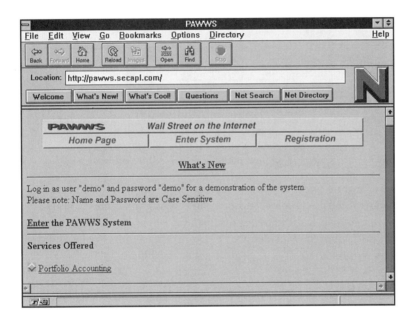

At this site you can choose from a variety of free and commercial market-related services, including quotes, a portfolio challenge, and National Discount Brokers' online survey about customer stock-trading needs.

The Reference Press Bookstore

http://www.hoovers.com

The Reference Press publishes regional and national company profiles for the mass market. From this site, you can find information about such companies as Time Warner, Starbucks, and Yamaha.

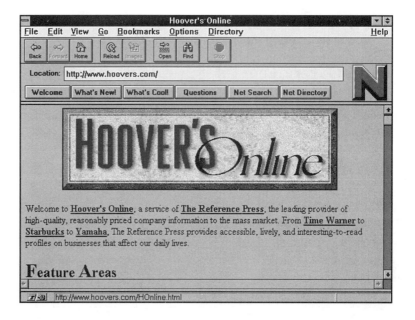

RISKWeb

http://riskweb.bus.utexas.edu/riskweb.htm

Dedicated to providing information about risk management and insurance, this server archives articles, papers, and employment opportunities from the RISKNet mailing list. Keyword searches of the databases are available. Other financial sites, including the University of Texas insurance home page and the American Risk and Insurance home page, are also on this site.

RSA Data Security

http://www.rsa.com

RSA is the leader in cryptography and other information-protection services. This page contains an archive of press releases, general corporate information, and a primer on cryptography.

Security APL

http://www.secapl.com

Security APL offers users not only product and service information about itself, but also stock quotes, news updates, and links to other finance-related sites.

Softbank Exposition/Conference Company

http://programs.digitalworld.com

Trade shows and conferences, both online and physical, are Softbank's specialty. Users will find the company's upcoming exhibitions described on this page.

Sprint Communications

http://www.sprintlink.net

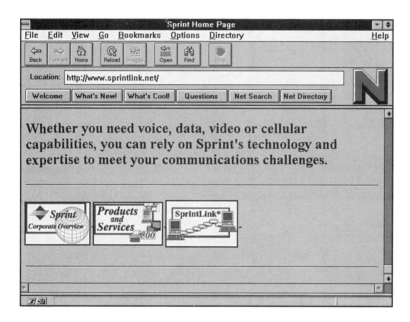

This is the server for Sprint Communications. Here you can find information about Sprint's communications products and services, including Internet access and networking.

Stanford Federal Credit Union

http://netmedia.com/cu/cu_home.html

In addition to a nice presentation of the credit union's products and services, this site provides links to university sponsors as well as to servers on the Stanford University campus.

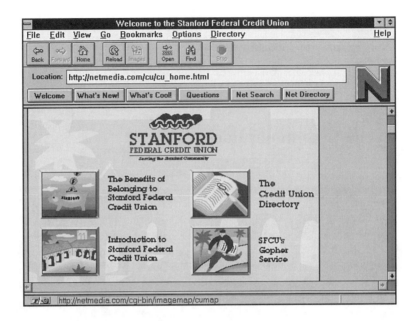

TechWeb

http://www.wais.com:80/techweb

The home page for CMP Publications, Inc., highlights this company's publishing, trade show organizing, and information marketing business. Use their search feature on more than 15 magazines to find articles about a specific subject.

Telemedia, Networks, and Systems Group

http://tns-www.lcs.mit.edu

This is a list of well-maintained and frequently updated commercial services and sites on the Web and Net.

Time Warner Electronic Publishing

http://www.timeinc.com/twep

Each week, this page highlights the new releases of books and electronic titles from Time Warner Electronic Publishing. Some recent excerpts include suggestions on how to drive your woman mad in bed, an illustrated screenplay by Harlan Ellison, and the work of best-selling author James Patterson.

Total Quality Management Gopher

http://deming.eng.clemson.edu

This is a collection of materials relating to the elimination of defects through comprehensive quality control in industry, government, and universities.

Toyo Engineering Corporation

http://www.toyo-eng.co.jp

This Japanese company's resource has good information about regional business issues. Toyo makes great use of graphics on this page.

WAIS, Inc.

http://server.wais.com

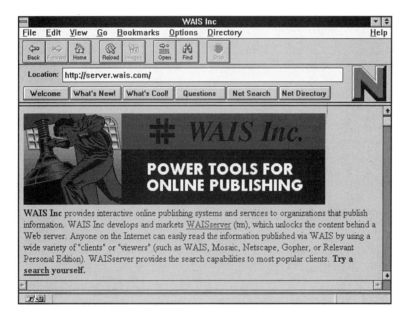

WAIS, Inc., provides online publishing systems and services to organizations that want to distribute information via the Internet.

Wells Fargo Bank

http://www.wellsfargo.com

In addition to general information about the company, this server provides information about the bank's services, such as small business banking, personal financial center, and information about "Commerce on the Internet."

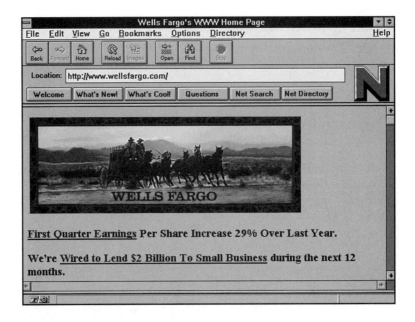

Yahoo Market and Investments

http://akebono.stanford.edu/yahoo/Economy/Markets_and_Investments

This comprehensive look at the current economic status covers a wide range of brokers and stocks.

Commercial

The following section contains a small sampling of some of the best commercial sites on the World Wide Web.

Access Plus Communications

http://www.deltanet.com/accessplus/access.html

Access Plus was founded in order to bid on broadband *Personal Communications Services* (PCS) licenses. The licenses are offered in the Entrepreneurs' Blocks during the FCC auction in the Spring of 1995. Access Plus has brought together an experienced team of professionals to bid on and win PCS licenses and then to operate the businesses. Users will find information about Access Plus and the FCC auctions from this site.

ELVIS+, Co.

http://www.elvis.msk.su

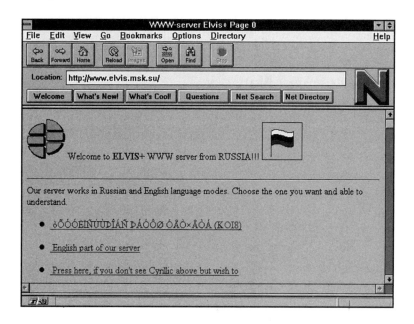

Come to this Russian site to find exchange rates, a Russian-English dictionary, fax service to Moscow, advertisements, and an index of other Russian Web sites. Use the search engine to search on keywords.

PC Index

http://ici.proper.com/1/pc

From this server you can jump to the best and most action-packed PC-related FTP, Gopher, and Web sites. Issues of several of the best online magazines can be downloaded. You can also connect to the American Computer Exchange to get the latest prices on used PCs and related equipment.

Employment

Looking for a new job? The Web is the place to go for information on career options and trends, as well as current job listings. The following sites represent a small sampling of the many employment sites that the Web has to offer.

American Employment Weekly

http://branch.com:1080

In this publication you can find the position that best suits you, particularly if you are in the accounting, banking, engineering, human resources, or sales professions.

Interactive Employment Network

http://www.espan.com/ienhome.html

This resource for job hunters and employers provides a career manager, job library, and a human resources library.

Jobnet

http://www.westga.edu:80/~coop

Jobnet is a great starting point in your job search. Jobnet contains links to a number of other employment-related sites, and maintains a growing number of international databases as well.

Shopping

You can buy, sell, or trade nearly anything over the Web. The following sites give you some idea of the amazingly wide range of products that are offered over the Web.

Book Stacks Unlimited

http://www.books.com

Books. Books. Books. More than 240,000 books are available for users to browse through and buy online. The Book Stacks server allows searches by author, title, subject, keyword, or ISBN.

Catalog Mart Home Page

http://catalog.savvy.com

This site offers a searchable database of over 10,000 free catalogs in more than 800 categories. Orders are taken online, and the catalogs are delivered to your home.

Condom Country

http://www.ag.com/condom/country

Safe sex on the Web! This is the place to browse and order from an online catalog of condoms and other sexual aids and devices. Check out the history of our latex friends and find out how your favorite condom rates.

FTD Internet

http://www.novator.com/FTD-Catalog/FTD-Internet.html

This is the Web site for FTD florists. You can have flowers delivered just about anywhere in the world. First view the different arrangements, then use the online form to order your favorite "picks."

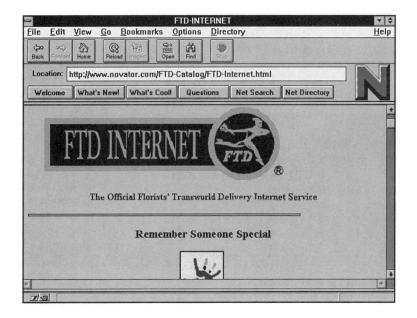

InfoWeb

http://infoweb.net

InfoWeb is a virtual mall where you not only can shop online, but you can find a source of news, classified ads, help wanted ads, and links to other Web sites.

InteliQuest

http://voyager.enet.net/iquest/index.html

At this site you can order audio, video, and multimedia-based educational programs from InteliQuest's online catalog.

Internet Mall

http://www.mecklerweb.com/imall/imall.htm

Come to this virtual mall to shop for furniture, clothes, services, computer hardware and software, media, and automotive products. There is even a food court!

Krema Nut Company

http://www.infinet.com/~schapman/mwow.cmh/krema/homepage.html

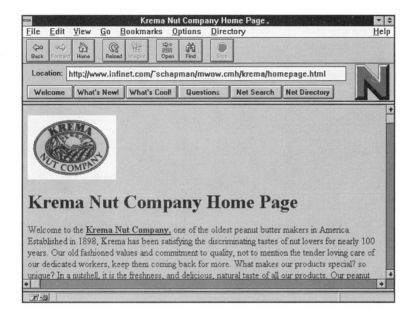

This is a site for nut nuts. View this company's online brochure and place an order.

Los Gatos Coffee Roasting Company

http://www.los-gatos.scruznet.com/los_gatos/businesses/los_gatos_coffee/storefront.html

Here you can learn all about roasting coffee and then order online a variety of beans and strengths.

MacZone Interactive

http://www.geo.net:8240

From this site you can find MacZone's online catalog, which contains information about Power Macintosh products and Software Toolworks CD-ROMs.

The Market Basket

http://www.glaci.com/market/brewing/homepage.html

This is the place to get your brewing products, from leaf hop plugs to freeze-dried beer yeast to wine concentrates.

Nine Lives

http://chezhal.slip.netcom.com

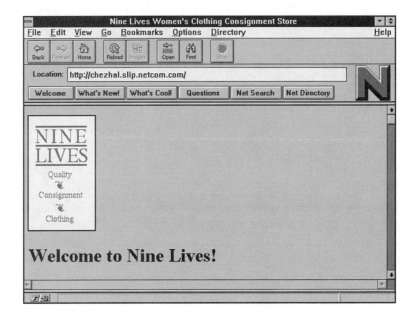

This women's clothing consignment store provides a personal assistant during business hours. Browse their catalog online.

NSTN CyberMall

http://www.nstn.ns.ca

This Canada-based virtual mall provides Internet-related information and services, and is a good starting point to begin exploring the Web.

Paper Direct

http://www.imn.net/paperdirect/index.html

This is the site for a paper and related products mail-order company. Browse the catalog and order online. Also available are software and fonts, and a "how-to" guide for presentations.

Pathfinder

http://www.timeinc.com/pathfinder

Pathfinder is a service of Time Warner. In addition to company highlights, this page provides information about the magazines they publish, current updates of late-breaking news events, online chat areas, search functions, and shopping.

Photopia

http://www.solutionsrc.com/PHOTOPIA

The Photopia server contains stock photos you can browse and order online. Their database is searchable, and product delivery is made on a Syquest disk to your home.

Speak to Me

http://www.clickshop.com:80/speak

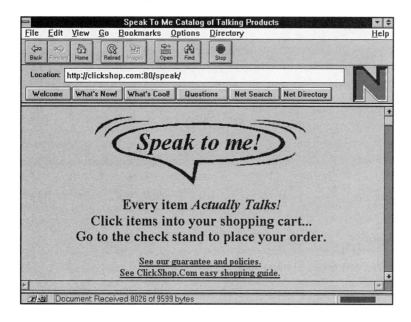

This online catalog of talking products is one of the most unique places on the Web. The catalog is arranged by type of product. Just click and listen!

STUFF.com

http://www.stuff.com

Browse and order Internet-related tees, CD-ROMs, and other…well…stuff. Sign up for their mailing list of new product announcements.

United Distillers

http://www.os2.iaccess.za/ud

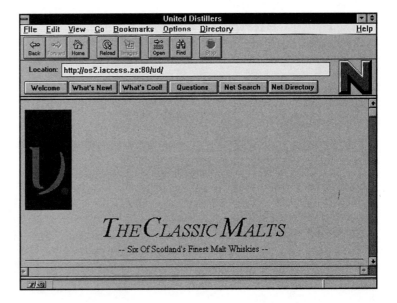

This page presents a virtual tour of the heart of Scotland. While there, you can also learn about some of its best malt whiskies.

The UWI Shopping Maul

http://kzsu.stanford.edu/uwi/maul.html

Yes, it's spelled right! The items and products from this site include, as their home page states, "freak-o stuff, but from the heart! Don't worry, this is far from commercialization of the net—most of these people lose money doing what they do." Some product listings include Lunatic Fringe (zine), The Ann Arbor Edge (music), and Synergy (zine).

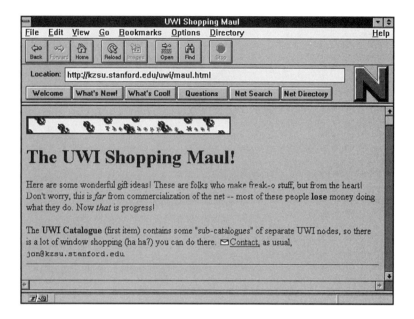

WorldWide Marketplace

http://www.cygnus.nb.ca

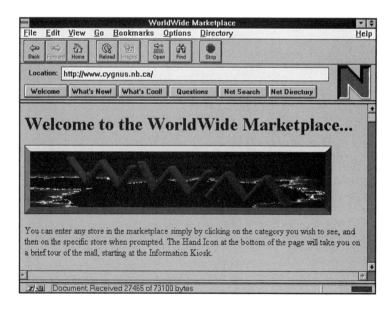

The WorldWide Marketplace, an online mall, offers an assortment of interesting products and services for purchase.

Part VIII

Appendix

APPENDIX

Using the Inside the World Wide Web CD-ROM

The *Inside the World Wide Web* CD-ROM is designed to give you a healthy cross-section of Web-related software utilities. Web users should be able to try out browsers, HTML text editors, file-viewing programs, and other Web tools in order to more fully learn just how much can be done on the Web.

It also helps to have these tools even if you're hitting the Web from a Unix or Macintosh machine. While relatively few Web tools exist for these operating systems, more are being written regularly. Keep looking for them—and add them to the ones you get here.

Because of our efforts to obtain as much useful material as possible for the *Inside the World Wide Web* CD-ROM, New Riders found itself adding programs even after the book went to the printer.

Some software was late in arriving; other matters, such as obtaining the proper software distribution rights, could not be resolved until after the book went into printing. All of which is to say, in order to see a truly comprehensive list, with descriptions, of what's on the CD-ROM, you'll need to see the Readme directory on the CD. There you'll find the following files:

◆ **Readme1.txt**   Readme1.txt is a text file that contains a list of all of the software programs on the CD-ROM. First is a basic list of the programs and files by directory; following this list is a brief description of each software product on the CD.

◆ **Readme2.txt**   Readme2.txt contains information about New Riders Publishing.

Categories of Software on the CD

The CD-ROM software can be broken into four main categories.

Browsers

These programs enable you to actually interface with the Web. All browsers use a form of code derived from the NCSA Mosaic Internet Web browser. Netscape is currently the most widely used Web browser, but several others exist. Try them out and see which ones have the features that work best for your needs.

Compression/Decompression Tools

These tools enable you to download compressed files from the Internet, via the Web, and decompress (re-expand) the files on your hard drive for use.

TCP/IP Programs

TCP/IP software allows you to access the Internet and transfer files in different ways. You'll get to explore non-Web Internet interfaces using some of these programs.

Operating System Additions

This includes Microsoft's Win32s freeware program, which enables Windows and Windows for Workgroups to run 32-bit Windows programs such as NCSA Mosaic.

Microsoft Internet Assistant/HTML Editors

Hyper Text Mark-up Language is the "programming" language of Web authoring—even though it's actually closer to simply being a kind of formatting system. Several programs are featured that enable you to manipulate text for use on the Web.

If you've heard about Microsoft's new Web page authoring system, Internet Assistant, and wanted to check it out, look no further. Internet Assistant enables you to easily turn Word 6 for Windows .doc files into HTML Web pages.

World Wide Web Servers

When you decide you want to increase your Web presence to the point of providing access to others, you'll need the software to do so. These shareware and freeware programs can help you implement Web access effectively.

Web File Viewers/Adobe Acrobat Reader/ Paint Shop Pro

All kinds of files are available from the Web for downloading or viewing. The trouble is, you may not have the software to enable you to actually see graphics files, or listen to audio files, or check out animation files, and so on.

We've provided viewer programs for audio, video, graphics (the award-winning Paint Shop Pro 3.0), and even Word for Windows .doc files (Microsoft Word Viewer).

If you haven't heard of Adobe's Acrobat Reader, you'll be amazed at the program; Acrobat enables cross-platform reading of text and graphics files.

Other Sundry and Useful Software

Look for mail programs, security software, speech recognition, and more.

Understanding Freeware and Shareware Concepts

One of the great things about the Internet and the Web and the computing community in general is that there are talented people out there who work very hard producing really useful software—and then they actually give it away.

Well, not always...

One of the most unfortunate misunderstandings about downloadable software is that not all of it is "free" ware. You really do have an obligation to pay for the right to continue to use the software known as shareware.

What Is Freeware?

Freeware is basically just what it sounds like—a developer writes a program and uploads it to a public place (like the Web) and attaches a message to it that says, "Here's something I made. Anybody who wants to can have a copy of this, no charge. Enjoy!"

What Is Shareware?

Shareware follows the previous concept concerning freeware up to a point. But with shareware, the author's message says something like, "Here's something I made. Anybody who wants to can *try out* a copy of this, no charge. If you like it and decide to keep using it, *please recognize the usefulness of the product I spent effort on producing and pay me for it.*"

You need to take this seriously. From an ethical point of view, it's only right to hold up your end of the bargain by paying for the software you continue to use. And from a more pragmatic angle, if programmers don't get money for creating this great shareware, they stop making it, which leaves us all a little poorer.

You can usually find out if software is shareware or freeware by opening the text or write file(s) that come with each program.

Index

M

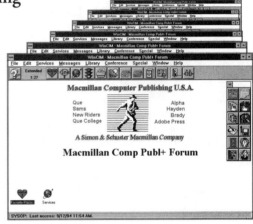

YOUR WAY TO REACH THE WORLD

Worried about making your presence known on the Internet?

Vyne Communications, Inc. is a fully integrated Internet service, design and marketing company.

- We provide **24 hour technical services** based on **World Wide Web** Servers, anonymous **FTP servers, automated email**, and information distribution systems.
- We design, build, oversee—and **provide user analysis** of—a wide variety of Internet communications and promotional sites.
- We are the home of world-wide marketing data services, technical newsletters, and information **wire services** for **science and technology** news.

Far-reaching, ever-changing and growing with the world's technology, Vyne makes it easy and affordable for you to set up shop on the Internet. We have the foresight, information and talent to let your Internet identity evolve as the Information Superhighway does. Make world-wide contact. Communicate, market, promote. We customize according to your needs—and your budget.

Feel free to check out our home page at **http://www.vyne.com/**

For more information, feel free to call us at: 212-293-VYNE

OPEN THE DOOR TO THE
INTERNET!

DO BUSINESS ON THE
WEB!

EarthLink Network™, Southern California's largest Internet access provider, is your Internet business partner. EarthLink offers all of the services you need to establish a presence for your business in cyberspace.

World Wide Web Server Services

"A one-stop provider for World Wide Web commerce."

–Cover Story: "EarthLink's Web Solution: Low-cost Web sites and high-speed access" from Interactive Age, March 27, 1995.

EarthLink's Web server services allow you to build your own electronic storefront, so you can conduct marketing and commerce on the Internet, without the layout of capital needed to establish and run your own Internet servers. We provide space on our Internet-connected servers for you to put up your Web documents. You get daily reports of activity to your pages.

High-Speed Connectivity

EarthLink Network offers direct access to the Internet using leading-edge technologies such as ISDN and Frame Relay. With these services, you can connect your workstation or LAN to the Internet at 56kb to 1,544kb per second.

Contact our trained sales staff to find out what level of connectivity is right for your needs.

TotalAccess™ to the Internet is just minutes away!

EarthLink Network™ is proud to announce the release of TotalAccess, a complete software and Internet connection package for Windows. TotalAccess makes accessing the Internet easier than ever. TotalAccess includes Netscape Navigator™, award-winning Internet access software, Eudora™, the most popular Internet email software in the world, and everything you need to register for complete Internet access in 5 minutes. Best of all, the software is FREE with your registration!

CALL NOW! 213-644-9500

EarthLink Network, Inc. 3171 Los Feliz Boulevard, Suite 203
Los Angeles, CA 90039 Fax: 213-644-9510
Via the web: http://www.earthlink.net Via email: info@earthlink.net
Live human via email: sales@earthlink.net

REGISTRATION CARD

Inside the World Wide Web

Name _____ Title _____

Company _____ Type of business _____

Address _____

City/State/ZIP _____

Have you used these types of books before? ☐ yes ☐ no

If yes, which ones? _____

_____

How many computer books do you purchase each year? ☐ 1–5 ☐ 6 or more

How did you learn about this book? _____

Where did you purchase this book? _____

Which applications do you currently use? _____

_____

Which computer magazines do you subscribe to? _____

_____

What trade shows do you attend? _____

_____

Comments: _____

_____

_____

Would you like to be placed on our preferred mailing list? ☐ yes ☐ no

☐ **I would like to see my name in print!** You may use my name and quote me in future New Riders products and promotions. My daytime phone number is: _____

New Riders Publishing   201 West 103rd Street ◆ Indianapolis, Indiana 46290 USA

Fax to **317-581-4670**   Orders/Customer Service **1-800-653-6156**   Source Code **NRP95**

Fold Here

BUSINESS REPLY MAIL

FIRST-CLASS MAIL PERMIT NO. 9918 INDIANAPOLIS IN

POSTAGE WILL BE PAID BY THE ADDRESSEE

NEW RIDERS PUBLISHING
201 W 103RD ST
INDIANAPOLIS IN 46290-9058

Installing the Inside the World Wide Web CD-ROM

The *Inside the World Wide Web* CD-ROM is designed to give you a healthy cross-section of Web-related software utilities. Web users should be able to try out browsers, HTML text editors, file-viewing programs, and other Web tools in order to more fully learn just how much can be done on the Web.

It also helps to have these tools even if you're hitting the Web from a Unix or Macintosh machine. While relatively few Web tools exist for these operating systems, more are being written regularly. Keep looking for them—and add them to the ones you get here.

Because of our efforts to obtain as much useful material as possible for the *Inside the World Wide Web* CD-ROM, New Riders found itself adding programs even after the book went to the printer.

Some software was late in arriving; other matters, such as obtaining the proper software distribution rights, could not be resolved until after the book went into printing. All of which is to say, in order to see a truly comprehensive list, with descriptions, of what's on the CD-ROM, you'll need to see the Readme directory on the CD. There you'll find the following files:

◆ **Readme1.txt**   Readme1.txt is a text file that contains a list of all of the software programs on the CD-ROM. First is a basic list of the programs and files by directory; following this list is a brief description of each software product on the CD.

◆ **Readme2.txt**   Readme2.txt contains information about New Riders Publishing.